THE KÀVYAPRAKÀSHA

OF

MAMMATA

THE KÀVYAPRAKÀSHA

OF

MAMMATA

TRANSLATOR

GANGANATHA JHA

GYAN

Published by

Gyan Publishing House
5, Ansari Road
Daryaganj, New Delhi-110002
Phone: 011-47034999, 9811692060
E-mail: books@gyanbooks.com

Distribution Network
gyanbooks.com
India, USA, Canada, UK, Australia

ISBN: 978-93-6780-097-3 (PB)

First Published, 1925

2nd Impression 2024

Printed at: Gyan Press, Delhi.

THE KÀVYAPRAKÀSHA OF MAMMATA
Translator: GANGANATHA JHA

KĀVYAPRAKĀSHA

OF

MAMMATA

WITH

ENGLISH TRANSLATION

(REVISED)

(Chapters I to X)

(*With Index & Appendices*)

By

Mahamahopadhyaya Dr. Sir Ganganatha Jha,

M. A, D. Litt, LL. D, *Vidyā-Sāgara, Ex Vice-Chancellor*

Allahabad University

FOREWORD

The famous English "Translation" of Kavya-Prakāsha by late Mahamahopadhyaya Dr. Sir Ganganatha Jha had been out of print for the last several years and the scholars from all over the world have been persistently craving for its re-issue. The same is being done with the concurrence of Dr. Adityanath Jha, Vacaspati, I. C. S. Lieutenant-Governor of Delhi, the only surviving son of the illustrious translator.

Although Sir Ganganatha Jha called his work merely a translation in all humility, it is really a highly learned commentary as well, since attempt has been made here not only for reproduction in English of the Sanskrit text and commentary, but also towards their further elucidation, and for this the illustrious savant has supported his stand by references to different authorities and by providing supplementary notes. Although the work, as published hitherto, did not contain the text in the present edition the same has been added for the convenience of the readers. Dr Jha had said in the previous editions that he had followed the text of Vāmanī, but at so many places it is not so, and so effort has been made to present the readings as followed by the learned translator, and not that by Vāmanāchārya.

In the meantime a copy of the manuscript of the Kāvya Prakāsha-Kārikā was discovered in the Saraswati Bhavana Library, Varanasi. Its opening stanza is significant in as much as it mentions expressly that Mammata was the Vṛttikāra, without mentioning about his being the author of the Kārikā In addition the stanza, in which Śānta is mentioned as a Rasa (31), is missing in this manuscript. The writer of this manuscript has in another stanza, where Śānta (26) is mentioned in other manuscripts, a text that does not have the word śānta. In the present edition not only the Kārikās have been reproduced, but the readings where this manuscript differs from those of Vāmanāchārya have also been mentioned.

While effort has been made to preserve the method of transcription of the translator, a deviation has been made especially in respect of the anusvāra. Dr. Jha had *m* for both म and anusvāra, but in the present edition, anusvāra is being indicated by ṁ. Certain misprints of the text, particularly in the Prakrit passages, have been rectified. Readers will find that श is transcribed in some places by *sh* and at others by *ś*.

The work is being issued in two parts, Part I consisting of the first seven chapters and Part II of the remaining chapters with indices including a biography of Dr. Sir Ganganatha Jha.

Dr. Adityanatha Jha has left to the charge of this humble student the honourable task of arranging for re-publication of the works of his father. In consequence thereof through the interest taken in the project by the energetic proprietor of Messess Bharatiya Vidya Prakashan Shri Kishore Chand Jain the first work of Dr. Jha that he had originally written as a university student is being published presently. It is now for scholars to see how far success has been attained in the matter of faithful reproduction of the work of the master. If this edition receives approbation of scholars, other works of Dr. Jha will follow in succession. and the second work to be published is the Prābhākara School of Pūrva-Mīmāṁsā.

In execution of this work Pt. Shri Ahi Bhushan Bhattacharya, Principal. C. M. Anglo Bengali College, Varanasi, the worthy son of one of the greatest Sanskritists of the time, namely late Mahamahopadhyaya Pandit Phanibhushan Bhattacharya, has ungrudingly cooperated in correcting the proofs, although for all shortcomings the responsibility rests with

Subhadra Jhā.

Vārāṇasī, 13. 12. 1966.

श्रीः पातु

प्रास्ताविकम्

काव्यानुशासनविवेचनकोविदाना
प्रज्ञासुवर्णनिकषोपलतां दधान ।
स्वल्पै पदैर्विवृतभूरिगभीरतत्त्व-
काव्यप्रकाश इह कस्य न सुप्रशस्य ॥ १ ॥

यन्निर्मितिप्रजनिता भुवि मम्मटस्य
वाग्देवतापुरुषरूपतया प्रसिद्धि ।
श्रीश्रीधरादिविबुधै रसवेदसख्या
व्याख्याश्च सविदधिरे यदुपाश्रयेण ॥ २ ॥

सङ्गृह्य पूर्वविवृतीरथ वामनाख्या
ऽऽचार्येण चारु रचितास्य विभाति टीका ।
लोकप्रिय सकलसूरिसमाजसेव्य
साहित्यरत्नकलश स विराच्चकास्ति ॥ ३ ॥

दोषा गुणा ध्वनिरलङ्कृतय समस्ता
शास्त्रान्तरीयमनुवन्धि तथाऽर्थतत्त्वम् ।
काव्यप्रकाशमुकुरे प्रतिबिम्बकल्प
प्राकाशि मम्मटबुधेन नवक्रमेण ॥ ४ ॥

यत्सूरिभिर्निगदित पद - वाक्य - मान -
शास्त्रेषु काव्यसहकारि विचारहारि ।
स्फोटादि जैमिनिनयानुगतञ्च किञ्चित्
बौद्धोदितञ्च विनिवेशितमत्र युक्त्या ॥ ५ ॥

सूक्ष्मेक्षिकासमधिगम्यमुपेयवस्तु
सूत्रात्मकं गुरुगभीरगिरा प्रवाहे ।
आस्वादयन् सहृदयान् विशद यशस्व
श्रीमम्मट स्फटिकमन्दिरवच्चकार ॥ ६ ॥

एतद्ग्रन्थमनोज्ञताञ्चितमतिर्विद्वत्कुलाम्भोजिनी–
तिग्मांशु स महादिमाङ्कितमहोपाध्यायभूषाचित ।
गङ्गानाथसुधीर्मदीयजनको लोकोपकारक्षमा
व्याख्यामाङ्गलगिराऽस्य निर्मलपदन्यासोत्तमा निर्ममे ॥ ७ ॥

श्रीभारतीयविद्याप्रकाशन काशिकानिलयम् ।
काव्यप्रकाशसेन प्रकाशयत् काशता स्वगुणैं ॥ ८ ॥

पितृचरणवच श्रीदेवनद्या प्रवाहे
विबुधनिवहहंसोत्तमसान्निध्यहृद्ये ।
सविनयनतिशाली पुष्पमेतत्सुवर्णं
विसृजति मिथिलाभूः श्रीमदादित्यनाथः ॥ ९ ॥

GOVINDA !

It was at your instance that this translation was done in 1891, and it is at your persistent insistence that it has been re-written in 1924. May you find it more satisfactory than its predecessor—is the fervent hope of

Your own,

GANGA.

KĀVYAPRAKĀSHA

'Light of Poesy'

PREFACE TO THE SECOND EDITION

It was in a fit of juvenile enthusiasm that I permitted the first edition of my translation of the *Kāvyaprakāsha* to appear in the 'Pandit' of Benares; otherwise, under ordinary circumstances, it would be sheer audacity on the part of a boy of eighteen to put himself forward as the interpreter of a book which, apart from its subject-matter, is regarded, in point of style and expression, as one of the tersest, and hence the most difficult, in the Sanskrit language. The boy of eighteen, however, had his justification; he had written out a rough translation of the work in course of his preparation for the M A. Examination; and when, on passing that examination, he had his ambition for authorship aroused by the example and precept of his late lamented tutor, Dr. Arthur Venis of Benares, he sent his aforesaid translation to him and asked him if he thought it fit for publication. Apparently with a view to encouraging his pupil, the doctor wrote to him—"room could be found in the *Pandit* for your translation of the *Kāvyaprakāsha*", and the work was allowed to go forth to the public. The boy of eighteen has since grown to be an old man of fifty, and numerous have been the volumes with which he has thrust himself before an indulgent public; and after all these years, when he came to look into his earlier work, he felt that he owed it to the public to revise at least such of his works as had secured a number of readers. Foremost among these appeared to be the *Kāvyaprakātha*, the translation of which, imperfect as it is, has had to be read, more or less, by numerous candidates for the M. A. degree, for whom the original is prescribed by almost every University in India Thus it is in the spirit of repaying a debt long over-due that I am setting my hand to doing what is practically the rewriting of the translation of the work which, during all the centuries that have elapsed since it was written in far-off Kāshmir, has held the supreme position in the world of Sanskrit rhetorical literature.

With a view to interesting the modern reader, I requested my son, Amaranatha Jha of the University of Allahabad to add some notes, which would help the comparative study of this interesting subject After he had done this work over Chapter I, it was found that matter available for these notes was so abundant that if it were to appear in the form of foot-notes, the original work would become hugely encumbered. He has therefore decided to incorporate all this material for comparative study in a separate book that he is writing on the subject, and to include in this volume only a few notes.—My own notes on the text I have embodied in the Text itself, distinguishing them from the text either by using square brackets (in the case of short notes) or by employing a smaller type (in the case of longer ones).

I hope the reader will find this revised translation less defective than its forerunner.

THE UNIVERSITY :
ALLAHABAD,
February 22, 1924.

GANGANATHA JHA.

Preface to the First Edition

This is the second Sanskrit work on the Science of Poetry that is being offered to the English-reading public in an English garb— if we do not count the Bhāshā-Bhūshaṇa, a Hindi work on the same subject, which was rendered into English and published in the pages of the Indian Antiquary in 1894, by Dr. Grierson, whose labours in the cause of Hindi literature rival those of the late Mr. Growse. The first was the Sāhitya-Darpaṇa of Vishwanātha Kavirāja, which was placed over twenty years ago before the public by Rai Bahadur Pramadā Dāsa Mittra, in an English form, that still remains a model of scholarly and excellent translation. It is time that another work on the subject, expounding more or less different views on important points, should be published. Indeed it is surprising that so little attention should have been directed to this department of Sanskrit learning by Oriental Scholars. For, as it seems to the present writer, the *Sāhitya* literature of India is remarkably full and complete, and contains perhaps as many useful ideas worth the acceptance of foreign scholars as the literature of philosophy.

With the growth of interest and study in metaphysics and psychology there has undoubtedly grown on parallel lines, in Europe, interest in and study of the philosophy of other sciences. And we see excellent books issued from the press day after day, which seek to clear up the fundamental ideas of Law, of History, of Politics, of the Physical Sciences and of the various branches of Art. In short there has been a general growth of introspective "Intelligence" on all matters ; and an effort is perceptible everywhere to locate every portion of knowledge in its proper place in a universal scheme. There has been no philosopher worthy of the name, who has left an impress other than merely ephemeral on subsequent literature, and has not endeavoured so to organise the whole of human knowledge into one complete whole, or not matured ideas on all matters interesting to humanity. But it must be confessed that the literature on the science and philosophy of poetry is not excessively rich in English. Works on poets, dramatists, novelists, and on the history of literature abound ; and naturally many of such works, principally biographical, critical, appreciative, or descriptive, yet incidentally, enunciate directly, or indicate indirectly, very useful and instructive ideas on the basic questions of the subjects concerned. But scientific works, professedly confining themselves to the principles which underlie all literature (in the special sense of the term, viz. *belles lettres*), are few. Prof. Bain's works on Rhetoric and Composition and On Teaching English are what might have been expected from him, a clear thinker and philosopher and scholar of "encyclopedical learning" in the well-judged language of Mill But they stand almost by themselves , Prof. Bain himself says in his prefaces, with reference to the department of Figures of Speech, that "never before has that branch received so large a share of attention", and again, adverting to the emotional qualities of style, that his "is the first attempt at a methodical and exhaustive account of these qualities". And they are not final nor complete, as the Professor himself admits beforehand. Thus, though it would probably be presumptuous at this date, to hint that India had anything new to teach Europe, still it may perhaps be excusable to say that Indian books on *Sāhitya* might help to clear up ideas if only by affording the occasion for a further and deeper study of the subject.

The first and most important question of the science is as to what constitutes the essence of poetry. The long accepted answer in India is that Emotion constitutes that essence—a conclusion which British investigators are only now approaching, and with still hesitating steps ; as Dr. Bain tentatively says (On Teaching English, p. 214)—"to emotion we must come at last, in any precise definition" of poetry. Of course there are more or less slight differences in the details as discussed by different writers. The author of the work now translated has formulated his answer to the question in language which may appear at first sight to be even radically different from the accepted view ; and students will find interesting points of resemblance in his treatment of the subject and Prof. Bain's, who also, at least in the form of his book on Rhetoric, treats of all connected questions as subsidiary to Style. But this innovation of our author's too is only apparent; and is perhaps due to nothing else than an exaggerated desire to be original. He tacitly reverts to the general position in his treatment of the auxiliary subjects,—herein again offering a point of resemblance to Dr. Bain. And this is the essence and the net result of the teaching of the *Sāhitya Shāstra* : *viz*. that the expression of the emotions, in their infinite forms and their combinations developed by the infinite forms and situations of human life, is the business of literature; and that those writers are the greatest, and those works the most permanent and the most prominent that have seized and embodied the most permanent and prominent emotions of humanity in the most remarkable manner.

It is interesting and instructive to compare Dr. Bain's classification of the emotions admissible into poetry with those of the Sanskrit authors, and their respective arguments in support of them. The secret of the true reason, why Pathos plays such an important part in all literature, why रसेषु करुणो रसः ("amongst the poetical emotions the supreme is Pathos ") in the words of the ancient Indian poet, and why " our sweetest songs are those that tell of saddest thought " in the words of the modern English poet, is still to seek. Neither Mammata nor Bain, etc., are quite satisfactory on this point. The student might try and invent an explanation for himself. If he can, further, satisfy himself as to why "the Furious" "the Terrible" and " the Disgusting " should find a place in poetry, he will have discovered a deeper reason than Dr. Max Nordau, for the amazing outbreak of these in the literature, whose aberrations he so trenchantly, if not sufficiently deeply, exposes in his book entitled " Degeneration ".

Another notable point is that the *form* of the *Kāvya* is assigned a very secondary place in *Sāhitya*. While in the West, metre, and to a less extent, rhyme, have been held to be essentials, they are of very minor importance in India. Prof. Bain and J. S. Mill before him (*vide* his Dissertations), apparently approximate to the Indian view which allows of such famous *gadya-kāvyas* (prose-poems) as *Kādambarī*, *Vāsavadattā*, &c., and of course includes the drama under poetry at large, as one of its species , Walt Whitman and his imitators also recognise in practice the accuracy of it. It must be confessed, however, that this view is only correct in principle and as a theory. In practice the powerful additions made to the pleasures of poetry by metre and rhyme have checked the growth of prose-poems considerably, and thrown into the shade all but the very best. For similar reasons, just as the metrical poem is an advance upon the prose-poem, so "recited poetry" and the drama constitute an advance upon the metrical poem, to the musical effects of metre and rhyme which enlist the services of the ear in furthering the pleasures of poetry, the drama adds the scenic effects, which engage the eye also. And hence the dictum काव्येषु नाटकं श्रेष्ठम् (of poems the drama is the highest). Thus it appears that *Sāhitya* treats of the principles of poetry and it treats of Words and Style only in so far as they express more fitly or otherwise the appropriate emotion The treatment of the metre form it leaves to Prosody for metre and rhyme, and to *Nātya Shāstra* for dramaturgy. Sanskrit Prosody has little interest for the general English reader; but the science of Mimetics obviously has, and there is no work on the subject yet, for a wonder, in the land of Shakespeare,—the one or two books like Hammerton's "The Actor's Art," that are just beginning to come out, being scarcely entitled to rank as scientific books. If opportunities are favourable, the present writer hopes to bring out some day a translation of Bharata's *Nātya Shāstra*, the oldest work available on the subject.

The history of the science of poetry in India, like that of all others, is lost in antiquity. Tradition speaks of original aphorisms by Çauddhodani, by Bharata and by Vāmana These aphorisms too are lost for the present, except the last which has been recently printed by the enterprising publishers of the *Kāvyamālā*. Vāmana's Sūtras are not old, that is to say, not much older than 800 A. C. Fragments of the other two are met with in the form of quotations by later writers. It is possible and to be hoped that they may be recovered some day; for not very old authors refer to them as having formed the subject of their studies, before they began their own works; and it is very much to be desired that they may be so recovered, for the Sūtra—literature shows a finality of statement, so far as general principles are concerned, which could result only from a perfect grasp of the completed "circle of knowledge," and it is not likely that any future races will succeed in improving upon these statements of final principles, however much they may and will make fuller the contents of the general ideas in consequence of more varied experience in larger circles of life.

Shauddhodani appears to have been one of the first to definitely formulate the view that emotion is the essence of poetry—

वाक्यं रसादिमत् काव्यम्—(utterance embodying emotion is poetry), according to a quotation in *Alaṁkāra Shekhara.* It is only a matter of conjecture whether he belonged to the genuine Sūtra period of Sanskrit literature—the period immediately following Vyāsa, the great organiser of Sanskrit learning

The outlines and the elementary principles of Sāhitya are given in the Agni Purāna also as now extant , but as to the authorship, authenticity and antiquity of the work grave doubts are entertained by those learned in these matters.

As regards Bharata, a tradition says that the Kārikās (memorial verses), of the Kāvya-Prakāça, themselves are the work of Bharata, and that Mammata wrote only the prose portion of the text in the form of a commentary. But another tradition, as also the fact that Mammata refers to Bharata in one place, in the fourth Chapter of the work, in support of the doctrine stated in the Kārikā, goes against this. The truth, as usual, probably lies between, and Mammata seems to have made large use of the Sūtras of Bharata in fashioning his verses, and has perhaps incorporated therein large pieces of them bodily, thus giving rise to the first mentioned tradition.

Mammata himself was undoubtedly a Brāhmana of Kashmir and lived and wrote his famous work certainly before the 12th century A. C , about the time when English literature was just beginning to be born. The earliest commentary on his work now available and apparently the earliest in fact also, is, that of Mānikya-Chandra, and that is expressedly dated by Mānikya-Chandra himself, in the colophon, with the *Saṁvat* year 1216, corresponding with 1159 A. C. At the same time there is no reason to believe that the author of the Kāvya-Prakāsha lived earlier than the eleventh century A. C.; for he quotes a verse in his 10th Chapter from Bhoja, who reigned in the earlier half of that century , for a tradition has it that his younger brother Uvvata attended the court of this very Bhoja at his capital Avanti for some time; and he was probably the medium of the quotation. It is easy to understand that the Court-Pandit should have gladly seized on the first opportunity that offered of paying an elegant compliment to the literary merits of his really deserving master, by securing for a production of his a gratifying reference and quotation in the masterpiece of his famous brother, and of, at the same time, and by the same stroke of policy, obtaining for that masterpiece an introduction under the most favourable circumstances to the court of his royal patron.

Mammaṭa was a member of a true Pandit family ; he was the son of Jayyata, the joint author with Vāmana of the celebrated grammatical treatise, the Kāshikā; and the brother of Kayyata, the author of the standard gloss on Patañjali's Great Commentary and of the above-mentioned Uvvaṭa, the author of a Bhāshya on the Vedas and other Vedic works, which, however, have been superseded by the later works of Sāyaṇa and Mādhava. Mammata is said, by Bhīmasena in the opening verses of his commentary on the Kāvya-Prakāsha to have travelled to Benares for purposes of study. The times of Mammaṭa seem to have been times of a general outburst of literature and learning in Kashmir, which had most likely something to do with the Buddhist literature and learning, then on its way out of India to its present Tibetan home across the Himālayas. A lot of literary names ending with the characteristic syllable ṭa are to be found in the books of this period, Vajjraṭa, Rudrata, Bhallaṭa, Vābhaṭa, Allaṭa, &c. How these outbursts and revivals travel about from place to place is a phenomenon which is observable in the literary history of ancient and modern Europe also. Sāhitya in India appears to have passed on from Kashmir to Mithilā, and thence to Bengal ; it is now almost confined to the Deccan.

The mention of Allaṭa leads us to the fact that the Kāvya-Prakāsha could not be completed by Mammaṭa, notwithstanding the inevitable *maṅgalācharana*, the propitiation of the appropriate Goddess of Speech. Apparently in accordance with the very satisfactory explanation of the ingenious *Naiyāyika*, the past evil *karma* of Mammaṭa's previous births was too voluminous to be dispelled by the amount of *maṅgalācharaṇa* he made, and so the thread of his life broke short ! But it broke short when he was in sight of his goal ; and he has practically completed his work. About a third of the last chapter on Figures,—or rather as they are more becomingly named in Sanskrit, Ornaments of Speech—which third amounts roughly to a tenth of the whole work,—was written by Allaṭa, from the second half of the 118th verse onwards, (page 244 of the translation*). This is expressly stated by Anand in his commentary entitled the *Nidarshana* on the *Kāvya-Prākāshu*, who again, in explaining the last verse of the work

*Not in the present edition.

refers to the same fact in this wise, " although this 10th chapter has been written by two authors, still the appreciating I will miss no pleasure of true excellence . indeed the general experience is that the mango fruit bred out of crossed varieties is even more luscious (than the fruit of either of its original parents)." Other commentators also interpret the *shloka* above referred to, to the same effect

Of commentaries and glosses on the *Kāvya Prākāsha* the number is legion. Verses current amongst the Pandits refer to this fact thus—

काव्यप्रकाशस्य कृता गृहे गृहे टीका तथाप्येष तथैव दुर्गमः ।।

(commentaries on the Kāvya-Prakāsha have been done up in every house, and yet it remains as difficult to understand as ever !)

Or again—

काव्यप्रकाशे टिप्पण्यः सहस्रं सन्ति तद्यपि ।

(although there are thousands of glosses on the Kāvya-Prakāsha still, &c. &c.). There is no other Sanskrit work so much be-commented, except perhaps the *Paribhāshendu-Shekhara* of Nāgesha Bhaṭṭa It might be worth mention in this connection that Vishwanātha Kavirāja, the author of the other most famous work on Sāhitya, referred to at the outset of this preface, thought fit to write an elaborate commentary on the Kāvya-Prakāsha *after* composing his own independent work, as is evident from the frequent references to the latter in the former. Indeed the work seems to have excited a most singular emulation amongst all classes of writers to show their appreciation of it by means of comments; famous Naiyāyikas like Jagadīsha and Gadādhara, leaders in Vyākaraṇa like Nāgesha Bhatta, renowned Tāntrikas like Gokula-Nātha and Kalyāna Upādhyāya, have all tried their hands at it. This gives us an idea of the high honour in which the Kāvya-Prakāsha has always been held throughout India, as an authority on its subject, and as a work, the careful study of which is indispensable to every Pandit who aspires to be regarded as a " Sāhityāchārya ".

A very full account of principal commentaries* on the work is

---

*Though no less than forty-six commentaries are enumerated, there, three more commentaries have been found of which no mention is made : (1) By one "Pandita-Rāja" (identified by Pandits with Raghunandana Rāya, the renowned disciple of Mahesha Thakkura. This commentary begins thus : रघुवंशजलधिचन्द्रं रावणवनदन्तिपारीन्द्रम् ।

to be found in the elaborate Sanskrit Introduction (from which many of the facts stated above have been taken) to his edition of it. (with his own—the latest, perhaps the best, and certainly the fullest commentary), by the eminently learned Mahāmahopadhyāya Pandit Vāmanāchārya Zhalkikar of Poona.

In bringing the above remarks to a conclusion, I have to thank the gentlemen who have, in one way or another, helped me in the

---

मीतामुदितमयूरीमुदिरमुदारमहं कलये ॥ १ ॥ मौलौ निधाय पाणी वाणीमनिशं नमस्कृत्य । पण्डितराजः कुरुते टीकां काव्यप्रकाशस्य ॥ २ ॥ इयताऽपि बुद्धिविभवेन मोहतो यदमुष्य भावशतवर्णनोद्यमः । अपि सत्सु सत्सु गुणभावगौरवादवधेहि वाणि करवाणि साहसम् ॥३॥ बलिशादपि वक्रहृदः कुलिशादपि कठिनकर्माणः । गरलादपि मर्मभिदो ये केचन तान्नमस्कुर्मः ॥४॥ हरमौलिगलितगङ्गावीचिविचित्राशया सुधियः । मत्कृतिमतिदीर्घकृपादृक्पातसुधारसेन सिञ्चन्तु ॥ ५ ॥ प्रथमतः प्रेक्षावत्प्रवृत्तिनिमित्तत्वेन प्रयोजनाभिधेयसम्बन्धस्याभिधातुमुचितस्यानभिधानाद् भारतीस्तुतिमत्यात्मकमङ्गलस्य समाप्तौ व्यभिचारात् फलान्तरस्याभावात् ... प्रथमश्लोकमवतारयति ग्रन्थारम्भ इति ॥ and ends thus : उल्लासमुपसंहरति तदेत इति । इतीति ग्रन्थसमाप्तौ ॥ इति महामहोपाध्यायश्रीमत्पण्डितराजविरचिताकाव्यप्रकाशटीकाया दशमोल्लासः ॥ The MS. found is dated शाके १५५९ (A. C. 1637) (2) By Mahāmahopādhyāya Gokula-Nātha Upādhyāya. This begins thus : नत्वा परमात्मानं श्रीगोकुलनाथशर्मणा रचिता । काव्यप्रकाशिकायटीका प्रीत्यै सुनामस्तु ॥ १ ॥ कारिकानिबद्धमङ्गलश्लोकानुवचनादेवानुषङ्गिकविघ्नध्वंससिद्धौ वृत्तिकारो न मङ्गलम् प्रणीतवान् न चोपनिबबन्ध । किन्तु कारिकाप्रबन्धमारिप्समानस्य ग्रन्थकृत प्रथमम् मङ्गलमाचरतो निबध्नतश्च निष्फलकर्मकर्तृत्वादनवधेयवचनत्वशङ्कामपाकर्तुमवतारयन्नानुषङ्गिकमङ्गलसम्पत्तये मौलम्पद्यमनुवदति ग्रन्थेत्यादिना जयतीत्यन्तेत । अधिकरणसमूहः शास्त्रम् . .. ॥

The MS. found does not extend to the end.[1] (3) By Kallyāna Upādhyāya—only fragments of this work have been found.

In a foot-note in connection with commentary No 25, the Sanskrit Introduction says that it is by Vāchaspati Mishra, the "सर्वतन्त्रज्ञः" I venture to point out that this is an oversight : because the Vāchaspati Mishra, who is generally styled 'सर्वतन्त्रज्ञ'—the author of "Bhamatī" &c.—is much older than Mammaṭa, and further, this author has enumerated all his works at the end of "Bhāmatī" where no mention is made of any commentary on the Kāvya-Prakāsha. The Vāchaspati Mishra who wrote a commentary on the Kāvya-Prakāsha, is the *legist*, the author of a series of Dharmasāshstra works—Āchāra-chintāmaṇi, &c.

[1. Fragment extending up to the chapter V edited by Kavi-shekhara Badarinatha Jha and published by the Sanskrit University, Varanasi 1961.]

translation. First among these comes Pandit Jayadeva Mishra, Professor of Vyākarana in the "Darbhanga Pāthashālā," Benares, from whom I got my first lessons in Kāvya-Prakāsha, and then Rai Bahadur Pramadā Dāsa Mittra of Benares, already mentioned, who not only encouraged me in the work, but also took upon himself the trouble of correcting an important portion of it. My thanks are also due to my honoured tutor, late Mr. Arthur Venis. M. A. Principal of the Queen's College, Benares, without whose encouraging words and example, I should probably have never ventured upon literary work, and to whose kind help is due the publication of the present translation. The last person, but not the least, whom I cannot leave unmentioned, is Babu Govinda-Dāsa of Benares, who has ever been the guiding spirit of literary life

DARBHANGA
April, 1918

GANGĀNĀTHA JHĀ.

KĀVYAPRAKĀSHA

CONTENTS

Text with translation, etc.

CHAPTER III

CHAPTER IV

CHAPTER V

CHAPTER VI

CHAPTER VII

CHAPTER VIII

Excellences गुणा:

CHAPTER IX

Verbal Figures of Speech शब्दालंकारा:

CHAPTER X

The Ideal Figures of Speech अर्थालंकारा:

APPENDICES

ॐ नमः शिवाय ।

काव्यप्रकाश-

कारिकावली

नियतिकृतनियमरहितां ह्लादैकमयीमनन्यपरतन्त्राम् ।
नवरसरुचिरां निर्मितिमादधती भारती कवेर्जयति ॥ १ ॥
काव्यं यशसेऽर्थकृते व्यवहारविदे शिवेतरक्षतये ।
सद्यः परनिर्वृतये कान्तासंमिततयोपदेशयुजे ॥ २ ॥
शक्तिर्निपुणता लोकशास्त्रकाव्याद्यवेक्षणात् ।
काव्यज्ञशिक्षयाभ्यास इति हेतुस्तदुद्भवे ॥ ३ ॥
तददोषौ शब्दार्थौ सगुणावनलंकृती पुनः क्वापि ।
इदमुत्तममतिशयिनि व्यङ्ग्ये वाच्याद्ध्वनिर्बुधैः कथितः ॥४॥
अतादृशि गुणीभूतव्यङ्ग्यं व्यङ्ग्ये तु मध्यमम् ।
शब्दचित्रं वाच्यचित्रमव्यङ्ग्यं त्ववरं स्मृतम् ॥ ५ ॥
स्याद्वाचको लाक्षणिकः शब्दोऽत्र व्यञ्जकस्त्रिधा ।
वाच्यादयस्तदर्थाः स्युस्तात्पर्यार्थोऽपि केषुचित् ॥ ६ ॥
सर्वेषां प्रायशोऽर्थानां व्यञ्जकत्वमपीष्यते ।
साक्षात्संकेतितं योऽर्थमभिधत्ते स वाचकः ॥ ७ ॥
सङ्केतितश्चतुर्भेदो जात्यादिर्जातिरेव वा ।
स मुख्योऽर्थस्तत्र मुख्यो व्यापारोऽस्याभिधोच्यते ॥ ८ ॥
मुख्यार्थबाधे तद्योगे रूढितोऽथ प्रयोजनात् ।
अन्योऽर्थो लक्ष्यते यत्सा लक्षणारोपिता क्रिया ॥ ९ ॥
स्वसिद्धये पराक्षेपः परार्थं स्वसमर्पणम् ।
उपादानं लक्षणं चेत्युक्ता शुद्धैव सा द्विधा ॥ १० ॥

सारोपान्या तु यत्रोक्तौ विषयी विषयस्तथा ।
विषय्यन्तःकृतेन्यस्मिन् सा स्यात्साध्यवसानिका ॥ ११ ॥
भेदाविमौ च सादृश्यात्सम्बन्धान्तरतस्तथा ।
गौणौ शुद्धौ च विज्ञेयौ लक्षणा तेन षड्विधा ॥ १२ ॥
व्यङ्ग्येन रहिता रूढौ सहिता तु प्रयोजने ।
तच्च गूढमगूढं वा तदेषा कथिता त्रिधा ॥ १३ ॥
तद्भूर्लाक्षणिकस्तत्र व्यापारो व्यञ्जनात्मकः ।
यस्य प्रतीतिमाधातुं लक्षणा समुपास्यते ॥ १४ ॥
फले शब्दैकगम्येत्र व्यञ्जनान्नापरा क्रिया ।
नाभिधा समयाभावाद्धेत्वभावान्न लक्षणा ॥ १५ ॥
लक्ष्यं न मुख्यं नाप्यत्र बाधो योगः फलेन नो ।
न प्रयोजनमेतस्मिन् न च शब्दः स्खलद्गतिः ॥ १६ ॥
एवमप्यनवस्था स्याद् या मूलक्षयकारिणी ।
प्रयोजनेन सहितं लक्षणीयं न युज्यते ॥ १७ ॥
ज्ञानस्य विषयो ह्यन्यः फलमन्यदुदाहृतम् ।
विशिष्टे लक्षणा नैवं विशेषाः स्युस्तु लक्षिते ॥ १८ ॥
अनेकार्थस्य शब्दस्य वाचकत्वे नियन्त्रिते ।
संयोगाद्यैरवाच्यार्थधीकृद्व्यापृतिरञ्जनम् ॥ १९ ॥
तद्युक्तो व्यञ्जकः शब्दो यत्सोर्थान्तरयुक् तथा ।
अर्थोपि व्यञ्जकस्तत्र सहकारितया मतः ॥ २० ॥
अर्थाः प्रोक्ताः पुरा तेषामर्थव्यञ्जकतोच्यते ।
वक्तृबोद्धव्यकाकूनां वाक्यवाच्यान्यसन्निधेः ॥ २१ ॥
प्रस्तावदेशकालादेर्वैशिष्ट्यात् प्रतिभाजुषाम् ।
योर्थस्यान्यार्थधीहेतुर्व्यापारो व्यक्तिरेव सा ॥ २२ ॥
शब्दप्रमाणवेद्योर्थो व्यनक्त्यर्थान्तरं यतः ।
अर्थस्य व्यञ्जकत्वे तच्छब्दस्य सहकारिता ॥ २३ ॥

अविवक्षितवाच्यो यस्तत्र वाच्यं भवेद्ध्वनौ ।
अर्थान्तरे सङ्क्रमितमत्यन्तं वा तिरस्कृतम् ॥ २४ ॥
विवक्षितं चान्यपरं वाच्यं यत्रापरस्तु सः ।
कोऽप्यलक्ष्यक्रमव्यङ्ग्यो लक्ष्यव्यङ्ग्यक्रमः परः ॥ २५ ॥
रसभावतदाभावभावशान्त्यादिरक्रमः ।
भिन्नो रसाद्यलङ्कारादलङ्कार्यतया स्थितः ॥ २६ ॥
कारणान्यथ कार्याणि सहकारीणि यानि च ।
रत्यादेः स्थायिनो लोके तानि चेन्नाट्यकाव्ययोः ॥ २७ ॥
विभावा अनुभावास्तत् कथ्यन्ते व्यभिचारिणः ।
व्यक्तः स तैर्विभावाद्यैः स्थायी भावो रसः स्मृतः ॥ २८ ॥
शृङ्गारहास्यकरुणरौद्रवीरभयानकाः ।
बीभत्साद्भुतसंज्ञौ चेत्यष्टौ नाट्ये रसाः स्मृताः ॥ २९ ॥
रतिर्हासश्च शोकश्च क्रोधोत्साहौ भयं तथा ।
जुगुप्सा विस्मयश्चेति स्थायिभावाः प्रकीर्तिताः ॥ ३० ॥
निर्वेदग्लानिशङ्काख्यास्तथासूया मदश्रमाः ।
आलस्यं चैव दैन्यं च चिन्ता मोहः स्मृतिर्धृतिः ॥ ३१ ॥
व्रीडा चपलता हर्ष आवेगो जडता तथा ।
गर्वो विषाद औत्सुक्यं निद्रापस्मार एव च ॥ ३२ ॥
सुप्तं प्रबोधोऽमर्षश्चाप्यवहित्थमथोग्रता ।
मतिर्व्याधिस्तथोन्मादस्तथा मरणमेव च ॥ ३३ ॥
त्रासश्चैव वितर्कश्च विज्ञेया व्यभिचारिणः ।
त्रयस्त्रिंशदमी भावाः समाख्यातास्तु नामतः ॥ ३४ ॥
निर्वेदस्थायिभावोऽस्ति शान्तोऽपि नवमो रसः ।
रतिर्देवादिविषया व्यभिचारी तथाञ्जितः ॥ ३५ ॥
भावः प्रोक्तस्तदाभासा अनौचित्यप्रवर्त्तिताः ।
भावस्य शान्तिरुदयः सन्धिः शबलता तथा ॥ ३६ ॥

मुख्ये रसेपि तेङ्गित्वं प्राप्नुवन्ति कदाचन ।
अनुस्वानाभसंलक्ष्यक्रमव्यङ्ग्यस्थितिस्तु यः ॥ ३७ ॥
शब्दार्थोभयशक्त्युत्थस्त्रिधा स कथितो ध्वनिः ।
अलङ्कारोथ वस्त्वेव शब्दाद्यत्रावभासते ॥ ३८ ॥
प्रधानत्वेन स ज्ञेयः शब्दशक्त्युद्भवो द्विधा ।
अर्थशक्त्युद्भवोप्यर्थो व्यञ्जकः संभवी स्वतः ॥ ३९ ॥
प्रौढोक्तिमात्रात्सिद्धो वा कवेस्तेनोम्भितस्य वा ।
वस्तु वालंकृतिर्वेति षड्भेदोसौ व्यनक्ति यत् ॥ ४० ॥
वस्त्वलंकारमथवा तेनायं द्वादशात्मकः ।
शब्दार्थोभयभूरेको भेदा अष्टादशास्य तत् ॥ ४१ ॥
रसादीनामनन्तत्वाद्भेद एको हि गण्यते ।
वाक्ये द्व्युत्थः पदेप्यन्ये प्रबन्धेप्यर्थशक्तिभूः ॥ ४२ ॥
पदैकदेशरचनावर्णेष्वपि रसादयः ।
भेदास्तदेकपञ्चाशत्तेषां चान्योन्ययोजने ॥ ४३ ॥
संकरेण त्रिरूपेण संसृष्ट्या चैकरूपया ।
वेदखाब्धिवियच्चन्द्राः शरेषुयुगलेन्दवः ॥ ४४ ॥
अगूढमपरस्याङ्गं वाच्यसिद्ध्यङ्गमस्फुटम् ।
सन्दिग्धतुल्यप्राधान्ये काक्वाक्षिप्तमसुन्दरम् ॥ ४५ ॥
व्यङ्ग्यमेवं गुणीभूतव्यङ्ग्यस्याष्टौ भिदाः स्मृताः ।
एषां भेदा यथायोगं वेदितव्याश्च पूर्ववत् ॥ ४६ ॥
सालङ्कारैर्ध्वनेस्तैश्च योगः संसृष्टिसङ्करैः ।
अन्योन्ययोगादेवं स्याद्भेदसंख्यातिभूयसी ॥ ४७ ॥
शब्दार्थचित्रं यत्पूर्वं काव्यद्वयमुदाहृतम् ।
गुणप्राधान्यतस्तत्र स्थितिश्चित्रार्थशब्दयोः ॥ ४८ ॥
मुख्यार्थहतिर्दोषो रसश्च मुख्यस्तदाश्रयाद्वाच्यः ।
उभयोपयोगिनः स्युः शब्दाद्यास्तेन तेष्वपि सः ॥ ४९ ॥

दुष्टं पदं श्रुतिकटु च्युतसंस्कृत्यप्रयुक्तमसमर्थम् ।
निहतार्थमनुचितार्थं निरर्थकमवाचकं त्रिधाऽश्लीलम्॥५०॥
सन्दिग्धमप्रतीतं ग्राम्यं नेयार्थमथ भवेत् क्लिष्टम् ।
अविमृष्टविधेयांशं विरुद्धमतिकृत्समासगतमेव ॥ ५१ ॥
अपास्य च्युतसंस्कारमसमर्थं निरर्थकम् ।
वाक्येपि दोषाः सन्त्येते पदस्यांशेपि केचन ॥ ५२ ॥
प्रतिकूलवर्णमुपहतलुप्तविसर्गं विसन्धि हतवृत्तम् ।
न्यूनाधिककथितपदं पतत्प्रकर्षं समाप्तपुनरात्तम् ॥ ५३ ॥
अर्धान्तरैकवाचकमभवन्मतयोगमनभिहितवाच्यम् ।
अपदस्थपदसमासं संकीर्णं गर्भितं प्रसिद्धिहतम् ॥ ५४ ॥
भग्नप्रक्रममक्रममममतपरार्थं च वाक्यमेव तथा ।
अर्थोपुष्टः कष्टो व्याहतपुनरुक्तदुष्क्रमग्राम्याः ॥ ५५ ॥
संदिग्धो निर्हेतुः प्रसिद्धिविद्याविरुद्धश्च ।
अनवीकृतः सनियमानियमविशेषा विशेषपरिवृत्ताः ॥ ५६ ॥
साकाङ्क्षोपदयुक्तः सहचरभिन्नः प्रकाशितविरुद्धः ।
विध्यनुवादायुक्तत्यक्तपुनःस्वीकृतोश्लीलः ॥ ५७ ॥
कर्णावतंसादिपदे कर्णादिध्वनिनिर्मितिः ।
संनिधानादिबोधार्थं स्थितेष्वेतत्समर्थनम् ॥ ५८ ॥
ख्यातेर्थे निर्हेतोरदुष्टतानुकरणे तु सर्वेषाम् ।
वक्त्राद्यौचित्यवशाद्दोषोपि गुणः क्वचित्क्वचिन्नोभौ ॥५९॥
व्यभिचारिरसस्थायिभावानां शब्दवाच्यता ।
कष्टकल्पनया व्यक्तिरनुभावविभावयोः ॥ ६० ॥
प्रतिकूलविभावादिग्रहो दीप्तिः पुनः पुनः ।
अकाण्डे प्रथनच्छेदावङ्गस्याप्यतिविस्तृतिः ॥ ६१ ॥
अङ्गिनोननुसंधानं प्रकृतीनां विपर्ययः ।
अनङ्गस्याभिधानं च रसे दोषाः स्युरीदृशाः ॥ ६२ ॥

न दोषः स्वपदेनोक्तावपि संचारिणः क्वचित् ।
संचार्यादेर्विरुद्धस्य बाध्यस्योक्तिर्गुणावहा ॥ ६३ ॥
आश्रयैक्ये विरुद्धो यः स कार्यो भिन्नसंश्रयः ।
रसान्तरेणान्तरितो नैरन्तर्येण यो रसः ॥ ६४ ॥
स्मर्यमाणो विरुद्धोपि साम्येनाथ विवक्षितः ।
अङ्गिन्यङ्गत्वमाप्तौ यौ तौ न दुष्टौ परस्परम् ॥ ६५ ॥
ये रसस्याङ्गिनो धर्माः शौर्यादय इवात्मनः ।
उत्कर्षहेतवस्ते स्युरचलस्थितयो गुणाः ॥ ६६ ॥
उपकुर्वन्ति तं सन्तं येङ्गद्वारेण जातुचित् ।
हारादिवदलंकारास्तेनुप्रासोपमादयः ॥ ६७ ॥
माधुर्यौजःप्रसादाख्यास्त्रयस्ते न पुनर्दश ।
आह्लादकत्वं माधुर्यं शृङ्गारे द्रुतिकारणम् ॥ ६८ ॥
करुणे विप्रलम्भे तच्छान्ते चातिशयान्वितम् ।
दीप्त्यात्मविस्तृतेर्हेतुरोजो वीररसस्थिति ॥ ६९ ॥
बीभत्सरौद्ररसयोस्तस्याधिक्यं क्रमेण च ।
शुष्केन्धनाग्निवत् स्वच्छजलवत्सहसैव यः ॥ ७० ॥
व्याप्नोत्यन्यत् प्रसादोसौ सर्वत्र विहितस्थितिः ।
गुणवृत्त्या पुनस्तेषां वृत्तिः शब्दार्थयोर्मता ॥ ७१ ॥
केचिदन्तर्भवन्त्येषु दोषत्यागात्परे श्रिताः ।
अन्ये भजन्ति दोषत्वं कुत्रचिन्न ततो दश ॥ ७२ ॥
तेन नार्थगुणा वाच्याः प्रोक्ताः शब्दगुणाश्च ये ।
वर्णाः समासो रचना तेषां व्यञ्जकतामिताः ॥ ७३ ॥
मूर्ध्नि वर्गान्त्यगाः स्पर्शा अटवर्गा रणौ लघू ।
आवृत्तिर्मध्यवृत्तिर्वा माधुर्ये घटना तथा ॥ ७४ ॥
योग आद्यतृतीयाभ्यामन्त्ययो रेण तुल्ययोः ।
टादिः शषौ वृत्तिदैर्घ्यं गुम्फ उद्धृत ओजसि ॥ ७५ ॥

श्रुतिमात्रेण शब्दात्तु येनार्थप्रत्ययो भवेत् ।
साधारणः समग्राणां स प्रसादो गुणो मतः ॥ ७६ ॥
वक्तृवाच्यप्रबन्धानामौचित्येन क्वचित्क्वचित् ।
रचनावृत्तिवर्णानामन्यथात्वमपीष्यते ॥ ७७ ॥
यदुक्तमन्यथा वाक्यमन्यथान्येन योज्यते ।
श्लेषेण काक्वा वा ज्ञेया सा वक्रोक्तिस्तथा द्विधा ॥ ७८ ॥
वर्णसाम्यमनुप्रासश् छेकवृत्तिगतो द्विधा ।
सोनेकस्य सकृत्पूर्व एकस्याप्यसकृत्परः ॥ ७९ ॥
माधुर्यव्यञ्जकैर्वर्णैरुपनागरिकोच्यते ।
ओजःप्रकाशकैस्तैस्तु परुषा कोमला परैः ॥ ८० ॥
केषांचिदेता वैदर्भीप्रमुखा रीतयो मताः ।
शाब्दस्तु लाटानुप्रासो भेदे तात्पर्यमात्रतः ॥ ८१ ॥
पदानां सः पदस्यापि वृत्तावन्यत्र तत्र वा ।
नाम्नः स वृत्त्यवृत्त्योश्च तदेवं पञ्चधा मतः ॥ ८२ ॥
अर्थे सत्यर्थभिन्नानां वर्णानां सा पुनः श्रुतिः ।
यमकं पादतद्भागवृत्ति तद्यात्यनेकताम् ॥ ८३ ॥
वाच्यभेदेन भिन्ना यद् युगपद्भाषणस्पृशः ।
श्लिष्यन्ति शब्दाः श्लेषोसावक्षरादिभिरष्टधा ॥ ८४ ॥
भेदाभावात्प्रकृत्यादेर्भेदोपि नवमो भवेत् ।
तच्चित्रं यत्र वर्णानां खड्गाद्याकृतिहेतुता ॥ ८५ ॥
पुनरुक्तवदाभासो विभिन्नाकारशब्दगा ।
एकार्थतेव शब्दस्य तथा शब्दार्थयोरयम् ॥ ८६ ॥
साधर्म्यमुपमा भेदे पूर्णा लुप्ता च साग्रिमा ।
श्रौत्यार्थी च भवेद्वाक्ये समासे तद्धिते तथा ॥ ८७ ॥
तद्वद् धर्मस्य लोपे स्यान्न श्रौती तद्धिते पुनः ।
उपमानानुपादाने वाक्यगाथ समासगा ॥ ८८ ॥

वादेर्लोपे समासे सा कर्माधारक्यचि क्यङि ।
कर्मकर्त्रोर्णमुल्येतद्द्विलोपे क्विप्समासगा ॥ ८९ ॥
धर्मोपमानयोर्लोपे वृत्तौ वाक्ये च दृश्यते ।
क्यचि वाद्युपमेयासे त्रिलोपे च समासगा ॥ ९० ॥
उपमानोपमेयत्वे एकस्यैवैकवाक्यगे ।
अनन्वयो विपर्यास उपमेयोपमा तयोः ॥ ९१ ॥
संभावनमथोत्प्रेक्षा प्रकृतस्य समेन यत् ।
ससंदेहस्तु भेदोक्तौ तदनुक्तौ च संशयः ॥ ९२ ॥
तद्रूपकमभेदो य उपमानोपमेययोः ।
समस्तवस्तुविषयं श्रौता आरोपिता यदा ॥ ९३ ॥
श्रौता आर्थाश्च ते यस्मिन्नेकदेशविवर्ति तत् ।
साङ्गमेतन् निरङ्गं तु शुद्धं माला तु पूर्ववत् ॥ ९४ ॥
नियतारोपणोपायः स्यादारोपः परस्य यः ।
तत्परंपरितं श्लिष्टे वाचके भेदभाजि वा ॥ ९५ ॥
प्रकृतं यन्निषिध्यान्यत् साध्यते सा त्वपह्नुतिः ।
श्लेषः स वाक्य एकस्मिन् यत्रानेकार्थता भवेत् ॥ ९६ ॥
परोक्तिर्भेदकैः श्लिष्टैः समासोक्तिर्निदर्शना ।
अभवन्वस्तुसंबन्ध उपमापरिकल्पकः ॥ ९७ ॥
स्वस्वहेत्वन्वयस्योक्तिः क्रिययैव च सापरा ।
अप्रस्तुतप्रशंसा या सा सैव प्रस्तुताश्रया ॥ ९८ ॥
कार्ये निमित्ते सामान्ये विशेषे प्रस्तुते सति ।
तदन्यस्य वचस्तुल्ये तुल्यस्येति च पञ्चधा ॥ ९९ ॥
निगीर्याध्यवसानं तु प्रकृतस्य परेण यत् ।
प्रस्तुतस्य यदन्यत्वं यद्यर्थोक्तौ च कल्पनम् ॥१००॥
कार्यकारणयोर्यश्च पौर्वापर्यविपर्ययः ।
विज्ञेयातिशयोक्तिः सा प्रतिवस्तूपमा तु सा ॥ १०१ ॥

सामान्यस्य द्विरेकस्य यत्र वाक्यद्वये स्थितिः ।
दृष्टान्तः पुनरेतेषां सर्वेषां प्रतिबिम्बनम् ॥ १०२ ॥
सकृद्वृत्तिस्तु धर्मस्य प्रकृताप्रकृतात्मनाम् ।
सैव क्रियासु बह्वीषु कारकस्येति दीपकम् ॥ १०३ ॥
मालादीपकमाद्यं चेद्यथोत्तरगुणावहम् ।
नियतानां सकृद्धर्मः सा पुनस्तुल्ययोगिता ॥ १०४ ॥
उपमानाद्यदन्यस्य व्यतिरेकः स एव सः ।
हेत्वोरुक्तावनुक्तीनां त्रये साम्ये निवेदिते ॥ १०५ ॥
शब्दार्थाभ्यामथाक्षिप्ते श्लिष्टे तद्वत्त्रिरष्ट तत् ।
निषेधो वक्तुमिष्टस्य यो विशेषाभिधित्सया ॥ १०६ ॥
वक्ष्यमाणोक्तविषयः स आक्षेपो द्विधा मतः ।
क्रियायाः प्रतिषेधेपि फलव्यक्तिर्विभावना ॥ १०७ ॥
विशेषोक्तिरखण्डेषु कारणेषु फलावचः ।
यथासंख्यं क्रमेणैव क्रमिकाणां समन्वयः ॥ १०८ ॥
सामान्यं वा विशेषो वा तदन्येन समर्थ्यते ।
यत्तु सोर्थान्तरन्यासः साधर्म्येणेतरेण वा ॥ १०९ ॥
विरोधः सोविरोधेपि विरुद्धत्वेन यद्वचः ।
जातिश्चतुर्भिर्जात्याद्यैर्विरुद्धा स्याद्गुणैस्त्रिभिः ॥ ११० ॥
क्रिया द्वाभ्यामपि द्रव्यं द्रव्येणैवेति ते दश ।
स्वभावोक्तिस्तु डिम्भादेः स्वक्रियारूपवर्णनम् ॥ १११ ॥
व्याजस्तुतिर्मुखे निन्दा स्तुतिर्वा रूढिरन्यथा ।
सा सहोक्तिः सहार्थस्य बलादेकं द्विवाचकम् ॥ ११२ ॥
विनोक्तिः सा विनान्येन यत्रान्यः सन्न नेतरः ।
परिवृत्तिर्विनिमयो योर्थानां स्यात्समासमैः ॥ ११३ ॥
प्रत्यक्षा इव यद्भावाः क्रियन्ते भूतभाविनः ।
तद्भाविकं काव्यलिङ्गं हेतोर्वाक्यपदार्थता ॥ ११४ ॥

पर्यायोक्तं विना वाच्यवाचकत्वेन यद्वचः ।
उदात्तं वस्तुनः संपत् महतां चोपलक्षणम् ॥ ११५ ॥
तत्सिद्धिहेतावेकस्मिन् यत्रान्यत्तत्करं भवेत् ।
समुच्चयोसौ स त्वन्यो युगपद् या गुणक्रियाः ॥ ११६ ॥
एकं क्रमेणानेकस्मिन् पर्यायोन्यस्ततोन्यथा ।
अनुमानं तदुक्तं यत् साध्यसाधनयोर्वचः ॥ ११७ ॥
विशेषणैर्यत्साकूतैरुक्तिः परिकरस्तु सः ।
व्याजोक्तिश्छद्मनोद्भिन्नवस्तुरूपनिगूहनम् ॥ ११८ ॥
किंचित् पृष्टमपृष्टं वा कथितं यत् प्रकल्पते ।
तादृगन्यव्यपोहाय परिसंख्या तु सा स्मृता ॥ ११९ ॥
यथोत्तरं चेत् पूर्वस्य पूर्वस्यार्थस्य हेतुता ।
तदा कारणमाला स्यात् क्रियया तु परस्परम् ॥ १२० ॥
वस्तुनोर्जननेन्योन्यमुत्तरश्रुतिमात्रतः ।
प्रश्नस्योन्नयनं यत्र क्रियते तत्र वा सति ॥ १२१ ॥
असकृद् यदसंभाव्यमुत्तरं स्यात् तदुत्तरम् ।
कुतोपि लक्षितः सूक्ष्मोप्यर्थोऽन्यस्मै प्रकाश्यते ॥ १२२ ॥
धर्मेण केनचिद् यत्र तत् सूक्ष्मं परिचक्षते ।
उत्तरोत्तरमुत्कर्षो भवेत्सारः परावधिः ॥ १२३ ॥
भिन्नदेशतयात्यन्तं कार्यकारणभूतयोः ।
युगपद्धर्मयोर्यत्र ख्यातिः सा स्यादसंगतिः ॥ १२४ ॥
समाधिः सुकरं कार्यं कारणान्तरयोगतः ।
समं योग्यतया योगो यदि संभावितः क्वचित् ॥ १२५ ॥
क्वचिद्यदतिवैधर्म्यान्न श्लेषो घटनामियात् ।
कर्तुः क्रियाफलावाप्तिर्नैवानर्थश्च यद्भवेत् ॥ १२६ ॥
गुणक्रियाभ्यां कार्यस्य कारणस्य गुणक्रिये ।
क्रमेण च विरुद्धे यत् स एष विषमो मतः ॥ १२७ ॥

महतोर्यन्महीयांसावाश्रिताश्रययोः क्रमात् ।
आश्रयाश्रयिणौ स्यातां तनुत्वेप्यधिकं तु तत् ॥ १२८ ॥
प्रतिपक्षमशक्तेन प्रतिकर्तुं तिरस्क्रिया ।
या तदीयस्य तत्स्तुत्यै प्रत्यनीकं तदुच्यते ॥ १२९ ॥
समेन लक्ष्मणा वस्तु वस्तुना यन्निगूह्यते ।
निजेनागन्तुना वापि तन्मीलितमिति स्मृतम् ॥ १३० ॥
स्थाप्यतेपोह्यते वापि यथापूर्वं परं परम् ।
विशेषणतया यत्र वस्तु सैकावली द्विधा ॥ १३१ ॥
यथानुभवमर्थस्य दृष्टे तत्सदृशे स्मृतिः ।
स्मरणं भ्रान्तिमानन्यसंवित्तत्तुल्यदर्शने ॥ १३२ ॥
आक्षेप उपमानस्य प्रतीपमुपमेयता ।
तस्यैव यदि वा कल्प्या तिरस्कारनिबन्धनम् ॥ १३३ ॥
प्रस्तुतस्य यदन्येन गुणसाम्यविवक्षया ।
ऐकात्म्यं बध्यते योगात्तत्सामान्यमिति स्मृतम् ॥ १३४ ॥
विना प्रसिद्धमाधारमाधेयस्य व्यवस्थितिः ।
एकात्मा युगपद्वृत्तिरेकस्यानेकगोचरा ॥ १३५ ॥
अन्यत् प्रकुर्वतः कार्यमशक्यस्यान्यवस्तुनः ।
तथैव करणं चेति विशेषस्त्रिविधः स्मृतः ॥ १३६ ॥
स्वमुत्सृज्य गुणं योगादत्युज्ज्वलगुणस्य यत् ।
वस्तु तद्‌गुणतामेति भण्यते स तु तद्‌गुणः ॥ १३७ ॥
तद्रूपाननुहारश्चेदस्य तत् स्यादतद्‌गुणः ।
यद्यथा साधितं केनाप्यपरेण तदन्यथा ॥ १३८ ॥
तथैव यद्विधीयेत स व्याघात इति स्मृतः ।
सेष्टा संसृष्टिरेतेषां भेदेन यदिह स्थितिः ॥ १३९ ॥
अविश्रान्तिजुषामात्मन्यङ्गाङ्गित्वं तु संकरः ।
एकस्य च ग्रहे न्यायदोषाभावादनिश्चयः ॥ १४० ॥

स्फुटमेकत्र विषये शब्दार्थालंकृतिद्वयम् ।
व्यवस्थितं च तेनासौ त्रिरूपः परिकीर्तितः ॥ १४१ ॥
एषां दोषा यथायोगं संभवन्तोपि केचन ।
उक्तेष्वन्तर्भवन्तीति न पृथक् प्रतिपादिताः ॥ १४२ ॥

॥ इति काव्यप्रकाशीयकारिकावली समाप्ता ॥

Variant Readings from the MS No. 42290 of the काव्यप्रकाशकारिकावली of the सरस्वतीभवन Library of the वाराणसेय-संस्कृत-विश्वविद्यालय

कारिका No. (According to the MS.)	Readings in the Printed texts.	Readings in the manuscript No. 42290.
१	There is no मङ्गलश्लोक	दुर्धीदूषणनागेन्द्रमृगेन्द्रस्य गुरोः पदम् । नत्वा व्यातन्यते वृत्तिर्मम्मटेन विपश्चिता ।
२३	व्यञ्जकत्वे तच्छब्दस्य सहकारिता।	व्यञ्जकत्वे हि तदन्यसहकारिता ।
२६	(क) रसभावतदाभावभावशान्त्यादिरक्रमः। (ख) रसभावतदाभासभाव—	रसभास-तदाभास-भावभासादिरक्रमः ।
२७	रत्यादेः	रसादेः ।
३२	जडता तथा	जडता मता
३३	प्रबोधोमर्षश्च	सुसंविबोधोमर्षश्च
३५	निर्वेदस्थायिभावोस्ति शान्तोपि नवमो रसः ।	It is wanting in this MS.

३६	तदाभासा अनौचित्यप्रवर्त्तिकाः ।	–भासानौचित्यप्रवर्तिताः ।
३९	अर्थशक्त्युद्भवोप्यर्थः ।	अर्थशक्त्युद्भवेप्यर्थो ।
४२	अनन्तत्वात् ।	अनंत्यत्वात् ।
४८	चित्रार्थशब्दयोः ।	शब्दार्थचित्रयोः
४९	शब्दाद्यास्तेन तेष्वपि सः ।	शब्दाद्या तेष्वपि सः ।
५१	समासगतमेव ।	समासगतमेव । वाक्येप्याह ।
५४	समासं संकीर्णम् ।	समाससंकीर्णम् ।
	परार्थं च वाक्यमेव तथा ।	परार्थं वाक्यमेव च तथा । अर्थदोषान् विशदयति ।
५६	निर्हेतुः	निर्हेतु ।
५९	दोषोपि गुणःक्वचित्क्वचिन्नोभौ ।	दोषोपि गुणः क्वचिन्नोभौ । रसदोषानाह ।
६०	०भावानां शब्दवाच्यता ।	०भावानां व्यभिशब्दवाच्यता ।
६१	अङ्गस्याप्यतिविस्तृतिः ।	अंगस्याप्यतिविस्मृतिः ।
६२		श्लोकमध्ये रसदोषापवादमाह ।
६७	येङ्गद्वारेण	योगद्वारेण ।
		श्लोकान्ते गुणानाह ।

६७		श्लोकान्ते—एषां लक्षणमाह ।
७०	शुष्केन्धनाग्निवत् ।	शुष्केन्धननादिवत् ।
७१	दोषत्यागात्परे श्रिताः ।	दोषत्यागात्परोस्थिता ।
७४	आद्यतृतीयाभ्याम् ।	आद्ययोगतृतीयाभ्याम्
७६	गुणोमतः	गुणः स्मृतः —
७७		अष्टमः—अथ शब्दालङ्कारः ।
७८	वर्णसाम्यमनुप्रासः	सवर्णसाम्यमनुप्रासः ।
८०	केषांचिदेता वैदर्भी ।	एषांचिदेता वैदर्भी ।
८७	तद्धिते तथा ।	तद्धिते यथा ।
९०	विपर्यास उपमेयोपमा तयोः ।	विपर्यास उपमानोपमेययोः ।
९४	परस्य यः ।	परस्परः ।
९५	श्लेषः स वाक्य एकस्मिन् ।	श्लेषः स वाच्य एकस्मिन् ।
९६	अभवन् वस्तु०	अभवंत्वस्तु० ।
९७	क्रिययैव च सापरा ।	क्रिययैव हि सापरा ।
१०६	०विषयः ।	०विषये ।

१०८	वा तदन्येन समर्थ्यते ।	वा यदन्यो न समर्थ्यते । यत्र
११२	सन्न नेतरः ।	सन्न चेतरः ।
११४	०वाचकत्वेन यद्वचः ।	वाचकत्वेन वस्तु यत् ॥
११७	परिकरस्तु सः ।	परिकरस्तथा ।
१२६	गुणक्रिये ।	गुणे क्रियाभ्याम्
१२९	समेन लक्ष्मणा वस्तुवस्तुना यन्निगूह्यते ।	समेनवलक्षणा वस्तु वस्तुना यद्विगूह्यते ।
१३०	परंपरम् । विशेषणतया यत्र वस्तु ।	परस्परम् । विशेषणतया न तद्वस्तु ।
१३१	यथानुभवमर्थस्य ।	यथानुभवदृष्टस्य ।
१३६	स्वमुत्सृज्य गुणं योगादत्युज्ज्वल-गुणस्य यत् ।	स्वमुत्सृज्य गुणा योगादित्युज्ज्वलगुणस्य तत् ।
१३८	यदिह स्थितिः ।	यदिहा स्थितिः ।
१४०	स्फुटमेकत्र विषये ।	स्फुटमेकार्थविषये ।
१४२	तमसंख्यकः श्लोकोयं नास्ति मुद्रितेषु ग्रन्थेषु ।	इत्येष मार्गोभिन्नोप्यभिन्नरूपो भासते यत् । न तद्विचित्रं यदमुत्र सम्यक्विनिर्मितिः संघटनेन हेतुः ।

काव्यप्रकाशः

प्रथम उल्लासः

ग्रन्थारम्भे विघ्नविघाताय समुचितेष्टदेवता ग्रन्थकृत् परामृशति–

नियतिकृतनियमरहितां ह्लादैकमयीमनन्यपरतन्त्राम् ।
नवरसरुचिरां निर्मितिमादधती भारती कवेर्जयति ॥ १ ॥

नियतिशक्त्या नियतरूपा सुखदुःखमोहस्वभावा परमाण्वाद्युपादानकर्मादिसहकारिकारणपरतन्त्रा षड्रसा न च हृद्यैव तैः, तादृशी ब्रह्मणो निर्मितिर्निर्माणम् । एतद्विलक्षणा तु कविवाङ्-निर्मितिः । अत एव जयति । जयत्यर्थेन च नमस्कार आक्षिप्यते इति तां प्रत्यस्मि प्रणत इति लभ्यते ॥१॥

KĀVYAPRAKĀŚA

CHAPTER I

[OF THE AIM, SOURCE AND KINDS OF POETRY.]

In the beginning, the author invokes the appropriate divinity for the destruction of all obstacles.

Splendid is the poet's speech, comprehending a creation which is without the restraints of Nature's laws, full of pleasure alone, independent of other helps, rejoicing in a nine-fold Rasa.—(1)

Brahmā's creation is subject to the laws of Nature, is full of pleasure, pain and delusion, is dependent upon material and co-operative causes, such as atoms and actions (matter and motion) respectively—has only six tastes, and these, too, not always of an agreeable nature. The creation of the poet's speech, on the contrary, is different, and hence is 'splendid'—an expression which implies reverence to it. 1.

इहाभिधेयं सप्रयोजनमित्याह—

काव्यं यशसेऽर्थकृते व्यवहारविदे शिवेतरक्षतये ।
सद्यः परनिर्वृतये कान्तासंमिततयोपदेशयुजे ॥ २ ॥

कालिदासादीनामिव यश श्रीहर्षादेर्धावकादीनामिव धनम् राजादिगतोचिताचारपरिज्ञानम् आदित्यादेर्मयूरादीनामिवानर्थनिवारणम् ।

सकलप्रयोजनमौलिभूतं समनन्तरमेव रसास्वादनसमुद्भूतं विगलितवेद्यान्तरमानन्दम् प्रभुसंमितशब्दप्रधानवेदादिशास्त्रेभ्य. सुहृत्संमितार्थतात्पर्यवत्पुराणादीतिहासेभ्यश्च शब्दार्थयोर्गुणभावेन रसाङ्गभूतव्यापारप्रवणतया विलक्षणं

The author now states the subject-matter, together with its aims :

Poetry brings fame and riches, knowledge of the ways of the world and relief from evils, instant and perfect happiness, and counsel sweet as from the lips of a beloved consort.—(2)

Fame—as to Kālidāsa and others , wealth—as to Dhāvaka and other poets, from Śrī Harsa and other kings ; knowledge of rights and usages proper to kings and others ; relief from evils—as to Mayūra, whose hymn to the sun brought him a cure.

The chief aim of poetry, however, is the attainment of the pure unmixed pleasure that follows instantaneously on the sensing of Rasa. When poetry exercises its full functions, it helps the development of the various Rasas (Emotions), sublating the direct effects of the word and its meaning. As such poetry differs from the Veda, in which the word, in the form of a master's command, predominates ; it differs also from the Purānas, in which the predominant element is friendly counsel (not to be

यत् काव्य लोकोत्तरवर्णनानिपुणकविकर्म तत् कान्तेव सरसतापादनेनाभिमुखीकृत्य रामादिवद्वर्तितव्यं न रावणादिवदित्युपदेशं च यथायोगं कवेः सहृदयस्य च करोतीति सर्वथा तत्र यतनीयम् ॥२॥

एवमस्य प्रयोजनमुक्त्वा कारणमाह—

शक्तिर्निपुणता लोकशास्त्रकाव्याद्यवेक्षणात् ।
काव्यज्ञशिक्षयाभ्यास इति हेतुस्तदुद्भवे ॥ ३ ॥

शक्तिः कवित्वबीजरूपः संस्कारविशेषः यां विना काव्यं न प्रसरेत् प्रसृतं वा उपहसनीयं स्यात् । लोकस्य स्थावरजङ्गमात्मकलोकवृत्तस्य । शास्त्राणा छन्दोव्याकरणाभिधानकोशकलाचतुर्वर्गगजतुरगखड्गादिलक्षणग्रन्थानाम् । काव्यानां

---

followed literally). Such poetry is the work of poets, clever in depicting things in a manner passing the comprehension of ordinary men, it offers to other poets and cultured men counsel most persuasively, like a beloved wife, by means of a moving tenderness in the manner of it (that is, in the words)—counsel such as that one should behave like Rāma and not like Rāvana. As such, poetry is by all means to be studied and cultivated. 2

Having defined the aims, the author now states the source of poetry.

Poetic genius, knowledge born of a study of the world, of sciences and of poems, and the practice of the teachings of those versed in writing poetry—these three together constitute the source of poetry. (3)

(1) Poetic genius, which may be called the germ of poetry. This is a peculiar faculty, without which there could either be no poetical work or, if there were, would be ridiculous.

च महाकविसंबन्धिनाम् । आदिग्रहणादितिहासाना च विमर्शनाद्व्युत्पत्ति. । काव्यं कर्तुं विचारयितु च ये जानन्ति तदुपदेशेन करणे योजने च पौनःपुन्येन प्रवृत्तिरिति । त्रयः समुदिता. न तु व्यस्ताः तस्य काव्यस्योद्भवे निर्माणे समुल्लासे च हेतुर्न तु हेतवं ॥३॥

एवमस्य कारणमुक्त्वा स्वरूपमाह—

तददोषौ शब्दार्थौ सगुणावनलंकृती पुनः क्वापि ।

दोषगुणालंकारा. वक्ष्यन्ते । क्वापीत्यनेनैतदाह यत् सर्वत्र सालंकारौ क्वचित्तु स्फुटालंकारविरहेपि न काव्यत्वहानि. । यथा

---

(2) Facility in composition, arising from a careful study of—'objects,' *i. e.*, of all kinds of objects, animate as well as inanimate ; of the sciences, such as prosody, grammar, lexicons, fine arts, the sciences dealing with the four ends of life, and the sciences dealing with the distinguishing qualities of elephants, horses and the various weapons of warfare , and of poems, the works of great poets. The word 'ādi' implies 'history' and the rest.

(3) Frequent attempt at writing poetry, under the direction of men capable of writing and appreciating it.

The above three *conjointly*, and not *singly*, constitute the *source*, and not the *sources*, of poetry. 3.

Having thus stated the cause, the author next describes the nature or character of poetry :

It consists in word and sense—without faults and with merits and excellences of style—which may at times be without Figures of Speech. (4)

यः कौमारहरः स एव हि वरस्ता एव चैत्रक्षपास्-
ते चोन्मीलितमालतीसुरभयः प्रौढाः कदम्बानिलाः ।
सा चैवास्मि तथापि तत्र सुरतव्यापारलीलाविधौ
रेवारोधसि वेतसीतरुतले चेतः समुत्कण्ठते ॥ १ ॥

अत्र स्फुटो न कश्चिदलंकारः। रसस्य च प्राधान्यान्नालंकारता।

तद्भेदान् क्रमेणाह—

इदमुत्तममतिशयिनि व्यङ्ग्ये वाच्याद्ध्वनिर्बुधैः कथितः ॥४॥

The faults (grammatical and other mistakes), merits (*mādhurya*, etc.) and ornaments of speech (*Upamā*, etc.) will be described later on (chapters VII, VIII, IX and X)

The words 'at times' mean that, while generally, poetry has some Figure or other, yet, if in some case there be no figure directly expressed, that omission alone need not make the composition unpoetical. For instance—

" My husband is the same as when from me he
stole my virginity ; these lovely Chaitra-nights
are the same ; this breeze, too, comes, as of old
from the Kadamba grove, laden with the fragrance
of Mālatī blooms ; and I, too, am the same.
Yet still my heart longs for Love's dalliances
amidst the citron-bowers of Revā's banks."

In this verse, there is no explicit figure of speech The Rasa (erotic) being the primary element, there cannot be said to be a Figure (because, as the *Pradīpa* says, the Rasa is not in a subordinate position, and therefore, there is no *Rasavadalankāra* , a Rasa is called a Figure only when it occupies a subordinate position) 3

The author next states the divisions of poetry.

इदमिति काव्यम् । बुधैर्वैयाकरणैः प्रधानभूतस्फोट-रूपव्यङ्ग्यव्यञ्जकस्य शब्दस्य ध्वनिरिति व्यवहारः कृतः । ततस्तन्मतानुसारिभिरन्यैरपि न्यग्भावितवाच्यव्यङ्ग्यव्यञ्जन-क्षमस्य शब्दार्थयुगलस्य । यथा—

निःशेषच्युतचन्दनं स्तनतटं निर्मृष्टरागोऽधरो
नेत्रे दूरमनञ्जने पुलकिता तन्वी तवेयं तनुः ।
मिथ्यावादिनि दूति बान्धवजनस्याज्ञातपीडागमे
वापी स्नातुमितो गतासि न पुनस्तस्याधमस्यान्तिकम् ॥२॥

अत्र तदन्तिकमेव रन्तु गतासीति प्राधान्येनाधमपदेन व्यज्यते ॥४॥

The poetry in which the suggested meaning dominates the expressed is poetry of the best kind, called 'Dhvani' by the learned—(4)

By the learned—that is by the grammarians, that word is called *Dhvani* which suggests the *sphota*, which is all-important (inasmuch as it is through this *sphota* that a word conveys its meaning), others carry this theory of the grammarians farther still, and apply the word *Dhvani* not only to words, but also to sense, capable of suggesting meanings other than the directly expressed ones. As an instance of *Dhvani*, we have—

"The sandal-paste has vanished from thy breast, its colour has fled from thy lip; thine eyes have lost their jetty fringing dye—and all thy slender frame is quivering with hair on end. Thus I learn, O false friend, that knowest not the approach of thy friend's sufferings, that thou hast been only to the tank to bathe and not to that mean wretch."

Here the words 'mean wretch' suggest the real meaning 'thou hadst gone to dally in my lover's company.' 4.

अतादृशि गुणीभूतव्यङ्ग्यं व्यङ्ग्ये तु मध्यमम् ।

अतादृशि वाच्यादनतिशायिनि । यथा—

ग्रामतरुणं तरुण्या नववञ्जुलमञ्जरीसनाथकरम् ।
पश्यन्त्या भवति मुहुर्नितरां मलिना मुखच्छाया ॥ ३ ॥

अत्र वञ्जुललतागृहे दत्तसंकेता न गतेति व्यङ्ग्यं गुणीभूतं तदपेक्षया वाच्यस्यैव चमत्कारित्वात् ॥

शब्दचित्रं वाच्यचित्रमव्यङ्ग्यं त्ववरं स्मृतम् ॥ ५ ॥

चित्रमिति गुणालंकारयुक्तम् । अव्यङ्ग्यमिति स्फुट-प्रतीयमानार्थरहितम् । अवरम् अधमम । यथा—

स्वच्छन्दोच्छलदच्छकच्छकुहरच्छातेतराम्वुच्छटा-
मूर्छन्मोहमहर्षिहर्षविहितस्नानाह्निकाह्नाय वः ।

When the suggested meaning is not dominant, as described above, the poetry is but of middle excellence, and is called the Poetry of Subordinate Suggestion—(5)

Example.—"There is a cloud on the face of the young damsel at the sight of the country youth, with a bunch of fresh Vañjula flowers."

Here the suggested meaning—'thou hadst promised to bear me company in the Vañjula-bower, but thou never didst go there,' is subordinate to the more beautiful expressed meaning 'cloud on the face.'

Non-suggestive poetry, consisting of fanciful words and meanings, is of the inferior kind called 'Fanciful' by the learned.—(5)

Fanciful—that, is possessing 'merits' and 'figures,' non-suggestive, *i.e.*, devoid of any clearly suggested meaning, 'inferior'—of the lowest kind. Example:

svachchhandochchhaladachchhakachchhakuharachchhātetarāmbuchchhaṭā mūrchhanmohamaharṣiharṣavihitasnānāhnikāhnāya vaḥ ।

भिद्यादुद्यदुदारदर्दुरदरीदीर्घादरिद्रद्रुम-
द्रोहोद्रेकमहोर्मिमेदुरमदा मन्दाकिनी मन्दताम् ॥ ४ ॥

विनिर्गतं मानदमात्ममन्दिराद् भवत्युपश्रुत्य यदृच्छयापि यम् ।
ससंभ्रमेन्द्रद्रुतपातितार्गला निमीलिताक्षीव भियामरावती ॥ ५ ॥

इति काव्यप्रकाशे काव्यस्य प्रयोजनकारणस्वरूपविशेष-
निर्णयो नाम प्रथम उल्लास. ॥ १ ॥

---

bhıdyādudyadudāradardıı adarī dı ghādaı īdradı ıma-
dı ohodrekamahoı mımedıı amadā mandākınī mandatām ॥

"May Gangā, the dıvıne, all your doubts and errors remove !—Gangā, on whose sacred banks the happy Rsıs perform theır daıly rıtes who have theır delusıons washed away by the lovely sparklıng of water dashıng agaınst the rocky bank-holes full of bıg frogs, whose pııde ıs enhanced by the hıgh waves rısıng on account of the wıde-spreadıng trees havıng fallen ın."

And agaın :—*vınırgataın mānadamātmamandıı ād*
bhavatyupaśı utya yadrıhıbhayāpı yam ।
sasaınbhı amendı adrutapātıtārgalā
nımīlıtākṣīva bhıyāmaı āvatī ॥

(Full of fear as soon as Amaıāvatī heaıs that he has moved beyond hıs palace-gates—the pııde of all the Demon race—though ıt may be put for a pleasure stroll, her gates are baıred up ın all haste and hurıy by agitated Indıa and she wears the aspect of a maıden wıth closed eyes.) 5.

Thus ends Chapter I, ın whıch are determıned the aım, source and natuıe of Poetry.

द्वितीय उल्लास:

क्रमेण शब्दार्थयो स्वरूपमाह–

स्याद्वाचको लाक्षणिक: शब्दोत्र व्यञ्जकस्त्रिधा ।

अत्रेति काव्ये । एषां स्वरूप वक्ष्यते ।।

वाच्यादयस्तदर्था: स्यु:

वाच्यलक्ष्यव्यङ्ग्या. ।।

तात्पर्यार्थोपि केषुचित् ।। ६ ।।

आकाङक्षायोग्यतासंनिधिवशाद्वक्ष्यमाणस्वरूपाणां पदार्थानां समन्वये तात्पर्यार्थो विशेषवपुरपदार्थोपि वाक्यार्थ समुल्लसतीत्यभिहितान्वयवादिना मतम् ।।

वाच्य एव वाक्यार्थ इत्यन्विताभिधानवादिन. ।।६।।

CHAPTER II

[OF THE NATURE OF WORDS AND THEIR MEANINGS.]

The author desciibes, in due oidei, the nature of words and their sense :—

Words heie aie of three kinds—the Expressive, the Indicative and the Suggestive.

'*Here*' in poetiy ,—the exact nature of these is going to be defined later on.

The meanings thereof are the Expressed and so forth.

That is, the *Expressed*, the *Indicated* and the *Suggested*.

According to some, the Import also—(6)

The opinion held by the *Abhihitānvayavādin Mīmāṃsakas* (the followeis of Kumārila) is that when the denotations of a number of words—which aie going to be described later on—become related together, through 'mutual requiiement,' 'compatibility' and 'proximity,' there appeais a iesultant in the shape of the 'meaning of the sentence,'—which is not expiessed by any single word constituting that sentence, and which, being, on that account, of a peculiar character, comes to be called by the name '*Tātparyārtha*' or 'Import'.

The *Anvitābhidhānavādins* (followers of Prabhākara) on the other hand, hold that the 'meaning of the sentence' is the *expressed* meaning of the words themselves.

सर्वेषां प्रायशोऽर्थानां व्यञ्जकत्वमपीष्यते ।

तत्र वाच्यस्य यथा—

माए घरोवअरणं अज्ज हु णत्थि त्ति साहिअं तुमए ।
ता भण कि करणिज्जं एमेअ ण वासरो ठाइ ॥ ६ ॥

अत्र स्वैरविहारार्थिनीति व्यज्यते ।

लक्ष्यस्य यथा—

साहेन्ती सहि सुहअं खणे खणे दुम्मिआसि मज्झकए ।
सब्भावणेहकरणिज्जसरिसअं दाव विरइअं तुमए ॥ ७ ॥

[By the former view, each word of the sentence expresses its meaning, and these word-meanings, becoming related together, give rise to the 'meaning of the sentence',—while by the latter view the connected meaning of the sentence is also expressed by the words themselves, as, according to this view, words have no meaning apart from the sentence in which they occur]

Almost all the various kinds of meanings are held to be suggestive also.

As an example of 'suggestion' by the *Expressed* meaning, we have the following :—

"You said, O mother, that house-hold requisites are wanting. Say, then, what is to be done? Day-light will not long continue";—where the meaning *suggested* is that the woman speaking is desirous of roaming about for enjoyment. 6.

[This suggestion has been inferred through the character of the speaker, who is known to be *a woman of loose character*, if it came from a virtuous person, the speech would convey no such suggestion at all.]

As an example of suggestion by the *Indicated* meaning, we have the following :—

अत्र मत्प्रियं रमयन्त्या त्वया शत्रुत्वमाचरितमिति लक्ष्यम् । तेन च कामुकविषयं सापराधत्वप्रकाशनं व्यङ्ग्यम् । व्यङ्ग्यस्य यथा—

उअ णिच्चलणिप्पंदा भिसिणीपत्तम्मि रेहइ वलाआ ।
णिम्मलमरगअभाअणपरिट्ठिआ संखसुत्तिव्व ॥ ८ ॥

अत्र निष्पन्दत्वेन आश्वस्तत्वम् । तेन च जनरहितत्वम् । अतः संकेतस्थानमेतदिति कयाचित् कंचित्प्रत्युच्यते । अथवा मिथ्या वदसि न त्वमत्रागतोभूरिति व्यज्यते ॥

"O friend ! you have for my sake been put to great trouble in having to pursue that handsome man ; but what you have done was prompted only by your goodness, kindness and affection for me ;"—where the meaning *Indicated* (by the clear marks of infidelity perceived by the speaker) that ' by giving the pleasure of your company to my beloved, you have acted like my enemy ' ;—and what is *suggested* by this indicated meaning is that the lover has proved unfaithful to his own beloved (by misbehaving with her friend).

[This suggestion is based upon the fact of the speaker being the beloved of the man to whom she had sent messages through her friend.]

As an example of *suggestion* by the *Suggested* meaning we have the following :—

" See, the white crane, still and unperturbed, is shining on the lotus-leaf like a conch-shell resting on a dish of flawless emerald." The speaker says *expressly* that the bird is sitting quiet, unmoved, and *suggests* thereby the security of the spot, betokening the absence of intruders ; the *suggestion*, therefore, is that the spot is just suited for their meeting. On the other hand, the suggestion

वाचकादीनां क्रमेण स्वरूपमाह

साक्षात्संकेतितं योर्थमभिधत्ते स वाचकः ॥ ७ ॥

इहागृहीतसंकेतस्य शब्दस्यार्थप्रतीतेरभावात्संकेतसहाय एव शब्दोर्थविशेष प्रतिपादयतीति यस्य यत्राव्यवधानेन संकेतो गृह्यते स तस्य वाचकः ॥७॥

सङ्केतितश्चतुर्भेदो जात्यादिर्जातिरेव वा ।

यद्यप्यर्थक्रियाकारितया प्रवृत्तिनिवृत्तियोग्या व्यक्तिरेव तथाप्यानन्त्याद व्यभिचाराच्च तत्र संकेतः कर्तुं न युज्यत इति गौः शुक्लश्चलो डित्थ इत्यादीना विषयविभागो न प्राप्नोतीति च । तदुपाधावेव संकेतः ।

---

may be, "since the bird is sitting so peacefully, you could not have come here ere this; your protestation that you had come here is consequently false."

[This suggestion is based upon the fact of the two interlocutors being lovers.]

The author now proceeds to describe in due order the character of the *Expressive* and other kinds of words :—

That which denotes the direct conventional meaning is the 'Expressive' word.—(7)

As a matter of fact, in ordinary parlance, there is no comprehension of the meaning of a word, the convention regarding whose denotation is not known; thus it is only when the word is helped by its *usage* that it expresses a certain meaning; and when the conventional denotation is apprehended directly, without the intervention of any other agency, the word is said to be 'expressive' of that denotation or meaning. 7.

The conventional denotation is four-fold, consisting of Community and the rest,—or (according to some) Community alone.

उपाधिश्च द्विविध·—वस्तुधर्मो वक्तृयदृच्छासंनिवेशितश्च। वस्तुधर्मोपि द्विविध.–सिद्धः साध्यश्च। सिद्धोपि द्विविधः—पदार्थस्य प्राणप्रदो विशेषाधानहेतुश्च। तत्राद्यो जातिः। उक्तं हि वाक्यपदीये—"न हि गौः स्वरूपेण गौर्नाप्यगौः। गोत्वाभिसंबन्धात्तु गौः" इति।

Though in every case it is the individual that is endowed with intelligent activity, and as such capable of acting and desisting from action ;—yet it is not right to restrict the conventional denotation to that alone, as this would make the convention either indefinite (if it were applied to *all* individuals, whose number is infinite) or wrong (if it were restricted to any one or only a few individuals, and hence not applicable to other individuals) ; and also because (if the convention were restricted to individuals alone), no such distinction or differentiation would be possible as we have in the expression—'This (*a*) *ox* (community) which is (*b*) *white* (attribute) and (*c*) *Ḍittha* (by name) is (*d*) *walking* (action).'

[As *per hypotheses*, every one of these four words would denote the individual only, which is one and the same.]

For these reasons the only reasonable course is to take the conventional denotation as appertaining only to the characteristic appurtenant to the individual.

This characteristic of things is of two kinds—(*a*) that which belongs to the thing by its very nature and (*b*) that which is fastened upon it by the speaker ; the former of these again is of two kinds—(*c*) that which is an accomplished entity and (*d*) that which has got to be accomplished ; the former of these again, is of two kinds—(*e*) that which constitutes the very essence of the thing denoted by the word and (*f*) that which is the means of the

द्वितीयो गुणः। शुक्लादिना हि लब्धसत्ताक वस्तु विशिष्यते। साध्यः पूर्वापरीभूतावयवः क्रियारूपः।

डित्थादिशब्दानामन्त्यबुद्धिनिर्ग्राह्यं संहृतक्रमं स्वरूपं वक्त्रा यदृच्छया डित्थादिष्वर्थेषूपाधित्वेन संनिवेश्यत इति सोयं संज्ञारूपो यदृच्छात्मक इति।

---

imposition upon it of some distinguishing feature; of these latter two, the former *i. e.* (*e*) is the *Community*,—as has been declared in *Vākyapadīya*, 'By itself the ox is neither an *ox* nor a *non-ox*, it is only by reason of its being related to the community *ox* that it is called an "ox" [which means that the community is the very essence of the thing denoted];'—the latter [*i. e.* (*f*)] is the *quality*, because when the thing has obtained its *essence* (become an entity), it is the quality of *whiteness* and so forth, that serves to distinguish it;—(*d*) that which has got to be accomplished is the action, consisting of a series of steps appearing one after the other;—lastly, when the speaker, of his own accord, fastens upon a particular object the distinguishing characteristic in the shape of any such haphazard group of letters as '*Dittha*', '*Ḍavittha*' and so forth, solely as a collocation of letter-sounds ending with the last syllable, and not as occurring in any distinct order of sequence, this group of letters is what forms the name of the object concerned, and is what is classed as a proper noun (b). This is what the author of the *Mahābhāsya* (on Pāṇini-sūtra, '*ṛlk*') has declared in the following words—'The denotation of words is foufold, as signified in the expression," the ox which is white and named Ḍittha is walking."

As regards the Atomic Dimension and such other Eternal Qualities (as, e.g. the Infinite Dimension, Sound

"गौःशुक्लश्चलो डित्थ इत्यादौ चतुष्टयी शब्दानां प्रवृत्तिः" इति महाभाष्यकारः । परमाण्वादीना तु गुणमध्यपाठात् पारिभाषिकं गुणत्वम् । गुणक्रियायदृच्छाना वस्तुत एकरूपाणामप्याश्रयभेदाद् भेद इव लक्ष्यते। यथैकस्य मुखस्य खड्गमुकुरतैलाद्यालम्बनभेदात् ।

---

and so forth) which, being eternal qualities, are coeval with the substances to which they belong, of which latter, on that account, they are the very 'essence', and as such included under the category of 'community',—these have even so been classed under the category of 'quality' (and not under 'community'), only in view of the fact that they have been classed (by the *Vaiśeṣikas*) under 'qualities'; but in reality they can be called 'quality' only in a figurative or indirect sense.

As for qualities, actions and proper names, even though each of them is, in reality one only (there being only one *whiteness*, only one act of *walking* and only one proper name 'Dittha', each of these being comprehensive respectively of all individual shades of *whiteness*, of all kinds of *walking* and of all instances of the utterance of the particular name by several persons), yet it appears as if there were some diversity in them, the reason whereof lies in the fact of their subsisting in diverse individuals; just as, for instance, though the face reflected is one only, yet when it is reflected in diverse reflecting substances,—such as the polished sword, the mirror, the oil and so forth,—it has the appearance of being diverse.

[Hence as the diversity in the case of quality, action and name is only *apparent*, not *real*, the denotation of these does not involve either 'vagueness' or 'wrongness' which has been found in the case of the denotation of individuals.]

हिमपयःशङ्खाद्याश्रयेषु परमार्थतो भिन्नेषु शुक्लादिषु यद्वशेन शुक्लः शुक्ल इत्याद्यभिन्नाभिधानप्रत्ययोत्पत्तिस्तत् शुक्लत्वादि सामान्यम् । गुडतण्डुलादिपाकादिष्वेवमेव पाकत्वादि । बालवृद्धशुकाद्युदीरितेषु डित्थादिशब्देषु च प्रतिक्षणं भिद्यमानेषु डित्थाद्यर्थेषु वा डित्थत्वाद्यस्तीति सर्वेषां शब्दानां जातिरेव प्रवृत्तिनिमित्तमित्यन्ये । तद्वान् अपोहो वा शब्दार्थः कैश्चिदुक्त इति ग्रन्थगौरवभयात् प्रकृतानुपयोगाच्च न दर्शितम् ।।७।।

Some people (i. e. the Mīmāṁsakas) have argued as follows :—"(a) Even though the quality of *whiteness* subsisting in such varied substances as the snow, the milk, the conch and other things is in reality diverse, yet there is something in them by virtue of which all of them are spoken of and comprehended under the single common name 'whiteness'; and this something is what has been called the 'community of *whiteness*',—(b) similarly, in the *cooking* of such diverse things as molasses, rice and so forth, there is the 'community of *cooking*';—(c) as also in the name '*Ḍittha*' as pronounced by such diverse individuals as the boy, the grown up man, the parrot and so forth ; or as applied to such and such objects named '*Ḍittha*' as are undergoing transformation at every moment, there is the 'community of the *name Ḍittha*';—and from all this it is clear that the denotation of the word consists (in all cases) in the *community* only (and not in quality, action and name also.)"—7

There is another view held by others (*i.e.* the *Naiyāyikas*) viz., that what is denoted by the word is the *Individual as belonging to the Community*.

Yet others (*Bauddhas*) have held the view that what is

स मुख्योर्थस्तत्र मुख्यो व्यापारोस्याभिधोच्यते ॥ ८ ॥
स इति साक्षात्संकेतितः । अस्येति शब्दस्य ॥ ८ ॥

मुख्यार्थबाधे तद्योगे रूढितोथ प्रयोजनात् ।
अन्योर्थो लक्ष्यते यत्सा लक्षणारोपिता क्रिया ॥ ९ ॥

'कर्मणि कुशल.' इत्यादौ दर्भग्रहणाद्ययोगात् 'गङ्गाया घोषः' इत्यादौ च गङ्गादीनां घोषाद्याधारत्वासंभवात् मुख्यार्थस्य बाधे विवेचकत्वादौ सामीप्ये च सवन्धे रूढितः प्रसिद्धेः तथा

---

denoted by the word is the '*Apoha*', *i.e.*, 'the negation of the contrary'.

[*e. g.*, what the word 'ox' denotes is 'the negation of the 'non-ox', this view being in accordance with the Bauddha theory that there is absolutely no *positive entity* in the world.]

All these various views are not set forth here, as it would unduly prolong our work, and it would not serve any useful purpose in regard to the real subject-matter of the treatise.

That is the primary meaning; and this is the primary function of it (the word), called 'denotation'.—(8)

'*That*'—*i.e.*, the directly conventional;—'*of it*', of the word. 8.

When the primary meaning is precluded (by incompatibility), another meaning, in affinity therewith, comes to be implied,—either on the basis of usage or for a special purpose,—this process of imposed implication is called 'Indication', Lakṣaṇā.—(9)

(a) In the expression '*karmaṇi kuśalaḥ*', (used in the sense of 'expert in his work') the primary meaning of the word '*kuśalaḥ*' is 'grass-chopper', and this idea of 'grass-chopping' is not compatible with the sense of the sentence;—similarly in the expression

2

गङ्गातटे घोष इत्यादेः प्रयोगात् येषां न तथा प्रतिपत्तिः तेषां पावनत्वादीना धर्माणां तथाप्रतिपादनात्मनः प्रयोजनाच्च मुख्येन अमुख्योर्थो लक्ष्यते यत् स आरोपितः शब्दव्यापार. सान्तरार्थनिष्ठो लक्षणा ॥ ९॥

'*gangāyāṁ ghosah*' (used in the sense of 'the ranch in the Gangā') the primary meaning of the term '*Gangā*' is the *river* itself, and this is incompatible as the location for the *ranch* ;—hence in both these cases 'the primary meaning is barred'; and 'another' secondary meaning comes to be implied by the primary meaning in each of these two cases,—(a) the term '*kuśala*', implying the sense of the 'expert', which is 'in affinity with' the primary sense of 'grass-chopping,' in this that just as the '*expert* in business is possessed of discrimination so is the *grass-chopper* also (who cuts what he needs and rejects what he does not need),—and (b) the term '*Gaṅgā*' implying the sense of 'the bank,' which is 'in affinity with' the primary sense of the 'river' in this that it is situated in close proximity ,—and while in (a), the case of the term '*kuśala*', the said implication is based upon 'usage' (by which the term is generally used in the sense of 'expert'), while in (b), in that of the term 'Gangā,' the said implication proceeds on the basis of the 'purpose' of pointing out those properties of 'sanctity' and the rest which could not be expressed by the use of such expressions as '*gangā-tate ghosah*' ('the ranch on the bank of the Gaṅgā'); this function of indirect implication is 'imposed' upon the word, in the sense that it is not direct (from the word to the meaning), but indirect, through certain intervening factors (in the shape of the 'incompatibility of the primary meaning' and the rest mentioned in the text). 9.

स्वसिद्धये पराक्षेपः परार्थं स्वसमर्पणम् ।
उपादानं लक्षणं चेत्युक्ता शुद्धैव सा द्विधा ॥ १० ॥

'कुन्ताः प्रविशन्ति' 'यष्टयः प्रविशन्ति' इत्यादौ कुन्तादिभिरात्मनः प्रवेशसिद्ध्यर्थं स्वसंयोगिनः पुरुषा आक्षिप्यन्ते । तत उपादानेनेयं लक्षणा।

"गौरनुबन्ध्यः" इत्यादौ श्रुतिचोदितमनुबन्धनं कथं मे स्यादिति जात्या व्यक्तिराक्षिप्यते न तु शब्देनोच्यते "विशेष्यं

'Pure' Indication is of two kinds—(a) the 'Inclusive', in which there is implication of the other (the secondary) meaning for the purpose of completing (the logical connection of) the primary meaning itself, and (b) the 'Indicative' in which the primary meaning surrenders itself for the sake of the other (the secondary meaning)—(10).

(a) An example of the 'Inclusive' Indication we have in the expression '*kuntāh pravisanti*' ('the lances enter'), where the 'primary meaning,' the 'lances,' implies the *men holding the lances*, for the purpose of establishing the logical connection of the *lances* themselves with the act of 'entering' (which could not be done by the lances, except through the men holding them).

Some people have cited as an example of 'Inclusive' Indication, the expression '*gauranubandhyah* ('the ox is to be sacrificed'), where, they explain, the primary meaning of the term 'ox'—which is the 'community' *ox*—implies an *individual* ox, for the purpose of establishing its connection with the act of 'being sacrificed' enjoined by the said Vedic expression; and they go on, this *individual ox* could not be regarded as directly denoted by the word itself, because of the principle 'the denotation of a word, having its force spent up in the *qualifying adjunct* (which, in this

नाभिधा गच्छेत् क्षीणशक्तिर्विशेषणे" इति न्यायादित्युपादान-लक्षणा तु नोदाहर्तव्या । न ह्यत्र प्रयोजनमस्ति न वा रूढि-रियम् । व्यक्त्यविनाभावित्वात्तु जात्या व्यक्तिराक्षिप्यते । यथा क्रियतामित्यत्र कर्ता । कुर्वित्यत्र कर्म । प्रविश पिण्डी-मित्यादौ गृहं भक्षयेत्यादि च ।

---

case, is the *community*), is unable to proceed to the *qualified* (which is the *Individual*).'

This however is not a right example of 'inclusive' indication ; because in this case, there is neither any 'purpose' (served by the indirect implication, which could not be got by direct denotation), nor any 'usage' (and these alone have been declared to be the basis for indirect implication). What really happens in the case cited is that the individual is implied by the community by reason of their invariable concomitance ; just as there is in the case of the imperative passive form '*kriyatām*', where the *agent* is implied by reason of his being invariably concomitant with an action,—or in that of the imperative word '*kuru*', the *object* is implied by reason of its being inseparable from every transitive verb,—or in the case of the word '*praviśa*,' 'enter,' which implies the 'house' to be entered, as *what is entered* is inseparable from the act of *entering*,—or in the case of the word '*piṇḍim*' 'cake' (in the accusative), some such verb as 'eat' is implied, as without some such transitive verb , there could be no *object*.

The expression 'fat Devadatta eats not during the day' as implying his *nocturnal feeding* has been regarded by some people as an example of 'Indication'; but in this case the *nocturnal feeding* is not 'indicated' by the words

'पीनो देवदत्तो दिवा न भुङ्क्ते' इत्यत्र च रात्रिभोजनं न लक्ष्यते श्रुतार्थापत्तेरर्थापत्तेर्वा तस्य विषयत्वात्।

'गङ्गायां घोषः' इत्यत्र तटस्य घोषाधिकरणत्वसिद्धये गङ्गाशब्दः स्वार्थमर्पयति इत्येवमादौ लक्षणेनैषा लक्षणा। उभयरूपा चेयं शुद्धा। उपचारेणामिश्रितत्वात्।

---

at all ; it is simply cognised either through 'Verbal Presumption' (of the expression 'he eats at night' as held by the *Bhātta*), or through pure presumption (of the *fact* of the nocturnal feeding, as held by the *Prābhākara*).

(*b*) An example of the 'Indicative' Indication we have in the expression '*gangāyām ghoṣah*' ("the ranch in the Gangā"); here, for the purpose of obtaining for the *Bank* (which is the secondary meaning indicated by the term '*Gangāyām*') the character of being the location of the ranch, the term '*Gangāyām*' 'surrenders its primary meaning' (*i. e.* the *river*) ; and in this case the process of Indication is called 'Indicative.'

Both of these kinds here exemplified (*a* and *b*) belong to the category of 'pure' Indication,—so called because they do not involve or require any auxiliary agency (in the shape of some sort of *similitude* between the Primary and Secondary meanings).

It is not true (as some people have asserted) that in cases of 'pure' Indication—like those just cited—there is a clear 'difference' manifested between the *indicated* (secondary) and the *indicative* (primary) meanings,—this 'difference' being technically called '*tātasthya*' 'aloofness' —[while in cases of Indication other than the 'pure,' there is 'non-difference' manifested between the two meanings.]—This, we say, is not true ; because as a matter of

अनयोर्लक्ष्यस्य लक्षकस्य च न भेदरूपं ताटस्थ्यम् । तटादीनां गङ्गादिशब्दैः प्रतिपादने तत्त्वप्रतिपत्तौ हि प्रतिपिपादयिषितप्रयोजनसंप्रत्ययः । गङ्गासंबन्धमात्रप्रतीतौ तु गङ्गातटे घोष इति मुख्यशब्दाभिधानाल्लक्षणायाः को भेदः ॥१०॥

सारोपान्या तु यत्रोक्तौ विषयी विषयस्तथा ।

आरोप्यमाणः आरोपविषयश्च यत्रानपह्नुतभेदौ सामानाधिकरण्येन निर्दिश्येते सा लक्षणा सारोपा ॥

---

fact, in a case where the *Bank* is spoken of by means of the word '*Gaṅgā*,' it is done clearly for the purpose of expressing some definite notion (such as that of 'sanctity' in the present case); and this purpose can be accomplished only when the two (the *indicated* 'bank' and the *indicative* 'river') are comprehended as absolutely identical *i. e.*, the sanctity of the 'bank' is recognised only when the 'bank' is identified with the 'river' whose sanctity is already well-known. If this were not so, and if all that was intended to be expressed was some sort of connection with the 'river,' then as this could be done equally well by the ordinary expression '*gangātate ghosaḥ*' ('the ranch on the banks of the river *Gaṅgā*'), —what difference would there be between the expression of that idea by this direct assertion and the indirect 'indication' of the same (by the indirect expression '*gangāyām ghosaḥ*') ? 10.

There is however another (kind of Indication) called the 'Super-imponent', wherein the 'imposed' as well as 'that imposed upon' are both distinctly expressed.

That Indication is called 'Super-imponent' in which what is 'imposed' and what is 'imposed upon' are both mentioned as correlated and as clearly distinct from one another.

विषय्यन्तःकृतेन्यस्मिन् सा स्यात्साध्यवसानिका ॥ ११ ॥

विषयिणारोप्यमाणेनान्तःकृते निगीर्णे अन्यस्मिन्नारोपविषये सति साध्यवसाना स्यात् ॥ ११ ॥

भेदाविमौ च सादृश्यात्सम्बन्धान्तरतस्तथा ।
गौणौ शुद्धौ च विज्ञेयौ

इमावारोपाध्यवसानरूपौ सादृश्यहेतू भेदौ 'गौर्वाहीक.' इत्यत्र 'गौरयम्' इत्यत्र च ।

अत्र हि स्वार्थसहचारिणो गुणा जाड्यमान्द्यादयो लक्ष्यमाणा अपि गोशब्दस्य परार्थाभिधाने प्रवृत्तिनिमित्तत्वमुपयान्ति

That same (Indication) would be called 'Introsusceptive' when what is 'imposed' swallows the other (that is 'imposed upon').—(11)

Where the '*viṣayin*', what is 'imposed' 'swallows'—*i. e.*, takes within itself—'the other'—*i. e.*, that which is 'imposed upon',—it is a case of 'Introsusceptive' Indication. 11.

These two kinds of Indication (a) when based upon similitude, are known as 'qualitative'; and (b) as 'pure' when they are based upon other kinds of relationship.

(*A*) As examples respectively of the 'Superimponent' and 'Introsusceptive' Indication, based upon similitude (and hence 'qualitative'), we have the two expressions (*a*) '*gaurvāhīkaḥ*') ('the ploughman is an ox'), and (*b*) '*gaurayam*' ('he is the ox itself').

[In (*a*) the character of the 'ox' is what is 'imposed', and the 'ploughman' is the one 'imposed upon', and both these being mentioned as distinct from one another, it is a case of 'superimponent' Indication; while in (*b*) the character imposed, *i. e.* the 'ox', 'swallows' up the ***man*** upon whom it is imposed, the man loses his distinct individuality and becomes merged, as it were, in the 'ox', hence this becomes a case of the 'introsusceptive' Indication.]

इति केचित् । स्वार्थसहचारिगुणाभेदेन पदार्थगता गुणा एव लक्ष्यन्ते न परार्थोभिधीयते इत्यन्ये । साधारणगुणाश्रयत्वेन परार्थ एव लक्ष्यते इत्यपरे ।

उक्तं चान्यत्र "अभिधेयाविनाभूतप्रतीतिर्लक्षणोच्यते । लक्ष्यमाणगुणैर्योगाद्वृत्तेरिष्टा तु गौणता" इति ।

अविनाभावोत्र संबन्धमात्रं न तु नान्तरीयकत्वम् । तत्त्वे हि 'मञ्चाः क्रोशन्ति' इत्यादौ न लक्षणा स्यात् । अविनाभावे चाक्षेपेणैव सिद्धेर्लक्षणाया नोपयोग इत्युक्तम् ।

The exact process of Indication in these cases is thus explained by some people :—When the 'ploughman' is spoken of as the 'ox', this latter word *indicates* the qualities of stupidity, dullness and the like which belong to the animal denoted by that word, and through these qualities (thus indirectly indicated) the word 'ox' comes to denote the *man* (and it is thus that the co-ordination between the *man* and the *ox* is secured).—According to others, however, what happens is, *not* that the word 'ox' directly expresses the *man* (through its qualities of *stupidity* and *dullness*), but that it indirectly indicates similar qualities in the *man*.—But according to others again (men of our way of thinking), the word 'ox' indicates the *man* himself, as being the substratum of those same qualities that belong to the *ox* also.

This has been declared elsewhere also (in the *Ślokavārttika*)—'Indication is the name given to the cognition of what is invariably concomitant with what is directly expressed by the word ; and this process is called 'qualitative' on account of the indication being based upon the presence of certain *qualities*.'

'आयुर्घृतम्' 'आयुरेवेदम्' इत्यादौ च सादृश्यादन्यत् कार्यकारणभावादि संबन्धान्तरम् । एवमादौ च कार्यकारण-भावादिलक्षणपूर्वे आरोपाध्यवसाने ।

अत्र गौणभेदयोर्भेदेपि ताद्रूप्यप्रतीति. सर्वथैवाभेदावगमश्च प्रयोजनम । शुद्धभेदयोस्त्वन्यवैलक्षण्येनाव्यभिचारेण च कार्यकारित्वादि ।

In this passage what is meant by 'invariable concomitance' is only relationship, and not actual (inseparable) concomitance, for if the latter were meant, there could be no indication in the case of such expressions as '*mañchāḥ krośanti*' ('the platforms are shouting').

[As there is no *inseparable* concomitance between the *platform* and the *men* on the platform.]

In fact it has been rightly observed that in cases where there is actual *invariable concomitance* (between the *indicated* and the *indicator*), one naturally implies the other, and there is no need for the indicative process at all.

(*b*) Examples of the 'superimponent' and 'introsusceptive' Indication, based upon factors other than 'similitude,' (and hence 'pure') we have in the two expressions '*Āyurghṛtam*' ('clarified butter is longevity') and '*Āyurevedam*' ('It is longevity itself'); —where the factor upon which the indication is based is some such relationship as that between cause and effect, and the like and in all such cases the two kinds of Indication—'superimponent' and 'introsusceptive'—are such as are actually preceded (and brought about) by the said relationships of 'cause and effect' and the like.

क्वचित् तादर्थ्यादुपचारः । यथा इन्द्रार्था स्थूणा इन्द्रः । क्वचित् स्वस्वामिभावात् । यथा राजकीयः पुरुषो राजा । क्वचित् अवयवावयविभावात् । यथा अग्रहस्त इत्यत्राग्रमात्रेवयवे हस्तः । क्वचित् तात्कर्म्यात् । यथा अतक्षा तक्षा ॥

Now here, in the case of the two kinds of 'qualitative' Indication, the purpose served [(*a*) in the case of the 'superimponent' variety, *e. g.*, 'the ploughman is an ox'] is the bringing about of the cognition of similarity between the two things recognised as different from one another,—and [(*b*) in the case of the 'introsusceptive' variety, *e. g.*, 'he is verily an ox'] it is the bringing about of the notion of absolute identity between the two things. In the case of the two kinds of 'pure' Indication [*e g.*, (*J*) 'Butter is longevity' and (*b*) 'It is longevity itself'], on the other hand, the purpose served is the bringing about of the notion that the thing spoken of is one that accomplishes a certain object *in a way better than anything else* [in the case of (*a*)] or *infallibly* [in the case of (*b*)] .

In some cases the Indication is based upon the relation of 'subserviency ;' *e.g.*, the *pillar* that subserves the purpose of (the worship of) Indra is called '*indra*';—sometimes it is based upon the relationship of 'master and servant'; *e. g.* when the king's servant is spoken as the 'king';—in some cases it is based upon the relationship of 'whole and part'; *e. g.* in the expression '*agrahastaḥ*' ('foremost hand') as applied to any and every *foremost limb*, this latter is indicated by the word 'hand' ;—in other cases again it is based upon the relationship of 'doing the same work'; *e. g.*, when one who is not a *carpenter* is spoken of as 'carpenter' (on account of his doing the carpenter's work).

लक्षणा तेन षड्विधा ॥ १२ ॥

आद्यभेदाभ्या सह ॥ १२ ॥

सा च

व्यङ्ग्येन रहिता रूढौ सहिता तु प्रयोजने ।

प्रयोजनं हि व्यञ्जनव्यापारगम्यमेव ॥

तच्च गूढमगूढं वा

तच्चेति व्यङ्ग्यम् । गूढं यथा

मुखं विकसितस्मितं वशितवक्रिम प्रेक्षितं

समुच्छलितविभ्रमा गतिरपास्तसस्था मतिः ।

Thus Indication is of six kinds.—(12).

That is, (the four kinds mentioned in 11 and 12) along with the first two kinds (described in 10) 12.

This (Indication)—

When based upon usage, is without any 'suggested' meaning; but when it is based upon some purpose, it is accompanied by a 'suggested' meaning.

In fact the recognition of the *purpose* (in the case of Indication) is obtained only through the process of 'suggestion'.

And it may be either abstruse or explicit.

'It'—the suggested meaning.

It is 'abstruse' in the following passage—

'Oh! The first tide of youth is exuberant in the body of the moon-faced one : her face is blooming with smiles, her glances have acquired the graceful arch, her gait evinces a rising gracefulness, her thoughts have relinquished steadiness, the bosom shows the budding breasts, and her thighs are plump and efficient.'

[Here we have the primary meaning of the following words barred by incompatibility with the context—(*a*) the word 'is exuberant' (as applied to *tide of youth*, which is inanimate),—(*b*) 'blooming' (applied to *smile*, though it is really applicable to *flowers*),—(*c*) 'acqui-

उरो मुकुलितस्तनं जघनमंसबन्धोद्धुरं
बतेन्दुवदनातनौ तरुणिमोद्गमो मोदते ॥ ९ ॥

अगूढं यथा

श्रीपरिचयाज्जडा अपि भवन्त्यभिज्ञा विदग्धचरितानाम् ।
उपदिशति कामिनीनां यौवनमद एव ललितानि ॥ १० ॥

अत्रोपदिशतीति ॥

---

ing' (as applied to the *glances*, which are inanimate),—(*d*) 'rising' (as applied to *gracefulness*, which is not a material substance and hence cannot do any *rising*),—*e*) 'relinquishing steadiness' (as applied to *thoughts* which are not *sentient*),—(*f*) 'budding' (as applied to *breasts*, though really applicable to *flowers*,)—and (*g*) 'efficient' (as applied to the *thighs* which are inanimate), and hence they are taken as *indicating* the (figurative) meaning in which the words are understood in the passage, *e g* (*a*) 'exuberance' indicates *excellence* and what is *suggested* is 'desirability',—(*b*) 'blooming' indicates unrestrained *manifestation*, and what is suggested is 'sweet odour' and so forth,—(*c*) 'acquiring' indicates *mastery* and it *suggests* the 'appearance of the loved person',—(*d*) 'rising' indicates *profuseness*, which *suggests* 'heart-ravishing character';—*e*) 'relinquishing steadiness' indicates *impatience*, which *suggests* 'the increasing influence of love',—(*f*) 'budding' indicates *unflabbiness*, which *suggests* 'fitness for embrace',—(*g*) 'efficiency' indicates *capacity for spirited intercourse*, which *suggests* 'loveliness.'—And all this, not capable of being comprehended by ordinary men, is very 'abstruse']

As an example of the 'explicit' suggested meaning, we have the following—

'Coming into contact with prosperity' even dull persons become conversant with the functions of the clever : the intoxication of youth itself teaches the graces to lovely women.'

Here the work 'teaches' (having its direct meaning barred, in relation to the 'intoxication of youth,' which is inanimate), indicates 'manifestation', which suggests 'spontaneous attainment of the graces'; and this suggestion is quite *explicit*).

तदेषा कथिता त्रिधा ॥ १३ ॥

अव्यङ्ग्या गूढव्यङ्ग्या अगूढव्यङ्ग्या च ॥ १३ ॥

तद्भूर्लाक्षणिकः

शब्द इति संबध्यते । तद्भूस्तदाश्रयः ॥

तत्र व्यापारो व्यञ्जनात्मकः ।

In this way Indication has been declared to be of three kinds.—(13).

That is, (1) that in which there is no suggested meaning, (2) that in which the suggested meaning is abstruse, and (3) that in which the suggested meaning is explicit.

That which contains the said (indication) is the 'Indicative'—

'Word', '*śabdaḥ*', has to be construed here (from Text 6).

'*Tadbhūḥ*'—That which contains, is the substratum of, the Indication.

[Having described the 'expressive word' (in the Text 7) and the 'indicative word' (in the foregoing Text), the author now turns to the description of the 'suggestive word' As in the other two cases, however, so here also, before describing the 'suggestive word,' it is necessary to explain the process of 'suggestion.' This *suggestion* is of two kinds—'Verbal', based upon the word, and 'Ideal', based upon the meaning, as the present context is dealing with *words*, the author takes up Verbal suggestion here, the other kind being dealt with in Chapter III. The Verbal suggestion also is of two kinds, that based upon the directly expressed meaning of the word, 'denotative', and that based upon the indicated meaning of the word, 'indicative'. And as he has been just dealing with Indication, he takes up the 'Indicative' suggestion first]—13

Of the Indicative Word, that function (which brings about the cognition of the 'purpose' of the indication) is of the nature of 'Suggestion'.

"Why so ?"

कुत इत्याह

यस्य प्रतीतिमाधातुं लक्षणा समुपास्यते ॥ १४ ॥
फले शब्दैकगम्येऽत्र व्यञ्जनान्नापरा क्रिया ।

प्रयोजनप्रतिपिपादयिषया यत्र लक्षणया शब्दप्रयोगस्तत्र नान्यतस्तत्प्रतीतिरपि तु तस्मादेव शब्दात् । न चात्र व्यञ्जनादृतेऽन्यो व्यापारः ॥

तथाहि

नाभिधा समयाभावात्

[*Answer.*]

In regard to that intended idea for bringing about the cognition whereof one has recourse to Indication, (14) *and which is cognisable through the word only,—the function (of the word) can be none other than 'Suggestion.'*

A word is used indicatively only when it is intended to convey the notion of the 'purpose' (which could not be cognised through the direct denotation of the word);—and yet the said notion is obtained from that same word, and not from anything else ; and in this function the word is none other than *Suggestion* ;—because

(*a*) *it cannot be direct denotation, as there is no usage to that effect* ;—

In the case of the expression 'the ranch in the Gangā', the 'sanctity' and such other qualities are recognised as belonging to the bank ; and yet there is no usage of the word 'Gangā in that sense :—

(*b*) *nor can it be Indication because the necessary conditions are wanting.*—(15).

गङ्गायां घोष इत्यादौ ये पावनत्वादयो धर्मास्तटादौ प्रतीयन्ते न तत्र गङ्गादिशब्दाः संकेतिताः ॥

हेत्वभावान्न लक्षणा ॥ १५ ॥

मुख्यार्थबाधादित्रयं हेतुः ॥ १५ ॥

तथा च

लक्ष्यं न मुख्यं नाप्यत्र बाधो योगः फलेन नो ।

न प्रयोजनमेतस्मिन् न च शब्दः स्खलद्गतिः ॥ १६ ॥

That is the three conditions described above—the primary meaning being barred and so forth (see Text 9). For instance—

What is 'indictated' is not the primary meaning; nor is that meaning incompatible; nor has it any connection with the intended idea; nor again is there any purpose served by it (i. e., by making the intended idea an object of further Indication), nor lastly is the word itself wanting in the requisite force. (16).

In the expression 'the ranch in the Gaṅgā', the word 'Gangā' is taken as *indicating* the 'bank', because its primary meaning of 'river' is found incompatible;—if, in the same manner, the sense of the 'bank' also were incompatible, then alone could it be taken as *indicating* the intended idea (of 'sanctity' and so forth);—as a matter of fact however, in the first place, the bank does not form the primary meaning of the word 'Gangā', nor is it incompatible, [so that the first condition of Indication is not fulfilled],—secondly there is no affinity between the 'bank' as indicated by the word '*Gangā*' with 'sanctity' and the other qualities that would be *indicated* (by the *bank*) [so that the second condition of Indication is not fulfilled];—thirdly, there is no further purpose served by making the intended idea of 'sanctity' and the rest the object of a further indication;—nor lastly, is the word '*Gangā*' incapable (without the intervention

यथा गङ्गाशब्द स्रोतसि सबाध इति तटं लक्षयति तद्वत् यदि तटेऽपि सबाध स्यात् तत प्रयोजनं लक्षयेत । न च तटं मुख्योर्थ. । नाप्यत्र बाधः । न च गङ्गाशब्दार्थस्य तटस्य पावनत्वाद्यैर्लक्षणीयै संबन्ध· । नापि प्रयोजने लक्ष्ये किञ्चित् प्रयोजनम् । नापि गङ्गाशब्दस्तटमिव प्रयोजनं प्रतिपादयितुमसमर्थः ॥१६॥

एवमप्यनवस्था स्याद् या मूलक्षयकारिणी ।

---

of the indicative process) of bringing about the notion of 'sanctity' and the rest, as it is of denoting the *bank*.

[The word '*Gaṅgā*' is incapable of denoting the *bank*, hence for the purpose of bringing about the notion of the *bank*, it has to seek the help of Indication, but as regards 'sanctity' and the rest, the idea of these can be brought about by the word '*Gaṅgā*' itself, through 'suggestion']—16

Further, in this manner, there would be an infinite regress, which would strike at the very root (of the intended comprehension).

If the purpose for which the original Indication has been adopted were itself the object of a further Indication,—then for the second Indication there would be another purpose; and in connection with the Indication of this latter, there would be yet another purpose; and so on and on, there would be an infinite regress, and the result of this would be that the desired comprehension would not be got at.

An objection is raised :—"What the word '*Gaṅgā*' indicates may be the *bank as possessed of the qualities of sanctity* and the rest; and the purpose served by this indication is the bringing about of a notion that could not be got at by the expression 'the ranch on the bank of the *Gaṅgā*'; and thus as Indication itself would provide the comprehension of the *bank along with the qualities*, where would be the need for having any 'suggestion' at all ?"

एवमपि प्रयोजनं चेल्लक्ष्यते तत् प्रयोजनान्तरेणेति तदपि प्रयोजनान्तरेणेति प्रकृताप्रतीतिकृत् अनवस्था भवेत् ॥

ननु पावनत्वादिधर्मयुक्तमेव तटं लक्ष्यते । 'गङ्गायास्तटे घोषः' इत्यतोधिकस्यार्थस्य प्रतीतिश्च प्रयोजनमिति विशिष्टे लक्षणा तत्किं व्यञ्जनयेत्याह—

प्रयोजनेन सहितं लक्षणीयं न युज्यते ॥ १७ ॥

कुत इत्याह—

ज्ञानस्य विषयो ह्यन्यः फलमन्यदुदाहृतम् ।

प्रत्यक्षादेर्नीलादिर्विषयः फलं तु प्रकटता संवित्तिर्वा ॥

[The answer to this is given by the following Text.]

It is not right to make the 'indicated' meaning include the intended idea (for the sake of which Indication is admitted.—(17)

"Why not?"

Because the object of a cognition is one thing, and its resultant is said to be another.

For instance, the 'object' of the perceptional cognition is the *blue thing*, while the 'resultant' of that cognition is the 'apprehendedness' of that thing (as held by the *Mīmāṁsaka*), or the 'representative cognition' ('I perceive the blue thing,'—this is according to the *Naiyāyika*).

[Similarly the *object* of the cognition obtained by Indication is the 'bank', and the idea of 'sanctity' and the rest is only its *resultant*, which, therefore, being different from the 'object', cannot be coupled with the former.—There is no doubt that such is the meaning of the text, and the commentators have had recourse to a subtle and laboured explanation only on account of their being unable to reconcile the clear meaning of the text with their own conceptions] 17

Thus Indication cannot apply to the thing along with its qualities.

This has been already explained.

विशिष्टे लक्षणा नैवम्

व्याख्यातम् ॥

विशेषाः स्युस्तु लक्षिते ॥ १८ ॥

तटादौ ये विशेषाः पावनत्वादयस्ते चाभिधातात्पर्यलक्षणाभ्यो व्यापारान्तरेण गम्याः । तच्च व्यञ्जनध्वननद्योतनादिशब्दवाच्यमवश्यमेषितव्यम् ॥ १८ ॥

It is only after something has been indicated that special qualities come (to be recognised) as belonging to it.—(18).

Thus after the *bank* has been *indicated* (by the word 'Gangā), the special qualities of 'sanctity' and the rest come to be recognised as belonging to it; and the recognition of these qualities can be brought about by the word through a function that is different from Denotation and Indication; and this function must necessarily be held to be that which is spoken of by such names as '*vyañjana*' (suggestion), '*dhvanana*' (echo), '*dyotana*' (illumination) and so forth. 18.

Suggestion *based upon Indication* has been described; the author now proceeds to describe that *based upon Denotation*—

> *When a word having several primary meanings has the range of its denotation restricted by 'connection' and such other conditions,—if there appears the cognition of a meaning other than the denoted (or directly expressed) one, that function which brings about this cognition is 'Suggestion.'*—(19).

[Says the *Vākyapadīya*] (*a*) 'Connection, (*b*) Disjunction, (*c*) Association, (*d*) Enmity, (*e*) Purpose, (*f*) Context, (*g*) Peculiarity, (*h*) Proximity of another word, (*i*) Capacity, (*j*) Compatibility, (*k*) Place, (*l*) Time, (*m*) Gender, (*n*) Accent and so forth,—these are the conditions that serve to bring about the idea of a particular meaning of a word, when there is an uncertainty as to its actual meaning in a particular context';—and it is in accordance with this that one particular meaning, out of a number of meanings, of a word is understood to be intended, in each of the following expressions respectively :—

(*a*) In the expression '*Hari* with conch and discus' the exact meaning of the word '*hari*', which has many meanings, is restricted to Visnu, through 'connection', [as of all the things denoted by the word '*hari*', it is Viṣṇu alone who has any connection with 'the conch and the discus'] ;—(*b*) similarly in the expression 'Hari without the conch and the discus', [as it is only one who has had 'connection' with a thing that can be 'disjoined' from it, this 'disjunction' restricts the meaning of '*hari*' to Viṣṇu];—(*c*) in the expression '*Rāmalaksmaṇau*,' the meaning of the word 'Rāma', is restricted to that Rāma who was the son of Daśaratha [and this on account of the 'association' of Lakṣmaṇa] ; (*d*) while in the expression 'the behaviour of these two combatants is like that of Rāma and Arjuna', the meaning of 'Rāma' is restricted to Paraśurāma, and that of 'Arjuna' to the son of Kṛtavīrya [and this through the well-known 'enmity' between these two persons]; —(*e*) in the expression 'worship *Sthāṇu* for the purpose of removing the shackles of the world', the meaning of the word '*Sthāṇu*' is restricted to Śiva [as the 'purpose' mentioned can be fulfilled by the worship of that God only];—(*f*) in the expression 'Deva knows everything', the meaning of the word 'deva' is restricted to '*you*' [and this is done through the 'context',

एवं लक्षणामूलं व्यञ्जकत्वमुक्तम् ॥ अभिधामूलं त्वाह—

the words being addressed to the *king*]; (*g*) in the expression 'Makaradhvaja is angry', the meaning of the word '*Makaradhvaja*' is restricted to the Love-God [as the 'peculiarity' mentioned, *being angry*, can apply to that God alone, and not to the *ocean*, which is also called '*Makaradhvaja*'];—(*h*) in '*devasya purārāteḥ*', the meaning of the word, '*deva*' is restricted to Śiva [through the 'proximity of the word' '*purārāti*', which can apply to Śiva, and to no other God];—(*i*) in 'the *kokila* bird is intoxicated by *Madhu*'. the meaning of the word '*Madhu*' is restricted to the *Spring* [as that alone, and not honey or wine, has the 'capacity' to intoxicate the bird]; (j)—in '*pātu vo dayitāmukham*,' the meaning of the word '*pātu*' (which can mean *drink* and *protect* also) is restricted to *confrontation* [as this alone is 'compatible' with the 'beloved's face'];—(*k*) in 'Parameśvara shines here', the meaning of the word '*Parameśvaraḥ*' is restricted to the *king*, through the 'place' referred to being the King's capital;—(*l*) in '*Chitrabhānu* is shining,' the meaning of the word '*Chitrabhānu*' is restricted to the *Sun*, if the words are uttered during the day, and to *fire*, if they are uttered at night, and this is done through 'time';—(*m*) in the expression '*Mitra shines*', if the word 'Mitra' is used in the neuter 'gender', its meaning becomes restricted to the *friend*, but if in the masculine 'gender', then to the Sun;—(*n*) in the expression '*Indraśatru*,' the meaning becomes restricted by the 'accent' [if the accent is put on the first word of the compound, it has to be taken as *Bahuvrīhi*, and then its meaning is he 'whose killer is Indra,' but if the accent is put on the second word it has to be taken as *Tatpurusa*, which means 'the killer

अनेकार्थस्य शब्दस्य वाचकत्वे नियन्त्रिते ।
संयोगाद्यैरवाच्यार्थधीकृद्व्यापृतिरञ्जनम् ॥ १९ ॥

"संयोगो विप्रयोगश्च साहचर्यं विरोधिता ।
अर्थः प्रकरणं लिङ्गं शब्दस्यान्यस्य संनिधिः ॥
सामर्थ्यमौचिती देशः कालो व्यक्तिः स्वरादयः ।
शब्दार्थस्यानवच्छेदे विशेषस्मृतिहेतवः ॥"

इत्युक्तदिशा

सशङ्खचक्रो हरिः अशङ्खचक्रो हरिरित्युच्यते । रामलक्ष्मणाविति दाशरथौ । रामार्जुनगतिस्तयोरिति भार्गवकार्तवीर्ययोः । स्थाणु भज भवच्छिदे, इति हरे । सर्वं जानाति देव इति युष्मदर्थे । कुपितो मकरध्वज इति कामे । देवस्य पुरारातेरिति शंभौ । मधुना मत्तः कोकिल इति वसन्ते । पातु वो दयितामुखमिति सांमुख्ये । भात्यत्र परमेश्वर इति राजधानीरूपात् देशाद्राजनि । चित्रभानुर्विभातीति दिने रवौ रात्रौ वह्नौ । मित्रं भातीति सुहृदि मित्रो भातीति रवौ । इन्द्रशत्रुरित्यादौ वेदे एव न काव्ये स्वरो विशेषप्रतीतिकृत् ।

---

of Indra ']. But it is only in the case of Vedic expressions that accent serves the purpose of restricting the denotation of words.—The verse quoted from the *Vākyapadīya* contains at the end the term '*ādi*', 'and so forth'; this is meant to include (*o*) *Gesture*, which serves to restrict the meaning in such passages as—'During all these days her breasts have been reduced to *this* (marked by a gesture) size, her eyes have shrunk to *this*, and her condition has become like *this*.'

Now, in some cases, it is found that though the signification of the word has been restricted in the manner described above, and the other significations are pre-

आदिग्रहणात्

एद्दहमेत्तत्थणिआ एद्दहमेत्तेहि अच्छिवत्तेहिं ।
एद्दहमेत्तावत्था एद्दहमेत्तेहिँ दिअएहिं ॥ ११ ॥

इत्यादावभिनयादयः ।

इत्थं संयोगादिभिरर्थान्तराभिधायकत्वे निवारितेप्यनेकार्थस्य शब्दस्य यत् क्वचिदर्थान्तरप्रतिपादनं तत्र नाभिधा नियमनात्तस्याः । न च लक्षणा मुख्यार्थबाधाद्यभावात् । अपि त्वञ्जनं व्यञ्जनमेव व्यापारः । यथा

भद्रात्मनो दुरधिरोहतनोर्विशाल
वंशोन्नतेःकृतशिलीमुखविग्रहस्य ।
यस्यानुपप्लुतगतेः परवारणस्य
दानाम्बुसेकसुभगः सततं करोभूत् ॥ १२ ॥ १९ ॥

---

cluded,—yet the word, which has several meanings, may even so succeed in bringing about the cognition of a meaning other than that to which the signification has been restricted ;—and this could not be done by the *denotative* function of the word, as that has been restricted and hence precluded from the meaning cognised ; nor could it be done by its *indicative* function, as the 'incompatibility of the primary meaning' and other conditions of Indication would be wanting ; the only function by which it can be done is 'suggestion.'

An example of this we have in the following verse :—

'Bhadrātmano duradhirohatanorviśāla—
Vaṁśonnateḥ kṛtaśilīmukhavigrahasya
Yasyānupaplutagateḥ paravāraṇasya
Dānāmbusekasubhagaḥ satataṅkarobhūt.'

['The hand (trunk) of this destroyer of enemies (large elephant),—who is high-souled (belongs to the 'bhadra' species of elephants), whose body is irrepressible (who

तद्युक्तो व्यञ्जकः शब्दः

तद्युक्तो व्यञ्जनयुक्तः

यत्सोर्थान्तरयुक् तथा ।

अर्थोपि व्यञ्जकस्तत्र सहकारितया मतः ॥ २० ॥

तथेति व्यञ्जकः ॥ २० ॥

इति काव्यप्रकाशे शब्दार्थस्वरूपनिर्णयो नाम द्वितीय उल्लासः ॥२॥

---

can be mounted with difficulty), the nobility of whose race is high (who is as tall as a bamboo), who has become an expert in the use of arrows (who has a host of bees hovering round him), whose insight is undimmed (whose gait is steady),—was always beautified by the water poured in the formal making of gifts (by the ichor flowing from his temples)].

[Here we find that the words are so skilfully chosen that they are applicable to the king as also to the elephant; the fact however that it is addressed to the king restricts the meaning of the words to him alone; and yet the idea of the 'elephant' also is cognisable throughout; and this idea is the result of *Suggestion.*] 19.

The word endowed with that (i. e. the said function of suggestion) is the 'suggestive word.'

'*Endowed with that,*' *i. e.* endowed with the function of suggestion.

Inasmuch as the word is 'suggestive' only when it has other meanings, the meaning also is held to be so (i. e. 'suggestive' by virtue of its helping the process. (20).

'*So*'—*i. e.* suggestive. 20.

तृतीय उल्लासः

अर्थाः प्रोक्ताः पुरा तेषाम्

अर्थाः वाच्यलक्ष्यव्यङ्ग्याः। तेषां वाचकलाक्षणिकव्यञ्जकानाम्॥

अर्थव्यञ्जकतोच्यते ।

कीदृशीत्याह—

वक्तृबोद्धव्यकाकूनां वाक्यवाच्यान्यसन्निधेः॥ २१ ॥
प्रस्तावदेशकालादेर्वैशिष्ट्यात् प्रतिभाजुषाम् ।
योऽर्थस्यान्यार्थधीहेतुर्व्यापारो व्यक्तिरेव सा॥ २२ ॥

बोद्धव्यः प्रतिपाद्यः। काकुर्ध्वनेर्विकारः। प्रस्तावः प्रकरणम्।

CHAPTER III

THE SUGGESTIVENESS OF MEANING

The meanings of these have been described before.

'*Meanings*'—*i. e.* the Expressed, the Indicated and the Suggested.

'*Of these*',—*i. e.* of the Expressive, the Indicative and the Suggestive words.—(*Vide* Text 6, above).

The suggestiveness of Meanings in now described.

The author next states the nature of the said suggestiveness of words.—

'*Suggestion*' *is that function of the meaning which brings about the cognition of another meaning, by persons endowed with imaginative intuition,—through peculiarities of* (*a*) *the speaker,* (*b*) *the person spoken to,* (*c*) *intonation,* (*d*) *the sentence,* (*e*) *the expressed meaning,* (*f*) *the presence of another,* (*g*) *context,* (*h*) *place,* (*i*) *time and so forth.*—(21-22).

'*The person spoken to*'—*i. e.* one for whose sake the

अर्थस्य वाच्यलक्ष्यव्यङ्ग्यात्मनः।

क्रमेणोदाहरणानि ।

अइपिहुलं जलकुंभं घेत्तूण समागदह्मि सहि तुरिअं ।

समसेअसलिलणीसासणीसहा वीसमामि खणं ॥ १३ ॥

अत्र चौर्यरतगोपनं गम्यते ।

ओण्णिद्दं दोब्बल्लं चिंता अलसत्तणं सणीससिअं ।

मह मंदभाइणीए केरं सहि तुह वि अहह परिहवइ ॥१४॥

---

words are used ;—'*Intonation*'—variation of tone;—'*context*'—the occasion ;—'*of the meaning*'—*i. e.* of the expressed, the indicated or the suggested meaning.

Examples are cited in due order—(*a*) 'O Friend! having taken up a heavy jar of water, I have come walking fast, I feel fatigued and languid through perspiration and breathlessness ; I shall rest awhile.'

Here what is suggested is that the speaker is trying to conceal her stolen amours.

[What the woman describes are the physical signs that may be caused either by hard physical work or by amorous flirtations ; but on account of *the character of the speaker* being known to be that of a woman with loose morals, what is suggested is that the signs described have been due to dalliance, and she is trying to conceal this by attributing them to her having carried a heavy jar of water.]

(*b*) 'Oh my friend! for the sake of wretched me, thou also art suffering from sleeplessness, weakness, anxiety, lassitude and breathlessness !'

Here what is suggested is that the friend, who has been acting as an intermediary between the separated lovers, has herself been enjoying the company of her friend's lover.

[The physical effects described are such as may be caused, either by constant moving about from one party to the other for the purpose

अत्र दूत्यास्तत्कामुकोपभोगो व्यज्यते ।

तथाभूतां दृष्ट्वा नृपसदसि पाञ्चालतनयां
वने व्याधैः सार्धं सुचिरमुषितं वल्कलधरैः ।
विराटस्यावासे स्थितमनुचितारम्भनिभृतं
गुरुः खेदं खिन्ने मयि भजति नाद्यापि कुरुषु ॥१५॥

अत्र मयि न योग्यः खेदः कुरुषु तु योग्य इति काक्वा प्रकाश्यते । न च वाच्यसिद्ध्यङ्गमत्र काकुरिति गुणीभूतव्यङ्ग्यत्वं शङ्क्यम् । प्रश्नमात्रेणापि काकोर्विश्रान्तेः ।

---

of bringing the lovers together, or by dalliance; but the *friend addressed* being known to be prone to misbehaviour, the suggested meaning is that the symptoms described are due to her secret intercourse with her friend's lover.]

(*c*) 'Having seen the Princess of Pāñchāla subjected to indescribable indignity in the assembly of kings,—having observed the way in which for a long time we lived in the forest, clad in tree-bark, along with the foresters,—and having witnessed how we lived in Virāṭa's house, secretly and engaged in unbecoming acts,—having seen all it is still towards *myself*, sorely afflicted as I am, that our eldest brother bears anger, and not even now towards the Kurus!'

Here what is suggested by the 'Intonation' (the emphasis laid upon the pronoun 'myself') is that 'it is not right for the king to bear anger towards me, it is time now that he were angry with the Kurus'.

It will not be right to argue here that, inasmuch as the Intonation only serves to complete the directly expressed meaning of the sentence, this is a case of the suggested meaning being subservient (to the expressed meaning).—This, we say, will not be right; the Intonation does really serve to complete the meaning of the sentence; but this

तइआ मह गंडत्थलणिमिअं दिट्ठि ण णेसि अण्णत्तो ।
एण्हि सच्चेअ अहं ते अ कवाला ण सा दिट्ठी ॥१६॥

अत्र मत्सखीं कपोलप्रतिबिम्बितां पश्यतस्ते दृष्टिरन्यैवाभूत् चलितायां तु तस्यामन्यैव जातेत्यहो प्रच्छन्नकामुकत्वं ते इति व्यज्यते ।

उद्देशोयं सरसकदलीश्रेणिशोभातिशायी
कुञ्जोत्कर्षाङ्कुरितरमणीविभ्रमो नर्मदायाः ।
किं चैतस्मिन् सुरतसुहृदस्तन्वि ते वान्ति वाता
येषामग्रे सरति कलिताकाण्डकोपो मनोभूः ॥१७॥

---

it does only in so far as it *expresses* the question (' does the king bear anger towards me, and not towards the Kurus ? —and not as it *suggests* the further meaning of the *impropriety* of anger towards the speaker).

[Hence in so far as the *suggestion* by the Intonation is concerned, there is no ' subserviency to the expressed meaning ', specially as the *suggestion* appears after the *expressed* meaning has been duly comprehended.]

(*d*) ' At that time you did not turn away your eyes fixed as they were upon my cheeks ; now however, even though I am the same, and the cheeks are the same, yet that look of yours is no more.'

Here the meaning suggested is—' while my friend was sitting by me her face being reflected in my cheek, the way in which you looked towards that reflection was of quite a different character ; when however she has gone away, it has completely changed,—what a stealthy lover you are !'

[The *suggestion* is due to the fact of the *sentences* containing the terms ' at that time ' and ' now'.]

(*e*) ' This spot on the bank of the Narmadā is redolent with the beauty of fresh plantain-groves, and excites,

अत्र रतार्थं प्रविशेति व्यङ्ग्यम् ।

णोल्लेइ अणोल्लमणा अत्ता मं घरभरम्मि सअलम्मि ।
खणमेत्तं जइ संझाइ होइ ण व होइ वीसामो ॥१८॥

अत्र संध्या संकेतकाल इति तटस्थं प्रति कयाचिद्द्योत्यते ।

सुव्वइ समागमिस्सदि तुज्झ पिओ अज्ज पहरमेत्तेण ।
एमे अ कित्ति चिट्ठसि ता सहि सज्जेसु करणिज्जं ॥१९॥

---

through the loveliness of its bowers, the sportive graces of the lovely woman ! and further, O delicate one ! here are blowing breezes favourable to love-making, led as they are by the God of Love flurried with unaccountable excitement.'

Here the meaning suggested is—'let us enter the bower for the purpose of love-making.'

[This *suggestion* is due to the *expressed meaning* of the following words—(1) '*Tanvi*', which expresses *delicacy* brought about by the influence of love,—(2) '*Narmadā*,' the literal meaning of which is 'that which gives pleasure',—3) '*uddeśa*' which means 'that which can only be pointed out, and not easily reached, hence free from intrusion,'—(4) '*sarasa*' denotes freshness of the leaves, hence freedom from all fear of any shuffling sound being made,—(5) '*śreṇi*' denotes thickness of the grove, and hence invisibility from outside.]

(*f*) 'My hard-hearted mother-in-law is always urging me to all household work ; it is only in the evening that I get some respite, if any at all'.

Here a woman suggests to the person close by that evening is the only time at which assignation could be made.

[The expressed meaning is that the woman has no time except in the evening, and by reason of the proximity of her lover who is waiting for assignation, this simple statement suggests the evening as the time at which she agrees to meet him.]

(*g*) 'We hear your husband is coming here in three hours' time ; why then are you sitting idle ? O, friend, make your preparations'.

अत्रोपपतिं प्रत्यभिसर्तुं प्रस्तुता न युक्तमिति कयाचिन्निवार्यते ।

अन्यत्र यूयं कुसुमावचायं कुरुध्वमत्रास्मि करोमि सख्यः ।
नाहं हि दूरं भ्रमितुं समर्था प्रसीदतायं रचितोञ्जलिर्वः ॥२०॥

अत्र विविक्तोयं देश इति प्रच्छन्नकामुकस्त्वयाभिसार्यतामिति आश्वस्तां प्रति कयाचिन्निवेद्यते ।

गुरुअणपरवस पिअ किं भणामि तुइ मंदभाइणी अहअं ।
अज्ज पवासं वच्चसि वच्च सअं जेव्व सुणसि करणिज्जं ॥२१॥

अत्राद्य मधुसमये यदि व्रजसि तदाहं तावत् न भवामि तव तु न जानामि गतिमिति व्यज्यते । ॥

A woman who is on the point of going out to meet her lover, is warned by another woman that it would not be right to do so.

[The expressed meaning is that the woman should make preparations for meeting her husband who will soon be arriving ; but this being said on the *occasion* of the woman going out to meet a lover, *suggests* the said meaning.]

(*h*) ' O dear friends, you please do the flower-picking in some other place ; I am doing it here ; I am unable to wander farther off ; do me, therefore, this favour ; here I am beseeching you with joined palms '.

What is suggested by the speaker to her confidante is—' This place being quite solitary, please bring in my lover.'

[The expressed meaning is simply a request to her companions to leave her alone ; the sequestered position of the *spot* where the speech is made *suggests* the aforesaid request to the confidante.]

(*i*) 'O my beloved, you are bound to obey the wishes of your elders ; what shall I say to you, unfortunate as I am ! If you have to go on your journey, you may go ; you will hear what I am going to do.'

आदिग्रहणाच्चेष्टादेः । तत्र चेष्टाया यथा—
द्वारोपान्तनिरन्तरे मयि तया सौन्दर्यसारश्रिया
प्रोल्लास्योरुयुगं परस्परसमासक्तं समासादितम् ।
आनीतं पुरतः शिरोंशुकमधः क्षिप्ते चले लोचने
वाचस्तत्र निवारितं प्रसरणं संकोचिते दोर्लते ॥२२॥

The meaning suggested is—'The spring-season having arrived (when lovers should be united), if you are going away from home, I shall not be alive any longer and shall, therefore, not know where you may be.'

[This *suggestion* is due to the fact of the speech being made during *spring-time*.]

(*j*) The phrase 'and so forth' (in Text 22) is meant to include gesture and such other details. An example of suggestion by expressed meaning, through the peculiarity of *gesture*, we have in the following—

'While I was standing close to the door, she, resplendent with the very essence of beauty, having dilated her thighs, pressed them together; she brought down the veil over her face, cast unsteady glances, suppressed her speech and drew her arms together.'

Here the various gestures described *suggest* to the lover the wishes of the speaker.

[(1) The movement of the thighs suggests her desire for inverted intercourse, (2) the bringing down of the veil suggests that the lover should come secretly,—(3) the unsteady glances suggest that her passion of love has been aroused,—(4) the suppression of speech suggests that there should be no talk regarding the meeting,—(5) and the bringing together of the arms suggests that when he comes to her he will receive her embraces.]

Whenever occasion presents itself, examples are cited again and again for the purpose of explaining the subject

अत्र चेष्टया प्रच्छन्नकान्तविषय आकूतविशेषो ध्वन्यते ।

निराकाङ्क्षप्रतिपत्तये प्राप्तावसरतया च पुनः पुनरुदाह्रियते । वक्त्रादीनां मिथःसंयोगे द्विकादिभेदेन । अनेन क्रमेण लक्ष्यव्यङ्ग्ययोश्च व्यञ्जकत्वमुदाहार्यम् ।। २१–२२ ।।

शब्दप्रमाणवेद्योर्थो व्यनक्त्यर्थान्तरं यतः ।
अर्थस्य व्यञ्जकत्वे तच्छब्दस्य सहकारिता ।। २३ ।।

शब्देति । नहि प्रमाणान्तरवेद्योर्थो व्यञ्जकः ।। २३ ।।

इति श्रीकाव्यप्रकाशेर्थव्यञ्जकतानिर्णयो नाम
तृतीय उल्लासः ।।३।।

---

so fully as to leave nothing to be desired on the part of the enquirer.

Sometimes we have suggestion based upon the peculiarity of two or more of the conditions of the 'speaker' and the rest enumerated here.

The suggestiveness of the 'indicated' and 'suggested' meanings also may be illustrated in the same manner (as that of the 'expressed' meaning.) 22.

Inasmuch as the meaning that suggests another meaning is itself cognisable by means of the word,—the word also is helpfful in the suggestiveness of the meaning.—(23).

'*By means of the word*',—That is, anything cognised through any other means of knowledge is never *suggestive*. 23.

चतुर्थ उल्लासः

यद्यपि शब्दार्थयोर्निर्णये कृते दोषगुणालंकाराणां स्वरूपमभिधानीयं तथापि धर्मिणि प्रदर्शिते धर्माणां हेयोपादेयता ज्ञायत इति प्रथमं काव्यभेदान् आह—

अविवक्षितवाच्यो यस्तत्र वाच्यं भवेद्ध्वनौ ।
अर्थान्तरे सङ्क्रमितमत्यन्तं वा तिरस्कृतम् ॥ २४ ॥

लक्षणामूलगूढव्यङ्ग्यप्राधान्ये सत्येव अविवक्षितं वाच्यं यत्र स 'ध्वनौ' इत्यनुवादात् ध्वनिरिति ज्ञेयः । तत्र च वाच्यं क्वचिदनुपयुज्यमानत्वादर्थान्तरे परिणमितम् । यथा

CHAPTER IV

SUGGESTIVE POETRY.

'Word' and 'meaning' having been defined, the next subject to be dealt with should be the exact nature of 'defects,' 'excellences' and 'figures of speech' [in view of the form in which the definition of 'poetry' has been worded]; but it is only when the *object* to which the properties belong has been described that it can be ascertained whether certain *properties* of it are fit to be rejected or admitted; for this reason the author now proceeds to describe the various kinds of *poetry* (of which the defects, excellences and figures are *properties*.)

In that 'suggestive' poetry where the 'expressed' meaning is not meant to be applicable,—the 'expressed meaning' is either (*a*) *transformed into another meaning or* (*b*) *entirely rejected.*—(24).

त्वामस्मि वच्मि विदुषां समवायोत्र तिष्ठति ।
आत्मीयां मतिमास्थाय स्थितिमत्र विधेहि तत् ॥२३॥

अत्र वचनादि उपदेशादिरूपतया परिणमति ।
क्वचिदनुपपद्यमानतया अत्यन्तं तिरस्कृतम् । यथा—
उपकृतं बहु तत्र किमुच्यते सुजनता प्रथिता भवता परम् ।
विदधदीदृशमेव सदा सखे सुखितमास्स्व ततः शरदां शतम् ॥२४॥

The 'expressed meaning' is 'not meant to be applicable' only in cases where predominance attaches to that *abstruse* 'suggested meaning' which is based upon Indication ;—and it is such instances that should be understood as '*Dhvani*', 'suggestive poetry'; since they have been referred to in the text by the expression '*dhvanau*,' 'in suggestive poetry'.—(*a*) In this 'suggestive poetry,' the 'expressed meaning', being found to have no useful significance, becomes, in some cases, 'transformed into another meaning';—*e. g.* in the following—

'I tell you here sits an assembly of learned men ; you should, therefore, remain here with your mind fully alert.'

Here, mere *telling* (having no significance at all) becomes transformed into *advising* (the suggestion being 'I advise you that in this assembly of learned men, you should keep your mind alert, or else you will make yourself ridiculous').

(*b*) While in other cases, the 'expressed meaning,' being found to be inapplicable, becomes 'entirely rejected';—*e. g* in the following—

'Much benefit has been conferred upon me ;—what shall I say ?—Extreme gentlemanliness has been evinced by you ! May you, therefore, O friend, live in happiness for a hundred years, always behaving as you have done !'

एतद् अपकारिणं प्रति विपरीतलक्षणया कश्चिद्वक्ति ॥ २४ ॥

विवक्षितं चान्यपरं वाच्यं यत्रापरस्तु सः ।

अन्यपरं व्यङ्ग्यनिष्ठम् ॥ एष च

कोऽप्यलक्ष्यक्रमव्यङ्ग्यो लक्ष्यव्यङ्ग्यक्रमः परः ॥ २५ ॥

अलक्ष्येति । न खलु विभावानुभावव्यभिचारिण एव रसः । अपि तु रसस्तैः इत्यस्ति क्रमः । स तु लाघवान्न लक्ष्यते ॥ २५ ॥

अत्र

This is addressed to a person who has caused much injury to the speaker, who addresses to him these words in an ironical sense.

[The gratitude expressed by the words is altogether inapplicable to one who has done harm ; hence it is 'entirely rejected,' and its contrary is suggested.] 24.

[Suggestive Poetry *based upon Indication* having been described, the author proceeds to describe that *based upon denotation.*]

That (suggestive poetry), however, where the 'expressed meaning' is meant to be applicable, and is yet subservient to another meaning,—is the other kind.

'*Subservient to another*'—*i. e.* implies the 'suggested meaning'.

This 'other kind' of suggestive poetry is of two varieties—

(*a*) *One in which the order of sequence of the 'suggested meaning' is imperceptible. and* (*b*) *the other in which the order of sequence of the 'suggested meaning' is perceptible.* 25.

'*Imperceptible*';—there is this 'order of sequence' (in the case of all 'passionate' poetry, which is of the 'suggestive' kind) that the Excitants, the Ensuants and the Variables (which are 'expressed' by the words)

रसभावतदाभासभावशान्त्यादिरक्रमः ।
भिन्नो रसाद्यलङ्कारादलङ्कार्यतया स्थितः ॥ २६ ॥

आदिग्रहणाद् भावोदयभावसंधिभावशबलत्वानि । प्रधानतया यत्र स्थितो रसादिस्तत्रालंकार्यः यथोदाहरिष्यते । अन्यत्र तु प्रधाने वाक्यार्थे यत्राङ्गभूतो रसादिस्तत्र गुणीभूतव्यङ्ग्ये

---

do not themselves constitute the '*Rasa*' or 'Passion' (which is the 'suggested' meaning),—but this latter is *manifested* by them [and thus there is a distinct order of sequence, *first* the Excitant and the rest, and *then* the Passion]; but this sequence, being extremely subtle, is *not perceptible* in the case of the first kind of poetry here described. 25.

(a) Passion (b) Emotion (c) Aberrations of these, and the (d) Allayment of Emotion and the rest, constitute that in which the sequence is imperceptible ;—and all this, appearing in the form of something to be embellished, is distinct from those embellishments (Figures of Speech), *which are known as the* '*Passionate*' (Rasavat) *and the like.*

'*And the rest*'—this is meant to include (*a*) the *manifestation* of emotions, (*b*) the conjuncture of emotions, and (*c*) the *admixture* of emotions.

In cases where the Passion and the rest appear as the predominant factor, they are *to be embellished* ; as is going to be illustrated later on. In other cases, where the literal meaning of the sentence forms the predominant factor, and the Passion comes in only as a secondary element, the suggested meaning is subordinated, these same (passion and the rest), become *embellishments*, known as (*a*) '*Rasavat*' (Passionate), [where the Passion forms the subordinate factor], (*b*) '*Preya*' (agreeable) [where emotion forms the

रसवत्प्रेयऊर्जस्विसमाहितादयोलंकाराः । ते च गुणीभूतव्यङ्ग्या-भिधाने उदाहरिष्यन्ते ॥ २६ ॥

तत्र रसस्वरूपमाह–

कारणान्यथ कार्याणि सहकारीणि यानि च ।
रत्यादेः स्थायिनो लोके तानि चेन्नाट्यकाव्ययोः ॥ २७ ॥
विभावा अनुभावास्तत् कथ्यन्ते व्यभिचारिणः ।
व्यक्तः स तैर्विभावाद्यैः स्थायी भावो रसः स्मृतः ॥ २८ ॥

उक्तं हि भरतेन "विभावानुभावव्यभिचारिसंयोगाद् रसनिष्पत्तिः" इति ।

एतद्विवृण्वते— "विभावैर्ललनोद्यानादिभिरालम्बनोद्दीपन-कारणैः रत्यादिको भावो जनितः अनुभावैः कटाक्षभुजाक्षेपप्रभृतिभिः कार्यैः प्रतीतियोग्यः कृतः व्यभिचारिभिर्निर्वेदादिभिः सहकारिभिरुपचितो मुख्यया वृत्त्या रामादावनुकार्ये तद्रूपसंधानान्नर्तकेपि प्रतीयमानो रसः" इति भट्टलोल्लटप्रभृतयः ।

---

subordinate factor], (*c*) '*ūrjasvi*' (Forceful) [where the aberration of Passion forms the subordinate factor], (*d*) '*Samāhita*' Quiescent [where the allayment of emotion forms the subordinate factor].—Instances of these are to be cited under the sections dealing with 'Poetry of Subordinated Suggestion' (under Chapter V). 26.

The author now describes the nature of 'Passion'—

Text—What are known, in ordinary language, as (a) 'causes' (b) 'effects' and (c) 'auxiliaries' of the 'latent emotion' of Love and the like,—come to be spoken of as (a) 'excitants', (b) 'ensuants' and (c) 'variants', when found in Drama and Poetry; and when the latent emotion comes to be manifested by these, it is known as 'Rasa', '*Passion*'.—(27-28).

राम एवायम् अयमेव राम इति 'न रामोयम्' इत्यौत्तर-कालिके बाधे रामोयमिति रामः स्याद्वा न वायमिति राम-सदृशोयमिति च सम्यङ्मिथ्यासंशयसादृश्यप्रतीतिभ्यो विलक्षणया चित्रतुरगादिन्यायेन रामोयमिति प्रतिपत्त्या ग्राह्ये नटे

This is what has been thus declared by Bharata (in his *Nāṭyaśāstra*)—" There is accomplishment of Passion through the conjunction of the excitant, the ensuant and the variant."

[Four different interpretations of this assertion have been propounded, and each of these interpretations forms the basis of a distinct theory regarding the genesis of Rasa].

(A) The first interpretation is that given by Bhaṭṭa-Lollaṭa and his followers ; it is as follows :—The (latent) sentiment of love (and the like) is (*a*) *generated* by the *excitants—i. e.,* the basic cause, in the shape of the woman, and the inflaming cause, in the shape of the garden and so forth—(*b*) rendered cognisable by the *ensuants—i. e.,* effects, in the form of amorous glances, embraces and so forth,—and (*c*) consummated by the *variants*—such as self-disparagement and the like ;—this emotion, though primarily and really subsisting in the character personated—*e. g.* Rāma—comes to be recognised as subsisting in the personating actor by reason of his having assumed that character ; and when thus recognised, it is called ' Rasa ', ' passion '.

[This theory is open to the objection that it fails to explain the emotion that arises in the mind of the spectator of the dramatic representation; as according to it, the sentiment is generated in the *personated* character and secondarily recognised in the *personating* actor.]

'सेयं ममाङ्गेषु सुधारसच्छटा सुपूरकर्पूरशलाकिका दृशोः ।
मनोरथश्रीर्मनसः शरीरिणी प्राणेश्वरी लोचनगोचरं गता ॥२५॥
दैवादहमद्य तया चपलायतनेत्रया वियुक्तश्च ।
अविरलविलोलजलदः कालः समुपागतश्चायम्' ॥ २६ ॥

इत्यादिकाव्यानुसंधानबलाच्छिक्षाभ्यासनिर्वर्तितस्वकार्यप्रकटनेन च नटेनैव प्रकाशितैः कारणकार्यसहकारिभिः

(B) The second interpretation put forward by Śrī Śaṅkuka is as follows :—When an actor is personating Rāma, the spectator has with regard to him, the idea that 'this is Rāma himself'; but this idea is of a peculiar kind, being of the same nature as the idea of 'horse' that one has in regard to the picture of a horse ; it is different from all the four kinds of ordinary notions : (1) it is not of the nature of the ordinary right notion that one has in the case of the real Rāma. 'Rāma is the person', which is also confirmed by the subsequent cognition 'this is Rāma himself' [the cognition in question cannot be of this kind as Rāma is not present there] ;—(2) it is different also from the ordinary wrong cognition 'this is Rāma', which appears in regard to one who is not really Rāma, and which is sublated by the subsequent cognition 'this is not Rāma' [the cognition in question cannot be of this nature, as there is no such sublation in this case] ;—(3) nor is it of the same nature as the doubtful cognition 'this may or may not be Rama';—(4) nor lastly is it of the nature of the cognition of mere similarity, 'he is like Rāma' [the cognition in question cannot be of the nature of these last two cognitions, as it partakes of the notion of identification] ;—and this actor gives expression to the causes, effects and auxiliaries by the display of his art acquired

कृत्रिमैरपि तथानभिमन्यमानैर्विभावादिशब्दव्यपदेश्यैः 'संयोगात्, गम्यगमकभावरूपात् अनुमीयमानोपि वस्तुसौन्दर्यबलाद्रसनीयत्वेनान्यानुमीयमानविलक्षणः स्थायित्वेन संभाव्यमानो रत्यादिर्भावस्तत्रासन्नपि सामाजिकानां वासनया चर्व्यमाणो रस इति श्रीशङ्कुकः ।

---

through instruction and practice, and pondering over such poetry as the following—

'That lady, the mistress of my life, a splash of nectar to my body, unguent of camphor to my eyes, the very embodiment of the glorious longings of my heart, glided within the range of my vision';—

'Unfortunately I have to-day been separated from her, with eyes large and unsteady ; and that season has arrived wherein clouds are constantly flitting about';

Though all these causes, effects and auxiliaries are only artificially assumed, yet they are not regarded as such, and hence they are spoken of as 'excitants,' 'ensuants' and 'variants';—the '*saṁyoga*', 'conjunction', of these three,—*i. e.*, through the relation of 'the indicative and the indicated', subsisting between these three and the resultant feeling—leads to the *inference* of the 'latent emotion', of Love *e. g.*;—though thus *inferred*, the emotion is by reason of the peculiar charm, different from all other objects of inference ; and hence it is recognised as something subsisting latently ; and as, though thus *inferred*, this emotion is recognised, through its peculiar charm, as something *relished*, and as such different from other ordinary *inferred* things ; it is imagined to be subsisting latently in the actor ; and even though not really present in him, it is relished by the spectators through their predisposed tendencies.

न ताटस्थ्येन नात्मगतत्वेन रसः प्रतीयते नोत्पद्यते नाभिव्यज्यते अपि तु काव्ये नाट्ये चाभिधातो द्वितीयेन विभावादिसाधारणीकरणात्मना भावकत्वव्यापारेण भाव्यमानः स्थायी सत्त्वोद्रेकप्रकाशानन्दमयसंविद्विश्रान्तिसतत्त्वेन भोगेन भुज्यते इति भट्टनायकः ।

[Under this view, the causes, effects and auxiliaries are the invariable concomitants of the emotion,—and hence when they are perceived, in the Actor, they lead to the inference of the emotion; and the inference of this non-existent emotion is explained as being due to the predisposition of the audience.]

[The objection against this view is that inference is a purely intellectual process, and hence cannot account for the highly complex emotional phenomena involved in *Rasa*.]

(C) The third interpretation, that of Bhaṭṭa-nāyaka, is as follows :—'Passion' is not cognised (inferred), or generated, or manifested,—either unconcernedly (as not concerning the spectator at all, as held by Bhaṭṭa-Lollaṭa), or as subsisting in the spectator himself (relished by him, as held by Śrī-Śaṅkuka);—what happens is that in poetry and drama words are endowed with a peculiar presentative potency, distinct from direct Denotation (and indirect Indication)—which tends to generalise the Excitants, Ensuants and Variants, and thereby presents to consciousness the 'latent emotion', which thereupon comes to be relished by a process of delectation abounding in enlightenment and bliss, due to the plenitude of the quality of Harmony (*Sattva*).

[According to this view the relishing of Passion is the outcome of the purely verbal process of 'generalised presentation'. This is open to the objection that it makes the unwarrantable assumption of this last mentioned verbal process.]

लोके प्रमदाभिः स्थाय्यनुमानेऽभ्यासपाटववतां काव्ये नाट्ये च तैरेव कारणत्वादिपरिहारेण विभावनादिव्यापारवत्त्वादलौकिकविभावादिशब्दव्यवहार्यैर्ममैवैते शत्रोरेवैते तटस्थस्यैवैते न ममैवैते न शत्रोरेवैते न तटस्थस्यैवैते इति संबन्धविशेषस्वीकारपरिहारनियमानध्यवसायात् साधारण्येन प्रतीतैरभिव्यक्तः सामाजिकानां वासनात्मतया स्थितः स्थायी

(D) The fourth explanation, propounded by the revered Āchārya Abhinavagupta, is as follows :—

In the mind of such spectators as are proficient in the art of feeling emotion, a particular emotion is already present, in the form of 'predisposition';—lying thus latent, it becomes patently manifested by such agencies as those of women and other things, which, in ordinary parlance are known as 'causes', (effects and auxiliaries); but in poetry and drama, they renounce these names by reason of their being endowed with the faculty of *exciting* and so forth, and, on this account, come to be spoken of by the extraordinary names of 'Excitants', 'Ensuants' and 'Variants' ;—these Excitants and the rest being recognised in their most generalised forms, not partaking of any restrictions due to either the affirmation or negation of any of those specific relationships that are involved in such conceptions as (1) 'this is mine' or 'this is my enemy's', or 'this belongs to a disinterested person' (where specific relationship is *affirmed*) or (2) 'this is not mine', 'this is not my enemy's', 'this does not belong to a disinterested person' (where specific relationship is *denied*);—though the said emotion actually subsists in the particular spectator himself, yet, by reason of the generalised form in which it is presented, the man loses, for the moment, all sense of his separate personality and has his

रत्यादिको नियतप्रमातृगतत्वेन स्थितोपि साधारणोपायबलात् तत्कालविगलितपरिमितप्रमातृभाववशोन्मिषितवेद्यान्तरसंपर्क-शून्यापरिमितभावेन प्रमात्रा सकलसहृदयसंवादभाजा साधा-रण्येन स्वाकार इवाभिन्नोपि गोचरीकृतश्चर्व्यमाणतैकप्राणो

---

consciousness merged in the universal ; and this representing the mental condition of all men of poetic sensibility, he apprehends the said emotion ; though, having been manifested in its most generalised form, it has no existence apart from its own apprehension ; in fact its sole essence consists in its *being relished*, and it lasts as long as the Excitants, Ensuants and Variants continue to exist ;—it is relished in the same manner as a mixed beverage ; and when it is relished, it appears as if it were vibrating before the eyes, entering the inmost recesses of the heart, inspiriting the entire body, and eclipsing everything else ; it makes one feel the rapturous bliss of Brahman ;—the emotion thus manifested becomes the source of transcendent charm and is spoken of as '*rasa*', 'Passion'.—This Passion is not an *effect*, something produced (by the excitants and the rest) ; for if it were an effect, it would continue to exist even after these excitants and the rest had ceased to exist. [As the jar continues to exist even after the destruction of the stick and other causes that had operated in its production.] Nor is it something *to be made known* (by the excitants etc.); as it is never an accomplished entity (like the jar, and it is only an accomplished entity that can be made known) ;—in reality, it is only *manifested* by the Excitants, Ensuants and Variants, and is something *to be relished*.—Against this, the question may be asked—" where has anything been seen to exist apart from *what produces* and from what *makes*

विभावादिजीवितावधिः पानकरसन्यायेन चर्व्यमाणः पुर इव परिस्फुरन् हृदयमिव प्रविशन् सर्वाङ्गीणमिवालिङ्गन् अन्यत् सर्वमिव तिरोदधत् ब्रह्मास्वादमिवानुभावयन् अलौकिक-चमत्कारकारी शृङ्गारादिको रसः। स च न कार्यः। विभावादि-विनाशेपि तस्य संभवप्रसङ्गात्। नापि ज्ञाप्यः सिद्धस्य तस्या-संभवात्। अपि तु विभावादिभिर्व्यञ्जितश्चर्वणीयः। कारक-ज्ञापकाभ्यामन्यत् क्व दृष्टमिति चेत् न क्वचिद्दृष्टमित्यलौकि-कसिद्धेर्भूषणमेतन्न दूषणम्। चर्वणानिष्पत्त्या तस्य निष्पत्तिरुप-चरितेति कार्योऽप्युच्यताम्। लौकिकप्रत्यक्षादिप्रमाणताटस्थ्याव-बोधशालिमितयोगिज्ञानवेद्यान्तरसंस्पर्शरहितस्वात्ममात्रपर्यवसि-

---

known ?"—Our answer to this is that the fact that what occurs in the case of Passion has not been seen anywhere else only serves to confirm, not vitiate, the transcendental nature of Passion. It may however be spoken of as an 'effect' by virtue of its being *accomplished* by the accomplishment of its relishing ; and it may also be regarded as 'to be known', 'cognised', in the sense that it forms the object of a super-physical consciousness, which differs (1) from Perception and other ordinary forms of cognition, (2) from the cognition of the imperfect *Yogin*, which is independent of the ordinary means of cognition and (3) also from the cognition of the perfect *Yogin*, which is self-centered and free from all touch of any other cognisable thing.—Further the cognition that apprehends it cannot be of the 'indeterminate' kind, a due recognition of the excitants, ensuants and variants forming an important element in it ; nor can it be of the 'determinate' kind, because what is merely *relished* as transcendent bliss depends entirely upon its own realisation (which is not the case with determinate cognitions).—Here also as before,

तपरिमितेतरयोगिसंवेदनविलक्षणलोकोत्तरस्वसंवेदनगोचर इति प्रत्येयोप्यभिधीयताम् । तद्ग्राहकं च न निर्विकल्पकं विभावादिपरामर्शप्रधानत्वात् । नापि सविकल्पकं चर्व्यमाणस्यालौकिकानन्दमयस्य स्वसंवेदनसिद्धत्वात् । उभयाभावस्वरूपस्य चोभयात्मकत्वमपि पूर्ववल्लोकोत्तरतामेव गमयति न तु विरोधमिति श्रीमदाचार्याभिनवगुप्तपादाः ॥

व्याघ्रादयो विभावा भयानकस्येव वीराद्भुतरौद्राणाम् अश्रुपातादयोनुभावाः शृङ्गारस्येव करुणभयानकयोः चिन्तादयो व्यभिचारिणः शृङ्गारस्येव वीरकरुणभयानकानामिति पृथगनैकान्तिकत्वात् सूत्रे मिलिता निर्दिष्टाः ।

---

the fact that it is neither the one nor the other, and yet it partakes of the nature of both, only confirms its transcendental character, and does not vitiate it.

[The difference between the *fourth* and the *third* explanations lies in the fact that according to the *third*, there is relishing of the emotion which is not present in the spectator's mind, while according to the *fourth*, it is present in his mind in the form of *predisposition*. The propriety of this explanation is further strengthened by the fact that the spectator whose mind is free from such predisposition does not feel the passion,]

The 'excitants, ensuants and variants' have been spoken of in the *Sūtra* (of Bharata) in a general way, because as a rule they are not related specifically to any particular Passion ; for instance, the Tiger is an *excitant* of the 'Frightful', as also of the 'Heroic', the 'Marvellous' and the 'Furious'; the shedding of tears is an *ensuant* of the 'Erotic', as also of the 'Pathetic' and the 'Frightful'; painful reflection is the *variant* of the 'Erotic', as also of the 'Heroic', the 'Pathetic' and the 'Frightful.'

वियदलिमलिनाम्बुगर्भमेघं
मधुकरकोकिलकूजितैर्दिशां श्रीः ।
धरणिरभिनवाङ्कुराङ्कटङ्का
प्रणतिपरे दयिते प्रसीद मुग्धे ॥२७॥

इत्यादौ

परिमृदितमृणालीम्लानमङ्गं प्रवृत्तिः
कथमपि परिवारप्रार्थनाभिः क्रियासु ।
कलयति च हिमांशोर्निष्कलङ्कस्य लक्ष्मी-
मभिनवकरिदन्तच्छेदकान्तः कपोलः ॥२८॥

इत्यादौ

दूरादुत्सुकमागते विवलितं संभाषिणि स्फारितं
संश्लिष्यत्यरुणं गृहीतवसने किंचाञ्चितभ्रूलतम् ।
मानिन्याश्चरणानतिव्यतिकरे बाष्पाम्बुपूर्णेक्षणं
चक्षुर्जातमहो प्रपञ्चचतुरं जातागसि प्रेयसि ॥२९॥

In the following verses—

(*a*) 'The sky is overcast with heavy clouds dark as the black bee ; the atmosphere has acquired loveliness through the warbling of the cuckoo and the bee ; the earth bears on her lap the shoots of tender sprouts ; young woman ! be reconciled to your lover who is so devoted in his affections !' ;—

(*b*) 'Her body withered and languid like the squeezed lotus-stalk, her activity due to the expostulations of her attendants, her cheek lovely like a piece of fresh ivory, bears the sheen of the stainless moon';—

(*c*) 'Her lover having given cause for offence, the eyes of the self-respecting woman became skilled in giving expression to varied emotions—being anxious on seeing

इत्यादौ च

यद्यपि विभावानामनुभावानामौत्सुक्यव्रीडाहर्षकोपासूयाप्रसादानां च व्यभिचारिणां केवलानामत्र स्थितिः, तथाप्येतेषामसाधारणत्वमित्यन्यतमद्वयाक्षेपकत्वे सति नानैकान्तिकत्वमिति ॥ २८ ॥

तद्विशेषानाह—

शृङ्गारहास्यकरुणरौद्रवीरभयानकाः ।
बीभत्साद्भुतसंज्ञौ चेत्यष्टौ नाट्ये रसाः स्मृताः ॥ २९ ॥

---

her lover at a distance, averted on his drawing near her, beaming on being spoken to, blushing on embrace, curving the brows on her clothes being touched, filling with tears on his falling on her feet,'—

We find that the first (*a*) mentions the excitants only (in the shape of the woman, the season and so forth ; and makes no mention of any ensuants or variants),—the second (*b*) mentions the ensuants alone (in the shape of the languishing of the body and so forth),—and the third (*c*) mentions only the variants, in the shape of Anxiety, Modesty, Joy, Anger, Aversion and Conciliation ; [and as such it would appear to be not right to say that Passion is manifested by the excitants, ensuants and variants collectively, as the *Sūtra* declares].—But what each of the cited examples directly mentions—are the exceptional elements of each case, and the other two factors are also indirectly implied ; so that they do not vitiate the truth of the general proposition (propounded by Bharata). 28.

The Author next mentions the particular kinds of Passion.—

(1) *The Erotic,* (2) *the Comic,* (3) *the Pathetic,* (4) *the Furious,* (5) *the Heroic,* (6) *the Frightful,* (7) *the Disgustful,*

तत्र शृङ्गारस्य द्वौ भेदौ । संभोगो विप्रलम्भश्च । तत्राद्यः परस्परावलोकनालिङ्गनाधरपानपरिचुम्बनाद्यनन्तत्वादपरिच्छेद्य एक एव गण्यते । यथा

शून्यं वासगृहं विलोक्य शयनादुत्थाय किंचिच्छनै-
र्निद्राव्याजमुपागतस्य सुचिरं निर्वर्ण्य पत्युर्मुखम् ।
विस्रब्धं परिचुम्ब्य जातपुलकामालोक्य गण्डस्थलीं
लज्जानम्रमुखी प्रियेण हसता बाला चिरं चुम्बिता ॥३०॥

तथा

त्वं मुग्धाक्षि विनैव कञ्चुलिकया धत्से मनोहारिणीं
लक्ष्मीमित्यभिधायिनि प्रियतमे तद्वीटिकासंस्पृशि ।
शय्योपान्तनिविष्टसस्मितसखीनेत्रोत्सवानन्दितो
निर्यातः शनकैरलीकवचनोपन्यासमालीजनः ॥ ३१ ॥

---

and (8) *the Marvellous have been described as the eight Passions in the Drama.*—(29).

Of the Erotic there are two varieties—(1) in union and (2) in privation ; of these the former is counted as *one* only, any classification of it being impossible by reason of the endless variety of its manifestations, in the form of mutual glances, kissing, embraces, and so forth. Examples—

(*a*) 'Finding the love-chamber empty, she rose gently from the couch and having intently gazed at the face of her husband who was feigning sleep, she kissed him with confidence ; but noticing a tremor in his cheeks, she hung her head through shame and was repeatedly kissed by her smiling lover'. [Here the first overture comes from the woman].—

(*b*) " 'O thou of lovely eyes, thou appearest heart-ravishing without the bodice '—saying this the lover

अपरस्तु—अभिलापविरहेर्ष्याप्रवासशापहेतुक इति पञ्चविधः । क्रमेणोदाहरणम्—

प्रेमार्द्राः प्रणयस्पृशः परिचयादुद्गाढरागोदया-
स्तास्ता मुग्धदृशो निसर्गमधुराश्चेष्टा भवेयुर्मयि ।
यास्वन्तःकरणस्य बाह्यकरणव्यापाररोधी क्षणा-
दाशंसापरिकल्पितास्वपि भवत्यानन्दसान्द्रो लयः ॥ ३२ ॥

अन्यत्र व्रजतीति का खलु कथा नाप्यस्य तादृक् सुहृद्
यो मां नेच्छति नागतश्च हहहा कोयं विधेः प्रक्रमः ।
इत्यल्पेतरकल्पनाकवलितस्वान्ता निशान्तान्तरे
बाला वृत्तविवर्तनव्यतिकरा नाप्नोति निद्रां निशि ॥ ३३ ॥

---

touched the knot of the bodice ; whereupon her friends, delighted at the look of rapture in the eyes of their smiling companion seated upon the couch, went out on various pretexts." [Here the overture comes from the man].

The other kind of the Erotic (that in Privation), is of five kinds, the feeling being due to (*a*) longing, (*b*) separation, (*c*) jealousy, (*d*) residence abroad, and (*e*) curse. Examples in order—

(*a*) 'May the behaviour of the fair-eyed one towards me be steeped in affection and full of love and naturally sweet !, that behaviour in which love has been intensified by ripening acquaintance, and the mere thought of which immerses the heart in a flood of joy, suspending the functioning of all external organs.'

(*b*) 'Has he gone elsewhere ?—What possibility is there of that ? He has no such friend as does not want me. And yet he has not come ! Oh ! What an irony of fate !—Having her heart devoured by these considerable vascillations, the girl rolls about in her bed and does not obtain sleep.'

एषा विरहोत्कण्ठिता ।

सा पत्युः प्रथमापराधसमये सख्योपदेशं विना
नो जानाति सविभ्रमाङ्गवलनावक्रोक्तिसंसूचनम् ।
स्वच्छैरच्छकपोलमूलगलितैः पर्यस्तनेत्रोत्पला
बाला केवलमेव रोदिति लुठल्लोलालकैरश्रुभिः ॥ ३४ ॥

प्रस्थानं वलयैः कृतं प्रियसखैरस्रैरजस्रं गतं
धृत्या न क्षणमासितं व्यवसितं चित्तेन गन्तुं पुरः ।
यातुं निश्चितचेतसि प्रियतमे सर्वे समं प्रस्थिता
गन्तव्ये सति जीवित प्रियसुहृत्सार्थः किमु त्यज्यते ॥ ३५ ॥

त्वामालिख्य प्रणयकुपितां धातुरागैः शिलाया-
मात्मानं ते चरणपतितं यावदिच्छामि कर्तुम् ।
अस्रैस्तावन्मुहुरुपचितैर्दृष्टिरालुप्यते मे
क्रूरस्तस्मिन्नपि न सहते संगमं नौ कृतान्तः ॥ ३६ ॥

The girl depicted here is anxious in separation.

(*c*) 'On the occasion of her husband's first delinquency, not having been instructed by her friend, she knows not how to make any graceful gestures or poignant remarks ; all that she does is to turn away her lotus-like eyes and weep with tears flowing down her cheeks and rolling over her dishevelled tresses'.

(*d*) 'The Bracelets have gone ; your dear friends the Fears have freely departed ; Patience stayed not for a moment ; the Mind determined to go forward ;—on my beloved having made up his mind to depart, all these have started together ; O Life ! as you also have to go, why are you losing the company of your dear friends ?'

(*e*) 'Having painted thee in a mood of loving displeasure, on a slab of stone with mineral pigments,—as

हास्यादीनां क्रमेणोदाहरणम्—

आकुञ्च्य पाणिमशुचिं मम मूर्ध्नि वेश्या
मन्त्राम्भसां प्रतिपदं पृषतैः पवित्रे ।
तारस्वनं प्रथितथूत्कमदात्प्रहारं
हाहा हतोहमिति रोदिति विष्णुशर्मा ॥ ३७ ॥

हा मातस्त्वरितासि कुत्र किमिदं हा देवताः क्वाशिषः
धिक् प्राणान् पतितोशनिर्हुतवहस्तेङ्गेषु दग्धे दृशौ ।
इत्थं घर्घरमध्यरुद्धकरुणाः पौराङ्गनानां गिर-
श्चित्रस्थानपि रोदयन्ति शतधा कुर्वन्ति भित्तीरपि ॥३८॥

---

soon as I think of representing myself as fallen upon thy feet, my vision becomes blurred by the frequent outburst of tears ; cruel Fate brooks not our union even in the picture !'

[This is cited as an instance of ' privation due to curse', as it describes a lover who was separated from his lady by reason of a curse of banishment pronounced upon him by his master.]

The following are examples, in due order, of the Comic and other passions :—

(1) " Clenching her dirty hands, the harlot struck with a loud thumping sound upon my head, sanctified with drops of water consecrated with incantations ; —Ah ! I am damned !"—so cries Viṣṇu Śarman." —(The *Comic*).

(2) " O mother, whereto hast thou hastened away ? What is this ? O Gods, where be the blessings ? Fie on our lives ! Thunderous fire has fallen on thy limbs ! Eyes scorched !"—These loud and pathetic lamentations of the female citizens make even statues weep and shatter even walls into hundreds of pieces'.—(The *Pathetic*).

कृतमनुमतं दृष्टं वा यैरिदं गुरुपातकं
मनुजपशुभिर्निर्मर्यादैर्भवद्भिरुदायुधैः ।
नरकरिपुणा सार्धं तेषां सभीमकिरीटिना-
मयमहमसृङ्मेदोमांसैः करोमि दिशां बलिम् ॥३९॥
क्षुद्रा संत्रासमेते विजहत हरयः क्षुण्णशक्रेभकुम्भा
युष्मद्देहेषु लज्जां दधति परममी सायका निष्पतन्तः ।
सौमित्रे तिष्ठ पात्रं त्वमसि न हि रुषां नन्वहं मेघनादः
किंचिद्भ्रूभङ्गलीलानियमितजलधिं राममन्वेषयामि ॥४०॥
ग्रीवाभङ्गाभिरामं मुहुरनुपतति स्यन्दने बद्धदृष्टिः
पश्चार्धेन प्रविष्टः शरपतनभयाद्भूयसा पूर्वकायम् ।
दर्भैरर्धावलीढैः श्रमविवृतमुखभ्रंशिभिः कीर्णवर्त्मा ।
पश्योदग्रप्लुतत्वाद्वियति बहुतरं स्तोकमुर्व्यां प्रयाति ॥४१॥

---

(3) 'O you dishonourable beasts of men wielding weapons, by whom this heinous crime has been committed, sanctioned or witnessed! Here I am going to make to the Quarters an offering of the blood, fat and flesh of all these along with Bhīma and Arjuna and Kṛṣṇa'.—(The *Furious*).

(4) 'Poor monkeys! Give up your fears; these arrows that have shattered the temple of Indra's elephant feel ashamed to fall upon your bodies;—O son of Sumitrā, stand where you are; you are not a fit object of my wrath; —I, Meghanāda, am looking for Rāma, who has bound down the ocean by a mere curving of his eye-brows!'—(The *Heroic*).

(5) 'Behold! The deer, owing to the great speed at which it is running, is moving more in the sky than on the earth; with a graceful turn of its neck, it is casting backward glances at the pursuing chariot; through fear

उत्कृत्योत्कृत्य कृत्तिं प्रथममथ पृथूत्सेधभूयांसि मांसा-
न्यंसस्फिक्पृष्ठपिण्डयाद्यवयवसुलभान्यग्रपूतीनि जग्ध्वा ।
आर्त्तः पर्यस्तनेत्रः प्रकटितदशनः प्रेतरङ्कः करङ्का-
दङ्कस्थादस्थिसंस्थं स्थपुटगतमपि क्रव्यमव्यग्रमत्ति ॥४२॥
चित्रं महानेष बतावतारः क्व कान्तिरेषाभिनवैव भङ्गिः ।
लोकोत्तरं धैर्यमहो प्रभावः काप्याकृतिर्नूतन एष सर्गः ॥४३॥
एषां स्थायिभावानाह—

रतिर्हासश्च शोकश्च क्रोधोत्साहौ भयं तथा ।
जुगुप्सा विस्मयश्चेति स्थायिभावाः प्रकीर्तिताः ॥ ३० ॥

---

of the falling of the arrow, it has much of its hinder part contracted within the fore-part ; and it scatters on the path half-chewed morsels of grass out of its mouth gaping with fatigue'.—(The *Frightful*).

(6) 'Having first torn and stripped off the skin, and then devoured the swollen and fearfully stinking lumps of flesh that could be easily got at from such parts of the body as the shoulder, the back and the buttocks, the beggarly ghost casts its glances all round, and displaying its teeth, is leisurely devouring the flesh that remains on the bones and joints of the skeleton lying on its lap.'—(*The Disgustful*).

(7) 'How wonderful ! A superb incarnation this ! What effulgence ! An unprecedented grace ! Supernatural equanimity ! Marvellous majesty ! An indescribable figure ! Quite a novel creation !'—(The *Marvellous*). 29.

The author now mentions the 'basic feelings' of the above-mentioned Passions—

Love, Mirth, Sorrow, Resentment, Heroism, Fear, Loathing and Wonder have been declared to be the 'Basic Feelings.'—(30)

स्पष्टम् ॥ ३० ॥

व्यभिचारिणो ब्रूते—

निर्वेदग्लानिशङ्काख्यास्तथासूया मदश्रमाः ।
आलस्यं चैव दैन्यं च चिन्ता मोहः स्मृतिर्धृतिः ॥ ३१ ॥
व्रीडा चपलता हर्ष आवेगो जडता तथा ।
गर्वो विषाद औत्सुक्यं निद्रापस्मार एव च ॥ ३२ ॥
सुप्तं प्रबोधोमर्षश्चाप्यवहित्थमथोग्रता ।
मतिर्व्याधिस्तथोन्मादस्तथा मरणमेव च ॥ ३३ ॥
त्रासश्चैव वितर्कश्च विज्ञेया व्यभिचारिणः ।
त्रयस्त्रिंशदमी भावाः समाख्यातास्तु नामतः ॥ ३४ ॥

निर्वेदस्यामङ्गलप्रायस्य प्रथममनुपादेयत्वेप्युपादानं व्यभिचारित्वेपि स्थायिताभिधानार्थम् । तेन

He next describes the *Variants*—

(1) *Self-disparagement,* (2) *Debility,* (3) *Apprehension,* (4) *Hatred,* (5) *Intoxication,* (6) *Lassitude,* (7) *Indolence,* (8) *Depression,* (9) *Painful Reflection,* (10) *Distraction,* (11) *Recollection,* (12) *Serenity,* (13) *Shame,* (14) *Unsteadiness,* (15) *Joy,* (16) *Flurry,* (17) *Stupefaction,* (18) *Arrogance,* (19) *Despondency,* (20) *Impatience,* (21) *Drowsiness,* (22) *Dementedness,* (23) *Dreaming,* (24) *Awakening,* (25) *Animosity,* (26) *Constraint,* (27) *Irascibility,* (28) *Resolve,* (29) *Sickness,* (30) *Mental Derangement,* (31) *Demise,* (32) *Alarm and* (33) *Trepidation,—these are the thirty-three Variants described by name.*—(31-34).

Though 'self-disparagement' is an almost inauspicious feeling, and as such should not have been mentioned first, yet it has been so mentioned with a view to indicate that though it is a 'variant', it serves as a 'basic emotion' also ; hence it is that—

निर्वेदस्थायिभावोस्ति शान्तोपि नवमो रसः ।

यथा

अहौ वा हारे वा कुसुमशयने वा दृषदि वा
मणौ वा लोष्टे वा बलवति रिपौ वा सुहृदि वा ।
तृणे वा स्त्रैणे वा मम समदृशो यान्ति दिवसाः
क्वचित्पुण्यारण्ये शिव शिव शिवेति प्रलपतः ॥ ४४ ॥

रतिर्देवादिविषया व्यभिचारी तथाञ्जितः ॥ ३५ ॥
भावः प्रोक्तः

आदिशब्दान्मुनिगुरुनृपपुत्रादिविषया । कान्ताविषया तु व्यक्ता शृङ्गारः ।

The Quietistic is the ninth Passion, of which Self-disparagement is the basic feeling.

Example.—

'May my days pass in some sacred forest, while I am muttering *Śiva, Śiva,* with an equal eye towards a snake or a necklace, a flower-bed or a stone-slab, a jewel or a clod of earth, a powerful enemy or a friend, a straw or a woman !'

[Having provided a full account of 'Passion,' the author proceeds to define 'Emotion' and the other subdivisions of 'suggestion with imperceptible sequence,' mentioned in Text 26.]

'Love' (and the other feelings) towards a god or such other beings, as also a 'Variant' when suggested (as a primary factor), is described as 'Bhāva', 'Emotion'.

[The 'Basic Feeling,' when not sufficiently developed into 'Passion,'—*e.g.* when the feeling of Love is towards a god or some such superior being,—it is known simply as 'Emotion,' *Bhāva,* as distinguished from the 'Latent Emotion,' *Sthāyī Bhāva.*]

'Such other beings' refers to sages, preceptors, king, son and so forth ; when Love is manifested towards a woman, it becomes the 'Erotic' *passion.*

उदाहरणम्

कण्ठकोणविनिविष्टमीश ते कालकूटमपि मे महामृतम् ।
अप्युपात्तममृतं भवद्वपुर्भेदवृत्ति यदि मे न रोचते ॥ ४५ ॥
हरत्यघं संप्रति हेतुरेष्यतः शुभस्य पूर्वाचरितैः कृतं शुभैः ।
शरीरभाजां भवदीयदर्शनं व्यनक्ति कालत्रितयेऽपि योग्यताम् ॥ ४६ ॥

एवमन्यदप्युदाहार्यम् ।

अञ्जितव्यभिचारी यथा

जाने कोपपराङ्मुखी प्रियतमा स्वप्नेऽद्य दृष्टा मया
मा मां संस्पृश पाणिनेति रुदती गन्तुं प्रवृत्ता पुरः ।
नो यावत्परिरभ्य चाटुशतकैराश्वासयामि प्रियां
भ्रातस्तावदहं शठेन विधिना निद्रादरिद्रीकृतः ॥ ४७ ॥

Example (of the said 'Emotion')—

(*a*) 'O Lord ! Even the deadly poison, though hidden within Thy throat, is pure nectar to me ; while nectar itself (in the shape of the moon), even though held high (on Thy head), pleases me not, as it does not form part of Thy body',—(*Love towards a God*).

(*b*) 'It destroys sin at the present time, it is the cause of forthcoming blessings, and is brought about by (and indicative of) virtuous acts of the past : thus does your visit to all corporeal beings bear testimony to their excellent character at all the three periods of time'.
—(*Love towards a sage,* Nārada).

Example of the Variant suggested (as the predominant factor).—

'My best loved one was seen by me to-day in a dream, having her face turned away through anger, weeping and saying "don't, don't touch me with your hand," and proceeding to go away ; as soon as I was going to em-

अत्र विधिं प्रत्यसूया ।

तदाभासा अनौचित्यप्रवर्त्तिताः ।

तदाभासा रसाभासा भावाभासाश्च ।

तत्र रसाभासो यथा

स्तुमः कं वामाक्षि क्षणमपि विना यं न रमसे
विलेभे कः प्राणान् रणमखमुखे यं मृगयसे ।
सुलग्ने को जातः शशिमुखि यमालिङ्गसि बलात्
तपःश्रीः कस्यैषा मदननगरि ध्यायसि तु यम् ।। ४८ ।।

अत्रानेककामुकविषयमभिलाषं तस्याः स्तुम इत्याद्यनुगतं बहुव्यापारोपादानं व्यनक्ति ।

---

brace and pacify her with sweet and loving words, I was, O brother, deprived by wicked Fate of sleep.'

Here Hatred towards Fate is what is meant to be suggested.

The 'aberrations of these' are these same when improperly manifested.

'*Aberrations of these*' *i. e.,*—'aberration of Passion' and 'Semblance of Emotion.'

An example of the 'semblance of Passion' we have in the following.—

'O fair-eyed one ! Which is the man whom I should adore, without whom thou art not happy even for a moment ? Who gave up his life in battle, whom thou art seeking ? Who is born in an auspicious moment, whom thou O moon-faced one, embracest firmly ? Who is the man with such glorious religious merit as thạt thou thinkest of him, O abode of Cupid !'

In this verse the various sentences—'whom I should adore' and so forth—are indicative of the manifold

भावाभासो यथा

राकासुधाकरमुखी तरलायताक्षी
सा स्मेरयौवनतरङ्गितविभ्रमाङ्गी ।
तत् किं करोमि विदधे कथमत्र मैत्रीं
तत्स्वीकृतिव्यतिकरे क इवाभ्युपायः ।। ४९ ।।

अत्र चिन्ता अनौचित्यप्रवर्तिता । एवमन्येप्युदाहार्याः ।।

भावस्य शान्तिरुदयः सन्धिः शबलता तथा ।। ३६ ।।

---

activities of the woman, which show that she entertains the feeling of love towards several lovers.

[And the love of the speaker towards such a woman, on that account, and also on account of her not entertaining any such feeling towards himself, not reaching the high degree of 'Passion,' becomes manifested only as an 'aberration' thereof.]

The following is an example of the 'Aberration of Emotion'—

'She has a face like the full moon ; her eyes are large and unsteady ; her body is vibrating with budding youth ; what shall I do ? How should I proceed to win her favour ? What is the means whereby she would accept me ?'

Here we have 'Reflection' 'improperly manifested.'

[The impropriety is lying in the fact that the love proceeds from the man before it has arisen in the woman, which is not the conventional process.]

Similarly examples of the other 'aberrations' may be cited.

Of Emotion, there are (a) 'Allayment,' (b) 'Manifestation', (c) 'Conjuncture' and (d) 'Admixture'—(36).

Examples in due order—

(*a*) '"Why are you concealing, under the pretence of falling on my feet, your chest bearing the marks of

क्रमेणोदाहरणम्

तस्याः सान्द्रविलेपनस्तनतटप्रश्लेषमुद्राङ्कितं
किं वक्षश्चरणानतिव्यतिकरव्याजेन गोपाय्यते ।
इत्युक्ते क्व तदित्युदीर्य सहसा तत् संप्रमार्ष्टुं मया
साश्लिष्टा रभसेन तत्सुखवशात्तन्व्या च तद्विस्मृतम् ॥५०॥

अत्र कोपस्य ।

एकस्मिञ्छयने विपक्षरमणीनामग्रहे मुग्धया
सद्यो मानपरिग्रहग्लपितया चाटूनि कुर्वन्नपि ।
आवेगादवधीरितः प्रियतमस्तूष्णीं स्थितस्तत्क्षणं
मा भूत्सुप्त इवेत्यमन्दवलितग्रीवं पुनर्वीक्षितः ॥ ५१ ॥

अत्रौत्सुक्यस्य ।

उत्सिक्तस्य तपःपराक्रमनिधेरभ्यागमादेकतः
सत्संगप्रियता च वीररभसोत्फालश्च मां कर्षतः ।
वैदेहीपरिरम्भ एष च मुहुश्चैतन्यमामीलयन्
आनन्दी हरिचन्दनेन्दुशिशिरस्निग्धो रुणद्ध्यन्यतः ॥ ५२ ॥

---

the embrace of her sandal-painted breasts ?"—After she had said this, I said 'where is it ?'—and embraced her suddenly and quickly, for the purpose of wiping off the mark ; and the tender one forgot all about it under the fervent bliss ensuing from that embrace'.

Here we have the 'allayment' of Anger.

(*b*) 'When the young woman lying on the same bed had her indignation aroused on the naming of her rival, she firmly disdained him with all his advances and loving assurances ; and he, having lain silent for a moment, the girl looked back upon him, fearing that he might go to sleep'.

अत्रावेगहर्षयोः ।

क्वाकार्यं शशलक्ष्मणः क्व च कुलं भूयोपि दृश्येत सा
दोषाणां प्रशमाय न श्रुतमहो कोपेपि कान्तं मुखम् ।
किं वक्ष्यन्त्यपकल्मषाः कृतधियः स्वप्नेपि सा दुर्लभा
चेतः स्वास्थ्यमुपैहि कः खलु युवा धन्योधरं धास्यति ॥ ५३ ॥

अत्र वितर्कौत्सुक्यमतिस्मरणशङ्कादैन्यधृतिचिन्तानां शबलता । भावस्थितिस्तूक्ता उदाहृता च ॥ ३६ ॥

मुख्ये रसेपि तेऽङ्गित्वं प्राप्नुवन्ति कदाचन ।

Here we have the 'manifestation' of Impatience.

(*c*) 'On one side attract me my love for good company and sudden outburst of heroism on seeing this receptacle of austerity and prowess ; on the other, the exquisite embrace of Sītā, cooling and soft like celestial sandal and like the moon, lulls my consciousness and keeps me back'.

Here we have the 'conjuncture' of Flurry and Joy.

(*d*) 'Where on one side is this unblemished lunar dynasty, and where, on the other, this improper act ?—May she be seen again ! Our learning is meant to be a check upon evil tendencies ;—her face lovely even in anger ! What shall the wise and pure ones say ?—She is difficult to be got at even in a dream ! O, heart, be calm ;—what blessed young man will kiss her lips !'

Here we have the 'admixture' of Trepidation, Impatience, Resolve, Recollection, Anxiety, Depression, Serenity and Painful Reflection.

The mere *presence* of 'emotion' has already been described and illustrated (*vide* above—'*Jāne kopaparaṅmukhī etc.*') 36.

Though it is Passion that is the predominant factor, yet these also acquire predominance sometimes.

ते भावशान्त्यादयः । अङ्गित्वं राजानुगतविवाहप्रवृत्तभृत्यवत् ॥

अनुस्वानाभसंलक्ष्यक्रमव्यङ्ग्यस्थितिस्तु यः ॥ ३७ ॥

शब्दार्थोभयशक्त्युत्थस्त्रिधा स कथितो ध्वनिः ।

शब्दशक्तिमूलानुरणनरूपव्यङ्ग्यः, अर्थशक्तिमूलानुरणनरूपव्यङ्ग्यः, उभयशक्तिमूलानुरणनरूपव्यङ्ग्यश्चेति त्रिविधः ॥३७॥

'*These*'—*i. e.*, the Allayment (Manifestation, Conjuncture and Admixture) of Emotions.

'*Predominance*'.—This occasional predominance is like that of the King's servant whose marriage is attended by the King (who, for the time, occupies a position subordinate to that of the servant).

[Having described the suggestion 'with imperceptible sequence,' the author proceeds to describe that in which the sequence is perceptible.]

That suggestion in which the (suggested meaning has its sequence to the suggestive word) clearly perceptible, in the manner of a reverberating echo, has been said to be of three kinds—(1) *that arising from the force of the word,* (2) *that arising from the force of the meaning, and* (3) *that arising from the force of both.* 37.

The three kinds are—(1) that in which the reverberating suggested meaning is based on the force of the word, (2) that in which the suggested meaning is based upon the force of the meaning, and (3) that in which the suggested meaning is based upon the force of both.

[Whether in a certain case the suggestion proceeds from the word or from its expressed meaning is determined by the possibility or otherwise of its being got at even by the changing of the word : If it is found that the suggestion remains unaffected even when we substitute other synonyms of the word, then it is regarded as based upon the *meaning*, while if the slightest change in the word vitiates the suggestion, then it is regarded as based upon the *word*.] 37.

तत्र

अलङ्कारोथ वस्त्वेव शब्दाद्यत्रावभासते ॥ ३८ ॥
प्रधानत्वेन स ज्ञेयः शब्दशक्त्युद्भवो द्विधा ।

वस्त्वेति, अनलंकारं वस्तुमात्रम् । आद्यो यथा

उल्लास्य कालकरवालमहाम्बुवाहं
देवेन येन जरठोर्जितगर्जितेन ।
निर्वापितः सकल एव रणे रिपूणां
धाराजलैस्त्रिजगति ज्वलितः प्रतापः ॥ ५४ ॥

Suggestion based upon the force of the word is of two kinds,—according as what is principally represented by the word is (a) a figure of speech or (b) a bare matter of fact. 38.

'*Bare matter of fact*,'—*i. e.* the simple statement of a fact, without any ornamental figure of speech.

(*a*) As an example of the former we have the following—

'*Ullāsya kālakarabālamahāmbuvāham*
Devena yena jaraṭhorjitagarjitena
Nirvāpitaḥ sakala eva raṇe ripūṇām
Dhārājalaistrijagati jvalitaḥ pratāpaḥ.'

Here the literal meaning of the sentence would be distinctly irrelevant ; hence with a view to avoiding this, it has to be assumed that what is intended is to describe the similarity between the directly mentioned subject (the king) and the one only indirectly implied (Indra) ; and thus what comes to be suggested here is the figure of speech known as 'Simile'.

The full meaning of the sentence being 'Just as Indra brings up the cloud, dark and fresh, and accompanied by fierce thundering, extinguishes, by means of torrents of rain, the heat of the destructive fires pervading over the three worlds,—in the same manner has this king

अत्र वाक्यस्यासंबद्धार्थाभिधायकत्वं मा प्रसाङ्क्षीदिति प्राकरणिकाप्राकरणिकयोरुपमानोपमेयभावः कल्पनीय इत्यत्रोपमालंकारो व्यङ्ग्यः ।

तिग्मरुचिरप्रतापो विधुरनिशाकृद्विभो मधुरलीलः
मतिमानतत्त्ववृत्तिः प्रतिपदपक्षाग्रणीर्विभाति भवान् ।।५५।।

अत्रैकैकस्य पदस्य द्विपदत्वे विरोधाभासः ।

---

with a fierce roar, lifted his sharp sword, and by means of its flickering edge, has destroyed the glory of his enemies, which was extending over the three worlds.' And this suggestion is held to be 'based upon the force of the word,' because the words used here lend themselves to the above interpretation only because they have double meanings; and this effect would be lost if they were replaced by their synonyms.]

(Another example of the same)—(*a*) *Tigmaruchirapratāpo*, (*b*) *Vidhuraniśākṛd vibho*, (*c*) *madhuratlīlaḥ*, (*d*) '*Matimānatattvavṛttiḥ*, *and* (*e*) *Pratipadapakṣāgraṇīrvibhāti bhavān*.'

Here, if each of the five terms (*a*, *b*, *c*, *d* and *e*) is resolved into two terms, we get the suggestion of the figure of speech known as 'Seeming Contradiction.'

['*Vibho bhavān vibhāti*,' 'O' Lord, you are resplendent', is the principal sentence, the other five terms are epithets of 'bhāvan'. (*a*) '*Tigmaruchirapratāpaḥ*', When taken as one word, means 'he whose splendour is *tigma*, fierce, and *ruchira*, sweet'; but when it is resolved into two words, it means '*tigmaruchiḥ*, with fierce splendour' and '*apratāpaḥ*, wanting in splendour, which expresses two contradictory qualifications ;—(*b*) '*vidhuraniśākṛt*,' taken as one word, means 'capable of bringing about the *nishā*, extinction, of his *vidhura*, enemies ;' but when resolved into two words, it means '*vidhuḥ*' the moon, and '*aniśākṛt*, not the night making moon,' an apparent contradiction; (c) '*madhurlīlaḥ*', when taken as one word, means 'he whose *līlā*, operations, are *madhura*, sweet, pleasing'; but when resolved into words, it means '*madhu*' the spring-time,' and *alīlaḥ*,

अमितः समितः प्राप्तैरुत्कर्षैर्हर्षद प्रभो ।
अहितः सहितः साधुयशोभिरसतामसि ॥ ५६ ॥

अत्रापि विरोधाभासः ।

निरुपादानसंभारमभित्तावेव तन्वते ।
जगच्चित्रं नमस्तस्मै कलाश्लाघ्याय शूलिने ॥ ५७ ॥

अत्र व्यतिरेकः ।

---

devoid of beauty,' a contradiction ;—(*d*) '*matimānatattvavṛttiḥ*', taken as one word, means 'who acts with *mati*, intelligence, and *māna*, magnanimity ;' but when resolved into two terms, it means '*matimān*, intelligent' and '*atattvavṛttiḥ*, acting blankly,' an apparent contradiction ;—(*e*) '*pratipadapakṣāgraṇīḥ*', as one term, means the '*agraṇīḥ*, of your *pakṣa*, party, *pratipada*, at each step' ; but when it is resolved into two terms, it means '*pratipat*, the first day of the fortnight, and '*apakṣāgraṇīḥ*, not the opening day of the fortnight', an apparent contradiction.]

[Here also the suggestion of 'Seeming Contradiction' would be lost if other synonyms were substituted ; hence it is held to be 'based upon the force of words'.]

[Another example of the same kind]

'Amitaḥ samitaḥ prāptairutkarṣaiṭharṣada prabho
Ahitaḥ sahitaḥ sādhu-yashobhirasatāmasi.'

Here also Seeming Contradiction is the figure suggested.

[The meaning is '*prabho*, O Lord, *harṣada*, you who are the *giver* of joy, (*harsam dadāti*) and also the *destroyer* of joy (*harsam dyati*),—through the glories attained *in battle* (*samitaḥ*) you are '*amitaḥ*' immeasureably great, (you are both *samitaḥ*, measureable, and *amitaḥ*, immeasureable) ; being endowed, *sahitaḥ*, with good fame, you are the *ahitaḥ*, enemy, of all wicked men.' The epithets are so chosen as to imply, in their *second intention*, an apparent contradiction.]

[Another example of the same kind.]

'Salutation to that Trident-bearer whose art is so praiseworthy that he paints the mundane picture without aboard and without the painting brush or other accessories:'

अलंकार्यस्यापि ब्राह्मणश्रमणन्यायेनालंकारता ।

वस्तुमात्रं यथा

पंथिअ ण एत्थ सत्थरमत्थि मणं पत्थरत्थले गामे ।
उण्णअपओहरं पेक्खिऊण जइ वससि ता वससु ॥ ५८ ॥

अत्र यद्युपभोगक्षमोसि तदा आस्स्वेति व्यज्यते ।

शनिरशनिश्च तमुच्चैर्निहन्ति कुप्यसि नरेन्द्र यस्मै त्वम् ।
यत्र प्रसीदसि पुनः स भात्युदारोनुदारश्च ॥ ५९ ॥

Here the figure of speech suggested is the *Vyatireka*, Dissimilitude (between the god described and the ordinary painter.)

Though in the examples cited the figure suggested is the predominant factor, and hence something *to be embellished* (*alaṅkārya* ; and for that reason, it cannot be right to call it, as the text has done, an *alaṅkāra*, an *embellishment*, a figure of speech), yet it is so called on the analogy of the expression '*brāhmaṇaśramaṇa*.'

[When one has become a '*śramaṇa*,' a Buddhist monk, he has no caste ; and yet the expression '*brāhmaṇa śramaṇa*' is used in the sense 'the monk that was, under other circumstances, a Brāhmaṇa' ; similarly in the case in question, what is meant by the suggested meaning being a *figure*, an '*alaṅkāra*,' is that, under other circumstances, —*i. e.* when *expressed* directly by the word and not only *suggested*,—it would be so, even though in the instances cited it is not so.]

(*b*) The following is the example of that where what is suggested is a bare matter of fact.—

'O traveller, in this village of stones, there is not a bedding to be had ; yet, seeing the rising clouds (*unnatapayodhara*, my blossoming breasts), if you decide to lodge here, you may do so.'

Here what is suggested is—'if you are fit to enjoy my company, then you may stay here.'

अविरुद्धावपि त्वदनुवर्तनार्थमेकं कार्यं कुरुत इति ध्वन्यते ।

अर्थशक्त्युद्भवोप्यर्थो व्यञ्जकः संभवी स्वतः ॥ ३९ ॥
प्रौढोक्तिमात्रसिद्धो वा कवेस्तेनोम्भितस्य वा ।
वस्तु वालंकृतिर्वेति षड्भेदोसौ व्यनक्ति यत् ॥ ४० ॥
वस्त्वलंकारमथवा तेनायं द्वादशात्मकः ।

स्वतःसंभवी न केवलं भणितिमात्रनिष्पन्नो यावद्बहिरप्यौचित्येन संभाव्यमानः । कविना प्रतिभामात्रेण बहिरसन्नपि निर्मितः कविनिबद्धेन वक्त्रेति वा द्विविधोपर इति त्रिविधः ।

[Another example of the same kind]—

'O King, when you are angry with a man, both *Śani* (the evil planet Saturn) and *Aśani* (the thunderbolt) strike him fiercely ; while when you are pleased with a man, he shines nobly (*udāra*) and has his wife obedient to him (*anudāra*)'.

Here what is suggested is that even mutually contradictory forces (*Śani—Aśani*, and *Udāra—Anudāra*) co-operate in obeying your wishes.

Inasmuch as the suggestive object 'based upon the force of the meaning' is either (a) self-existent or (b) owing its existence to the bold assertion of the poet or (c) owing its existence to the bold assertion of some character portrayed by the poet ;—each of these three being either a figure of speech or a bare fact, it comes to be of six kinds (39-40) ; *and since each of these suggests a figure or a fact, it comes to be of twelve kinds.*

(*a*) '*Self-existent*'—Not only created by the words of the poet, but having a real existence in the world ;—(*b*) created by the poet's imagination, and having no real existence in the external world ;—(*c*) created by the imagination of a speaker portrayed by the poet ;—these two non-existent varieties along with the former make the

वस्तु वालंकारो वासाविति षोढा व्यञ्जकः । तस्य वस्तु वालंकारो वा व्यङ्ग्य इति द्वादशभेदोर्थशक्त्युद्भवो ध्वनिः । क्रमेणोदाहरणम्—

अलसशिरोमणि धुत्ताणं अग्गिमो पुत्ति धणसमिद्धिमओ ।
इअ भणिएण णअङ्गी पप्फुल्लविलोअणा जाआ ॥ ६० ॥

अत्र ममैवोपभोग्य इति वस्तुना वस्तु व्यज्यते ।

धन्यासि या कथयसि प्रियसंगमेपि
विस्रब्धचाटुकशतानि रतान्तरेषु ।
नीवीं प्रति प्रणिहिते तु करे प्रियेण
सख्यः शपामि यदि किंचिदपि स्मरामि ॥ ६१ ॥

---

three kinds. This being either a fact or a figure of speech, the *suggestive* object comes to be of six kinds. What is *suggested* by this is again either a fact or a figure. Thus suggestion 'based upon the force of meaning' has twelve varieties.

Examples in due order—

(1) "He is the most indolent, foremost among proficient men, and O child, he is possessed of immense wealth ;"—When this was said, she hung down her head and her eyes bloomed.—(The *self-existent fact suggesting the self-existent fact*).

Here the mere *fact*—'the person referred to is just the one suited for receiving my love'—is suggested (by the *fact* of the blooming of the girl's eyes).

(2) 'Thou art really fortunate, that on meeting your lover, you can, even during the intervals of dalliance utter endless sweet and coquettish words ! O Friends, as for me I swear I do not remember anything after my beloved places his hand on the knot of my waist-cloth.'—(*The self-existent fact suggesting a figure*).

अत्र त्वमधन्या अहं तु धन्येति व्यतिरेकालंकारः ।

दर्पान्धगन्धगजकुम्भकपाटकूट-
संक्रान्तिनिघ्नघनशोणितशोणशोचिः ।
वीरैर्व्यलोकि युधि कोपकषायकान्तिः
कालीकटाक्ष इव यस्य करे कृपाणः ।। ६२ ।।

अत्रोपमालंकारेण सकलरिपुबलक्षयः क्षणात् करिष्यते इति वस्तु ।

गाढकान्तदशनक्षतव्यथासंकटादरिवधूजनस्य यः ।
ओष्ठविद्रुमदलान्यमोचयन्निर्दशन् युधि रुषा निजाधरम् ।।६३।।

अत्र विरोधालंकारेणाधरनिर्दंशनसमकालमेव शत्रवो व्यापादिता इति तुल्ययोगिता मम क्षत्याप्यन्यस्य क्षतिर्निवर्तंतामिति

Here the meaning being—'I am fortunate, you are unfortunate'—we have the *figure* 'Dissimilitude' (suggested by the *facts* described).

(3) 'In whose hand the sword was seen by the heroes in battle, resembling the wrath-red glances of the goddess Kālī ; since it shone red through the thick blood on being struck against the hard surface of the forehead of redolent elephants blinded with intoxication.' (*The self-existent figure suggesting a fact.*)

Here the *fact* that 'all the enemies would be killed in a trice' is suggested by the *figure* 'Simile'.

(4) 'Who, biting with rage his own underlip in battle, freed the coral lips of his enemy's wives from the pain arising from the deep wound inflicted by the teeth of their husbands.' (*The self-existent figure suggesting a figure*).

Here the *figure* of 'Seeming Contradiction' (involved in the statement that the *biting* of the lips relieved the lips of pain) suggests either the *figure* of 'Equal Pairing,' in the implication that 'the enemies were killed at the very

तद्वुद्धिरुत्प्रेक्ष्यते इत्युत्प्रेक्षा च ।

एषूदाहरणेषु स्वतःसंभवी व्यञ्जकः ।

कैलासस्य प्रथमशिखरे वेणुसंमूर्छनाभिः
श्रुत्वा कीर्तिं विबुधरमणीगीयमानां यदीयाम् ।
स्रस्तापाङ्गाः सरसबिसिनीकाण्डसंजातशङ्का
दिङ्मातङ्गा श्रवणपुलिने हस्तमावर्तयन्ति ॥ ६४ ॥

अत्र वस्तुना येषामप्यर्थाधिगमो नास्ति तेषामप्येवमादिबुद्धिजननेन चमत्कारं करोति त्वत्कीर्तिरिति वस्तु ध्वन्यते ।

केसेसु बलामोडिअ तेण अ समरम्मि जअसिरी गहिआ ।
जह कन्दराहिँ विहुरा तस्स दढं कंठअम्मि संठविआ ॥६५॥

---

moment in which the king bit his lips in rage',—or the *figure* 'Poetic Fancy', in the implication that 'the king desires to relieve the pain of others even by hurting himself'.

In all these (four) examples, the suggestive factor is something that is really *Self-existent*.

(5) 'Hearing his fame sung by the nymphs on the highest peak of mount Kailāsa, to the accompaniment of the melodies of the flute,—the Elephants of the quarters, casting side-long glances, mistake it to be the juicy lotus-root (on account of its pure whiteness), and hence extend their trunk to their ears (in order to reach the Fame which has reached the ears).' (*A fact, the creation of the poet's fancy, suggests a fact*).

Here the *fact* that—' even such beings as do not comprehend the meaning of the song sung are affected in the manner described,—such is the wonderful effect of your fame'—is suggested (by the imaginary *fact* of the elephants extending their trunks to the ears).

(6) 'Victory was so forcibly held by her locks by the king that his discomfited enemies were drawn by the caves to their necks.'—(*Figure suggested by a fact created by the poet's imagination*).

अत्र केशग्रहणावलोकनोद्दीपितमदना इव कन्दरास्तद्विधुरान् कण्ठे गृह्णन्ति इत्युत्प्रेक्षा। एकत्र संग्रामे विजयदर्शनात्तस्यारयः पलाय्य गुहासु तिष्ठन्तीति काव्यहेतुरलंकारः। न पलाय्य गतास्तद्वैरिणोपि तु ततः पराभवं संभाव्य तान् कन्दरा न त्यजन्तीत्यपह्नुतिश्च।

गाढालिंगणरहसुज्जअम्मि दइए लहु समोसरइ।
माणंसिणीण माणो पीलणभीअ व्व हिअआहिं ॥ ६६ ॥

अत्रोत्प्रेक्षया प्रत्यालिङ्गनादि तत्र विजृम्भते इति वस्तु।

Here we have the (*a*) *figure* 'Poetic Fancy', in the implication that 'the caves (females) had their sexual passion aroused by looking at the locks of the lady, Victory, being held (in dalliance, as it were) and hence embraced the enemies (males)';—also (*b*) the *figure* 'Poetic Reason', in the implication that 'the enemies fled away to hide themselves in caves on seeing that the king had attained victory in battle';—as also (*c*) the *figure* 'Concealment', in the implication that 'it was not that the enemies fled to the caves, but what happened was that the caves, fearing that the said enemies would suffer at the hands of the king, did not allow them to go out'.

[And all this is suggested by the imaginary fact that the king caught hold of the locks of one lady and the enemies were embraced by other ladies.]

(7) 'On the lover preparing to embrace them, the feelings of indignation gently depart from the hearts of the high-minded girls, being, as it were, afraid of the pressure of the embrace'—(*Fact suggested by Figure created by the poet's fancy*).

जा ठेरंव्व हसन्ती कइवअणंबुरुहबद्धविणिवेसा ।
दावेइ भुअणमंडलमण्णं विअ जअइ सा वाणी ॥ ६७ ॥

अत्रोत्प्रेक्षया चमत्कारैककारणं नवं नवं जगत् अजडासनस्था निर्मिमीते इति व्यतिरेकः । एषु कविप्रौढोक्तिमात्रनिष्पन्नो व्यञ्जकः ।

जे लंकागिरिमेहलासु खलिआ संभोगखिण्णोरइ-
फारुप्फुल्लफणावलीकवलणे पत्ता दरिद्दत्तणं ।
ते एह्लि मलआनिला विरहिणीणीसाससंपक्किणो
जादा झत्ति सिसुत्तणे वि बहला तारुण्णपुण्णा विअ ॥ ६८ ॥

Here the *fact* that 'the embraces began to be returned' is suggested by the *figure* 'Poetic Fancy' herein set forth.

(8) 'Ever glorious is that Goddess of Speech who has taken up her abode in the lotus of the poet's mouth, exhibiting a universe of unique character, and who is, as it were, ridiculing the old Fogey'.—(*Figure suggested by an imaginary figure*).

Here the *figure* of 'Poetic Fancy' set forth in the verse suggests the *figure* of 'Dissimilitude', in the implication that 'the goddess of speech has an *animate* seat (in the shape of the poet's mouth, while Brahmā, the creator of the world is seated upon the *inanimate* lotus), and creates a world (of poetic imagination) which is always new and the source of unmixed charm (while the creator's world is old and not always beautiful)'.

In the last four examples the suggestive agent is the creation of the poet's bold assertion.

(9) 'The winds from the Malaya, which had become emaciated by being inhaled in the large and rising hoods of the female serpents lying exhausted in dalliance on the lower ranges of the Hemakūṭa mountain, attain the exu-

अत्र निःश्वासैः प्राप्तैश्वर्या वायवः किं किं न कुर्वन्तीति वस्तुना वस्तु व्यज्यते ।

सहि विरइऊण माणस्स मज्झ धीरत्तणेण आसासं ।
पिअदंसणविहंखलेलक्खणम्मि सहसत्ति तेण ओसरिअं ॥६९॥

अत्र वस्तुनाकृतेपि प्रार्थने प्रसन्नेति विभावना प्रियदर्शनस्य सौभाग्यबलं धैर्येण सोढुं न शक्यते इत्युत्प्रेक्षा वा ।

ओल्लोल्लकरअरअक्खएहि तुह लोअणेसु मह दिण्णं ।
रत्तंसुअं पसाओ कोवेण पुणो इमे ण अक्कमिआ ॥ ७० ॥

---

berance of youth,—even though only new born—by contact with the sighs of women suffering from the pangs of separation from their lovers.'—(*Fact suggested by Fact, based upon the bold assertion of an imaginary person*).

Here the *fact* that 'the winds strengthened by the sighs become capable of doing anything' is suggested by the *fact* (that the 'Malaya-winds have become youthful', which is purely imaginary, being set forth by the particular person, the lady's friend, portrayed by the poet).

(10) 'Self-possession, after having encouraged my self-respect, suddenly vanished at the exciting moment of my lover's visit'.—(*Figure suggested by fact asserted by an imaginary person*).

Here, either (*a*) the *figure* of 'Peculiar Causation,—in the implication that 'the lady became reconciled to her lover even before he made his protestations'.—or (*b*) the *figure* of 'Poetic Fancy',—in the implication that 'self-possession cannot withstand the force of the charm of the lover's visit',—is suggested by the *fact* (that the indignant lady became reconciled) [and this is asserted by the imaginary female character portrayed by the poet]'.

(11) 'These eyes of mine are not seized by anger; in fact they have received the red clothing as a reward from

अत्र किमिति लोचने कुपिते वहसि इति उत्तरालंकारेण न केवलमार्द्रनखक्षतानि गोपायसि यावत्तेषामहं प्रसादपात्रं जातेति वस्तु ।

महिलासहस्सभरिए तुह हिअए सुहअ सा अमाअन्ती ।
अणुदिणमणण्णकम्मा अङ्गं तणुअं वि तणुएइ ।।७१।।

अत्र हेत्वलंकारेण तनोस्तनूकरणेपि तव हृदये न वर्तते इति विशेषोक्तिः । एषु कविनिबद्धवक्तृप्रौढोक्तिमात्रनिष्पन्न-

---

the fresh marks of nails and teeth on your body'.—(*Fact suggested by figure set forth by an imaginary character*).

On the question (being put by the lover)—'why are your eyes looking angry ?'—the lady makes her answer, in the above form, which involves the *figure* of 'Reply'; and this *figure* suggests the *fact* that 'the lover is not only trying to hide the fresh marks, they are also rewarding the lady (by enabling her to detect the lover's infidelity)'. [and the said figurative assertion comes from an imaginary character delineated by the poet].

(12) 'O blessed one ! All the place in your heart being taken up by thousands of women, she is unable to find place in it ; hence, giving up all other work, she is making her already thin body still thinner and thinner day by day'.—(*Figure suggested by Figure in the assertion of an imaginary character*).

Here the *figure* of 'Poetic Reason' (in the implication that 'the reason for her getting thinner lies in her attempt to make herself thin enough to find room in your filled-up heart') suggests the *figure* of 'Peculiar Allegation', in the implication that 'even though she is making herself thinner and thinner, she finds no room in your heart'.

शरीरो व्यञ्जकः । एवं द्वादश भेदाः ॥

शब्दार्थोभयभूरेकः

अतन्द्रचन्द्राभरणा समुद्दीपितमन्मथा ।

तारकातरला श्यामा सानन्दं न करोति कम् ॥ ७२ ॥

अत्रोपमा व्यङ्ग्या ॥

In these last four examples the suggestive factor is based upon the assertion of an imaginary character delineated by the poet.

These are the twelve varieties (of Suggestion Based upon the Force of Meaning).

That (suggestion) based upon both Word and Meaning is one only.

For example—

'*Atandrachandrābharaṇā samuddīpitamanmathā.*
Tārakātaralā śyāmā sānandaṁna karoti kaṁ'.

'Whom does the young woman not please—adorned as she is, with a bright head-jewel, arousing love, and with unsteady glances—being like the night adorned with the bright moon, arousing thoughts of love, and glimmering with stars ?'

Here the figure of 'Simile' is suggested.

[And all this is suggested by the imaginary fact that the king caught hold of the locks of one lady and the enemies were embraced by other ladies.]

[And this suggestion is based upon the power of both word and meaning ; the *former*, because the entire similitude rests upon the double meanings of the words '*śyāmā*,' '*chandra*' and '*tārākā*,' which cannot be replaced by their synonyms without destroying the said effect ; and the *latter* because the other words are such as can be easily replaced by other synonyms without spoiling the effect.]

भेदा अष्टादशास्य तत् ॥ ४१ ॥

अस्येति ध्वनेः ॥ ४१ ॥

ननु रसादीनां बहुभेदत्वेन कथमष्टादशेत्यत आह ।

रसादीनामनन्तत्वाद्भेद एको हि गण्यते ।

अनन्तत्वादिति । तथाहि–नव रसाः । तत्र शृङ्गारस्य द्वौ भेदौ । संभोगो विप्रलम्भश्च । संभोगस्यापि परस्परावलोकनालिङ्गनपरिचुम्बनादिकुसुमोच्चयजलकेलिसूर्यास्तमयचन्द्रोदयषड्-

---

Thus there are eighteen varieties of it.

'*of it*'—*i. e.* of Suggestion. 41.

Objection :—" There being many varieties of Passion (Emotion and so forth),—why are the varieties of suggestion said to be *eighteen* only ?"

The answer to this is as follows :—

The varieties of 'Passion' and other forms being endless, these (Passion, Emotion, etc.) are counted as a single variety.

'*Endless*'.—For instance, there are nine Passions ;—of the Erotic Passion there are two varieties —that in union and that in privation ;—the former has several varieties, in the form of 'mutual glances', 'embrace', 'kissing', 'flower-picking,' 'amorous water-sports', descriptions of sunset, rise of the moon, the six seasons and so forth ;—the Erotic *in privation* again has been already described as being of several kinds, such as *longing* and so forth ;—then again, these two kinds of the Erotic vary with the variations in the particular Excitants, Ensuants and Variants ;—the hero again is of three kinds, noble, ignoble and middling ;—these vary with the peculiarities of time, place and other circumstances ;—so that of the single Passion of the Erotic there are 'endless' varieties ;—not to speak of others ?

ऋतुवर्णनादयो बहवो भेदाः । विप्रलम्भस्याभिलाषादय उक्ताः । तयोरपि विभावानुभावव्यभिचारिवैचित्र्यम् । तत्रापि नायकयोरुत्तममध्यमाधमप्रकृतित्वम् । तत्रापि देशकालावस्थादि-भेदा इत्येकस्यैव रसस्यानन्त्यम् । का गणना त्वन्येषाम् । असंलक्ष्य-क्रमत्वं तु सामान्यमाश्रित्य रसादिध्वनिभेद एक एव गण्यते ।।

वाक्ये द्व्युत्थः

द्व्युत्थ इति शब्दार्थोभयशक्तिमूलः ।।

पदेप्यन्ये

अपिशब्दाद्वाक्येपि । एकावयवस्थितेन भूषणेन कामिनीव पदद्योत्येन व्यङ्ग्येन वाक्यव्यङ्ग्यापि भारती भासते । तत्र पदप्रकाश्यत्वे क्रमेणोदाहरणानि–

The suggestion, however, of all these, Passion and the rest, is counted as one 'kind' only, on the basis of the common characteristic of having the 'sequence imperceptible'.

[Having described the eighteen varieties of suggestion, the author proceeds to differentiate among them by pointing out that while the one variety—that based upon the force of both word and meaning—is found in sentences, only the other seventeen are found in sentences as well as in single words.]

That arising from both is present in the sentence only.

'Arising from both'—*i. e.* suggestion based upon the force of both word and meaning.

[*Example* cited above—'*Atandrachandrābharaṇā*' etc.]

The others in the word also.

The term 'also' indicates that they are also found in the sentence. Even though a certain statement is such as is suggested by the sentence, yet it acquires additional charm through what is suggested by a word occurring in that sentence, just as a lovely woman does by an ornament worn on one part of her body.

यस्य मित्राणि मित्राणि शत्रवः शत्रवस्तथा ।
अनुकम्प्योऽनुकम्प्यश्च स जातः स च जीवति ॥७३॥ (१)

अत्र द्वितीयमित्रादिशब्दा आश्वस्तत्वनियन्त्रणीयत्वस्नेहपात्रत्वादिसंक्रमितवाच्याः ।

खलववहारा दीसन्ति दारुणा जहवि तहवि धीराणं ।
हिअअवअस्सवहुमआ ण हु ववसाआ विमुज्झन्ति ॥७४॥(२)

अत्र विमुह्यन्तीति ।

लावण्यं तदसौ कान्तिस्तद्रूपं स वचःक्रमः ।
तदा सुधास्पदमभूदधुना तु ज्वरो महान् ॥ ७५ ॥

The following are the examples in order of the seventeen kinds of suggestion as *based upon the word* :—

(1) [Transference of the expressed meaning to another by a word]—'He alone is really born and lives whose friends are friends, foes, foes and the affable, affable'.

Here the expressed meaning of the second term—'friends'—is altered into (stands for) *reliability*, that of the second 'enemies' into *reprehensibility*, and that of the second 'affable' into *lovability*.

(2) [The expressed meaning entirely ignored, in a word]—

'Even though the behaviour of the wicked is always found to be terrible, the efforts of the wise are never stupefied, being always approved by their heart, as if by a friend'.

Here the suggestion lies in the single word 'stupefied'. [*Stupefaction*, which is impossible for the inanimate 'efforts,' stands for *being impeded*.]

(3) [The 'suggestion of imperceptible sequence', in a single word].

अत्र तदादिपदैरनुभवैकगोचरा अर्थाः प्रकाश्यन्ते । यथा वा

मुग्धे मुग्धतयैव नेतुमखिलः कालः किमारभ्यते
मानं धत्स्व धृतिं बधान ऋजुतां दूरे कुरु प्रेयसि ।
सख्यैवं प्रतिबोधिता प्रतिवचस्तामाह भीतानना
नीचैः शंस हृदि स्थितो हि ननु मे प्राणेश्वरः श्रोष्यति॥७६॥ (३)

अत्र भीताननेति । एतेन हि नीचैःशंसनविधानस्य युक्तता गम्यते ।
भावादीनां पदप्रकाश्यत्वेधिकं न वैचित्र्यमिति न तदुदाह्रियते ।

'That loveliness, that brilliancy, that beauty, and that sweetness of speech,—were all like nectar at that time; but now it is all a terrible fever'.

Here the term, 'that' used several times, suggests that the things spoken of are such as can be only seen (and cannot be described).

Another example of the same—

"O beautiful one, why do you proceed to pass the whole time in mere simplicity? Have self-respect; hold out with patience; set aside your artless behaviour towards your lover";—on being thus exhorted by her friend, the girl, replied with fear-stricken face—"Talk low, lest the Lord of my life residing in my heart should overhear what your are saying".

Here the epithet 'with fear-stricken face' suggests the propriety of 'talking low'.

Emotion [and Aberration of Passion, Aberration of Emotion, Allayment of Emotion, Conjuncture of Emotions and Admixture of Emotions] do not acquire any additional charm, when suggested by a single word [to the same extent as that of 'Passion' does]; hence examples of these have not been cited.

रुधिरविसरप्रसाधितकरवालकरालरुचिरभुजपरिघः ।
झटिति भ्रुकुटिविटङ्कितललाटपट्टो विभासि नृप भीम ॥७७॥ (४)

अत्र भीषणीयस्य भीमसेन उपमानम् ।

भुक्तिमुक्तिकृदेकान्तसमादेशनतत्परः ।
कस्य नानन्दनिस्यन्दं विदधाति सदागमः ॥७८॥ (५)

काचित् संकेतदायिनमेवं मुख्यया वृत्त्या शंसति ।

---

(4) [*Suggestion of perceptible process by a word—founded on the power of words—of figure by fact*]—

'O King, thou awe-inspiring one (*Bhīma*) ! Thou art resplendent, with thy bolt-like arm pleasing and terrible through the sword reddened with the flow of blood, and with thy broad forehead marked with creases caused by the sudden curvature of the eye-brows.'

The similitude (Simile) of the awe-inspiring King to Bhīmasena is suggested (by the *fact* of the King's sword being reddened with blood and so forth, and this is done through the force of the *single word* '*bhīma*,' the replacing of which by its synonym would spoil the whole effect).

(5) [*Suggestion of perceptible process—founded on the power of a word—of fact by fact.*]

'To whom does *Sadāgama*, (*a*) true scripture, [(*b*) lover's visit] not bring continued bliss,—(a) always offering salutary advice and leading to heavenly pleasure and beatitude [(b) always bent upon indicating secluded rendezvous, and bringing about enjoyment and deliverance from the pangs of separation] ?' "

The woman is conveying (her acquiescence) to the lover suggesting a meeting-place, by means of *suggestion*.

[And this is done through the double meanings of the words chosen ; it is the suggestion of the *fact* of her acceptance by the *fact* described.]

सायं स्नानमुपासितं मलयजेनाङ्गं समालेपितं
यातोस्ताचलमौलिमम्बरमणिर्विस्रब्धमत्रागतिः ।
आश्चर्यं तव सौकुमार्यमभितः क्लान्तासि येनाधुना
नेत्रद्वन्द्वममीलनव्यतिकरं शक्नोति तेनासितुम् ॥७९॥ (६)

अत्र वस्तुना कृतपुरुषपरिचया क्लान्तासीति वस्तु अधुनापद-द्योत्यं व्यज्यते ।

तदप्राप्तिमहादुःखविलीनाशेषपातका ।
तच्चिन्ताविपुलाह्लादक्षीणपुण्यचया तथा ॥ ८० ॥
चिन्तयन्ती जगत्सूतिं परब्रह्मस्वरूपिणम् ।
निरुच्छ्वासतया मुक्तिं गतान्या गोपकन्यका ॥८१॥ (७)

---

(6) [*Suggestion of perceptible process—by word—founded on the force of meaning—of fact by self-existent fact*]—

'In the evening thou hadst recourse to bath and anointed thy body with sandal-paste; the ethereal gem has passed the crest of the setting mount; and thy coming here has been unflurried; [thus there being no external cause for fatigue], astonishing then is thy tenderness by virtue of which thou art at this time so completely exhausted that thy eyes cannot help being closed frequently.'

Here the *fact* that 'thou art exhausted by reason of having met a paramour' is suggested, through the implication of the term 'at this time', '*adhunā*'.

(7) [*Suggestion of perceptible process—by word—founded on the force of meaning—of figure by a self-existent fact*]—

'Meditating upon the Origin of the World, the incarnation of supreme Brahma (*i. e.* 'Kṛṣṇa), another milkmaid had her breath suspended and obtained beatitude; all her sins being dissolved by the great suffering caused

अत्र जन्मसहस्रैरुपभोक्तव्यानि दुष्कृतसुकृतफलानि वियोग-दुःखचिन्तनाह्लादाभ्यामनुभूतानीत्युक्तम् । एवं चाशेषचय-पदद्योत्ये अतिशयोक्ती ।

क्षणदासावक्षणदा वनमवनं व्यसनमव्यसनम् ।
बत वीर तव द्विषतां पराङ्मुखे त्वयि पराङ्मुखं सर्वम् ॥८२॥ (८)

अत्र शब्दशक्तिमूलविरोधाङ्गेनार्थान्तरन्यासेन 'विधिरपि त्वामनुवर्तते' इति सर्वपदद्योत्यं वस्तु ।

---

by her not meeting him, and the store of her spiritual merit exhausted in the deep joy of contemplating upon Him.'

What is meant here is that the sins and spiritual merit, the fruition of which would ordinarily extend over thousands of lives, were passed through merely by the pangs of separation and the joy of contemplation ; and thus the figure of Hyperbole is *suggested* by the two terms 'all' and 'store' (by the fact of the girl having attained beatitude).

(8) [*Suggestion of perceptible process—by word—based on force of meaning of fact by self-existent figure*]—

'O heroic king! When you become contrary to your enemies, every thing of theirs becomes contradictory—*Kṣaṇadā* [(*a*) night] becomes *akṣaṇadā* [(*a*) non-night, (*b*) uneasy], *vana* (forest) becomes *a-vana* [(*a*) *non-vana*, (*b*) shelter], and *vyasana* (occupation) becomes *a-vyasana* [(*a*) *non-vyasana*, (*b*) sheep-tending]. [*i.e.* They pass uncomfortable nights, fly to the forest and take to the tending of sheep].'

Through the implication of the term 'everything' the *fact* that 'even Fate follows your lead' is suggested by the Figure of 'Transition', which subserves the figure

तुह् वल्लहस्स गोसम्मि आसि अहरो मिलाणकमलदलो ।
इअ णववहुआ सोऊण कुणइ वअणं महिसँमुहं ॥८३॥ (९)

अत्र रूपकेण त्वयास्य मुहुर्मुहुः परिचुम्बनं तथा कृतं येन म्लानत्वमिति मिलाणादिपदद्योत्यं काव्यलिङ्गम् । एषु स्वतः-संभवी व्यञ्जकः ।

राईसु चंदधवलासु ललिअमप्फालिऊण जो चावं ।
एकच्छत्तं विअ कुणइ भुअणरज्जं विजंभंतो ॥८४॥ (१०)

अत्र वस्तुना येषां कामिनामसौ राजा स्मरस्तेभ्यो न कश्चि-दपि तदादेशपराङ्मुख इति जाग्रद्भिरुपभोगपरैरेव तैर्निशाति-

---

of 'Contradiction', which is based on the force of the words with double meanings, which cannot be replaced by others.

(9) *Suggestion of perceptible process,—based on the force of meaning—of Figure by self-existent Figure.*]—

"In the morning your lover's lips were withered lotus-leaves,"—on hearing this, the young bride cast her face towards the ground."

The Figure of 'Metaphor' involved in the term 'withered lotus-leaves' suggests the 'Poetic Reason', in the implication that 'your lover's lips looked faded on account of your having continued to kiss him frequently (till the very morning).'

In these examples the suggestive factor is self-existent.

(10) [*Suggestion of perceptible process—based on the force of meaning—of fact by imaginary fact.*]—

'He who, brandishing his beautiful bow, during moon-lit nights, brings the three worlds under his own undisputed sway.'

The (imaginary) *fact* (of Cupid's undisputed sway over the world), expressed by the term 'sway over the three worlds', suggests the *fact* that 'not a single one of those

7

वाह्यते इति भुअणरज्जपदद्योत्यं वस्तु प्रकाश्यते ।

निशितशरधियार्पयत्यनङ्गो
दृशि सुदृशः स्वबलं वयस्यराले ।
दिशि निपतति यत्र सा च तत्र
व्यतिकरमेत्य समुन्मिषन्त्यवस्थाः ॥ ॥८५॥ (११)

अत्र वस्तुना युगपदवस्थाः परस्परविरुद्धा अपि प्रभवन्तीति व्यतिकरपदद्योत्यो विरोधः ।

वारिज्जंतो वि पुणो संदावकदत्थिएण हिअएण ।
थणहरवअस्सएण विसुद्धजाई ण चलइ से हारो ॥८६॥ (१२)

अत्र विशुद्धजातित्वलक्षणहेत्वलंकारेण हारोनवरतं कम्पमान

---

persons over whom Cupid has his sway ever goes against his orders, hence they spend the nights in wakeful dalliance.'

(11) *Suggestion of perceptible process—of Figure by an imaginary Fact.*]—

'Regarding it as his sharp arrow, the Bodiless God (Cupid) lends all his force to the glance of the beautiful-eyed woman at her saucy age; whenever on whatever side it falls, it produces quite an admixture of conditions.'

The *Figure* of 'Contradiction',—in the implication that 'even mutually incompatible conditions appear simultaneously'—involved in the term 'admixture', is suggested by the (imaginary) *fact* (of Cupid lending his forces to the arrow and bringing about mixed conditions).

(12) [*Suggestion of perceptible process—of a fact by an imaginary Figure.*]—

'Even though forbidden by the heart suffering from pain (due to the impediment to embrace caused by the presence of the ornament), the necklace, being of pure breed, does not abandon its friends, the breasts.'

The (imaginary) Figure of 'Poetic Reason' involved

एवास्ते इति ण चलइ-पदद्योत्यं वस्तु ।

सो मुद्धसामलंगो धम्मिल्लो कलिअललिअणिअदेहो ।
तीए खंधाहि बलं गहिअ सरो सुरअसंगरे जअइ ॥८७॥ (१३)

अत्र रूपकेण मुहुर्मुहुराकर्षणेन तथा केशपाशः स्कन्धयोः प्राप्तो यथा रतिविरतावप्यनिवृत्ताभिलाषः कामुकोभूदिति खंध-पदद्योत्या विभावना ॥

एषु कविप्रौढोक्तिमात्रनिष्पन्नशरीरः ॥

णवपुण्णिमामिअंकस्स सुहअ को तं सि भणसु मह सच्चं ।
का सोहग्गसमग्गा पओसरअणिव्व तुह अज्ज ॥८८॥ (१४)

---

in the epithet 'being of pure breed' (which accounts for the constancy of the heart) suggests the Fact that 'the necklace remained constantly scintillating', which is expressed by the phrase 'abandons not.'

(13) [*Suggestion of perceptible process—of a Figure by an imaginary Figure*]—

'Cupid has, as it were, regained his beautiful body in the shape of the black and lovely tresses of the girl, and having borrowed strength from here shoulder, triumphs in the b:ttle of dalliance.'

The Figure of 'Peculiar Causation', involved in the word 'shoulder', and implying that 'when the lover pulled the locks frequently they fell upon her shoulder in such a ravishing way that, even at the close of the intercourse, the man's passion did not cease',—is suggested by the Metaphor (involved in the comparing of 'dalliance' to 'battle' and of 'Cupid' to the 'tresses').

In the last four examples the suggestion is reared entirely by the imaginary assertion of the poet.

(14) [*Suggestion of fact by fact, founded upon the assertion of an imaginary person.*]—

अत्र वस्तुना मयीवान्यस्यामपि प्रथममनुरक्तस्त्वं न तत इति णवेत्यादि-पओसेत्यादिपदद्योत्यं वस्तु व्यज्यते ॥

सहि णवणिहुवणसमरम्मि अंकवालीसहीए णिविडाए ।
हारो णिवारिओ विअ उच्छेरन्तो तदो कहं रमिअं ॥८९॥ (१५)

अत्र वस्तुना हारच्छेदानन्तरमन्यदेव रतमवश्यमभूत् तत्कथय कीदृगिति व्यतिरेकः कहंपदगम्यः ॥

'O beautiful one, tell me truly how you are related to the moon newly risen on the fullmoon night, and who is the lady that enjoys your love as the early evening does that of the moon.'

[During the early part of the evening the full moon appears 'red'; this redness, is regarded figuratively, as representing the moon's love towards the evening; it is fleeting, disappearing with the advent of night ; and the indignant wife insinuates that her husband's love for his new found lady will be as fleeting.]

The *fact* (described in the verse) suggests the fact that 'you are attached to this other lady only now in the beginning, and you will not remain so much longer, just as it was in my case,'—this suggestion being based upon the terms 'newly risen', 'early evening.'

(15) [*Suggestion of perceptible process—of Figure by fact asserted by the fanciful assertion of an imaginary person.*]—

'O friend'! When in the battle of dalliance, your necklace snapped, on being restrained (from intruding) by your fast friend in the shape of the lover's embrace,—in what manner did your enjoyment proceed ?'

The figure of 'Dissimilitude', indicated by the term 'in what manner', and implying that 'after the snapping of the necklace, the form of the enjoyment must have been peculiarly sweet',—is suggested by the *fact* (described in the verse).

प्रविसंती घरवारं विवलिअवअणा विलोइऊण पहं ।
खंधे घेत्तूण घडं हा हा णट्ठोत्ति रुअसि सहि किंति ॥९०॥

अत्र हेत्वलंकारेण संकेतनिकेतनं गच्छन्तं दृष्ट्वा यदि तत्र गन्तुमिच्छसि तदा अपरं घटं गृहीत्वा गच्छेति वस्तु किंति-पद-द्योत्यम् । यथा वा

विहलंखलं तुमं सहि दट्ठूण कुडेण तरलतरदिट्ठिं ।
वारप्फंसमिसेण अ अप्पा गुरुओत्ति पाडिअ विहिण्णो॥९१॥(१६)

अत्र नदीकूले लतागहने कृतसंकेतमप्राप्तं गृहप्रवेशावसरे पश्चादागतं दृष्टवा पुनर्नदीगमनाय द्वारोपघातव्याजेन बुद्धिपूर्वं व्याकुलतया त्वया घटः स्फोटित इति मया चिन्तितं तत्किमिति

---

(16) [*Suggestion of perceptible process—of a fact by a figure resting upon the fanciful assertion of an imaginary person.*]—

'O friend! You were entering your house-door, with the jar on your shoulders, and turning your face and looking towards the road, you say " the jar is broken " and are weeping :—why is this ?'

The *Figure* of 'Poetic Reason' (implying 'you are weeping *because* the jar is broken'), suggests the following *fact*—'on seeing your lover going to the place of appointment, if you wish to go there, then you take up another jar and go there', which is implied by the expression 'why is this'.

Another example of the same—

'The jar, seeing that you were exhausted and your eyes were unsteady, thought itself too heavy for you, and therefore, it has broken itself under the pretext of having struck against the door.'

The *Figure* of 'concealment', involved in the expression 'under the pretext of having struck against the door',

नाश्वसिषि तत्समीहितसिद्धये व्रज अहं ते श्वश्रूनिकटे सर्वं समर्थयिष्ये इति द्वारस्पर्शनव्याजेनेत्यपह्नुत्या वस्तु ।

जोह्णाइं महुरसेण अ विइण्णतारुण्णुच्छुअमणा सा ।
वुड्ढावि णवोढव्विअ परवहुआ अहह हरइतुह हिअअं॥९२॥ (१७)

अत्र काव्यलिङ्गेन वृद्धां परवधूं त्वमस्मानुज्झित्वाभिलषसीति त्वदीयमाचरितं वक्तुं न शक्यमित्याक्षेपः परवहूपदप्रकाश्यः ।

---

suggests the following *fact*—'you had made an appointment with your lover that you would meet him in the bower on the river-bank,—you went there but he was not there ; so you returned ; but entering the house you found that he had come to the place after you had left ;—so in order to be able to return to the river you have intentionally broken the jar under the pretext of striking against the door ;—all this I have understood ; why then don't you take heart ? Go and fulfil your desires, I justify everything to your mother-in-law.'

(17) *Suggestion of perceptible process—of figure by figure based upon the fanciful assertion of an imaginary person.*

'What a pity that your concubine captivates your heart, like a young girl, even though she is an old hag, to whose mind youthful sensuality is lent by moonlight and wine'.

The *figure* of 'Poetic Reason' (involved in the statement that the fact of her being the concubine, and not your wife, is the *reason* why she captivates your heart) suggests the *figure* of 'Hint', on the following implication—'you neglect young girls like myself and go after old women who are the wives of other men,—this conduct of yours is simply inexplicable'; all this being indicated by the word 'concubine'.

एषु कविनिबद्धवक्तृप्रौढोक्तिमात्रनिष्पन्नशरीरः ॥

वाक्यप्रकाश्ये तु पूर्वमुदाहृतम् ॥

शब्दार्थोभयशक्त्युद्भवस्तु पदप्रकाश्यो न भवतीति पञ्चत्रिंशद्भेदाः ॥

प्रबन्धेऽप्यर्थशक्तिभूः ॥ ४२ ॥

यथा गृध्रगोमायुसंवादादौ ।

अलं स्थित्वा श्मशानेऽस्मिन् गृध्रगोमायुसंकुले ।
कङ्कालबहुले घोरे सर्वप्राणिभयंकरे ॥ ९३ ॥

In these last examples the suggestion is based entirely upon the fanciful assertion of a person portrayed by the poet.

Suggestion manifested by a sentence has already been exemplified before (in the commentary on Text 24)—'*Tvāmasmi vachmi etc.*'

That arising from *both* word and meaning is never manifested by a word ; hence there are *thirty-five* varieties of Suggestion.

[*Eighteen* manifested by sentence and *seventeen* manifested by word.]

That (suggestion) which is based upon the force of meaning occurs in Context also.—(42).

As is found in the following dialogue of the Vulture and the Jackal.—

Says the vulture to the men (who have brought the dead body of a boy to the cremation ground and are mourning over it) whom it is anxious to send away, while it is yet day, in order to enable it to feed upon the body which it could do during the day only—

'There is no necessity for staying in this horrible crematorium crowded with vultures and jackals, abounding in skeletons, frightful and full of terror to all living

न चेह जीवितः कश्चित् कालधर्ममुपागतः ।
प्रियो वा यदि वा द्वेष्यः प्राणिनां गतिरीदृशी ॥ ९४ ॥

इति दिवा प्रभवतो गृध्रस्य पुरुषविसर्जनपरमिदं वचनम् ॥

आदित्योयं स्थितो मूढाः स्नेहं कुरुत सांप्रतम् ।
बहुविघ्नो मुहूर्तोयं जीवेदपि कदाचन ॥ ९५ ॥
अमुं कनकवर्णाभं बालमप्राप्तयौवनम् ।
गृध्रवाक्यात्कथं मूढास्त्यजध्वमविशङ्किताः ॥ ९६ ॥

इति निशि विजृम्भमाणस्य गोमायोर्जनव्यावर्तननिष्ठं च वचनमिति प्रबन्ध एव प्रथते ॥

---

beings; when once one has fallen a victim to death, one never revives, whether one be loved or hated ; such is the end of all living beings'.

This is followed by the following from the jackal who can feed on the body only when night has arrived and who tries to dissuade the people from going away early—

'O foolish men ! the sun is still up ; satisfy your affections yet ; the present may be an inauspicious moment, and it is just possible the dead may come back to life after sometime ; how is it that like fools you are without any hesitation, merely on the word of the vulture, leaving behind this boy of golden complexion who has scarcely attained youth ?'

Exactly what is meant by the two speakers here is indicated only by the *context*.

The other *eleven* varieties of this suggestion (through Context) are not illustrated here ; as that would make our work too prolix ; they can be easily followed from the definition itself.

अन्ये त्वेकादश भेदा ग्रन्थविस्तरभयान्नोदाहृताः स्वयं तु लक्षणतोनुसर्तव्याः ॥

अपिशब्दात्पदवाक्ययोः ॥४२॥

पदैकदेशरचनावर्णेष्वपि रसादयः ।

तत्र प्रकृत्या यथा

रइकेलिहिअणिवसणकरकिसलअरुद्धणअणजुअलस्स ।

रुद्दस्स तइअणअणं पव्वईपरिचुंबिअं जअइ ॥ ९७ ॥

अथ जयतीति न तु शोभते इत्यादि । समानेपि हि स्थगनव्यापारे लोकोत्तरेणैव व्यापारेणास्य पिधानमिति तदेवोत्कृष्टम् ।

'*Also*';—this means that the said suggestion is found in word and sentence also. 42.

Passion (Emotion, Aberrations of Passion, Aberrations of Emotion, Allayment of Emotion, Conjunction of Emotions and Admixture of Emotions) are (suggested imperceptibly) also (a) by parts of words, (b) by style and (c) by individual letters.

(*a*) Example of suggestion by the base of a word—
Ratikelihṛtanivasanakarakisalayaruddhanayanayugalasya.
Rudrasya tṛtīyanayanaṁ pārvatīparichumbitañjayati.

'The two eyes of Śiva having been closed by her two lotus-like hands when she was deprived of her cloth,—His third eye being (closed by being) kissed by Pārvatī scores a triumph.'

Here the suggestion of the Erotic 'Passion' lies in the use of the root '*ji*' in the verb '*jayati*', 'scores a triumph', in preference to the verb '*shobhate*', 'appears beautiful';—the implication of the particular root being that, 'though the action of being *closed* was common to all the three eyes, yet there is a distinct superiority in the third eye, the manner of whose closing was entirely unique.'

यथा वा

प्रेयान् सोयमपाकृतः सशपथं पादानतः कान्तया
द्वित्राण्येव पदानि वासभवनाद्यावन्न यात्युन्मनाः ।
तावत्प्रत्युत पाणिसंपुटगलन्नीविनिबन्धं धृतो
धावित्वेव कृतप्रणामकमहो प्रेम्णो विचित्रा गतिः ॥९८॥

अत्र पदानीति न तु द्वाराणीति ॥

तिङ्सुपोर्यथा

पथि पथि शुकचञ्चूचारुराभाङ्कुराणां
दिशि दिशि पवमानो वीरुधां लासकश्च ।
नरि नरि किरति द्राक् सायकान् पुष्पधन्वा
पुरि पुरि विनिवृत्ता मानिनीमानचर्चा ॥ ९९ ॥

Another example of the same kind of suggestion—

Preyān soyamapākṛtaḥ saśapatham pādānātaḥ kāntayā.
Dvitrāṇyeva padāni vāsabhavanād yāvanna yātyunmanāḥ.
Tāvat pratyuta pāṇisampuṭagalannīvīnibandhandhṛto.
Dhāvitveva kṛtapraṇāmakamaho premṇo vichitrā gatiḥ.

'Though when the lover lay adjuringly at her feet, he was rejected by his beloved, yet no sooner does he, in a dejected mood, go two or three *steps* out of the love-chamber, than she runs up to him with her loosened cloth held in her hands and falling on his feet, embraces him.'

Here the *suggestion* (of loving anxiety) lies in the use of the noun '*pada*' (steps) instead of '*dvāra*' (gates.)

[The suggestion being that she was so anxious that he may not go away that she could not bear his moving away even a few *steps* to the door of the room itself.]

Suggestion by verbal and nominal affixes—

Pathi pathi śukachañchūchārurābhāṅkurāṇāṁ
Dishi dishi pavamāno vīrudhāṁ lāsakaścha.
Nari nari kirati drāk sāyakān puṣpadhanvā
Puri puri vinivṛttā māninīmānacharchā.

अत्र किरतीति किरणस्य साध्यमानत्वं निवृत्तेति निवर्तनस्य सिद्धत्वं तिङा सुपा च तत्रापि क्तप्रत्ययेनातीतत्वं द्योत्यते। यथा वा

लिखन्नास्ते भूमिं बहिरवनतः प्राणदयितो
निराहाराः सख्यः सततरुदितोच्छूननयनाः।
परित्यक्तं सर्वं हसितपठितं पञ्जरशुकैः
तवावस्था चेयं विसृज कठिने मानमधुना ॥१००॥

'On every way-side there is the sheen of sprouts resembling the parrot's beak ; on every side the breeze is making the creepers dance ; on every male is the Flower-bowed God showering his arrows ; and in every town has ceased the very talk of self-restraint on the part of affronted women.'

The present tense form '*kirati*,' 'is showering,' indicates, by the conjugational affix, that the act of *showering arrows* is still only in the course of accomplishment, and the past-participle form '*vinivṛttā*,' 'has ceased,' indicates by the nominative ending, that the action of *ceasing* has become a thing accomplished already ; and further, the past-participle affix '*kta*' (in 'vinivṛttā) indicates that the action (*of ceasing*) is past.

[And the suggestion here is that the circumstances described are so effective in exciting the Erotic Passion that they accomplish their purpose even before they are themselves accomplished.]

Another example of the same—

Likhannāste bhumim vahiravanataḥ prāṇadayito
Nirāhārāḥ sakhyaḥ satataruditochchhūnanayanāḥ.
Parityaktam sarvam hasitapaṭhitam pañjaraśukais-
Tavāvasthā cheyam visrja kaṭhine mānamadhunā.

अत्र लिखन्निति न तु लिखतीति तथा आस्ते इति न तु आसीत इति अपि तु प्रसादपर्यन्तमास्ते इति भूमिमिति न तु भूमाविति न हि बुद्धिपूर्वकमपरं किंचिल्लिखतीति तिङ्सुब्विभक्तीनां व्यङ्ग्यम् ।

संबन्धस्य यथा

गामारुहम्हि गामे वसामि णअरट्ठिइं ण जाणामि ।
णाअरिआणं पइणो हरेमि जा होमि सा होमि ॥१०१॥

'The beloved of thy life sits outside, depressed, scratching the ground; thy friends with eyes swollen by constant weeping, have been without food; all amusing talk has been given up by the parrots in the cages; thy own condition is this; even now, O cruel one, give up thy sense of dignity injured.'

Here we have (*a*) the form '*likhan*' ('scratching,' the present participle in which suggests the continuity of an *aimless* act) and not '*likhati*' ('writes,' in the present tense, which would indicate writing *with a purpose*);—again (*b*) '*āste*' ('stays') which suggests that the man will continue to so stay till reconciliation, and not '*āsīta*' ('is seated,' which would indicate an accomplished act, without regard to anything else);—again (*c*) '*bhūmim*' (with the Accusative ending), —which suggests that he is scratching the ground aimlessly—and not '*bhūmau*' (with the locative ending, which would indicate that the act was done with some purpose.) Thus we have here suggestion by verbal and nominal affixes.

Example of suggestion by relationship (denoted by the genitive ending)—

I am born in the village and live in the village, and know not the ways of the city; whatever I am, I capture the husbands *of city-women*.'

अत्र नागरिकाणामिति षष्ठ्याः ।

रमणीयः क्षत्रियकुमार आसीत् इति कालस्य ।

एषा हि भग्नमहेश्वरकार्मुकं दाशरथिं प्रति कुपितस्य भार्गवस्योक्ति। वचनस्य यथा ।

ताणँ गुणग्गहणाणं ताणुक्कंठाणं तस्स पेम्मस्स ।
ताणँ भणिआणं सुंदर एरिसिअँ जाअमवसाणं ॥१०२॥

अत्र गुणग्रहणादीनां बहुत्वं प्रेम्णश्चैकत्वं द्योत्यते ॥

पुरुषव्यत्ययस्य यथा

The suggestion here lies in the genitive ending in 'of city-women,' '*nāgarīkāṇām*.'

[The use of the expression 'husbands of city-women,' instead of city-men, suggests the extreme cleverness of the speaker, who is able to capture, not the ordinary men of the city, but those men of the city who have acquired much cleverness by their connection with the very clever 'city-women.']

In the sentence 'lovely *was* this Kṣattriya boy,' the suggestion lies in the tense ; it is said by the enraged Bhārgava with reference to Rāma who has broken the bow of Shiva.

[The suggestion by the use of the Past Tense being that the boy is as good as already killed by me and exists no more.]

The following is an example of suggestion by number—

'O beautiful one ! such has been the end of *those* appreciations of good qualities, of *those* longings, of *that* love and of *those* conversations !'

What is suggested here (by the plural number in 'appreciations', 'longings' and 'conversations' and the singular number in 'love') is that though the appreciation and the rest (which aroused the love) have been many

रे रे चञ्चललोचनाञ्चितरुचे चेतः प्रमुच्य स्थिर-
प्रेमाणं महिमानमेणनयनामालोक्य किं नृत्यसि ।
किं मन्ये विहरिष्यसे बत हतां मुञ्चान्तराशामिमाम्
एषा कण्ठतटे कृता खलु शिला संसारवारांनिधौ ॥१०३॥

अत्र प्रहासः ।

पूर्वनिपातस्य यथा

येषां दोर्बलमेव दुर्बलतया ते संमतास्तैरपि
प्रायः केवलनीतिरीतिशरणैः कार्यं किमुर्वीश्वरैः ।

---

and multifarious, the Love (aroused by them) is *one* and uniform.

The following is an example of suggestion by the change of 'Person.'

'O thou my heart, in whom has been aroused a hankering after the fickle-eyed woman ! Why dost thou relinquish that exalted position of lasting devotion and begin to dance at the sight of the fawn-eyed one ? *I think*—you will dally ! Ah ! give up this despicable desire ; this is a piece of stone tied to one's neck in the ocean of the world.'

Here ridicule (is suggested by the sudden change into the First Person in 'I think,' '*manye*,' according to Pāṇini's rule 1.4.106 whereby the First Person singular affix added to the root '*man*' to 'think' implies ridicule).

The following is an example of suggestion by 'irregular priority.'—

Those men who have only the strength of arms have been regarded as weak ; what useful work again can be done by those kings who take shelter in mere statesmanship ? O terrestrial Indra ! Those who, like you, have

ये क्ष्माशक्र पुनः पराक्रमनयस्वीकारकान्तक्रमास्--
ते स्युर्नैव भवादृशास्त्रिजगति द्वित्राः पवित्राः परम् ॥१०४॥

अत्र पराक्रमस्य प्राधान्यमवगम्यते ।

विभक्तिविशेषस्य यथा

प्रधनाध्वनि धीरधनुर्ध्वनिभृति विधुरैरयोधि तव दिवसम् ।
दिवसेन तु नरप भवानयुद्ध विधिसिद्धसाधुवादपदम् ॥१०५॥

अत्र दिवसेनेत्यपवर्गतृतीया फलप्राप्तिं द्योतयति ।

भूयो भूयः सविधनगरीरथ्यया पर्यटन्तं
दृष्ट्वा दृष्ट्वा भवनवलभीतुङ्गवातायनस्था ।
साक्षात्कामं नवमिव रतिर्मालती माधवं यत्
गाढोत्कण्ठालुलितलुलितैरङ्गकैस्ताम्यतीति ॥१०६॥

---

their actions guided by both *valour and statesmanship* ("*parākramanaya*"),—of those there may, or may not be, even two or three in all the three worlds !"

Here the placing of '*parākrama*' (valour) before 'naya' (statesmanship) in the compound [which is irregular in view of the rule that the shorter term should precede the longer] suggests the superior importance of *Valour.*

Pradhanādhvani dhīradhanurdhvanibhṛti vidhurairayodhi tava divasam.

Divasena tu narapa bhavānayuddha vidhisiddhasādhuvādapadam.

'O protector of men ! in the battle resounding with the twanging of bows wielded by the brave, thy enemies fought *all the day long*; you, on the other hand, fought *by the day* in such a way as to win encomiums from all good men.'

The Instrumental ending in '*divasena*' ('by the day'), which denotes 'success' (according to Pāṇini 2.3.6)), suggests that the king addressed attained the object for which he fought.

'Seated in the high window of her mansion, whenever Mālatī, who resembles Rati, sees Mādhava, who is a new

अत्रानुकम्पावृत्तेः करूपतद्धितस्य ।

परिच्छेदातीतः सकलवचनानामविषयः
पुनर्जन्मन्यस्मिन्ननुभवपथं यो न गतवान् ।
विवेकप्रध्वंसादुपचितमहामोहगहनो
विकारः कोप्यन्तर्जडयति च तापं च कुरुते ॥१०७॥

अत्र प्रशब्दस्योपसर्गस्य ।

कृतं च गर्वाभिमुखं मनस्त्वया
किमन्यदेवं निहताश्च नो द्विषः ।
तमांसि तिष्ठन्ति हि तावदंशुमान्
न यावदायात्युदयाद्रिमौलिताम् ॥१०८॥

---

personification of the Love-god himself, passing by the adjacent highway, she suffers from her *poor limbs* (*aṅgakaiḥ*) being charmingly affected by deep longings.'

Here the suggestion (of the fragility of the limbs due to the Erotic Passion) is made by the nominal affix '*Ka*' (in '*aṅgakaiḥ*') which signifies *pitiableness.*

'An indescribable feeling benumbs and inflames my heart,—a feeling above all measure and beyond all power of expression, which has never in this life come within the range of experience, and which, owing to the *entire destruction* ('*pradhvamsāt*') of my discriminative faculty, has become deep and has brought about extreme stupor.'

Here the suggestion (of the Erotic in privation) is made by the prefix '*pra*' (in '*pradhvamsāt*', which means *entire*).

'You turned your mind towards glory, and—what else ?—our enemies were destroyed [*kṛtañcha garvābhimukham manastvayā...nihatāshcha no dviṣah*] ;—Darkness prevails only so long as the sun does not reach the crest of the Rising Mount.'

अत्र तुल्ययोगिताद्योतकस्य 'च' इति निपातस्य ।

रामोसौ भुवनेषु विक्रमगुणैः प्राप्तः प्रसिद्धिं परा-
मस्मद्भाग्यविपर्ययाद्यदि परं देवो न जानाति तम् ।
बन्दीवैष यशांसि गायति मरुद्यस्यैकबाणाहति-
श्रेणीभूतविशालतालविवरोद्गीर्णैः स्वरैः सप्तभिः ॥१०९॥

Here the suggestion of Heroic Passion is made by the Indeclinable '*cha*' ('and'), which implies the figure of 'Equal Pairing' [the simultaneity of the *king's thinking of glory* and the *destruction of the enemies*.]

Rāmosau bhuvaneṣu vikramaguṇaiḥ prāptaḥ prasiddhiṁ parāṁ
Asmadbhāgyaviparyayād yadi paraṁ devo na jānāti tam.
Bandīvaiṣa yaśāṁsi gāyati marud yasyaikabāṇāhati—
Śreṇībhūtaviśālatālavivarodgīrṇaiḥ svaraiḥ saptabhiḥ.

'Through his valour and other excellences, this Rāma has attained great renown in the worlds ; through the reversal of our fortune, your majesty does not yet recognise him ; his fame is being sung, as if by a bard, by the wind, in all the seven notes of music issuing forth from the holes made by the stroke of a single arrow in the seven huge palm-trees standing in a line.'

The passion of the Heroic is suggested here—(*a*) by the pronoun '*asau*', 'this' (which indicates that the person is well-known), (*b*) by the basic noun '*bhuvaneṣu*' 'in the worlds' (which mean that the person's fame is not confined to any particular province or country), (*c*) by the number in '*guṇaiḥ*' (which means that he is famous not only for one or two qualities but for many), (*d*) by the use of the term '*asmat*' (our) in preference to '*tvat*' (your) or '*mat*' (mine) [in the compound '*asmadbhāgya*'...], which implies that the misfortune is of all the persons

8

अत्रासाविति भुवनेष्विति गुणैरिति सर्वनामप्रातिपदिकवचनानां न त्वदिति न मदिति अपि अस्मदित्यस्य सर्वाक्षेपिणः भाग्यविपर्ययादित्यन्यथासंपत्तिमुखेन न त्वभावमुखेनाभिधानस्य।

तरुणिमनि कलयति कलामनुमदनधनुर्भ्रुवोः पठत्यग्रे ।
अधिवसति सकलललनामौलिमियं चकितहरिणचलनयना ।।११०।।

अत्र इमनिजव्ययीभावकर्मभूताधाराणां स्वरूपस्य तरुणत्वे, इति धनुषः समीपे, इति मौलौ वसतीति त्वादिभिस्तुल्ये, एषां वाचकत्वे, अस्ति कश्चित् स्वरूपस्य विशेषो यश्चमत्कारकारी स एव व्यञ्जकत्वं प्राप्नोति।

---

concerned,—and (*e*) by the term '*bhāgyaviparyayāt*,' 'reversal of fortune,' which means that it is not only that we have no fortune or luck, but that our fortune has taken an entirely wrong turn.

Taruṇimani kalayati kalāmanumadanadhanurbhruvoḥ paṭhatyagre.

Adhivasati sakalalalanāmaulimiyam chakitahariṇachalanayanā.

'On youthfulness being fully developed in vivacity, and the eye-brows having become instructed in liveliness under the guidance of Cupid's Bow, she with eyes unsteady like that of the fawn occupies the highest position among damsels.'

Here the Erotic Passion is suggested by the *form* (*a*) of the '*imanich*' affix (in '*taruṇimani*'), (*b*) of the *Avyayībhāva* compound ('*anumadanadhanuḥ*'), (*c*) of the locative used accusatively (in '*maulim*'). The expressed meaning of each of these would be exactly the same as that respectively of (*a*) '*taruṇatve*', with the nominal affix '*tva*' (instead of '*imanich*'), (*b*) '*madanadhanuṣaḥ samīpe*,' and

एवमन्येषामपि बोद्धव्यम् ।

वर्णरचनानां व्यञ्जकत्वं गुणस्वरूपनिरूपणे उदाहरिष्यते अपिशब्दात् प्रबन्धेषु नाटकादिषु ।

एवं रसादीनां पूर्वगणितभेदाभ्यां सह षड् भेदाः ।

भेदास्तदेकपञ्चाशत्

व्याख्याताः ॥

(c) '*maulau*'; and yet there is something distinctly charming in the use of the *forms* used by the poet ; and it is in these forms that there lies the said suggestiveness.

Suggestion by other (parts of words) may be similarly explained.

The suggestiveness of Letters and Style is going to be described in the section dealing with Qualities (under Chapter VIII).

Thus, along with the two kinds previously enumerated, there are six varieties of Suggestion of Passion and the rest.

[*i. e.* As suggested by (1) Sentence, (2) Word, (3) Part of Word, (-4) Style, (5) Letter and (6) Context].

Thus there are fifty-one varieties.

These have been already described.

(*A*) That where the expressed meaning is not intended has two varieties—(*a*) That in which the expressed meaning is transferred into another and (*b*) in which it is entirely ignored, and each of these belonging to *word* and meaning, make up *Four* varieties ;—(*B*) that where the expressed meaning is intended to be subservient to another, and the suggestive process is imperceptible, belongs to word, sentence, part of word, style, letters and context, makes up *six* varieties ;—(*c*) The same where the suggestive process is perceptible has *forty-one* varieties as follows :—2 varieties of that, based on word and each belonging to word and sentence, make *four*,—12 varieties of that based on meaning and each belonging to word, sentence and context, make *thirty-six*; and one variety of that based on both word and meaning; and 4+6+41 make 51.

तेषां चान्योन्ययोजने ॥ ४३ ॥
संकरेण त्रिरूपेण संसृष्टया चैकरूपया ।

न केवलं शुद्धा एवैकपञ्चाशद्भेदा भवन्ति । यावत्तेषां स्वप्रभेदैरेकपञ्चाशता संशयास्पदत्वेनानुग्राहकतयैकव्यञ्जकानुप्रवेशेन चेति त्रिविधेन संकरेण परस्परनिरपेक्षरूपयैकप्रकारया संसृष्टया चेति चतुर्भिगुणने ।

वेदखाब्धिवियच्चन्द्राः
शुद्धभेदैः सह
शरेषुयुगखेन्दवः ॥ ४४ ॥

By the mutual combination of these, in the three forms of commixture and one form of uniform conjunction, they come to the number made up of (*a*) *the Vedas* (4), (*b*) *the sky* (0), (*c*) *the oceans* (4). (*d*) *the sky* (0) *and the moon* (1) [*i. e.* 10404].

There are not only the 51 simple varieties ; each of these 51 has its own 51 varieties, and each of these combines with the other in three ways (in which there is mutual dependency)—*viz*. (1) where it is doubtful which one is the predominant factor, (2) where one distinctly helps the other (and is hence the predominant factor, and (3) where both form part of a single suggestive factor—and also in one another way (in which both are independent of each other) ; and thus by multiplying by 4 the *fifty-one times fifty-one* varieties) the number becomes 10404.

These mixed varieties along with the (51) pure varieties make the number—

made up of—(*a*) *arrows* (5), (*b*) *arrows* (5), (*c*) *age-cycles* (4), (*d*) *sky* (0) *and* (*e*) *the Moon* (1)—*i. e.* 10455.

तत्र दिङ्मात्रमुदाह्रियते ।

खणपाहुणिआ देअर जाआए सुहअ किंपि दे भणिआ ।
रुअइ पडोहरवलहीघरम्मि अणुणिज्जउ वराई ॥१११॥

अत्रानुनयः किमुपभोगलक्षणेर्थान्तरे संक्रमितः किमनुरण-
नन्यायेनोपभोगे एव व्यङ्ग्ये व्यञ्जकः इति संदेहः ।

स्निग्धश्यामलकान्तिलिप्तवियतो वेल्लद्बलाका घनाः
वाताः शीकरिणः पयोदसुहृदामानन्दकेकाः कलाः ।
कामं सन्तु दृढं कठोरहृदयो रामोस्मि सर्वं सहे
वैदेही तु कथं भविष्यति ह हा हा देवि धीरा भव ॥११२॥

These are illustrated only partially—

'O brother! Has the girl, a guest for the moment, been told something by your wife? She is weeping behind the house; go, console the poor creature'.

Here it is *doubtful* whether the 'consoling' is meant to be transformed into something else, in the form of *dalliance*, (thus making the suggestion one of 'transferred denotation'), or it itself suggests, in the manner of an echo, the dalliance (making the suggestion one in which the expressed meaning, while applicable, is subservient to another meaning).

'The clouds have overspread the sky with dense black lustre, and are adorned with lines of cranes; the wind is blowing in sprays; there is joyous shrieking of the friends of clouds (Peacocks).—Let all these be! I am surely Rāma of the hard heart and shall bear all; but how will Vaidehī be keeping? Ah! O Lady, bear up with fortitude!'

Here (*a*) in the terms 'overspread' and 'friends of clouds' we have the 'conjunction' (mutually indepen-

अत्र लिप्तेति पयोदसुहृदामिति च अत्यन्ततिरस्कृतवाच्ययोः संसृष्टिः । ताभ्यां सह रामोस्मीत्यर्थान्तरसंक्रमितवाच्यस्यानुग्राहकभावेन रामपदलक्षणैकव्यञ्जकानुप्रवेशेन चार्थान्तरसंक्रमितवाच्यरसध्वन्योः संकरः । एवमन्यदप्युदाहार्यम् ॥

इति काव्यप्रकाशे ध्वनिनिर्णयो नाम चतुर्थ उल्लासः ॥ ४ ॥

---

dent) of the two suggestions (where the expressed meaning is entirely ignored) ;—and (*b*) again with these two there is 'commixture' with the suggestion in the expression 'I am Rāma', whose expressed meaning is transformed into something else (*i. e.* disregard for himself, who is known to be the receptacle of constant sufferings); in which commixture (of the second kind) the two factors help each other,—and another 'commixture' (of the third kind) of the suggestion (by the whole sentence) of the 'erotic in privation' and that (by the single word '*rāmaḥ*') of 'self-abnegation', in both of which the Expressed meaning is transformed, and both of which form part and parcel of what is indicated by the single word '*rāmaḥ*'.

The other varieties may be similarly illustrated. 43-44.

[Here ends the chapter IV entitled Description of Suggestion of the Kāvyaprakāśa.]

अथ पञ्चम उल्लासः

एवं ध्वनौ निर्णीते गुणीभूतव्यङ्ग्यप्रभेदानाह ।

अगूढमपरस्याङ्गं वाच्यसिद्ध्यङ्गमस्फुटम् ।
सन्दिग्धतुल्यप्राधान्ये काक्वाक्षिप्तमसुन्दरम् ॥ ४५ ॥
व्यङ्ग्यमेवं गुणीभूतव्यङ्ग्यस्याष्टौ भिदाः स्मृताः ।

कामिनीकुचकलशवत् गूढं चमत्करोति । अगूढं तु स्फुटतया वाच्यायमानमिति गुणीभूतमेव ।

CHAPTER V

POETRY OF SUBORDINATE SUGGESTION

(POETRY OF INTERMEDIATE ORDER).

Suggestive Poetry having been described, the author proceeds to describe the varieties of 'Poetry of Subordinate Suggestion'—

There are eight varieties of the Poetry of Subordinate Suggestion, according as the suggested meaning is—(1) *obvious,* (2) *subservient to something else,* (3) *subservient to the accomplishment of the 'expressed' meaning,* (4) *abstruse,* (5) *of doubtful prominence (in comparison to the expressed meaning),* (6) *of equal importance (with the expressed meaning),* (7) *rendered manifest by intonation, or* (8) *not beautiful.*

Like the breasts of a young girl, suggestion has a charm only while it is concealed; when it is not concealed, it becomes too obvious and hence as prosaic as the expressed meaning; this is what is meant by its being 'subordinate'.

अगूढं यथा

यस्यासुहृत्कृततिरस्कृतिरेत्य तप्त-
सूचीव्यधव्यतिकरेण युनक्ति कर्णौ ।
काञ्चीगुणग्रथनभाजनमेष सोस्मि
जीवन्न संप्रति भवामि किमावहामि ॥११३॥

अत्र जीवन्नित्यर्थान्तरसंक्रमितवाच्यस्य ।

उन्निद्रकोकनदरेणुपिशङ्गिताङ्गा
गायन्ति मञ्जु मधुपा गृहदीर्घिकासु ।
एतच्चकास्ति च रवेर्नवबन्धुजीव-
पुष्पच्छदाभमुदयाचलचुम्बि बिम्बम् ॥११४॥

अत्र चुम्बनस्यात्यन्ततिरस्कृतवाच्यस्य ।

---

(1) Example of *obvious* suggestion—

'In former times the taunts of an enemy always appeared in my ears like piercing hot needles,—and now that same I have been reduced to this position that I am entrusted with the work of knitting the girdle-zones of ladies! Even though existing, I am not alive! What can I do?'

Here the suggestion lies in the term 'existing,' which has *its expressed meaning* of 'living' *transformed into something else* (*i. e., ignominious existence*) [and this is too 'obvious' to be charming].

Another example—

'Among the house-hold pools, the black bees, are humming sweetly, their bodies rendered tawny with the dust of the full-blown red lotus; and here shines the Sun, bright as the petals of the Bandhujīva flower, kissing the Rising Mount.'

Here the suggestion of dawn lies in the term 'kissing',

अत्रासीत् फणिपाशबन्धनविधिः शक्त्या भवद्देवरे
गाढं वक्षसि ताडिते हनुमता द्रोणाद्रिरत्राहृतः ।
दिव्यैरिन्द्रजिदत्र लक्ष्मणशरैर्लोकान्तरं प्रापितः
केनाप्यत्र मृगाक्षि राक्षसपतेः कृत्ता च कण्ठाटवी ॥११५॥ (१)

अत्र केनाप्यत्रेत्यर्थशक्तिमूलानुरणनरूपस्य । 'तस्याप्यत्र' इति युक्तः पाठः ।

अपरस्य रसादेर्वाच्यस्य वा (वाक्यार्थीभूतस्य) अङ्गं रसादि अनुरणनरूपं वा । यथा

---

which has its *expressed meaning entirely ignored*, [and this is too ' obvious '.]

Another example—

'Here occurred the act of being bound in the serpentine noose ; here was the Droṇa mountain brought by Hanuman when your younger brother-in-law was wounded by the missile in his chest ; here was Indrajit sent to the regions of the dead by the celestial arrows of Lakṣmaṇa ; and O fawn-eyed one, here was cut down by some one the line of heads of the Demon-king.'

Here the suggestion of the *speaker* himself lies in the term ' by some one ', where *the suggestive reverberation is based upon the force of the meaning.* [And this is too ' obvious '.]

' *Tasyāpyatra* ' (of that) would be the better reading (in which case the suggestion would not be too obvious or subordinated).

(2) Example of that Passion (Emotion and so forth) which is ' subservient to—a mere echo of—' something else '—i. e., of another Passion (Emotion and so forth), or of the expressed meaning, denoted by a sentence,—

अयं स रशनोत्कर्षी पीनस्तनविमर्दनः ।
नाभ्यूरुजघनस्पर्शी नीवीविस्रंसनः करः ॥११६॥

अत्र शृङ्गारः करुणस्य ।

कैलासालयभाललोचनरुचा निर्वर्तितालक्तक-
व्यक्तिः पादनखद्युतिर्गिरिभुवः सा वः सदा त्रायताम् ।
स्पर्धाबन्धसमृद्धयेव सुदृढं रूढा यया नेत्रयोः
कान्तिः कोकनदानुकारसरसा सद्यः समुत्सार्यते ॥११७॥

अत्र भावस्य रसः ।

अत्युच्चाः परितः स्फुरन्ति गिरयः स्फारास्तथाम्भोधय-
स्तानेतानपि बिभ्रती किमपि न क्लान्तासि तुभ्यं नमः ।

'This is that same hand which used to pull (my) girdle-zone, press the plump breasts, touch the navel, the thighs and the hips and loosen the cloth-knot.'

Here the Erotic is 'subservient' to the Pathetic.

[It is the speech of the wife of a hero in the Māhābhārata war, addressed on seeing the dead body of her husband].

Another example—

'May the sheen of the foot-nails of Pārvatī ever protect you,—the red paint wherein has become heightened by the (red) light emanating from the eye on the forehead of Śiva (who has fallen upon her feet for the purpose of propitiating her) ; and this sheen, urged by emulation as it were, speedily and steadily sets aside the red-lotus-like lustre of her eyes (by depriving them of the redness due to her anger which has ceased upon her husband falling at her feet)'.

Here the Passion (Erotic) is 'subservient' to the Emotion (the poet's devotion to the goddess).

आश्चर्येण मुहुर्मुहुः स्तुतिमिति प्रस्तौमि यावद्भुव-
स्तावद्बिभ्रदिमां स्मृतस्तव भुजो वाचस्ततो मुद्रिताः॥११८॥

अत्र भूविषयो रत्याख्यो भावो राजविषयस्य रतिभावस्य ।

बन्दीकृत्य नृप द्विषां मृगदृशस्ताः पश्यतां प्रेयसां
श्लिष्यन्ति प्रणमन्ति लान्ति परितश्चुम्बन्ति ते सैनिकाः ।
अस्माकं सुकृतैर्दृशोर्निपतितोस्यौचित्यवारांनिधे
विध्वस्ता विपदोखिलास्तदिति तैः प्रत्यर्थिभिः स्तूयसे॥११९॥

अत्र भावस्य रसाभासभावाभासौ प्रथमार्धद्वितीयार्धद्योत्यौ ।

Another example—

"On all sides there rise these lofty mountains and wide-expanding oceans,—though thou bearest all these, yet thou feelest not the slightest fatigue,—all reverence to thee !"—While, struck with wonder, I was thus singing the praises of the Earth, I remembered your arm, O King, bearing, as it does, the burden even of this earth, and thereupon my speech became sealed'.

The feeling of veneration for the earth is 'subservient' to the same feeling for the king.

Another example—

'O King, your soldiers, having captured the fawn-eyes wives of your enemies, embrace them, court them, carry them about and kiss them, even while their husbands are looking on ;—and yet those same enemies of yours are praising you in the following strain—"O ocean of propriety, it is by virtue of our past good deeds that you have come before our eyes and all our troubles have been destroyed." '

The 'Aberration of the Passion' (of the Erotic, appearing in the soldiers)—which is implied in the first half of the verse,—and the 'Aberration of the feeling' of venera-

अविरलकरवालकम्पनैर्भ्रुकुटीतर्जनगर्जनैर्मुहुः ।
दददृशे तव वैरिणां मदः स गतः क्वापि तवेक्षणे क्षणात् ॥१२०॥

अत्र भावस्य भावप्रशमः ।

साकं कुरङ्गकदृशा मधुपानलीलां
कर्तुं सुहृद्भिरपि वैरिणि ते प्रवृत्ते ।
अन्याभिधायि तव नाम विभो गृहीतं
केनापि तत्र विषमामकरोदवस्थाम् ॥१२१॥

अत्र त्रासोदयः ।

---

tion (for the king, on the part of his enemies)—implied in the second half—are 'subservient' to the (poet's) feeling of veneration for the king.

Another example—

'The haughtiness of your enemies was seen in the constant brandishing of swords, in the curvature of the eye-brows and in frequent roaring ; but at sight of you, it instantly disappeared'.

The 'Allayment of the Feeling' (of pride) is subservient to the (poet's) feeling (of veneration for the king).

Another example—

'On the occasion of your enemy setting about a drinking revelry in the company of the fawn-eyed girl and his friends,—your name, even though mentioned by some one in another connection, filled him with distress'.

Here the 'appearance of the feeling of fear' (is subservient to the poet's feeling of veneration for the king).

असोढा तत्कालोल्लसदसहभावस्य तपसः
कथानां विश्रम्भेष्वथ च रसिकः शैलदुहितुः ।
प्रमोदं वो दिश्यात् कपटबटुवेषापनयने
त्वराशैथिल्याभ्यां युगपदभियुक्तः स्मरहरः ॥१२२॥

अत्रावेगधैर्ययोः संधिः ॥

पश्येत्कश्चिच्चल चपल रे का त्वराहं कुमारी
हस्तालम्बं वितर ह ह हा व्युत्क्रमः क्वासि यासि ।
इत्थं पृथ्वीपरिवृढ भवद्विद्विषोरण्यवृत्तेः
कन्या कंचित् फलकिसलयान्याददानाभिधत्ते ॥१२३॥

Another example—

'May the Destroyer of Kāma (Śiva) ordain your happiness,—He who, being unable to bear any longer the zealousness of Pārvatī's austerities, and fondly gratified at her confidently loving manner of address, was seized simultaneously by both precipitancy and languor'.

Here we have the 'Conjunction' of the feelings of Flurry and Equanimity, (which is 'subordinate' to the poet's feeling of devotion to the king).

Another example—

'"O impetuous one! Some one might be looking! Move aside.—What is the hurry?—I a virgin!—Offer me the support of your arms.—Ah! Ah! this perverted order of things!—Where are you? Whither are you going?"—O Lord of the earth, thus does the daughter of your enemy who has retired to the forest address some man while she is collecting fruits and leaves'.

Here there is the 'Commixture' of the feelings of Apprehension ('some one might be looking'), Calmness ('what is the hurry?'), Remembrance ('I, a virgin'), Lan-

अत्र शङ्कासूयाधृतिस्मृतिश्रमदैन्यविबोधौत्सुक्यानां शबलता।

एते च रसवदाद्यलंकाराः। यद्यपि भावोदयभावसंधिभावशबलत्वानि नालंकारतया उक्तानि तथापि कश्चित् ब्रूयादित्येवमुक्तम्।

यद्यपि स नास्ति कश्चिद्विषयः यत्र ध्वनिगुणीभूतव्यङ्ग्ययोः स्वप्रभेदादिभिः सह संकरः संसृष्टिर्वा नास्ति तथापि प्राधान्येन व्यपदेशा भवन्तीति क्वचित्केनचिद्व्यवहारः।

---

guor ('offer me the support of your arms'), Depression ('Ah, ah'), Determination ('what a perverted order of things'), and Longing ('whither are you going?'),—(which is 'subordinate' to the poet's regard for the king).

These [(1) Passion, (2) Feeling, (3) Aberration of Passion, (4) Aberration of Feeling, (5) Manifestation of Feeling, (6) Conjunction of Feeling and (7) Commixture of Feeling—as 'subordinate' to another Passion or Feeling] are what are known as the Figures of Speech [called (1) the Sentimental, (2) the Agreeable, (3) the Forcible, (4) the Quiescent, (5) Manifested Feeling, (6) Conjunct Feeling and (7) Commingled Feeling respectively].

Though as a matter of fact, 'Manifested Feeling', 'Conjunct Feeling' and 'Commingled Feeling' (the last three of those just mentioned) have nowhere been spoken of as 'Figures', yet, we have made the above assertion (including these also) in view of the possibility of some one describing them as such.

Though there is no single case where there is no commixture of both 'Suggestive Poetry' and 'Poetry of Subordinate Suggestion' and their respective varieties—where one or the other is the more prominent or where both are of equal importance [and hence no example can

जनस्थाने भ्रान्तं कनकमृगतृष्णान्धितधिया
वचो वैदेहीति प्रतिपदमुदश्रु प्रलपितम् ।
कृतालंकाभर्तुर्वदनपरिपाटीषुघटना
मयाप्तं रामत्वं कुशलवसुता न त्वधिगता ॥१२४॥

अत्र शब्दशक्तिमूलानुरणनरूपो रामेण सहोपनानोपमेय-भावो वाच्याङ्गतां नीतः ।

---

be cited as a pure unmixed example of any one kind],—yet we classify the examples as of one or the other, according as one or the other happens to be the prominent factor; and this is done in accordance with the principle that appellations are applied to things in accordance with what happens to be their most prominent element.

[Example of Suggested Figure subservient to the expressed meaning]—

Janasthāne bhrāntam kanakamṛgatṛṣṇāndhitadhiyā
Vacho vai-dehīti pratipadamudaśru pralapitam
Kṛtā-laṅkābhartturvadanaparipāṭīṣughaṭanā
Mayāptam rāmatvaṁ kuśalavasutā na tvadhigatā

'I wandered *among men's haunts* [in the Janasthāna forest], with my mind blinded *by a miragic solicitude for gold* [by a desire for the golden deer];—at every step, with tearful eyes, I said the words "*Please give me*" ["O Vaidehī"];—*enough attempt was made by me at flattering the meanly rich people* [I directed my arrows at the serried heads of the king of Laṅkā];—thus though I attained the position of Rāma, yet I did not obtain *perfect affluence* [the mother of Kuśa and Lava, Sītā].'

Here the similitude between the speaker and Rāma, which is suggested through the force of the reverberating

आगत्य संप्रति वियोगविसंष्ठुलाङ्गी
मम्भोजिनीं क्वचिदपि क्षपितत्रियामः ।
एतां प्रसादयति पश्य शनैः प्रभाते
तन्वङ्गि पादपतनेन सहस्ररश्मिः ॥१२५॥ (२)

अत्र नायकवृत्तान्तोर्थशक्तिमूलो वस्तुरूपो निरपेक्ष-रविकमलिनीवृत्तान्ताध्यारोपेणैव स्थितः ॥

वाच्यसिद्ध्यङ्गं यथा

भ्रमिमरतिमलसहृदयतां प्रलयं मूर्छां तमः शरीरसादम् ।
मरणं च जलदभुजगजं प्रसह्य कुरुते विषं वियोगिनीनाम् ॥१२६॥

---

echo of the words (with double meanings), has been made subservient to the expressed meaning.

[Since all that the suggested similitude does is to justify the assertion 'I have attained the position of Rāma'.]

[Example of the 'Suggestion of Fact' being made subservient to the expressed meaning].

'See, O delicate lady, the Sun, having passed the night somewhere else, is propitiating the Lotus withered through separation from him, by falling at her feet.'

Here the *fact* of the lover (propitiating his lady-love),—which is suggested by the force of the meaning of the word,—appears merely as an imposition upon (as lending additional charm to) the entirely different fact of the Lotus (blooming on the contact of the Sun's rays).

(3) Example of 'suggestion subservient to the accomplishment of the expressed meaning,'—

'The *rain* (poison) emanating from the serpent-like clouds forcibly brings about, in ladies separated from

अत्र हालाहलं व्यङ्ग्यं भुजगरूपस्य वाच्यस्य सिद्धिकृत् ।

यथा वा

गच्छाम्यच्युत दर्शनेन भवतः किं तृप्तिरुत्पद्यते
किं त्वेवं विजनस्थयोर्हतजनः संभावयत्यन्यथा ।
इत्यामन्त्रणभङ्गिसूचितवृथावस्थानखेदालसाम्
आश्लिष्यन् पुलकोत्कराञ्चिततनुर्गोपीं हरिः पातु वः ।।१२७।। (३)

अत्राच्युतादिपदव्यङ्ग्यमामन्त्रणेत्यादिवाच्यस्य ।

एतच्चैकत्र एकवक्तृगतत्वेन अपरत्र भिन्नवक्तृगतत्वेनेत्यनयोर्भेदः ।।

अस्फुटं यथा

---

their lovers, vertigo, apathy, lassitude, insensibility, coma, stupefaction, physical prostration and death.'

Here the suggestion of 'poison' only serves to complete the expressed meaning (*serpent*) of the term '*bhujaga*.'

Another example—

"O Achyuta (Immovable One), I am going; is any satisfaction to be obtained from merely looking at you? In fact, if we remain together in this solitary place, wretched people will think quite otherwise;"—after the cowgirl signified her depression and languor due to her futile stay by the special form of address, Kṛṣna embraced her and the hairs on his body were thrilled;—may Kṛṣna, in this condition, protect you.'

Here the suggestion (of unperturbability) made by the term '*achyuta*' ('looking on' and so forth) only serves to help in the fulfilment of what is expressed by the expression "having signified....form of address."

The difference between the two examples just cited lies in the fact that the former consists of the speech

अदृष्टे दर्शनोत्कण्ठा दृष्टे विच्छेदभीरुता ।
नादृष्टेन न दृष्टेन भवता लभ्यते सुखम् ॥१२८॥ (४)

अत्रादृष्टो यथा न भवसि वियोगभयं च यथा नोत्पद्यते तथा कुर्या इति क्लिष्टम् ॥

संदिग्धप्राधान्यं यथा

हरस्तु किंचित्परिवृत्तधैर्यश्चन्द्रोदयारम्भ इवाम्बुराशिः ।
उमामुखे बिम्बफलाधरोष्ठे व्यापारयामास विलोचनानि ॥१२९॥५

अत्र परिचुम्बितुमैच्छदिति किं प्रतीयमानं किं वा विलोचनव्यापारणं वाच्यं प्रधानमिति संदेहः ॥

---

of only one speaker (the poet) while the latter consists of the speeches of two persons (the poet and the cow-girl).

(4) Example of the *Abstruse Suggestion.*

'While you are not seen, there is longing to see you, and when you are seen, there is fear of separation ; there is no comfort either on seeing you or not seeing you.'

What is sugested here is that 'you should act in such a way that you may not remain unseen and yet there may be no fear of separation,'—and this is *not very clear* (abstruse).

(5) Example of the suggestion 'of doubtful prominence.'—

'Śiva, having his equanimity slightly perturbed, like the ocean at the appearance of the moon, directed his eyes towards Pārvatī's face with bimba-like lips.'

Here it is doubtful whether prominence attaches to the *suggested* meaning that 'he wished to kiss her.' or to the *expressed* meaning that 'the eyes were turned towards the face.'

तुल्यप्राधान्यं यथा

ब्राह्मणातिक्रमत्यागो भवतामेव भूतये ।
जामदग्न्यस्तथा मित्रमन्यथा दुर्मनायते ॥१३०॥ (६)

अत्र जामदग्न्यः सर्वेषां क्षत्रियाणामिव रक्षसां क्षणात् क्षयं करिष्यतीति व्यङ्ग्यस्य वाच्यस्य च समं प्राधान्यम् ॥

काक्वाक्षिप्तं यथा

मथ्नामि कौरवशतं समरे न कोपात्
दुःशासनस्य रुधिरं न पिबाम्युरस्तः ॥
संचूर्णयामि गदया न सुयोधनोरू
संधिं करोतु भवतां नृपतिः पणेन ॥१३१॥ (७)

अत्र मथ्नाम्येवेत्यादि व्यङ्ग्यं वाच्यनिषेधसहभावेन स्थितम् ॥

---

(6) Example of the suggestion 'of equal prominence'—

'To abandon insulting the Brāhmaṇas will be conducive to your welfare ; otherwise your well-known friend Paraśurāma will become displeased.'

Here the *suggested* meaning—'Paraśurāma will exterminate the Rākṣasas in the same manner as he did the Kṣattriyas'—and the directly *expressed* one [that 'he will be angry']—are both equally charming.

(7) Example of suggestion 'rendered manifest by intonation,'—

'I shall not wrathfully batter the hundred Kauravas ! I shall not drink the blood from Duḥśāsana's heart ! I shall not smash Duryodhana's thighs ! Let your king make peace by an amicable settlement.'

Here what is *suggested* is—'I shall surely batter etc., etc.; and this, appearis by the side of the negation (of *battering* &c.), which is directly *expressed* [is got at only through the peculiar intonation in which the words are uttered].

असुन्दरं यथा

वाणीरकुञ्जुड्डीणसउणिकोलाहलं सुणंतीए ।
घरकम्मवावडाए बहुए सीअन्ति अंगाइं ॥१३२॥ (८)

अत्र दत्तसंकेतः कश्चिल्लतागहनं प्रविष्ट इति व्यङ्ग्यात् सीदन्त्यङ्गानीति वाच्यं सचमत्कारम् ॥

एषां भेदा यथायोगं वेदितव्याश्च पूर्ववत् ॥ ४६ ॥

यथायोगमिति

"व्यज्यन्ते वस्तुमात्रेण यदालंकृतयस्तदा ।
ध्रुवं ध्वन्यङ्गता तासां काव्यवृत्तेस्तदाश्रयात् ॥"

इति ध्वनिकारोक्तदिशा वस्तुमात्रेण यत्रालंकारो व्यज्यते न तत्र गुणीभूतव्यङ्ग्यत्वम् ।

---

(8) Example of the 'not beautiful' suggestion—

"When she heard the chatter of parrots flying from the Vetasa-bower, on account of her being engaged in her house-hold work, her limbs began to writhe.'

Here the directly *expressed* meaning—that 'her limbs are suffering (from her deep longing for her lover)' is more charming than the *suggested* meaning (that into the bower has entered a lover with whom she had made an engagement].

The varieties of these (eight kinds of Poetry of Sub-ordinate Suggestion should be understood to be, as far as possible, like those of what has gone before (i. e. Suggestive Poetry).—(46).

'*As far as possible.*'—This has been added with a view to the fact that there is no 'subordination of suggestion' in a case where a Figure is manifested by a mere Fact;—as has been declared by the author of the *Dhvani* in the following passage—"Whenever Figures

सालङ्कारैर्ध्वनेस्तैश्च योगः संसृष्टिसङ्करैः ।

सालंकारैरिति तैरेवालंकारैः अलंकारयुक्तैश्च तैः । तदुक्तं ध्वनिकृता

"स गुणीभूतव्यङ्ग्यैः सालंकारैः सह प्रभेदैः स्वैः ।
संकरसंसृष्टिभ्यां पुनरप्युद्द्योतते बहुधा ।।" इति ।

अन्योन्ययोगादेवं स्याद्भेदसंख्यातिभूयसी ।। ४७ ।।

---

of Speech are suggested by a mere Fact, they only serve the purpose of making it regarded as 'Suggestive Poetry'; because the existence of poetry rests upon those Figures (which, therefore, cannot be regarded as 'Subordinate' to the expressed meaning). 46.

There is a combination of 'Suggestive Poetry, with these (eight varieties of Poetry of Subordinate Suggestion) (a) as transformed into 'Figures' (the 'sentimental,' the 'agreeable' and so forth), and also (b) as accompanied (embellished) by (other) Figures (directly expressed),—this combination being per subserviency as also per equality.

The term '*sālaṅkāraiḥ*' is to be expounded as '*alaṅkāraiḥ*'—'with these as themselves transformed into, assuming the character of, Figures of speech,'—and '*alaṅkārayuktaiḥ*,' 'with those as embellished by other figures of speech.'

The following declaration has been made by the author of the *Dhvani* :—

'This (Suggestive Poetry),—combining, *per* subserviency and *per* equality, with its own varieties, as also with the varieties of Poetry of Subordinate Suggestion, along with the Figure of Speech,—appears in many forms'.

Thus by mutual combination the number of its varieties becomes very large.—(47).

एवमनेन प्रकारेण अवान्तरभेदगणनेतिप्रभूततरा गणना। तथाहि–शृङ्गारस्यैव भेदप्रभेदगणनायामानन्त्यम्। का गणना तु सर्वेषाम्।

संकलनेन पुनरस्य ध्वनेस्त्रयो भेदाः। व्यङ्ग्यस्य त्रिरूपत्वात्। तथाहि–किंचिद्वाच्यतां सहते किंचित्त्वन्यथा। तत्र वाच्यतासहम् अविचित्रं विचित्रं चेति। अविचित्रं वस्तुमात्रं विचित्रं त्वलंकाररूपम्। यद्यपि प्राधान्येन तदलंकार्यं तथापि ब्राह्मणश्रमणन्यायेन तथोच्यते। रसादिलक्षणस्त्वर्थः स्वप्नेपि न वाच्यः।

'*Thus*',—in the manner described,—by counting all the sub-divisions,—the number becomes very large; *e. g.* the varieties of the Erotic Passion itself are endless,—not to speak of others.

Thus, briefly, of Suggestive Poetry there are three varieties, there being three kinds of what is *suggested* (according as it happens to be a *Fact* or a *Figure* or Passion, Feeling and the rest) ;—of these again, some (*i. e. Figure* and *Fact*) are such as can be *expressed* also, while others (*e. g.* Passion and the rest) can never be *expressed*. Of those that can be also *expressed*, some are *fanciful*, while others are *not fanciful*; what is not *fanciful* is the mere *fact*, and what is *fanciful* is the *Figure*.—Though, in this connection the Figure (when suggested) is really what is itself *embellished* (and hence cannot be called a 'figure', 'embellishment,' in the exact sense of the term), yet it is called by the name of 'figure,' on the same principle as the Brāhmaṇa, who has become a mendicant and thereby has ceased to be a real Brāhmaṇa, is still called a 'Brāhmaṇa' in view of his having formerly been a Brāhmaṇa. Passion and the rest, however, cannot be regarded even in a dream to

स हि रसादिशब्देन शृङ्गारादिशब्देन वाभिधीयेत । न चाभिधीयते तत्प्रयोगेपि विभावाद्यप्रयोगे तस्याप्रतिपत्तेस्तदप्रयोगेपि विभावादिप्रयोगे तस्य प्रतिपत्तेश्चेत्यन्वयव्यतिरेकाभ्यां विभावाद्यभिधानद्वारेणैव प्रतीयते इति निश्चीयते ।

तेनासौ व्यङ्ग्य एव । मुख्यार्थबाधाद्यभावान्न पुनर्लक्षणीयः ।

---

be directly *expressed*. If these were *expressed*, they could be so, either by the (generic) words 'rasa' (Passion) and the rest, or by the (particular) words '*śṛṅgāra*' (erotic) and the rest ; as a matter of fact they are not so expressed ; as is clear from the facts (*a*) that even though these words are used, the Passion and the rest are not cognised, so long as the excitants (ensuants and variants) are not mentioned, and (*b*) that even when those words are *not* used, if the excitants (ensuants and variants) are mentioned, there *is* due cognition of Passion and the rest ; and from these two premises—both affirmative and negative—it follows that what brings about the cognition of these latter is the mention of the excitants (ensuants and variants) (and not any verbal expressions at all).

It is for this reason that Passion and the rest can be only *suggested*, and not even *indicated*, because the necessary conditions of Indication,—such as *incompatibility of the primary meaning* and so forth—are wanting. Then again, it has been already explained how there can be no 'Indication' without that kind of 'suggestion of Fact in which the expressed meaning is either transformed into something else or entirely ignored. In that 'suggestion' which is based upon the force of the words, the denotation itself being restricted, any other that may be denoted,

अर्थान्तरसंक्रमितात्यन्ततिरस्कृतवाच्ययोर्वस्तुमात्ररूपं व्यङ्ग्यं विना लक्षणैव न भवतीति प्राक् प्रतिपादितम् । शब्दशक्तिमूले तु अभिधाया नियन्त्रणेनानभिधेयस्यार्थान्तरस्य तेन सहोपमादेररलंकारस्य च निर्विवादं व्यङ्ग्यत्वम् ।

अर्थशक्तिमूलेपि विशेषे संकेतः कर्तुं न युज्यते इति सामान्यरूपाणां पदार्थानामाकाङ्क्षा-संनिधि-योग्यतावशात्परस्परसंसर्गो यत्रापदार्थोऽपि विशेषरूपो वाक्यार्थस्तत्राभिहितान्वयवादे का वार्ता व्यङ्ग्यस्याभिधेयतायाम् ।

---

as also the Simile or any other figure of speech that may be perceptible, must doubtless be regarded as 'suggested'.

In cases of 'suggestion' based upon the force of meaning also, how can there be any possibility of the 'suggested' meaning being regarded as 'expressed' or 'denoted', when,—in accordance with the '*Abhihitānvaya*' theory—what is expressed by a sentence is the mutual relationship among the denotation of the component words based upon their mutual need, proximity and capability; and as such it must be confined to particular individuals, and hence cannot be 'denoted' by any single word, whose denotation must always pertain to *Universals* only, for the simple reason that convention, upon which alone 'denotation' is based, can never pertain to *particular individuals*.

['Suggestion' being shown to be inevitable according to the *Bhāṭṭa* theory of '*Abhihitānvaya*,' the author proceeds to show that it must be accepted under the *Prābhākara* theory of '*Anvitābhidhāna*' also; and for this purpose he sets forth this latter theory, as bearing upon the matter under consideration.]

यप्याहुः
"शब्दवृद्धाभिधेयांश्च प्रत्यक्षेणात्र पश्यति ।
श्रोतुश्च प्रतिपन्नत्वमनुमानेन चेष्टया ॥ १ ॥
अन्यथानुपपत्त्या तु बोधेच्छक्तिं द्वयात्मिकाम् ।
अर्थापत्त्यावबोधेत संबन्धं त्रिप्रमाणकम् ॥ २ ॥

इति प्रतिपादितदिशा देवदत्त गामानय इत्याद्युत्तमवृद्धवाक्यप्रयोगाद्देशाद्देशान्तरं सास्नादिमन्तमर्थं मध्यमवृद्धे नयति सति अनेनास्माद्वाक्यादेवंविधोर्थः प्रतिपन्नः इति तच्चेष्टयानुमाय

The upholders of the '*Anvitābhidhāna*' theory have offered the following explanation of the process of denotation:—(*a*)

"The word, the experienced elderly man uttering it, and the object denoted by the word, these three things the young child *perceives* by his senses,—(*b*) that the young man to whom the word has been addressed has understood its meaning, he deduces by *inference* from the action of the young man,—(*c*) and the two-fold potency (of the word to denote and of the object to be denoted) he recognises by means of presumption based upon 'apparent inexplicability;'—thus the denotative relationship (of the word and its meaning) is cognised through three means of cognition."—

According to this account what happens is that—(*a*) the elder person utters the words 'bring the cow,'—(*b*) upon which the younger person (to whom the words are addressed) is found to bring from one place to another an animal with the dewlap and other distinguishing features,—(*c*) the youngest person (the child) then deduces from this action that 'such and such a meaning has been understood by the younger person from the words that have been uttered';—(*d*) thus he comes to recognise the de-

तयोरखण्डवाक्यवाक्यार्थयोरर्थापत्त्या वाच्यवाचकभावलक्षणं संबन्धमवधार्य बालस्तत्र व्युत्पद्यते । परतः चैत्र गामानय देवदत्त अश्वमानय देवदत्त गां नय इत्यादिवाक्यप्रयोगे तस्य तस्य शब्दस्य तं तमर्थमवधारयतीति अन्वयव्यतिरेकाभ्यां प्रवृत्ति-निवृत्तिकारि वाक्यमेव प्रयोगयोग्यमिति वाक्यस्थितानामेव

---

notative relationship subsisting between the said sentence and its meaning as one impartible whole, and thereby he himself comes to comprehend its signification ;—(*e*) after sometimes he hears such sentences as 'Chaitra, bring the cow,' 'Devadatta, bring the horse.' 'Devadatta, take away the cow,' and so forth, and thence deduces the meaning of the several words and expressions. Thus it is clear from positive as well as negative concomitance that what is really significant and hence capable of being used is the *sentence* only ; so that the denotative convention pertaining to each individual word is cognised only when it occurs in a sentence, and is connected with other words ; so that the meaning of the sentence consists only in the denotations of its component words as related to one another ; and it is not that each word expresses its own meaning and then these several meanings become correlated (through proximity etc.) ; though it is true that individual words when found to be used in other sentences become recognised as the same (as the one that was heard for the first time). Thus what forms the subject of denotative convention is the denotation of a single word only as correlated to the denotation of other words ; thus though, when the said convention comes to be comprehended, it is comprehended in a particular form, yet this particular form is one that is always overshadowed

पदानामन्वितैः पदार्थैरन्वितानामेव संकेतो गृह्यते इति विशिष्टा एव पदार्था वाक्यार्थः ।

न तु पदार्थानां वैशिष्ट्यम् ।

---

by the corresponding generic character (a notion of the *particular* being impossible without that of the corrrespond-ing *universal*) ; and this for the simple reason that those word-meanings that are inter-related are always of the said character (*i. e.*, the particular over-shadowed by the universal)."

According to this view also, the subject of Conven-tion is only such word-meaning as appears in a *particular* form, but *over-shadowed by the corresponding universal* ; from which it follows that when a word occurs in a sentence, what is denoted by it forms part of the denotation of the sentence as a whole, and as such what it expresses is some-thing that is very much restricted to an extremely specific form (in which it is correlated to the other words of the particular sentence) and this very specific form which is expressed by the word, not being the subject of convention (which appertains to particulars only as overshadowed by universals), cannot be regarded as directly 'denoted' by the word. And thus when the ordinary meaning of a word also cannot be 'denoted' by it, it is a far cry to what we hold to be the objects of 'suggestion,' which are totally different from the direct meaning of the words employed ;—*e. g.*, in the verse 'The Sandal paint over thy breasts is entirely rubbed of...thou hast *not* gone to that wretched man,' what is 'suggested' is that the person addressed *has gone* to the man, while the direct meaning of the words is quite the opposite.

Thus it is found that—(*a*) according to the '*Abhi-hitānvayavāda*', what is 'denoted' by the word is some-

यद्यपि वाक्यान्तरप्रयुज्यमानान्यपि प्रत्यभिज्ञाप्रत्ययेन तान्येवैतानि पदानि निश्चीयन्त इति पदार्थान्तरमात्रेणान्वितः पदार्थः संकेतगोचरः । तथापि सामान्यावच्छादितो विशेष-रूप एवासौ प्रतिपद्यते व्यतिषक्तानां पदार्थानां तथाभूतत्वादि-त्यन्विताभिधानवादिनः ।

तेषामपि मते सामान्यविशेषरूपः पदार्थः संकेतविषय इत्यतिविशेषभूतो वाक्यार्थान्तर्गतोसंकेतितत्वादवाच्य एव यत्र पदार्थः प्रतिपद्यते तत्र दूरे अर्थान्तरभूतस्य निःशेषच्युतेत्यादौ विध्यादेश्चर्चा ।

अनन्वितोर्थोभिहितान्वये पदार्थान्तरमात्रेणान्वित-स्त्वन्विताभिधाने अन्वितविशेषस्त्ववाच्य एव इत्युभयन येप्यपदार्थ एव वाक्यार्थः ।

यदप्युच्यते नैमित्तिकानुसारेण निमित्तानि कल्प्यन्ते इति ।

---

thing not correlated to anything else, and (*b*) according to the '*Anvitābhidhānavāda*', what is 'denoted' is something only correlated in a general way with what is expressed by other words ; so that in either case the particular object as related to another particular object is what is never 'denoted'; and hence under both these theories the meaning of the sentence can never be the object of direct verbal 'denotation'.

Some people have urged the following arguments (against the 'suggestion-theory')—"In every case causes are inferred from their effects. So that when we find an expression producing a certain idea, we conclude that that expression is possessed of the potency necessary for expressing that idea ; consequently, whether the idea be expressed directly or indirectly, the fact remains that it has been expressed by the word ; and hence every case can be

तत्र निमित्तत्वं कारकत्वं ज्ञापकत्वं वा शब्दस्य। प्रकाशकत्वान्न कारकत्वम्। ज्ञापकत्वं तु अज्ञातस्य कथम्। ज्ञातत्वंच संकेतेनैव स चान्वितमात्रे एवं च निमित्तस्य नियतनिमित्तत्वं यावन्न निश्चितं तावन्नैमित्तिकस्य प्रतीतिरेव कथम् इति 'नैमित्तिकानुसारेण निमित्तानि कल्प्यन्ते इत्यविचारिताभिधानम्।

---

regarded to be of the word *expressing* an idea ; and there is no ground for making any such distinction as that into 'expression', 'indication' and 'suggestion'."

In answer to this we ask—What is meant by the *word* being the 'cause' here ? Does it mean that it *produces* the idea ? or that it *makes it known* ? It cannot be said to *produce* the idea, as what the word does is to *give expression* to an idea, it can never *produce* one. As regards its *making* (the idea) *known*, how can the power to do this belong to what is itself *not known* or understood ?

[*i. e.* So long as the meaning of the word itself has not been understood, it cannot *give expression* to anything else.]

As a matter of fact, the word itself can be understood only through convention ; and this convention is (as shown above) only in regard to such words as are correlated to others. Thus then, so long as the precise extent of causal potency of the cause has not been ascertained, how can the cause itself be recognised as such ? So that the assertion that 'causes are inferred from their effects' is extremely ill-conceived.

Others again urge the following argument—"The action of the word is like that of an arrow, its reach being prolonged further and further; so that in whatever sense a word may be used, that is the meaning *expressed* or *denoted* by it. Thus then (even in the case of the verse 'the

ये त्वभिदधति सोयमिषोरिव दीर्घदीर्घतरो व्यापारः इति यत्परः शब्दः स शब्दार्थः इति विधिरेवात्र वाच्य इति। तेप्यतात्पर्यज्ञास्तात्पर्यवाचोयुक्तेर्देवानांप्रियाः । तथाहि 'भूतभव्यसमुच्चारणे भूतं भव्यायोपदिश्यते' इति कारक-पदार्थाः क्रियापदार्थेनान्वीयमानाः प्रधानक्रियानिर्वर्तकस्व-क्रियाभिसंबन्धात् साध्यायमानतां प्राप्नुवन्ति । ततश्चा-दग्धदहनन्यायेन यावदप्राप्तं तावद्विधीयते। यथा ऋत्विक्प्रचरणे

---

sandal-paint has been entirely ...... thou hast *not* gone to that wretched man'), the *affirmation* ('thou *hast* gone',—which has been held to be the *suggested* meaning) is what is really only *expressed* or *denoted* by it."

These ignorant people also do not understand what is meant by a word being 'used in a certain sense'. It is a well-established principle that 'when an *accomplished* entity (*i. e.*, substance) is spoken of along with *what is to be accomplished* (*i. e.* an action), the former is mentioned as subserving the purposes of the latter; and according to this principle, when substantives become correlated to verbs (*e. g.* in the expression 'bring the cow'), they themselves acquire the character of 'what is to be accomplished,' inasmuch as they have to be the substratum of their own action of *walking* which helps in the accomplishment of the principal action (of *bringing*) [as the *bringing of the cow* can be accomplished only when she herself does the *walking*]; and in this case (where the *accomplished entity*, cow, is tainted with the character of *what is to be accomplished, i. e.* its *walking*), the direction in question ('bring the cow') involves the injunction or predication of that factor alone which is not already accomplished. For example in the case of the sentence—'The red-turbaned

प्रमाणान्तरात् सिद्धे "लोहितोष्णीषा ऋत्विजः प्रचरन्ति" इत्यत्र लोहितोष्णीषत्वमात्रं विधेयं हवनस्यान्यतः सिद्धेः "दध्ना जुहोति" इत्यादौ दध्यादेः करणत्वमात्रं विधेयम् ॥

क्वचिदुभयविधिः क्वचित्त्रिविधिरपि यथा 'रक्तं पटं वयः' इत्यादौ एकविधिर्द्विविधिस्त्रिविधिर्वा। ततश्च 'यदेव विधेयं तत्रैव तात्पर्यम्' इत्युपात्तस्यैव शब्दस्यार्थे तात्पर्यं न तु प्रतीतमात्रे एवं हि 'पूर्वो धावति' इत्यादावपराद्यथपि क्वचित्तात्पर्यं स्यात्।

---

priests move along,'—it being found that the 'moving of the priests' is already accomplished (through another injunction),—all that the sentence does is to enjoin that they shall wear red turbans. Similarly in the sentence 'one shall pour the libation of curds,' the *pouring of the libation* having been got at from other sources, this sentence enjoins that the libation is to be of curds. In some cases the injunction applies to two factors, and sometimes to three factors ; *e. g.*, when one says 'weave the red cloth,' this may involve the injunction of one or two or three things.

[(*a*) If the direction is addressed to the weaver for the first time, it involves the injunction of (1) the *weaving* —of (2) the *cloth*—which (3) should be *red* (*b*) if the man has been previously told to *weave*, the injunction applies to (1) the *cloth* and (2) its *red colour* (*c*) if the *weaving of the cloth* has been enjoined before, the present injunction applies to the *red colour* only].

Thus every direction is said to 'have its sense' in the injunction of that particular factor only which forms its direct objective. So that the 'sense' or 'import' can apply only to what is directly expressed by the word actually used, and not to anything and everything that may be implied (by it); otherwise (if everything implied were to

यत्तु 'विषं भक्षय मा चास्य गृहे भुङ्क्थाः' इत्यत्र 'एतद्गृहे न भोक्तव्यम्' इत्यत्र तात्पर्यमिति स एव वाक्यार्थ इति, उच्यते तत्र चकार एकवाक्यतासूचनार्थः न चाख्यातवाक्ययोर्द्वयोरङ्गाङ्गिभाव इति विषभक्षणवाक्यस्य सुहृद्वाक्यत्वेनाङ्गता कल्पनीयेति 'विषभक्षणादपि दुष्टमेतद्गृहे भोजनमिति सर्वथा मास्य गृहे भुङ्क्थाः' इति, उपात्तशब्दार्थे एव तात्पर्यम् ।

---

be included in the 'sense' or 'import' of a certain word, then) the expression 'the former man is running' would have to be regarded as having its 'sense' applying to the notion of the 'latter' also [as the notion of the 'latter', is implied by that of the 'former,' which is the word pronounced].

Then again, it has been urged that in the case of the sentences, 'Eat poison, and don't eat in that man's house,' the *sense* is that 'you should not eat in that man's house,' and this is accepted as the *meaning* of the sentence [though it is only *implied* and not directly *expressed*].

But what happens in the case of this sentence is that the conjunctive particle 'and' indicates that the two sentences have to be construed together,—and as between the two sentences themselves, there can be no justification, (without sufficient reason) for taking one as subordinate to the other ;—but it is found that there is such reason in the shape of the fact that the admonition coming from a friend, the first sentence 'Eat poison' (being incompatible, in its direct meaning) must be regarded as subordinate to the second one,—the meaning of the two sentences taken together being 'Eating in that man's house is worse than eating poison, therefore you should never eat in his house.' And when we accept this to be the sense or import of the sentence, it is only what is expressed by the

यदि शब्दश्रुतेरनन्तरं यावानर्थो लभ्यते तावति शब्दस्याभिधैव व्यापारः ततः कथं 'ब्राह्मण पुत्रस्ते जातः ब्राह्मण कन्या ते गर्भिणी' इत्यादौ हर्षशोकादीनामपि न वाच्यत्वम्। कस्माच्च लक्षणा लक्षणीयेप्यर्थे दीर्घदीर्घतराभिधाव्यापारेणैव प्रतीतिसिद्धेः। किमिति च श्रुतिलिङ्गवाक्यप्रकरणस्थानसमाख्यानां पूर्वपूर्वबलीयस्त्वम् इत्यन्विताभिधानवादेपि विधेरपि सिद्धं व्यङ्ग्यत्वम् ॥

---

words of the sentence itself (by Indication, if not by direct Denotation).

[The distinction between such 'Indication' and the 'Suggestion' under dispute is that the *indicated* meaning is apprehended immediately from the words themselves, while what is *suggested* comes to be grasped some time after the direct *denoted* meaning has been comprehended].

Further, if we were to accept the view that in regard to anything and everything that happens to be perceived on the hearing of a certain word, the action of the word is always 'Denotation' only,—then, in the case of the words 'O Brāhmaṇa, a son has been born to you—and your unmarried daughter is *enciente*'—why should not joy and dejection that become manifested on the face of the man to whom they are addressed be regarded as the meaning of the words? 'Why too, in that case, admit of 'Indication' either (as a Secondary Verbal process)? For in the case of 'Indication' also, the gradually extending reach of 'Denotation' itself could account for the desired signification.—Why again should there be any gradually descending authority attaching to 'Direct Vedic Declaration', 'Indicative Power', 'Syntactical Connection', 'Context', 'Position' and 'Name' (as the means of ascertaining what accessory is subservient to what sacrificial act)?

From all this it follows that under the theory of the '*Anvitābhidhāna*' also, 'the affirmation (implied by the

10

किं च 'कुरु रुचिम्' इति पदयोर्वैपरीत्ये काव्यान्तर्वर्तिनि कथं दुष्टत्वम् । न ह्यत्रासभ्योऽर्थः पदार्थान्तरैरन्वितः इत्यनभिधेय एवेति एवमादि अपरित्याज्यं स्यात् ।

यदि च वाच्यवाचकत्वव्यतिरेकेण व्यङ्ग्यव्यञ्जकभावो नाभ्युपेयते तदासाधुत्वादीनां नित्यदोषत्वं कष्टत्वादीनामनित्य-

---

verse 'The sandal paint......thou hast not gone to the wretched man') must be regarded as the object of suggestion.'

Further, in the case of the expression '*kuru ruchim*' ('have the pleasure'), it has been held that if in a poem, the order of the two words is inverted, and we have the form '*ruchiṅkuru*', it becomes defective [by reason of the unseemly *suggestion* by the word '*chiṅku*,' which would be heard in the middle of the said expression, and which is the name of a private part of the female body] ;—now why should the said expression be defective ? [Even though a particular sound-combination may have an unseemly significance, yet] the unseemly meaning is not correlated to any other words of the expression ; and not being so correlated, it would be as good as *not denoted* (according to the view that there is no other verbal signification except 'denotation' and the denotation of a word must always be correlated to the denotation of other words) ; and thus there would be no ground for avoiding the use of such expressions as the one noted above (which are to be avoided only on account of the unseemly meaning *suggested* by the particular sound-combination).

Then again, if the suggestive process be not accepted as distinct from the denotative process, it would be im-

दोषत्वमिति विभागकरणमनुपपन्नं स्यात् । न चानुपपन्नं सर्वस्यैव विभक्ततया प्रतिभासात् । वाच्यवाचकभावव्यतिरेकेण व्यङ्ग्यव्यञ्जकताश्रयणे तु व्यङ्ग्यस्य बहुविधत्वात् क्वचिदेव कस्यचिदेवौचित्येनोपपद्यत एव विभागव्यवस्था ॥

'द्वयं गतं संप्रति शोचनीयतां समागमप्रार्थनया कपालिनः ।'

---

possible to make any such distinction among 'Defects' as that 'grammatical mistake' and others like it are permanent defects (*always* defective), while 'Harshness 'and the like are *impermanent* defects (*sometimes* defective and sometimes not so).

[Harshness is regarded as an *excellence* when occurring in words depicting the Heroic Passion, but a *defect* in those portraying the Pathetic; and the reason for this lies in the idea that the *suggestions* made by the *harsh* sounds are helpful in the delineation of Heroism, but mar the effect of the Pathetic Passion. There is no difference in the *denotation* or expressed meaning of a word, be its letters harsh or sweet. Hence if denotation were the only verbal process, there could be no ground for regarding the mere sound as either helpful or prejudicial to the sentiment depicted.]

And yet we know that such distinction is not impossible; in fact we find such distinction made by all men. If, on the other hand, the suggestive process is accepted as distinct from the denotative, the suggested meaning of words being manifold, some of these only may be appropriate in a certain instance ; and as such the said distinction (among defects) would be quite permissible.

Then again in the line—'The brilliant digit of the Moon and Thyself (Pārvatī), who art like moon-light to the eyes of people, are the two things that have become pitiable by reason of seeking association with the *Holder*

इत्यादौ पिनाक्यादिपदवैलक्षण्येन किमिति कपाल्यादि-पदानां काव्यानुगुणत्वम् ।

अपि च वाच्योर्थः सर्वान् प्रतिपत्तॄन् प्रति एकरूप एवेति नियतोसौ। न हि 'गतोस्तमर्कः' इत्यादौ वाच्योर्थः क्वचिदन्यथा भवति । प्रतीयमानस्तु तत्तत्प्रकरणवक्तृप्रतिपत्त्रादिविशेष-सहायतया नानात्वं भजते । तथा च 'गतोस्तमर्कः' इत्यतः सपत्नं प्रत्यवस्कन्दनावसर इति अभिसरणमुपक्रम्यतामिति प्राप्तप्रायस्ते प्रेयानिति कर्मकरणान्निवर्तामह इति सांध्यो

---

of the Begging-bowl (Śiva),'—what is that peculiar charm that is added by the use of the particular name '*kapālin*' (Holder of the Begging-bowl), in preference to such other names as 'Pinākin' (Holder of the Pināka bow) ?

[Both '*Kapālin*' and '*Pinākin*' are the names of Śiva; so that there is no difference in their *denotation*; and yet there is a peculiar charm in the use of the former name, which lies in its suggestion of *poverty*, which heightens the 'pitiable' character spoken of].

Further, the denoted meaning of a word is one and the same for all persons bearing it ; so that it is fixed and uniform ; the denoted or directly *expressed* meaning of the words 'the sun has set' never varies (is fixed), while its *suggested* meaning varies with the variation in such accessory conditions as the context, the character of the speaker, the character of the person spoken to, and so forth. For instance, the words 'the sun has set' suggests (1) the idea that 'now is the opportunity to attack the enemy' (when they are addressed by the general to the king) ;—(2) that you should set forth to meet your lover' (when addressed by the *confidant* to the girl in love),—(3) that 'your lover is just coming' (when addressed by a friend

विधिरुपक्रम्यतामिति दूरं मा गा इति सुरभयो गृहं प्रवेश्यन्तामिति संतापोधुना न भवतीति विक्रेयवस्तूनि संहियन्तामिति नागतोद्यापि प्रेयानित्यादिरनवधिर्व्यङ्ग्योर्थः तत्र तत्र प्रतिभाति ।

वाच्यव्यङ्ग्ययोः निःशेषेत्यादौ निषेधविध्यात्मना

"मात्सर्यमुत्सार्य विचार्य कार्यमार्याः समर्यादमुदाहरन्तु ।
सेव्या नितम्बाः किमु भूधराणामुतस्मरस्मेरविलासिनीनाम् ॥१३३"

---

to a girl who is eagerly awaiting the arrival of her lover),—(4) that 'we shall rest from our labours' (when addressed by one labourer to another),—(5) 'let us betake ourselves to our twilight prayers' (when addressed by one religious student to another),—(6) 'don't go very far' (when addressed to a way-farer),—(7) 'let the cows enter their fold' (when addressed to the cowherd),— (8) 'we shall not suffer from heat now' (when addressed by one way-farer to another),—(9) 'let us pack up our merchandise' (when addressed by one salesman to another),—(10)' my love has not come even to-day' (when spoken by an impatient girl waiting for her beloved's return from a journey) ; thus, in fact, there is no end to the number of suggested meanings.

As a matter of fact, the *suggested* and the *expressed* meanings differ on the following (*seven*) points :—

(1) *In point of character*:—*e. g.*, (*a*) in the verse 'the sandal-paint is entirely rubbed out ... thou hast not gone to the wretched man', the *expressed* meaning is *negative*, while the *suggested* one is *affirmative* ('thou *hast* gone').—(*b*) Or in the verse—' you noble men, give up all partiality and after due consideration say whether one should have

इत्यादौ संशयशान्तशृङ्गार्यन्तरगतनिश्चयरूपेण,

"कथमवनिप दर्पो यन्निशातासिधारा-
दलनगलितमूर्ध्ना विद्विषां स्वीकृता श्रीः।
ननु तव निहतारेरप्यसौ किं न नीता
त्रिदिवमपगताङ्गैर्वल्लभा कीर्तिरेभिः ॥१३४॥"

इत्यादौ निन्दास्तुतिवपुषा स्वरूपस्य।

पूर्वपश्चाद्भावेन प्रतीतेः कालस्य शब्दाश्रयत्वेन शब्दतदेकदेशतदर्थवर्णसंघटनाश्रयत्वेन च आश्रयस्य शब्दानुशासनज्ञानेन प्रकरणादिसहायप्रतिभानैर्मल्यसहितेन तेन चावगम इति

---

recourse to the outskirts of mountains or to the waists of beautiful women smiling with love,'—the *expressed* meaning is the mere *doubt* (whether one should have recourse to the one or the other), while what is suggested is the definite assertion, that 'one should have recourse to women' (when the speaker or the person addressed is inclined to be *erotic*),—or that 'one should retire to the mountains' (when the persons concerned are of the *quietistic* temperament).—(*c*) Or again, in the verse—'why should you feel proud of your having appropriated to yourself the property of your enemies, whose heads were cut off by the sharp edge of your sword? When you had killed your enemies, was not your Fame, so loved of you, been taken away to heaven by those enemies, even when they had lost their bodies';—what is *expressed* is *reproach*, while what is *suggested* is *praise*.

(2) *In point of times* :—The suggested meaning is comprehended *after* the *expressed* meaning.

(3) *In point of the conveying medium* :—The *expressed* meaning is conveyed by the word, while the *suggested* meaning may be conveyed by the word, by a part of the

निमित्तस्य बोद्धृमात्रविदग्धव्यपदेशयोः प्रतीतिमात्रचमत्कृत्योश्च करणात् कार्यस्य "गतोस्तमर्कः" इत्यादौ प्रदर्शितनयेन संख्यायाः

"कस्स व ण होइ रोसो दट्ठूण पिआइ सव्वणं अहरं।
सभमरपडमग्घाइणि वारिअवामे सहसु एण्हि ॥१३५॥"

---

word, by the expressed meaning of the word, by the letters, and by the style.

(4) *In point of the means (of knowing)* :—The *expressed* meaning is understood with the help of grammatical rules, while the suggested meaning is understood with the help of those as also with that of *context* and other conditions (described above).

(5) *In point of their effects* :—The *expressed* meaning brings about a simple comprehension and that also in every one who hears the word, while the *suggested* meaning brings about a certain charm in the minds of such persons as are entitled to the name of 'cultured'.

(6) *In point of number* :—As has been found in the case of the expression 'the sun has set' (where the *expressed* meaning is *one* only and the *suggested* meanings are *ten* or more).

(7) *In point of the person addressed* :—In the verse—'who will not be annoyed at seeing the lips of his wife bitten ? I warned you not to smell the lotus with the bee inside it !'—while the *expressed* meaning is conveyed to the girl-friend [who, on appearing before her husband, has her lips bearing the mark of her paramour's kiss, and feels disconcerted at the husband's notice of it,] while the *suggested* meaning (that the mark on the lips of my friend

इत्यादौ सखीतत्कान्तादिगतत्वेन विषयस्य च भेदेपि यद्येकत्वम् तत् क्वचिदपि नीलपीतादौ भेदो न स्यात्। उक्तं हि "अयमेव हि भेदो भेदहेतुर्वा यद्विरुद्धधर्माध्यासः कारण-भेदश्च" इति।

वाचकानामर्थापेक्षा व्यञ्जकानां तु न तदपेक्षत्वमिति न वाचकत्वमेव व्यञ्जकत्वम्। किं च "वाणीरकुडंग-" इत्यादौ प्रतीयमानमर्थमभिव्यज्य वाच्यं स्वरूप एव यत्र विश्राम्यति तत्र

---

is one made by the sting of the bee in the lotus, and not by a man's kiss) is conveyed to the husband.

Even when differing in so many points, if the two are to be regarded as one and the same, then there can be no difference at all, even in the case of such things as the blue and the yellow colour and so forth. In fact, it has been declared that—"The *difference*, or the *ground of difference*, (between any two things) consists in their having contrary properties and in having different causes' [and both these conditions are fulfilled in the case of the *expressed* and *suggested* meanings].

Then again, purely *denotative* or *expressive* words require (in the act of *denoting* their meaning) the aid of an actually existent meaning (fixed by convention), while *suggestive* words do not stand in need of any such meaning (as *suggestion* very often lies in mere letters or syllables, which have no meaning at all). For this reason also *suggestiveness* cannot be the same as *denotativeness*.

Further, in the verse quoted above—'Hearing the chattering of parrots in the Vetasa bower etc.,'—where, it has been shown, the *expressed* meaning rests within itself after having signified the *suggested* meaning,—and which, on that account, has been regarded as an instance

गुणीभूतव्यङ्ग्येतात्पर्यभूतोप्यर्थः स्वशब्दानभिधेयः प्रतीतिपथमवतरन् कस्य व्यापारस्य विषयतामवलम्बतामिति ।

ननु 'रामोस्मि सर्वं सहे' इति 'रामेण प्रियजीवितेन तु कृतं प्रेम्णः प्रिये नोचितम्' इति 'रामोसौ भुवनेषु विक्रमगुणैः प्राप्तः प्रसिद्धिं पराम्' इत्यादौ लक्षणीयोप्यर्थो नानात्वं भजते विशेषव्यपदेशहेतुश्च भवति। तदवगमश्च शब्दार्थायत्तः प्रकरणादिसव्यपेक्षश्च इति कोयं नूतनः प्रतीयमानो नाम ।

---

of 'subordinated suggestion,'—it is found that a meaning, which is not denoted by the words and which does not fall within their import, is yet brought within the range of cognizance ;—and under what operation of the word would the meaning thus cognised fall (if *Suggestion* is not admitted) ?

[The following question is raised by one who admits of 'Indication' as distinct from 'Denotation', but does not accept 'Suggestion.']—"In such instances as (*a*) 'I am Rāma and shall bear everything', (*b*) 'O beloved one, Rāma is so fond of his life that he has not done what befits love', and (*c*) 'This Rāma has attained high fame for the excellence of his valour' and so forth, we find that the 'indicated' meaning (of the single word 'Rāma') is manifold and also capable of having the several peculiar appellations [' with the expressed meaning transformed', 'with the expressed meaning entirely ignored' and others that have been described above as pertaining to 'suggestion' and 'suggested meaning'],—the comprehension also of such 'indicated' meaning is based (like that of the 'suggested' meaning) upon both words and meanings, and is also dependent upon *context* and other conditions ; so that (all these conditions being fulfilled by the 'Indicated' mean-

उच्यते—लक्षणीयस्यार्थस्य नानात्वेपि अनेकार्थशब्दाभिधेयवन्नियतत्वमेव । न खलु मुख्येनार्थेनानियतसंबन्धो लक्षयितुं शक्यते । प्रतीयमानस्तु प्रकरणादिविशेषवशेन नियत संबन्धः अनियतसंबन्धः संबद्धसंबन्धश्च द्योत्यते ।

न च

"अत्ता एत्थ णिमज्जइ एत्थ अहं दिअहए पलोएहि ।
मा पहिअ रत्तिअन्धअ सेज्जाए मह णिमज्जहिसि ॥१३६॥"

---

ing), what is this new kind of meaning that is called 'suggested' ?"

Our answer to this is as follows :—

Firstly, even though a word may have several 'indicated' meanings, yet their number must be limited, just like the expressed meaning of a word which has many meanings.—*Secondly*, what is 'indicated' can never be such as has no definite connection with the primary (denoted) meaning, while the 'suggested' meaning, under the influence of 'context' and other circumstances, may have a definite connection (with the expressed meaning), or it may have only an indefinite (vague) connection with it, or it may be only indirectly connected (being connected with something else which is connected with the expressed meaning).—*Thirdly*, the primary (expressed) meaning is not 'barred' by (incompatibility) in the case of 'suggestion', in such instances as—'my mother-in-law lies here, and here myself, mark this well while there is daylight ; lest, O wayfarer, you tumble into our beds at night';—so that (the very first condition of 'Indication' being wanting) how can this be regarded as a case of 'Indication' ?—*Fourthly*, it has been already shown (under Chapter II) that in the process of 'Indication' also, 'Suggestion' comes in as an essential factor.

इत्यादौ विवक्षितान्यपरवाच्ये ध्वनौ मुख्यार्थबाधः । तत्कथमत्र लक्षणा । लक्षणायामपि व्यञ्जनमवश्यमाश्रयितव्यमिति प्रतिपादितम् ।

यथा च समयसव्यपेक्षा अभिधा तथा मुख्यार्थबाधादित्रयसमयविशेषसव्यपेक्षा लक्षणा । अत एवाभिधापुच्छभूता सेत्याहुः ।

न च लक्षणात्मकमेव ध्वननं तदनुगमेन तस्य दर्शनात् । न च तदनुगतमेव अभिधावलम्बनेनापि तस्य भावात् । न चोभयानुसार्येव अवाचकवर्णानुसारेणापि तस्य दृष्टेः । न च शब्दानुसार्येव अशब्दात्मकनेत्रत्रिभागावलोकनादिगतत्वेनापि तस्य प्रसिद्धेः इति अभिधातात्पर्यलक्षणात्मकव्यापारत्रयातिवर्ती ध्वननादिपर्यायो व्यापारोनपह्नवनीय एव ॥

—*Fifthly*, just as 'Denotation' is dependent upon convention, so is 'Indication' also upon the particular convention relating to the three conditions of 'the primary meaning being barred' and the rest (described under Chapter II); and it is on this account that 'Indication' has been called the 'tail of Denotation.' [Hence it is just as impossible for 'Suggestion' to be included under 'Indication' as under 'Denotation.']—

Sixthly, 'Suggestion' is not exactly of the nature of 'Indication', because in some cases Suggestion follows on the wake of Indication; nor indeed does Suggestion always follow on the wake of Indication, as in several instances Suggestion is based upon Denotation itself nor again is Suggestion always based upon these two; (Denotation and Indication), as it is found to emanate even from mere letters and syllables which do not 'denote' anything at all,—or even from such entirely *non-verbal* sources as side-long glances and other mere gestures.

तत्र "अत्ता एत्थ" इत्यादौ नियतसंबन्धः "कस्स व ण होइ रोसो" इत्यादौ, अनियतसंबन्धः ।

"विपरीअरए लच्छी बम्हं दटठूण णाहिकमलट्ठं ।
हरिणो दाहिणणअणं रसाउला झत्ति ढक्केइ ॥१३७॥"

इत्यादौ संबद्धसंबन्धः । अत्र हि हरिपदेन दक्षिणनयनस्य सूर्यात्मकता व्यज्यते। तन्निमीलनेन सूर्यास्तमयः । तेन पद्मस्य संकोचः । ततो ब्रह्मणः स्थगनम् । तत्र सति गोप्याङ्गस्यादर्शनेन अनिर्यन्त्रणं निधुवनविलसितमिति ।

From all this it follows that we cannot reject 'Suggestion' as a process which functions far beyond the three processes of 'Denotation', 'Import' and 'Indication'.

(*a*) In the verse referred to above—'my mother-in-law lies here &c.'—the 'suggested' meaning is one that bars a definite relationship (to the expressed meaning); (*b*) while in the verse 'who will not get annoyed etc., (quoted above) the relationship is extremely vague and (*c*) in the following verse—

'On the occasion of......when Lakṣmī saw Brahmā seated on the naval-lotus of her husband, she, being too immersed in her passion, closed the right eye of Viṣṇu (her husband)',

—the suggested meaning is related to the expressed indirectly through something else related to it ; *e. g.* the term '*Hari*' (Viṣṇu) suggests the fact of his right eye being the Sun (the Sun and the Moon being described as the two eyes of Viṣṇu), hence the closing of that eye signifies *sunset*, which signifies the closing of the lotus and the consequent hiding of Brahmā seated upon it, which, lastly, suggests the fact that her secret parts being rendered invisible to anyone, her pleasure would continue unmolested.

'अखण्डबुद्धिनिर्ग्राह्यो वाक्यार्थं एव वाच्यः वाक्यमेव च वाचकम्' इति येप्याहुः तैरप्यविद्यापदपतितैः पदपदार्थकल्पना कर्तव्यैवेति तत्पक्षेप्यवश्यमुक्तोदाहरणादौ विध्यादिर्व्यङ्ग्य एव ।

ननु वाच्यादसंबद्धं तावन्न प्रतीयते यतः कुतश्चित् यस्य कस्यचिदर्थस्य प्रतीतेः प्रसङ्गात् । एवं च संबन्धात् व्यङ्ग्य-

---

Others again (the Vedāntins) have held the view that —" It is the *meaning of the sentence* which, comprehended through a single indivisible cognition, is what is 'expressed' or 'denoted', and it is the *sentence* alone that is *denotative*".

But even these men, when they descend to the regions of 'Illusion', have to take into account 'words' and 'meanings of words'; so that according to these people also, in the examples cited above '(' The sandal-paint over thy breasts has been......thou hast *not* gone to that wretched man') the *affirmation* and such other meanings must be regarded as being 'suggested'.

[The logician starts off with another objection to the 'Suggestion theory']—" What is *suggested* is not something entirely unconnected with the *expressed* meaning; if it were, then anything could be suggested by any word, without any restriction. In view of some such connection being essential, there can be no *suggestiveness* in the absence of some restrictive relationship; and thus what really happens in the case of 'Suggestion' is that there is (1) a constant relation (between the *suggested* and the *suggester*), (2) the relation is such that the *suggester* is never concomitant with the contrary of the *suggested*, and (3) the *suggester* subsists in the *suggested*; so that the suggester fulfilling the three conditions of the 'Inferential Problems',

व्यञ्जकभावोप्रतिबन्धेवश्यं न भवतीति व्याप्तत्वेन नियतधर्मिनिष्ठत्वेन च त्रिरूपाल्लिङ्गाल्लिङ्गिज्ञानमनुमानं यत् तद्रूपः पर्यवस्यति । तथाहि—

"भम धम्मिअ वीसद्धो सो सुणओ अज्ज मारिओ तेण ।
गोलाणइकच्छकुडंगवासिणा दरिअसीहेण ॥१३८॥"

अत्र गृहे श्वनिवृत्त्या भ्रमणं विहितं गोदावरीतीरे सिंहोपलब्धेरभ्रमणमनुमापयति । यत् यत भीरुभ्रमणं तत्तद्भयकारणनिवृत्त्युपलब्धिपूर्वकं गोदावरीतीरे च सिंहोपलब्धिरिति व्यापकविरुद्धोपलब्धिः ।

अत्रोच्यते—भीरुरपि गुरोः प्रभोर्वा निदेशेन प्रियानुरागेण अन्येन चैवंभूतेन हेतुना सत्यपि भयकारणे भ्रमतीत्यनैकान्तिको

---

our knowledge of the *suggested* meaning comes to be purely *inferential* in character. For instance, in the following verse—'My good man, roam about as you choose ; the dog has been killed by the lion living in the cave of the banks of the Godāvarī',—what is advised is the safety of roaming about due to the removal of the dog from the house, and this leads to the *inference* of the danger involved in wandering on the banks of the Godāvarī, by reason of the presence of the lion. The 'roaming of a coward' is invariably concomitant with the certainty of 'the absence of all cause of fear' ;—on the banks of the Godāvarī 'the cause of fear' is present ; and so this 'presence' is the contrary of the aforesaid 'absence' with which the said roaming is invariably concomitant. Hence the said 'presence' leads to the deduction of what is contrary to the aforesaid 'roaming', *i. e.* the *impropriety of roaming*".

Our answer to the above is as follows :—(*a*) As a matter of fact, even a coward is found going to places where

हेतुः शुनो बिभ्यदपि वीरत्वेन सिंहान्न बिभेतीति विरुद्धोपि गोदावरीतीरे सिंहसद्भावः प्रत्यक्षादनुमानाद्वा न निश्चितः। अपि तु वचनात्। न च वचनस्य प्रामाण्यमस्ति । अर्थेनाप्रतिबन्धादित्यसिद्धश्च तत्कथमेवंविधाद्धेतोः साध्यसिद्धिः ।

तथा "निःशेषच्युत-" इत्यादौ गमकतया यानि चन्दनच्यवनादीन्युपात्तानि तानि कारणान्तरतोपि भवन्ति। अतश्चात्रैव स्नान-

---

there is danger, under certain circumstances, such as by the order of his preceptor or master, under the influence of his love for his beloved ; so that the inferential *probans* (premise) is ' inconclusive ' (the ' coward's roaming ' being *not* invariably concomitant with the ' absence of danger ');—(*b*) and again, it is possible that the person addressed may be a brave man who, even though fearing the *dog*, would not fear the *lion*, and thus the premise is also ' contradictory ' (the '*presence of the lion*' not necessarily involving the impossibility of the ' fearing man ' not roaming that way) ;—(*c*) further, ' the presence of the lion ' on the banks of the Godāvarī is not something known either by direct Perception or by Inference, it is learnt only from the *words* (of the speaker), and since no reliability belongs to the mere word (of a stray person), until it has been found to be consonant with facts, the *probans* is ' unknown ' also.—Thus the *probans* being vitiated by three fallacies, how can it lead to any valid inference of the conclusion ?—Further, in the case of the verse ' the sandal-paint over thy breasts has been entirely rubbed out...... thou hast not gone to the wretched man ', the marks—rubbing out of the sandal-paint and so forth—which have been set forth as suggestive (of the conclusion ' thou hast gone ') are such as could be brought out by (and hence be indicative of) other circumstances also ; in fact even in

कार्यत्वेनोक्तानीति नोपभोगे एव प्रतिबद्धानीत्यनैकान्तिकानि।

व्यक्तिवादिना चाधमपदसहायानामेषां व्यञ्जकत्वमुक्तम्। न चात्राधमत्वं प्रमाणप्रतिपन्नमिति कथमनुमानम्। एवंविधादर्थादेवंविधोर्थ उपपत्त्यनपेक्षत्वेपि प्रकाशते इति व्यक्तिवादिनः पुनस्तत् अदूषणम्॥

इति काव्यप्रकाशे ध्वनिगुणीभूतव्यङ्ग्यसंकीर्णभेदनिर्णयो नाम पञ्चम उल्लासः॥५॥

---

the verse itself they are described as brought about by *bathing*; so that they are not invariably concomitant with the 'dalliance' (of the person addressed, which is held to be *suggested*).

According to the upholder of the 'Suggestion' theory, on the other hand, the said *suggestion* has been explained as brought about by the marks described, through the aid of the epithet 'wretched' (applied to the lover, which suggests his infidelity in having dallied with the messenger).—Nor could this 'wretchedness' be made the basis of any *Inference*, for the simple reason that it is not something that is already cognised through any (other) valid means of cognition. As for the fact that a certain set of words gives rise to the notion of things (not actually expressed by them), without any rhyme or reason,—this cannot be effectively urged against the upholder of the 'Suggestion' theory (who takes pride in the suggestion of such meanings). 47.

Thus ends Chapter V dealing with the sub-divisions of Suggestive Poetry and the Poetry of Subordinate Suggestion.

अथ षष्ठ उल्लासः

शब्दार्थचित्रं यत्पूर्वं काव्यद्वयमुदाहृतम् ।
गुणप्राधान्यतस्तत्र स्थितिश्चित्रार्थशब्दयोः ॥ ४८ ॥

न तु शब्दचित्रे अर्थस्याचित्रत्वमर्थचित्रे वा शब्दस्य ।

तथा चोक्तम्

"रूपकादिरलंकारस्तस्यान्यैर्बहुधोदितः ।
न कान्तमपि निर्भूषं विभाति वनितानम् ॥
रूपकादिमलंकारं बाह्यमाचक्षते परे ।
सुपां तिङां च व्युत्पत्तिं वाचां वाञ्छन्त्यलंकृतिम् ॥

CHAPTER VI

LOWEST KIND OF POETRY

OF FANCIFUL WORD AND FANCIFUL MEANING

In the two kinds of Poetry spoken of above—that of Fanciful Word and that of Fanciful Meaning,—subordinacy and predominance belong respectively to the fanciful meaning and the fanciful word.

It is not that in the Poetry of Fanciful Word, there is no fanciful meaning or *vice versa.*

[All that the division means is that though in any individual instance, we may have both fanciful word and fanciful meaning, yet it is regarded as the Poetry 'of Fanciful Word' when the fanciful *word* (*i. e.*, the *Verbal Figure of Speech*) is more prominent than the fanciful *meaning* (*i. e.*, the *Ideal Figure of Speech*) ; and it is regarded as 'of fanciful *meaning*' when the fanciful meaning is the more prominent of the two].

[In support of this commixture of both] we have the following declaration :—

'(*a*) Some writers have spoken of Metaphor and the other (*ideal*) Figures of Speech as the real 'embellishments'

तदेतदाहुः सौशब्द्यं नार्थव्युत्पत्तिरीदृशी ।
शब्दाभिधेयालंकारभेदादिष्टं द्वयं तु नः ॥" इति ॥

शब्दचित्रं यथा

"प्रथममरुणच्छायस्तावत्ततः कनकप्रभ-
स्तदनु विरहोत्ताम्यत्तन्वीकपोलतलद्युतिः ।
उदयति ततो ध्वान्तध्वंसक्षमः क्षणदामुखे
सरसबिसिनीकन्दच्छेदच्छविर्मृगलाञ्छनः" ॥१३९॥

---

of Poetry ; even the face of a woman, though beautiful in itself, does not appear charming when it is without any ornaments [similarly Poetry, however beautiful in itself is not charming unless it is embellished by a Figure of Speech] ;—(*b*) others regard Metaphor and the other *Ideal* Figures of Speech as something *foreign* to Poetry, and they hold that the real embellishment consists in the elegant placing of nouns and verbs ; it is this that they call 'elegance of composition'; no such elegance (or charm) attaches to the mere *Ideal* figure (the fanciful meaning);—(*c*) we however accept both kinds of embellishments ro figures—the *Verbal* and the *Ideal*'.

Example of the 'Fanciful Word' (*Verbal* Figure of Speech)—

Prathamamaruṇachchhāyastāvattataḥ kanakaprabhas.
Tadanu virahottāmyattanvī kapolataladyutiḥ.
Udayati tato dhvāntadhvamsakṣamaḥ kṣaṇadāmukhe
Sarasabisinīkandachchhedachchhavirmṛgalāñchhanaḥ.

'The Moon rises at first with a shade of red ; then he takes the golden hue ; after that he has the lustre of the cheeks of the slender woman pining under separation ; then towards night he takes the splendour of the bulbous

अर्थचित्रं यथा

ते दृष्टिमात्रपतिता अपि कस्य नात्र
क्षोभाय पक्ष्मलदृशामलकाः खलाश्च ।
नीचाः सदैव सविलासमलीकलग्ना
ये कालतां कुटिलतामिव न त्यजन्ति ॥१४०॥

यद्यपि सर्वत्र काव्येन्ततः विभावादिरूपतयैव पर्यवसानं तथापि स्फुटस्य रसस्यानुपलम्भादव्यङ्ग्यमेतत्काव्यद्वयमुक्तम् ।

---

root of the fresh lotus-stock and is then capable of dispersing darkness'.

[Here the charm, lies in alliteration, which is more prominent and charming than the series of similes involved].

Example of the 'Fanciful Meaning' (Ideal Figure of Speech)—

'Whom do not (*a*) the locks of the woman with fair-lashed eyes—and (*b*) *the wicked people* —not perturb,—when they (*a*) curl over the eyes [(*b*) *are seen*], (*a*) hanging low [(*b*) *mean*], (*a*) lying beautifully on the forehead [(*b*) *delighting in telling lies*], and never abandon their (*a*) blackness [(*b*) *fraudulence*] and (*a*) *curls* [(*b*) *crookedness, dishonesty*]'.

[Here we have the *ideal* figure 'Combination' aided by 'Paranomasia' and 'Simile]'.

Though in reality, in the case of all kinds of Poetry, everything ultimately turns upon the Excitants, Ensuants and Variants (and the Passion manifested by these) [and hence in Fanciful Poetry also there is bound to be some suggestion of Passion], yet what happens in the two kinds of Fanciful Poetry just described is that no real 'Passion' is clearly discernible and it is on that ground

अत्र च शब्दार्थालंकारभेदाद्बहवो भेदाः ते चालंकारनिर्णये निर्णेष्यन्ते ॥

इति काव्यप्रकाशे शब्दार्थचित्रनिरूपणं नाम षष्ठ उल्लासः ॥६॥

---

that they are regarded as 'devoid of suggestiveness' [and hence 'inferior'].

The varieties of this kind of Poetry are many, in accordance with the number of Figures of Speech—*ideal and verbal* ; and these are going to be described under the section treating of the 'Figures of Speech' (Chapters IX and X). 48.

Thus ends Chapter VI dealing with the Poetry of Fanciful Word and Meaning.

अथ सप्तम उल्लासः

काव्यस्वरूपं निरूप्य दोषाणां सामान्यलक्षणमाह

मुख्यार्थहतिर्दोषो रसश्च मुख्यस्तदाश्रयाद्वाच्यः ।
उभयोपयोगिनः स्युः शब्दाद्यास्तेन तेष्वपि सः ॥ ४९ ॥

हतिरपकर्षः । शब्दाद्याः इत्याद्यग्रहणाद्वर्णरचने ।

विशेषलक्षणमाह

दुष्टं पदं श्रुतिकटु च्युतसंस्कृत्यप्रयुक्तमसमर्थम् ।
निहतार्थमनुचितार्थं निरर्थकमवाचकं त्रिधाऽश्लीलम्॥५०॥

CHAPTER VII

OF DEFECTS

Having described the form of Poetry, the author states the general definition of defects (the absence of which he has made a necessary condition in all poetry) :—

Defect is the repressor of the principal meaning ; the 'principal meaning' being the Passion, as also the Expressed Meaning, which is essential for the manifestation of the Passion ;—both of these requiring the aid of Word and the rest, Defects pertain to these latter also. 49.

'*Repressing*' is hindering the agreeableness.

'*Word and the rest.*—The phrase 'and the rest' is meant to include Letters and Syntactical construction (*i. e. Sentence*).

The author now proceeds to add specific definitions of particular Defects.—

The defective Word is such as—(1) *unpleasant to the ear,* (2) *lacking correctness,* (3) *unconventional,* (4) *incapable*

सन्दिग्धमप्रतीतं ग्राम्यं नेयार्थमथ भवेत् क्लिष्टम् ।
अविमृष्टविधेयांशं विरुद्धमतिकृत्समासगतमेव ॥ ५१ ॥

(१) 'श्रुतिकटु' परुषवर्णरूपं दुष्टम् ।

यथा

अनङ्गमङ्गलगृहापाङ्गभङ्गितरङ्गितैः ।
आलिङ्गितः स तन्वङ्ग्या कार्तार्थ्यं लभते कदा ॥१४१॥

अत्र कार्तार्थ्यमिति ॥

(२) 'च्युतसंस्कृति' व्याकरणलक्षणहीनम्

---

of giving sense, (5) *having its meaning suppressed,* (6) *having an improper signification,* (7) *useless,* (8) *not expressive,* (9) *indecorous in three ways,* (10) *ambiguous,* (11) *unintelligible,* (12) *vulgar,* (13) *and one whose meaning has to be guessed ;—and it is* (14) *obscure, or* (15) *having the predicative factor not discriminated, or* (16) *of repugnant implication,—only when occurring in a compound.* 51.

[Examples of each of the above sixteen defects]—(1) The word that has the defect of being 'unpleasant to the ear',—*i. e.* consisting of harsh letters,—is found in the following—

'*Anaṅgamaṅgalagṛhāpāṅgabhaṅgitaraṅgitaiḥ*
Āliṅgitaḥ sa tanvaṅgyā kārtārthyaṁ labhate kadā'.

'When will he attain the fulfilment of his desires, on being embraced by the slender-bodied girl, lovely through the graces of her glance, the auspicious abode of the Love-god himself ?'.

Here the word '*kārtārthyam*' is 'unpleasant to the ear' (Harsh).

(2) The following contains an example of the word 'lacking in correctness', *i. e.* not according with the rules of grammar.—

यथा

एतन्मन्दविपक्वतिन्दुकफलश्यामोदरापाण्डर-
प्रान्तं हन्त पुलिन्दसुन्दरकरस्पर्शक्षमं लभ्यते ।
तत् पल्लीपतिपुत्रि कुञ्जरकुलं कुम्भाभयाभ्यर्थना-
दीनं त्वामनुनाथते कुचयुगं पत्रावृतं मा कृथाः ॥१४२॥

अत्रानुनाथते इति । 'सर्पिषो नाथते' इत्यादावाशिष्येव नाथतेरात्मनेपदं विहितम् । "आशिषि नाथः" इति । अत्र तु याचनमर्थः । तस्मात् 'अनुनाथति स्तनयुगम्' इति पठनीयम् ।

'*Etanmanda* ....
Dīnaṁtvāmanunāthate ....

'O thou, the daughter of the chief of the settlement ! the herd of elephants, seeking safety from danger (at the hands of young foresters), is begging you not to cover your breasts with leaves,—breasts that resemble the half ripe *Tinduka* fruit in being dark in the centre and slightly white all round, and which deserve to be fondled by Shabara-youths'.

[The sense is that if the girl does not cover her breasts the hunting youths would be attracted nearer towards them than towards the heads of the elephants.]

Here the verb '*anunāthate*' is grammatically incorrect. In accordance with Pāṇini's Sūtra 2.3.15, the root '*nāth*' can take the *Ātmanepada*-ending only when it is used in the sense of *benediction* (hope or expectation), as in the expression '*sarpiṣo nāthate*' (' he expects to obtain butter'); while in the verse cited, the word '*anunāthate*' has the sense of *begging*. Hence the correct reading should have been '*anunāthati stanayugam*'.

(३) 'अप्रयुक्तं तथा आम्नातमपि कविभिर्नादृतम् ।
यथा
यथायं दारुणाचारः सर्वदैव विभाव्यते ।
तथा मन्ये दैवतोस्य पिशाचो राक्षसोथ वा ॥१४३॥

अत्र दैवतशब्दो "दैवतानि पुंसि वा" इति पुंस्याम्नातोपि न केनचित्प्रयुज्यते ॥

(४) 'असमर्थं' यत्तदर्थं पठ्यते न च तत्रास्य शक्तिः ।
यथा
तीर्थान्तरेषु स्नानेन समुपार्जितसत्कृतिः ।
सुरस्रोतस्विनीमेष हन्ति संप्रति सादरम् ॥१४४॥

अत्र हन्तीति गमनार्थम् ॥

---

(3) The following is an example of the 'unconventional',—*i. e.* a word, which though quite correct formally, is one that has not been admitted by poets into usage—

'*yathāyaṁ......................daivatosya*'

'Inasmuch as this person is always cruel in his actions, it seems as if his guiding spirit were a ghost or a demon'.

Though the form '*daivataḥ*' is formally correct,—it being mentioned in the lexicons as belonging both to the masculine and neuter genders—yet as a matter of fact, it has never been used in its masculine form.

(4) The following is an example of the word incapable of giving sense', *i. e.* one used in a sense to which its denotative potency does not extend.

'*Tīrthāntareṣu......hanti samprati sādaram*'

'After having acquired merit from bathing in other sacred places, he now reverentially repairs to the Celestial River.'

Here the verb '*hanti*' has been used in the sense of *going* (which it is incapable of denoting).

[In the Dhātupāṭha the root *han* is mentioned to have the meanings "to kill" and "to go".]

(५) 'निहतार्थं' यदुभयार्थमप्रसिद्धेर्थे प्रयुक्तम् ।

यथा

यावकरसार्द्रपादप्रहारशोणितकचेन दयितेन ।

मुग्धा साध्वसतरला विलोक्य परिचुम्बिता सहसा ॥१४५॥

अत्र शोणितशब्दस्य रुधिरलक्षणेनार्थेनोज्ज्वलीकृतत्वरूपोर्थो व्यवधीयते ॥

(६) 'अनुचितार्थं' यथा

तपस्विभिर्या सुचिरेण लभ्यते प्रयत्नतः सत्त्रिभिरिष्यते च या ।

प्रयान्ति तामाशु गतिं यशस्विनो रणाश्वमेधे पशुतामुपागताः ॥१४६॥

---

(5) The following is an example of a word which has its meaning 'suppressed'—*i. e.* used in a sense which, though formally correct, is not generally known—

'*Yāvakarasārdra.........shoṇitakachena.........*

.......................parichumbitā sahasā.

'When the lover, who had his locks made ruddy by the touch of her feet painted with red *alakta*, saw that the young girl was flurried through fright (caused by the suspicion that the redness might be due to blood), he kissed her vehemently'.

Here the intended meaning of the word '*shoṇita*' *i. e.* 'made ruddy'—is 'suppressed' by its better known meaning, 'blood'.

(6) In the following we have an example of the word 'with an improper signification'—

'*Tapasvibhiryā.......................*

...........raṇāshvamedhe pashutāmupāgatāḥ'

'The glorious men who have become beasts offered in the sacrifice of battle quickly attain that condition which is attained by ascetics by prolonged austerities, and which is eagerly sought after by performers of sacrifices.'

अत्र पशुपदं कातरतामभिव्यनक्तीत्यनुचितार्थम् ॥

(७) 'निरर्थकं पादपूरणमात्रप्रयोजनं चादिपदम् ।

यथा

उत्फुल्लकमलकेसरपरागगौरद्युते मम हि गौरि ।
अभिवाञ्छितं प्रसिद्ध्यतु भगवति युष्मत्प्रसादेन ॥१४७॥

अत्र हिशब्दः ॥

(८) 'अवाचकं' यथा

अवन्ध्यकोपस्य विहन्तुरापदां भवन्ति वश्याः स्वयमेव देहिनः ।
अमर्षशून्येन जनस्य जन्तुना न जातहार्देन न विद्विषादरः ॥१४८॥

Here the word '*pashu*', 'beast',—indicating (in its proper denotation) as it does, *cowardliness*—conveys a sense that is 'improper' (and repugnant to the context).

[The meaning is that those who lose their lives in battle attain heaven more quickly than others ; this has been figuratively expressed by means of the words ' men who are killed in battle as beasts are offered in sacrifice ',—and this implies that the men are possessed of the qualities of the 'beasts' ; and these qualities are quite the reverse of bravery and other qualities which are generally associated with the heroes of *war*.]

(7) In the following we have an example of the 'useless' (redundant) word.—

'*Utphulla*...............................*mama* *hi* *gauri*
.... *yuṣmatprasōdena*'

'O blessed Gauri, whose complexion is bright like the pollen of the full-blown lotus, may my desired object be accomplished by your kindness !'

Here the particle '*hi*' is entirely superfluous.

(8) In the following we have an example of the 'in-expressive' word—

(*a*) '*Abandhyakopasya* ....
.... *jantunā* ....*daraḥ*.'

अत्र जन्तुपदमदातर्यर्थे विवक्षितं तत्र च नाभिधायकम् । यथा वा
हाधिक् सा किल तामसी शशिमुखी दृष्टा मया यत्र सा
तद्विच्छेदरुजान्धकारितमिदं दग्धं दिनं कल्पितम् ।
किं कुर्मः कुशले सदैव विधुरो धाता न चेत्तत्कथं
तादृग्यामवतीमयो भवति मे नो जीवलोकोधुना ॥१४९॥

'To him whose anger is never futile and who is ever able to destroy his own troubles, people surrender themselves of their own accord ; on the other hand, if one is devoid of resentment, men do not mind his enmity, nor do they care for his friendship, if he is *not generous*'.

Here the word '*jantu*' (which means 'animal'), is used in the sense of 'not generous', which it never expresses.

[A distinction is made between the 'inexpressive' word and the word 'incapable of giving sense' (4) on the ground that while the latter, though incapable of expressing the intended meaning in its entirety, does express a portion of it, the former is absolutely unable to express any portion of it at all : that is of the two factors of the intended meaning, the *object* and its *qualities*, while the 'Incapable word' may signify one or the other, though not both, the 'Inexpressive word' signifies neither.]

Another example of the "Inexpressive Word"—

Hā dhik....................
.... *dagdhaṁ dinaṁ* ...
....
....*jīvaloko dhunā*'.

'Woe to me ! That time when I saw the Moon-faced one is said to have been (dark) *night*, and this present time, darkened as it is by the pangs of her separation, is held to be (light) *day* ! What shall I do ? The Dispenser is ever averse to my welfare ! Or else, why was not the entire living world transformed for me into that same night.'

अत्र दिनमिति प्रकाशमयमित्यर्थेवाचकम् ।

यच्चोपसर्गसंसर्गादर्थान्तरगतम्

यथा

जङ्घाकाण्डोरुनालो नखकिरणलसत्केसरालीकरालः
प्रत्यग्रालक्तकाभाप्रसरकिसलयो मञ्जुमञ्जीरभृङ्गः ।
भर्तुर्नृत्तानुकारे जयति निजतनुस्वच्छलावण्यवापी-
संभूताम्भोजशोभां विदधदभिनवो दण्डपादो भवान्याः ॥१५०॥

अत्र दधदित्यर्थे विदधदिति ॥

Here the word '*dinam*' is not quite expressive of *brightness* [in the same manner as '*tāmasī*' is of *darkness*.]

Another example of this same defect we have in a case where (though the verbal root is quite expressive of the intended meaning), the meaning becomes changed by the particular prefix added to it ; as in the following—

'*Jaṅghā*..................
......*vidadhadabhinavo*...*bhavānyāḥ*'

'Glorious is the *Daṇḍapāda* attitude struck up by Bhavānī when imitating her husband's dance,—the attitude (of the legs) which bears the splendour of the lotus grown in the tank of the exquisite charm of her body, having the thighs for its stalk, the lustrous nails for its filaments, the bright red paints on the feet for its petals, and the jingling anklets for the bees hovering round it.'

Here the word '*vidadhat*' has been used in the sense of '*dadhat*,' 'bears.'

[The form '*dadhat*' without the prefix ' means 'bearing'; with the said prefix, it means 'ordaining,' 'encompassing' and so forth.]

(९) 'अश्लीलम्' त्रिधेति व्रीडाजुगुप्सामङ्गलव्यञ्जकत्वात् ।
यथा
साधनं सुमहद्यस्य यन्नान्यस्य विलोक्यते ।
तस्य धीशालिनः कोन्यः सहतारालितां भ्रुवम् ॥१५१॥ (१)
लीलातामरसाहतोन्यवनितानिःशङ्कदष्टाधरः
कश्चित्केसरदूषितेक्षण इव व्यामील्य नेत्रे स्थितः ।
मुग्धा कुड्मलिताननेन ददती वायुं स्थिता तत्र सा
भ्रान्त्या धूर्ततयाथ वा नतिमृतेतेनानिशं चुम्बिता॥१५२॥ (२)

---

(9) The 'indecorous' word is of three kinds, implying either (*a*) indecency or (*b*) disgust or (*c*) inauspiciousness ; we have an example of (*a*) in the following :—

'*Sādhanaṁ* ....
.... *bhruvam*'

'He whose vast *sādhana* (army—the male organ) is one that is not found with any one else,—of such an intelligent person who can bear the eyebrows curved (in anger) ?'

There is an *indecent* implication in the double meaning of the word '*sādhanaṁ*'.

An example of (*b*) we have in the following—

'*Līlātāmarasā* ....
......*dadatī vayuṁ*......*chumbitā*'

'He who had his lips bearing the marks of the freely bestowed kisses of a strange woman, on being struck (in anger) by his wife with her sporting lotus, stood rubbing his eyes, as if they were hurt by the dust of the flower falling into them ; the simple-minded young girl (taking pity on him) stood there puffing air into the eyes with her budded mouth ; thereupon, either through mistake or through cunningness, the man kissed her repeatedly (thus becoming reconciled), without having had to throw himself at her feet (and seek her forgiveness)'.

मृदुपवनविभिन्नो मत्प्रियाया विनाशाद्
घनरुचिरकलापो निःसपत्नोद्य जातः ।
रतिविगलितबन्धे केशपाशे सुकेश्याः
सति कुसुमसनाथे कं हरेदेष बर्ही ॥१५३॥ (३)
एषु साधनवायुविनाशशब्दाः व्रीडादिव्यञ्जकाः ॥

(१०) 'संदिग्धं' यथा

आलिङ्गितस्तत्रभवान् संपराये जयश्रिया ।
आशीःपरंपरां वन्द्यां कर्णे कृत्वा कृपां कुरु ॥१५४॥

The phrase '*vāyuṁ dadatī*', has an implication that arouses *disgust*.

(*c*) '*Mṛdupavana......vināshāt*
..............*barhī*'.

'By the disappearance of my beloved, this dense and lovely train of the peacock, ruffled by mild breeze, has been left without a rival ; for in the presence of the hair-braid of that fair-tressed one, interspersed with flowers, and ruffled in dalliance, whom could this peacock captivate ?'

Here the term '*vināśāt*' has an *inauspicious* implication (as it denotes *death*).

(10) In the following we have an example of the 'ambiguous' word—

'*Āliṅgitastatra*..............
.........*vandyāṁ*.........*kuru*'.

'Embraced by glorious victory, may you, revered Sire, receive in your ears reverent and continuous benedictions, and extend your mercy !'

The exact signification of the word '*vandyāṁ*' is ambiguous ; it being doubtful whether it means 'forcibly

अत्र वन्द्यां किं हठहृतमहिलायां किं वा नमस्यामिति संदेहः ।।

(११) 'अप्रतीतं' यत्केवले शास्त्रे प्रसिद्धम् । यथा

सम्यग्ज्ञानमहाज्योतिर्दलिताशयताजुषः ।
विधीयमानमप्येतन्न भवेत्कर्मबन्धनम् ।।१५५।।

अत्राशयशब्दो वासनापर्यायो योगशास्त्रादावेव प्रयुक्तः ।।

(१२) 'ग्राम्यं' यत्केवले लोके स्थितम् । यथा

राकाविभावरीकान्तसंक्रान्तद्युति ते मुखम् ।
तपनीयशिलाशोभा कटिश्च हरते मनः ।।१५६।।

---

captured women' (in which case the sentence would mean 'may you extend your mercy *towards the captive woman*'), or 'reverent' (in which case it would qualify '*āśīḥparam-parām*').

(11) The following is an example of the 'unintelligible' word,—i. e. one that is used in a technical sense attaching to it only in scientific literature :—

'*Samyagjñāna ...... dalitāshayatājuṣaḥ ....*
.................bandhanam.'

'One who has his desires destroyed by the supreme light of True Wisdom,—to him an act, even though done, does not act as a bondage.'

Here the term '*āshhaya*' in the sense of *desire* or *longing* is a technicality of the Yoga and other technical philosophical literature.

(12) In the following we have an example of the 'vulgar' word, *i. e.* one that is used only by the lower order of men.

'*Rākā.................*
..................kaṭiśhcha harate manaḥ.'

'Thy face which has taken to itself the lustre of the

अत्र कटिरिति ॥

(१३) 'नेयार्थम्'।

"निरूढा लक्षणाः काश्चित् सामर्थ्यात् अभिधानवत् ।
क्रियन्ते सांप्रतं काश्चित् काश्चिन्नैव त्वशक्तितः ॥" इति यन्निषिद्धं लाक्षणिकम् । यथा

शरत्कालसमुल्लासिपूर्णिमाशर्वरीप्रियम् ।
करोति ते मुखं तन्वि चपेटापातनातिथिम् ॥१४७॥

---

full moon, and these thy buttocks resembling a block of gold, captive the heart'.

The word '*kaṭi*' (is one that is used only in vulgar parlance.)

(13) The following is an example of the word 'whose meaning has to be guessed out',—*i. e.* which is used in such a secondary or figurative sense as is not permissible, in accordance with the law (stated by Kumārila) that (*a*) 'Some forms of figurative use are such as are as well recognised as direct denotation itself, being based upon the inherent potency of the words, (*b*) there are others adopted for the moment, for some special purpose, (*c*) while there are some that are absolutely incapable of affording the required sense and are hence inadmissible.' [And it is this third kind of figurative use that is meant in the present context].

'*Sharatkāla........................chapeṭāpātanātithim*'.

'Thy face, O slender one, makes the Moon, who is the beloved of the autumnal Full-moon night, the recipient of a slap'.

Here the 'giving of a slap' is meant to be indicative of *surpassing* [and this indication is not based upon either convention or upon any special purpose to be served].

अत्र चपेटापातनेन निर्जितत्वं लक्ष्यते ।

अथ समासगतमेव दुष्टमिति संबन्धः, अन्यत् केवलं समासगतं च ॥

(१४) 'क्लिष्टं' यतः अर्थप्रतिपत्तिर्व्यवहिता । यथा

अत्रिलोचनसंभूतज्योतिरुद्गमभासिभिः ।
सदृशं शोभतेत्यर्थं भूपाल तव चेष्टितम् ॥१५८॥

अत्रात्रिलोचनसंभूतस्य चन्द्रस्य ज्योतिरुद्गमेन भासिभिः कुमुदैरित्यर्थः ॥

(१५) 'अविमृष्टविधेयांशम्' अविमृष्टः प्राधान्येनानिर्दिष्टो विधेयांशो यत्र तत् । यथा

'*Samāsagatameva*' (in the text) is to be construed as meaning that the three defects that are mentioned last are so *only* when occurring in a compound, the others being defective both when occurring in a single word and in a compound.

(14) The following one contains an example of the 'obscure' word,—*i. e.* where the comprehension of the intended meaning is impeded :—

'*Atrilochanasambhūtajyotirudgamabhāsibhiḥ* ।
'*Sadṛsham̐ shobhatetyartham̐ bhūpāla tava cheṣṭitam* ॥

'Thy conduct looms bright like those that bloom in the light of him who was born of the eyes of the sage Atri'.

What are meant here are the white 'lilies', which bloom in the light of the *Moon*, who is described as being born out of the eyes of the sage Atri. [And this is extremely *obscure*].

(15) The following is an example of (a compound) where 'the predicative factor is not discriminated,'—i. e. not sufficiently emphasised as the principal factor,—

मूर्द्ध्नामुद्वृत्तकृत्ताविरलगलगलद्रक्तसंसक्तधारा-
धौतेशाङ्घ्रिप्रसादोपनतजयजगज्जातमिथ्यामहिम्नाम् ।
कैलासोल्लासनेच्छाव्यतिकरपिशुनोत्सर्पिदर्पोद्धुराणां
दोष्णां चैषां किमेतत् फलमिह नगरीरक्षणे यत् प्रयासः ॥१५९॥

अत्र मिथ्यामहिमत्वं नानुवाद्यम् अपि तु विधेयम् । यथा वा

Mūrdhnāmud..
Dhauteshāṅghriprasādopanatajayajagajjātamithyāmahimnām......
....
.... *prayāsaḥ*'.

'What is the use of these my heads and arms, if I have to make an effort even for the protecting of the city ?—the heads whose false glory was trumpeted to the world through victories gained by the favour of Shiva's feet, washed as they were with the unimpeded flow of blood issuing from them when they were majestically cut off by myself ;—and the arms full of intense pride manifested in the deep longing for the lifting of the Kailāsha mountain.'

Here the defect lies in the compound ending with *mithyāmahimnām*', where '*mithyā*' 'false', forming the first term of the qualitative compound, appears only as a *qualifying adjunct* (*anuvādya*, referred to for the sake of, and hence subordinate) to something else (*i. e.* 'greatness'), while in reality it is meant to be the *predicative factor*, and the predominant element.

[The meaning being that 'the greatness *had turned out to be false*, inasmuch as I have to make an effort to guard my city'. In this manner there is a logical connection between the assertion of *falsity* and the subsequent statement; in the other case the two statements stand separately —(*a*) 'my heads have false greatness' and (*b*) 'I have to guard the city'; and there is no logical connection between the two.]

स्रस्तां नितम्बादवरोपयन्ती पुनः पुनः केसरदामकाञ्चीम् ।
न्यासीकृतां स्थानविदा स्मरेण द्वितीयमौर्वीमिव कार्मुकस्य ॥१६०॥

अत्र द्वितीयत्वमात्रमुत्प्रेक्ष्यम् । मौर्वीं द्वितीयामिति युक्तः पाठः ।
यथा वा

वपुर्विरूपाक्षमलक्ष्यजन्मता दिगम्बरत्वेन निवेदितं वसु ।
वरेषु यद्बालमृगाक्षि मृग्यते तदस्ति किं व्यस्तमपि त्रिलोचने॥१६१॥

अत्र 'अलक्षिता जनिः' इति वाच्यम् । यथा वा

Another example of the same we have in the following :—

'*Srastām.........dvitīyamaurvīmiva.................*'

'She again and again tucked up the girdle of Bakula-flowers which slid down from her waist,—the girdle that resembled the second bow-string kept in her charge by the Love-God who knows the proper place to deposit things'.

What is meant to be emphasised here is the fact of the girdle being the *second* ;

[As it is only when it is the *second*, that there can be any possibility of its being *deposited* ; —and this fact of its being the *second* is subordinated in the compound, where '*dvitīya*', 'second,' appears only as a subordinate factor.]

The right reading, therefore, would be '*maurvīṁ dvitīyāmiva*' [where '*dvitīyām*'' standing by itself, the fact of being 'second' becomes duly emphasised].

Another example of the same defect :—

'*Vapurvirūpākṣamalakṣyajanmatā.................*
.. trilochane.

'His body contains disfigured eyes, he is of unknown birth, and his wealth is indicated by his having no dress; O thou fawn-eyed one, is there in Shiva, even singly any of those qualities that one seeks for in a bridegroom ?'

आनन्दसिन्धुरतिचापलशालिचित्त-
संदाननैकसदनं क्षणमप्यमुक्ता ।
या सर्वदैव भवता तदुदन्तचिन्ता
तान्ति तनोति तव संप्रति धिग्धिगस्मान् ॥१६२॥

अत्र 'न मुक्ता' इति निषेधो विधेयः । यथा

नवजलधरः संनद्धोयं न दृप्तनिशाचरः
सुरधनुरिदं दूराकृष्टं न तस्य शरासनम् ।
अयमपि पटुर्धारासारो न बाणपरंपरा
कनकनिकषस्निग्धा विद्युत् प्रिया न ममोर्वशी ॥१६३॥

What is meant to be emphasised here is that 'his birth *is unknown*' [and this has been made a subordinate factor in the compound '*alakṣyajanmatā*]. The right reading would thus have been '*alakṣitā janiḥ.*'

Yet another example of the same defect.—

'*Ānanda*.................
.................*kṣaṇamapyamuktā*
....
.................*dhigdhigasmān*'

'Being the ocean of bliss, the one abode of the force enchaining the fickle heart, she was not left by you even for one moment; and now her very name brings disgust in you,—woe to us!'

What is meant to be emphasised or predicated here is the *negation*—'*not* left';—and hence the negative particle should have stood by itself, as '*na muktā*',—as it is in the verse '*navajaladharaḥ.........na dṛptanishācharaḥ, ... suradhanūridam...na tasya sharāsanam, ... ayamapi...... dhārāsāro na bāṇaparamparā,.........vidyut priyā na mamorvashī*'—'This is the fresh dense cloud, *not* a vainglorious demon;

'इत्यत्र। न त्वमुक्ततानुवादेनान्यदत्र किंचिद्विहितम्। यथा

जुगोपात्मानमत्रस्तो भेजे धर्ममनातुरः।
अगृध्नुराददे सोर्थानसक्तः सुखमन्वभूत् ॥१६४॥

इत्यत्र अत्रस्तत्वाद्यनुवादेनात्मनो गोपनादि ॥

(१६) 'विरुद्धमतिकृत्' यथा

सुधाकरकराकारविशारदविचेष्टितः।
अकार्यमित्रमेकोसौ तस्य किं वर्णयामहे ॥१६५॥

---

this is the celestial bow, *not* the bow of that demon ; this is the downpour of rain ; *not* the flight of arrows ; this is the lightning bright like the hue of gold on a touch-stone, and *not* my beloved Urvashī ;—while, in the passage quoted before we have the negative particle appearing as the subordinate factor in the compound '*amuktā*', which would have been justified only if there were something else predicated in reference to the 'non-abandoning', as is found to be the case with the following—'*jugopātmānamatrasto* ; *bheje dharmamanāturaḥ* ; *agṛdhnurādade sorthān* ; *asaktaḥ sukhamanvabhūt* ;—' Though unterrified, he guarded himself ; though untroubled, he had recourse to righteousness ; though not greedy, he received wealth ; and though unattached, he enjoyed pleasures;' [where the *self-guarding* is predicated with reference to the fact of the king being *unterrified* and so forth, which justifies the compounding of the negative particle.]

(16) The following is an example of 'repugnant suggestion',—

'*sudhā*.................

akāryamitra.................*varṇayāmahe*'

'What shall I say of him who is a *disinterested* friend, his conduct being as pure as the rays of the moon.'

अत्र 'कार्यं विना मित्रम्' इति विवक्षितम् 'अकार्ये मित्रम् इति' तु प्रतीतिः । यथा वा

चिरकालपरिप्राप्तलोचनानन्ददायिनः ।
कान्ता कान्तस्य सहसा विदधाति गलग्रहम् ॥१६६॥

अत्र 'कण्ठग्रहम्' इति वाच्यम् । यथा वा

न त्रस्तं यदि नाम भूतकरुणासंतानशान्तात्मनः
तेन व्यारुजता धनुर्भगवतो देवाद्भवानीपतेः ।
तत्पुत्रस्तु मदान्धतारकवधाद्विश्वस्य दत्तोत्सवः
स्कन्दः स्कन्द इव प्रियोहमथ वा शिष्यः कथं विस्मृतः ॥१६७॥

Here the sense meant to be conveyed by the word '*akāryamitram*' is that he is friendly without any selfish motive—a disinterested friend; whereas the word has also the other (repugnant) signification—that 'he is a *mitra*, a companion, an associate, in *akārya*, evil deeds.'

Another example—

'*Chirakāla*...........

................*galagraham*'

'Meeting after a long time her lover rejoicing her eyes, the loving girl suddenly offers him her embrace.'

Here the right word to use would have been '*Kaṇṭhagraham*', 'falling on his neck'.

[The word that is used, however, '*galagraham*', is better known as the name of a particular disease of the neck, and as such it *has* a most repugnant implication in the present context.]

Another example—

'*Na trastam*........

....................*bhavānīpateḥ*

.........................*vismṛtaḥ*.'

'When Rāma broke the bow of the husband of Bhavānī, he did not fear that God himself, because his heart

अत्र भवानीपतिशब्दो भवान्याः पत्यन्तरे प्रतीतिं करोति । यथा वा

गोरपि यद्वाहनतां प्राप्तवतः सोपि गिरिसुतासिंहः ।
सविधे निरहंकारः पायाद्वः सोम्बिकारमणः ॥१६८॥

अत्राम्बिकारमण इति विरुद्धां धियमुत्पादयति ॥

'श्रुतिकटु' ससासगतं यथा

---

is quiescent through his mercy on all living creatures ; the son of that God, Skanda, also, was the source of joy to the universe by reason of his having killed the haughty demon Tāraka (and hence he also could not be feared) ; but how is it that he did not think of myself, the disciple of the God Śiva, and as dear to him as his son Skanda ?'

Here the word '*bhavānīpati*', literally meaning 'the husband of Bhava's wife' ('*bhavānī*' meaning the 'wife of Bhava' another name for Shiva,) has the repugnant signification that the Goddess had a husband other than Shiva, the God spoken of.

Another example—

'*Gorapi.....................ambikāramaṇaḥ*'

'May Ambikā's husband protect you,—he near whom even Gaurī's lion becomes freed from all ill-feeling towards the bull that is used as a conveyance by that God.'

Here the word '*ambikāramaṇaḥ*' has a repugnant signification (its literal meaning 'one who enjoys the company of '*Ambikā*', *Mother*).

[Having dealt with the defects found in compounds only, the author proceeds to deal with the other defects described before, the 'disagreeable to the ear' and the rest which are held to occur in single words as also in compounds.]

But he gives an example of only one of them, the 'disagreeable to the ear,' as occurring in a compound—

सा दूरे च सुधासान्द्रतरङ्गितविलोचना ।
बर्हिनिर्ह्रादनार्होयं कालश्च समुपागतः ॥१६९॥

एवमन्यदपि ज्ञेयम् ॥

अपास्य च्युतसंस्कारमसमर्थं निरर्थकम् ।
वाक्येपि दोषाः सन्त्येते पदस्यांशेपि केचन ॥ ५२ ॥

केचन न पुनः सर्वे । क्रमेणोदाहरणम्

सोध्यैष्ट वेदांस्त्रिदशानयष्ट पितॄनताप्सींत्समममंस्त बन्धून् ।
व्यजेष्ट षड्वर्गमरंस्त नीतौ समूलघातं न्यवधीदरींश्च ॥१७०॥

'*Sā dūre..............................*
Barhinirhrādanārhoyaṁ......gataḥ'

'Far away is she of the lovely and graceful glances, and here has arrived the season resounding with the cry of the peacocks !'

[Here the compound in the second line is harsh-sounding].

The other defects (as occurring in compounds) may be similarly exemplified. 51.

Excepting (*a*) '*lack of correctness*', (*b*) '*incapability of giving sense*' *and* (*c*) '*uselessness*'—*these* (*aforesaid*) *defects occur in a sentence also; and some of them in parts of words as well.* 52.

'*Some of them*',—not all.

The following are the examples in due order—

(1) [The *sentence* 'disagreeable to the ear']—

'*Sodhyaiṣṭa vedāṁstridashānayaṣṭa*
'*Pitṝnatārpsīt samamaṁsta bandhūn*
'*Vyajeṣṭa ṣaḍvargamaraṁsta nītau*
'*Samūlaghātaṁ nyavadhīdarīṁshcha*'.

'He studied the Vedas, offered sacrifices to the Gods and oblations to the Pitṛs, honoured his friends, subjugated the 'sixfold group' (of Desire, Anger, Avarice, Delu-

स रातु वो दुश्च्यवनो भावुकानां परंपराम् ।
अनेडमूकताद्यैश्च द्यतु दोषैरसंमतान् ॥१७१॥

अत्र दुश्च्यवन इन्द्रः अनेडमूको मूकबधिरः ॥

सायकसहायबाहोर्मकरध्वजनियमितक्षमाधिपतेः ।
अब्जरुचिभास्वरस्ते भातितरामवनिप श्लोकः ॥१७२॥

---

sion, Pride and Envy), took delight in statesmanship, and rooted out his enemies'.

[Though in most cases cited as exemplifying the defects as *occurring in a sentence* the defects are actually found to lie in *words* only,—as here the *harshness* lies in the words '*adhyaiṣṭa*', '*ayaṣṭa*' and so forth,—yet the distinction is justified on the ground that where the defect lies in a *single* word in the sentence, it is regarded as occurring *in the word*, while where it occurs in more than one word, it is taken as occurring *in the sentence*.]

(2) [The 'unconventional']—
'*Sa rātu vo dushchyavano bhāvukānāṁ paraṁparām*
'*Aneḍamūkatādyaishcha dyatu doṣairasaṁmatān*'.

'May Indra bring you a continuity of prosperity! May he strike your enemies with deafness, dumbness and other disabilities !'

Here the word '*dushchyavana*' for *Indra*, and '*aneḍa-mūka*' for 'deaf and dumb', are such as are *not used*, are 'unconventional.'

(3) [The 'suppressed meaning']—
'*Sāyakasahāyabāhormakaradhvajaniyamitakṣamādhipateḥ*
'*Abjaruchibhāsvaraste bhātitarāmavanipa shlokaḥ*'

'You, O King, who are the master of the Ocean-bounded Earth, and have the sword for your companion, have your fame shining resplendent like the moon'.

Here the words '*sāyaka*', '*makaradhvaja*', '*kṣamā*', '*abja*' and '*shloka*' have been used in the sense, respec-

अत्र सायकादयः शब्दाः खड्गाब्धिभूचन्द्रयशःपर्यायाः शराद्यर्थतया प्रसिद्धाः ॥

कुविन्दस्त्वं तावत्पटयसि गुणग्राममभितो
यशो गायन्त्येते दिशि दिशि च नग्नास्तव विभो ।
शरज्ज्योत्स्नागौरस्फुटविकटसर्वाङ्गसुभगा
तथापि त्वत्कीर्तिर्भ्रमति विगताच्छादनमिह ॥१७३॥

अत्र कुविन्दादिशब्दोऽर्थान्तरं प्रतिपादयन्नुपश्लोक्यमानस्य तिरस्कारं व्यनक्तीत्यनुचितार्थः ।

---

tively, of *sword*, *ocean*, *earth*, *moon*, and *fame*,—while they are better known as having the sense of *arrow*, *love-god*, *forgiveness*, *lotus* and *verse*, *respectively* [and hence the desired signification of all these words is 'suppressed'].

(4) ['Improper signification']

Kuvindastvaṁ tāvat paṭayasi guṇagrāmamabhito
Yasho gāyantyete dishi dishi cha nagnāstava vibho
Sharajjyotsnāgaurasphuṭavikaṭasarvāṅgasubhagā
Tathāpi tvatkīrtirbhramati vigatāchchhādanamiha'.

'As Lord of the Earth, you are spreading on all sides hosts of good qualities ; these bards are singing your fame on all sides ; and yet thy renown, beautiful and resplendent as the autumnal moon, wanders about unfurled.'

Here there is an 'improper signification,' inasmuch as some of the words—*e. g.* '*kuvinda*' ['*paṭayasi*', '*nagna*', '*yasha*'] have a second meaning which indicates disrespect towards the person described.

['*Kuvinda*' means a *weaver*, '*guṇam paṭayasi*' means '*weave yarn*, '*nagna*' means *naked*, '*yashaḥ* is capable of being read or construed as '*ayaśaḥ*,' so that the person addressed comes to be described as a weaver weaving cloth and so forth.]

प्राभ्रभ्राड्विष्णुधामाप्य विषमाश्वः करोत्ययम् ।
निद्रां सहस्रपर्णानां पलायनपरायणाम् ॥१७४॥

अत्र प्राभ्रभ्राड्विष्णुधामविषमाश्वनिद्रापर्णशब्दाः प्रकृष्टजलद-गगनसप्ताश्वसंकोचदलानामवाचकाः ॥

भूपतेरुपसर्पन्ती कम्पना वामलोचना ।
तत्तत्प्रहरणोत्साहवती मोहनमादधौ ॥१७५॥

अत्रोपसर्पणप्रहरणमोहनशब्दा व्रीडादायित्वादश्लीलाः ।

तेन्यैर्वान्तं समश्नन्ति परोत्सर्गं च भुञ्जते ।
इतरार्थग्रहे येषां कवीनां स्यात्प्रवर्तनम् ॥१७६॥

---

(5) [The 'Inexpressive']—

'*Prābhrabhrāḍ viṣṇudhamāpya viṣamāshvaḥ karotyayam*
Nidrāṁ sahasraparṇānāṁ palāyanaparāyaṇām.

'Having reached the beautifully clouded sky, the sun puts to flight the sleep of the lotuses.'

Here the words '*prābhrabhrāṭ*,' *viṣṇudhāma*,' '*viṣamāshva*', '*nidrā*' and '*parṇa*' have been used in the sense, respectively, of 'beautiful cloud', 'sky' 'sun', 'closing' and 'petal',—while, as a matter of fact they do not express or denote these things.

(6) [Indecorous—shameful]—

'*Bhūpaterupasarpantī kampanā vāmalochanā*
Tattatpraharaṇotsāhavatī mohanamādadhau'.

'The angry army of the king brought about the stupefaction (of the enemy) by marching and energetically striking'.

Here the words '*upasarpantī*', '*praharaṇa*' and '*mohana*' give rise to feelings of shame by reason of their second meanings (women in love, embraces and passionate love, respectively), and are 'therefore' 'indecorous'.

[Indecorous—Disgusting]—

Tenyairvāntam samashnanti···parotsargaṁcha bhuñjate.

अत्र वान्तोत्सर्गप्रवर्तनशब्दा जुगुप्सादायिनः ।

पितृवसतिमहं व्रजामि तां सह परिवारजनेन यत्र मे ।
भवति सपदि पावकान्वये हृदयमशेषितशोकशल्यकम्॥१७७॥

अत्र पितृगृहमित्यादौ विवक्षिते श्मशानादिप्रतीतावमङ्गलार्थत्वम् ।

सुरालयोल्लासपरः प्राप्तपर्याप्तकम्पनः ।
मार्गणप्रवणो भास्वद्भूतिरेष विलोक्यताम् ॥१७८॥

'Those who are prone to making use of the ideas of other poets eat out of other people's vomitings and sluttings.'

Here the words 'vomiting', 'slutting' and 'excreting' (which is another meaning of *pravartana*) are productive of *disgust.*

[Indecorous—Inauspicious]—

'*Pitṛvasatimahaṁ vrajāmi tāṁ saha parivārajanena yatra me*
'*Bhavati sapadi pāvakānvaye hṛdayamashesitashokashalyakam*'.

'With all my family I shall repair to my father's house, where in the purifying family, my heart shall have all its darts of grief removed.'

Here the words '*pitṛvasati*' (and '*pāvaka*') intended to convey the meaning of 'father's house' (and 'purifying'), signify also the *crematorium* (and *fire*), and are for that reason 'inauspicious.'

(7) [The 'Ambiguous']—

'*Surālayollāsaparaḥ prāptaparyāptakampanaḥ*
Mārgaṇapravaṇo bhāsvadbhūtireṣa vilokyatām.'

It is doubtful whether (*a*) the words '*surālaya*', '*kampana*', '*mārgaṇa*' and '*bhūti*' are meant to signify 'abode of the gods', 'army', 'arrow' and 'glory' [in which case the passage would mean—'Look at this king, who is bent upon Heaven, is equipped with sufficient

अत्र किं सुरादिशब्दा देवसेनाशरविभूत्यर्थाः किं मदिराद्यर्थाः इति संदेहः ॥

तस्याधिमात्रोपायस्य तीव्रसंवेगताजुषः ।
दृढभूमिः प्रियप्राप्तौ यत्नः स फलितः सखे ॥१७९॥

अत्राधिमात्रोपायादयः शब्दा योगशास्त्रमात्रप्रयुक्तत्वादप्रतीताः ॥

ताम्बूलभृतगल्लोयं भल्लं जल्पति मानुषः ।
करोति खादनं पादं सदैव तु यथा तथा ॥१८०॥

---

army, clever in the use of arrows and of resplendent glory'], or (*b*) 'wine-shop', 'trembling', 'begging' and 'destruction' [in which case the meaning would be—'Look at this man, ever bent upon wine-shops, constantly trembling, efficient in begging and with destruction facing him'].

(8) [The 'Unintelligible']—

'*Tasyādhimātropāyasya*
Tīvrasaṁvegatājuṣaḥ
Dṛḍhabhūmiḥ prīyaprāptau
Yatnaḥ sa phalitaḥ sakhe'.

'The powerful efforts of the man have succeeded in helping him to attain what he desired,—he having employed the methods (of self-control and the rest) conducive to true wisdom, and practising intense renunciation'.

Here the words '*adhimātra*' ('*tīvrasaṁvega*' and '*dṛḍhabhūmi*') are used in their technical sense found in Yoga literature only, and as such they are not intelligible'.

(9) ['The Vulgar']—

'*Tāmbūlabhṛtagalloyaṁ bhallaṁ jalpati mānuṣaḥ*'
'*Karoti khādanaṁ pānaṁ sadaiva tu yathā tathā*'.

'Having his cheeks filled with betel-leaves, and eating and drinking always, he goes on talking rapidly'.

अत्र गल्लादयः शब्दाः ग्राम्याः ॥

वस्त्रवैदूर्यचरणैः क्षतसत्त्वरजःपरा ।
निष्कम्पा रचिता नेत्रयुद्धं वेदय सांप्रतम् ॥१८१॥

अत्राम्बररत्नपादैः क्षततमा अचला भूः कृता नेत्रद्वन्द्वं बोधयेति नेयार्थता ॥

The words '*galla*' (and '*bhalla*') are 'vulgar'.

(10) ['Whose meaning is to be guessed']

'*Vastravaidūryacharaṇaiḥ*
Kṣatasattvarajaḥparāḥ
Niṣkampā rachitā netra—
Yuddhaṁ vedaya sāmpratam'.

'This *unshaking thing* (*i. e.* the earth) has its *third besides Harmony and Energy* (*i. e.* Darkness) dispelled by the *feet* (*i. e.* rays) of the *emerald* (*i. e.* gem) of the *vastra* (*i. e.* '*ambara*', *viz* : sky) [*i. e.* the sun]; so open now the *battle* (*i. e.* pair) of your eyes'.

The meaning intended to be conveyed here is that 'the sun having dispelled darkness from the earth, the eyes should be opened'; and this can only be guessed out of the words used.

[(*a*) '*Vastra*' has another synonym in '*ambara*', which means the *sky*,—'*vaidūrya*' denotes the emerald, which is one kind of *gem*,—'*charaṇa*' is synonymous with '*pada*', which also means 'rays',—hence the compound '*vastravaidūryacharaṇa*' the rays of the gem of the sky *i.e.* the sun;—'*Sattva*', *Rajas* and *Tamas* are the three cosmic attributes,—so that the third besides Rajas and Sattva is Tamas, which denotes *darkness*,—so that the compound '*kṣatasattvarajaḥparāḥ*' means 'whose darkness has been dispelled;'—'*niṣkampā*' meaning *unshaking*, is used for the immovable Earth;—'*yuddha*' is synonymous with '*dvandva*', which also means 'pair',—hence the compound '*netrayuddham*' means 'pair of eyes'.]

धम्मिल्लस्य न कस्य प्रेक्ष्य निकामं कुरङ्गशावाक्ष्याः ।
रज्यत्यपूर्वबन्धव्युत्पत्तेर्मानसं शोभाम् ॥१८२॥

अत्र धम्मिल्लस्य शोभां प्रेक्ष्य कस्य मानसं न रज्यतीति संबन्धे क्लिष्टत्वम् ॥

न्यक्कारो ह्ययमेव मे यदरयस्तत्राप्यसौ तापसः
सोप्यत्रैव निहन्ति राक्षसकुलं जीवत्यहो रावणः ।
धिग्धिक् शक्रजितं प्रबोधितवता किं कुम्भकर्णेन वा
स्वर्गग्रामटिकाविलुण्ठनवृथोच्छूनैः किमेभिर्भुजैः ॥१८३॥

---

(11) [The 'obscure'.]—

'*Dhammillasya na kasya preksya nikāmaṁ kuraṅgashāvakṣyāḥ*
Rajyatyapūrvabandhavyutpattermānasam shobhām'.

'Whose heart does not become enamoured on seeing the loveliness of the beautifully-braided locks of the fawn-eyed one ?'

The syntactical connection intended here—

'*Dhammillasya shobhāṁ preksya kasya mānasaṁ na rajyati*',—is difficult to get at, 'obscure [by reason of the order in which the words are placed].

(12) ['The predicative factor not discriminated']—
'*Nyakkārohyayameva me yadarayastatrāpyasau tāpasaḥ*

....

Svargagrāmaṭikāviluṇṭhanavṛthochchhūnaīḥ kimebhirbhujaiḥ'.

'It is a disgrace that I have enemies ; and even that an ascetic, who is slaughtering the host of demons ; and that at this very place ; and yet Rāvaṇa is living ; woe, woe, to Meghanāda ! What has come out of Kumbhakarṇa having been awakened. What too has been the use of these my arms that have become uselessly fattened by plundering the tiny hamlet of heaven ?'

अत्र 'अयमेव न्यक्कारः' इति वाच्यम् । उच्छूनत्वमात्रं चानुवाद्यम्, न वृथात्वविशेषितम् । अत्र च शब्दरचना विपरीता कृतेति वाक्यस्यैव दोषो न वाक्यार्थस्य ।

यथा वा

अपाङ्गसंसर्गि तरङ्गितं दृशोर्भ्रुवोररालान्तविलासि वेल्लितम् ।
विसारि रोमाञ्चनकञ्चुकं तनोस्तनोति यो सौ सुभगे तवागतः।।
॥१८४॥

What is intended is that 'that I have enemies is itself a disgrace', and the proper order of words would be '*ayameva nyakkārah*'; and secondly, what should have been merely referred to, is the mere *fattening* of the arms, for the purpose of predicating its *uselessness*, which should not have been made a mere qualifying adjunct in the compound.

[The meaning intended is that the fattening of my arms has been *of no use*; *being of no use*, therefore, being the predicated factor, should have stood by itself, while it has been made a subordinate adjunct by being placed in the middle of a compound.]

Inasmuch as the fault here lies in the order of the words being reversed, the defect is attributed to the *sentence*, not to the *meaning* of the sentence.

Another example (of 'non-discrimination of the predicative factor')—

'*Apāṅgasaṁsargi taraṅgitaṁ dṛshorbhruvorarālāntavilāsi-vellitam*
Visāri romāñchanakañchukaṁ tanostanoti yosau subhage tavāgataḥ'

'Here has come—*one who* brings a tremor to your eyes, an elegant curvature to your eye-brows and a bodice of thrilling hairs to your body'.

अत्र योसाविति पदद्वयमनुवाद्यमात्रप्रतीतिकृत् ।

तथाहि—प्रक्रान्तप्रसिद्धानुभूतार्थविषयस्तच्छब्दो यच्छब्दोपादानं नापेक्षते ।

क्रमेणोदाहरणम् ।

कातर्यं केवला नीतिः शौर्यं श्वापदचेष्टितम् ।
अतः सिद्धिं समेताभ्यामुभाभ्यामन्वियेष सः ॥१८५॥

द्वयं गतं संप्रति शोचनीयतां समागमप्रार्थनया कपालिनः ।
कला च सा कान्तिमती कलावतस्त्वमस्य लोकस्य च नेत्रकौमुदी ॥१८६॥

Here the two pronouns '*yaḥ* and *asau*' only serve to point out the person as merely *referred* to [and the *predicative* pronoun '*he*', '*saḥ*', is wanting].

It is the pronoun '*tat*', 'that', which, standing as it does for (*a*) what has been spoken of before, or (*b*) what is well-known, or (*c*) what has been already seen or heard of, does not require the corresponding pronoun '*yat*', 'which' or 'what'; as for example—

(*a*) '*Kātaryaṁ*..................*saḥ*'.—'Regarding pure statesmanship as a weakness, and sheer valour to be beast-like, *he* always sought to attain success by both these means';—[Here the pronoun '*saḥ*', 'he', stands for the king spoken of before, and hence the corresponding 'who' is not required];—

(*b*) '*Dvayaṁ*......*kalā cha sā*......*kaumudī*—'By seeking to be associated with the God of the Begging Bowl, two things have become objects of concern—*that* resplendent digit of the moon and thyself, who art like moonlight to the eyes of this world;'—[Here the pronoun '*sā*' referring to the well-known digit of the moon on Śiva's forehead, does not require the corresponding '*yā*'];—

उत्कम्पिनी भयपरिस्खलितांशुकान्ता
ते लोचने प्रतिदिशं विधुरे क्षिपन्ती ।
क्रूरेण दारुणतया सहसैव दग्धा
धूमान्धितेन दहनेन न वीक्षितासि ॥१८७॥

यच्छब्दस्तूत्तरवाक्यानुगतत्वेनोपात्तः सामर्थ्यात्पूर्ववाक्यानुगतस्य तच्छब्दस्योपादानं नापेक्षते । यथा

साधु चन्द्रमसि पुष्करैः कृतं मीलितं यदभिरामताधिके ।
उद्यता जयिनि कामिनीमुखे तेन साहसमनुष्ठितं पुनः ॥१८८॥

प्रागुपात्तस्तु यच्छब्दस्तच्छब्दोपादानं विना साकाङ्क्षः ।

(c) '*Utkampinī......te lochane........vīkṣitāsi*';—'Trembling and having the clothing gliding off through fear, and casting *those* timid glances all round, thou wert burnt by the cruel fire blinded by smoke, and wert no longer seen';—[Here the pronoun '*te*', 'those', standing for the glances that the speaker has seen before, does not stand in need of the corresponding '*ye*'].

The pronoun '*yat*', (*who* or *which*) also, when occurring in the latter of two correlated clauses, does not require the corresponding '*tat*' in the preceding clause, because by reason of its inherent power (it always implies a preceding '*tat*'); as we find in the following example—'*Sādhu...yadabhirāmatādhike...punaḥ*;'—'On the rising of the lovelier moon the lotuses did well that they closed themselves; but this moon has behaved most arrogantly when he has risen even on the appearance of the face of the lovely woman, which is far superior to her'. [Here '*yat mīlitam*' implies the corresponding '*tat sādhu kṛtam*', and hence the actual presence of this latter pronoun is not necessary in the preceding clause].

But in cases when the pronoun '*yat*' occurs in the

यथा अत्रैव श्लोके आद्यपादयोर्व्यत्यासे । द्वयोरुपादाने तु निराकाङ्क्षत्वं प्रसिद्धम् । अनुपादानेपि सामर्थ्यात्कुत्रचिद्द्वयमपि गम्यते । यथा

ये नाम केचिदिह नः प्रथयन्त्यवज्ञां
जानन्ति ते किमपि तान् प्रति नैष यत्नः ।
उत्पत्स्यतेस्ति मम कोपि समानधर्मा
कालो ह्ययं निरवधिर्विपुला च पृथ्वी ॥१८९॥

---

preceding clause, it is always deficient (wanting in essentials), if the corresponding '*tat*' is not actually present; as for example in the verse just quoted, if we reverse the order of the two clauses [reading '*mīlitaṁ yadabhirāmatādhike sādhu chandramasi puṣkaraiḥ kṛtam*'] we find that it gives no sense.

(*a*) In cases where both the pronouns are used, of course, there is nothing wanting, as every one knows; and (*b*) in certain cases, even when neither is present, *both* are implied by the force of the sentence. *e. g.*

(*a*) '*Ye nāma kechidiha naḥ prathayantyavajñāṁ*
Jānanti te kimapi tān prati naiṣa yatnaḥ;
(*b*) *Utpatsyatesti mama kopi samānadharmā*
Kālo hyayaṁ niravadhirvipulā cha pṛthvī'.

'*Who* would deride me in this attempt, know something perhaps,—for *them* this effort of mine is not intended; some one possessed of qualities similar to mine may yet be born,—or he may even be living now,—time is interminable and the earth immense'.

Here in the second half both '*yat*' and '*tat*' are understood, the meaning intended being 'the person *who* will be born, for *him* is this mark of mine meant'.

अत्र य उत्पत्स्यते तं प्रतीति ।

एवं च तच्छब्दानुपादानेत्र साकाङ्क्षत्वम् । न चासाविति तच्छब्दार्थमाह ।

असौ मरुच्चुम्बितचारुकेसरः प्रसन्नताराधिपमण्डलाग्रणीः ।
वियुक्तरामातुरदृष्टिवीक्षितो वसन्तकालो हनुमानिवागतः॥१९०॥

अत्र हि न तच्छब्दार्थप्रतीतिः ।

[The first half of the verse is an example of this correct use of both '*yat*' and '*tat*' and the second half that of the correct suppression of both.]

[Having thus discussed the correct use of the relative pronouns '*yat*' and '*tat*', the author takes up the thread of his remarks on the verse '*apāṅgasaṁsargi*' &*c*.', see above]. Thus in the above-mentioned verse, the absence of the pronoun '*tat*' causes a deficiency, and leaves something wanting to complete the sentence.—It cannot be said that the pronoun '*asau*' has the same sense at '*tat*'; because in such sentences as the following we do not find the word '*asau*' conveying the sense of '*tat*'—

'*Asau maruchchumbita ......āgataḥ*'

'Like Hanumān, (*a*) having his beautiful locks kissed by the Wind-god (his father), (*b*) the leader of the army of the Lord of Tārā (Sugrīva), and (*c*) eagerly looked up to by Rāma, separated from his wife,—has this springtime season arrived, (*a*) having its flower-pollen wafted by the breeze, (*b*) beautified by the bright moon, and (*c*) eagerly looked upon by women separated from their lovers.'

In fact if the pronoun '*asau*' conveyed the same sense as '*tat*', then the use of the pronoun '*sa*' (the masculine

प्रतीतौ वा

करवालकरालदोः सहायो युधि योसौ विजयार्जुनैकमल्लः ।
यदि भूपतिना स तत्र कार्ये विनियुज्येत ततः कृतं कृतं स्यात् ॥१९१॥

अत्र स इत्यस्यानर्थक्यं स्यात् ।

अथ

योविकल्पमिदमर्थमण्डलं पश्यतीश निखिलं भवद्वपुः ।
आत्मपक्षपरिपूरिते जगत्यस्य नित्यसुखिनः कुतो भयम् ॥१९२॥

---

nominative form of '*tat*') in the following example would be entirely superfluous :—

'*Karabāla......yosau......*

'*Yadi.........sa tatra......syāt*'

'If this person, who is the only equal of Arjuna, attended by his sword, were employed by the King in this work, then would it be perfectly accomplished'.

It might be argued that the pronoun '*asau*' in the passage in question may be taken in the sense of '*tat*' (even though it may not be quite synonymous with it) ; just as we find, in the following passage the pronoun '*asya*' (the genitive form of '*idam*') used in the sense of '*tat*' ('that', though its ordinary meaning is 'this')—'*yovikalpa............asya.........bhayam*'—'For one who perceives, without any doubt, your body in all this world, where is there any fear in this universe, filled as it is with his own self ?'

Our answer to this is that if in the passage in question the pronoun '*asau*' were really intended to convey the sense of '*tat*', (as '*idam*' is in the passage just quoted), then it would have been used in a clause other than the one in which the pronoun '*yat*' ('*yaḥ*') occurs,—as in the passage just quoted, '*asya*' occurs in a separate clause,—

इतीदंशब्दवददःशब्दस्तच्छब्दार्थमभिधत्ते इति उच्यते। तर्ह्यत्रैव वाक्यान्तरे उपादानमर्हति न तत्रैव। यच्छब्दस्य हि निकटे स्थितः प्रसिद्धि परामृशति। यथा

यत्तदूर्जितमत्युग्रं क्षात्रं तेजोस्य भूपतेः।
दीव्यताक्षैस्तदानेन नूनं तदपि हारितम् ॥१९३॥

इत्यत्र तच्छब्दः।

ननु कथम्

कल्याणानां त्वमसि महसां भाजनं विश्वमूर्ते
धुर्यां लक्ष्मीमथ मयि भृशं धेहि देव प्रसीद।
यद्यत्पापं प्रतिजहि जगन्नाथ नम्रस्य तन्मे
भद्रं भद्रं वितर भगवन् भूयसे मङ्गलाय ॥१९४॥

---

and not in the same clause (as it does in the passage in question, where we have the two pronouns appearing in juxtaposition, '*yosau*'). In fact when pronouns like '*tat*' and '*adas*', appear in close juxtaposition to '*yat*', they signify the *well-known* character of the thing spoken of [and they are not used predicatively];—*e. g.* in the passage—'*yattadūrjita.........hāritam*'—'Even that well-known virile and glorious warlike spirit of the king was lost in the gambling,'—where the pronoun '*tat*' signifies the *well-known* character of the 'spirit.'

It might be argued that, if such be the rule (that the pronoun '*yat*' in one clause must be followed by a corresponding '*tat*' in a subsequent clause), then how is it that in the following passage, though the preceding clause contains the pronoun '*yat*' repeated twice—'*yat-yat*'—the corresponding '*tat*' occurs only once in the subsequent clause—'*Kalyāṇām......yadyat pāpaṁ......tanme...... maṅgalāya*'—'Oh Thou of form universal! Thou art

अत्र यद्यदित्युक्त्वा तन्मे इत्युक्तम् । उच्यते——यद्यदिति येन केनचिद्रूपेण स्थितं सर्वात्मकं वस्त्वाक्षिप्तं तथाभूतमेव तच्छब्देन परामृश्यते ।

यथा वा

किं लोभेन विलङ्घितः स भरतो येनतदेवं कृतं
मात्रा स्त्रीलघुतां गता किमथ वा मातैव मे मध्यमा ।
मिथ्यैतन्मम चिन्तितं द्वितयमप्यार्यानुजोसौ गुरु-
र्माता तातकलत्रमित्यनुचितं मन्ये विधात्रा कृतम् ॥१९५॥

---

the receptacle of the most auspicious effulgence ! Be pleased to ordain for me the highest prosperity ! O Lord of the world ! destroy whatever sin there is in me,—I bow down to thee ! O Blessed Lord ! bestow upon me for my welfare, everything that is good !'

Our answer to this is that '*yad—yat*' stands for anything and everything that exists, that is the entire world regarded as a single entity, and it is this single entity that is referred to in the subsequent clause by the pronoun '*tat*' [so that there is perfect co-ordination].

[Finding that the example of the defect cited by him above has given rise to difficulties, the author cites another example of the defect, whereby the *predicative factor is not discriminated.*]

Kiṁ lobhena...āryānujosau......tātakalatraṁ...kṛtam'.

'Was Bharata beset with greed that he got this done through his mother ? Or , did my second mother herself succumb to the meanness common among women ?—Both these ideas of mine are wrong ; as he (Bharata) is the younger brother of my noble brother, and she, my revered mother, is my father's wife. So I think that this improper deed is the work of Providence itself.'

Here stress is meant to be laid upon the terms '*ārya*' and '*tāta*' [the idea being that '*it is of my noble brother*

अत्रार्यस्येति तातस्येति च वाच्यम् । न त्वनयोः समासे गुणीभावः कार्यः । एवं समासान्तरेप्युदाहार्यम् ॥
विरुद्धमतिकृद्यथा

श्रितक्षमा रक्तभुवः शिवालिङ्गितमूर्तयः ।
विग्रहक्षपणेनाद्य शेरते ते गतासुखाः ॥१९६॥

अत्र क्षमादिगुणयुक्ताः सुखमासते इति विवक्षिते हता इति विरुद्धा प्रतीतिः ॥

Rāma, that Bharata is the younger brother ;' and '*it is of my father* that Kaikeyī is the wife,' and 'it is not possible for a brother of Rāma or for the wife of my father to do anything wrong'], [and hence these two being the predicative factors] the proper expressions should have been '*āryasyānujosau*' '*tātasya kalatram*'; and it was not right to make both these the subordinate factors of compounds.

Similar examples may be cited of this defect occurring in other compounds.

(13) The following is an example of 'repugnant implication.'—

'*Shritakṣamā raktabhuvaḥ*
'*Śhivāliṅgitamūrtayaḥ*
'*Vigrahakṣapaṇenādya*
'*Sherate te gatāsukhāḥ*'

'They, having recourse to forgiveness, with the world attached to them, and their bodies embraced by all that is good, lie down, with all their troubles gone through the removal of all quarrels.'

Here the meaning intended is that 'persons of forgiving nature remain happy' (as translated above), but the words chosen have another signification, which is entirely repugnant to this ['Lying down on the ground (*shṛtakṣamāḥ*),

पदैकदेशे यथासंभवं क्रमेणोदाहरणम्

अलमतिचपलत्वात्स्वप्नमायोपमत्वात्
परिणतिविरसत्वात्संगमेनाङ्गनायाः ।
इति यदि शतकृत्वस्तत्त्वमालोचयाम-
स्तदपि न हरिणाक्षीं विस्मरत्यन्तरात्मा ॥१९७॥

अत्र त्वादिति । यथा वा

तद्गच्छ सिद्ध्यै कुरु देवकार्यमर्थोयमर्थान्तिरलभ्य एव ।
अपेक्षते प्रत्ययमङ्गलब्ध्यै बीजाङ्कुरः प्रागुदयादिवाम्भः ॥१९८॥

---

having reddened the earth with their blood (*raktabhuvaḥ*), their bodies tossed about by jackals (*shivāliṅgitamūrtayaḥ*), they lie down with their life and organs all gone (*gatāsukhāḥ*), through the destruction of their body (*vigrahakṣapaṇena*)'.]

The text has said that 'some of those defects occur in parts of words also ;' the following are the examples—

(1) [The 'Disagreeable to the ear']

'*Alamatichapalatvāt*
Svapnamāyopamatvāt
Pariṇativirasatvāt
..............*ātmā*'

"Have done with this association with women, which is extremely fickle, resembling dreamy illusion, and leads to unpleasant consequences ;"—even though this truth I ponder over hundreds of times, yet my inner soul forgets not the fawn-eyed one'.

Here the repetition of the syllable '*tvāt*' is 'unpleasant to the ear'.

Another example of the same—

'*Tad gachchha siddhyai*.........*labdhyai*.........*vāmbhaḥ*'.

'Thus you go forward to success, do the work of the gods ; this end in view, which can be attained only

अत्र द्ध्यै ब्ध्यै, इति कटु ॥
यश्चाप्सरोविभ्रममण्डनानां संपादयित्रीं शिखरैर्बिभर्ति ।
बलाहकच्छेदविभक्तरागामकालसंध्यामिव धातुमत्ताम् ॥१९९॥
अत्र मत्ताशब्दः क्षीबार्थे निहतार्थः ॥
आदावञ्जनपुञ्जलिप्तवपुषां श्वासानिल्लोल्लासित-
प्रोत्सर्पद्विरहानलेन च ततः संतापितानां दृशाम् ।
संप्रत्येव निषेकमश्रुपयसा देवस्य चेतोभुवो
भल्लीनामिव पानकर्म कुरुते कामं कुरङ्गेक्षणा ॥२००॥

---

through something else, stands in need of an operative agent, just as the sprouting of the seed, before it appears, needs water'.

Here the repetition of '*ddhyai*' and *bdhai* is 'unpleasant to the ear'.

(2) [The 'suppressed meaning']—

'*Yashchāpsaro..............dhātumattām*'.

'Who bears on his (snowy) summits a supply of (red) minerals which help in making up the coquettish toilet of celestial women,—as if it were the red hue of the suddenly falling evening, interspersed with pieces of (white clouds)'.

The term '*mattā*' (which forms part of the word '*dhātumattā*') is better known in the sense of 'intoxicated,' (which suppresses the sense of the possessive, which is intended).

(3) ['The useless'.]—

Ādāvañjana..............dṛshāṁ :

...........*kurute kāmaṁ kuraṅgekṣaṇā*'

'Her eyes having been painted with collyrium, and then heated by the fire of the pangs of separation formed by the hot sighs, the fawn-eyed one is now sprinkling her tears, and thereby is doing, as it were,the sharpening of the arrows of the Love-god'.

अत्र दृशामिति बहुवचनं निरर्थकम् कुरङ्गेक्षणाया एकस्या एवोपादानात् । न चालसवलितैरित्यादिवत् व्यापारभेदाद्-बहुत्वम् व्यापाराणामनुपात्तत्वात् । न च व्यापारेत्र दृक्शब्दो वर्तते । अत्रैव 'कुरुते' इत्यात्मनेपदमप्यनर्थकम् । प्रधानक्रिया-फलस्य कर्त्रसंबन्धे कर्त्रभिप्रायक्रियाफलाभावात् ॥

चापाचार्यस्त्रिपुरविजयी कार्तिकेयो विजेयः
शस्त्रव्यस्तः सदनमुदधिर्भूरियं हन्तकारः ।

[In sharpening a weapon, the mechanic smears it with acid and ashes, then heats it and then sprinkles water over it ;—the eyes being the love-god's arrows these arrows are sharpened in the manner described.]

Here the plural number in '*dṛshām*' is 'useless' or meaningless, as only one 'fawn-eyed girl' is spoken of. It is true that in certain cases,—*e. g.*, in the verse '*alasavalitaiḥ etc.*,'—the plural number is used in view of the multiplicity or manifoldness of functions ; but in the present instance it cannot be due to any such manifoldness ; as no such manifold functions are mentioned ; nor does the term '*dṛk*' ('eye') denote any *functions*.

Then again, in this same verse the *Ātmanepada* ending in '*kurute*' is also 'useless', because the effect of the action connoted does not belong to the subject ('woman'), and hence the condition necessary for the use of the *Ātmanepada* ending—that the result of the action should pertain to the subject—is not fulfilled.

(4) [The 'Inexpressive']

'*Chāpāchāryas.... [illegible]*

......................chandrahāsaḥ.'

'Your preceptor in archery is the victor of the three cities (Śhiva), Kārtikeya is your subduable, the ocean,

अस्त्येवैतत् किमु कृतवता रेणुकाकण्ठबाधां
बद्धस्पर्धस्तव परशुना लज्जते चन्द्रहासः ॥२०१॥

अत्र विजेय इति कृत्यप्रत्ययः क्तप्रत्ययार्थेवाचकः ॥

अतिपेलवमतिपरिमितवर्णं लघुतरमुदाहरति शठः ।
परमार्थतः स हृदयं वहति पुनः कालकूटघटितमिव ॥२०२॥

अत्र पेलवशब्दः ॥

यः पूयते सुरसरिन्मुखतीर्थसार्थ-
स्नानेन शास्त्रपरिशीलनकीलनेन ।
सौजन्यमान्यजनिरूर्जितमूर्जितानां
सोयं दृशोः पतति कस्यचिदेव पुंसः ॥२०३॥

---

forced back by your weapons, is your abode, and the earth is for you an object to be given away ; though all this is so, yet my sword *Chandrahāsa* is ashamed at being pitted against your axe which cut off Reṇukā's head !'

The verbal potential affix ('*yat*') in '*vijeya*' has been used in the sense of the past participle affix '*kta*', which sense it can never have.

[What is meant is that Kartikeya has been *subdued* by you, while the word used is '*vijeya*' which means 'subduable'.]

(5) [The 'Indecorous']—

(*a*) '*Atipelava.........ghaṭitamiva*'

'A rogue always speaks very little, and that softly and gently; in reality 'however' he has his heart full of poison.'

Here the term '*pelava*' is 'indecorous' (being the name in the Lāṭa language of a secret part of the human body).

(*b*) '*Yaḥ pūyate.........puṁsaḥ*'

'Rare is the person before whose eyes comes a great man like this, who is sanctified by bathing in the Gaṅgā apu other sacred places, and also by the consolidation of

अत्र पूयशब्दः ॥

विनयप्रणयैककेतनं सततं योभवदङ्ग तादृशः ।
कथमद्य स तद्वदीक्ष्यतां तदभिप्रेतपदं समागतः ॥२०४॥

अथ प्रेतशब्दः ॥

कस्मिन् कर्मणि सामर्थ्यमस्य नोत्तपतेतराम् ।
अयं साधुचरस्तस्मादञ्जलिर्बध्यतामिह ॥२०५॥

अत्र किं पूर्वं साधुः उत साधुषु चरतीति संदेहः ॥

---

this knowledge of the scriptures,—of noble and respectable birth, the personified spirit of all that is spirited.'

The term '*pūyā*' is 'indecorous' (as it denotes *pus*).

(*c*) '*Vinaya......tadabhipretapadaṁ samāgataḥ*'.

'O friend! he who used to be the one receptacle of humility and love,—how can be looked upon as the same, when he has attained the position he desired (of becoming the lover of another woman)?'

Here the term '*preta*' is 'indecorous' (as it denotes the 'departed dead').

(6) [The 'Ambiguous']—

'*Kasmin karmaṇi sāmarthyam...ayaṁ sādhucharaḥ...iha*'.

'In what action does his capacity not shine?—And he is of virtuous character; so salute him.'

The exact meaning of the part ('*chara*') of the word '*Sādhucharaḥ*' is 'ambiguous';—'*chara*' is an affix denoting 'something that is past', and in that sense '*Sādhucharaḥ*' means 'who *was* good in the past'; on the other hand, '*chara*' may be a noun derived from the root '*chara*' (to behave), in which case the compound '*Sādhucharaḥ*' would mean 'he who behaves virtuously'

किमुच्यतेस्य भूपालमौलिमालामहामणेः ।
सुदुर्लभं वचोबाणैस्तेजो यस्य विभाव्यते ॥२०६॥

अत्र वचःशब्देन गीःशब्दो लक्ष्यते । अत्र खलु न केवलं पूर्वपदम् यावदुत्तरपदमपि पर्यायपरिवर्तनं न क्षमते । जलध्यादावुत्तरपदमेव वडवानलादौ पूर्वपदमेव ॥

---

(7) ['The meaning having to be guessed']—

'*Kimuchyate......vachobāṇaiḥ...vībhāvyate.*'

'What is to be said to this central crest-jewel of kings !—whose splendour is such as is difficult even for the gods to attain !'

Here the term '*vachaḥ*' (in '*vachobāṇaiḥ*') is meant to indicate its synonym '*gīḥ*' (which gives the word '*gīrbāṇa*',—which is one of the names of the *gods*), and thus the meaning of the compound '*vachobāṇaiḥ*' is such as can be 'guessed' with difficulty].

In fact the compound word '*gīrbāṇa*' (as a name of the *gods*) is such that it is not only the first term of the compound that does not admit of being replaced by a synonym; the second term also does not admit of being so replaced [*i.e.* just as we cannot have '*vachobāṇa*' so also we cannot have '*gīḥ-śara*']. As compound names where the second term does not admit of being replaced by a synonym, we have such words as '*jaladhi*' (ocean) and the like (which become entirely altered in sense by being transformed into '*jaladhara*', which means *cloud*) ; and as instances of compound names in which the first term does not admit of being replaced by a synonym, we have such words as '*vāḍavānala*' (the submarine fire) [which, when changed into '*aśvānala*' does not mean the same thing].

यद्यप्यसमर्थस्यैवाप्रयुक्तादयः केचन भेदाः तथाप्यन्यैरालंकारिकैर्विभागेन प्रदर्शिता इति भेदप्रदर्शनेनोदाहर्तव्या इति च विभज्योक्ताः ॥५२॥

प्रतिकूलवर्णमुपहतलुप्तविसर्गं विसन्धि हतवृत्तम् ।
न्यूनाधिककथितपदं पतत्प्रकर्षं समाप्तपुनरात्तम् ॥ ५३ ॥
अर्धान्तरैकवाचकमभवन्मतयोगमनभिहितवाच्यम् ।
अपदस्थपदसमासं संकीर्णं गर्भितं प्रसिद्धिहतम् ॥ ५४ ॥
भग्नप्रक्रममक्रमममतपरार्थं च वाक्यमेव तथा ।

(१) रसानुगुणत्वं वर्णानां वक्ष्यते। तद्विपरीतं प्रतिकूलवर्णम् ।

Though the words classed as 'unconventional' and the rest are only sub-classes of what is 'incapable of giving sense', yet they have been described separately, because some rhetoricians have treated of them as separate and hence it was thought proper to cite separate examples of them. 52.

That sentence is defective which (1) *contains discordant letters,* (2) *has the visarga blunted,* (3) *has the visarga deleted,* (4) *involves an unharmonious euphony,* (5) *involves a marred metre,* (6) *is deficient in words,* (7) *is redundant in words,* (8) *contains repeated words,* (9) *has its excellence receding,* (10) *resumes the concluded,* (11) *has a word isolated in a distinct half,* (12) *is devoid of intended connection,* (13) *omits a necessary statement,* (14) *has a word misplaced,* (15) *has a compound misplaced,* (16) *is confused,* (17) *is parenthetical,* (18) *is oppossed to usage,* (19) *has its uniformity broken,* (20) *has no uniformity and* (21) *has an undesirable second meaning.*

(1) It is going to be explained later on (Ch. VIII) how certain letters are in consonance with the delineation of certain particular Passions; and letters that are

यथा शृङ्गारे

अकुण्ठोत्कण्ठया पूर्णमाकण्ठं कलकण्ठि माम् ।
कम्बुकण्ठ्याः क्षणं कण्ठे कुरु कण्ठार्तिमुद्धर ।।२०७।।

रौद्रे यथा

देशः सोयमरातिशोणितजलैर्यस्मिन् ह्रदाः पूरिताः
क्षत्त्रादेव तथाविधः परिभवस्तातस्य केशग्रहः ।
तान्येवाहितहेतिघस्मरगुरूण्यस्त्राणि भास्वन्ति मे
यद्रामेण कृतं तदेव कुरुते द्रोणात्मजः क्रोधनः ।।२०८।।

---

not in such consonance are called 'discordant'. For example in the following delineation of the *Erotic*—

'*Akuṇṭhotkaṇṭhayā pūrṇamākāṇṭhaṁ kalakaṇṭhi mām*
Kambukaṇṭhyāḥ kṣaṇaṁ kaṇṭhe kuru kaṇṭhārtimuddhara.'

'O sweet-voiced one ! Do place me, who am full up to the throat with unimpeded longing, on the neck of the conch-necked one, and thereby remove the pangs of my neck';—

[The frequent repetition of the harsh letter *ṇṭha* is highly discordant with the sentiment depicted].

Or, in the following delineation of the *Furious*—

'*Deśaḥ soyamarātiśoṇitajalairyasmin hradāḥ pūritāḥ*
Kṣattrādeva tathāvidhaḥ paribhavastātasya keśagrahaḥ
Tānyevāhītahetighasmaragurūṇyastrāṇi bhāsvanti me
Yad rāmeṇa kṛtantadeva kurute droṇātmajaḥ krodhanaḥ'.

'This land is the same where pools were filled (by Paraśurāma) with the blood of slaughtered enemies ; insult at the hands of a Kṣattriya, in the shape of the father's locks being pulled, is also similar ; these resplendent weapons of mine also are similarly famous as being destructive of the weapons of enemies ; the wrathful son of

अत्र हि विकटवर्णत्वं दीर्घसमासत्वं चोचितम् । यथा

प्रागप्राप्तनिशुम्भशांभवधनुर्द्वेधाविधाविर्भवत्-
क्रोधप्रेरितभीमभार्गवभुजस्तम्भापविद्धः क्षणात् ।
उज्ज्वालः परशुर्भवत्वशिथिलस्त्वत्कण्ठपीठातिथि-
र्येनानेन जगत्सु खण्डपरशुर्देवो हरः ख्याप्यते ॥२०९॥

यत्र तु न क्रोधस्तत्र चतुर्थपादाभिधाने तथैव शब्दप्रयोगः ॥

Droṇa is going to do precisely what was done by Paraśurāma '.—

What would have been in consonance with the sentiment depicted would be [not the soft letters and simple words used, but] harsh sounding letters and long compounds ; as in the following—

' *Prāgaprāptanishumbhashāmbhava-*
dhanurdvedhāvidhāvirbhavat-
Krodhapreritabhīmabhārgavabhuja-
stambhāpaviddhaḥ kṣaṇāt
Ujjvālaḥ parashurbhavatvashithilas-
tvatkaṇṭhapīṭhātithir-
Yenānena jagatsu khaṇḍaparashur-
devo haraḥ khyāpyate '.

' May this blazing and powerful axe of mine, by reason whereof the god Shiva is known as 'the god of the broken axe,' (He having bestowed a part of his axe to me), be the guest of the back of your neck,—being wielded by my pillar-like terrific arms urged into action by the wrath excited by the breaking of the ever unbent bow of Śiva ';—

[We find long compounds and harsh-sounding words] ; but in the last quarter of the verse, where no anger is expressed (but only a deferential reference to the God Shiva), we have words suited to the sentiment.

(२) उपहत उत्वं प्राप्तो (३) लुप्तो वा विसर्गो यत्र तत्। यथा

धीरो विनीतो निपुणो वराकारो नृपोत्र सः।
यस्य भृत्या बलोत्सिक्ता भक्ता बुद्धिप्रभाविताः ॥२१०॥

(४) विसंधि संधेर्वैरूप्यम् विश्लेषोऽश्लीलत्वं कष्टत्वं च।

तत्राद्यं यथा

राजन्विभान्ति भवतश्चरितानि तानि
इन्दोर्द्युतिं दधति यानि रसातलेन्तः।
धीदोर्बले अतितते उचितानुवृत्ती
आतन्वती विजयसंपदमेत्य भातः ॥२११॥

---

(2) and (3) The following is an example of the '*visarga* blunted',—*i. e.,* transformed into 'o',—as also of the '*visarga* deleted'—

'*Dhīro vinīto nipuṇo*
varākāro nṛpotra saḥ—(2)
Yasya bhṛtyā balotsiktā
bhaktā buddhiprabhāvitāḥ'—(3)

'This king is dignified, modest, efficient and of handsome presence; his dependants are strong in intelligence, devoted to their master and proud of their strength.'

[In the first half the *visarga* is transformed into 'o' no less than five times; and in the second half it is *deleted* thrice.]

(4) The '*Cacophonous*' is that which involves a discordant euphony,—this discordance manifesting itself in three ways : (*a*) in disjunction, (*b*) in indecorousness and (*c*) in harshness.

(*a*) The following is an example of the euphony of discordant- disjunction—

'*Rājan...tāni indor......dhīdorbale atitate uchitānuvṛttī ātanvatī........bhātaḥ*'...

यथा वा

तत उदित उदारहारहारिद्युतिरुच्चैरुदयाचलादिवेन्दुः ।।
निजवंश उदात्तकान्तकान्तिर्बत मुक्तामणिवच्चकास्त्यनर्घः।।२१२।।

'O King! thy deeds shine resplendent even in the nethermost regions, resembling the sheen of the moon; and the power of thy intellect and arms, functioning in the right manner, brings about thy victory and glory and shines in the world'.

[Here the disjunction between *'tāni'* and *'indoḥ'*, between *'bale'* and *'atitate'* and *'uchitānuvṛtti'* and *'ātanvati'* even though grammatically correct, is highly *discordant'*.]

Or in the following—

'Tata udita udārahāra......nijavaṁsha-
.........udātta...........narghaḥ'.

'That great man of the exquisitely fascinating splendour rises resplendent in his family, resembling the pearl (appearing from the bamboo); and having his resplendence enhanced by the beautiful pearl-necklace, he resembles the moon (whose sheen is like that of the flawless pearl)'.

[Here the visarga is deleted twice after *'tataḥ'* and *'uditaḥ*.]

In this connection it has to be borne in mind that there are two conditions under which the disjunction in euphony is grammatically permissible,—in the first place, there is the very wide rule which makes all euphonious combination purely optional, and secondly in the case of the preceding word being a noun with a dual termination ending in the vowel '*ī*' or '*ū*', where according to *'Pāṇini* (1.1.11 and 6.1.125), no conjunction takes place. Now if the disjunction in euphony is of the former kind, then even a single instance makes the sentence defective; while if it belongs

संहितां न करोमीति स्वच्छया सकृदपि दोषः प्रगृह्यादिहेतुकत्वे त्वसकृत् ॥

वेगादुड्डीय गगने चलण्डामरचेष्टितः ।
अयमुत्तपते पत्त्री ततोऽत्रैव रुचिङ्कुरु ॥२१३॥

अत्र संधावश्लीलता ॥

उर्व्यसावत्र तर्वाली मर्वन्ते चार्ववस्थितिः ।
नात्रर्जु युज्यते गन्तुं शिरो नमय तन्मनाक् ॥२१४॥

(५) हतं लक्षणानुसरणेप्यश्रव्यम्। अप्राप्तगुरुभावान्तलघु रसाननुगुणं च वृत्तं यत्र तत् हतवृत्तम् । क्रमेणोदाहरणम्——

---

to the latter class, then it renders the sentence defective if it occurs more than once.

(*b*) '*Vegā......chalaṇḍāmara.........ruchiṅkuru*' 'This bird of unrestrained activity, flying in the sky with great force, finds it extremely hot; so take your rest here.'

Here the euphonious combination (involved in the expressions '*chalaṇḍāmara*' and '*ruchiṅkuru*') lead to indecorousness (in this that they give rise to sounds manifesting the terms '*laṇḍa*' and '*chiṅku*' respectively, both of which are the names of certain private parts of the human body).

(*c*) '*Urvyasāvatra tarvālī*
marvante charvavasthitiḥ
nātrārju............manāk'.

'Hence on the outskirts of a sandy desert the ground is covered by a line of trees affording a nice resting place; it is not right to go through it standing; so just lower your head a little.'

[Here the euphonious combination becomes *harsh*.]

(5) The 'marred metre' is of three kinds—(*a*) Though technically satisfying the formal conditions, it may be

अमृतममृतं कः संदेहो मधून्यपि नान्यथा
मधुरमधिकं चूतस्यापि प्रसन्नरसं फलम् ।
सकृदपि पुनर्मध्यस्थः सन् रसान्तरविज्जनो
वदतु यदिहान्यत्स्वादु स्यात्प्रियादशनच्छदात् ॥२१५॥

अत्र 'यदिहान्यत्स्वादु स्यात्' इत्यश्रव्यम् । यथा वा

जं परिहरिउं तीरइ मणअंपि ण सुन्दरत्तणगुणेण ।
अह णवरँ जस्स दोसो पडिपक्खेहिं पि पडिवण्णो ॥२१६॥

अत्र द्वितीयतृतीयगणौ सकारभकारौ ।

---

unpleasant to the ear, unmelodious,—(*b*) it may not have the last syllable of the foot elongated,—and (*c*) it may not be in harmony with the sentiment depicted.

The following are the examples of each of these three.

(*a*) '*Amṛtam.........vadatu yadihānyat svādu......chhadāt.*' What doubt is that nectar is really nectar; honey also is not otherwise; the fruit of the mango also is very sweet and of pleasing flavour; yet let any disinterested person, who is capable of appreciating the various kinds of flavours; say if anything in this world is sweeter than the lips of one's beloved !'

In the fourth line the portion '*yadihānyat svādu syāt*' (though formally correct) is not pleasant to the ear.

Or again in the following—

'*Jaṁ pari.........paḍivaṇṇo*'.

'That by reason of their very fascinating character affairs of love cannot be avoided is their one defect, which has been admitted even by their opponents'.

Here the close proximity of the group of three letters '*ha-ri-uṁ*'—which is technically named '*sa*' (*i. e.* the group of three in which, the first two letters are short and the third long),—to the next group, '*tī—ra-i*'—which is technically called '*bha*' (*i. e.* one long letter followed by

विकसितसहकारतारहारिपरिमलगुञ्जितपुञ्जितद्विरेफः ।
नवकिसलयचारुचामरश्रीहरति मुनेरपि मानसं वसन्तः ॥२१७॥

अत्र हारिशब्दः । हारिप्रमुदितसौरभेति पाठो युक्तः । यथा वा

अन्यास्ता गुणरत्नरोहणभुवो धन्या मृदन्यैव सा
संभाराः खलु तेन्य एव विधिना यैरेष सृष्टो युवा ।
श्रीमत्कान्तिजुषां द्विषां करतलात् स्त्रीणां नितम्बस्थलात्
दृष्टे यत्र पतन्ति मूढमनसामस्त्राणि वस्त्राणि च ॥२१८॥

---

two short ones),—is unmelodious [as has been recognised by standard writers on metrics also].

(*b*) '*Vikasitasahakāratārahāriparimala*........................
....................................*vasantaḥ*'.

'The spring bearing the fascinating fragrance of the blossoming mangoes, having swarms of black bees humming about, and beautified by chowries in the shape of the fresh leaves of trees—captivates the heart of even the ascetic'.

Here the metre is halting at '*hāri*' [where the last vowel is not elongated]. The right reading would be '*hāri—pramudita etc. etc.*'

Or, as in the following—

'*Anyāstā*.......................*vastrāṇi cha*'.

'Wonderful must have been the mines that produced these jewels of qualities ! wonderful too that blessed clay, as also the accessories, wherewith this young man has been created by God ! Since at his appearance, the weapons fall off from the hands of his rich and elegant enemies, and clothes slur away from the waists of beautiful women,—both of these having their hearts benumbed (the former through fear and the latter through love)'.

अत्र 'वस्त्राण्यपि' इति पाठे लघुरपि गुरुतां भजते ॥

हा नृप हा बुध हा कविबन्धो विप्रसहस्रसमाश्रय देव ।
मुग्धविदग्धसभान्तररत्न क्वासि गतः क्व वयं च तवैते ॥२१९॥

हास्यरसव्यञ्जकमेतद्वृत्तम्

(६) न्यूनपदं यथा

तथाभूतां दृष्ट्वा नृपसदसि पाञ्चालतनयां
वने व्याधैः सार्धं सुचिरमुषितं वल्कलधरैः ।
विराटस्यावासे स्थितमनुचितारम्भनिभृतं
गुरुः खेदं खिन्ने मयि भजति नाद्यापि कुरुषु ॥२२०॥

[Here the short syllable '*cha*' at the end is such as cannot take the long accent]. If the reading were '*ṇyapi*' (instead of '*ṇi cha*'), the '*pi*', even though short, could have taken the long accent (by virtue of its being preceded by the conjunct consonant "*ṇya*").

(*c*) '*Hā nṛpa.........tavaite*'.

'O king ! O wise one ! O patron of poets, the patron of hundreds of Brāhmaṇas ! O godlike one, jewel of the assembly of the learned and the wise ! Whereto have you gone ?—and where are we, your very own ?'

The metre adopted here is suited to the delineation of the *Comic* (and not of the *Pathetic*, to which it is employed here).

(6) The following is an example of the 'deficient in words'—

'*Tathābhūtāṁ dṛṣṭvā nṛpasadasi pāñchālatanayāṁ*
Vane vyādhaiḥ sārdhaṁ suchiramuṣitaṁ valkaladharaiḥ
Virāṭasyāvāse sthitamanuchitārambhanibhṛtaṁ
Guruḥ khedaṁ khinne mayi bhajati nādyāpi kuruṣu.

(See translation above in Chapter III.)

अत्रास्माभिरिति "खिन्न" इत्यस्मात्पूर्वमित्थमिति च ॥

(७) अधिकं यथा

स्फटिकाकृतिनिर्मलः प्रकामं प्रतिसंक्रान्तनिशातशास्त्रतत्त्वः ।
अविरुद्धसमन्वितोक्तियुक्तिः प्रतिमल्लास्तमयोदयः स कोपि ॥
॥२२१॥

अत्र आकृतिशब्दः । यथा वा

इदमनुचितमक्रमश्च पुंसां यदिह जरास्वपि मान्मथा विकाराः ।
यदपि च न कृतं नितम्बिनीनां स्तनपतनावधि जीवितं रतं वा ॥२२२॥

Here, in the first sentence the word '*asmābhiḥ*' is wanting (without which the sentence is left without a nominative) ; similarly before '*khinne*', the adverb '*ittham*' 'in this manner' is wanting [the intended meaning being 'he bears anger towards me, who have suffered *in the manner described*'].

(7) The following in an example of the 'Redundant word'—

'*Sphaṭikākṛti......sa kopi*'

'Truly marvellous is this King !—clean like the form of the rock-crystal, all the most abstruse principles of the sciences fully reflected in himself, his statements consistent and closely reasoned, and the source of the destruction of his adversaries.'

Here the term '*ākṛti*' ('form') is entirely superfluous.

Another example—

'*Idamanuchitaṁ.........*

Yadapi cha na kṛtaṁ......rataṁ vā'.

'It is improper and unnatural that men should evince sexual desires even in old age ; as also that of women, either life itself or sexual enjoyment was not made to end with the fall of their breasts'.

अत्र कृतमिति। कृतं प्रत्युत प्रक्रमभङ्गमावहति। तथा च 'यदपि' च न कुरङ्गलोचनानाम्' इति पाठे निराकाङ्क्षैव प्रतीतिः॥

(८) कथितपदं यथा

अधिकरतलतल्पं कल्पितस्वापलीला-
परिमिलननिमीलत्पाण्डिमा गण्डपाली।
सुतनु कथय कस्य व्यञ्जयत्यञ्जसैव
स्मरनरपतिलीलायौवराज्याभिषेकम्॥२२३॥

अत्र लीलेति॥

(९) पतत्प्रकर्षं यथा

कः कः कुत्र न घुर्घुरायितघुरीघोरो घुरेत्सूकरः
कः कः कं कमलाकरं विकमलं कर्तुं करी नोद्यतः।

Here the term '*kṛtam*' is superfluous; in fact its insertion breaks the uniformity (of the two statements). If the reading were '*yadapi cha na kuraṅgalochanānām*', the intended sense would be quite complete.

(8) The following is an example of the 'Repeated Word'—

'*Adhikara......līlā—*
Smaranarapatilīlā......ṣekam'

'The paleness of your cheek is waning on account of the pressure of your arms upon which it rested during sleep; tell me, O beautiful one! of what young man does this (cheek) indicate the coronation as the Prince of the sportings of King Cupid.'

Here the word '*līlā*' is needlessly repeated.

(9) The following is the example of 'Receding Excellence'—

'*Kaḥ kaḥ kutra na ghurghurāyitaghurīghoro ghuret sūkaraḥ*
Kaḥ kaḥ kaṁ kamalākaraṁ vikamalaṁ kartuṁ karī nodyataḥ

के के कानि वनान्यरण्यमहिषा नोन्मूलयेयुर्यतः
सिंहीस्नेहविलासबद्धवसतिः पञ्चाननो वर्तते ॥२२४॥

(१०) समाप्तपुनरात्तं यथा

क्रेङ्कारः स्मरकार्मुकस्य सुरतक्रीडापिकीनां रवः
झङ्कारो रतिमञ्जरीमधुलिहां लीलाचकोरीध्वनिः ।
तन्व्याः कञ्चुलिकापसारणभुजाक्षेपस्खलत्कङ्कण-
क्वाणः प्रेम तनोतु वो नववयोलास्याय वेणुस्वनः ॥२२५॥

Ke ke kāni vanānyaraṇyamahiṣā nonmūlayeyuryataḥ
Siṁhīsnehavilāsabaddhavasatiḥ pañchānano vartate'

'What boar and where would not make the terrible *ghur ghur* sound?—What elephant would not deprive the lotus-ponds of its lotuses?—What wild buffalo would not uproot the forests?—Now that the lion lies captivated by the love of the lioness!'

[Here the climax is not maintained to the end; it breaks off after the third line. The destructiveness of one animal is described in the first foot, greater destructiveness is described in the second foot, and still greater destructiveness is described in the third foot; this climax would have been rightly maintained, if the lion were described, in the last foot, as bringing greater destruction than that wrought by all the aforesaid animals. What is done on the other hand is that the fierce destructiveness of animals is toned down towards the end to the quiescent lying down of the lion under the captivating influence of feminine charms.]

(10) The following is the example of 'Resuming the Concluded'—

'*Kreṅkāraḥ.........veṇusvanaḥ*'.

'Like unto the twang of Cupid's bow, the sweet singing of the cuckoo of dalliance, the humming of bees in the blossom of love, the sound of the partridge of graceful sportiveness,—may the jingling of the slender

(११) द्वितीयार्धगतैकवाचकशेषप्रथमार्धं यथा
मसृणचरणपातं गम्यतां भूः सदर्भा
विरचय सिचयान्तं मूर्ध्नि घर्मः कठोरः ।
तदिति जनकपुत्री लोचनैरश्रुपूर्णैः
पथि पथिकवधूभिर्वीक्षिता शिक्षिता च ॥२२६॥

(१२) अभवन् मतः (इष्टः) योगः (संबन्धः) यत्र तत् । यथा

---

girl's bangles dropped in the shaking of her arms at the time of the attempt to remove her bodice, expand your love !—the jingling resembling the ring of the flute, played to the dancing of youthfulness !'

[The last qualification is thrown in, after the sentence has been completed, without materially adding to the beauty of the description.]

(11) The following is an example of the 'Isolation, in the second part of a word required by the first half'—

'*Masṛṇa*...........*bhūḥ sadarbhā*

....

Taditi.......................

.................*shikṣitā cha*'.

'The ground is covered with grass-shoots, *therefore*, weak with soft foot-steps ; the sun is strong overhead, therefore place a piece of cloth on your head ;—thus was Jānakī on her way exhorted and looked upon with tearful eyes by the wives of fellow-travellers'.

[The construction here is '*bhūḥ sadarbhā*—'(the ground is covered with shoots) *tat* (therfore) *gamyatām* (walk with soft tread etc. etc.); and the term '*tat*' which is required in the first half of the verse has been placed in the second half, with which it has no syntactical connection.]

(12) The following is an example of what is 'devoid of intended connection', *i.e.* where the desired connection is wanting—

येषां तास्त्रिदशेभदानसरितः पीताः प्रतापोष्मभि-
र्लीलापानभुवश्च नन्दनवनच्छायासु यैः कल्पिताः ।
येषां हुंकृतयः कृतामरपतिक्षोभाः क्षपाचारिणां
किं तैस्त्वत्परितोषकारि विहितं किंचित्प्रवादोचितम् ॥२२७॥

अत्र "गुणानां च परार्थत्वादसंबन्धः समत्वात्स्यात्" इत्युक्तनयेन यच्छब्दनिदश्यानामर्थानां परस्परमसमन्वयेन यैरित्यत्र विशेषस्याप्रतीतिरिति । 'क्षपाचारिभिः' इति पाठे युज्यते समन्वयः ।

(a)
'*Yeṣāṁ tāstridashebhadānasaritaḥ*
pītāḥ pratāpoṣmabhiḥ
Līlāpānabhuvashcha nandanavana-
(b)
chchhāyāsu yaiḥ kalpitāḥ
(c)
Yesāṁ huṁkṛtayaḥ kṛtāmarapati-
kṣobhāḥ kṣapāchārīṇāṁ
Kiṁ taistvatparitoṣakāri vihitaṁ
kiñchit pravādochitam'.

'By the fire of whose glory was dried the ichor-flow of the celestial elephants,—by whom were established drinking booths in the shady groves of the Nandana garden,—of which demons the slightest sound of displeasure brought up perturbation in the mind of the king of the gods,—what satisfactory act has been done by them which could be spoken of?'

Here it is not comprehensible what is the antecedent (qualified and referred to) of the pronoun '*yaiḥ*' (there being no noun with the instrumental ending),—it being not possible to co-ordinate it with '*yeṣām*' and thus correlate it with the 'demons' (*kṣapāchāriṇām*' with the

यथा वा

त्वमेवंसौन्दर्या स च रुचिरतायाः परिचितः
कलानां सीमानं परमिह युवामेव भजथः ।
अपि द्वन्द्वं दिष्टया तदिति सुभगे संवदति वाम्
अतः शेषं यत्स्याज्जितमिह तदानीं गुणितया ।।२२८।।

अत्र यदित्यत्र तदिति तदानीमित्यत्र यदेति वचनं नास्ति ।

---

genitive ending, which is the antecedent of the pronoun '*yeṣām*'), because, according to the dictum of Jaimini (Mimā. Sū. 3.1.22), when there are several subordinate factors (in the present case, the pronouns '*yeṣām*', in the first line, '*yaiḥ*' in the second line and '*yeṣām*' in the third line), they are all equally subservient to something else, and as such cannot be mutually correlated. The necessary co-ordination (and antecedent) would be got at, if we read '*kṣapāchāribhiḥ*', (with the instrumental ending, in place of '*kṣapāchāriṇāṁ*'.

Another example of the same defect we have in the following—

'*Tvamevaṁ saundaryāḥ sa cha ruchiratāyāḥ parichitaḥ*
Kalānāṁ sīmānaṁ paramiha yuvāmeva bhajathaḥ
Api dvandvaṁ diṣṭyā taditi subhage saṁvadati vām
Ataḥ sheṣaṁ yat syāj jitamiha tadānīṁ guṇitayā'.

'You are endowed with such beauty, and he is not unfamiliar with handsomeness ; both of you possess the highest proficiency in the finer arts ; thus fortunately the pair of you two is quite compatible ; if the subsequent issue were what it should be, then indeed would the endowment of qualities become duly glorified.'

Here the relative pronoun '*yat*' (in the fourth line) requires a corresponding '*tat*', and the term '*tadānīm*'

'चेत्स्यात्' इति युक्तः पाठः । यथा वा

संग्रामाङ्गणमागतेन भवता चापे समारोपिते
देवाकर्णय येन येन सहसा यद्यत्समासादितम् ।
कोदण्डेन शराः शरैररिशिरस्तेनापि भूमण्डलं
तेन त्वं भवता च कीर्तिरतुला कीर्त्या च लोकत्रयम् ॥२२९॥

अत्राकर्णनक्रियाकर्मत्वे कोदण्डं शरानित्यादि वाक्यार्थस्य कर्मत्वे कोदण्डः शरा इति प्राप्तम् । न च यच्छब्दार्थस्तद्विशेषणं वा कोदण्डादि । न च केन केनेत्यादि प्रश्नः ।

---

requires a corresponding '*yadānīm*'; but both these are absent [and hence the desired connection becomes impossible]. The right reading would be '*chet syāt*' (for '*yat syāt*').

Another example of the same.

'*Saṅgrāmāṅgaṇamāgatena bhavatā chāpe samāropite*
'*Devākarṇaya yena yena sahasā yad yat samāsāditam*
Kodaṇḍena sharāḥ sharairarishirastenāpi bhūmaṇḍalaṁ
Tena tvaṁ bhavatā cha kīrtiratulā kīrtyā cha lokatrayam'.

'O king ! listen to what was attained by what, when you came to the field of battle and stringed your bow : The bow obtained the arrows,—the arrows, the enemy's head,—this head, the earth,—the earth, yourself (for its master),—you, unrivalled fame,—and the fame, all the three worlds.'

As objectives of the verb 'listen', all the nouns mentioned should have the accusative ending—'*Kodaṇḍam sharān*' and so forth. If the whole of the subsequent sentence were to be treated as the objective of the said verb, then the form would be '*Kodaṇḍaḥ sharāḥ*' [as what

यथा वा

"चापाचार्यस्त्रिपुरविजयी कार्तिकेयो विजेयः
शस्त्रव्यस्तः सदनमुदधिर्भूरियं हन्तकारः ।
अस्त्येवैतत् किमु कृतवता रेणुकाकण्ठबाधां
बद्धस्पर्द्धस्तव परशुना लज्जते चन्द्रहासः" ॥२३०॥

इत्यादौ भार्गवस्य निन्दायां तात्पर्यम् । कृतवतेति परशौ सा प्रतीयते । 'कृतवतः' इति तु पाठे मतयोगो भवति ।

---

are meant to be 'listened' to are (1) the thing that attains, and (2) the thing attained; and in any enumeration of these, both of them should be spoken of by means of nouns with the nominative ending].—Nor is it possible for the 'Bow' and other things to be regarded either as included in the denotation of the pronoun '*yat*' (in the first line, which is the objective of the verb to *listen*), or as a qualification of that denotation. Nor lastly is there any such question as—'what was attained by what?'—'*kena kena kim kim*'—(which would have established the intended connection between the two sets of sentences).

Another example of the same defect—

'*Chāpāchāryastripuravijayī kārtikeyo vijeyaḥ*
Shastravyastaḥ sadanamudadhirbhūriyaṁ hantakāraḥ
Astyevaitat kimu kṛtavatā reṇukā-kaṇṭhabādhāṁ
Baddhaspardhastava parashunā lajjate chandrahāsaḥ'

(For translation see above, stanza No. 201)

What is intended here is the deprecation of Parashurāma himself (for having killed his mother); while the term '*kṛtavatā*' qualifying the *axe*, makes the said deprecation appliable to this latter. The reading '*kṛtavataḥ*' (which would qualify '*tava*') would afford the intended connection.

यथा वा

चत्वारो वयमृत्विजः स भगवान् कर्मोपदेष्टा हरिः
संग्रामाध्वरदीक्षितो नरपतिः पत्नी गृहीतव्रता ।
कौरव्याः पशवः प्रियापरिभवक्लेशोपशान्तिः फलं
राज्यन्योपनिमन्त्रणाय रसति स्फीतं हतो दुन्दुभिः ॥२३१॥

अत्राध्वरशब्दः समासे गुणीभूत इति न तदर्थः सर्वैः संयुज्यते । यथा वा

जङ्घाकाण्डोरुनालो नखकिरणलसत्केसरालीकरालः
प्रत्यग्रालक्तकाभाप्रसरकिसलयो मञ्जुमञ्जीरभृङ्गः ।

Another example—

Chatvāro vayamṛtvijaḥ sa bhagavān karmopadeṣṭā hariḥ
Saṁgrāmādhvaradīkṣito narapatiḥ patnī gṛhītavratā
Kauravyāḥ pashavaḥ priyāparibhavakleshopashāntiḥ phalaṁ
Rājanyopanimantraṇāya rasati sphītaṁ hato dundubhiḥ.'

'We four are the sacrificial priests ; the blessed Hari is the spiritual adviser ; the king has been initiated for the battle-ritual ; and his wife is keeping the vows ; the Kurus are the animals (to be sacrificed) ; the result aimed at is the allayment of the pain caused by the molestation of our beloved wife ; the battle-drum is being sounded for the purpose of inviting the Kṣattriyas (to the sacrifice)'.

Here the term '*adhvara*', 'sacrifice', has been made a subordinate member of the compound, and hence what is denoted by it fails to be connected with all the sacrificial details mentioned.

The following is yet another example ;—

'*Jaṅghākāṇḍorunālo nakhakiraṇalasatkesarālīkarālaḥ*
Pratyagrālaktakābhāprasarakisalayo mañjumañjīrabhṛṅgaḥ

भर्तुर्नृत्तानुकारे जयति निजतनुस्वच्छलावण्यवापी-
संभूताम्भोजशोभां विदधदभिनवो दण्डपादो भवान्याः ॥२३२॥

अत्र दण्डपादगता निजतनुः प्रतीयते भवान्याः संबन्धिनी तु विवक्षिता ॥

(१३) अवश्यवक्तव्यमनुक्तं यत्र । यथा

अप्राकृतस्य चरितातिशयैश्च दृष्टै-
रत्यद्भुतैरपहृतस्य तथापि नास्था ।
कोप्येष वीरशिशुकाकृतिरप्रमेय-
सौन्दर्यसारसमुदायमयः पदार्थः ॥२३३॥

अत्र 'अपहृतोस्मि' इत्यपहृतत्वस्य विधिर्वाच्यः तथापीत्यस्य द्वितीयवाक्यगतत्वेनैवोपपत्तेः । यथा वा

Bharturnṛttānukāre jayati nijatanusvachchhalāvaṇyāvāpī-
Saṁbhūtāmbhojashobhāṁ vidadhadabhinavo daṇḍapādo bhavānyāḥ.

(Translated above as stanza No. 150)

Here the expression '*nijatanu*', appearing in the compound, is understood as refering to the *Daṇḍapāda*, while it is intended to refer to *Bhavānī*.

(13) In the following we have an example of the 'Omission of a necessary Statement'.—

'*Aprākṛtasya charitātishayaishcha dṛṣṭair*
Atyadbhutairapahṛtasya tathāpi nāsthā
Kopyeṣa vīrashishukākṛtiraprameya-
Saundaryasārasamudāyamayaḥ padārthaḥ'.

'Though I am captivated by the apparently excellent and marvellous deeds of this extraordinary person, yet I have no faith (in the fact that the bow has been broken by him) ; for this is an indescribable entity constituted by the very essence of illimitable beauty, appearing in the shape of a heroic boy.'

Here what should have been expressly stated was the

15

एषोहमद्रितनयामुखपद्मजन्मा
प्राप्तः सुरासुरमनोरथदूरवर्ती ।
स्वप्नेनिरुद्धघटनाधिगताभिरूप-
लक्ष्मीफलामसुरराजसुतां विधाय ॥२३४॥

अत्र मनोरथानामपि दूरवर्तीत्यप्यर्थो वाच्यः। यथा वा
त्वयि निबद्धरतेः प्रियवादिनः प्रणयभङ्गपराङ्मुखचेतसः ।
कमपराधलवं मम पश्यसि त्यजसि मानिनि दासजनं यतः ॥२३५॥

---

direct affirmation of his having 'become captivated',—the right reading being '*apahṛtosmi*' (for '*apahṛtasya*'); specially as the use of the expression '*tathāpī*' could be justified only as occurring in a totally different sentence [hence it is essential that there should be a finite verb in the preceding sentence, without which there would not be two distinct sentences.]

Another example of the same :—

'*Eṣohamadritanayāmukhapadmajanmā*
Prāptaḥ surāsuramanorathadūravartī
Svapneniruddhaghaṭanādhigatābhirūpa-
Lakṣmīphalāmasurarājasutāṁ vidhāya'.

'I, born of the lotus-face of Pārvatī, who am beyond the reach of the longings of gods and demons, have come here, after having made the daughter of the demon-king such as has her exquisite beauty rendered fruitful through association, in a dream, with Aniruddha.'

[Here the sense intended to be conveyed is that 'I am beyond *even* the longings of the gods and demons ;' [and this idea the words used fail to convey].

Similarly in the following verse also—

Tvayi nibaddharateḥ priyavādinaḥ
Praṇayabhaṅgaparāṅmukhachetasaḥ
Kamaparādhalavaṁ mama pashyasi
Tyajasi mānini dāsajanaṁ yataḥ.

अत्र 'अपराधस्य लवमपि' इति वाच्यम् ।।

(१४) अस्थानस्थपदं यथा

प्रियेण संग्रथ्य विपक्षसंनिधा-
वुपाहितां वक्षसि पीवरस्तने ।
स्रजं न काचिद्विजहौ जलाविलां
वसन्ति हि प्रेम्णि गुणा न वस्तुषु ।।२३६।।

अत्र 'काचिन्न विजहौ' इति वाच्यम् । यथा वा

'O proud one ! what trace of fault do you find in me, which makes you abandon me, your servant ?—I, whose love is centered in you, who always talk to you affectionately and whose mind is ever averse to any breach of endearment.'

Here also what is meant to be expressed is '*even* the slightest trace of a fault.'

(14) The following is an example of the 'Misplaced Word'—

'*Priyeṇa saṅgrathya vipakṣasannidhā-*
Vupāhitāṁ vakṣasi pīvarastane
Srajaṁ na kāchid vijahau jalāvilāṁ
Vasanti hi premṇi guṇā na vastuṣu.'

'The lover had carefully knitted a garland and placed it over her chest covered with her high breasts, in the presence of her rivals ; and though this garland had become sullied with water, yet not a certain girl did remove it ; the value lies, not in the presented object, but in the love that prompts it.'

What is intended to be expressed is that 'a certain woman did not remove the garland ;' and to this end the '*na*' should have come before '*vijahau*'.

लग्नः केलिकचग्रहश्लथजटालम्बेन निद्रान्तरे
मुद्राङ्कः शितिकन्धरेन्दुशकलेनान्तःकपोलस्थलम् ।
पार्वत्या नखलक्ष्मशङ्कितसखीनर्मस्मितह्रीतया
प्रोन्मृष्टः करपल्लवेन कुटिलाताम्रच्छविः पातु वः ॥२३७॥

अत्र नखलक्ष्मेत्यतः पूर्वं 'कुटिलताम्र०' इति वाच्यम् ॥

(१५) अस्थानस्थसमासं यथा

अद्यापि स्तनशैलदुर्गविषमे सीमन्तिनीनां हृदि
स्थातुं वाञ्छति मान एष धिगिति क्रोधादिवालोहितः ।

[As it stands, the expression means 'not some one,—but all—removed the garland.']

Another example of the same—

Lagnaḥ kelikachagrahashlathajaṭālambena nidrāntare
Mudrāṅkaḥ shitikandharendushakalenāntaḥkapolasthalam
Pārvatyā nakhalakṣmashaṅkitasakhīnarmasmitahrītayā
Pronmṛṣṭaḥ karapallavena kuṭilātāmrachhaviḥ pātu vaḥ.

'May the curved red mark made on Pārvatī's cheek by Shiva's moon-digit, while she slept on his matted locks, tired during dalliance, protect you !—the marks wiped off by her tender hands, when she was abashed by the smiles of her companion who suspected the mark to be of nails.'

The epithet '*kuṭilātāmrachchhaviḥ*' ('red and curved') should have been placed before the term '*nakhalakṣma etc.*'

[As it is the 'curvature and redness' that supply the grounds for the companion's suspicion.]

(15) The following is an example of the 'Misplaced Compound'—

'*Adyāpi stanashailadurgaviṣame sīmantinīnāṁ hṛdi*
Sthātuṁ vāñchhati māna eṣa dhigiti krodhādivālohitaḥ

प्रोद्यद्दूरतरप्रसारितकरः कर्षत्यसौ तत्क्षणात्
फुल्लत्कैरवकोशनिःसरदलिश्रेणीकृपाणं शशी ।।२३८।।

अत्र क्रुद्धस्योक्तौ समासो न कृतः कवेरुक्तौ तु कृतः ।।

(१६) संकीर्णम् यत्र वाक्यान्तरस्य पदानि वाक्यान्तरमनुप्रविशन्ति । यथा

किमिति न पश्यसि कोपं पादगतं बहुगुणं गृहाणेमम् ।
ननु मुञ्च हृदयनाथं कण्ठे मनसस्तमोरूपम् ।।२३९।।

Prodyaddūrataraprasāritakaraḥ karṣatyasau tatkṣaṇāt
Phullatkairavakoshanissarodalishreṇīkṛpāṇam shashī'.

'Even yet this pride wishes to stay in the hearts of women, fortified by the hill-like breasts! Woe be to me!—Saying this, and becoming reddened with rage, the moon immediately puts forth his arms (rays) far and wide and draws the sword in the shape of the line of black bees issuing forth from the blooming lily.'

Here the first line represents the speech of the enraged moon, and the rest that of the poet; the long compounds however, appear in the latter and not in the former (where it would have been more in keeping with the sentiment expressed).

(16) The following is an example of 'Confusion',—*i.e.,* where the words of one sentence are found in the midst of another—

'Kimiti na pashyasi kopaṁ pādagataṁ bahugūṇaṁ gṛhāṇemam
Nanu muñcha hṛdayanāthaṁ kaṇṭhe manasastamorūpam.'

'Why do you not look upon your heart's lord, the receptacle of many good qualities, fallen upon your feet? Embrace him on the neck and renounce your anger, which hangs like a gloom on your heart'.

अत्र पादगतं बहुगुणं हृदयनाथं किमिति न पश्यसि । इमं कण्ठे गृहाण मनसस्तमोरूपं कोपं मुञ्चेति । एकवाक्यतायां तु क्लिष्टमिति भेदः ॥

(१७) गर्भितम् यत्र वाक्यस्य मध्ये वाक्यान्तरमनुप्रविशति । यथा

परापकारनिरतैर्दुर्जनैः सह संगतिः ।
वदामि भवतस्तत्त्वं न विधेया कथञ्चन ॥२४०॥

अत्र तृतीयपादो वाक्यान्तरमध्ये प्रविष्टः । यथा वा

लग्नं रागावृताङ्ग्या सुदृढमिह ययैवासियष्टयारिकण्ठे
मातङ्गानामपीहोपरि परपुरुषैर्या च दृष्टा पतन्ती ।

The sentences meant here are—'*Atra pādagataṁ bahuguṇaṁ hṛdayanāthaṁ kimiti na pashyasi,—imaṁ kaṇṭhe gṛhāṇa,—manasastamorūpaṁ kopaṁ muñcha.*'

The difference between this (confusion) and 'obscurity' lies in the fact that in the latter it is the words of a single sentence that appear in a confused order (while in the former they appear in several sentences).

(17) In the following we have an example of the 'Parenthetical Expression'—

'*Parāpakāraniratairdurjanaiḥ saha saṅgatiḥ*'
Vadāmi bhavatastattvaṁ na vidheyā kathañchana

'Association with bad men bent upon injuring others, —I tell you the truth,—should never be maintained.' Here the third foot of the verse ('*vadāmi bhavatastattvam*') occurs in the middle of a sentence.

Another example of the same—

Lagnaṁ rāgāvṛtāṅgyā sudṛḍhamiha
yayaivāsiyaṣṭyārikaṇṭhe
Mātaṅgānāmapīhopari parapuruṣair-
yācha dṛṣṭā patantī

तत्सक्तोयं न किंचिद्गणयति विदितं तेस्तु तेनास्मि दत्ता
भृत्येभ्यः श्रीनियोगाद्गदितुमिव गतेत्यम्बुधिं यस्य कीर्तिः ॥२४१॥

अत्र 'विदितं तेस्तु' इति एतत्कृतम्। प्रत्युत लक्ष्मीस्ततोपसरतीति विरुद्धमतिकृत् ॥

(१८) "मञ्जीरादिषु रणितप्रायं पक्षिषु च कूजितप्रभृति ।
स्तनितमणितादि सुरते मेघादिषु गर्जितप्रमुखम् ॥

Tatsaktoyaṁ na kiṁchid gaṇayati viditaṁ
testu tenāsmi dattā
Bhṛtyebhyaḥ shrīniyogād gaditumiva gate—
tyambudhiṁ yasya kīrtiḥ'

'Whose fame repaired to the ocean to deliver the following message to him under orders from the Goddess of Wealth—"This Sword (woman), corroded with blood (full of passion) fell upon the neck [(*a*) in the act of cutting, (*b*) in the act of embracing] of the enemy, and which was seen by strangers to fall upon elephants (to repair to Chāṇḍālas),—being attached to this same Sword (woman), this king cares for nothing else, and—be this known to you—I am being given away by him to his dependents".

Here the clause '*viditaṁ testu*', 'be this known to you', is unnecessarily inserted; in fact it has the implication that 'the Goddess of Wealth is going to desert the king', which is entirely repugnant to the context.

(18) 'Opposed to Usage or Convention' is that which contravenes such conventions as the following—"The sound of the anklet and such ornaments is to be described as '*raṇita*' (jingling), that of birds as '*kūjita*' (warbling), those produced at the time of embraces, as '*stanita*' (murmur), '*maṇita*' (cooing) and so forth, and that of clouds as '*garjita*' (thundering)".

इति प्रसिद्धिमतिक्रान्तम् । यथा

महाप्रलयमारुतक्षुभितपुष्करावर्तक-
प्रचण्डघनगर्जितप्रतिरुतानुकारी मुहुः ।
रवः श्रवणभैरवः स्थगितरोदसीकन्दरः
कुतोद्य समरोदधेरयमभूतपूर्वः पुरः ॥ २४२ ॥

अत्र रवो मण्डूकादिषु प्रसिद्धो न तूक्तविशेषे सिंहनादे ॥

(१९) भग्नः प्रक्रमः प्रस्तावः यत्र । यथा

नाथे निशाया नियतेर्नियोगादस्तं गते हन्त निशापि याता ।
कुलाङ्गनानां हि दशानुरूपं नातःपरं भद्रतरं समस्ति ॥२४३॥

We have an example of this in the following—

‘ *Mahāpralayamārutakṣubhitapuṣkarāvartaka—*
Prachaṇḍaghanagarjitapratirutānukārī muhuḥ
Ravaḥ shravaṇabhairavaḥ sthagitarodasīkandaraḥ
Kutodya samarodadherayamabhūtapūrvaḥ puraḥ’.

‘ Whence this unprecedented ear-splitting sound of the ocean of battle, pervading the entire valley between the earth and the heavens, and resembling the echo of the thundering of clouds tossed about by storms during universal dissolution ?’

The word ‘ *rava* ’ (sound) that is used here is generally used in the sense of the noise made by frogs and such animals, and not in that of the particular *leonine roar*, here referred to.

(19) The following is an example of ‘ Broken Uniformity ’, *i. e.* where the ‘ uniformity’, *i. e.* continuity of sequence, is broken :—

‘ *Nāthe nishāyā niyaterniyogād*
Astaṁ gate hanta nishāpi yātā
Kulāṅganānāṁ hi dashānurūpaṁ
Nātaḥ paraṁ bhadrataraṁ samasti.’

अत्र 'गते' इति प्रकान्ते 'याता' इति प्रक्रुतेः ।

'गता निशापि' इति तु युक्तम् ।

ननु 'नैकं पदं द्विः प्रयोज्यं प्रायेण' इत्यन्यत्र कथितपदं दुष्टमिति चेहैवोक्तम् । तत्कथमेकस्य पदस्य द्विःप्रयोगः । उच्यते । उद्देश्यप्रतिनिर्देश्यव्यतिरिक्तो विषय एकपदप्रयोगनिषेधस्य । तद्वति विषये प्रत्युत तस्यैव पदस्य सर्वनाम्नो वा प्रयोगं विना दोषः । तथाहि—

'Under the ordination of destiny, the Lord of Night having gone to set, it is well that the Night also has departed ; for noble women, there is no better condition and more in keeping with the state of things than this'.

The statement, having opened with '*gata*' (gone), ends with '*yāta*' (departed) ; thus violating the uniformity of the *verbal root*. The right reading would have been '*gatā nishāpi*',

[which would have been more appropriate in describing the exact following by the wife in the foot-steps of her lord.]

Objection :—"In another work (Vāmana's sūtras) it has been laid down that *no word should be repeated twice*, and in this work itself the Repetition of words has been described as a Defect ; how then should it be regarded advisable to repeat the same word *gatā*') as suggested ?"

Our answer is as follows :—The prohibition of the repeating of a word is meant to apply to cases other than the one where what is spoken of subsequently is meant to be precisely the same that has been mentioned previously ; [as in the case in question the going of the night is meant to be precisely the same as the going of the moon] where, on the other hand, such identity is meant, it would be a positive defect if the same noun were not repeated, either

उदेति सविता ताम्रस्ताम्र एवास्तमेति च ।
संपत्तौ च विपत्तौ च महतामेकरूपता ।। २४४ ।।

अत्र रक्त एवास्तमेतीति यदि क्रियेत तदा पदान्तरप्रतिपादितः स एवार्थोर्थान्तिरतयेव प्रतिभासमानः प्रतीतिं स्थगयति ।।

यथा वा

यशोधिगन्तुं सुखलिप्सया वा मनुष्यसंख्यामतिवर्तितुं वा ।
निरुत्सुकानामभियोगभाजां समुत्सुकेवाङ्कमुपैति सिद्धिः ।।२४५।।

---

by itself, or by a corresponding pronoun ; as for instance, in the folllwing—

'*Udeti savitā tāmrastāmra evāstameti cha*
Sampattau cha vipattau cha mahatāmekarūpatā'.

'The sun rises red, and sets red also ; great beings retain the same condition both in prosperity and adversity'.

Here if the form adopted in the second clause were '*rakta evāstameti*', though the meaning would be the same expressed in different words, yet it would not afford the idea intended (*of unchangeableness*),—the use of different words giving rise to the notion that the condition spoken of is different from that spoken of before.

The following is an example of the 'Violation of Uniformity', as realating to the *affix*—

'*Yashodhigantuṁ sukhalipsayā vā*
Manusyasaṅkhyāmativartituṁ vā
Nirutsukānāmabhiyogabhājāṁ
Samutsukevāṅkamupaiti siddhiḥ'.

'To those who exert themselves without flurry,—either to obtain fame, or with a desire to obtain pleasure, or to surpass ordinary humanity,—success comes to the lap, as if it were anxious to reach him'.

अत्र प्रत्ययस्य। 'सुखमीहितुं वा' इति युक्तः पाठः ।

ते हिमालयमामन्त्र्य पुनः प्रेक्ष्य च शूलिनम् ।
सिद्धं चास्मै निवेद्यार्थं तद्विसृष्टाः खमुद्ययुः ॥ २४६ ॥

अत्र सर्वनाम्नः। 'अनेन विसृष्टाः' इति तु वाच्यम् ।

महीभृतः पुत्रवतोपि दृष्टिस्तस्मिन्नपत्ये न जगाम तृप्तिम् ।
अनन्तपुष्पस्य मधोर्हि चूते द्विरेफमाला सविशेषसङ्गा ॥२४७॥

Here the uniformity of the *affix* (Infinitive) is broken. The right reading would be '*sukhamīhitum vā*'.

In the following we have an example of the 'Violation of the Uniformity' of the *Pronoun*—

'*Te himālayamāmantrya punaḥ preksya cha shūlinam*
Siddhaṁchāsmai nivedyārthaṁ tadvisṛṣṭāḥ khamudyayuḥ'

'Having asked Himālaya and seen Shiva, communicated to him the fulfilment of the purpose, and, having obtained his leave, repaired to the skies'.

Here the uniformity of the pronoun is broken; the right form would have been '*anena visṛṣṭāḥ*' (in place of '*tadvisṛṣṭāḥ*', which latter points to some one different from the person, Shiva, just mentioned).

In the following we have an example of the 'Violation of the Uniformity' of the *synonym*—

'*Mahībhṛtaḥ putravatopi dṛṣtis—*
Tasminnapatye na jagāma tṛptim
Anantapuṣpasya madhorhi chūte
Dvirephamālā savisheṣāsaṅgā'.

'Though he had sons, yet his eyes were never tired of feasting upon that child; though spring is full of endless flowers, yet the line of black bees has a special attachment for the mango.'

अत्र पर्यायस्य । 'महीभृतोपत्यवत्तोपि' इति युक्तम् । 'अत्र सत्यपि पुत्रे कन्यारूपेप्यपत्ये स्नेहोभूत्' इति केचित्समर्थयन्ते ।

विपदोभिभवन्त्यविक्रमं रहयत्यापदुपेतमायतिः ।
नियता लघुता निरायतेरगरीयान्न पदं नृपश्रियः ॥२४८॥

अत्रोपसर्गस्य पर्यायस्य च । 'तदभिभवः कुरुते निरायतिम् ।

The right reading would have been '*mahibhṛtopatyavatopi*' (which would be in keeping with '*apatya*' in the second line).

Some people defend the original reading on the ground that it affords the meaning that—'though he had *sons*, male children, yet, he had special love for the daughter, the female child'. [A meaning which will not be available if the suggested emendation were made].

In the following we have an example of the 'Violation of the Uniformity' of the *prefix*, as also of the *synonym*—

'*Vipadobhibhavantyavikramaṁ*
Rahayatyāpadupetamāyatiḥ
Niyatā laghutā nirāyater—
Agarīyānna padannṛpashriyaḥ.'

'Calamities press upon one who is devoid of courage; future prospects desert one who is beset with calamities; disrespect is the certain lot of one who is deprived of future prospects; and he who commands no respect is not the receptacle of kingly splendour.'

[In the first sentence we have the term '*vipat*', which is replaced in the second sentence by '*āpat*' the *prefix* being changed; again in the preceding sentence we have the term '*laghutā*', whose place in the following sentence is taken by its synonym '*agariyān*'.]

The right reading would be—

(*a*) '*Tadabhibhavaḥ kurute nirāyatim*'

लघुतां भजते निरायतिर्लघुतावान्न पदं नृपश्रियः ।। इति युक्तम् ।
काचित्कीर्णा रजोभिर्दिवमनुविदधौ मन्दवक्त्रेन्दुलक्ष्मी-
रश्रीकाः काश्चिदन्तर्दिश इव दधिरे दाहमुद्भ्रान्तसत्त्वाः ।
भ्रेमुर्वात्या इवान्याः प्रतिपदमपरा भूमिवत्कम्पमानाः
प्रस्थाने पार्थिवानामशिवमिति पुरो भावि नार्यः शशंसुः ।।२४९।।

(*b*) '*Laghutām bhajate nirāyatiḥ*'

(*c*) '*Laghutāvanna padannṛpashriyaḥ*' (fourth line)

In the following we have an example of the 'Violation of the Uniformity' of *number*.

'*Kāchit kīrṇā rajobhirdivamanuvidadhau mandavaktrendu-lakṣmīr-*

Ashrīkāḥ kāśchidantardisha iva dadhire dāhamudbhrān-tasattvāḥ

Bhremurvātyā ivānyāḥ pratipadamaparāḥ bhūmivat kam-pamānāḥ

Prasthāne pārthivānāmashivamiti puro bhāvi nāryaḥ shashaṁsuḥ.'

'At the time of the king's departure the women fore-boded impending calamity ;—while one was beset with menstrual impurity and had her moon-like face bedimmed, thereby resembling the atmosphere (dusty and with a dull moon, a sign of coming trouble),—others, devoid of all splendour and their minds unsteady under the fire of the pangs of separation, resembled the quarters (dull and amazing all animals by their red glare, another inauspicious sign);—others again flitted about like storms (an inauspici-ous sign), and another shook like the earth (earth-quake being a premonition of impending disaster).'

[In the first we have the noun in the *Singular* number, while throughout the following sentences of the verse, the *Plural* number is used, and in the last sentence again we find the *Singular* number.]

अत्र वचनस्य । 'काश्चित्कीर्णा रजोभिर्दिवमनुविदधुर्मन्दवक्त्रेन्दुशोभा निःश्रीकाः' इति 'कम्पमानाः' इत्यत्र 'कम्पमापुः' इति च पठनीयम् ।

गाहन्तां महिषा निपानसलिलं शृङ्गैर्मुहुस्ताडितं
छायाबद्धकदम्बकं मृगकुलं रोमन्थमभ्यस्यताम् ।
विश्रब्धैः क्रियतां वराहपतिभिर्मुस्ताक्षतिः पल्वले
विश्रान्तिं लभतामिदं च शिथिलज्याबन्धमस्मद्धनुः ॥२५०॥

अत्र कारकस्य । 'विश्रब्धा रचयन्तु शूकरवरा मुस्ताक्षतिम्' इत्यदुष्टम् ।

The right reading would be—

'*Kāshchit kīrṇā rajobhīrdivamanuvidadhurmaṇdavaktrendushobhāḥ, niḥshrīkāḥ &c., &c..................kampamāpuḥ*'

In the following we have an example of 'Violation of the Uniformity' of the *case-termination*—

'*Gāhantāṁ mahiṣā nipānasalilaṁ shṛṅgairmuhustāḍitam*
Chhāyābaddhakadambakaṁ mṛgakulaṁ romanthamabhyasyatām
Vishrabdhaiḥ kriyatāṁ varāhapatibhirmustākṣatiḥ palvale
Vishrāntiṁ labhatāmidaṁ cha shithilajyābandhamasmaddhanuḥ'.

'The wild buffaloes may now dabble in the pools, striking the water frequently with their horns ; the deer herded under the shade may practise rumination ; the huge boars may fearlessly destroy the long grass along the tanks ;—this very bow also may obtain rest on having its string slackened.'

[While we have the *Active* nominative ending throughout the verse, in the third line we have the *Passive* nominative ending].

The right reading would be—

'*Viṣhrabdhā rachayantu shūkaravarā mustākṣatim.*'

अकलिततपस्तेजोवीर्यप्रथिम्नि यशोनिधा-
ववितथमदाध्माते रोषान्मुनावभिगच्छति ।
अभिनवधनुर्विद्यादर्पक्षमाय च कर्मणे
स्फुरति रभसात्पाणिः पादोपसंग्रहणाय च ॥२५१॥

अत्र क्रमस्य । पादोपसंग्रहणायति पूर्वं वाच्यम् । एवमन्य-दप्यनुसर्तव्यम् ॥

(२०) अविद्यमानः क्रमो यत्र । यथा

In the following we have 'Violation of the Uniformity' of *sequence* —

'*Akalitatapastejovīryaprathimni yashonidhā-*
Vavitathamadādhmāte roṣānmunāvabhigachchhati
Abhinavadhanurvidyādarpakṣamāya cha karmaṇe
Sphurati rabhasātpāṇiḥ pādopasaṅgrahaṇāya cha.'

'On the arrival of this sage, who is endowed with greatness due to illimitable ascetic virtue, and is the receptacle of fame, puffed with real haughtiness—my arms suddenly throb for such action as would be in keeping with the efficiency newly acquired in the science of archery, and also for clasping his feet.'

The presence of 'ascetic virtue' is mentioned before that of 'haughtiness', hence in the corresponding passage, 'the clasping of the feet' '*pādopasaṅgrahaṇāya*,' which would be the correlative of the presence of ascetic virtue, should have been mentioned first (before the 'efficiency in Archery' which would correspond with the sage's 'haughtiness'.)

Other similar examples may be cited.

(20) In the following we have the example of the 'Absence of Uniformity'.

द्वयं गतं संप्रति शोचनीयतां
समागमप्रार्थनया कपालिनः ।
कला च सा कान्तिमती कलावतः
त्वमस्य लोकस्य च नेत्रकौमुदी ॥२५२॥

अत्र त्वंशब्दानन्तरं चकारो युक्तः । यथा वा

शक्तिर्निस्त्रिंशजेयं तव भुजयुगले नाथ दोषाकरश्री-
र्वक्त्रे पार्श्वे तथैषा प्रतिवसति महाकुट्टनी खड्गयष्टिः ।
आज्ञेयं सर्वगा ते विलसति च पुरः किं मया वृद्धया ते
प्रोच्येवेत्थं प्रकोपाच्छशिकरसितया यस्य कीर्त्या प्रयातम् ॥२५३॥

'*Dvayaṅgataṁ samprati shochanīyatāṁ*
Samāgamaprārthanayā kapālinaḥ
Kalā cha sā kāntimatī kalāvatas-
Tvamasya lokasya cha netrakaumudī.'

(For translation, see above stanza No. 186).

The presence of the particle '*cha*' after '*tvam*' would be proper (making the two correlated clauses more uniform).

Another example of the same—

'*Shaktirnistriṁshajeyaṁ tava bhujayugale nātha doṣākaraśrīr*
Vaktre pārshve tathaiṣā prativasati mahākuṭṭanī khaḍgayaṣṭiḥ
Ājñeyaṁ sarvagā te vilasati cha puraḥ kiṁ mayā vṛddhayā te
Prochyevetthaṁ prakopāchchhashikarasitayā yasya kīrtyā prayātam.'

'"O Lord! you have in your hands (in your arms, in your embrace) this strength of your long sword (a prostitute); in your face you have the splendour of the moon (the receptable of blemishes); by your side hangs this sword, a mighty slaughterer (a pandering woman); your command, all-pervading (going to all men) dances before you;—what use can you have of myself, overgrown

अत्र 'इत्थं प्रोच्येव' इति न्याय्यम् । तथा

'लग्नं रागावृताङ्ग्या० ॥ २५३ (क) ॥

इत्यादौ 'इति श्रीनियोगात्' इति वाच्यम् ॥

(२१) अमतः प्रकृतविरुद्धः परार्थो यत्र । यथा

राममन्मथशरेण ताडिता दुःसहेन हृदये निशाचरी ।
गन्धवद्रुधिरचन्दनोक्षिता जीवितेशवसतिं जगाम सा ॥२५४॥

अत्र प्रकृते रसे विरुद्धस्य शृङ्गारस्य व्यञ्जकोपरोऽर्थः ॥५४॥

अर्थदोषानाह

अर्थोऽपुष्टः कष्टो व्याहतपुनरुक्तदुष्क्रमग्राम्याः ॥ ५५ ॥
संदिग्धो निर्हेतुः प्रसिद्धिविद्याविरुद्धश्च ।
अनवीकृतः सनियमानियमविशेषा विशेषपरिवृत्ताः ॥ ५६ ॥

(old) as I am"—Having said this the king's Fame, white as the moon's rays, went forth, as if in a rage.'

Here the proper order of words would have been '*ittham prochyeva.*'

Another example of the same defect we have in the verse '*Lagnam rāgavṛtāngyā etc.*' (quoted above, stanza No. 241); where the proper form would have been '*iti shrīniyogāt*'.

(21) In the following we have an example of 'Undesirable Second Meaning'; *i.e.* where the words have an implication repugnant to the context :—

'The demoness, struck in her heart by the unbearable arrows of the Cupid-like Rāma, went to the abode of the Lord of Life, being smeared all over with her own sandal-like stinking blood.'

Here the sentiment desired to be described is that of Disgust,—and repugnant to this is the erotic sentiment which is implied by the words used. 54.

The author now describes the *defects of meaning* (*Ideal* Defects, as distinguished from *Verbal* Defects described above).

साकाङ्क्षोपदयुक्तः सहचरभिन्नः प्रकाशितविरुद्धः ।
विध्यनुवादायुक्तस्त्यक्तपुनःस्वीकृतोऽश्लीलः ॥ ५७ ॥

दुष्ट इति संबध्यते । क्रमेणोदाहरणम्—

(१) अतिविततगगनसरणिप्रसरणपरिमुक्तविश्रमानन्दः ।
मरुदुल्लासितसौरभकमलाकरहासकृद्रविर्जयति ॥२५५॥

अत्रातिविततत्वादयोनुपादानेपि प्रतिपाद्यमानमर्थं न बाधन्त इत्यपुष्टाः न त्वसंगताः पुनरुक्ता वा ॥

The meaning is—(1) *irrelevant*, (2) *obscure*, (3) *inconsistent*, (4) *tautophonous*, (5) *irregular*, (6) *vulgar*, (7) *dubious*, (8) *inconsequential*, (9) *opposed to prevailing notions*, (10) *opposed to scientific notions*, (11) *monotonous*, (12) *too unspecific*, (13) *too specific*, (14) *too restricted*, (15) *too unrestricted*, (16) *incomplete*, (17) *misplaced*, (18) *mismatched*, (19) *of repugnant implication*, (20) *with improper predicate*, (2) *with improper adjunct*, (22) *resuming the concluded*, *and* (23) *indecorous*. 55-57

The 'meaning' here referred to is to be understood as the 'defective' meaning.

The following are the examples of the *defects of meaning* in due order :—

(1) 'Having renounced the pleasures of ease during his constant journey through the very wide-spread ethereal path, and making to smile the lotus which has its fragrance wafted by the breeze—the sun shines resplendent.'

The epithets 'very wide-spread' ('path') and the rest are such that even if they were dropped, there would be no harm done to the sense ; hence they are 'irrelevant'—not 'inconsistent' or 'tautological'.

(२) सदा मध्ये यासामियममृतनिस्यन्दमधुरा
सरस्वत्युद्दामा वहति बहुमार्गा परिमलम् ।
प्रसादं ता एता घनपरिचिताः केन महतां
महाकाव्यव्योम्नि स्फुरितमधुरा यान्तु रुचयः ॥२५६॥

अत्र यासां कविरुचीनां मध्ये सुकुमारविचित्रमध्यमात्मक-त्रिमार्गा भारती चमत्कारं वहति ताः गम्भीरकाव्यपरिचिताः कथमितरकाव्यवत् प्रसन्ना भवन्तु । यासामादित्यप्रभाणां मध्ये

---

(2) The following is an example of the 'obscure' meaning—

'*Sadā madhye yāsāmiyamamṛtanisyandamadhurā*
Sarasvatyuddāmā vahati bahumārgā parimalam
Presādaṁ tā etā ghanaparichitāḥ kena mahatāṁ
Mahākāvyavyomni sphuritamadhurā yāntu ruchayaḥ.'

'How can the imaginative flashes of great poets attain simplicity, when within them flows untramelled the Goddess of Speech rendered sweet and passionate with the flow of nectar, decked in various styles and carrying a peculiar charm,—flashes which, assiduously practised, waft sweetness in the atmosphere of Poetry ?—How too (*second entendre*) can the rays of the Twelve Sons become pleasant, when in their midst flows untramelled the river Sarasvatī sweet with flowing water, running in diverse directions and spreading sweet fragrance,—the rays accompanied by clouds and wafting sweet water in the atmosphere ?'

The meaning of this, expressed too succinctly is as follows—(*a*) 'The flashes of the poet's imagination, wherein speech produces a peculiar charm through the styles—the lucid, the picturesque and the medium,—and which are found in deep poetry,—how can these be easy, like ordinary poetry ?—(*b*) 'The sun's rays,

त्रिपथगा वहति ता मेघपरिचिताः कथं प्रसन्ना भवन्तीति संक्षेपार्थः ॥

(३) जगति जयिनस्ते ते भावा नवेन्दुकलादयः
प्रकृतिमधुराः सन्त्येवान्ये मनो मदयन्ति ये ।
मम तु यदियं याता लोके विलोचनचन्द्रिका
नयनविषयं जन्मन्येकः स एव महोत्सवः ॥२५७॥

अत्रेन्दुकलादयो यं प्रति पस्पशप्रायाः स एव चन्द्रिकात्वमुत्कर्षार्थमारोपयतीति व्याहतत्वम् ॥

(४) कृतमनुमतमित्यादि ॥२५८॥

अत्रार्जुनार्जुनेति भवद्भिरिति चोक्ते सभीमकिरीटिनामिति

---

among whom flows the Triple stream (Gaṅgā), which are interspersed with clouds,—how can these be pleasant ?'

[And this, second meaning, is extremely *obscure*].

(3) [Example of the Inconsistent]—

'In the universe there are several most excellent things,—such as the fresh lustre of the moon and so forth—which are, by their very nature, sweet and which enrapture the heart ; but for me, the one ubilant event in my life has been this that she, who is like moonlight to the eye, has come within the range of my vision.'

Here, the very person to whom moonshine and other things are described (in the first sentence) as being very insignificant, regards the woman's likeness to moonlight as a ground of excellence ; and herein lies the inconsistency.

(4) In the verse '*kṛtamanumatam* &c.' (see above, stanza No. 39), the mention of Arjuṇa in the compound '*sabhīmakirīṭinām*' is 'tautophonous,' where the speaker

किरीटिपदार्थः पुनरुक्तः । यथा वा

अस्त्रज्वालावलीढप्रतिबलजलधेरन्तरौर्वायमाणे ।
सेनानाथे स्थितेऽस्मिन्मम पितरि गुरौ सर्वधन्वीश्वराणाम् ।
कर्णालं संभ्रमेण व्रज कृप समरं मुञ्च हार्दिक्य शङ्कां
ताते चापद्वितीये वहति रणधुरं को भयस्यावकाशः ॥२५९॥

अत्र चतुर्थपादवाक्यार्थः पुनरुक्तः ॥

(५) भूपालरत्न निर्दैन्यप्रदानप्रथितोत्सव ।
विश्राणय तुरङ्गं मे मातङ्गं वा मदालसम् ॥२६०॥

अत्र मातङ्गस्य प्राङ्निर्देशो युक्तः ।

---

has already mentioned the name of Arjuṇa twice in the words preceding the verse.

Another example of the same we have in the following :—

'While my father, the preceptor of all the foremost archers, is acting like the submarine fire in the midst of the ocean of the enemy-warriors licked by the flame of his weapons, remains the commander of the army,—there is no ground, O Karṇa ! for this flurry ! O Kṛpa repair to the fray ! O Kṛtavarman, give up all fear ! While my father, aided by his bow, is bearing the brunt of the battle, where can there be any room for fear ?'

Here what is said in the last foot of the verse is a needless repetition.

(5) [Example of the 'Irregular']—

'O best of kings, who are known to rejoice in the bestowing of wealth,—give to me a horse, or an elephant in lethargic intoxication.'

The correct order would have been to mention the 'elephant' (the larger gift) first.

(६) स्वपिति यावदयं निकटे जनः स्वपिमि तावदहं किमैपति ते ।
तदपि सांप्रतमाहर कूर्परं त्वरितमूरुमुदञ्चय कुञ्चितम्॥२६१॥

एषोविग्दग्धः ॥

(७) मात्सर्यमुत्सार्येत्यादि ॥२६२॥

अत्र प्रकरणाद्यभावे संदेहः शान्तशृङ्गार्यन्यतराभिधाने तु निश्चयः ॥

(८) गृहीतं येनासीः परिभवभयान्नोचितमपि
प्रभावाद्यस्याभून्न खलु तव कश्चिन्न विषयः ।
परित्यक्तं तेन त्वमसि सुतशोकान्न तु भया-
द्विमोक्ष्ये शस्त्र त्वामहमपि यतः स्वस्ति भवते ॥२६३॥

---

(6) [Example of the 'Vulgar']—

'While this person is asleep, I sleep by your side; what do you lose by that?—So, you may remove your elbows and spread out your thighs.'

The speaker here is entirely vulgar (in the expression of his desire). 55.

(7) In the verse '*mātsaryamutsārya etc.*' (see above, stanza No. 133), the meaning is 'dubious' or doubtful until there is some determining factor in the form of context and the like. When, on the other hand, it is known whether the speaker is a man of the erotic or the quietistic temperament, there is no doubt regarding the meaning.

(8) [Example of the 'Inconsequential']

'O weapon! though such conduct was not consistent with his caste, yet thou wert taken up by my father to guard against ill-treatment; through his valour, there was nothing that did not fall within thy range; now thou hast been relinquished by him, not through fear, but through grief for his son;—I also am going to leave thee in a place, where all may go well with thee!'

अत्र शस्त्रमोचने हेतुर्नोपात्तः ॥

(९) इदं ते केनोक्तं कथय कमलातङ्कवदने
यदेतस्मिन् हेम्नः कटकमिति धत्से खलु धियम् ।
इदं तद् दुःसाधाक्रमणपरमास्त्रं स्मृतिभुवा
तव प्रीत्या चक्रं करकमलमूले विनिहितम् ॥२६४॥

अत्र कामस्य चक्रं लोकेप्रसिद्धम् । यथा वा

(९ अ) उपपरिसरं गोदावर्याः परित्यजताध्वगाः
सरणिमपरो मार्गस्तावद्भवद्भिरिहेक्ष्यताम् ।
इह हि विहितो रक्ताशोकः कयापि हताशया
चरणनलिनन्यासोदञ्चन्नवाङ्कुरकञ्चुकः ॥२६५॥

अत्र पादाघातेनाशोकस्य पुष्पोद्गमः कविषु प्रसिद्धो न पुनरङ्कुरोद्गमः ।

This supplies no reason why the speaker is giving up his weapon.

(9) [Example of what "is contrary to prevalent notions"]—

'O thou, whose face abashes the lotus! who has told you this, by virtue of which thou entertainest the notion that this thing is a bangle of gold? In reality, it is the *disc* of the Love-god placed, through his love for you, on your wrist, as the weapon capable of striking the most invulnerable of men!'

The idea of the Love-god holding a *disc* is 'contrary to all prevalent notions' regarding him.

Another example—

'O travellers! Give up this path that passes along the Godāvarī, and look out for another path; as on this spot the red Aśoka tree has grown fresh sprouts through the action of the lotus-feet of some mischievous woman'.

(सुसितवसनालंकारायां कदाचन कौमुदी-
महसि सुदृशि स्वैरं यान्त्यां गतोस्तमभूद्विधुः ।
तदनु भवतः कीर्तिः केनाप्यगीयत येन सा
प्रियगृहमगान्मुक्ताशङ्का क्व नासि शुभप्रदः ॥२६६॥

अत्रामूर्तापि कीर्तिः ज्योत्स्नावत्प्रकाशरूपा कथितेति लोक-विरुद्धमपि कविप्रसिद्धेर्न दुष्टम् ॥)

(१०) सदा स्नात्वा निशीथिन्यां सकलं वासरं बुधः ।
नानाविधानि शास्त्राणि व्याचष्टे च शृणोति च ॥२६७॥

What is known as a poetical convention is that the touch of woman's feet leads to the appearance of *blossoms*,—and not *sprouts*—on the Aśoka tree.

In cases where what is described is in keeping with poetic convention, it is not defective, even though it may be contrary to popular notions. For example, in the following verse, though Fame, which is popularly known to be *formless*, has been described as having the *form* of light,—and to that extent it is contrary to popular notions,—yet it is not regarded as defective, as it is in keeping with poetic conventions.—

'While a certain beautiful-eyed woman, decked in white garments and ornaments, was proceeding fearlessly in the bright moon-light, the moon went down; after that your fame was sung by some one, whereby she proceeded unhesitatingly to the house of her lover ;—where is it that you are not a source of happiness ?'

(10) [An example of what is 'Unscientific.']—

(*a*) 'The learned man always bathes at midnight and expounds and listens to lectures upon the various scriptures throughout the day.'

ग्रहोपरागादिकं विना रात्रौ स्नानं धर्मशास्त्रेण विरुद्धम् ।

(१० अ) अनन्यसदृशं यस्य बलं बाह्वोः समीक्ष्यते ।
षाड्गुण्यानुसृतिस्तस्य सत्यं सा निष्प्रयोजना ॥२६८॥

एतत् अर्थशास्त्रेण ।

(१० आ) विधाय दूरे केयूरमनङ्गाङ्गणमङ्गना ।
बभार कान्तेन कृतां करजोल्लेखमालिकाम् ॥२६९॥

अत्र केयूरपदे नखक्षतं न विहितमिति । एतत्कामशास्त्रेण ।

(१० इ) कष्टाङ्गयोगपरिशीलनकीलनेन
दुःसाधसिद्धिसविधं विदधद्विदूरे ।
आसादयन्नभिमतामधुना विवेक-
ख्यातिं समाधिधनमौलिमणिर्विमुक्तः ॥२७०॥

Bathing at night, except on the occasion of an eclipse, is contrary to the Scriptural Code.

(*b*) 'In the case of the king the strength of whose arms is unequalled, the following of the dictates of 'the Science of Six Limbs' (Political Science) is entirely useless.'

This is contrary to the Code of Polity.

(*c*) 'The woman, who is the very altar of the Love-god, threw away her armlet, and wore (in its stead) the series of nail-marks made by her lover.'

Nail-marks are not laid down as to be made on the place where the armlet is worn ; hence what is said here is contrary to the Science of Erotics.

(*d*) 'By the strenuous practice of the eight-limbed Yoga, having laid aside the whereabouts of the unattainable success,—the chief of Yogins obtained the desired discriminative wisdom and became released.'

अत्र विवेकख्यातिस्ततः संप्रज्ञातसमाधिः पश्चादसंप्रज्ञातस्ततो मुक्तिर्न तु विवेकख्यातौ। एतत् योगशास्त्रेण ॥

एवं विद्यान्तरैरपि विरुद्धमुदाहार्यम् ॥

(११) प्राप्ताः श्रियः सकलकामदुघास्ततः किम्
दत्तं पदं शिरसि विद्विषतां ततः किम् ।
संतर्पिताः प्रणयिनो विभवैस्ततः किम्
कल्पं स्थितं तनुभृतां तनुभिस्ततः किम् ॥२७१॥

अत्र ततः किमिति न नवीकृतम् । तत्तु यथा

यदि दहत्यनलोत्र किमद्भुतं यदि च गौरवमद्रिषु किं ततः ।
लवणमम्बु सदैव महोदधेः प्रकृतिरेव सतामविषादित ॥२७२॥

The doctrine of the Science of Yoga being that—*first* of all one obtains discriminative wisdom, then concrete meditation, then abstract meditation and then Release; and Release is not obtained immediately after discriminative wisdom. Hence what is here stated is opposed to the Science of Yoga.

Similar examples of opposition to other Sciences may be cited.

(11) [Example of 'Monotony']—

'All-affording wealth has been attained;—what then? The foot has been placed on the head of the enemy;—what then? Friends have been fully supplied with riches;—what then? The bodies of men have lasted for a whole cycle;—what then?'

Here the frequent repetition of 'what then' is *monotonous*. This 'monotony' is avoided in the following—

'If fire burns,—what is the wonder? If mountains are full of gravity,—what then? The water of the ocean is ever salty. To great beings freedom from depression comes naturally.'

(१२) यत्रानुल्लिखितार्थमेव निखिलं निर्माणमेतद्विधेर्-
उत्कर्षप्रतियोगिकल्पनमपि न्यक्कारकोटिः परा ।
याताः प्राणभृतां मनोरथगतीरुल्लङ्घ्य यत्संपदस्
तस्याभासमणीकृताश्मसु मणेरश्मत्वमेवोचितम्॥२७३॥

अत्र 'छायामात्रमणीकृताश्मसु मणेस्तस्याश्मतैवोचिता' इति सनियमत्वं वाच्यम् ॥

(१३) वक्त्राम्भोजं सरस्वत्यधिवसति सदा शोण एवाधरस्ते
बाहुः काकुत्स्थवीर्यस्मृतिकरणपटुर्दक्षिणस्ते समुद्रः ।

---

(12) [Example of the 'Too unspecific' or 'Too generalised']—

"In view of the *Chintāmaṇi* jewel, the entire creation of God becomes purposeless ; any mention of its excellences would be the highest insult to it ; and its plentiful richness has exceeded the bounds of human desire ; and yet when it gets mixed up with pebbles, which have been rendered gem-like through its reflection, it should be regarded as a *pebble* only'.

Here some such *specification* as 'through its *mere* reflection' is necessary ; and the right reading of the last foot therefore should be—'*chhāyāmātramaṇīkṛtāshmasu maṇestasyāshmataivochitā.*'

[Such *specification* would imply that the other gems belong to an inferior category; and the absence of this specification places the *Chintāmaṇi* on the same level as the other gems, which is not what is intended by the poet.]

(13) [Example of the 'Too specific']—

'The Sarasvatī river (Goddess of Learning) resides permanently in your lotus-like mouth ; your under-lip is the Shoṇa (red) itself ; your arm , which is capable of reminding people of the valour of 'Kākutstha, is the

वाहिन्यः पार्श्वमेताः क्षणमपि भवतो नैव मुञ्चन्त्यभीक्ष्णं
स्वच्छेन्तर्मानसेस्मिन् कथमवनिपते तेम्बुपानाभिलाषः ॥२७४॥
अत्र 'शोण एव' इति नियमो न वाच्यः ॥
(१४) श्यामां श्यामलिमानमानयत भोः सान्द्रैर्मषीकूर्चकैर्
मन्त्रं तन्त्रमथ प्रयुज्य हरत श्वेतोत्पलानां श्रियम् ।
चन्द्रं चूर्णयत क्षणाच्च कणशः कृत्वा शिलापट्टके
येन द्रष्टुमहं क्षमे दश दिशस्तद्वक्त्रमुद्राङ्किताः ॥२७५॥
अत्र 'ज्यौत्स्नीम्' इति श्यामाविशेषो वाच्यः ॥
(१५) कल्लोलवेल्लितदृषत्परुषप्रहारै
रत्नान्यमूनि मकरालय मावमंस्थाः ।
किं कौस्तुभेन विहितो भवतो न नाम
याच्ञाप्रसारितकरः पुरुषोत्तमोपि ॥२७६॥

---

southern ocean (adorned with rings); these rivers (armies) never leave your side even for a moment; your inside being the pure Mānasa lake (your inner heart being clean),—how can there be any thirst of water for you ?'

Here the specification—'Shoṇa *itself*'—is one that should not have been made.

(14) [Example of the 'Too unrestricted']—

'Make the night black with brushes of dense ink; destroy the beauty of the white lotuses by means of incantations or herbs; smash the moon to pieces on a slab of stone; so that I may be able to look upon all the quarters marked with the stamp of her face.'

Here the 'night' should have been restricted to the 'bright, moon-lit.'

(15) [Example of the 'Too restricted']—

'O, thou abode of alligators! do not ill-treat these gems by striking them with stones thrown about by the

अत्र 'एकेन किं न विहितो भवतः स नाम' इति सामान्यं वाच्यम् ।

(१६) अर्थित्वे प्रकटीकृतेपि न फलप्राप्तिः प्रभोः प्रत्युत
द्रुह्यन् दाशरथिर्विरुद्धचरितो युक्तस्तया कन्यया ।
उत्कर्षं च परस्य मानयशसोर्विस्रंसनं चात्मनः
स्त्रीरत्नं च जगत्पतिर्दशमुखो देवः कथं मृष्यते ॥२७७॥

अत्र स्त्रीरत्नम् 'उपेक्षितुम्' इत्याकाङ्क्षति । नहि परस्येत्यनेन संबन्धो योग्यः ॥

---

waves; was it not due to the Kaustubha-gem that even Lord Viṣṇu himself was made to appear before you with hands spread out to beg ?'

[Here the restricted mention by name of one particular gem, the *Kaustubha*, is not very effective]:—the statement should appear in a more generalised form—'was it not due to *one of these* gems that even Lord etc.'

(16) [Example of the 'Incomplete']

'*Arthitve prakaṭīkṛtepi na phalaprāptiḥ prabhoḥ pratyuta*
Druhyan dāsharathirviruddhacharito yuktasatayā kanyayā
Utkarṣaṁ cha parasya mānayashasorvisbraṁsanañchātmanaḥ
Strīratnaṁ cha jagatpatirdashamukho devaḥ kathaṁ mṛṣyate'

'O Lord ! even though you exhibited beggarliness, yet the desired object has not been attained ; on the contrary, to her has been wedded the son of Dasharatha, your enemy, who hates you. How can you, the ten-faced lord of the world, bear this superiority of the enemy, and the derogation of your own pride and fame,—as also the jewel among women ?'

Here the intended assertion is—'How can you bear the *idea of giving up the* jewel among women'; and inasmuch as the passage as the term '*strīratnam*' only, it is, to that extent, 'incomplete.' It might be urged that the term

(१७) आज्ञा शक्रशिखामणिप्रणयिनी शास्त्राणि चक्षुर्नवं
भक्तिर्भूतपतौ पिनाकिनि पदं लङ्केति दिव्या पुरी ।
उत्पत्तिर्द्रुहिणान्वये च तदहो नेदृग्वरो लभ्यते
स्याच्चेदेष न रावणः क्व नु पुनः सर्वत्र सर्वे गुणाः ॥२७८॥

अत्र 'स्याच्चेदेष न रावणः' इत्यत्र एव समाप्यम् ॥

(१८) श्रुतेन बुद्धिर्व्यसनेन मूर्खता मदेन नारी सलिलेन निम्नगा ।
निशा शशाङ्केन धृतिःसमाधिना नयेन चालंक्रियते नरेन्द्रता॥२७९॥

'*strīratnam*' may be construed with '*parasya*',—the sense being 'how can you bear the idea that the jewel among women *belongs to another*'. But such a construction is not possible, [the term '*parasya*' having been already construed with '*utkarṣam*']

(17) [Example of the 'Misplaced.']—

'His command is borne by Indra on his head; the sciences constitute his efficient organ of vision; his devotion rests in Shiva, the lord of beings; and beautiful Laṅkā is his residence; and his birth is in the family of Brahmā; thus, then, no such other bridegroom could be found :—only if he were not Rāvaṇa (the Terrible)! But wherein can all good qualities be found ?'

The sentence should have ended with 'only if he were not Rāvaṇa'.

[As what is meant is that this single disqualification nullifies all the aforesaid qualifications, and as such puts him out of court as a suitable bridegroom. This sense is prevented by the subsequent clause—'wherein &c.'—which is a sort of a palliative excuse for the presence of a single disqualification as against a large number of qualifications. which tends to indicate the suitability of Rāvaṇa].

(18) [Example of the 'Mismatched']—

'Intelligence is adorned by learning, illiteracy by frivolity, woman by lasciviousness, the river by water,

अत्र श्रुतादिभिरुत्कृष्टैः सहचरितैर्व्यसनमूर्खतयोर्निकृष्टयोर्भिन्नत्वम् ।

(१९) लग्नं रागावृताङ्गया० ॥२८०॥

इत्यत्र विदितं तेऽस्त्विवत्यनेन श्रीस्तस्मादपसरतीति विरुद्धं प्रकाश्यते ॥

(२०) प्रयत्नपरिबोधितः स्तुतिभिरद्य शेषे निशा-
मकेशवमपाण्डवं भुवनमद्य निःसोमकम् ।
इयं परिसमाप्यते रणकथाद्य दोःशालिना-
मपैतु रिपुकाननातिगुरुरद्य भारो भुवः ॥२८१॥

अत्र 'शयितः प्रयत्नेन बोध्यसे' इति विधेयम् । यथा वा

---

the night by the moon, steadiness by calmness, and kingship by policy.'

Here the excellent things, 'Learning' and the rest are wrongly associated with such inferior things as 'illiteracy' and 'frivolity'.

(19) In the verse '*lagnaṁ rāgāvṛtāṅgyā.*' (see above, stanza No. 241) we have an example of 'Repugnant Implication', as the clause 'might be known to you' implies that the Goddess of wealth is going to depart from the king.

(20) [Example of 'Improper Predication']—

'*Prayatnaparibodhitaḥ &c., &c.*'

'To-night you will sleep so soundly that you will be awakened with great effort by means of eulogising songs; the world is going to be deprived to-day of Kṛṣṇa, of Pāṇḍavas and of the entire Somaka-tribe; thus to-day is going to be finished all talk of war among the Kṣattriyas; may the burden of the forest of our enemies depart to-day from the surface of the earth!'

The right form of predication would have been 'when asleep it will be *with great effort that* you will be awakened.'

[With stress upon 'effort', which is lost when '*prayatna*' is made the subordinate factor in the compound *prayatna-paribodhitaḥ*].

वाताहारतया जगद्विषधरैराश्वास्य निःशषितं
ते ग्रस्ताः पुनरभ्रतोयकणिकातीव्रव्रतैर्बर्हिभिः ।
तेपि क्रूरचमूरुचर्मवसनैर्नीताः क्षयं लुब्धकैर्-
दम्भस्य स्फुरितं विदन्नपि जनो जाल्मो गुणानीहते॥२८२॥

अत्र वाताहारादित्रयं व्युत्क्रमेण वाच्यम् ॥

(२१) अरे रामाहस्ताभरण भसलश्रेणिशरण
स्मरक्रीडाव्रीडाशमन विरहिप्राणदमन ।

Another example of the same '(defect of improper predication' when the *impropriety* consists in the wrong order of the things spoken of)—

'The world was emptied by the snakes, who inspired confidence by living upon air; the snakes themselves were devoured by peacocks undergoing the difficult penance of living on rain-drops from the clouds; these latter again were consigned to destruction by the fowlers clad in deer-skin;—even knowing the effects of religious hypocrisy, foolish people expect to find excellent qualities (in such persons)'.

The three things mentioned here should have been mentioned in the reverse order.

[The austerities should have been mentioned in the ascending scale: the less difficult coming before the more difficult; in the passage however the most difficult austerity, living upon air, has been mentioned first, and the least difficult, wearing of deer-skin, comes last; this spoils the effect of the climax.]

(21) [Example of the 'Improper (unsuitable) Adjunct']—

'O my friend, the Blue Lotus—who is an ornament for the hands of women, and the shelter of the line of black bees, who serves to suppress all modesty during love-

सरोहंसोत्तंस प्रचलदल नीलोत्पल सखे
सखेदोहं मोहं श्लथय कथय क्वेन्दुवदना ॥२८३॥

अत्र 'विरहिप्राणदमन' इति नानुवाद्यम् ॥

(२२) लग्नं रागावृताङ्गयेत्यादि ॥२८४॥

अत्र 'विदितं तेस्तु' इत्युपसंहृतोपि तेनेत्यादिना पुनरुपात्तः ॥

(२३) हन्तुमेव प्रवृत्तस्य स्तब्धस्य विवरैषिणः ।
यथास्य जायते पातो न तथा पुनरुन्नतिः ॥२८५॥

अत्र पुंव्यञ्जनस्यापि प्रतीतिः ॥

---

dalliance, who destroys the lives of separated lover, who is an ornament of the best of lakes, and whose petals are moving ! I am grief-stricken ; remove my bewilderment and tell me where the moon-faced one is.'

Here the adjunct 'who destroys the lives of separated lovers' is highly improper.

[As one who does this can never be expected to help the lover in his difficulties, and it is such help that the speaker is seeking.]

(22) In the verse '*Lagnaṁ rāgāvṛtāṅgyā*' *&c.*' (see above, stanza No. 241) though the statement is 'concluded' at the clause 'be it known to you,'—yet it is resumed again in the clause 'by him &c.' [So this is an example of the 'resuming of the concluded].

(23) [Example of the 'Indecorous'].

'*Hantumeva pravṛttasya*
Stabdhasya vivaraiṣiṇaḥ
Yathāsya jāyate pāto
Na tathā punarunnatiḥ.'

'An evil person being always arrogant, bent upon mischief, given to fault-finding,—his fall, when it comes, is such that he can never rise again.'

यत्रैको दोषः प्रदर्शितस्तत्र दोषान्तराण्यपि सन्ति तथापि तेषां तत्राप्रकृतत्वात्प्रकाशनं न कृतम् ॥५५–५७॥

कर्णावतंसादिपदे कर्णादिध्वनिनिर्मितिः ।

संनिधानादिबोधार्थम्

अवतंसादीनि कर्णाद्याभरणान्येवोच्यन्ते । तत्र कर्णादिशब्दाः कर्णादिस्थितिप्रतिपत्तये । यथा

अस्याः कर्णावतंसेन जितं सर्वं विभूषणम् ।
तथैव शोभतेत्यर्थमस्याः श्रवणकुण्डलम् ॥२८६॥

The words used here have an implication which points to the male organ (and thus this becomes 'indecorous').

Though in several cases, a verse that has been cited as an example of a certain defect, contains other defects also, yet these latter have not been pointed out, as not being quite pertinent to the context. 55-57.

In such expressions as 'Karṇāvataṁsa' and the like, the introduction of the term 'karṇa' is for the purpose of expressing proximity.

Such words as '*avataṁsa*' and the like denote the *ear-ring* itself; the addition of the term '*karṇa*' '*ear*' (in the compound '*karṇāvataṁsa*') serves the purpose of expressing *proximity* [and hence it cannot be regarded as 'redundant'].

Examples of such use are found in the following verses—

'*Asyāḥ karṇāvataṁsena*
Jitaṁ sarvaṁ vibhūṣaṇam
Tathaiva shobhatetyartham
Asyāḥ shravaṇakuṇḍalam.

अपूर्वमधुरामोदप्रमोदितदिशस्ततः ।
आययुर्भृङ्गमुखराः शिरःशेखरशालिनः ॥२८७॥

अत्र कर्णश्रवणशिरःशब्दाः संनिधानप्रतीत्यर्थाः ॥

विदीर्णाभिमुखारातिकराले संगरान्तरे ।
धनुर्ज्याकिणचिह्नेन दोष्णा विस्फुरितं तव ॥२८८॥

अत्र धनुःशब्द आरूढत्वावगतये ॥

Apūrvamadhurāmoda-Pramoditadishastataḥ
Āyayurbhṛingamukharāḥ shiraḥshekharashālinaḥ.

'By her *ear-ornament on the ear*, all ornament has been subdued ; similarly does excellently shine her *ear-ring in the ear* :—The men came forward, rendering all the directions fragrant with excellent perfumes, with bees humming about them, and wearing *crown-jewels on their heads*.'

Here the terms '*karṇa*', '*shravaṇa*' and '*shiraḥ*' (when the terms '*avataṁsa*', '*kuṇḍala*' and '*shekhara*' denote respectively, the *ear-ornament*, the *ear-ring* and the *head-ornament*), serve the purpose of expressing *proximity* (*i.e.*, the fact of the ornament being actually worn on the occasion spoken of).

Similarly in the following verse—

'*Vidīrṇābhimukhārātikarāle saṅgarāntare*
Dhanurjyākiṇacihnena dosṇā visphuritaṁ tava',

'Throbbing was thy arm, hardened by the marks made by the bow-string of thy bow, and terrible through the rending of opponents during battle ';—the addition of the term '*dhanuḥ*,' 'bow' (when '*jyā*' itself denotes the *bow-string*) serves to indicate the fact of the string being *placed upon the bow*.

(That the addition of the term 'bow' is meant to

अन्यत्र तु

ज्याबन्धनिष्पन्दभुजेन यस्य विनिश्वसद्वक्त्रपरंपरेण ।
कारागृहे निर्जितवासवेन लङ्केश्वरेणोषितमा प्रसादात् ॥२८९॥

इत्यत्र केवलो ज्याशब्दः ।

प्राणेश्वरपरिष्वङ्गविभ्रमप्रतिपत्तिभिः ।
मुक्ताहारेण लसता हसतीव स्तनद्वयम् ॥२०९॥

अत्र मुक्तानामन्यरत्नामिश्रितत्वबोधनाय मुक्ताशब्दः ।

---

convey this additional idea is shown by the fact that) in other cases (where no such idea is meant to be conveyed), we find the term '*jyā*', 'bow-string,' used alone by itself; *e.g.*, in the following—

'*Jyābandhaniṣpandabhujena yasya*
Vinishvasadvaktraparamparеṇa
Kārāgṛhe nirjitavāsavena
Laṅkeshvareṇoṣitamāprasādāt.'

'In whose prison, there lived, till propitiation, the king of Laṅkā, the subduer of Indra, who had his arms paralysed by being tied up with the bowstring, and the line of his mouths panting.'

In the following.—

'*Prāṇeshvarapariṣvaṅgavibhramapratipattibhiḥ*
Muktāhāreṇa lasatā hasatīva stanadvayam'.

'The pair of breasts, beautified by the pearl-necklace is smiling as it were, under the consciousness of the joys of the embrace of her lover;'—the addition of the term '*muktā*', 'pearl' (when the term '*hāra*', 'necklace', itself signifies the presence of pearls) is meant to express the fact that no other gems were mixed with the pearls in the necklace.

सौन्दर्यसंपत् तारुण्यं यस्यास्ते ते च विभ्रमाः ।
षट्पदान् पुष्पमालेव कान् नाकर्षति सा सखे ॥२९१॥

अत्रोत्कृष्टपुष्पविषये पुष्पशब्दः । निरुपपदो हि मालाशब्दः पुष्पस्रजमेवाभिधत्ते ॥

स्थितेष्वेतत्समर्थनम् ॥ ५८ ॥

न खलु कर्णावतंसादिवज्जघनकाञ्चीत्यादि क्रियते ।
जगाद मधुरां वाचं विशदाक्षरशालिनीम् ॥२९२॥

Similarly in the following—

'*Saundaryasampat tāruṇyaṁ yasyāste te cha vibhramāḥ*
Ṣaṭpadān puṣpamāleva kān nākarṣati sā sakhe.

'She who is endowed with a richness of beauty, youth and excellent graces,—whom does she not captivate, O Friend ! in the same manner as a flower-garland attracts the bees ?'—

The term '*puṣpa*' 'flower', has been added in the sense of *excellent flowers*,—the word '*mālā*' 'garland', without a prefix, denoting merely a *string of flowers* (without any idea of the quality of the flowers strung).

This is a justification of only such instances as are actually found (in standard works). 58.

It is not meant to justify such usage by modern writes) ; so that it would not be right to use such expressions as '*jaghanakāñchī*', on the analogy of the expression '*Karṇāvataṁsa*' (justified above p. 258).

In such expressions as

'*jagāda madhurāṁ vāchaṁ vishadākṣarashālinīm*' ('uttered a speech, sweet and clearly worded'), it is not right

इत्यादौ क्रियाविशेषणत्वेपि विवक्षितार्थप्रतीतिसिद्धौ "गतार्थस्यापि विशेष्यस्य विशेषणदानार्थं क्वचित्प्रयोगः कार्यः" इति न युक्तम् । युक्तत्वे वा

चरणत्रपरित्राणरहिताभ्यामपि द्रुतम् ।
पादाभ्यां दूरमध्वानं व्रजन्नेष न खिद्यते ॥२९३॥

इत्युदाहार्यम् ॥५८॥

---

to justify (as Vāmana has done) the addition of the noun '*vācham*', 'speech', [which would appear to be superfluous on the ground of the verb '*jagāda*' '*uttered*', itself denoting the 'uttering *of speech*'], on the ground that 'even though the sense of the noun may have been obtained already, it is added for the purpose of adding qualifying epithets to it'; because the purpose sought to be served by the adding of these epithets could be more easily served by the use of adverbs (qualifying the verb itself) ; [So that the addition of the noun should not be necessary, even for that purpose].

[The expression with the adverbs could appear in the form '*jagāda madhuraṁ vidvān vishadākṣarashāli cha*].

As an example of the propriety of the justification suggested by Vāmana we have (not the aforesaid sentence cited by him, but) the following—

'*Charaṇatraparitrāṇarahitābhyāmapi drutam*
Pādābhyāṁ dūramadhvānaṁ vrajanneṣa na khidyate.

'He is not fatigued even when he *walks* long distances swiftly *with feet* deprived of shoes.'—[Where the purpose served by the addition of adjectival epithets to the noun '*charaṇa*' is such as could not be served by the addition of any adverbial expressions]. 58.

ख्यातेर्थे निर्हेतोरदुष्टता

यथा

चन्द्रं गता पद्मगुणान्न भुङ्क्ते पद्माश्रिता चान्द्रमसीमभिख्याम् ।
उमामुखं तु प्रतिपद्य लोला द्विसंश्रयां प्रीतिमवाप लक्ष्मीः ॥२९४॥

अत्र रात्रौ पद्मस्य संकोचः दिवा चन्द्रमसश्च निष्प्रभत्वं लोकप्रसिद्धमिति 'न भुङ्क्ते' इति हेतुं नापेक्षते ॥

अनुकरणे तु सर्वेषाम् ।

सर्वेषां श्रुतिकटुप्रभृतीनां दोषाणाम् । यथा

मृगचक्षुषमद्राक्षमित्यादि कथयत्ययम् ।
पश्यैष च गवित्याह सूत्रामाणं यजेत च ॥२९५॥

In cases where what is stated is a well-known fact, 'inconsequentiality' is not a defect.

As an example we have the following—

'Located in the Moon, grace does not imbibe the qualities of the lotus ; and when located in the lotus, it partakes not of the beauty of the Moon ; but when it rested in Umā's face, the fickle grace obtained the charm belonging to both (Moon and Lotus).'

The statement that grace 'does not imbibe &c. &c.' does not need an explanation ; as it is well-known that the lotus is closed up during the night, and the Moon is lustreless during the day.

In imitation, all the defects (cease to be defects).

'*All the defects*'—'unmelodiousness' and the rest.

As examples we have the following—

'*Mṛgachakṣuṣamadrākṣamityādi kathayatyayam*
Pashyaiṣa cha gavityāha sūtrāmāṇaṁ yajeta cha.'

'He says "I saw the fawn-eyed one' and so forth ; he says "see the cow" and also "offer sacrifices to Indra."

वक्त्राद्यौचित्यवशाद्दोषोपि गुणः क्वचित्क्वचिन्नोभौ ॥५९॥

वक्तृप्रतिपाद्यव्यङ्ग्यवाच्यप्रकरणादीनां महिम्ना दोषोपि क्वचिदगुणः क्वचिन्न दोषो न गुणः । तत्र वैयाकरणादौ वक्तरि प्रतिपाद्ये च रौद्रादौ च रसे व्यङ्ग्ये कष्टत्वं गुणः ।

क्रमेणोदाहरणम्—

दीधीङ्वेवीङ्समः कश्चिद्गुणवृद्ध्योरभाजनम् ।
क्विप्प्रत्ययनिभः कश्चिद्यत्र संनिहिते न ते ॥२१६॥

[(*a*) '*Mṛgachakṣuṣam*' is unmelodious ;—(*b*) '*gaviti*' is ungrammatical ;—and (*c*) '*sūtrāmāṇam*' is unconventional; but being only reproductions of what has been said by another person, they do not constitute defects in the reproduction.]

By virtue of the special character of the speaker and the rest, sometimes a defect becomes an excellence, and sometimes it is neither the one nor the other. 59.

By virtue of the importance attaching to the character of —(*a*) the speaker, (*b*) the person spoken to, (*c*) the meaning suggested, (*d*) the thing described, (*e*) the context and so forth,—a defect sometimes becomes an excellence ; and in certain cases it is neither a defect nor an excellence.

For instance, when a grammarian is the person speaking, or the person spoken to,—or when the passion of 'Fury' forms the suggested meaning,—the *Harshness* of words becomes an excellence.

Examples in order :—

(*a*) '*Dīdhiṅvevīṅsamaḥ kashchid*
Guṇavṛddhyorabhājanam
Kvippratayanibhaḥ kashchid
Yatra sannihite na te.'

यदा त्वामहमद्राक्षं पदविद्याविशारदम् ।
उपाध्यायं तदास्मार्षं समस्प्राक्षं च संमदम् ॥२९७॥

अन्त्रप्रोतबृहत्कपालनलकक्रूरक्वणत्कङ्कण-
प्रायप्रेङ्खितभूरिभूषणरवैराघोषयन्त्यम्बरम् ।
पीतच्छर्दितरक्तकर्दमघनप्राग्भारघोरोल्लस-
द्व्यालोलस्तनभारभैरववपुर्दर्पोद्धतं धावति ॥२९८॥

'Like the roots "*dīdhīṅ*" and "*vevīṅ*", some people are not amenable to excellence and prosperity (*eṅ* and *ai*, changes, to which the said roots are not subject) ; others again are like the "*kvip*" affix, by virtue of whose proximity, the said two things (excellence and prosperity) do not exist.

[Here since the speaker is a grammarian, the obscurity attaching to the expressions becomes an excellence.]

(*b*) '*Yadā tvāmahamadrākṣaṁ*
Padavidyāvishāradam
Upādhyāyaṁ tadāsmārṣaṁ
Samasprākṣaṁ cha saṁmadam.'

'When I saw you well-versed in grammatical lore, I was reminded of my own teacher and became elated with joy'.

[The person spoken to being a grammarian, obscurity is an excellence.]

(*c*) '*Āntraprotabṛhatkapālanalakakrūrakvaṇatkaṅkaṇa—*
Prāyapreṅkhitabhūribhūṣaṇaravairāghoṣayantyambaram
Pītachchharditaraktakardamaghanaprāgbhāraghorollasad-
Vyālolastanabhārabhairavavapurdarpoddhataṁ dhāvati'.

'She is rushing forward with proud arrogance, filling the atmosphere with the jingling of her dangling ornaments consisting of sculls and thighbones strung on the entrails,—her body appearing frightful on account of her dangling

वाच्यवशाद्यथा

मातङ्गाः किमु वल्गितैः किमफलैराडम्बरैर्जम्बुकाः
सारङ्गा महिषा मदं व्रजथ किं शून्येषु शरा न के ।
कोपाटोपसमुद्भटोत्कटसटाकोटेरिभारेः पुरः
सिन्धुध्वानिनि हुङ्कृते स्फुरति यत् तद्गर्जितं गर्जितम् ।।२९१।।

अत्र सिंहे वाच्ये परुषाः शब्दाः ।।

प्रकरणवशाद्यथा

---

breasts bespattered with the muddy blood that she has drunk and vomited.'

[The passion of disgust being suggested here, the harshness of the words becomes a source of excellence.]

(*d*). The following is an example where the defect (of Harshness) becomes an excellence by virtue of the character of the thing described.—

' *Mātaṅgāḥ kimu valgitaiḥ kimaphalaīrāḍambarairjambukāḥ*
Sāraṅgā mahiṣā madaṁ vrajata kiṁ shūnyeṣu shūrā na ke
Kopāṭopasamudbhaṭotkaṭasaṭākoṭeribhāreḥ puraḥ
Sindhudhvānini huṅkṛte sphurati yat tad garjitaṁ garjitaṁ'

' O elephants, what of your cries ! O jackals, what of these useless struttings ! O deer and buffaloes, wherefore are you so proud ? Who is not brave, in solitude ? Roaring would be real roaring, only in the presence of the ocean-like rumble of the lion with his name ruffled in anger.'

In the latter half of this verse, the lion being the thing described, the harsh-sounding words are a source of excellence.

(*e*) The following is an example of a defect becoming an excellence, by virtue of the context or occasion.

रक्ताशोक कृशोदरी क्व नु गता त्यक्त्वानुरक्तं जनं
नो दृष्टेति मुधैव चालयसि किं वातावधूतं शिरः ।
उत्कण्ठाघटमानषट्पदघटासंघट्टदष्टच्छद-
स्तत्पादाहतिमन्तरेण भवतः पुष्पोद्गमोयं कुतः ॥३००॥

अत्र शिरोधूननेन कुपितस्य वचसि ॥

क्वचिन्नीरसे न गुणो न दोषः । यथा

'Raktāshoka kṛshodarī kva nu gatā
tyaktvānuraktaṁjanaṁ
No dṛṣṭeti mudhaiva chālayasi kiṁ
vātāvadhūtaṁ shiraḥ
Utkaṇṭhāghaṭamānaṣaṭpadaghaṭāsaṅghaṭṭa-
daṣṭachchhadas-
Tatpādāhatimantareṇa bhavataḥ puṣpod-
gamoyaṅkutaḥ.'

'O red Ashoka tree, whereto has the slender-waisted one gone, leaving her lover ?—Why do you dishonestly shake your wind-blown head as if denying your having seen her ?—Without the touch of her feet, whence could there appear in you these blossoms, which have their petals bitten off by the swarms of black bees hovering round in their anxiety (to get at the flowers)'.

The latter half of the verse is spoken by the speaker on an occasion when he has become enraged by the dishonest behaviour of the tree shaking its head, [and hence the harshness of the words used is an excellence].

In some cases, where there is no Passion depicted, Harshness is neither a defect nor an excellence. For example—

शीर्णघ्राणाङ्घ्रिपाणीन् व्रणिभिरपघनैर्घर्घराव्यक्तघोषान्
दीर्घाघ्रातानघौघैः पुनरपि घटयत्येक उल्लाघयन् यः ।
घर्मांशोस्तस्य वोन्तर्द्विगुणघनघृणानिघ्ननिर्विघ्नवृत्तेर्
दत्तार्घाः सिद्धसंघैर्विदधतु घृणयः शीघ्रमंहोविघातम् ॥३०१॥

अप्रयुक्तनिहतार्थौ श्लेषादावदुष्टौ । यथा

येन ध्वस्तमनोभवेन बलिजित्कायः पुरा स्त्रीकृतो
यश्चोद्वृत्तभुजङ्गहारवलयोगङ्गां च योधारयत् ।

'*Shīrṇaghrāṇāṅghrīpāṇīn vraṇibhirapagha-*
nairghargharāvyaktaghoṣān
Dīrghāghrātānaghoghaiḥ punarapi ghaṭayat-
yeka ullāghayan yaḥ
Gharmāṁshostasya vontardviguṇaghanaghṛṇā-
nighnanirvighnavṛtter
Dattārghāḥ siddhasaṅghairvidadhatu ghṛṇayaḥ
shīghramaṁhovighātam.'

'May the rays of the sun, to whom water-offerings are made by the hosts of gods, bring about the destruction of your sins ;—the sun who restores and rejuvenates the bodies of lepers which, beset with hosts of sins, have the nose, legs and hands shattered and ulcerated, and whose voice is indistinct ; and whose disposition is affected by doubly intensified pity.'

[Here since no Passion of any kind is meant to be described, the high-sounding words do not constitute either a defect or an excellence.]

'Unconventionality' and 'Suppression of Meaning' are not defective in passages where we have the figure of Paronomasia. For instance, in the following verse :—

'*Yena dhvastamanobhavena balijitkāyaḥ purāstrīkṛto*
Yashchodvṛttabhujaṅgahāravalayogaṅgāṁ cha yodhārayat

यस्याहुः शशिमच्छिरोहर इति स्तुत्यं च नामामराः
पायात्स स्वयमन्धकक्षयकरस्त्वां सर्वदोमाधवः ॥३०२॥

अत्र माधवपक्षे शशिमदन्धकक्षयशब्दावप्रयुक्तनिहतार्थौ ॥

अश्लीलं क्वचिद्गुणः। यथा सुरतारम्भगोष्ठ्याम् "द्व्यर्थैः पदैः पिशुनयेच्च रहस्यवस्तु" इति कामशास्त्रस्थितौ

Yasyāhuḥ shashimachchhirohara iti stutyaṁ cha nāmāmarāḥ
Pāyāt sa svayamandhakakṣayakarastvāṁ sarvadomādhavaḥ.

(A) (Applied to *Kṛṣna*)—'May the all-giving husband of Lakṣmī protect you !—He who has destroyed the demon Shakaṭa, and himself unborn, conquered Balī, assumed a female form, subdued the serpent Kālīya ; in whom all sound becomes merged, who upheld the mountain and the earth, whose praiseworthy name the gods declare to be 'the chopper of the head of Rāhu', and who established the residence of the Andhaka race.'

(B) (Applied to *Shiva*)—'May the husband of Umā ever protect you !,—He, the destroyer of the mind-born Love-god, who turned into an arrow the body of Viṣṇu (the subduer of Balī), who has large serpents as his necklets and bangles, bears the Gaṅgā, and the moon also on his forehead, whose praiseworthy name declared by the gods is 'Hara', and who destroyed the demon Andhaka'.

In this verse the terms '*shashimat*' and '*andhakaṣaya*' are 'unconventional', when applied to Kṛṣṇa (but are not regarded as defective).

The 'Indecorous' is an excellence in certain cases ; for instance, in conversations leading upto sexual dalliance ; in accordance with the dictum of the Science of Erotics that 'secret matters are to be concealed by means of words with double meanings';—*e. g.*, in the following verse—

करिहस्तेन संबाधे प्रविश्यान्तर्विलोडिते ।
उपसर्पन् ध्वजः पुंसः साधनान्तर्विराजते ॥३०३॥

शमकथासु

उत्तानोच्छूनमण्डूकपाटितोदरसंनिभे ।
क्लेदिनि स्त्रीव्रणे सक्तिरकृमेः कस्य जायते ॥३०४॥

निर्वाणवैरदहनाः प्रशमादरीणां
नन्दन्तु पाण्डुतनयाः सह माधवेन।
रक्तप्रसाधितभुवः क्षतविग्रहाश्च
स्वस्था भवन्तु कुरुराजसुताः सभृत्याः ॥३०५॥

अत्र भाव्यमङ्गलसूचकम् ॥

Karihastena saṁbādhe pravishyāntarviloḍite
Upasarpan dhvajaḥ puṁsaḥ sādhanāntarvirājate.

Similarly also in conversation dealing with the quietistic sentiment ; *e.g.*

'*Uttānochchhūnamaṇḍūkapāṭitodarasannibhe*
Kledini strīvraṇe saktirakṛmeḥ kasya jāyate.'

Further, in the following verse, 'Indecorousness' is regarded as an excellence, by virtue of its affording a premonition of impending calamity—

'*Nirvāṇavairadahanāḥ prashamādarīṇāṁ*
Nandantu pāṇḍutanayāḥ saha mādhavena
Raktaprasādhitabhuvaḥ kṣatavigrahāshcha
Svasthā bhavantu kururājasutāḥ sabhṛtyāḥ'

'May the sons of Pāṇḍu along with Kṛṣṇa rejoice, on having the fire of animosity extinguished by the death (or peacefulness) of enemies ! and may the sons of the Kuru-king, along with their dependants, rest at peace (or

संदिग्धमपि वाच्यमहिम्ना क्वचिन्नियतार्थप्रतीतिकृत्त्वेन व्याजस्तुतिपर्यवसायित्वे गुणः । यथा

पृथुकार्तस्वरपात्रं भूषितनिःशेषपरिजनं देव ।
विलसत्करेणुगहनं संप्रति सममावयोः सदनम् ॥३०६॥

प्रतिपाद्यप्रतिपादकयोर्ज्ञत्वे सत्यप्रतीतं गुणः । यथा

---

in heaven), after having ruled over the world-kingdom attached to them (or, after having covered the earth with their blood), and having their quarrels set at rest (or having their bodies cut up).'

[Here the thing that is wished to happen is indicative of inauspiciousness.]

In cases where, the force of the character of the thing described tends to point to a definite meaning, 'Ambiguity' is regarded as an excellence, on account of its leading up to the Figure of Dissembling Eulogy. For instance, in the following versu—

'*Pṛthukārtasvarapātraṁ bhūṣitaniḥsheṣaparijanaṁ deva*
Vilasatkareṇugahanaṁ saṁprati samamāvayoḥ sadanaṁ'.—

'O Lord, at present the houses of both of us (you and I) are similar : yours being full of large golden vessels (and mine, full of the piteous shriekings of children), with all the servants decorated (mine, with all the inmates lying on the ground), and teeming with large elephants (mine, covered with mouse-dust);'—

[The fact of the words being addressed to the king point to the figure of Dissembling Eulogy, whereby the king's affluence is described]

In cases where the speaker and the person spoken to are both learned men, 'unintelligibility' is an excellence. For instance, in the following verse—

आत्मारामा विहितरतयो निर्विकल्पे समाधौ
ज्ञानोद्रेकाद्विघटिततमोग्रन्थयः सत्त्वनिष्ठाः ।
यं वीक्षन्ते कमपि तमसां ज्योतिषां वा परस्तात्
तं मोहान्धः कथमयममुं वेत्ति देवं पुराणम् ॥३०७॥

स्वयं वा परामर्शे । यथा

षडधिकदशनाडीचक्रमध्यस्थितात्मा
हृदि विनिहितरूपः सिद्धिदस्तद्विदां यः ।
अविचलितमनोभिः साधकैर्मृग्यमाणः
स जयति परिणद्धः शक्तिभिः शक्तिनाथः ॥३०८॥

'*Ātmārāmā vihitaratayo nirvikalpe samādhau*
Jñānodrekād vighaṭitatamogranthayaḥ sattvaniṣṭhāḥ
Yaṁ vīkṣante kimapi tamasām jyotiṣāṁ vā parastāt
Taṁ mohāndhaḥ kathamayamamuṁ vetti devaṁ purāṇam.

'How can this man (Duryodhana), blinded with delusion as he is, recognize the eternal God, whom only those perceive who, fixed in Goodness, have outgrown Darkness and Passion, and who have the knot of ignorance cut by the current of knowledge, given upto abstract meditation, and rejoicing in the contemplation of the god-head'.

[This is said by Bhīmasèna to Sahadeva, both highly educated princes : hence the use of Yoga technicalities is not a defect.]

In soliloquy also Unintelligibility is not a defect ; *e.g.*, in the following—

Ṣaḍadhikadashanāḍīchakramadhyasthitātmā
Hṛdi vinihitarūpaḥ siddhidastadvidāṁ yaḥ
Avichalitamanobhiḥ sādhakairmṛgyamāṇaḥ
Sa jayati pariṇaddhaḥ shaktibhiḥ shaktināthaḥ';—

'Glorious is Shiva, the Lord of the Female Divinity, possessed of manifold potentiality, having his soul located within the circle of the sixteenfold artery, who has his

अधमप्रकृत्युक्तिषु ग्राम्यो गुणः । यथा

फुल्लुक्करं कलमकूरणिहं वहन्ति
जे सिन्धुवारविडवा मह वल्लहा दे ।
जे गालिदस्स महिसीदहिणो सरिच्छा
दे किं च मुद्धविअइल्लपसूणपुञ्जा ॥३०९॥

अत्र कलमभक्तमहिषीदधिशब्दा ग्राम्या अपि विदूषकोक्तौ ॥

न्यूनपदं क्वचिद्गुणः । यथा

गाढालिङ्गनवामनीकृतकुचप्रोद्भूतरोमोद्गमा
सान्द्रस्नेहरसातिरेकविगलच्छ्रीमन्नितम्बाम्बरा ।

---

form in the heart, the ordainer of success to those who know Him, and who is looked up to by devotees with steady minds'.

'Vulgarity' is an excellence in the speeches of low-born persons.

e.g.—

'*Phullukkuraṁ kalamakūraṇihaṁ vahanti*
Je sindhubarabiḍavā mahaballahā de
Je gālidassa mahisīdahiṇo sarichchhā
De kiṁ cha muddhaviaillapasūṇapuñjā'.

'Those branches of the Sindhuvāra trees are dear to me, which bear fruits like rice ; as also are those masses of Mallikā flowers which resemble the squeezed curdled milk of a she-buffalo'.

In this the terms 'kalama', 'bhakta', 'kūra', 'mahiṣī' and 'dadhi', though *vulgar*, are not regarded as defective, as they occur in the speech of the clown.

'Verbal deficiency' is in some cases an excellence, *e. g.*, in the following :—

'*Gāḍhāliṅganavāmanīkṛtakuchaprodbhūtaromodgamā*
Sāndrasneharasātirekavigalachchhrīmannitambāmbarā

मा मा मानद माति मामलमिति क्षामाक्षरोल्लापिनी
सुप्ता किं नु मृता नु किं मनसि मे लीना विलीना नु किम् ।।३१०।।

क्वचिन्न गुणो न दोषः । यथा

तिष्ठेत्कोपवशात्प्रभावपिहिता दीर्घं न सा कुप्यति
स्वर्गायोत्पतिता भवेन्मयि पुनर्भावार्द्रमस्या मनः ।
तां हर्तुं विबुधद्विषोपि न च मे शक्ताः पुरोवर्तिनीं
सा चात्यन्तमगोचरं नयनयोर्यातेति कोयं विधिः ।।३११।।

Mā mā mānada māti māmalamiti kṣāmākṣarollāpinī
Suptā kiṁ nu mṛtā nu kiṁ manasi me līnā vilīnā nu kim '.

Her breasts dwarfed by firm embrace, and the body thrilling all over, her beautiful clothing slipping away from her waist, under the intensity of deep love, she uttered broken words—" Do not ! O ! do not ! my love ! not too much ! Ah me ! Enough !"—After which I know not if she went to sleep or was dead, or having entered into my heart, became assimilated therewith'.

[Here the broken utterance serve to intensify the feeling depicted.]

In certain cases the same defect of ' Verbal Deficiency ' is neither a defect nor an excellence ; *e.g.*, in the following—

' *Tiṣṭhet kopavashāt prabhāvapihitā dīrghaṁ na sā kupyati*
Svargāyotpatitā bhavenmayi punarbhāvārdramasyā manaḥ
Tāṁ hartuṁ vibudhaviṣopi na cha me shaktāḥ purovartinīṁ
Sā chātyantamagocharaṁ nayanayoryāteti koyaṁ vidhiḥ.'

' May she be lying concealed ?—She angers not for long ! Might she have flown to the heavens ?—Her heart bore deep affection towards me. Even the demons could not wrench her away from before me.—And yet she has passed completely beyond the range of my vision. What a process of fate !'

अत्र पिहिता इत्यतोनन्तरं 'नैतद्यतः' इत्येतैर्न्यूनैः पदैर्विशेषबुद्धेरकरणान्न गुणः । उत्तरा प्रतिपत्तिः पूर्वां प्रतिपत्तिं बाधते इति न दोषः ।।

अधिकपदं क्वचिद्गुणः । यथा ;

यद्वञ्चनाहितमतिर्बहुचाटुगर्भं
कार्योन्मुखः खलजनः कृतकं ब्रवीति ।
तत्साधवो न न विदन्ति विदन्ति किंतु
कर्तुं वृथा प्रणयमस्य न पारयन्ति ।।३१२।।

अत्र 'विदन्ति' इति द्वितीयमन्ययोगव्यवच्छेदपरम् ।

After '*pihitā*', 'concealed', there should have been the expression—'it is not so, because' and so forth; but this deficiency cannot be regarded as an excellence, because it does not afford any additional suggestion (as is done in the proceeding case); nor can it be regarded as a defect, because inasmuch as the second statement ('she angers not for long') by itself sets aside the first one, there is no real harm done by the omission of the words.

'Redundancy' is sometimes an excellence ; *e.g.* in the following—

'*Yadvañchanāhitamatirbahuchāṭugarbhaṁ*
Kāryonmukhaḥ khalajanaḥ kṛtakaṁ bravīti
Tatsādhavo na na vidanti vidanti kiṁtu
Kartuṁ vṛthā praṇayamasya na pārayanti'.

'The deceitful and cunning way in which evil people tell lies in business,—it is not that the good men do not know it, they do know it, even though they are unable to frustrate their hypocritical attachment'.

The second '*vidanti*', 'they do know', serves the purpose of excluding others from the knowledge in question [and as such the repetition is not a defect].

यथा वा

वद वद जितः स शत्रुर्न हतो जल्पंश्च तव तवास्मीति ।
चित्रं चित्रमरोदीद्धा हेति परं मृते पुत्रे ॥३१३॥

इत्येवमादौ हर्षभयादियुक्ते वक्तरि ॥

कथितपदं क्वचिद्गुणः लाटानुप्रासे अर्थान्तरसंक्रमितवाच्ये विहितस्यानुवाद्यत्वे च । क्रमेणोदाहरणम्—

सितकरकररुचिरविभा विभाकराकार धरणिधर कीर्तिः ।
पौरुषकमला कमला सापि तवैवास्ति नान्यस्य ॥३१४॥

Another example of the same—

'*Vada vada jitaḥ sa shatrur-na hato*
jalpaṁshcha tava tavāsmīti
Chitraṁ chitramarodīddhā heti paraṁ mṛte putre'.

'Say, say, if the enemy has been conquered';—'he was not killed, saying *I am yours*, *yours* and most curiously did he weep on the death of his son'.

Here the redundant words are not defective, as the speakers are under the influence of too much joy (in the first sentence), or too much fear (in the second).

Repetition also in some cases is an excellence. For instance, (*a*) in Lāṭa-alliteration, (*b*) where the expressed meaning is transferred to another meaning, and (*c*) where what has been asserted before is referred to again. For instance—

(*a*) '*Sitakarakararuchiravibhā-*
Vibhākarākāra dharaṇidhara kīrtiḥ
Pauruṣakamalā kamalā
Sāpi tavaivāsti nānyasya.'

'O Lord of the Earth, who resemblest the Moon, like the Moon's lovely sheen is thy fame ; thine alone too is the prosperity attendant upon valour'.

[Here the repetitions in *kara-kara*, *vibhā-vibhā* and *kamalā-kamalā* are not defective, since they serve to accomplish the Alliteration].

तालाजाअंति गुणा जाला दे सहिअएहिँ घेप्पन्ति ।
रइकिरणाणुग्गहिआइँ होन्ति कमलाइँ कमलाइँ ॥३१५॥
जितेन्द्रियत्वं विनयस्य कारणं गुणप्रकर्षो विनयादवाप्यते ।
गुणप्रकर्षेण जनोनुरज्यते जनानुरागप्रभवा हि संपदः ॥३१६॥
पतत्प्रकर्षमपि क्वचिद्गुणः। यथा उदाहृते प्रागप्राप्त-इत्यादौ।३१७।

(*b*) '*Tālā jāaṁti guṇāḥ*
Jālā de sahiaehiṁ gheppanti
Raïkiraṇāṇuggahiāïṁ
Honti kamalāïṁ Kamalāïṁ.

'Excellences appear when they are appreciated by really appreciative men. It is only when favoured by the Sun's rays that *lotuses* become *lotuses*'.

[Here the second 'lotuses' connotes *full-grown fragrance*, and hence having its expressed meaning transformed it is not a defect].

(*c*) '*Jitendriyatvaṁ vinayasya kāraṇaṁ*
Guṇaprakarṣo vinayādavāpyate
Guṇaprakarṣeṇa janonurajyate
Janānurāgaprabhavā hi saṁpadaḥ'.

Subjugation of the senses leads to humility ; by means of humility is excellence of qualities attained ; through excellent qualities, people become attached ; and prosperity follows from the attachment of the people'.

[The 'humility' described in the first sentence as the effect, is again referred to in the second sentence as the cause, and so on; and under the circumstances, the use of the same words and expressions only serves to lend force to the idea that what appears as the cause in the following sentence is precisely the same as that spoken of as the effect in the preceding sentence.]

'Receding Excellence', is sometimes an excellence ; as in the verse '*Prāgaprāpta*-&c'. (see above, stanza No. 209).

[Where the softer language adopted in the fourth line is only right and proper, as it involves the remembrance of the speaker's preceptor.]

समाप्तपुनरात्तं क्वचिन्न गुणो न दोषः। यत्र न विशेषण-मात्रदानार्थं पुनर्ग्रहणम् अपि तु वाक्यान्तरमेव क्रियते। यथा अत्रैव प्रागप्राप्त इत्यादौ ॥३१८॥

अपदस्थसमासं क्वचिद् गुणः। यथा उदाहृते रक्ताशोक-इत्यादौ ॥३१९॥

गर्भितं तथैव। यथा—

हुमि अवहत्थिअरेहो णिरंकुसो अह विवेअरहिओ वि।
सिविणे वि तुमम्मि पुणो पत्तिहि भत्तिं ण पसुमरामि ॥३२०॥

अत्र प्रतीहीति मध्ये दृढप्रत्ययोत्पादनाय। एवमन्यदपि लक्ष्याल्लक्ष्यम् ॥५९॥

'Resumption of the Concluded' is neither a defect nor an excellence in cases where the resumption is not for the purpose of adding a further epithet, but is introduced as a distinct statement; an example of this also we have in the verse just referred to ('*Prāgaprāpta*-etc. stanza No. 209).

'Misplaced Compound' is an excellence in certain cases; *e.g.*, in the verse '*Raktāshoka* &c'. (See above, stanza No. 300).

[Where, though the long compound is not quite appropriate in the delineation of the erotic passion, yet, as serving to intensify the displeasure felt by the suffering lover, it helps to heighten the said passion and becomes, as such, an excellence.]

Similarly the 'Parenthetical' also is an excellence in some cases; *e.g.*, in the following:

'*Humi avahatthiarebo*
Ṇiraṁkuso aha vivearahio vi
Siviṇevi tumammi puṇo.
Pattibi bhattiṁ ṇa pasumarāmi'.

'Though devoid of the steady decorum of behaviour, unrestrained and indiscreet, I do not even dream, *believe me*, of disobeying you'. 59.

व्यभिचारिरसस्थायिभावानां शब्दवाच्यता ।
कष्टकल्पनया व्यक्तिरनुभावविभावयोः ॥ ६० ॥
प्रतिकूलविभावादिग्रहो दीप्तिः पुनः पुनः ।
अकाण्डे प्रथनच्छेदावङ्गस्याप्यतिविस्तृतिः ॥ ६१ ॥
अङ्गिनोननुसंधानं प्रकृतीनां विपर्ययः ।
अनङ्गस्याभिधानं च रसे दोषाः स्युरीदृशाः ॥ ६२ ॥

(१) स्वशब्दोपादानं व्यभिचारिणो यथा

सव्रीडा दयितानने सकरुणा मातङ्गचर्माम्बरे
सत्रासा भुजगे सविस्मयरसा चन्द्रेमृतस्यन्दिनि ।
सेर्ष्या जह्नुसुतावलोकनविधौ दीना कपालोदरे
पार्वत्या नवसंगमप्रणयिनी दृष्टिः शिवायास्तु वः ॥३२१॥

The parenthetical clause 'believe me' is inserted for the purpose of emphasising the assertion.

So may others be illustrated.

(1) (2) (3)—*The mention by name of the variant sentiments, the Passion and of the latent sentiments,*—(4), (5) *Far-fetched Indication of the Ensuant and the Excitant,*—(6) *Admission of adverse Concomitants,*—(7) *Repeated Heightening,*—(8) *Untimely Introduction,*—(9) *Untimely Interruption,*—(10) *Excesive dilatation of the Subordinate Factor,*—(11) *Neglect of the Principal Factor,*—(12) *Perversion of Characters,* and (13) *Mention of what is not Germane; such are the defects in the delineation of Passion, Rasa.* 60-62.

(1) Example of the mention by name, of the variant emotions—

'*Savrīḍā dayitānane sakaruṇā mātaṅgacharmāmbare*
Satrāsā bhujage savismayarasā chandremṛtasyandini
Serṣyā jahnusutāvalokanavidhau dīnā kapālodare.
Pārvatyā navasaṅgamapraṇayiṇī dṛṣṭiḥ shivāyāstu vaḥ'.

अत्र व्रीडादीनाम् ।

'व्यानम्रा दयितानने मुकुलिता मातङ्गचर्माम्बरे
सोत्कम्पा भुजगे निमेषरहिता चन्द्रेमृतस्यन्दिनि ।
मीलद्भ्रूः सुरसिन्धुदर्शनविधौ म्लाना कपालोदरे'
इत्यादि तु युक्तम् ॥

(२) रसस्य स्वशब्देन शृङ्गारादिशब्देन वा वाच्यत्वम् । क्रमेणोदाहरणम्—

तामनङ्गजयमङ्गलश्रियं किंचिदुच्चभुजमूललोकिताम् ।
नेत्रयोः कृतवतोस्य गोचरे कोप्यजायत रसो निरन्तरः ॥३२२॥

'May the glance of Pārvatī, full of love at the first meeting of her husband, ordain your welfare ;—the glance which is affected by bashfulness when turned towards the face of her beloved,—imbued with pathos, when falling upon the dress of elephant's skin,—full of fear when turned towards the serpent,—struck by wonder at the nectar-dripping moon,—burning with jealousy when looking at the Gaṅgā,—and humiliated at the sight of the begging-bowl'.

Here the mention, by name, of 'bashfulness' and other variant emotions is defective. The right reading would be—

'*vyānamrā dayitānane mukulitā mātaṅgacharmāmbare*
sotkampā bhujage nimeṣarahitā chandremṛtasyandini
mīladbhūḥ surasindhudarshanavidhau mlānā kapālodare'

(where the same emotions are mentioned, not by their names, but by means of their physical effects).

(2) Example of the 'mention by name' of Passion,—(*a*) by the word 'passion,' '*rasa*', itself, and (*b*) by the names of the particular passions, the 'Erotic' and the rest.

आलोक्य कोमलकपोलतलाभिषिक्त
व्यक्तानुरागसुभगामभिराममूर्तिम् ।
पश्यैष बाल्यमतिवृत्य विवर्तमानः
शृङ्गारसीमनि तरङ्गितमातनोति ॥३२३॥

(३) स्थायिनो यथा

संप्रहारे प्रहरणैः प्रहाराणां परस्परम् ।
ठणत्कारैः श्रुतिगतैरुत्साहस्तस्य कोप्यभूत् ॥३२४॥

(*a*) '*Tāmanaṅgajayamaṅgalashriyaṁ*
Kiñchiduchchabhujamūlalokitām
Netrayoḥ kṛtavatosya gochare
Kopyajāyata raso nirantaraḥ

'When he got her within the range of his vision,—she, the auspicious glory of the victory of the Love-god, and having the slight elevation at the end of her arms rendered perceptible,—there became manifested in him a peculiar unimpeded *passion*.'

(*b*) '*Ālokya komalakopolatalābhiṣikta—*
Vyaktānurāgasubhagāmabhirāmamūrtim
Pashyaiṣa bālyamativṛtya vivartamānaḥ
Shṛṅgārasīmani taraṅgitamātanoti.'

'See how this young man, just passed his boyhood, behaves,—striking like waves as it were, on the boundaries of the *Erotic*, on seeing her of beautiful form, graceful and exquisitely handsome, through the loveful blush on her soft cheeks.'

(3) Example of the 'mention by name' of the Latent Emotion—

'*Samprahāre praharaṇaiḥ prahārāṇām parasparam*
Ṭhaṇatkāraiḥ shrutigatairutsāhastasya kopyabhūt.'

'When he heard the sound of weapons clashing in battle, there appeared in him a peculiar daring.'

अत्रोत्साहस्य ॥

(४) कर्पूरधूलिधवलद्युतिपूरधौत-
दिङ्मण्डले शिशिररोचिषि तस्य यूनः ।
लीलाशिरोंशुकनिवेशविशेषक्लृप्ति-
व्यक्तस्तनोन्नतिरभून्नयनावनौ सा ॥३२५॥

अत्रोद्दीपनालम्बनरूपाः शृङ्गारयोग्या विभावा अनुभाव-पर्यवसायिनः स्थिता इति कष्टकल्पना ॥

(५) परिहरति रतिं मतिं लुनीते स्खलति भृशं परिवर्तते च भूयः ।
इति बत विषमा दशास्य देहं परिभवति प्रसभं किमत्र कुर्मः॥३२६॥

Here the mention of '*utsāha*' (Daring) is defective.

(4) 'On the atmosphere being washed by the flood of the camphor-like bright light of the Moon,—she, having the appearance of her breasts brought about by a sportive manipulation of her veil, came within the range of the young man's vision.'

What are described here are the two kinds of excitants—(*a*) basic (in the shape of the woman) and (*b*) aggravative (in the shape of moonlight)—of the Erotic Passion ; and these do not serve to indicate the corresponding ensuants (in the young man, in the shape of thrilling and so forth) ; and it is with some difficulty that they become comprehended. This is what is meant by the ensuants being 'far-fetched.'

(5) 'He shuns pleasure, interrupts his thoughts, trembles and rolls about ; thus, Oh ! a violent condition is attacking his body ; what shall we do ?'

What are described here are the ensuants (certain effects produced in the young man) ; and it is only with some difficulty that one can comprehend that the loved woman

अत्र रतिपरिहारादीनामनुभावानां करुणादावपि संभवात्कामिनीरूपो विभावो यत्नतः प्रतिपाद्यः ॥

(६) प्रसादे वर्तस्व प्रकटय मुदं संत्यज रुषं
प्रिये शुष्यन्त्यङ्गान्यमृतमिव ते सिञ्चतु वचः ।
निधानं सौख्यानां क्षणमभिमुखं स्थापय मुखं
न मुग्धे प्रत्येतुं प्रभवति गतः कालहरिणः ॥३२७॥

अत्र शृङ्गारे प्रतिकूलस्य शान्तस्यानित्यताप्रकाशनरूपो विभावस्तत्प्रकाशितो निर्वेदश्च व्यभिचारी उपात्तः ॥

णिहुअरमणम्मि लोअणपहम्मि पडिए गुरुअणमज्झम्मि ।
सअलपरिहारहिअआ वणगमणं एव्व महइ वहू ॥३२८॥

---

is the *excitant* ; specially as the ensuants described are such as could be due to the Passion of Pathos also.

[This is what is meant by the excitant being 'farfetched']

(6*a*) 'Do be propitiated ; O my love ! give expression to joyfulness and give up anger ; let thy nectarine voice sprinkle my withering limbs. Just for a moment keep your face, the very fount of felicity, before me. O lovely damsel, past opportunities never come again.'

What is described here is : (1) an excitant, in the shape of the man's expression of the notion of the impermanence of pleasures, and also (2) a variant emotion, in the shape of self-disparagement,—both of which are concomitants helpful to the Quietistic Passion, but adverse to (and marring the effect of) the Erotic (which is the Passion described).

[Thus, this is an example of the admission of adverse concomitants in the shape of discordant excitant and *variants*.]

(6*b*) 'Her eyes having fallen upon her lover, while she was among her elders, she withdraws her heart from all work and is anxious to proceed to the forest.'

अत्र सकलपरिहारवनगमने शान्तानुभावौ । इन्धनाद्यानयनव्याजेनोपभोगार्थं वनगमनं चेत् न दोषः ।।

(७) दीप्तिः पुनः पुनर्यथा कुमारसंभवे रतिविलापे ।।

(८) अकाण्डे प्रथनं यथा वेणीसंहारे द्वितीयेऽङ्केनेकवीरक्षये प्रवृत्ते भानुमत्या सह दुर्योधनस्य शृङ्गारवर्णनम् ।

(९) अकाण्डे छेदो यथा वीरचरिते द्वितीयेऽङ्के राघवभार्गवयोर्धाराधिरूढे वीररसे 'कङ्कणमोचनाय गच्छामि' इति राघवस्योक्तौ ।।

The ensuants depicted here are the *losing of interest in all work* and *proceeding to the forest*; and both of these are helpful to the *quiestistic* Passion (and adverse to the Erotic.)

[Thus this is a case of the 'admission of adverse concomitants', in the shape of the *ensuant*.]

There would be nothing objectionable if there were something to indicate that the desire to proceed to the forest was for the purpose of meeting the lover, under the pretext of fetching fuel and such things.

(7) As an example of 'Repeated Heightening' we have '*Rati's Lament*' in the *Kumārasambhava*.

(8) An example of 'untimely introduction' we have in the Second Act of the *Veṇīsaṁhāra*, where, while the slaughter of numerous heroes is proceeding, the poet proceeds to describe the loving dalliances of Duryodhana with Bhānumatī.

(9) An example of 'untimely interruption' we have in the Second Act of the *Mahāvīracharita*, where the Heroic sentiment between Rāma and Parashurāma having reached the highest pitch, Rāma says—'I am going to unfasten the nuptial bracelet.'

(१०) अङ्गस्याप्रधानस्यातिविस्तरेण वर्णनम् । यथा हयग्रीववधे हयग्रीवस्य ॥

(११) अङ्गिनोननुसंधानम् । यथा रत्नावल्यां चतुर्थेङ्के बाभ्रव्यागमने सागरिकाया विस्मृतिः ॥

(१२) प्रकृतयो दिव्या अदिव्या दिव्यादिव्याश्च वीररौद्रशृङ्गारशान्तरसप्रधाना धीरोदात्तधीरोद्धतधीरललितधीरप्रशान्ताः उत्तमाधममध्यमाश्च । तत्र रतिहासशोकाद्भुतानि अदिव्योत्तमप्रकृतिवत् दिव्येष्वपि । किं तु रतिः संभोगशृङ्गाररूपा उत्तमदेवताविषया न वर्णनीया । तद्वर्णनं हि पित्रोः संभोगवर्णं निमवात्यन्तमनुचितम् ।

---

(10) 'Excessive Dilatation of the Subordinate Factor' we find in the lengthy description of Hayagrīva in the *Hayagrīvavadha—Kāvya.*

(11) 'Neglect of the Principal Factor' we find in the Fourth Act of the *Ratnāvalī*, where, on the approach of Bābhravya, Sāgarikā, the heroine, is completely ignored.

(12) 'Characters' are of three kinds—*Divine*, *Non-divine*, (Human) and *Humo-divine*. Each of these again is (*a*) firm-noble, (*b*) firm-haughty, (*c*) firm-gay, and (*d*) firm-calm, according as they are under the influence respectively of (*a*) the Heroic, (*b*) the Furious, (*c*) the Erotic and (*d*) the Quietistic Passions. [Thus there are 12 kinds]. Each of these again is either *High*, *Medium* or *Low*.—Now among these, Love, Mirth, Grief and Wonder are found in Divine as well as Human characters ; but it is not right to describe the Erotic Love-dalliances of a *High-Divine* character ; in fact such a description would be as highly improper as that of the love-dealings of one's own parents.

क्रोधं प्रभो संहर संहरेति यावद् गिरः खे मरुतां चरन्ति ।
तावत्स वह्निर्भवनेत्रजन्मा भस्मावशेषं मदनं चकार ॥३२९॥

इत्युक्तवत् भ्रुकुटयादिविकारवर्जितः क्रोधः सद्यःफलदः स्वर्गपातालगगनसमुद्रोल्लङ्घनाद्युत्साहश्च दिव्येष्वेव । अदिव्येषु तु यावदवदानं प्रसिद्धमुचितं वा तावदेवोपनिबन्द्धव्यम्। अधिकं तु निबध्यमानमसत्यप्रतिभासेन 'नायकवद्वर्तितव्यं न प्रतिनायकवत्' इत्युपदेशे न पर्यवस्येत् । दिव्यादिव्येषु उभयथापि ।

Further, it is only in the case of *Divine* characters that there can be either such *heroism* as involved in the undertaking of a journey to the Heavens or the nether regions, the jumping over the ocean and so forth, or such *anger* as is immediately effective, though not accompanied by any visible physical signs as the curvature of the brows and so forth ; such anger, for instance, as is delineated in the following verse—

' "O Lord, withdraw your wrath—do please withdraw it ",—by the time that these words of the gods go forth into the skies, the fire emanating from the eye of Shiva reduced the Love-god to ashes '. In the case of *non-divine or human* characters only such activity should be described as is known from past experience to have been possible ; if more than this were attributed to a human character, it would bear the stamp of untruth, and as such, fail to lead up to exhortation (which is the aim of poetry) that ' one should behave like the hero, and not like his opponent'.—Lastly in the case of *humo-divine* characters, both the above kinds of actions may be described.

This being the right course to adopt, if things are attributed to the *Divine* and other characters, or to the *Firm-noble* and the rest, which are not in keeping with the

एवमुक्तस्यौचित्यस्य दिव्यादीनामिव धीरोदात्तादीनामप्यन्यथा-वर्णनं विपर्ययः । तत्रभवन् भगवन्नित्युत्तमेन न अधमेन मुनिप्रभृतौ न राजादौ भट्टारक-इति नोत्तमेन राजादौ प्रकृतिविपर्ययापत्तेर्वाच्यम् । एवं देशकालवयोजात्यादीनां वेषव्यवहारादिकमुचितमेवोपनिबन्द्धव्यम् ॥

(१३) अनङ्गस्य रसानुपकारकस्य वर्णनम् । यथा कर्पूरमञ्जर्या नायिकया स्वात्मना च कृतं वसन्तवर्णनमनादृत्य बन्दिवर्णितस्य राज्ञा प्रशंसनम् ॥

"ईदृशाः" इति । नायिकापादप्रहारादिना नायककोपादिवर्णनम् ।

---

above-mentioned proprieties,—it involves the 'perversion' (of the characters). Similarly there is 'perversion of character' also in the case of the infringement of such rules as the following :—(*a*) such forms of address as '*tatrabhavān*' and '*bhagavān*' are to be used only by the *higher*, and never by the *lower* characters,—and these too, only with reference to sages, and never to kings ;—(*b*) the address '*bhaṭṭāraka*' is to be used, in reference to kings, only by such characters as do not belong to the *higher* order.—Similarly too the dress and actions of the characters are to be described in due accordance with the time, place, age, caste and such other circumstances. [And if this is not done, it involves 'perversion of character.']

(13) An example of 'what is *not germane*',—*i. e.*, not helpful in the delineation of the Passion concerned,—we have in the *Karpūramañjarī*, where the king ignores the description of the spring by the heroine and also that by himself, and goes on to praise that by the bard.

उक्तं हि ध्वनिकृता

"अनौचित्यादृते नान्यद् रसभङ्गस्य कारणम् ।
औचित्योपनिबन्धस्तु रसस्योपनिषत्परा ।।" इति ।।६०-६२।।

इदानीं क्वचिददोषा अप्येते इत्युच्यन्ते ।

न दोषः स्वपदेनोक्तावपि संचारिणः क्वचित् ।

यथा

औत्सुक्येन कृतत्वरा सहभुवा व्यावर्तमाना ह्रिया
तैस्तैर्बन्धुवधूजनस्य वचनैर्नीताभिमुख्यं पुनः ।
दृष्ट्वाग्रे वरमात्तसाध्वसरसा गौरी नवे संगमे
संरोहत्पुलका हरेण हसता श्लिष्टा शिवायास्तु वः ।।३३०।।

'*Such*' (in the text) is meant to include such descriptions as that of the Lover getting angry at being struck by the feet of his loved one and so forth.

(In regard to Defects) the Author of the *Dhvani* has made the following declaration—

'Apart from impropriety, there is nothing that mars the Passion ; as Propriety is the highest secret of the right delineation of the Passion'. 60-62.

In certain cases the said Defects are not defective. This is what is explained next.

In some cases the 'mention by name' of a variant emotion is not a defect.

For example, in the following—

'*Autsukyena kṛtatvarā sahabhuvā vyāvartamānā hriyā*
Taistairbandhuvadhūjanasya vachanairnītābhimukhyaṁ punaḥ
Dṛṣṭvāgre varamāttasādhvasarasā gaurī nave saṁgame
Saṁrohatpulakā hareṇa hasatā shliṣṭā shivāyāstu vaḥ'.

अत्रौत्सुक्यशब्द इव तदनुभावो न तथा प्रतीतिकृत् । अत एव 'दूरादुत्सुकम्' इत्यादौ व्रीडाप्रेमाद्यनुभावानां विवलितत्वादीनामिवोत्सुकत्वानुभावस्य सहसा प्रसरणादिरूपस्य तथा प्रतिपत्तिकारित्वाभावादुत्सुकमिति कृतम् ॥

संचार्यादेर्विरुद्धस्य बाध्यस्योक्तिर्गुणावहा ॥ ६३ ॥

'Hastening through longing, turning back from inborn modesty, carried before her husband by the exhortations of her female relatives, showing some fear on seeing her husband before her,—may Gaurī, on the occasion of her first meeting, embraced by smiling Shiva, and with her hairs thrilling, ordain your welfare !'

Here the variant emotion of *Autsukya*, '*Longing*', is mentioned by name, because the mere mention of the ensuants (the effects of the emotion) would not have been equally significant [as the said effects might be due to causes other than Longing ; hence the mention of the name of '*Autsukya*' is not regarded as a defect.]

Similarly in the verse—'*Dūrādutsukamāgate* &c.' (see above stanza No 29), though the poet has described the emotions of modesty, affection and the rest, through their respective ensuants, in the form of 'turning aside' and so forth, yet the emotion of 'Longing' has been mentioned by name '*utsuka*', because the mere mention of its ensuants, in the form of *approaching nearer*, would not be equally expressive of what is intended.

The mentioning of 'adverse concomitants' in the form of variant emotions (excitants and ensuants) is conducive to excellence, when they are spoken of as suppressed. 63.

That is, when they are mentioned in such a manner as to indicate that they are to be understood as being

बाध्यत्वेनोक्तिर्न परमदोषः यावत् प्रकृतरसपरिपोषकृत् । यथा

'क्वाकार्यं शशलक्ष्मणः क्व च कुलम्' इत्यादौ ॥३३१॥

अत्र वितर्कादिषु उद्गतेष्वपि चिन्तायामेव विश्रान्तिरिति प्रकृतरसपरिपोषः ॥

पाण्डु क्षामं वदनं हृदयं सरसं तवालसं च वपुः ।
आवेदयति नितान्तं क्षेत्रियरोगं सखि हृदन्तः ॥३३२॥

इत्यादौ साधारणत्वं पाण्डुतादीनामिति न विरुद्धम् ॥

सत्यं मनोरमा रामाः सत्यं रम्या विभूतयः ।
किं तु मत्ताङ्गनापाङ्गभङ्गलोलं हि जीवितम् ॥३३३॥

---

suppressed, such mention is not very defective; on the contrary, it serves to heighten the principal Passion depicted.

As an example we have the verse '*Kvākāryaṁ shashalakṣmaṇaḥ* &c'. (See above, stanza No. 53), where though the variants, ensuants and excitants, in the form of 'argumentation', 'doubt' and so forth (which are adverse to the Passion depicted) are mentioned as appearing, yet they are all represented as becoming merged into *painful reflection*, which tends to heighten the Passion depicted.

Similarly, in the following verse—

'O friend, thy face is pale and emaciated, and heart full of substance, and body languid; all this indicates the presence of an incurable disease of the heart'—

though Paleness and the other effects mentioned are in a sense adverse to the Erotic Passion depicted (inasmuch as they can be the effects of the Pathetic Passion also); —yet, inasmuch as they are common (to the Erotic and to the Pathetic), they cannot be regarded as entirely 'adverse.'

इत्यत्राद्यमर्धं बाध्यत्वेनैवोक्तम् । जीवितादपि अधिकमपाङ्ग-भङ्गस्यास्थिरत्वमिति प्रसिद्धभङ्गुरोपमानतयोपात्तं शान्तमेव पुष्णाति न पुनः शृङ्गारस्यात्र प्रतीतिस्तदङ्गाप्रतिपत्तेः । न तु विनेयोन्मुखीकरणमत्र परिहारः शान्तशृङ्गारयोर्नैरन्तर्यस्या-

---

Similarly again, in the verse—

'It is true that women are heart-ravishing, and riches also are pleasing; but life itself is as unsteady as the amorous glances of a love-intoxicated woman'.—

The first half (though adverse to the Quietistic Passion meant to be depicted) is spoken of only as something that is suppressed or negatived by the second half; the sense thus being that—'the glances' are more unsteady or transient than 'life'; and this mention of a parallel, which is universally known to be transitory, only serves to heighten the Quietistic Passion; which is what is depicted here, and not the *Erotic* (as has been held by the author of the Dhvani) because we do not recognise in the verse any such accessories as would point to this latter passion.—It has been argued (in support of the view that the Erotic is the passion depicted here) that it is the Erotic that is meant to be depicted, but only with a view to engaging the attention of the pupil addressed (by the depicting of a more agreeable subject, and through that, leading him on to the Quietistic).—But this can not be right; as there is such a large gap between the Erotic and the Quietistic (that one cannot lead on to the other).—Another explanation (in support of the view in question) is that the Erotic is depicted here with a view to lending a charm to the poetry.—But this also cannot be accepted; because charm could be added to the poetry either through

भावात् । नापि काव्यशोभाकरणं रसान्तरादनुप्रासमात्राद्वा तथाभावात् ॥६३॥

आश्रयैक्ये विरुद्धो यः स कार्यो भिन्नसंश्रयः ।
रसान्तरेणान्तरितो नैरन्तर्येण यो रसः ॥ ६४ ॥

वीरभयानकयोरेकाश्रयत्वेन विरोध इति प्रतिपक्षगतत्वेन भयानको निवेशयितव्यः । शान्तशृङ्गारयोस्तु नैरन्तर्येण विरोध इति रसान्तरमन्तरे कार्यम् यथा नागानन्दे शान्तस्य जीमूतवाहनस्य 'अहो गीतम् अहो वादित्रम्' इत्यद्भुतमन्तर्निवेश्य मलयवतीं प्रति शृङ्गारो निबद्धः ।

न परं प्रबन्धे यावदेकस्मिन्नपि वाक्ये रसान्तरव्यवधिना विरोधो निवर्तते । यथा

---

some other Passion than the Erotic (*i. e.*, through the Quietistic itself), or through mere Alliteration [so that for purposes of this charm also, it would not be necessary to introduce the Erotic]. 63.

If one Passion is repugnant to another when found together in the same substratum, they should be delineated in different substrata ; and if one Passion is repugnant to another when appearing in close contiguity, they should be separated by some other Passion. 64.

The Heroic and the Frightful are found to be repugnant to one another, when found in the same person ; hence the Frightful is to be depicted as subsisting in the hero's opponent (while the Heroic belongs to the hero himself).—And between the Erotic and the Quietistic, there is incompatibility only when they appear in close contiguity ; hence a third Passion should be made to intervene between these two. For instance, in the *Nāgā-*

भूरेणुदिग्धान् नवपारिजात-
मालारजोवासितबाहुमध्या ।
गाढं शिवाभिः परिरभ्यमाणान्
सुराङ्गनाश्लिष्टभुजान्तरालाः ॥३३४॥
सशोणितैः क्रव्यभुजां स्फुरद्भिः
पक्षैः खगानामुपवीज्यमानान् ।
संवीजिताश्चन्दनवारिसेकैः
सुगन्धिभिः कल्पलतादुकूलैः ॥३३४॥ (अ)॥
विमानपर्यङ्कतले निषण्णाः
कुतूहलाविष्टतया तदानीम् ।
निर्दिश्यमानान् ललनाङ्गुलीभिर्-
वीराः स्वदेहान् पतितानपश्यन् ॥३३५॥

---

nanda, when the Quietistic Jīmūtavāhana is described as falling in love with Malayavatī, the passion of Wonder is brought in between the two, by the sentences 'what a song ! what music !' ,

This incompatibility is warded off in this manner not only as occurring in course of a complete poetic work, but also in the same sentence. For instance, in the following verse :—

'The heroic men, lying upon magnificent beds in the flying cars, their chests perfumed by the pollens of the fresh Pārijāta-garlands, embraced by celestial nymphs, and fanned by silken cloths made out of the celestial trees, wet and fragrant,—saw their own bodies rolling in the dust of the earth, pointed to by the damsels through curiosity, embraced by jackals, and fanned by the flapping wings of the carnivorous birds dripping with blood',—

अत्र बीभत्सशृङ्गारयोरन्तर्वीररसो निवेशितः ॥६४॥

स्मर्यमाणो विरुद्धोपि साम्येनाथ विवक्षितः ।
अङ्गिन्यङ्गत्वमाप्तौ यौ तौ न दुष्टौ परस्परम् ॥ ६५ ॥

अयं स रशनोत्कर्षी पीनस्तनविमर्दनः ।
नाभ्यूरुजघनस्पर्शी नीवीविस्रंसनः करः ॥३३६॥

एतद् भूरिश्रवसः समरभुवि पतितं हस्तमालोक्य तद्वधूरभिदधौ । अत्र पूर्वावस्थास्मरणं शृङ्गाराङ्गमपि करुणं परिपोषयति ॥

दन्तक्षतानि करजैश्च विपाटितानि
प्रोद्भिन्नसान्द्रपुलके भवतः शरीरे ।
दत्तानि रक्तमनसा मृगराजवध्वा
जातस्पृहैर्मुनिभिरप्यवलोकितानि ॥३३७॥

---

the Heroic has been made to intervene between the Disgustful and the Erotic. 64.

Even if two Passions are incompatible, they do not mar each other,—(a) when one is merely remembered, or (b) when it is intended to be equal to the other (in importance), or (c) when the two become subservient to a third Principal (Passion). 65.

For instance, (*a*) in the following verse—'*Ayaṁ sa rashanotkarṣī &c.* 'This is that same hand &c.' (see above,)—which contains the speech of the wife of Bhūrishravas when she saw his hand lying on the battle field,—the remembrance of her past experience, even though savouring of the Erotic, only serves to heighten the Pathetic.

(*b*) In the following verse—

'The teeth-marks and the nail-tearings made in your thrilling body by the blood-thirsty (loving) lioness (woman), were looked at even by the sages, with coveting eyes'.

अत्र कामुकस्य दन्तक्षतादीनि यथा चमत्कारकारीणि तथा जिनस्य । यथा वा परः शृङ्गारी तदवलोकनात्सस्पृहस्तद्वत् एतद्दृशो मुनय इति साम्यविवक्षा ॥

क्रामन्त्यः क्षतकोमलाङ्गुलिगलद्रक्तैः सदर्भाः स्थलीः
पादैः पातितयावकैरिव गलद्बाष्पाम्बुधौताननाः ।
भीता भर्तृकरावलम्बितकरास्त्वच्छत्रुनार्योऽधुना
दावाग्निं परितो भ्रमन्ति पुनरप्युद्यद्विवाहा इव ॥३३८॥

The meaning is that the marks made on the body of the Buddha by the lioness looked as charming as those made on the body of the lover by his beloved woman; or that 'just as the erotically inclined man looks covetingly upon the marks of endearment made by a woman upon the body of another man, so did the sages look covetingly upon the marks upon Buddha's body made by the lioness'; and here both the Passions (the Heroic and the Erotic) are meant to be of equal importance.

(*c*) In the following verse—

'The frightened wives of your enemies sprinkle, with their feet on the grassy ground, blood issuing from their fingers, and appear as if dropping the red paint of their feet; their faces are washed with flowing tears; and supporting themselves on the hands of their husbands, they walk round the forest-fire, appearing as if they were again going through their marriage-rites'.—

The principal factor meant to be delineated by the clever statement is the speaker's regard for the king, and to this principal factor, both, the Pathetic as well as the Erotic, are equally subservient; and under the circumstances,

अत्र चाटुके राजविषया रतिः प्रतीयते । तत्र करुण इव शृङ्गारोप्यङ्गमिति तयोर्न विरोधः ।

यथा

एहि गच्छ पतोत्तिष्ठ वद मौनं समाचर ।
एवमाशाग्रहग्रस्तैः क्रीडन्ति धनिनोर्थिभिः ॥३३९॥

इत्यत्र एहीति क्रीडन्ति गच्छेति क्रीडन्तीति क्रीडनापेक्षयोः आगमनगमनयोर्न विरोधः ।

क्षिप्तो हस्तावलग्नः प्रसभमभिहतोप्याददानोंशुकान्तं
गृह्णन् केशेष्वपास्तश्चरणनिपतितो नेक्षितः संभ्रमेण ।
आलिङ्गन् योवधूतस्त्रिपुरयुवतिभिः साश्रुनेत्रोत्पलाभिः
कामीवार्द्रापराधः स दहतु दुरितं शांभवो वः शराग्निः ॥३४०॥

---

there is no incompatibility. Just as there is no incongruity in the mention of two mutually contradictory actions, when these are mentioned as subservient to a third act; *e.g.*, in the verse—"Come"—"go"—"fall down"—"rise"—"speak"—"keep quiet",—in this manner do the rich make fun of the needy men who are held in by hopes for 'getting something,'—'coming' and 'going' are both subservient 'to the act of making fun'.

Similarly in the following verse—

'May the fire of Shiva's arrows burn your sin,—the fire which, upon embracing the young ladies of Tripura, was shaken off by them with tearful eyes,—was thrown aside on touching their hands, was swiftly struck back, when catching hold of their cloth-end, —thrust aside, when touching their locks,—not even perceived, through flurry, when fallen on their feet; and thus appeared like a

इत्यत्र त्रिपुररिपुप्रभावातिशयस्य करुणोऽङ्गम्। तस्य तु शृङ्गारः। तथापि न करुणे विश्रान्तिरिति तस्याङ्गतैव। अथवा प्राक् यथा कामुक आचरति स्म तथा शराग्निरिति शृङ्गारपोषितेन करुणेन मुख्य एवार्थ उपोद्बल्यते।

उक्तं हि

'गुणः कृतात्मसंस्कारः प्रधानं प्रतिपद्यते।
प्रधानस्योपकारे हि तथा भूयसि वर्तते ॥' इति ॥

guilty lover of theirs,'—the principal object of delineation is the superior majesty of Tripura's enemy (Shiva); and to this is subservient the Pathetic, to which latter the Erotic is subservient; and even though in view of the Erotic being subservient to it, the Pathetic might be regarded as the predominant factor,—yet it has to be regarded as only a subordinate factor in view of the fact that the delineation of the Pathetic does not form the end of the describer. Or, the sense may be that—'the fire of the arrow behaved in the same manner as a guilty lover has done',—wherein the principal factor (greatness of Shiva) becomes heightened by the Pathetic as strengthened by the Erotic [so that in this sense also the Pathetic is not the end arrived at.]

In support of our view, we have the following statement—'It is only when it has undergone a purificatory process that the subordinate factor approaches its Principal, and it is only thus that it tends to help that principal.'

In this connection it has to be borne in mind that there can be no 'incompatibility' between one Passion and another,—when we understand Passion to be what it has been described to be above (under Ch. IV); nor can there

प्राक्प्रतिपादितस्य रसस्य रसान्तरेण न विरोधः नाप्यङ्गाङ्गिभावो भवति इति रसशब्देनात्र स्थायिभाव उपलक्ष्यते ॥६५॥

इति काव्यप्रकाशे दोषदर्शनो नाम सप्तम उल्लासः ॥७॥

be any relative subserviency between them ; hence in the present context, the term '*rasa*', 'passion', should be taken as standing for the corresponding '*Sthāyī-Bhāva*' 'Latent Feeling.' 65.

[Thus ends the Chapter VII dealing with the illustrations of Faults of Poetry in the Kāvya-Prakāśa.]

काव्यप्रकाशः

अथ अष्टम उल्लासः

एवं दोषानुक्त्वा गुणालंकारविवेकमाह—

ये रसस्याङ्गिनो धर्माः शौर्यादय इवात्मनः ।
उत्कर्षहेतवस्ते स्युरचलस्थितयो गुणाः ॥ ६६ ॥

आत्मन एव हि यथा शौर्यादयो नाकारस्य तथा रसस्यैव माधुर्यादयो गुणा न वर्णानाम् ॥

क्वचित्तु शौर्यादिसमुचितस्याकारमहत्त्वादेर्दर्शनात् 'आकार एवास्य शूरः' इत्यादेर्व्यवहारादन्यत्राशूरेऽपि विततकृतित्वमात्रेण 'शूरः' इति क्वापि शूरेऽपि मूर्तिलाघवमात्रेण 'अशूरः' इति अवि-

---

CHAPTER VIII

OF EXCELLENCES

Having described the Defects, the Author next proceeds to describe the difference between 'Excellences' and 'Ornaments' or 'Figures of speech'—

Those properties that belong to the Passion, the principal factor,—conducive to its maturity and having an unceasing existence,—are called 'Guṇas', 'Excellences', in the same manner as Bravery and such qualities belong to the Soul. 66.

Just as Bravery and such qualities belong to the *Soul,* not to the *body* ,—so Sweetness and the other Excellences belong to the *Passion,* not to the *letter.*

In some cases it so happens that people find bravery co-existing with the large-sized body, and come to speak of the body itself as '*brave*'; and hence in another case also, on seeing a large body, they are led to believe, from

श्रान्तप्रतीतयो यथा व्यवहरन्ति तद्वन्मधुरादिव्यञ्जकसुकुमारादिवर्णानां मधुरादिव्यवहारप्रवृत्तेरमधुरादिरसाङ्गानां वर्णानां सौकुमार्यादिमात्रेण माधुर्यादि मधुरादिरसोपकरणानां तेषामसौकुमार्यादेरमाधुर्यादि रसपर्यन्तविश्रान्तप्रतीतिबन्ध्या व्यवहरन्ति। अत एव माधुर्यादयो रसधर्माः समुचितैर्वर्णैर्व्यज्यन्ते न तु वर्णमात्राश्रयाः । यथैषां व्यञ्जकत्वम् तथोदाहरिष्यते ॥६६॥

---

the analogy of the former case, that this other man also must be brave ;—and thus, even a really brave man comes to be believed to be *not brave* on the ground of the smallness of his body ; and such beliefs are very common ;—in the same manner people (like Vāmana and others) have come to speak (*a*) of the soft—sounding *letters* as 'sweet', though in reality they are only suggestive of sweetness ;—and they come to speak of such passion and its accessories as are not really 'sweet', as 'sweet', simply by reason of the softness of the letters (expressing them) ; in the same manner, they also speak of the really 'sweet' passions and accessories as 'not sweet', when they are expressed in such words as are not soft-sounding ;—and in all this, they do not take into account the Passion at all (attributing as they do, the sweetness to the *letters*).

It is in view of all this divergent usage that it has been asserted (in the text) that sweetness and other excellences are properties really belonging to the Passion, and what the properly selected letters do is only to render such qualities perceptible ; and those qualities do not subsist in the letters entirely. In what manner the letters serve to manifest the qualities is going to be shown by means of examples. 66.

उपकुर्वन्ति तं सन्तं येऽङ्गद्वारेण जातुचित् ।
हारादिवदलंकारास्तेऽनुप्रासोपमादयः ॥ ६७ ॥

ये वाचकवाच्यलक्षणाङ्गातिशयमुखेन मुख्यं रसं संभविनमुपकुर्वन्ति ते कण्ठाद्यङ्गानामुत्कर्षाधानद्वारेण शरीरिणोपि उपकारका हारादय इवालंकाराः । यत्र तु नास्ति रसस्तत्रोक्तिवैचित्र्यमात्रपर्यवसायिनः । क्वचित्तु सन्तमपि नोपकुर्वन्ति । यथाक्रममुदाहरणानि—

अपसारय घनसारं कुरु हारं दूर एव किं कमलैः ।
अलमलमालि मृणालैरिति वदति दिवानिशं बाला ॥३४१॥

Those dualities which sometimes adorn the existing Passion, through its components,—just as the necklace and the like (do for the Soul, through the body),—are the ornaments (figures of speech), Alliteration, Simile and the rest. 67.

Those qualities that adorn the principal factor,—*i. e.* the Passion—where it exists,—by imparting excellence to its components, in the shape of the expressive words and their expressed meaning, are called 'ornaments', because they resemble the necklace and other things which, by imparting beauty to the neck and other parts of the body, come to adorn the soul also. Where, however, the Passion does not exist, the said ornaments tend to become merely fanciful expressions. In certian cases, even when the Passion is present, they do not serve to adorn it.

Examples in order :—

(1) In the following verse [and others] the ornament (Alliteration) adorns the Passion through the expressive words—

Apasāraya ghanasāraṁ kuru hāraṁ dūra eva kiṁ kamalaiḥ
Alamalamāli mṛṇālairiti vadati divānishaṁ bālā.

इत्यादौ वाचकमुखेन

मनोरागस्तीव्रं विषमिव विसर्पत्यविरतं
प्रमाथी निर्धूमं ज्वलति विधुतः पावक इव ।
हिनस्ति प्रत्यङ्गं ज्वर इव गरीयानित इतो
न मां त्रातुं तातः प्रभवति न चाम्बा न भवती ॥३४२॥

इत्यादौ वाच्यमुखेनालंकारौ रसमुपकुरुतः ॥

चित्ते चिहुट्टदि ण टुट्टदि सा गुणेसुं
सेज्जासु लोट्टदि विसप्पदि दिमुंहेसुं ।
बोलम्मि वट्टदि पवट्टदि कव्वबन्धे
झाणेण टुट्टदि चिरं तरुणी तरट्टी ॥३४३॥

"Remove the camphor ; throw away the garland ; what is the use of lotus-flowers ? O Friend, enough, enough of these lotus-stalks !"—Thus does the young girl go on speaking day and night.'

(2) In the following verse the Figure (Stringed Simile) adorns the Passion through the expressed meaning—

'The galling all-conquering love is freely circulating like poison ; it burns fiercely (smokelessly) like fire fanned by the wind; it afflicts every limb, like high fever; neither father nor mother nor your ladyship is able to save me from this.

In the following verse, the ornament (Alliteration) adorns only the *words* (and not the Passion depicted)—

'*Chitte cihuṭṭadi ṇa ṭuṭṭadi sā guṇesuṁ*
Sejjāsu loṭṭadi visappadi diṁmuhesuṁ
Bolammi vaṭṭadi pavaṭṭadi kavvabandhe
Jhbāṇeṇa tuṭṭadi chiraṁ taruṇī taraṭṭī.'

'The young woman acts sensibly ; she is not devoid of excellences ; she rolls about on the bed, moves all round and talks freely ; she engages in poetical composition, and

इत्यादौ वाचकमेव ।

मित्रे क्वापि गते सरोरुहवने बद्धानने ताम्यति
क्रन्दत्सु भ्रमरेषु वीक्ष्य दयितासन्नं पुरः सारसम् ।
चक्राह्वेन वियोगिना बिसलता नास्वादिता नोज्झिता
कण्ठे केवलमर्गलेव निहिता जीवस्य निर्गच्छतः ॥३४४॥

इत्यादौ वाच्यमेव न तु रसम् । अत्र बिसलता न जीवं रोद्धुं क्षमेति प्रकृताननुगुणोपमा ॥

एष एव च गुणालंकारप्रविभागः । एवं च "समवायवृत्त्या शौर्यादयः संयोगवृत्त्या तु हारादय इत्यस्तु गुणालंकाराणां भेदः ।

---

for long periods of time she does not break off her contemplation !'

(4) In the following verse, the Figure (Simile) adorns only the expressed meaning—and not the Passion depicted.

'When the sun had gone away,. the lotus had closed its mouth in anger, and the bees had begun to cry (in grief), the forlorn *Chakravāka* bird, seeing the Crane seated closed to his beloved, did not either eat or give up the lotus-fibre ; it was only retained in the throat, like a bar, as it were, to the outgoing life-breath.'

As a matter of fact, under the sorrowful circumstances depicted, a lotus-fibre cannot serve to keep back the breath ; so that the Simile, as it stands, only mars the effect of the Passion (Erotic—Privative) depicted (and does not help it).

Such is the actual difference between 'Excellence' and 'Ornament'. And this puts out of court all such assertions as the following (in the *Bhāmahavṛtti*, by Bhaṭṭodbhaṭa)—"The difference between such *Excellences* as Bravery and the rest, and such *Ornaments*, as necklace and

ओजःप्रभृतीनामनुप्रासोपमादीनां चोभयेषामपि समवायवृत्त्या स्थितिरिति गड्डलिकाप्रवाहेणैवैषां भेदः" इत्यभिधानमसत् ॥

यदप्युक्तम् "काव्यशोभायाः कर्तारो धर्मा गुणास्तदतिशयहेतवस्त्वलंकाराः" इति तदपि न युक्तम् । यतः किं समस्तैर्गुणैः काव्यव्यवहारः उत कतिपयैः । यदि समस्तैः तत्कथमसमस्तगुणा गौडी पाञ्चाली च रीतिः काव्यस्यात्मा ।
अथ कतिपयैः ततः

---

the rest, may be that while the former subsists by *inherence,* the latter is present only by *conjunction* ; [this may be true in the case of the Body and its excellences and ornaments but (in the case of Passion and its delineation) we find that both,—*excellences* like Floridity and the rest, as well as *ornaments*, like Simile, Alliteration and the rest—subsist by *inherence* only ; consequently any distinction drawn between these two must be regarded as merely based upon a blind tradition—a case of sheep blindly following another."

Then again, some people (Vāmana and his followers), have stated the distinction in the form that " while *Excellences* serve to *produce* charm in poetry, *Ornaments* serve to heighten the charm already produced."—This also is not right. Because the questions would arise—Is poetry to be regarded as such only through the presence of *all* the excellences, or through that of a few of these only ? If the former, how could the *Gauḍī* and *Pāñchālī* dictions, which are not possessed of *all* the excellences, constitute the 'soul of Poetry' (as has been held by Vāmana) ?—If, on the other hand, it is only the presence of a few of the Excellences that renders Poetry capable of being so regarded,—then, it would be permissible to regard as 'poetry',

अद्रावत्र प्रज्वलत्यग्निरुच्चैः प्राज्यः प्रोद्यन्नुल्लसत्येष धूमः ॥३४५॥

इत्यादावोजः प्रभृतिषु गुणेषु सत्सु काव्यव्यवहारप्राप्तिः ।

स्वर्गप्राप्तिरनेनैव देहेन वरवर्णिनी ।
अस्या रदच्छदरसो न्यक्करोतितरां सुधाम् ॥३४६॥

इत्यादौ विशेषोक्तिव्यतिरेकौ गुणनिरपेक्षौ काव्यव्यवहारस्य प्रवर्तकौ ॥६७॥

इदानीं गुणानां भेदमाह

माधुर्यौजःप्रसादाख्यास्त्रयस्ते न पुनर्दश ।

एषां क्रमेण लक्षणमाह

आह्लादकत्वं माधुर्यं शृङ्गारे द्रुतिकारणम् ॥ ६८ ॥

---

even such statements as—

'*adrāvatra prajvalatyagniruchchaiḥ*
prājyaḥ prodyannul lasatyeṣa dhūmaḥ.'

['In this hill fire burns high, because there arises thence a dense volume of smoke'],

where some of the Excellences, Floridity and the rest, are present.—

Further, in such verses as the following—

'This handsome woman represents the acquisition of the Heaven in this human form, and the loveliness of her lips puts nectar itself into the shade',—

we find that it *is* regarded as 'poetry', through the presence of the two Ornaments or Figures 'Peculiar Allegation' and 'Dissimilitude', independently of the presence of any excellences. 67.

The Author next proceeds to describe the varieties of *Excellences.*—

Sweetness, Floridity and Lucidity—they are these three, and not ten.

He states [one by one] the definition of each of these three—

'*Sweetness*' *is a source of delectability* ; *it is what leads to mollification in the case of the Erotic Passion.* 68.

शृङ्गारे अर्थात् संभोगे । द्रुतिर्गलितत्वमिव । श्रव्यत्वं पुनरोजः प्रसादयोरपि ॥६८॥

करुणे विप्रलम्भे तच्छान्ते चातिशयान्वितम् ।

[अतिशयान्वितमिति] अत्यन्तद्रुतिहेतुत्वात् ॥

दीप्त्यात्मविस्तृतेर्हेतुरोजो वीररसस्थिति ॥ ६९ ॥

चित्तस्य विस्ताररूपदीप्तत्वजनकमोजः ॥६९॥

बीभत्सरौद्ररसयोस्तस्याधिक्यं क्रमेण च ।

वीराद्बीभत्से ततो रौद्रे सातिशयमोजः ॥

शुष्केन्धनाग्निवत् स्वच्छंजलवत्सहसैव यः ॥ ७० ॥

व्याप्नोत्यन्यत् प्रसादोसौ सर्वत्र विहितस्थितिः ।

It leads to '*mollification*',—*i.e.*, soft flow or melting as it were,—in the case of the 'Erotic', *i.e.*, of the agreeable kind.

As for mere *melodiousness*, it belongs to Floridity and Lucidity also (and as such cannot form the differentia of *sweetness*, as has been held by Bhāskara). 68.

In the case of the Pathetic, the Privative—Erotic and the Quietistic, it (Sweetness) is present in an excessive degree.

'Present in an excessive degree'—because it leads to excessive mollification.

Floridity, the source of the lustrous expanding of the heart, resides in the Heroic Passion. 69.

[For the variant reading आत्मविस्मृतिः —Floridity the source of self-forgetfulness through illumination.]

Floridity brings about that *glow* of the heart which appears in the form of its expansion. 69.

It is present in an excessive degree in the Disgustful and Furious Passions, in order.

In the Disgustful, Floridity is present, in a greater degree than in the Heroic; and in a still greater degree in the Furious.

अन्यदिति । व्याप्यमिह चित्तम् । सर्वत्रेति । सर्वेषु रसेषु सर्वासु रचनासु च ॥

गुणवृत्त्या पुनस्तेषां वृत्तिः शब्दार्थयोर्मता ॥ ७१ ॥

गुणवृत्त्या उपचारेण। तेषांगुणानाम्। आकारे शौर्यस्येव॥७०-७१॥

कुतस्त्रय एव न दश इत्याह

केचिदन्तर्भवन्त्येषु दोषत्यागात्परे श्रिताः ।
अन्ये भजन्ति दोषत्वं कुत्रचिन्न ततो दश ॥ ७२ ॥

That which quickly pervades the other like fire among dry fuel, or like a clean stream of water, is Lucidity, whose presence is proper everywhere.

'*The other*'—*i. e.*, the heart. '*Every where*'—*i.e.*, in all Passions and in all forms of composition.

These (excellences) are held to subsist in words and their meanings only indirectly. 70-71.

'*Indirectly*'—*i. e.*, figuratively.

'*These*'—Excellences.

These excellences (really subsisting in Passion) are figuratively spoken of (even in Mammaṭa's own definition of Poetry) as subsisting in words and their meanings, in the same manner as Bravery and such qualities are attributed to the *body* (though really belonging to the *soul*). 70-71.

"Why should the number of these excellences be *three* only, and not *ten* (as described by Vāmana) ?"

The author answers this question—

(a) Some (of the ten) are included under these (three) ; (b) others are resolved into the mere negation of certain defects ; (c) the rest, in certain cases, have the character of Defects ;—for this reason they are not ten. 72.

बहूनामपि पदानामेकपदवद्भासनात्मा यः श्लेषः यश्चारोहावरोहक्रमरूपः समाधिः या च विकटत्वलक्षणा उदारता यश्चौजोमिश्रितशैथिल्यात्मा प्रसादः तेषामोजस्यन्तर्भावः । पृथक्पदत्वरूपं माधुर्यं भङ्ग्या साक्षादुपात्तम् । प्रसादेनार्थव्यक्तिर्गृहीता । मार्गाभेदरूपा समता क्वचिद्दोषः । तथाहि 'मातङ्गाः किमु वल्गितैः' इत्यादौ सिंहाभिधाने मसृणमार्गत्यागो गुणः । कष्टत्वग्राम्यत्वयोर्दुष्टताभिधानात्तन्निराकरणेनापारुष्यरूपं सौकुमार्यम् औज्ज्वल्यरूपा कान्तिश्च स्वीकृता ॥

(Among the ten enumerated by Vāmana) are—(1) *Shleṣa*, Coalescence, defined as that property whereby several words have the appearance of a single word,—(2) *Samādhi*, Smoothness, defined as consisting in the proper adjustment of ascent (high-flown language) and descent (simple language),—(3) *Udārartā*, Magnificence, consisting in the fanciful grouping of words,—(4) *Prasāda*, Simplicity, consisting in dullness mixed with floridity ;—and all these are included in 'Floridity' (as defined by ourselves) ;—(5) *Mādhurya*, Sweetness, consisting in the distinctness of words, has, in a way, been admitted by us also under the same name ;—(6) *Arthavyakti*, Clearness of Meaning, is included under 'Lucidity',—(7) *Samatā*, Uniformity, consisting in the sameness of style, is, in some cases, a defect ; *e. g.,* in such verses, '*mātaṅgāiḥ kimu &c.*' (see above stanza No. 229.), where too, the abandoning of the softer diction, in the description of the Lion (in the fourth line), is a positive excellence,—(8) *Saukumārya*, Softness, consisting in the absence of harshness, and (9) *Kānti*, Polish, consisting in the brightness of style, are admitted as the negations respectively of 'harshness' and 'vulgarity', which have been mentioned as defects.

एवं न दश शब्दगुणाः ॥

'पदार्थे वाक्यरचनं वाक्यार्थे च पदाभिधा ।

प्रौढिर्व्याससमासौ च साभिप्रायत्वमस्य च ॥'

इति या प्रौढिः ओज इत्युक्तं तद् वैचित्र्यमात्रम् न गुणः । तदभावेपि काव्यव्यवहारप्रवृत्तेः । अपुष्टार्थत्वाधिकपदत्वानवीकृतत्वामङ्गलरूपाश्लीलग्राम्याणां निराकरणेन च साभिप्रायत्वरूपमोजः अर्थवैमल्यात्मा प्रसादः उक्तिवैचित्र्यरूपं माधुर्यम् अपारुष्यरूपं सौकुमार्यम् अग्राम्यत्वरूपा उदारता च

Thus it follows that the number of excellences pertaining to *words* is not *ten*.

As regards those same Excellences as pertaining to the *meaning*, (1) the first (mentioned by Vāmana) is *Prauḍhi*, Boldness, also called (the first kind of '*ojas*' 'strength'), which has been defined as consisting (*a*) in the use of a sentence for the expressing of what can be expressed by a single word, (*b*) in using a single word for the expressing of what would be expressed by a sentence, (*c*) in expansion, (*d*) in brevity and (*e*) in the effectiveness of epithets. But this is merely a flourish of style, and not an 'excellence'; since expressions are regarded as 'poetical' even in the absence of the said (five kinds of) Boldness.—(1*a*) the second kind of '*ojas*', 'strength', which has been defined as consisting in *significance* (a pregnancy of meaning), is only the negation of the defect of Irrelevancy ;—(2) '*Prasāda*', consisting in clearness of meaning, is the negation of the defect of 'redundancy';—(3) '*Mādhurya*', consisting of fanciful expression, is the negation of the defect of 'monotony';—(4) *Saukumārya*, consisting of freedom from ruggedness, is the negation of the defect of 'Indecorous Inauspiciousness';—(5) *Udāratā*, consisting in the absence of vulgarity, is the

स्वीकृतानि । अभिधास्यमानस्वभावोक्त्यलंकारेण रसध्वनि-गुणीभूतव्यङ्ग्याभ्यां च वस्तुस्वभावस्फुटत्वरूपा अर्थव्यक्तिः, दीप्तरसत्वरूपा कान्तिश्च स्वीकृता । क्रमकौटिल्यानुल्बणत्वोपपत्तियोगरूपघटनात्मा श्लेषोपि विचित्रत्वमात्रम् । अवैषम्यस्वरूपा समता दोषाभावमात्रं न पुनर्गुणः । कः खल्वनुन्मत्तोन्यस्य प्रस्तावेन्यदभिदध्यात् । अर्थस्यायोनेरन्यच्छायायोनेर्वा यदि न भवति दर्शनं तत्कथं काव्यम् इत्यर्थदृष्टिरूपः समाधिरपि न गुणः ॥७२॥

---

negation of the defect of 'vulgarity.'—(6) *Arthavyakti*, consisting in the distinctness of the character of things, is included under the Figure of Svabhāvokti, 'natural description,'—going to be described later on ; (7) *Kānti*, consisting in the brilliance of Passion, is included under the 'Suggestion of Passion', either as the predominant or the subordinated factor.—(8) *Shleṣa*,—consisting of a combination of several circumstances, such as (*a*) sequence of several actions, (*b*) deceit (*c*) well-known character, and (*d*) statement of, reasons,—is only a flourish of the poetic fancy.—(9) *Samatā*, consisting in the non-relinquishment of continuity, is only the negation of a defect (of 'Broken Uniformity'), and not a positive *excellence* ; what man, unless he were mad, would ever begin with one thing and then speak of a totally different thing ?—(10) *Samādhi*, consisting in the true appreciation of the meaning (as being original or imitated), is not an *excellence* ; because unless one comprehends the true meaning of a poem, and recognises whether it is an original idea of the poet concerned, or has its source in the idea of some other poet,—how can the composition be regarded as 'poetry' at all ? 72.

तेन नार्थगुणा वाच्याः

न वाच्याः न वक्तव्याः ॥

प्रोक्ताः शब्दगुणाश्च ये ।
वर्णाः समासो रचना तेषां व्यञ्जकतामिताः ॥ ७३ ॥

के कस्य इत्याह

मूर्ध्नि वर्गान्त्यगाः स्पर्शा अटवर्गा रणौ लघू ।
अवृत्तिर्मध्यवृत्तिर्वा माधुर्ये घटना तथा ॥ ७४ ॥

टठडढवर्जिताः कादयो मान्ताः शिरसि निजवर्गान्त्ययुक्ताः तथा रेफणकारौ ह्रस्वान्तरिताविति वर्णाः समासाभावो मध्यमः

For these reasons, the excellences (held by others) as pertaining to the meaning should not be mentioned sep arately).

'*Should not be mentioned*'—do not deserve to be mentioned.

Those excellences that have been spoken of as pertaining (indirectly) to words, (though really belonging to Passion depicted)—these are suggested by Letters, compounds and diction. 73.

The *text* proceeds to describe what is suggestive of what excellence.—

(*a*) *The* '*sparsha*' [*mute*] *consonants, with the exception of those of the* '*ṭa*'*-group, combined with the last consonant of their group,—*(*b*) *the consonants* '*r*' *and ṇ*' *when short,—*(*c*) *expressions free compounds,—*(*d*) *compounds of medium length,—and* (*e*) *harmonious diction—are* (*suggestive*) *of Sweetness.* 74.

(*a*) All the consonants from *k* to *m*—except *ṭ*, *ṭh*, *ḍ* and *ḍh*—combined with the last letter of their respective groups, (*b*) *r* and ṇ combined with short vowels ; —these are the 'letters' (suggestive of *Sweetness*).

As for '*compounds*'—(*e*) '*expressions free from compounds*' or (*d*) '*compounds of medium length*' (are suggestive of *Sweetness*).

समासो वेति समासः तथा माधुर्यवती पदान्तरयोगेन रचना माधुर्यस्य व्यञ्जिका ॥ उदाहरणम्

अनङ्गरङ्गप्रतिमं तदङ्गं
भङ्गीभिरङ्गीकृतमानताङ्ग्याः ।
कुर्वन्ति यूनां सहसा यथैताः
स्वान्तानि शान्तापरचिन्तनानि ॥३४७॥७४॥॥

योग आद्यतृतीयाभ्यामन्त्ययो रेण तुल्ययोः ।
टादिः शषौ वृत्तिदैर्घ्यं गुम्फ उद्धत ओजसि ॥ ७५ ॥

वर्गप्रथमतृतीयाभ्यामन्त्ययोः द्वितीयचतुर्थयोः रेफेण अध उपरि उभयत्र वा यस्य कस्यचित् तुल्ययोः तेन तस्यैव

(*e*) '*Harmonious diction*'—*i. e.,* such diction in which the words are so combined as to make it soft—is also suggestive of *Sweetness.*

Example—

'*Anaṅgaraṅgapratimaṁ tadaṅgaṁ*
Bhaṅgībhiraṅgīkṛtamānatāṅgyāḥ
Kurvanti yūnāṁ sahasā yathaitāḥ
Svāntāni shāntāparachintanāni.'

'The exquisite body of the slender-bodied one, resembling the sportive altar of the Love-god, accompanied by graceful motions makes the innermost hearts of young men think of things other than the quietistic.' 74.

(*A*) *The combination—(a) of the first and of the third consonants of a group with the consonant following them,—(b) of any consonant with r,—and (e) of any two similar consonants ;—(B) the consonants beginning with ṭ —(C) the consonants sh and ṣ—(D) long compounds,—and (E) the bombastic diction,—these are suggestive of Floridity.* 75.

(*a*) The combination of the first and third letters of a group with those following them —*i.e.,* with the second and the fourth respectively ;—(*b*) any consonant

संबन्धः टवर्गोर्थात् णकारवर्जः शकारषकारौ दीर्घसमासः विकटा संघटना ओजसः ।

उदाहरणम्—मूर्ध्नामुद्वृत्तकृत्तइत्यादि ।।३४८।।७५।।

श्रुतिमात्रेण शब्दात्तु येनार्थप्रत्ययो भवेत् ।
साधारणः समग्राणां स प्रसादो गुणो मतः ।। ७६ ।।

समग्राणां रसानां संघटनानां च । उदाहरणम्

परिम्लानं पीनस्तनजघनसंगादुभयतस्-
तनोर्मध्यस्यान्तः परिमिलनमप्राप्य हरितम् ।
इदं व्यस्तन्यासं श्लथभुजलताक्षेपवलनैः
कृशाङ्ग्याः संतापं वदति बिसिनीपत्रशयनम् ।।३४९।।७६।।

---

having *r* either above or below it ;—(*c*) the combination of 'similar consonants' *i.e.,* that of a consonant with itself —(*d*) the entire *ṭ*—group with the exception of *ṇ* —(*e*) the consonants *sh* and *ṣ*—(*f*) long compounds —and (*g*) bombastic dictive ;—all these are suggestive of Floridity.

As an example we have the verse '*Mūrdhnāmudvṛtta &c.*' (see above stanza No. 285.)

Lucidity has been held to be that excellence, common to all, by virtue of which the comprehension of meaning of words follows on the mere hearing of it. 76.

'All'—*i. e.,* all Passions and all styles or diction. Example.—

'*Parimlānaṁ pīnastanajaghanasaṅgādubhayatas*
Tanor madhyasyāntaḥ parimilanamaprāpya haritam
Idaṁ vyastanyāsaṁ shlathabhujalatākṣepabalanaiḥ
Kṛshāṅgyāḥ santāpaṁ vadati bisinīpatrashayanam.'

'This bedding of lotus-leaves shows the distress of the slender-bodied one,—being as it is withered at its

यद्यपि गुणपरतन्त्राः संघटनादयस्तथापि

वक्तृवाच्यप्रबन्धानामौचित्येन क्वचित्क्वचित् ।
रचनावृत्तिवर्णानामन्यथात्वमपीष्यते ॥ ७७ ॥

क्वचिद्वाच्यप्रबन्धानपेक्षया वक्त्रौचित्यादेव रचनादयः । यथा

मन्थायस्तार्णवाम्भःप्लुतकुहरचलन्मन्दरध्वानधीरः
कोणाघातेषु गर्जत्प्रलयघनघटान्योन्यसंघट्टचण्डः ।
कृष्णाक्रोधाग्रदूतः कुरुकुलनिधनोत्पातनिर्घातवातः
केनास्मत्सिंहनादप्रतिरसितसखो दुन्दुभिस्ताडितोसौ ॥३५०॥

---

two ends where it has come into contact with the plump breasts and thighs—green in the middle where it did not come into contact with her slender waist—and ruffled by the throwing about of her unnerved arms.' 76.

[Although Construction, etc. are subservient to Excellence—]

The diction, the compounds and the letters are sometimes altered, in accordance with the nature of (a) the speaker, (b) the subject and (c) the form (of the composition). 77.

(*a*) In some cases the Diction &c., are made to accord with the nature of the *speaker*, irrespective of the subject or of the composition ; as an example of which we have the following—

Manthāyastārṇavāmbhaḥplutakuhara-chalanmandaradhvānadhīraḥ
Koṇāghāteṣu garjatpralayaghanaghaṭā-nyonyasaṅghaṭṭachaṇḍaḥ
Kṛṣṇākrodhāgradūtaḥ kurukulanidhanotpātanirghātavātaḥ
Kenāsmatsimhanādapratirasitasakho dundubhistāḍitosau.

'By whom has this trumpet been blown,—appearing as it does like the echo of my lion-roar, the forward messenger of Draupadī's wrath, the cyclone presaging the annihilation of the Kuru-race, resembling, at each stroke of the beating-stick, the terrible clash of the thundering

अत्र हि न वाच्यं क्रोधादिव्यञ्जकम् । अभिनेयार्थं च च काव्यमिति तत्प्रतिकूला उद्धता रचनादयः । वक्ता चात्र भीमसेनः ॥

क्वचिद्वक्तृप्रबन्धानपेक्षया वाच्यौचित्यादेव रचनादयः ॥

यथा

प्रौढच्छेदानुरूपोच्छलनरयभवत्सैंहिकेयोपघात-
त्रासाकृष्टाश्वतिर्यग्वलितरविरथेनारुणेनेक्ष्यमाणम् ।
कुर्वत् काकुत्स्थवीर्यस्तुतिमिव मरुतां कन्धरारन्ध्रभाजां
भांकारैर्भीममेतन्निपतति वियतः कुम्भकर्णोत्तमाङ्गम् ॥३५१॥

---

clouds at the time of universal dissolution, being as deep as the rumbling of the Mandara mountain tossed about and having its caves overflowing with the water of the sea thrown about, as it were, by the churning rod.'

Here the *subject* described , is not one suggestive of anger, or any such violent emotion ; the *form* of the work also is one to be staged ; so that the bombastic diction is not compatible with either of these two conditions ; and yet, since the speaker is Bhīmasena (well-known as a 'Furious' character) [the bombastic diction is quite suitable.]

In other cases the diction and other things are altered in accordance with the character of the *subject* portrayed, irrespective of the *speaker* or the *form*. For instance, in the following :—

'*Prauḍhachchhedānurūpochchhalanarayabhavatsaiṁhikeyopaghāta-*
Trāsākṛṣṭāshvatiryagvalitaravirathenāruṇenekṣyamāṇam
Kurvat kākutsthavīryastutimiva marutāṁ kandharārandhrabhājāṁ
Bhāṅkārairbhīmametannipatati viyataḥ kumbhakarṇottamāṅgam.'

'Here falls from the sky the head of Kumbhakarṇa, terrible on account of the curious humming of winds contained in the holes in his shoulders, and hence appearing

क्वचिद्वक्तृवाच्यानपेक्षाः प्रबन्धोचिता एव ते ॥

तथाहि—

आख्यायिकायां शृङ्गारेपि न मसृणवर्णादयः । कथायां रौद्रेपि नात्यन्तमुद्धताः । नाटकादौ रौद्रेपि न दीर्घसमासादयः ॥ एवमन्यदप्यौचित्यमनुसर्तव्यम् ॥७७॥

इति काव्यप्रकाशे गुणालंकारभेदनियतगुणनिर्णयो नाम

अष्टम उल्लासः ॥ ८ ॥

---

as it were, singing the praises of Rāma,—and being looked at by Aruṇa (the Sun's charioteer) wheeling about the sun's chariot and pulling up the horses on one side, fearing it to be Rāhu, on account of the force with which it has shot forth under the impact of the powerful stroke (of the sword).'

In other cases, the Diction &c. are altered in accordance with the nature of the *form*, irrespective of the *speaker* and the *subject*.—For instance in an *Ākhyāyikā* soft letters are not admissible even in the delineation of the Erotic Passion ;—in a *Kathā*, even in the delineation of the 'Furious', bombastic words are not used ;—and in dramas and works of that kind, long compounds are not used even in the depicting of the 'Furious'. Similarly in other cases, the proprieties are to vary with the circumstances. 77.

[Thus ends Chapter VIII dealing with the determination of Excellences as different from Ornaments (Figures of Speech).]

अथ नवम उल्लासः

गुणविवेचने कृतेलंकाराः प्राप्तावसराः इति संप्रति शब्दालंकारानाह—

यदुक्तमन्यथा वाक्यमन्यथान्येन योज्यते ।
श्लेषेण काक्वा वा ज्ञेया सा वक्रोक्तिस्तथा द्विधा ॥ ७८ ॥

तथेति श्लेषवक्रोक्तिः काकुवक्रोक्तिश्च। तत्र पदभङ्गश्लेषेण यथा

नारीणामनुकूलमाचरसि चेज्जानासि कश्चेतनो
वामानां प्रियमादधाति हितकृन्नैवाबलानां भवान् ।
युक्तं किं हितकर्तनं ननु बलाभावप्रसिद्धात्मनः
सामर्थ्यं भवतः पुरन्दरमतच्छेदं विधातुं कुतः ॥३५२॥

CHAPTER IX

THE VERBAL FIGURES OF SPEECH.

The Excellences having been examined, the author now describes the Verbal Figures of Speech.

(1)—*When what is said by one person in one sense is construed by another person in a different sense—either through punning or through intonation,—it is Equivoque* (*Vakrokti*) : *and thus it is of two kinds.* 78.

'*Thus*'—*i.e.*, (1) Equivoque based on Punning and (2) Equivoque based upon Intonation.

The following is an example of Equiyoque based upon pun due to the breaking up of words :—

'*Nārīṇāmanukūlamācharasi chejjānāsi kashchetano*
Vāmānāṁ priyamādadhāti hitakṛnnaivābalānāṁ bhavān
Yuktaṁ kiṁ hitakartanaṁ nanu balābhāvaprasiddhātmanaḥ,—
Sāmarthyaṁ bhavataḥ purandaramatachchhedaṁ vidhātuṁ kutaḥ.'

अभङ्गश्लेषेण यथा

अहो केनेदृशी बुद्धिर्दारुणा तव निर्मिता ।
त्रिगुणा श्रूयते बुद्धिर्न तु दारुमयी क्वचित् ॥३५३॥

"If you behave satisfactorily towards women, then you are wise".—"What intelligent person does what is agreeable to his enemies?" [This reply being based upon the pun involved in breaking up the term '*nārīṇām*', spoken by the first speaker in the sense of 'towards women', into two terms '*na-arīṇāṁ*', 'not to enemies']—"Then you are not a benefactor of the weaker sex." [This rejoinder takes the term '*vāmānāṁ*', used by the second speaker in the sense 'of enemies', in the sense 'of the weaker sex'.]—"Would it be proper to destroy the good of a person known to be weak?" [This answer is based upon the term '*hitakṛt*', used by the former speaker in the sense of *hitaṁ karoti* 'benefactor, one who does good', being taken in the sense of *hitaṁ* '*kṛntati*', 'one who destroys the good']. —"Whence can there be any power in you to bring about the destruction of what is desired by Indra?" [This reply is based on the expression '*balābhāvaprasiddhātmanaḥ*', used by the former speaker in the sense of 'one known to be weak', being taken by the latter in the sense of 'one who is known by his killing of the demon Bala, *i.e.,* Indra'.]

The following is an example of Equivoque based upon Paronomasia, not involving the breaking up of words.

'*Aho kenedṛshī buddhirdāruṇa tava nirmitā*
Triguṇā shrūyate buddhirna tu dārumayī kvachit'.

"Oh! By whom has this Intelligence of yours been made so cruel?"—"Intelligence is known to consist of the three attributes, and never of wood". [The reply

काक्वा यथा

गुरुजनपरतन्त्रतया दूरतरं देशमुद्यतो गन्तुम् ।
अलिकुलकोकिलललिते नैष्यति सखि सुरभिसमयेसौ ॥३५४॥७८॥

वर्णसाम्यमनुप्रासः ॥

स्वरवैसादृश्येपि व्यञ्जनसदृशत्वं वर्णसाम्यम् । रसाद्यनुगतः प्रकृष्टो न्यासोनुप्रासः ॥

---

is based upon the word '*dāruṇā*', used by the first speaker in the sense of 'cruel', being taken by the other in the sense of 'of wood'.]

The following is an example of Equivoque based on Intonation.

'*Gurujanaparatantratayā dūrataraṁ deshamudyato gantum*
Alikulakokilalalite naiṣyati sakhi surabhisamayesau'.

'Being obedient to his elders, he is prepared to go to a far remote country; and O friend! will he not come during the fragrant season (of spring), which is beautified by the presence of swarms of black bees and cuckoos?' [To this the friend is supposed to reply 'will he not come?' this reply in this sense being obtained by giving to the word '*naiṣyati*', 'will not come', the *intonation* of a question; so that the word used by the first speaker in the former sense is taken by the second in the latter sense, which carries the further meaning 'he is sure to come.']

Alliteration (Anuprāsa) consists in the similarity of letters.

The '*similarity of letters*' meant here is the sameness of the *consonants,* even though the vowels may be different.

The figure is called '*Anuprāsa*', because it consists in such '*prāsa*'—*prakṛṣṭa nyāsa, i.e., excellent allocation* (of letters)—as is '*anu*'—*anugata,* favourable, to the delineation of Passion and other things.

छेकवृत्तिगतो द्विधा ॥

छेकाः विदग्धाः। वृत्तिर्नियतवर्णगतो रसविषयो व्यापारः। गत इति छेकानुप्रासो वृत्त्यनुप्रासश्च ॥

किं तयोः स्वरूपम् इत्याह—

सोनेकस्य सकृत्पूर्वः ॥

अनेकस्य अर्थात् व्यञ्जनस्य सकृदेकवारं सादृश्यं छेकानुप्रासः। उदाहरणम्

ततोरुणपरिस्पन्दमन्दीकृतवपुः शशी ।
दध्रे कामपरिक्षामकामिनीगण्डपाण्डुताम् ॥३५५॥

It is of two kinds,—as pertaining to (a) chheka (experts) and (b) vṛtti (diction).

'*Chheka*'—Experts ; '*vṛtti*'—that function of letters which affects the delineation of Passion ;—'pertaining to' these,—*i.e.*, the two kinds of Alliteration are (*a*) '*chhekānuprāsa*' and (*b*) *Vṛttyanuprāsa*.'

[These are merely fanciful names, as is clear from the definitions that follow, according to which the two kinds may be called (*a*) 'Isolated' and (*b*) 'Complex' Alliteration.]

The author states the characteristics of these two kinds of Alliteration.—

The former is the single repetition of several.

When there is a single repetition of '*several*'—consonants, it is '*Chhekānuprāsa*', 'Isolated Alliteration.' Example—

'*Tato' ruṇaparispandamandīkṛtavapuḥ shashī*
Dadhre kāmaparikṣāmakāminīgaṇḍapāṇḍutām'.

'The Moon, having his body eclipsed by the advent of the Sun, bore the paleness of the cheek of a woman emaciated by the pangs of love.'

[Here we have 'single repetition of the consonants (*a*) 'n-d' and (*b*) 'ṇ-ḍ']

एकस्याप्यसकृत्परः ॥ ७९ ॥

एकस्य अपिशब्दादनेकस्य व्यञ्जनस्य द्विर्बहुकृत्वो वा सादृश्यं वृत्त्यनुप्रासः ॥७९॥

तत्र

माधुर्यव्यञ्जकैर्वर्णैरुपनागरिकोच्यते ।
ओजःप्रकाशकैस्तैस्तु परुषा ।
उभयत्रापि प्रागुदाहृतम् ।

कोमला परैः ॥ ८० ॥

परैः शेषैः । तामेव केचित् ग्राम्येति वदन्ति । उदाहरणम्

अपसारय घनसारं कुरु हारं दूर एव किं कमलैः ।
अलमलमालि मृणालैरिति वदति दिवानिशं बाला ॥३५६॥८०॥

The latter consists in several repetitions of one also. 79.

When there are 'several'—two or more—'repetitions' of 'one'—consonant—'also'—*i.e.*, or of several consonants,—we have the '*Vṛttyanuprāsa*', the 'Alliteration of Diction'. 79.

As regards '*Vṛtti*', 'Diction':—

(*a*) *That (Diction) which is characterised by consonants suggestive of sweetness is called 'Upanāgarikā' 'Polished'; and* (*b*) *that which is characterised by consonants suggestive of floridity is called 'Paruṣā', 'Harsh'.*

Examples of both these have been cited above (in Ch. VIII, under 'Sweetness' and 'Floridity').

(*c*) *That characterised by others is called 'komalā', 'soft'.* 80.

'*Others*'—Consonants other than the two kinds mentioned above.

This last diction some people also call '*grāmyā*', 'Vulgar.'

Example—

'*Apasāraya ghanasāraṁ kuru hāraṁ dūrameva kiṁ kamalaiḥ*
Alamalamāli mṛṇālairiti vadati divānishaṁ bālā.

For translatlon (see above stanza No. 341.) 80.

केषांचिदेता वैदर्भीप्रमुखा रीतयो मताः ॥

एतास्तिस्रो वृत्तयः वामनादीनां मते वैदर्भीगौडीपाञ्चाल्याख्या रीतयो मताः ॥

शाब्दस्तु लाटानुप्रासो भेदे तात्पर्यमात्रतः ॥ ८१ ॥

शब्दगतोनुप्रासः शब्दार्थयोरभेदेप्यन्वयमात्रभेदात् लाटजनवल्लभत्वाच्च लाटानुप्रासः। एष पदानुप्रास इत्यन्ये ॥८१॥

पदानां सः ।

स इति लाटानुप्रासः । उदाहरणम्

By some people these styles of diction have been called the 'Vaidarbhī' and the rest.

According to others—*i.e.,* Vāmana and his followers,—the three styles of diction just described have been called, respectively, (*a*) '*Vaidarbhī*', (*b*) '*Gauḍī*' and '*Pāñchālī*.'

The Lāṭānuprāsa is verbal; the difference lying only in the import. 81.

When there is Alliteration (repetition) of *words* (not mainly of single consonants as in the other two kinds of Alliteration),—and though the form and the meaning of the words thus repeated are the same, yet there is difference in the syntactical relation of the words,—it is '*Lāṭānuprāsa*,' so called because of its being popular among the inhabitants of the *Lāṭa* country.

Others have called this the 'Alliteration of Words.'

['Words' are here divided into the (A) verbal forms complete with the terminations; and (B) simple basic substantives. In the Alliteration of (A), there may be repetition either (*a*) of several words, or (*b*) of a single word; and in that of (B), the repetition may be either (*a*) in the same compound or (*b*) in different compounds. Each of these is next dealt with.] 81.

(*Aa*) *This pertains to several words.*

'*This*'—*i.e.* *The Lāṭānuprāsa.*

यस्य न सविधे दयिता दवदहनस्तुहिनदीधितिस्तस्य ।
यस्य च सविधे दयिता दवदहनस्तुहिनदीधितिस्तस्य ॥३५७॥

पदस्यापि ।

अपिशब्देन स इति समुच्चीयते । उदाहरणम्

वदनं वरवर्णिन्यास्तस्याः सत्यं सुधाकरः ।
सुधाकरः क्व नु पुनः कलङ्कविकलो भवेत् ॥३५८॥

वृत्तावन्यत्र तत्र वा ।

नाम्नः स वृत्त्यवृत्त्योश्च ।

Example—

'*Yasya na savidhe dayitā davadahanastuhinadīdhitistasya*
Yasya cha savidhe dayitā davadahanastuhinadīdhitistasya.'

'To one who has not his beloved near him, even the cool-rayed Moon is like the forest-conflagration; while to one who has his beloved near him, even the forest-conflagration is like the cool-rayed Moon.'

[Here we have the repetition of several words (a) '*yasya-savidhe dayitā*' and (a) '*davadahanaḥ-tuhinadīdhitiḥ-tasya*'.]

(*A*) *It pertains to a single word also.*

The particle '*api*', 'also', indicates that the pronoun '*saḥ*' of the preceding text is to be construed here also.

Example.—

'*Vadanaṁ varavarṇinyāṣtasyāḥ satyaṁ sudhākaraḥ*
Sudhākaraḥ kva nu punaḥ kalaṁkavikalo bhavet.'

'The face of the fair-complexioned one is really the Moon;—where else could the Moon be free from stains?'

[Here we have the repetition of the single word '*sudhākaraḥ*'.]

(B) *It is (repetition) of the same substantive base, either* (*a*) *in the same compound, or* (*b*) *in different compounds, or* (*c*) *once in a compound and once in a non-compound.*

एकस्मिन् समासे भिन्ने वा समासे समासासमासयोर्वा नाम्नः प्रातिपदिकस्य न तु पदस्य सारूप्यम् । उदाहरणम्

सितकरकररुचिरविभा विभाकराकार धरणिधर कीर्तिः ।
पौरुषकमला कमला सापि तवैवास्ति नान्यस्य ॥३५९॥

तदेवं पञ्चधा मतः ॥ ८२ ॥

अर्थे सत्यर्थभिन्नानां वर्णानां [सा पुनः श्रुतिः ।

यमकम् ।

समरसमरसोयमित्यादावेकेषामर्थवत्त्वे अन्येषामनर्थकत्वे भिन्नार्थानामिति न युज्यते वक्तुम् इति अर्थे सतीत्युक्तम् । सेति सरोरस इत्यादिवैलक्षण्येन तेनैव क्रमेण स्थिता ।

The repetition of the substantive *base*,—not of the *word* (with terminations),—either (*a*) in one and the same compound, or (*b*) in different compounds, or (*c*) occurring once in a compound and for the second time in a non-compound.

Example—

(*a*) *Sitakarakararuchiravibhā vibhākarākāra* (*b*) *dharaṇidhara kīrtiḥ*

(*c*) *Pauruṣakamalā kamalā sāpi tavaivāsti nānyasya'.*

(See above stanza No. 314).

[Here in (*a*) we have the repetition of the substantive '*kara*' in the same compound; in (*b*) we have the substantive '*vibhā*' occurring in two distinct compounds and in (*c*) the substantive '*kamalā*' occurs first in a compound and then by itself, not in a compound.]

Thus is Alliteration of five kinds :[82]: (3) *The repetition of letters in the same order, with a different meaning,—when there is meaning,—constitute 'Yamaka', 'Chime'.*

'*If there is meaning*';—this has been added in anticipation of the objection that—" in such expressions as '*samarasamarasoyam*' ('one whose passion for war is

पादतद्भागवृत्ति तद्यात्यनेकताम् ॥ ८३ ॥

प्रथमो द्वितीयादौ द्वितीयस्तृतीयादौ तृतीयश्चतुर्थे प्रथमस्त्रिष्वपीति सप्त । प्रथमो द्वितीये तृतीयश्चतुर्थे प्रथमश्चतुर्थे द्वितीयस्तृतीये, इति द्वे । तदेवं पादजं नवभेदम् । अर्धावृत्तिः श्लोकावृत्तिश्चेति द्वे ।

---

uniform'), the letters '*sa-ma-ra*', when occurring first, have the sense of 'war', but when repeated, the same letters have no sense, (as they form part of the compound '*samarasaḥ*'); so that it is not right to say that Chime consists in the repetition of letters *with a different meaning*."

'*Sā*', '*in the same order*',—this is meant to exclude such repetition, as in '*sarorasa*' (where the consonants are not repeated *in the same order*).

As occurring in the several feet of a verse or in several parts thereof,—it becomes manifold. 83.

(1) The first foot repeated in the second foot, (2) the first foot repeated in the third foot, (3) the first foot repeated in the fourth foot;—(4) the second foot repeated in the third foot, (5) the second foot repeated in the fourth foot;—(6) the third foot repeated in the fourth,—and (7) the first foot repeated in all the other three feet.—These make seven varieties.—Then there are two varieties—*viz*:—(8) the repetition of the first foot in the second foot, and that of the third in the fourth foot—and (9) the repetition of the first foot in the fourth and that of the second in the third.—Thus there are nine varieties of Chime as occurring in the several feet of a verse.—In addition to these there are two varieties—*viz*.,—(10) the repetition of one half of the verse and (11) the repetition of the entire verse.

द्विधा विभक्ते पादे प्रथमादिपादादिभागः पूर्ववत् द्वितीयादिपादादिभागेषु अन्तभागोनन्तभागेष्विति विंशतिर्भेदाः श्लोकान्तरे हि नासौ भागावृत्तिः। त्रिखण्डे त्रिंशत् चतुःखण्डे चत्वारिंशत्।

प्रथमपादादिगतान्त्यार्धादिभागो द्वितीयपादादिगते आद्यार्धादिभागे यम्यतें इत्याद्यन्वर्थतानुसरणेनानेकभेदम्। अन्तादिकम्। आद्यन्तिकम्। तत्समुच्चयः। मध्यादिकम्। आदिमध्यम्।

Then again, each foot of the verse being divided into two parts, there may be repetition of the first part of the first foot in the first part of the second foot and so forth,—and repetition of the second half of the first foot in the second half of the second foot and so forth ;—such partial repetition as occurring in different verses are not counted as such ;—so that in this way there are *twenty* varieties.

If each foot is divided into three parts, similar repetitions give rise to *thirty* varieties ; and when each foot is divided into four parts, there would be *forty* varieties.

The latter end of the second half of the first foot chiming with the former half of the second foot, and so forth, would give rise to several varieties. For instance, (1) The latter half of the first chiming with the former half of the second foot,—(2) the former half of the first chiming with the latter half of the second foot, and (3) the combination of these two ;—(4) (each of the feet being divided into three or more parts) the middle part of the first chiming with the first part of the second foot,—(5) the first part of the first foot chiming with the middle part of the second foot, (6) the third part of the first chiming with the middle part of the second foot,—(7) the middle part of the first chiming with the last part of the second

अन्तमध्यम् । मध्यान्तिकम् । तेषां समुच्चयः । तथा तस्मिन्नेव पादे आद्यादिभागानां मध्यादिभागे अनियते च स्थाने आवृत्ति-रिति प्रभूततमभेदम् । तदेतत्काव्यान्तर्गडुभूतम् इति नास्य भेदलक्षणं कृतम् । दिङ्मात्रमुदाह्रियते ।

सन्नारीभरणोमायमाराध्य विधुशेखरम् ।
सन्नारीभरणोमायस्ततस्त्वं पृथिवीं जय ॥३६०॥

विनायमेनो नयतासुखादिना विना यमेनोनयता सुखादिना ।
महाजनोदीयत मानसादरं महाजनोदी यतमानसादरम् ॥३६१॥

---

foot,—(8) the combination of the last three.—Similarly there can be repetition of the first and other parts in the middle, and other parts of the same foot,—or again, the repetition may be without any fixed order, any part of one foot being repeated in any part of another ; and so forth, there would be many varieties.

All this however is a mere excrescence in the body of poetry ; and hence any detailed definition of these varieties has not been attempted ; examples also we are citing of only a few kinds.—

(1)

Sannārībharaṇomāyastatastvaṁ pṛthivīṁ jaya.'

'Having worshipped the Moon-crested God, who has obtained the jewel of pure women, may you win the earth,—you, who are free from deceit and in whose battle your enemy's elephants have perished.'

(2) '*Vināyameno nayatāsukhādinā*
Vinā yamenonayatā sukhādinā
Mahājanodīyata mānasādaraṁ
Mahājanodī yatamānasādaraṁ.

स त्वारम्भरतोवश्यमबलं विततारवम् ।
सर्वदा रणमानैषीदवानलसमस्थितः ॥३६२॥
सत्त्वारम्भरतोवश्यमवलम्बिततारवम् ।
सर्वदारणमानैषी दवानलसमस्थितः ॥३६३॥
अनन्तमहिमव्याप्तविश्वां वेधा न वेद याम् ।
या च मातेव भजते प्रणते मानवे दयाम् ॥३६४॥
यदानतो यदा नतो नयात्ययं न यात्ययम् ।
शिवेहितां शिवे हितां स्मरामितां स्मरामि ताम् ॥३६५॥

'The soul-bird, great and destructive of the annoyers of the good, was estranged from the mind by the Death-god, who carries away people without fault, devours life and strips off all pleasure.'

(3) '*Satvārambharatovashyam—*
abalaṁ vitatāravam
Sarvādāraṇamānaiṣī—
davānalasamasthitaḥ.
Sattvārambharatovashyam—
avalambitatāravam
Sarvadāraṇamānaiṣī
davānālasamasthitaḥ.'

'The king, quick in action, devoted to Viṣṇu, always acting rightly, anxious to reach the heart of the people, and resembling the Submarine Fire,—always brought his enemies to battle, who were weak and noisy, who had not been subdued and hence resembled trees still standing upright.'

(4) *vedhā na veda yām*
Yā cha māteva bhajate praṇate mānave dayām

(5) '*Yadānatoyadānato nayātyayaṁ na yātyayaṁ*
Shivehitāṁ shive hitāṁ smarāmitāṁ smarāmi tām.'

(4) 'I meditate upon Pārvatī,—whose immanent

सरस्वति प्रसादं मे स्थितिं चित्तसरस्वति ।
सर स्वति कुरु क्षेत्रकुरुक्षेत्रसरस्वति ॥३६६॥
ससार साकं दर्पेण कन्दर्पेण ससारसा ।
शरन्नवाना बिभ्राणा नाबिभ्राणा शरन्नवा ॥३६७॥
मधुपराजिपराजितमानिनीजनमनःसुमनःसुरभि श्रियम् ।
अभृत वारितवारिजविप्लवं स्फुटितताम्रतताम्रवणं जगत् ॥३६८॥

---

majesty even Brahmā cannot fathom, and who, like a mother, bestows her grace upon devoted man.'

(5) 'I meditate upon Her who was sought after by Shiva,—by bowing to whom man, being auspiciously favoured by Her who is ever favourable to us, never goes beyond the bounds of propriety.'

(6) '*Sarasvati prasādaṁ me sthitiṁ chittasarasvati*
Sara svati kuru kṣetrakurukṣetrasarasvati.'

'O Sarasvatī, who art in the body, like the river Sarasvatī in Kurukṣetra ! Be propitiated and make the ocean of my heart thy splendid abode.

(7) '*Sasāra sākaṁ darpeṇa kandarpeṇa sasārasā*
Sharannavānā bibhrāṇā nāvibhrāṇā sharannavā

'The excellent autumn, accompanied by the lotus and fresh-looking carts, conducive to the ripening of the long grass, not devoid of the song of birds, slunk away along with the arrogant Love-god.'

(8) '*Madhuparājiparājitamāninī-*
janamanaḥsumanaḥ surabhi shriyam
Abhṛta vāritavārijaviplavaṁ
Sphuṭitatāmratatāmravaṇaṁ jagat.'

'The world acquired resplendence,—bearing the sweet fragrance of the flower-like hearts of love-quarrelled women subjugated by the appearance of lines of black

एवं वैचित्र्यसहस्रैः स्थितमन्यदुन्नेयम् ॥८३॥

वाच्यभेदेन भिन्ना यद् युगपद्भाषणस्पृशः ।
श्लिष्यन्ति शब्दाः श्लेषोसावक्षरादिभिरष्टधा ॥ ८४ ॥

'अर्थभेदेन शब्दभेदः' इति दर्शने 'काव्यमार्गे स्वरो न गण्यते' इति च नये वाच्यभेदेन भिन्ना अपि शब्दा यत् युगपदुच्चारणेन श्लिष्यन्ति भिन्नं स्वरूपमपह्नुवते स श्लेषः । स च वर्णपदलिङ्गभाषाप्रकृतिप्रत्ययविभक्तिवचनानां भेदादष्टधा ।

---

bees, discontinuing the destruction of the lotus and adorned with blossoming, tawny and wide-expanding mango-groves.'

In the above manner, we may deduce the examples of endless varieties of *Chime*. 83.

(IV) *When words that are different by reason of the difference in their denotations coalesce (become identified) through the sameness of their pronunciation, it is a case of Coalescence or Pun; and through Letter and other factors, it is of eight kinds.* 84.

There is the theory that words having different meanings must be regarded as different,—and also that in poetry, accents do not count ; and in accordance with the former theory, even though two words may be the same in their verbal form, yet they are regarded as different and in accordance with the latter, when these words (though differently accented, by reason of their meanings) come to be pronounced in exactly the same manner, they are regarded as 'coalescing', *i.e.*, as having their differences undiscernible ;—and when this happens, it is a case of Coalescence, *Pun*.

This Pun is of eight kinds, as based upon the eight different factors of (1) letters, (2) words, (3) gender, (4)

क्रमेणोदाहरणम्—

अलंकारः शङ्काकरनरकपालं परिजनो
विशीर्णाङ्गो भृङ्गी वसु च वृष एको बहुवयाः ।
अवस्थेयं स्थाणोरपि भवति सर्वामरगुरोर्-
विधौ वक्रे मूर्ध्नि स्थितवति वयं के पुनरमी ॥३६९॥
पृथुकार्तस्वरपात्रं भूषितनिःशेषपरिजनं देव ।
विलसत्करेणुगहनं संप्रति सममावयोः सदनम् ॥३७०॥
भक्तिप्रह्वविलोकनप्रणयिनी नीलोत्पलस्पर्धिनी
ध्यानालम्बनतां समाधिनिरतैर्नीतेहितप्राप्तये ।

---

dialect, (5) crude forms, (6) affixes, (7) terminations (declensional and conjugational) and (8) number.

The following are the examples in this same order :—

(1) '*Alaṅkāraḥ shaṅkākaranarakapālaṁ parījano*
Vishīrṇāṅgo bhṛṅgī vasu cha vṛṣa eko bahuvayāḥ
Avastheyaṁ sthāṇorapi bhavati sarvāmaraguror
Vidhau vakre mūrdhni sthitavati vayaṁ ke punaramī.

'For his ornament the fearful human skull ; for his attendant Bhṛṅgī of the broken limbs ; for his property, a single aged bull ;—when such is the condition of even Shiva, the revered of all the gods, when the *curved moon* (untoward Fate) stands on his head, who are we (that we should not suffer from untoward Fate) ?'

(2) '*Pṛthukārtasvarapātraṁ bhūṣitaniḥsheṣaparijanaṁ deva*
Vilasatkareṇugahanaṁ samprati samamāvayoḥ sadanaṁ

(See above stanza No. 306.)

(3) and (8)

'*Bhaktiprahvavilokanapraṇayinī nīlotpalaspardhinī*
Dhyānālambanatāṁ samādhiniratairnītehitaprāptaye

लावण्यस्य महानिधी रसिकतां लक्ष्मीदृशोस्तन्वती
युष्माकं कुरुतां भवार्तिशमनं नेत्रे तनुर्वा हरेः ॥३७१॥

एष वचनश्लेषोपि ।

महदेसुरसंधम्मे तमवसमासंगमागमाहरणे ।
हरबहुसरणं तं चित्तमोहमवसरउमे सहसा ॥३७२॥

Lāvaṁyasya mahānidhī rasikatāṁ lakṣmīdṛshostanvatī
Yuṣmākaṁ kurutāṁ bhavārtishamanaṁ netre tanurvā hareḥ.

'May (*a*) the eyes or (*b*) the body of Viṣṇu set at rest your worldly troubles !—(*a*) the eyes looking tenderly upon devotees, and (*a*) the body looked upon by persons in humble devotion,—(*a*) the eyes and (*b*) the body both vying with the lotus, mediated upon by yogins for the attainment of their highest ends,—the ocean of beauty, and producing charming sensations in the eyes of Lakṣmī.'

(2) Here again we have also the coalescence of the two numbers [Dual and Singular, the form of the various epithets being the same in both numbers ; the Neuter-Dual forms being the same the Feminine-Singular].

(4) '*Mahadesurasaṁdhaṁme*
tamavasamāsaṁgamāgamāharaṇe
Harabahusaraṇaṁ taṁ chittamoham-
avasaraume sahasā.'

[This couplet, when taken as *Sanskrit*, means—'O Umā, who ordains happiness, please safeguard my devotion to Vedic studies, which lead to union with the gods, and in proper time destroy the ever-growing delusion of my mind.'—

अयं सर्वाणि शास्त्राणि हृदि ज्ञेषु च वक्ष्यति ।
सामर्थ्यकृदमित्राणां मित्राणां च नृपात्मजः ॥३७३॥

रजनिरमणमौलेः पादपद्मावलोक-
क्षणसमयपराप्तापूर्वसंपत्सहस्रम् ।
प्रमथनिवहमध्ये जातुचित्त्वत्प्रसादाद्
अहमुचितरुचिः स्यान्नन्दिता सा तथा मे ॥३७४॥

And when taken as *Prakrit*, its meaning is as follows—'O Consort of Shiva ! produce in me a regard for virtue, and destroy my desire for birth and re-birth, which has its source in *Tamas* !—Thou art my sole refuge ; so please remove the delusion of my mind.'—

Thus in this case we have the coalescence of the two *dialects*.]

(5) '*Ayaṁ sarvāṇi shāstrāṇi hṛdi jñeṣu cha vakṣyati
Sāmarthyakṛdamitrāṇāṁ mitrāṇāṁ cha nṛpātmajaḥ*'.

['The son of the king shall (*a*) *bear in his heart*, and (*b*) *discuss* with the learned, all the sciences, and he shall be the (*a*) strength-giver to his friends and (*b*) the strength-*destroyer* of his foes.]

(6) '*Rajaniramaṇamauleḥ pādapadmāvaloka-
Kṣaṇasamayaparāptāpūrvasaṁpatsahasram
Pramathanivahamadhye jātuchittvatprasādād
Ahamuchitaruchiḥ syānnanditā sā tathā me.*'

'Having obtained a thousandfold splendour on the occasion of looking at the lotus-feet of the Moon-crested God, and having acquired the right devotion through your grace,—may I among Shiva's hosts, (*a*) become the joy-giver and (*b*) attain the position of Nandī, their leader !'

सर्वस्वं हर सर्वस्य त्वं भवच्छेदतत्परः ।
नयोपकारसांमुख्यमायासि तनुवर्तनम् ॥३७५॥८४॥

भेदाभावात्प्रकृत्यादेर्भेदोपि नवमो भवेत् ।

नवमोपीत्यपिर्भिन्नक्रमः । उदाहरणम्——

योसकृत्परगोत्राणां पक्षच्छेदक्षणक्षमः ।
शतकोटिदतां बिभ्रद्विबुधेन्द्रः स राजते ॥३७६॥

---

(7) *Sarvasvaṁ hara sarvasya*
Tvaṁ bhavachchhedatatparaḥ
Nayopakārasāṁmukhyam
Āyāsi tanuvartanam.

[This may be construed either (*a*) as addressed by a devotee to Śhiva, or (*b*) as addressed by a thief to his son :—(*a*) 'O Shiva ! you are the all in all of the entire universe,—addicted to the destruction of the world ; as such you have a body wherefrom emanates all that is conducive to good and virtue';—(*b*) 'O Son, take away all the property of all men ; employ yourself in cutting the walls ; do away with the idea of returning good for good ; and extend your livelihood at the cost of others.'—

[Here we have the coalescence (*a*) of the declensional termination, the vocative, and the conjugational termination, imperative, in the word '*hara*';—(*b*) of the conjugational termination, imperative and the declensional termination, the genitive, understood in the word '*bhava*'; also we have (*c*) the coalescence in the word '*āyāsi*', of the possessive ending '*ṇini*' and the conjugational termination, the present.] 84.

There is also the ninth kind (of Pun), where there is no difference in the crude form or other factors.

The particle '*api*', 'also', is to be construed with '*navamaḥ*', 'ninth'.

अत्र प्रकरणादिनियमाभावात् द्वावप्यर्थौ वाच्यौ ।।

ननु स्वरितादिगुणभेदाद् भिन्नप्रयत्नोच्चार्याणां तदभावादभिन्नप्रयत्नोच्चार्याणां च शब्दानां बन्धेलंकारान्तरप्रतिभोत्पत्तिहेतुः शब्दश्लेषोर्थश्लेषश्चेति द्विविधोप्यर्थालंकारमध्ये परिगणितोन्यैरिति कथमयं शब्दालंकारः ।

Example—

'Yosakṛtparagotrāṇāṁ pakṣachchhedakṣaṇakṣamaḥ
Shatakoṭidatāṁ bibhrad vibhudhendraḥ sa rājate.'

There being no defining factor in the shape of context and the rest, this couplet is equally capable of affording both. the meanings—(*a*) 'The *king of the learned* is resplendent, being capable of repeatedly destroying in a moment the prosperity of his enemy's people, and bearing the mark of having given away hundreds of millions';—(*b*) 'The king of the gods, Indra, is resplendent,—capable of cutting off in a moment, the wings of the great mountains, and bearing the character of striking with the thunderbolt.'

[Here we have a coalescence, where there is no difference in the two cases, in any one of the eight factors mentioned above.—This kind has been called the *'Abhaṅga-shleṣa'* 'Unbroken Pun', on the ground that it does not necessitate the *breaking up* of the words into its various factors;—the necessity of which breaking up leads to the above-mentioned eight kinds of Pun being called *'Sabhaṅga-shleṣa'*, 'Broken Pun.']

An objection is raised in this connection :—"A composition consists (*a*) of words that are pronouncible by diverse 'efforts' on account of the divergence in their accents, 'samāhāra' and other qualifications,—and also (*b*) of words that are pronouncible by similar 'efforts', by reason of there being no difference in the said qualifi-

उच्यते—इह दोषगुणालंकाराणां शब्दार्थगतत्वेन यो विभागः सः अन्वयव्यतिरेकाभ्यामेव व्यवतिष्ठते। तथाहि—कष्टत्वादिगाढत्वाद्यनुप्रासादयः व्यर्थत्वादिप्रौढ्याद्युपमादयस्तद्भावतदभावानुविधायित्वादेव शब्दार्थगतत्वेन व्यवस्थाप्यन्ते।

---

cations ; in such a composition, 'coalescence' serves the purpose of intimating the Simile and such other figures of speech ; the 'Coalescence' or 'Pun' is of two kinds, 'verbal' (based upon the forms of words) ; and 'ideal' (based upon the meanings of words) ; and since both these kinds of Pun have been included by others among 'Ideal Figures of Speech', why should it be treated as a *verbal* figure of speech (as it is done in the present context) ?"

The answer to the above is as follows :—

In the present connection, when we divide defects or excellences or figures of speech into 'verbal' and 'ideal'. such a division is based upon a consideration of concomitances, positive and negative.

[That is to say, when a certain defect pertains to and is concomitant with only the verbal form of words and takes no account of the meaning, it is classed as 'verbal'; while it if is found to be concomtant with and pertaining to the meaning of words and is not affected by the verbal forms, then it is classed as 'ideal'].

For instance, Harshness (defect), Floridity (excellence), Alliteration (figure of speech) and the rest are classed as 'verbal', because they are dependent entirely upon the presence or absence of the verbal forms of words ; and 'Irrelevancy' (defect), Boldness (excellence) and Simile (figure of speech) and the rest are classed as 'ideal', because they are dependent entirely upon the presence or

स्वयं च पल्लवाताम्रभास्वत्करविराजिता । इत्यभङ्गः
प्रभातसंध्येवास्वापफललुब्धेहितप्रदा ॥ ३७७॥ इति सभङ्गः
इति द्वावपि शब्दैकसमाश्रयाविति द्वयोरपि शब्दश्लेषत्वमुप-
पन्नं न त्वाद्यस्यार्थश्लेषत्वम् । अर्थश्लेषस्य तु स विषयः यत्र
शब्दपरिवर्तनेपि न श्लेषत्वखण्डना । यथा

---

absence of the meanings of words. For example, in the following two passages—

(*a*) '*Svayaṁ cha pallavātāmrabhāsvatkaravirājitā,*

(*b*) *prabhātasandhyevāsvāpaphalalubdhehitapradā.*'

['Gaurī—(1) adorned by hands red as the fresh leaf, and (2) fulfilling the desires of persons seeking for results hard to attain,—resembles the morn, which is (1) adorned by the shining sun red like the fresh leaf and fulfills the desires of persons intent upon performing the rites of the early dawn,' [—we have, in the first an instance of '*broken* pun'. [Since it involves the *breaking* up of the expression '*bhāsvatkaravirājitā*' into '*bhāsvat—kara-virājitā*' in one case, and into '*bhāsvatka—ravi—rājitā*' in the other], and in the second an instance of the '*unbroken* pun' [since the pun rests in the word '*asvāpa*', which retains the same form in both cases and has not got to be broken up].

[The commentators have made a hopeless muddle of this passage, being landed into it by the wrong reading whereby the first passage is spoken of as '*abhaṅga*' and the second as '*sabhaṅga*'; while, as a matter of fact, the case is just the reverse. The commentators say that '*asvāpa* involves a '*broken* pun'; but in both cases the word retaining the same form,—where is the *breaking* ?]

Since both these puns are based upon the verbal forms of the words, it is only right that they should be regarded as 'verbal'. It is not possible for even the first half to be regarded as 'ideal', because that Pun alone can be regarded

स्तोकेनोन्नतिमायाति स्तोकेनायात्यधोगतिम् ।
अहो सुसदृशी वृत्तिस्तुलाकोटेः खलस्य च ॥३७८॥

न चायमुपमाप्रतिभोत्पत्तिहेतुः श्लेषः अपि तु श्लेषप्रतिभोत्पत्तिहेतुरुपमा । तथाहि—यथा

'कमलमिव मुखं मनोज्ञमेतत्कचतितराम्' इत्यादौ गुणसाम्ये क्रियासाम्ये उभयसाम्ये वा उपमा । तथा 'सकलकलं पुरमेतज्जातं संप्रति सुधांशुबिम्बमिव' इत्यादौ शब्दमात्रसाम्येपि सा युक्तैव । तथा ह्युक्तं रुद्रटेन

---

as 'ideal', where the pun remains unaffected even when the words are changed ; as is the case in the verse—

'*Stokenonnatimāyāti stokenāyātyadhogatim*
aho susadṛshī vṛttistulākoṭeḥ khalasya cha']

['Rising with little and falling with little,—the character of the wicked is exactly like that of the balance-beam']—[where the Pun remains unaffected even when other synonyms are substituted for the words '*stokena*', '*unnatiṁ*' and '*adhogatiṁ*'.]

Nor would it be right to regard the instance cited above ('*svayañcha pallavā &c.*', stanza No. 377.) as only serving the purpose of indicating the Semblance of a Simile [as has been held by the objector], for in reality it is the Simile (the similitude between 'Gaurī's hands' and 'Morn') that serves the purpose of indicating the Semblance of the Pun. [It will not be right to urge that "the similitude between 'Gaurī's hands' and the 'Morn' resting merely on the fact of the verbal form of certain epithets being applicable to both, it can not be a case of *Simile*" ; because] even such instances as '*Sakalakalaṁ purametajjātaṁ saṁprati sudhāṁshubimbamiva*' ['This city has become *sakalakala*, full of humming voices, and hence resembles the disc of the Moon which is *sakalakala*, complete with all its

"स्फुटमर्थलिंकारावेतावुपमासमुच्चयौ किं तु ।
आश्रित्य शब्दमात्रं सामान्यमिहापि संभवतः ।।" इति ।

न च 'कमलमिव मुखम्' इत्यादिः साधारणधर्मप्रयोगशून्य उपमाविषय इति वक्तुं युक्तं पूर्णोपमाया निर्विषयत्वापत्तेः ।।

देव त्वमेव पातालमाशानां त्वं निबन्धनम् ।
त्वं चामरमरुद्भूमिरेको लोकत्रयात्मकः ।।३७९।।

---

digits'] [where the similitude lies in the verbal form of the epithet '*sakalakalam*' being applicable to both the city and the Moon],—it is just as right to regard it as a case of Simile, as in the case of such passages as '*kamalamiva mukhaṁ manojñametat kachatitarām*'] 'This face, blooms beautifully like the lotus'] where there is similitude of quality (beauty) or of action (blooming) or of both.—It has been well said by Rudraṭa—'Simile and Conjunction are clearly *ideal* figures; but in the case in question (of the passage '*sakalakalam etc.*') also they are possible, on the basis of the similitude in verbal expression only.'

Some people have held the following view :—" It is only those passages that do not contain any terms expressive of a common property—*e.g.*, 'the face is like the lotus'—that can be regarded as instances of Simile [and those that contain such terms fall under 'Pun'; so that the passage 'this face *blooms beautifully* like the lotus' should be regarded as a case of *Pun* pure and simple".

But this cannot be right; for if it were so, then there would be no instances of the *complete* Simile (where the expression of the common property is essential).

As regards Pun however, we have instances of it, which are entirely free from all tinge of Simile and the other figures of speech; *e.g.*, in the following :—

इत्यादि: श्लेषस्य चोपमाद्यलंकारविविक्तोस्ति विषय इति। द्वयोर्योगे संकर एव। उपपत्तिपर्यालोचने तु उपमाया एवायं युक्तो विषयः। अन्यथा विषयापहार एव पूर्णोपमायाः स्यात्।

न च 'अबिन्दुसुन्दरी नित्यं गलल्लावण्यबिन्दुका' इत्यादौ विरोधप्रतिभोत्पत्तिहेतुः श्लेषः अपि तु श्लेषप्रतिभोत्पत्ति-

---

Deva tvameva pātālamāshānāṁ tvaṁ nibandhanam
Tvaṁ chāmaramarudbhūmireko lokatrayātmakaḥ

[Which, (*a*) as addressed to Viṣṇu, means—'O Viṣṇu, you are the nether region, the bounds of space, and the land of the immortals;—thus centralising in yourself all the three regions':—and (*b*) as addressed to the king—'O king, you alone are the thorough protector, the fulfilment of all desires ; you are also the recipient of the wind flowing from the royal *chowries* ; thus though one, you are threefold'.] ;—

If, however, we admit the presence of both the figures here, it will have to be regarded as a case of 'combination' of figures. In reality however, on a full review of all the circumstances, the passage in question ('the face is blooming like the lotus') must be taken as an instance of Simile ; for if it were not so, there could be no instance of the 'Complete Simile' at all.

[As in the case of Simile, so in the case of Contradiction also] some people have held that in certain cases Pun is indicative of the 'semblance of Contradiction' also, *e.g.,* in the passage '*Abindusundarī nityaṁ galallāvaṇyabindukā.*' ('She is *dripping* with loveliness, and is (*a*) *beautiful as the Moon reflected in water* (*b*) beautiful *without drops*) the Pun contained in the word '*abindusundarī*' serves to indicate the 'semblance of contradiction' (as between 'without drops' and 'dripping'.)

हेतुर्विरोधः । न ह्यत्रार्थद्वयप्रतिपादकः शब्दश्लेषः द्वितीयार्थस्य प्रतिभातमात्रस्य प्ररोहाभावात्। न च विरोधाभास इव विरोधः श्लेषाभासः श्लेषः। तदेवमादिषु वाक्येषु श्लेषप्रतिभोत्पत्तिहेतुरलंकारान्तरमेव । तथा च

सद्वंशमुक्तामणिः ॥३८०॥

नाल्पः कविरिव स्वल्पश्लोको देव महान् भवान् ॥३८१॥

अनुरागवती संध्या दिवसस्तत्पुरःसरः ।
अहो दैवगतिश्चित्रा तथापि न समागमः ॥३८२॥

This, however, is not right; as here also the case is just the reverse: it is the Contradiction that serves to indicate the 'semblance of Pun'. And the reason for this lies in the fact that there is in reality no such *verbal* Pun as has a clear double meaning (which is the necessary element in all Puns), for the second meaning ('beautiful without drops') is merely hinted at and is not sufficiently complete or explicit (the epithet 'beautiful without drops' not being expressive enough to have any force). Nor is the mere *Semblance* of Pun a Figure of speech, in the same manner as the *Semblance of Contradiction* (Apparent Contradiction) is.

All this leads to the conclusion that in cases like those cited, it is the other figures of speech that are predominant and serve to indicate the mere *semblance* of Pun. For instance, in the following four passages—

(*a*) '*Sadvaṁshamuktāmaṇiḥ*'—'The pearl-gem *in the noble family* ['growing a nice bamboo'],—(*b*) '*Nālpaḥ kaviriva svalpashloko deva mahān bhavān,*'—'O king, you are great, and are not *of little fame*, like an inferior poet, whose poems are insignificant;'—

(*c*) '*Anurāgavatī sandhyā divasastatpurassaraḥ*
aho daivagatishchitrā tathāpi na samāgamaḥ;'—

आदाय चापमचलं कृत्वाहीनं गुणं विषमदृष्टिः ।
यश्चित्रमच्युतशरो लक्ष्यमभाङ्क्षीन्नमस्तस्मै ॥३८३॥

इत्यादावेकदेशविवर्तिरूपकश्लेषव्यतिरेकसमासोक्तिविरोधत्वमुचितं न तु श्लेषत्वम् ॥

शब्दश्लेष इति चोच्यते अर्थलिंकारमध्ये च लक्ष्यते इति कोयं नयः । किं च वैचित्र्यमलंकार इति य एव कविप्रतिभासं-

---

'The evening (girl) is red in the atmosphere (full of love), and the Day (her lover) goes before it (is present before her), and yet such is the curious way of Destiny that the two never meet ;'—

(*d*) '*Ādāya chāpamachalaṁ kṛtvāhīnaṁ guṇaṁ viṣamadṛṣṭiḥ, yashchitramachyutasharo lakṣyamabhāṅkṣīnnamastasmai*'.

'Having taken up the bow immovable (*in the shape of the Himālaya mountain*), putting to it a string *worn out* (*in the shape of the lord of serpents*), and having an arrow *which never moved* (in the shape of Viṣṇu), the Being *with deranged vision* (the *Three-eyed God*, Shiva), shattered his target in a strange manner;—salutation to Him !' ;—the Figure that is predominant is, *not* 'Pun', but respectively, (*a*) Partial Metaphor, (*b*) Dissimilitude based upon Pun, (*c*) Modal Metaphor and (*d*) Contradiction.

Then again, the objector calls the Figure in question '*Verbal* Pun', and yet he includes it among '*Ideal* Figures;' —what sort of principle is this ?

Further, a Figure of Speech is only a form of imagery or fancy,—and this imagery can belong to only that (word or idea) which forms the final goal of the poet's imagination ; and it is only this (Word or Idea) that forms the substratum of the Figure of Speech. [So that it cannot be right to say that all Pun is *Ideal*, as the objector has

रम्भगोचरस्तत्रैव विचित्रता इति सैवालंकारभूमिः । अर्थमुखप्रेक्षित्वमेतेषां शब्दानामिति चेत् अनुप्रासादीनामपि तथैवेति तेऽप्यर्थालंकाराः किं नोच्यन्ते । रसादिव्यञ्जकस्वरूपवाच्यविशेषसव्यपेक्षत्वेऽपि ह्यनुप्रासादीनामलंकारता । शब्दगुणदोषाणामप्यर्थापेक्षयैव गुणदोषता । अर्थगुणदोषालंकाराणां शब्दापेक्षयैव व्यवस्थितिरिति तेऽपि शब्दगतत्वेनोच्यन्ताम् । 'विधौ वक्रे मूर्ध्नि' इत्यादौ च वर्णादिश्लेषे एकप्रयत्नोच्चार्यत्वेऽर्थश्लेषत्वं शब्दभेदेऽपि प्रसज्यतामित्येवमादि स्वयं विचार्यम् ॥

---

held].—It might be argued that—"The words (in which the Pun rests) always look up to (depend upon) their meanings [so that in the long run, they must be regarded as *ideal*]."—But the same thing happens in the case of Alliteration and other Figures (which even the objector regards as *verbal*) ; so that why are not, these also called 'verbal'? As a matter of fact, even though Alliteration and the other verbal figures are dependent upon the meanings of words, and also upon all those factors that serve to suggest a Passion or Sentiment and the rest,—yet they are regarded as 'Figures of Speech'; [and according to the objector, these should have to be regarded as *Ideal*].—Further, the Excellences and Defects of words also are to be regarded only as bearing upon their meanings [so that according to the objector these should all be regarded as *ideal*, bearing upon the *meaning* only]. Further, even those Excellences, Defects and Figures that are regarded (by both parties) as belonging to the meaning or Idea are dependent upon the verbal form of the words ; so that, on the same principle, these latter should be held to belong to the *verbal* forms only.—Lastly in such passages as '*vidhau vakre mūrdhni &c.*' (See above stanza No. 369),

तच्चित्रं यत्र वर्णानां खड्गाद्याकृतिहेतुता ॥ ८५ ॥

संनिवेशविशेषेण यत्र न्यस्ता वर्णाः खड्गमुरजपद्माद्याकारमुल्लासयन्ति तच्चित्रं काव्यम्। कष्टं काव्यमेतदिति दिङ्मात्रं प्रदर्श्यते। उदाहरणम्—

मारारिशक्ररामेभमुखैरासाररंहसा ।
साराब्धस्तवा नित्यं तदार्तिहरणक्षमा ॥३८४॥
माता नतानां संघट्टःश्रियां बाधितसंभ्रमा ।
मान्याथ सीमा रामाणां शं मे दिश्यादुमादिमा ॥३८५॥
(खड्गबन्धः)

---

where the Pun rests in single letters, though the two words are entirely distinct (*e.g., 'vidhi'* and *'vidhu'*), yet on the mere ground of the word (' *vidhau* in both cases) being such as is pronouncible by the same ' effort ', it may be possible to speak of these as instances of ' *Ideal* ' Pun.

All these points have to be left to your intelligent consideration.

V. Where the letters assume the form of such objects as the sword and the like, it is the Figure Pictorial. 85.

In cases where the letters arranged in particular ways appear in the form of (*a*) the sword, (*b*) or the drum, (*c*) or the lotus and so forth, we have Pictorial Poetry (*i.e.* Poetry with the Pictorial Figures).

As this sort of poetry is extremely difficult, we are citing only a few examples—(*a*) The Sword

' *Mārārishakrārāmebhamukhairāsārarambhasā*
Sārārabdhastavā nityantadārtiharaṇakṣamā '

' May the primeval Umā,—eloquently eulogised by Shiva, Indra and Rāma,—always removing their troubles, the centre of majesty, free from all anxiety, esteemed by the best of women,—ordain our prosperity.'

सरला बहुलारम्भतरलालिबलारवा ।
वारलाबहुलामन्दकरलाबहुलामला ॥३८६॥
(मुरजबन्धः)

भासते प्रतिभासार रसाभाताहताविभा ।
भावितात्मा शुभा वादे देवाभा बत ते सभा ॥३८७॥
(पद्मबन्धः)

रसासार रसा सारसायताक्षक्षतायसा ।
सातावात तवातासा रक्षतस्त्वस्त्वतक्षर ॥३८८॥
(सर्वतोभद्रम्)

[The words of this verse lend themselves to being arranged in the form of the *Sword*; for which see Appendix-I.]

[The second stanza has not been translated with original tr*a*nslatic*o*n. It may be rendered us :—Mother of the humble, assemblage of prosperities, who has removed the fear, the Venerable, the model of women, the first of all beings, may such Umā make (me) happy.]

(*b*) The Drum

'Saralā bāhulārambhataralālibalāravā
Vāralābahulāmandakaralābahulāmalā'

'Clean, resounding with the humming of the active black bees, abounding in swans, with the royal officers fully alive to their duties, bright even during the darker fortnight—[may the Autumn ever prosper !]'

[This verse lends itself to being arranged in the form of the *Drum*, for which *see Appendix-I.*]

(*c*) The Lotus

'Bhāsate pratibhāsārarasābhātāhatāvibhā
Bhāvitātmā shubhā vāde devābhā bata te sabhā'

'O essence of genius ! your court shines resplendent with sentiments, undeterred, with undimmed lustre, in which the true nature of the soul has been recognized, ever expert in debâtes and equal to the gods.'

संभविनोप्यन्ये प्रभेदाः शक्तिमात्रप्रकाशका न तु काव्य-रूपतां दधतीति न प्रदर्श्यन्ते ॥८५॥

पुनरुक्तवदाभासो विभिन्नाकारशब्दगा ।
एकार्थतेव ॥

भिन्नरूपसार्थकानर्थकशब्दनिष्ठमेकार्थत्वेन मुखे भासनं पुनरुक्तवदाभासः । स च

शब्दस्य ॥

[This verse can be arranged in the form of the *Lotus* ; for which *see Appendix-I.*]

(*d*) The All-round Square

'*Rasāsararasāsārasāyatākṣakṣatāyasā*
Sātāvāta tavātāsā rakṣatastvastvataṁkṣara'.

'O essence of the Earth ! whose eyes are as large as the lotus, who has destroyed all illusion, and who is vastly generous ! when you protect her, may the Earth, destroy the wicked and remain free from harm !'

[This verse can be arranged in the form of the *Square* ; for which *see Appendix-I.*]

There are several possible varieties of this form of poetry ; but they only serve to display the (perverted) ingenuity of the poet, and do not attain to the dignity of real Poetry ; it is for this reason that we are not describing them here in detail. 85.

VI.—When it appears as if one and the same meaning is expressed by words in diverse forms,—it is Semblance of Repetition.

When, on the face of it, (there is by chance) an appearance of one and the same meaning, in words of diverse forms,—with or without meaning,—it is 'Semblance of Repetition'.

This—

(*a*) *Subsists in a word ;—*

सभङ्गाभङ्गरूपकेवलशब्दनिष्ठः । उदाहरणम्—

अरिवधदेहशरीरः सहसा रथिसूततुरगपादातः ।
भाति सदानत्यागः स्थिरतायामवनितलतिलकः ॥३८९॥
चकासत्यङ्गनारामाः कौतुकानन्दहेतवः ।
तस्य राज्ञः सुमनसो विबुधाः पार्श्ववर्तिनः ॥३९०॥

तथा शब्दार्थयोरयम् ॥ ८६ ॥

That is, it subsists merely in a word, either (1) broken or (2) unbroken. Example (*a*) *Semblance of Repetition* in '*broken* words'—

'*Arivadhadehasharīraḥ sahasā rathisūtaturagapādātaḥ*
Bhāti sadānatyāgaḥ sthiratāyāmavanitalatilakaḥ.

'The King, the ornament of the Earth, is glorious, through his meekness, being the leader of archers longing for the destruction of enemies, whose infantry and cavalry are kept compact by charioteers, and who is quite a mountain in his firmness.'

[Here we have 'Semblance of Repetition' in (1) '*deha—sharīra*', (2) '*sārathi—sūta*' and (3) '*dāna-tyāga*', and each of these cases involves the breaking of the words (1) '*vadhadeha*', (2) '*sahasā*' and (3) '*sadā*' respectively.]

(*b*) Example of 'Semblance of Repetition' in '*unbroken* words'—

'*Chakāsatyaṅganārāmāḥ kautukānandahetavaḥ*
Tasya rājñaḥ sumanaso vibudhāḥ pārshvavartinaḥ'.

'Resplendent are the king's attendants,—who are happy at home, who are the source of pleasure to him through their arts, well-disposed and learned.'

[Here we have the 'Semblance of Repetition' the words—(1) '*aṅganā—rāmā*', (2) '*kautuka-ānanda*', and (3) '*sumanaso—vibudhāḥ*', in neither of which there is a breaking up of any word.]

उदाहरणम्--

तनुवपुरजघन्योसौ करिकुञ्जररुधिररक्तखरनखरः ।
तेजोधाम महःपृथुमनसामिन्द्रो हरिर्जिष्णुः ॥३९१॥

अत्रैकस्मिन् पदे परिवर्तिते नालंकार इति शब्दाश्रयः अपरस्मिंस्तु परिवर्तितेपि स न हीयते इत्यर्थनिष्ठ इत्युभयालंकारोयम् ॥८६॥

इति काव्यप्रकाशे शब्दालंकारनिर्णयो नाम नवम उल्लासः ॥

And also in both Word and Meaning. 86.

Example—

'*Tanuvapurajaghanyosau karikuñjararudhiraraktakharanakharaḥ*
Tejodhāma mahaḥpṛthumanasāmindro harirjiṣṇuḥ'.

'This lion, though slim, is yet mighty,—having his sharp nails reddened with the blood of mighty elephants, the receptacle of glory, the leader of the glorious and the brave, and ever victorious.'

[Here we have the 'Semblance of Repetition' in—(1) '*tanu-vapuḥ*', (2) '*kari-kuñjara*', (3) '*rudhira-rakta*', (4) '*tejo-dhāma-mahaḥ*' *and* (5) '*indro-harir-jiṣṇuḥ*']; and among these some of the words—'*tanu*', '*kuñjara*', '*rakta*', '*dhāma*', '*hari*' and '*jiṣṇu*'—are such as cannot be altered without spoiling the effect of the Figure of Speech ; and to this extent the Figure subsists in *words*, and is '*verbal*' ;—while others—'*vapuḥ*', '*kari*', '*rudhira*' and '*indra*'—are such as can be replaced by their synonyms without spoiling the effect, and to this extent, the Figure subsists in the *meaning*, and is '*ideal*'. And thus the Figure belongs to both, Word and Meaning. 86.

Thus ends chapter IX of the Kāvya Prakāsha, dealing with the Verbal Figures of Speech.

अथ दशम उल्लास:

अथालंकारानाह—

साधर्म्यमुपमा भेदे ॥

उपमानोपमेययोरेव न तु कार्यकारणादिकयोः साधर्म्यं भवतीति तयोरेव समानेन धर्मेण संबन्ध उपमा ।

भेदग्रहणमनन्वयव्यवच्छेदाय ॥

पूर्णा लुप्ता च ॥

उपमानोपमेयसाधारणधर्मोपमाप्रतिपादकानामुपादाने पूर्णा । एकस्य द्वयोस्त्रयाणां वा लोपे लुप्ता ॥

CHAPTER X

THE IDEAL FIGURES OF SPEECH.

The author now describes the Ideal Figures of Speech—

I. U*pamā*—Simile.

I. When there is similarity of properties, while there is difference (between the objects themselves), it is Simile.

What the text is referring to is the similarity of the properties belonging to the two objects of comparison (the object compared and the object compared to),—and not those belonging to the cause and the effect, and such other correlatives ; so that it is a case of *Simile* when the said objects of comparison are related to some common property.

'*While there is difference*';—this has been added with a view to distinguish the Figure, *Ananvaya*, 'Comparison Absolute'.

[*Simile is of two kinds*]—*(a) Complete and (b) Elliptical.*

साग्रिमा ॥

श्रौत्यार्थी च भवेद्वाक्ये समासे तद्धिते तथा ॥ ८७ ॥

अग्रिमा पूर्णा ।

यथेवादिशब्दा यत्परास्तस्यैवोपमानताप्रतीतिरिति यद्यप्युपमानविशेषणान्येते तथापि शब्दशक्तिमहिम्ना श्रुत्यैव षष्ठीवत् संबन्धं प्रतिपादयन्तीति तत्सद्भावे श्रौती उपमा । तथैव "तत्र तस्येव" इत्यनेनेवार्थे विहितस्य वतेरुपादाने ॥

It is a case of *Complete* Simile when all the factors are mentioned—(1) the object compared, (2) the object compared to, (3) the common property, and (4) terms signifying similitude; and it is one of *Elliptical* Simile, when either one or two or three of these factors are omitted.

The former of these is (*a*) *directly expressed and* (*b*) *implied*; *and it appears* (1) *in sentence*, (2) *in a compound and* (3) *in a nominal affix*. 87.

'*Former*', *i.e.*, the *Complete Simile*

Such words as '*yathā*', '*iva*' and the like (meaning 'like', 'as', 'just as' and so forth.)

As a matter of fact, that object is recognised as the 'object compared to', in connection with which such terms (expressive of similitude) as '*yathā*', '*iva*' and so forth are used; and in this sense these terms serve to qualify the "object compared to'; but the force of these words such that, like the genitive case—ending, they directly express *relationship*; so that in a passage where these terms are present, it is a case of *Directly Expressed* Simile.—So also in cases where the affix '*vati*' is used in the sense of '*iva*', and other terms expressive of similitude in accordance with Pāṇini 5.1.116 (which prescribes the use of '*vati*' in the sense of *similarity*.)

'तेन तुल्यं मुखम्' इत्यादावुपमेये एव 'तत्तुल्यमस्य' इत्यादौ चोपमाने एव 'इदं च तच्च तुल्यम्' इत्युभयत्रापि तुल्यादिशब्दानां विश्रान्तिरिति साम्यपर्यालोचनया तुल्यताप्रतीतिरिति साधर्म्यस्यार्थत्वात्तुल्यादिशब्दोपादाने आर्थी तद्वत् 'तेन तुल्यं क्रिया चेद्वतिः' इत्यनेन विहितस्य वतेः स्थितौ ।

"इवेन नित्यसमासो विभक्त्यलोपः पूर्वपदप्रकृतिस्वरत्वं च" इति नित्यसमासे इवशब्दयोगे समासगा ।। क्रमेणोदाहरणम्—

On the other hand, it is a case of *Implied* Simile, where the similitude is *implied* by the presence of such terms as '*tulya*', 'equal' and the like; this *equality* as expressed by the term 'equal' and the like being comprehended by the due recognition of similarity (*a*) in the 'object compared',—where the expression used is in the form 'the face is equal to *that* (*i. e.* the lotus),' (*b*) in the 'object compared to', where the expression used is in the form 'that (lotus) is equal to this (face),' and (*c*) in both, where the expression is in the form 'this (face) and that (lotus) are equal.' So it is also in cases where the affix '*vati*' is used in accordance with Pāṇini 5.1.115 (which prescribes the use of the affix in the sense of *similarity of action*.)

We have the *directly expressed* Simile occurring in a compound, in cases where the compound is formed with the term '*iva*', in accordance with the *Vārttika* under Pāṇini 2.1.4 and 2.4.71—'There is *nitya* compounding with the term *iva*; where the case-termination of the preceding member is not dropped and where the preceding member takes the accent of its crude form.'

Examples are cited in order.

(1) [The *Directly Expressed Simile*, in a *Sentence*]—

स्वप्नेपि समरेषु त्वां विजयश्रीर्न मुञ्चति ।
प्रभावप्रभवं कान्तं स्वाधीनपतिका यथा ॥३९२॥

चकितहरिणलोललोचनायाः क्रुधि तरुणारुणतारहारिकान्ति ।
सरसिजमिदमाननं च तस्याः सममिति चेतसि संमदं विधत्ते ॥३९३॥

अत्यायतैर्नियमकारिभिरुद्धतानां
दिव्यैः प्रभाभिरनपायमयैरुपायैः ।
शौरिर्भुजैरिव चतुर्भिरदः सदा यो
लक्ष्मीविलासभवनैर्भुवनं बभार ॥३९४॥

Svapnepi samareṣu tvāṁ
Vijayashrīrna muñchati
Prabhāvaprabhavaṁ kāntaṁ
Svādhīnapatikā yathā.

'Victory in battle leaves you not, even in a dream, *just as* a woman to whom her husband is devoted leaves him not, who bestows deep affection upon her.'

(2) [The *Implied Simile*, in a *Sentence*]—

'*Chakitahariṇalolalochanāyāḥ*
Krudhi taruṇāruṇatārahārikānti
Sarasijamidamānanaṁcha tasyāḥ
Samamiti chetasi saṁmadam vidhatte.

'He goes into raptures when he finds that her face and the lotus are equal,—she with eyes like those of the frightened fawn, and face flushed with indignation and shining like a brilliant red necklace !

(3) [The *Directly Expressed Simile* in a *Compound*]—

'*Atyāyatairniyamakāṛibhiruddhatānāṁ*
Divyaiḥ prabhābhiranapāyamayairupāyaiḥ
Shaurirbhujairiva chaturbhiradaḥ sadā yo
Lakṣmīvilāsabhavanairbhuvanaṁ babhāra.'

अवितथमनोरथपथप्रथनेषु प्रगुणगरिमगीतश्रीः ।
सुरतरुसदृशः स भवानभिलषणीयः क्षितीश्वरो न कस्य ॥३९५॥
गाम्भीर्यगरिमा तस्य सत्यं गङ्गाभुजङ्गवत् ।
दुरालोकः स समरे निदाघाम्बररत्नवत् ॥३९६॥

'The king who held this world in sway through the four expedients, just as Viṣṇu does by his four arms,—the expedients and the arms both being '*atyāyata*' (the expedients *efficient*, and the arms *long*), subjugators of the wicked, glorious, resplendent and infallible, the abode of the sportings of the Goddess of Wealth.'

[Here the simile lies in '*bhujairiva*', which is a '*nitya*' compound does not drop the case-termination of the first term.]

(4) [The *Implied Simile*, in a *Compound*]—

'*Avitathamanorathapathaprathaneṣu*
praguṇa garimagītashrīḥ
Suratarusadṛshaḥ sa bhavān abhilaṣaṇīyaḥ
kṣitīshvaro na kasya'

'O King, who is there by whom you are not sought after ?—You who, having your great excellence sung as lying in the opening of the way for desires that never remain unfulfilled, are similar to the Celestial Tree.'

(5) and (6) [The *Directly Expressed* and the *Implied* Simile, in nominal Affixes]—

'*Gāmbhīryagarimā tasya satyaṁgaṅgābhujaṅgavat*
Durālokaḥ sa samare nidāghāmbararatnavat'

'The profundity of his depth is like that of the Gaṅga's Lover (Ocean) ; and in battle he is hard to look at, like the summer Sun.'

[In the first sentence, the similitude is *expressed* directly by the affix '*vati*' in '*bhujaṅgavat*', which is used in the sense of '*iva*', *like* ;—the term '*bhujaṅgavat*' being equivalent to '*bhujaṅgasya iva*' ;—and in

स्वाधीनपतिका कान्तं भजमाना यथा लोकोत्तरचमत्कारभूः तथा जयश्रीस्त्वदासेवनेनेत्यादिना प्रतीयमानेन विना यद्यपि नोक्तेर्वैचित्र्यम्। वैचित्र्यं चालंकारः। तथापि न ध्वनिगुणीभूतव्यङ्ग्यव्यवहारः। न खलु व्यङ्ग्यसंस्पर्शपरामर्शादत्र चारुताप्रतीतिः। अपि तु वाच्य वैचित्यप्रतिभासादेव॥ रसा-

the second half it is *implied only indirectly*, by the same affix in *'ratnavat'*, which is equivalent to *'ratnena tulyam'*, so that the affix '*vati*' in this case can only signify *similarity of action*; and through this is implied the similitude between the *entities acting*.]

[An *objection* is raised—" Fanciful Poetry has been defined in Ch. I as that which, " endowed with Excellences and Figures of Speech, is devoid of *suggestion* ;" and Figurative Poetry is Fanciful Poetry ; so that in poetry where there is a Figure of Speech, there should be no *suggestion* at all ; as a matter of fact, however, such is not found to be the case ; for instance.] Even in the first example cited, until we recognise the *suggested* meaning, that ' the constant attendance of Victory upon the King ' is as supremely charming as the attachment of the wife to the devoted husband ';—there is no *fancy*, in the verse ; and a Figure of Speech is nothing more than a ' fancy ' [so that every one of these examples should be regarded as instances, not of ' Fanciful Poetry, but of either Suggestive Poetry or Poetry of Subordinate Suggestion].'

The answer to this is that, though this is so, yet the examples are regarded as either ' Suggestive Poetry ' or ' Poetry of Subordinate Suggestion ', because in these cases the recognition of elegance follows, not from the perception of the tinge of *Suggestion* that may be present, but purely from the perception of the fanciful character of the *expressed* meaning itself.

दिस्तु व्यङ्ग्योर्थोलंकारान्तरं च सर्वत्राव्यभिचारीत्यगणयित्वैव तदलंकारा उदाहृताः । तद्रहितत्वेन तु उदाह्रियमाणा विरसतामावहन्तीति पूर्वापरविरुद्धाभिधानमिति न चोदनीयम् ॥८७॥

तद्वद् धर्मस्य लोपे स्यान्न श्रौती तद्धिते पुनः ।

धर्मः साधारणः । तद्धिते कल्पबादौ त्वार्थ्येव ॥ तेन पञ्च ॥

Then, as regards the presence of *suggestion* of Charm and other factors or of Figures of Speech other than the one, a particular verse is quoted to exemplify,—this will always be found in all cases. Hence when examples of particular Figures are cited, all these (concomitant issues) are entirely ignored.

In fact, if we were to cite examples entirely devoid of any *suggestion* (of charm and other factors), they would be extremely distasteful.

For these reasons, it would not be right to urge that in citing the above examples there is an inconsistency with what has been said before (regarding Figurative or Fanciful Poetry being devoid of suggestion).

[The 19 kinds of the Elliptical Simile are next described.] 87.

The property being omitted, this (form of Elliptical Simile) would be like the foregoing (Complete Simile); but in that case the Directly Expressed Simile would not occur in a word built with a nominal formative affix.

'*Property*'—*i. e.*, the common property. '*In a nominal formative affix*',—*i. e.*, in such affixes as '*kalpa*', '*vā*' and so forth; in connection with which we could have the *Implied* Simile only. It is thus of five kinds.

(1) Example [of the Elliptical Simile, omitting the common property, and directly expressed, *in a sentence*]

उदाहरणम्—

धन्यस्यानन्यसामान्यसौजन्योत्कर्षशालिनः
करणीयं वचश्चेतः सत्यं तस्यामृतं यथा ॥३९७॥
आकृष्टकरवालोसौ संपराये परिभ्रमन् ।
प्रत्यर्थिसेनया दृष्टः कृतान्तेन समः प्रभुः ॥३९८॥
करवाल इवाचारस्तस्य वागमृतोपमा ।
विषकल्पं मनो वेत्सि यदि जीवसि तत्सखे ॥३९९॥

Dhanyasyānanyasāmānyasaujanyotkarṣashālinaḥ
Karaṇīyaṁ vachashchetaḥ satyaṁ tasyāmṛtaṁ yathā

'He being generous and possessed of uncommon gentlemanly qualities, his words, true and like nectar as they are, should be acted up to.'

[Here the common property, *sweetness*, of *nectar* and *words*, has been omitted].

(2) [Example of the Elliptical Simile omitting the common property, *implied*.]

'*Ākṛṣṭakarabālosau saṁparāye paribhraman*
Pratyarthisenayā dṛṣṭaḥ kṛtāntena samaḥ prabhuḥ'

'Roaming in battle with the drawn sword, he was looked upon by the enemies, as equal to the Death-god.'

[Here the common property, *cruelty*, has been omitted; and as it is the sameness of *action* that is meant, the *Similitude* is 'implied.']

(3)-(4)-(5) [Example of the Elliptical Simile, omitting the common property, (*a*) directly expressed, in a compound, (*b*) implied, in a compound and (*c*) implied, in a nominal affix.]

'*Karavāla ivāchārastasya vāgamṛtopamā*
Viṣakalpaṁ mano vetsi yadi jīvasi tat sakhe'

'You will live if you know that (*a*) his behaviour is like that of the sword, (*b*) his speech is almost like nectar, and (*c*) his mind is like poison.'

उपमानानुपादाने वाक्यगाथ समासगा ॥ ८८ ॥

सअलकरणपरवीसामसिरिविअरणं ण सरसकव्वस्स ।
दीसइ अह वा णिसम्मइ सरिसं अंसंसमेत्तेण ॥४००॥

कव्वस्सेत्यत्र कव्वसममिति सरिसमित्यत्र च णूणमिति पाठे एषैव समासगा ॥८८॥

वादेर्लोपे समासे सा कर्माधारक्यचि क्यङि ।
कर्मकर्त्रोर्णमुलि ॥

[(*a*) '*Karabāla-iva*, is a 'nitya' compound, where the case-termination of the first member is not elided, and the common property of *murderousness* is omitted ;—(*b*) '*amṛtopamā*' omits the common property of *sweetness*, and the similitude is *implied*, the term '*upamā*' directly expressing merely *resemblance in general* ;—(*c*) '*viṣakalpam*' ends in the nominal affix '*kalpa*,' which denotes *approximate resemblance in general*, and hence the *Simile* is an *implied* one, and the common property of *harmfulness* has been omitted.]

(6) (7) *On the omission of the 'object compared to', the Simile occurs in a sentence and in a compound.*

(6) [Example of Elliptical Simile, omitting the object compared to, occurring in a sentence]—

'*Saalakaraṇaparavīsāmasiriviaraṇaṁ ṇa sarasakavvassa*
Dīsaï aha vā ṇisammaï sarisaṁ aṁsaṁsametteṇa'

''For affording pleasure to the highest senses, nothing is either known or seen to be equal to charming poetry, even in its smallest part.'

[The object to which Poetry is compared is not mentioned, and the similitude is *implied* by the sentence.]

(7) In this same verse if we read '*kavvasamaṁ*' for '*kavvassa*,' and '*ṇūṇaṁ*' for '*sarisaṁ*', we have an example of the same kind of Simile occurring in a compound. 88.

On the omission of 'vā' and such other terms (expressing similitude), it occurs (8) *in a compound,* (9) *in the affix*

वाशब्दः उपमाद्योतक इति । वादेरुपमाप्रतिपादकस्य लोपे षट् समासेन कर्मणोधिकरणाच्चोत्पन्नेन क्यचा कर्तुः क्यङा कर्मकर्त्रोरुपपदयोर्णमुला च भवेत् ॥

उदाहरणम्—

ततः कुमुदनाथेन कामिनीगण्डपाण्डुना ।
नेत्रानन्देन चन्द्रेण माहेन्द्री दिगलंकृता ॥४०१॥

तथा

असितभुजगभीषणासिपत्रो रुहरुहिकाहितचित्ततूर्णचारः ।
पुलकिततनुरुत्कपोलकान्तिः प्रतिभटविक्रमदर्शनेयमासीत् ॥४०२॥

'*kyach*' *as denoting the objective,* (10) *in the same affix as denoting location,* (11) *in the affix* '*kyan*', (12) *in the affix* '*ṇamul*' *used with a substantive used accusatively, and* (13) *in the same affix used with a substantive used nominatively.*

The term '*vā*' is expressive of similitude; and on the omission of this term '*vā*' and of others similarly expressive of similitude,—there are six kinds of Simile, as occurring—(8) in a compound, (9) in the affix '*kyach*' as used in the sense of the accusative, (10) in the affix '*kyach*' as used in the sense of the location; (11) in the affix '*kyan*' as used in the sense of the nominative, (12) in the affix '*ṇamul*' with a substantive used ccusatively, and (13) in the affix '*ṇamul*' with a substantive used nominatively.

Example of (8)—

'*Tataḥ kumudanāthena kāminīgaṇḍapāṇḍunā*
Netrānandena chandreṇa māhendrī digalaṅkṛtā

'The eastern quarter was thereupon adorned by the Moon, a joy to the eyes, pale like the cheeks of a love-stricken woman.'

पौरं सुतीयति जनं समरान्तरेसा-
वन्तःपुरीयति विचित्रचरित्रचुञ्चुः ।
नारीयते समरसीम्नि कृपाणपाणेर्
आलोक्य तस्य चरितानि सपत्नसेना ॥४०३॥
मृधे निदाघघर्मांशुदर्शं पश्यन्ति तं परे ।
स पुनः पार्थसंचारं संचरत्यवनीपतिः ॥४०४॥

Another example of the same—

'*Asitabhujagabhīṣaṇāsipatro ruharuhikābitachittatūrṇachāraḥ*
Pulakitatanurutkapolakāntiḥ pratibhaṭavikramadarshaneyamāsīt'

'This king, his sword-blade terrible like the black snake, and his movements inspired by energy, became thrilled, whereupon the freshness of his cheeks became manifested.'

(9)—(10)—(11)—

'*Pauraṁ sutīyati janaṁ samarantaresā-*
Vantaḥpurīyatī vichitracharitrachuñchuḥ.
Nārīyate samarasīmni kṛpāṇapāṇer
Ālokya tasya charitāni sapatnasenā.'

'He treats the citizens as his children ; famous for his wonderful deeds, he behaves in battlefield as if it were his harem; and the army of his enemies, seeing him, sword in hand, performing extraordinary feats in battle, come to behave like women.'

[(*a*) In '*sutīyatī*' we have the '*kyach*' affix in the accusative sense; (*b*) in '*antaḥpurīyati,*' we have the same affix used in the locative sense, and (*c*) in '*nārīyate,*' we have the affix '*kyaṅ*' in the nominative sense.]

(12)—(13)—

'*Mṛdhe nidāghāgharmāṁshudarshaṁ pashyanti taṁ pare*
Sa punaḥ pārthāsaṁchāraṁ sañcharatyavanīpatiḥ.'

एतद्द्विलोपे क्विप्समासगा ॥ ८९ ॥

एतयोर्धर्मवाद्योः । उदाहरणम्—

सविता विधवति विधुरपि सवितरति तथा दिनन्ति यामिन्यः ।
यामिनयन्ति दिनानि च सुखदुःखवशीकृते मनसि ॥४०५॥

परिपन्थिमनोराज्यशतैरपि दुराक्रमः ।
संपरायप्रवृत्तोसौ राजते राजकुञ्जरः ॥४०६॥८९॥

'In battle his enemies look upon him as they would upon the summer-sun; and the King himself moves about as if he were Arjuna.'

[In the first sentence the '*ṇamul*' affix has the force of the accusative and in the second that of the nominative.]

(14)—(15)—*On the omission of both these, it occurs in the 'kvip' affix and in a compound.* 89.

'*Of these two*'—*i. e.*, of the common property and the term expressive of similitude. (14) Example (of the Elliptical Simile, omitting both, occurring in the affix '*kvip*')—

'*Savitā vidhavati vidhurapi savitarati tathā dinanti yāminyaḥ*
Yāminayanti dināni cha sukhaduḥkha-vashīkṛte manasi'.

'When the mind is under the influence of pleasure, the sun becomes the moon and the nights become days; when, on the other hand, it is under the influence of pain, the moon becomes the sun and days become nights.'

[Here the Simile lies in the '*Kvip*' affix in the words '*vidhavati*', '*savitarati*', '*dinanti*' and '*yāminayanti*'.]

(15) [Of the same, in a compound]—

'*Paripanthimanorājyashatairapi durākramaḥ*
Samparāyapravṛttosau rājate rājakuñjaraḥ'.

धर्मोपमानयोर्लोपे वृत्तौ वाक्ये च दृश्यते ।

टुण्टुण्णन्तो मरिहिसि कण्टअकलिआइँ केअइवणाइँ ।
मालइकुसुमसरिच्छं भमर भमन्तो ण पाविहिसि ॥४०७॥

कुसुमेण सममिति पाठे वाक्यगा ।

क्यचि वाद्युपमेयासे ।

आसे निरासे ।

अरातिविक्रमालोकविकस्वरविलोचनः ।
कृपाणोदग्रदोर्दण्डः स सहस्रायुधीयति ॥४०८॥

'The chief of kings shines resplendent in battle, being unapproachable, as he is, by even the dreaming desires of his enemies.'

[Here the said Simile lies in the compound "*rājakuñjaraḥ*'.] 89.

(16)—(17)—

On the omission of the common property and the object compared to, it is found in a compound and in a sentence.

(16) '*Ṭuṇṭuṇṇanto marihisi kaṇṭaakaliāiṁ keaivaṇāiṁ*
Mālaikusumasarichchhaṁ bhamara bhamanto ṇa pāvihisi'

'O black bee ! thou shalt perish, wandering among Ketakī-bowers ; but however much thou mayst wander, thou shalt never find anything like the Mālatī-flower.'

[The Simile lies in the *compound* '*mālai-kusuma—sarichchaṁ*].'

(17) If we read '*kusumeṇa samaṁ*' (in place of '*kusuma-sarichchhaṁ*'), the same verse becomes an example of the same kind of compound as occurring in a *sentence.*

(18)—*On the omission of the term expressive of similitude and the object compared, it occurs in the affix* '*Kyach*'.

'*Āsā*' means "*nirāsā*', 'on the omission.' (18)—

[Example]—

'*Arātivikramālokavikasvaravilochanaḥ*
Kṛpāṇodagradordaṇḍaḥ sa sahasrāyudhīyati'

अत्रात्मा उपमेयः ।

त्रिलोपे च समासगा ॥ ९० ॥

त्रयाणां वादिधर्मोपमानानाम् । उदाहरणम्—

तरुणिमनि कृतावलोकना ललितविलासवितीर्णविग्रहा ।
स्मरशरविसराचितान्तरा मृगनयना हरते मुनेर्मनः ॥४०९॥

अत्र सप्तम्युपमानेत्यादिना यदा समासलोपौ भवतः । तदेदमुदाहरणम् ॥

'Having his eyes widely opened by the sight of his enemy's prowess, and arms terrible through his sword, he disports himself like the thousand-armed king Kārttavīrya.'

[Here the king's own self is the object compared; the Simile, occurring in the affix '*Kyach*' in the word '*Sahasrāyudhīyati*', means 'disports *himself* like the thousand-armed king'.]

(19)—*On the omission of the three, it occurs in a compound*. 90.

'*Three*'—the term expressing similitude, the common property and the object compared to.

Example—

'*Taruṇimani kṛtāvalokanā lalitavilāsavitīrṇavigrahā*
Smarasharavisarāchitāntarā mṛganayanā harate munermanaḥ.'

'Just peeping into youthfulness, surrendering her body to graceful dalliance, and having her heart pierced by a flight of Cupid's arrows, the fawn-eyed one captivates the heart of even the ascetic.'

This verse forms an apposite example only when the compound '*mṛganayanā*' is expounded in accordance with the *Vārtika* on Pāṇini 2.2.24 (as *mṛganayanā iva nayane yasyāḥ*), involving the elision [(1) of the former '*nayane*', which is the 'object compared to', and (2) of the term

क्रूरस्याचारस्यायःशूलतयाध्यवसायाद् अयःशूलेनान्विच्छति 'आयःशूलिकः' इत्यतिशयोक्तिर्न तु क्रूराचारोपमेयतैक्ष्ण्यधर्मवादीनां लोपे त्रिलोपेयमुपमा ।

एवमेकोनविंशतिर्लुप्ताः पूर्णाभिः सह पञ्चविंशतिः ॥

अनयेनेव राज्यश्रीर्दैन्येनेव मनस्विता ।
मम्लौ साथ विषादेन पद्मिनीव हिमाम्भसा ॥४१०॥

इत्यभिन्ने साधारणे धर्मे ॥

ज्योत्स्नेव नयनानन्दः सुरेव मदकारणम् ।
प्रभुतेव समाकृष्टसर्वलोका नितम्बिनी ॥४११॥

इति भिन्ने च तस्मिन् एकस्यैव बहूपमानोपादाने मालोपमा ।

'*iva*' expressive of similitude; in addition to these there is the omission (3) also of the *common property* of 'fickleness.']

The term *ayaḥshūlikaḥ*, 'one who behaves like a spear', has been taken by some people to be an example of that kind of Simile which omits the three factors of (1) the object compared—*the cruel person*, (2) the common property—*cruelty* and (3) the term expressive of similitude—'*vā*' and the rest. But this is not right; as what the term means is '*ayaḥshūlena anvichchhati*' 'who behaves like the spear,' and what is done here is that 'cruel behaviour' is spoken of as the 'spear', and this involves the figure of *Atishayokti*, Hyperbole,—and not that of *Simile with three factors omitted.*

These nineteen kinds of Elliptical Simile, along with the six kinds of the Complete Simile, make up the twenty-five varieties of Simile.

As regards other varieties of Simile that have been described by others, we find—(*a*) the *Mālopamā*, String-simile, where a single object is compared to several, with its two varieties—one in which the same common property

II–5

यथोत्तरमुपमेयस्योपमानत्वे पूर्ववदभिन्नधर्मत्वे
अनवरतकनकवितरणजललवभृतकरतरङ्गितार्थिततेः ।
भणितिरिव मतिर्मतिरिव चेष्टा चेष्टेव कीर्तिरतिविमला ॥४१२॥
मतिरिव मूर्तिर्मधुरा मूर्तिरिव सभा प्रभावचिता ।
तस्य सभेव जयश्रीः शक्या जेतुं नृपस्य न परेषाम् ॥४१३॥

इत्यादिका रशनोपमा च न लक्षिता एवंविधवैचित्र्य-सहस्रसंभवात् उक्तभेदानतिक्रमाच्च ॥९०॥

---

of *prowithering* appears throughout the 'string'—as in the verse.—' Like royal splendour,through injustice and corruption,—like prowess through poverty,—like the lotus through frost,—she has withered through sorrow ;' —and the other in which diverse common properties are involved,—*e. g.*, in the verse—' Like light, she is a joy to the eyes ; like wine, she is maddening; and like sovereignty, she attracts to herself all the world ;'—and (*b*) the *Rashanopamā*, the 'Girdle-simile', where the *object* compared in the preceding Simile becomes *the object compared to* in the succeeding one, with its two varieties, as before ; with the same or diverse common properties ; *e.g.*, (A) " When the King brings together hosts of supplicants like waves on his hand which is full of water used, in his continuous gifts of gold, his heart is like his words, like his heart his actions, and his fame pure like his actions ';—and (B) ' Of the King, the body is sweet like his heart, his court powerful as his body, and his victory irrepressible by enemies, like his court.'

But we have not described these, because in the first place there are thousands of such possible varieties, and secondly, they are not such as cannot be included under the varieties already described above. 90.

उपमानोपमेयत्वे एकस्यैवैकवाक्यगे ।
अनन्वयः ॥

उपमानान्तरसंबन्धाभावोनन्वयः । उदाहरणम्—

न केवलं भाति नितान्तकान्तिर्नितम्बिनी सैव नितम्बिनीव ।
यावद्विलासायुधलास्यवासास्ते तद्विलासा इव तद्विलासाः ॥४१४॥

विपर्यास उपमेयोपमा तयोः ॥ ९१ ॥

तयोः उपमानोपमेययोः । परिवृत्तिः अर्थात् वाक्यद्वये । इतरोपमानव्यवच्छेदपरा उपमेयेनोपमा इति उपमेयोपमा ।

II—*Ananvaya*—Comparison Absolute

When one and the same thing appears in a single sentence as both the 'object compared', and the 'object compared to' it is 'Comparison Absolute'.

'Comparison Absolute' means that there is no other thing to which the thing described could bear comparison.

Example—

'It is not only that possessed of exquisite loveliness, that woman shines as that woman herself; in fact, her graces also, which are the abode of the Cupid's blandishments, are like her own graces.'

III—*Upameyopamā—Reciprocal Comparison*

When there is alternation of these two, it is Reciprocal Comparison. 91.

'Of these two' *i. e.*, of the object compared and the object compared to;—there is '*alternation*', interchange, in two separate sentences,—this means that there is no third thing with which either of them could bear comparison, we have '*Upameyopamā—i. e.*, a figure, where there is '*Upamā*'—(comparison, of the object compared to) with the '*Upameya*' (object compared) itself.

उदाहरणम्—

कमलेव मतिर्मतिरिव कमला तनुरिव विभा विभेव तनुः ।
धरणीव धृतिर्धृतिरिव धरणी सततं विभाति बत यस्य ॥४१५॥९१॥

संभावनमथोत्प्रेक्षा प्रकृतस्य समेन यत् ।

समेन उपमानेन । उदाहरणम्–

उन्मेषं यो मम न सहते जातिवैरी निशायाम्
इन्दोरिन्दीवरदलदृशा तस्य सौन्दर्यदर्पः ।
नीतः शान्ति प्रसभमनया वक्त्रकान्त्येति हर्षाल्
लग्ना मन्ये ललिततनु ते पादयोः पद्मलक्ष्मीः ॥४१६॥

Example—

'His heart is like Lakṣmī,—Lakṣmī is like his heart; his splendour is like his body, and his body is like his splendour; his fortitude is like the earth, and the earth is like his fortitude.' 91.

IV—*Utprekṣā*—Poetic Fancy.

Poetic Fancy consists in the imagining of the thing described as (identical) with a similar thing.

'Similar thing'—*i.e.*, that to which it is meant to be compared.

Example—

'O beautiful one! I think that the beauty of the lotus attaches itself to your feet, on being happy at the idea that her born enemy the Moon, who brooks not her blossoming during the night, has had the pride of his beauty quickly suppressed by the splendour of the face of this lotus-eyed girl.

[Here the object compared is the beauty of the girl's feet, and this has been imagined to be the *beauty of the lotus fallen on her feet*, which, in reality, is the object to which the former is meant to be compared.]

लिम्पतीव तमोऽङ्गानि वर्षतीवाञ्जनं नभः ।
असत्पुरुषसेवेव दृष्टिर्विफलतां गता ।।४१७।।

इत्यादौ व्यापनादि लेपनादिरूपतया संभावितम् ।।

ससंदेहस्तु भेदोक्तौ तदनुक्तौ च संशयः ।। ९२ ।।

भेदोक्तौ यथा

अयं मार्तण्डः किं स खलु तुरगैः सप्तभिरितः
कृशानुः किं सर्वाः प्रसरति दिशो नैष नियतम् ।
कृतान्तः किं साक्षान्महिषवहनोसाविति चिरं
समालोक्याजौ त्वां विदधति विकल्पान् प्रतिभटाः ।।४१८।।

In the following verse—

'*Limpatīva tamoṅgāni varṣatīvāñjanaṁ nabhaḥ*
Asatpuruṣaseveva dṛṣṭirviphalatāṁ gatā'

'Darkness besmears the limbs as it were ; the sky is, as it were, showering soot ; and vision has become as useless as the service of a wicked master';—what is done is that the *pervading* (of darkness) has been *imagined* to be *besmearing*.

[And the *spreading of darkness* has been imagined to be the *showering of soot* : so that this is an instance of Poetical Fancy, and not *Simile*, as some people have taken it to be, having been misled to this view by the presence of the particle '*iva*']

V—*Sasandeha*—Doubtful.

The statement of a doubt constitutes the Doubtful,—the distinction being asserted or not asserted. 92.

For example, we have the 'difference stated', in the following verse—

'Is this the sun ?—But the sun is carried by seven horses. Is he the Fire ?—Surely, Fire never flames on all sides. Is he the Death-god ?—But the Death-god has the buffalo for his conveyance. Thus, O King, on

भेदोक्तावित्यनेन न केवलमयं निश्चयगर्भो यावन्निश्चयान्तोपि संदेहः स्वीकृतः ।

यथा

इन्दुः किं क्व कलङ्कः सरसिजमेतत् किमम्बु कुत्र गतम् ।
ललितसविलासवचनैर्मुखमिति हरिणाक्षि निश्चितं परतः॥४१९॥

किं तु निश्चयगर्भ इव नात्र निश्चयः प्रतीयमान इति उपेक्षितो भट्टोद्भटेन । तदनुक्तौ यथा

अस्याः सर्गविधौ प्रजापतिरभूच्चन्द्रो नु कान्तिप्रदः
शृङ्गारैकरसः स्वयं नु मदनो मासो नु पुष्पाकरः ।
वेदाभ्यासजडः कथं नु विषयव्यावृत्तकौतूहलो
निर्मातुं प्रभवेन्मनोहरमिदं रूपं पुराणो मुनिः ॥४२०॥९२॥

---

seeing you in battle, do your enemies entertain various doubts.'

Inasmuch as the definition speaks of the difference being stated, it follows that we have this Figure, not only when the certainty is left concealed (implied), but also when the cogitation leads on to certainty. *e.g.*—

'Is this the moon ?—But where is the dark stigma ? Is this the lotus ?—But where is the water gone to ? O Fawn-eyed one ! that what was seen was the face ascertained later on through the presence of sweet and elegant speech.'

But this variety of the *Doubtful* has been omitted by Rudraṭa, on the ground that in this case the certainty is not merely *suggested*, as it is in that variety where the certainty is left concealed [and hence it loses its effectiveness.]

The following is an example of the case where the difference is not stated—'In the creating of this woman, was the position of the creator occupied by the Moon,

तद्रूपकमभेदो य उपमानोपमेययोः ।

अतिसाम्याद् अनपह्नुतभेदयोः अभेदः ।

समस्तवस्तुविषयं श्रौता आरोपिता यदा ॥ ९३ ॥

आरोपविषया इव आरोप्यमाणाः यदा शब्दोपात्ताः तदा समस्तानि वस्तूनि विषयोऽस्येति समस्तवस्तुविषयम् । आरोपिता इति बहुवचनमविवक्षितम् । यथा

ज्योत्स्नाभस्मच्छुरणधवला बिभ्रती तारकास्थी-
न्यन्तर्धानव्यसनरसिका रात्रिकापालिकीयम् ।
द्वीपाद् द्वीपं भ्रमति दधती चन्द्रमुद्राकपाले
न्यस्तं सिद्धाञ्जनपरिमलं लाञ्छनस्यच्छलेन ॥३२१॥

---

the source of effulgence ? or was it the Love-god himself abounding in the erotic passion ? Or was it the season of spring ?—How else could the ancient sage, whose sensibility had been deadened by Vedic study and whose interest had been withdrawn from all objects, be able to create such a heart-ravishing body ?' 92.

VI—*Rūpaka*—Metaphor.

Where there is non-difference between the 'object compared to' and the 'object compared', it is Metaphor.

What is meant by 'non-difference' is that idea of non-difference which is based upon extreme likeness between two objects, whose difference is not entirely concealed.

(1) *In cases where what is imposed is directly expressed, it is Metaphor Universal.* 93.

In cases where, as the objects imposed upon, so the objects imposed also, are directly mentioned by words, it is that Metaphor which is called '*Universal*',—in the sense that the *whole* (*samasta*) *of what is imposed* (*nyasta*) is its expressed objective (*viṣaya*).

अत्र पादत्रये, अन्तर्धानव्यसनरसिकत्वमारोपितधर्मं एवेति रूपकपरिग्रहे साधकमस्तीति तत्संकराशङ्का न कार्या ॥९३॥

श्रौता आर्थाश्च ते यस्मिन्नेकदेशविवर्ति तत् ॥

केचिदारोप्यमाणाः शब्दोपात्ताः केचिदर्थसामर्थ्यादवसेयाः इत्येकदेशविवर्तनात् एकदेशविवर्ति । यथा

No significance attaches to the plural number, in the term '*āropitāḥ*'.

Example [of Metaphor Universal.]—

'This *Nun of the Night*, white with the painting of the *ash of light*, wearing the bones of *the stars*, and delighting in vanishing from view, is wandering from continent to continent, carrying in the *bowl of the lunar disc* the magic unguent, under the garb of the dark stigma.'

[Here we have the said Metaphor in the expressions '*jyotsnā-bhasma*', where there is 'non-difference' between *light* and *ashes*, (2) '*tārakāsthi*', where there is 'non-difference' between *stars* and *bones*, (3) in '*rātrikāpālikī*', where there is 'non-difference' between the *Night* and the *Nun*, and (4) in '*chandramudrakapāla*', where there is 'non-difference' between the *lunar disc* and the *bowl*.]

In connection with this verse, there is no justification for the suspicion that it is a case of the 'dubious commixture' [of Simile and Metaphor, on the ground that the compound expressions concerned are also capable of being construed as actually expressing similitude, and hence involving so many similes]; because in favour of its being regarded as 'Metaphor' there is the special reason that the property of 'delighting in vanishing from view' is one that (while actually belonging to the sentient *Nuns*) is imposed (upon the insentient *Night*). 93.

(2) *In a case where what is imposed is directly expressed as well as indirectly implied, it is the Partial Metaphor.*

जस्स रणंतेउरए करे कुणंतस्स मण्डलग्गलअं ।
रससंमुही वि सहसा परंमुही होइ रिउसेणा ॥४२२॥

अत्र रणस्यान्तःपुरत्वमारोप्यमाणं शब्दोपात्तम् मण्डलाग्रलतायाः नायिकात्वम् रिपुसेनायाश्च प्रतिनायिकात्वम् अर्थसामर्थ्यादवसीयते इति एकदेशे विशेषेण वर्तनादेकदेशविवर्ति ।

साङ्गमेतत् ॥

उक्तद्विभेदं सावयवम् ॥

Where some of the imposed factors are directly expressed by words, while some are cognised only through the force of the meanings of the words,—it is 'partial', *ekadeshavivarti*',—so called, because of its *functioning directly* (*vivartana*) *in one part* (*ekadesha*).

'*Jassa raṇaṁteurae kare kuṇaṁtassa maṇḍalaggalaaṁ*
Rasasaṁmuhī vi sahasā paraṁmuhī hoi riusenā'.

'When, in the harem of the battle-field, he takes in his arms the sword-blade (his beloved wife). the opposing army (her rival), even though passionate, turns away from him'.

Here the character of 'harem' as imposed upon the 'battlefield' is directly expressed by the words, while the fact of the 'sword-blade' being the 'beloved wife', as also that of the 'opposite army' being her 'rival', is comprehended only through the force of the meaning of the words employed; and thus the Metaphor, being particularly, explicit in only a part of it, is called 'partial'.

This is complex, with all its constituents.

The two kinds of Metaphor just described are equipped with all constituents.

[*i. e.* in these what is imposed is not only the object compared to, by itself alone, but along with all its accessories.]

निरङ्गं तु शुद्धम् ॥

यथा

कुरङ्गीवाङ्गानि स्तिमितयति गीतध्वनिषु यत्
सखीं कान्तोदन्तं श्रुतमपि पुनः प्रश्नयति यत् ।
अनिद्रं यच्चान्तः स्वपिति तदहो वेद्म्यभिनवां
प्रवृत्तोस्याः सेक्तुं हृदि मनसिजः प्रेमलतिकाम् ॥४२३॥

माला तु पूर्ववत् ॥ ९४ ॥

मालोपमायामिवैकस्मिन् बहव आरोपिताः । यथा

सौन्दर्यस्य तरङ्गिणी तरुणिमोत्कर्षस्य हर्षोद्गमः
कान्तेः कार्मणकर्म नर्मरहसामुल्लासनावासभूः ।

---

(3) *That which is devoid of constituents is the Pure Metaphor.*

[When the object alone by itself is imposed.]

Example—'While listening to songs, she keeps her limbs unmoved, like the doe ; asks her friend the news about her lover, even though she has already heard it ; she lies down within, without sleep ; from all this I gather that the Love-god has begun to water the fresh sprout of affection in her heart'.

[Here, all that is imposed upon the affection is the character of the sprout ; and nothing is said regarding any detailed properties of the latter.]

The 'String' is like the foregoing. 94.

Just as in the 'String Simile' so in the 'String Metaphor' also, the character of several objects is imposed upon a single object.

Example—'That beloved one is the stream of beauty, the joyous effusion of youthful exuberance, the touch-stone of resplendence, the abode of loving confidences,

विद्या वक्रगिरां विधेरनवधिप्रावीण्यसाक्षात्क्रिया
बाणाः पञ्चशिलीमुखस्य ललनाचूडामणिः सा प्रिया ॥४२४॥९४॥

नियतारोपणोपायः स्यादारोपः परस्य यः ।
तत्परंपरितं श्लिष्टे वाचके भेदभाजि वा ॥ ९५ ॥

यथा

विद्वन्मानसहंस वैरिकमलासंकोचदीप्तद्युते
दुर्गामार्गणनीललोहित समित्स्वीकारवैश्वानर ।
सत्यप्रीतिविधानदक्ष विजयप्राग्भावभीम प्रभो
साम्राज्यं वरवीर वत्सरशतं वैरिञ्चमुच्चैः क्रियाः ॥४२५॥

---

the tutoress of clever conversation, the direct evidence of the illimitable efficiency of the Creator, the arrows of the Love-god and the crest-jewel of lovely women'. 94.

(4). *Where as a means of the desired imposition, there is imposition of something else, it is the Consequential Metaphor; —where the expressive word is either 'coalescent' (in Pun) or 'distinct'.* 95.

Example

'*Vidvanmānasahaṁsa vairikamalāsaṁkochadīptadyute*
Durgāmārgaṇanīlalohita samitsvīkāravaishvānara
Satyaprītividhānadakṣa vijayaprāgbhāvabhīma prabho
Sāmrājyaṁ varavīra vatsarashataṁ vairiñchamuchchaiḥkriyāḥ

'O thou, who art like the swan in the *mind of the learned* [which is like the Mānasa-lake]; like the sun in the *shrivelling of the prosperity of your enemies* [which is like the blossoming of the lotus]; like Shiva is *not seeking the shelter of forts* [which is like the longing for Durgā]; like Fire *in accepting battle* [which is like the consuming of fuel]; like Dakṣa in *attachment to truth* [which is like displeasure with Satī]; like Bhīma in *the exuberance of victory* [which like being the elder brother of Arjuna];—bravest of the

अत्र मानसमेव मानसम् कमलायाः संकोच एव कमलानामसंकोचः दुर्गाणाममार्गणमेव दुर्गायाः मार्गणम् समितां स्वीकार एव समिधां स्वीकारः सत्ये प्रीतिरेव सत्यामप्रीतिः विजयः परपराभव एव विजयोर्जुनः एवमारोपणनिमित्तो हंसादेरारोपः।

यद्यपि शब्दार्थालंकारोयमित्युक्तं वक्ष्यते च तथापि प्रसिद्ध्यनुरोधादत्रोक्तः। एकदेशविवर्ति हीदमन्यैरभिधीयते ॥

---

brave! Mayst thou continue to sway your empire for a hundred years of Brahma!

Here (1) the character of the 'swan' is imposed upon the 'king', only as a means of imposing (through Pun) upon the 'mind' the character of the 'Mānasa lake';—(2) the character of the 'Sun' is imposed upon the 'king', only as a means of imposing (through Pun) the character of 'the blossoming of lotuses' upon 'the shrivelling of the enemy's prosperity';—(3) the character of 'Shiva' is imposed upon the 'king', only as a means of imposing (through Pun) the character of 'longing for Durgā' upon 'the not seeking of the shelter of forts';—(4) the character of 'fire' is imposed upon the 'king', only as a means of imposing (through Pun) the character of 'consuming fuel' upon 'the accepting of battle';—(5) the character of 'Dakṣa' is imposed upon the 'king' only as a means of imposing (through Pun) of the character of 'displeasure with Satī' upon the 'attachment to truth';—(6) the character of 'Bhīma' is imposed upon the 'king' as a means of imposing (through Pun) the character of 'being he elder brother of Arjuna' upon the 'exuberance of victory'.

Though (by reason of the Puns being such as do not admit of the replacing of the words used by their synonyms)

भेदभाजि यथा

आलानं जयकुञ्जरस्य दृषदां सेतुर्विपद्वारिधेः
पूर्वाद्रिः करवालचण्डमहसो लीलोपधानं श्रियः ।
संग्रामामृतसागरप्रमथनक्रीडाविधौ मन्दरो
राजन् राजति वीरवैरिवनितावैधव्यदस्ते भुजः ॥४२६॥

अत्र जयादेर्भिन्नशब्दवाच्यस्य कुञ्जरत्वाद्यारोपे भुजस्य आलानत्वाद्यारोपो युज्यते ।

---

this would be an instance of a *verbal* figure of speech, as has been already explained above, and as is going to be explained also later on,—yet it has been mentioned here, in accordance with usage (established by earlier writers on the subject), on the basis whereof some people have called this an instance of the *Partial* Metaphor.

The following is an example of the Consequential Metaphor where the expressive words are distinct (and not coalescing in a Pun)—

'O King! Ever glorious is thy arm, bringing about, as it does the widow-hood of the wives of the heroic enemies;—the arm, which is the post for the tying of the elephant of victory, the embankment against the ocean of adversity, the Rising Mount of the Sun of the Sword, the sporting fellow of the Goddess of Fortune, and the Mandara Mountain in the process of the churning of the nectar-ocean of Battle'.

Here the imposition of the character of the 'post' upon the arm is rendered possible by the imposition of the character of the 'elephant' upon 'Victory', both of these being mentioned by means of separate words; similarly also with the other impositions in the verse.

अलौकिकमहालोकप्रकाशितजगत्त्रयः ।
स्तूयते देव सद्वंशमुक्तारत्नं न कैर्भवान् ॥४२७॥

निरवधि च निराश्रयं च यस्य स्थितमनिवर्तितकौतुकप्रपञ्चम् ।
प्रथम इह भवान् स कूर्ममूर्तिर्जयति चतुर्दशलोकवल्लिकन्दः॥४२८॥

इति च अमालारूपकमपि परंपरितं द्रष्टव्यम् ॥

किसलयकरैर्लतानां करकमलैः कामिनां मनो जयति ।
नलिनीनां कमलमुखैः मुखेन्दुभिर्योषितां मदनः ॥४२९॥

इत्यादि रशनारूपकं न वैचित्र्यवदिति न लक्षितम् ॥९५॥

[The following is an example of the Punning Consequential Metaphor].

'*Alaukikamahālokaprakāshitajagattrayaḥ*
Stūyate deva sadvaṁshamuktāratnaṁ na kairbhavān.

'O King! brightening the three worlds with your superhuman resplendence, and being a pearl in the bamboo of a noble race, by whom are you not eulogised?'

[Here the imposition of the character of 'pearl' upon the king is made possible by the imposition of the character of the 'bamboo' upon the 'noble race,' both of these latter being expressed by the punning word '*sadvamsha*'],

[The following is an example of the non-punning Consequential Metaphor]—

'Ever glorious are you, the primeval Tortoise-shaped God! the root of the creeper of the fourteen regions, whose existence, infinite (in time) and unsupported. is never bereft of extraordinary phenomenon.'

[Here the imposition of the character of the 'root' upon the God is rendered possible by the imposition of the character of 'creeper' upon the 'fourteen regions,' both of these latter being expressed by distinct words.]

In both these cases we have the Consequential Metaphor, *not in the form of a 'string.'*

प्रकृतं यन्निषिध्यान्यत् साध्यते सा त्वपह्नुतिः ।

उपमेयम् असत्यं कृत्वोपमानं सत्यतया यत् स्थाप्यते सा तु अपह्नुतिः

उदाहरणम्—

अवाप्तः प्रागल्भ्यं परिणतरुचः शैलतनये
कलङ्को नैवायं विलसति शशाङ्कस्य वपुषि ।
अमुष्येयं मन्ये विगलदमृतस्यन्दशिशिरे
रतिश्रान्ता शेते रजनिरमणी गाढमुरसि ॥४३०॥

इत्थं वा

बत सखि कियदेतत् पश्य वैरं स्मरस्य
प्रियविरहकृशेऽस्मिन् रागिलोके तथा हि ।

There is 'Girdle-Metaphor' also, in such verses as—"The Love-god captivates the hearts of amorous men, by means (1) of the hand-like leaves of creepers, (2) of the lotus-like hands and moon-like faces of women, and (3) of the lotus-like faces of the lotus-pond.'

This, however, has not been described here as there is not much charm in it. 95.

VII—*Apahnuti*—Concealment.

When the object to be described is negatived and another is affirmed, it is Concealment.

Where the 'object compared' is 'negatived'—declared to be unreal,—and the 'object compared to' is 'affirmed' declared to be real, it is the Figure of *Concealment.*

Example—

'O Pārvatī! This that you see is not the fully developed stigma in the disc of the moon shining with full lustre; I think it is his beloved, Night, fatigued by dalliance, sleeping soundly on his chest, rendered cool by the drops of nectar.'

उपवनसहकारोद्भासिभृङ्गच्छलेन
प्रतिविशिखमनेनोट्टङ्कितं कालकूटम् ॥४३१॥

अत्र हि न सभृङ्गाणि सहकाराणि अपि तु सकालकूटाः शरा इति प्रतीतिः । एवं वा

अमुष्मिँल्लावण्यामृतसरसि नूनं मृगदृशः
स्मरः शर्वप्लुष्टः पृथुजघनभागे निपतितः ।
यदङ्गाङ्गाराणां प्रथमपिशुना नाभिकुहरे
शिखा धूमस्येयं परिणमति रोमावलिवपुः ॥४३२॥

अत्र न रोमावलिः धूमशिखेयमिति प्रतिपत्तिः ॥ एवमियं भङ्गयन्तरैरप्यूह्या ॥

Or again—

'O friend ! Just see the ill-will borne by the Love-god towards lovers already emaciated by separation from their beloved : Under the pretext of black bees hovering over the mango-trees in the garden. he has applied poison to each one of his arrows'.

Here the idea meant to be conveyed is that 'what are seen are not mango-trees with black bees hovering about them, but so many arrows dipped in poison'.

Yet another example—

'Verily, the Love-god, scorched by Shiva, has fallen upon the plump thighs of the Fawn-eyed one,—which are like the tank of the nectar of loveliness ; as from the hole of her naval there is proceeding a line of smoke, in the form of the line of hair, which is the first sign of the extinguishing of the fire-embers of his body.'

The idea conveyed here is that 'what we see is not the line of hair, but the line of smoke.'

श्लेषः स वाक्य एकस्मिन् यत्रानेकार्थता भवेत् ॥ ९६ ॥

एकार्थप्रतिपादकानामेव शब्दानां यत्रानेकोर्थः स श्लेषः ।

उदाहरणम्—

उदयमयते दिङ्मालिन्यं निराकुरुतेतरां
नयति निधनं निद्रामुद्रां प्रवर्तयति क्रियाः ।
रचयतितरां स्वैराचारप्रवर्तनकर्तनं
बत बत लसत्तेजःपुञ्जो विभाति विभाकरः ॥४३३॥

अत्राभिधाया अनियन्त्रणात् द्वावप्यर्कभूपौ वाच्यौ ॥९६॥

Thus may other ways of expressing this Figure be deduced.

VIII—*Shleṣa*—Paronomasia.

When in a single sentence, there are several meanings, it is Paronomasia. 96.

Where a set of words, expressive of one meaning, is found to have several meanings, it is Paronomasia.

Example—

'*Udayamayate diṅmālinyaṁ nirākurutetarāṁ*
Nayati nidhanaṁ nidrāmudrāṁ pravartayati kriyāḥ.
Rachayatitarāṁ svairāchārapravartanakartanaṁ
Vata vata lasattejaḥpuñjo vibhāti vibhākaraḥ'

'(*a*) The Sun, [(*b*) the king named Vibhākara], (*a*) the receptacle of effulgent light [(*b*) possessing exuberant energy],—who attains (*a*) the Rising Mount [(*b*) prosperity], sets aside (*a*) the darkness of the quarters [(*b*) the poverty-stricken appearance of the people], destroys (*a*) sleepiness [(*b*) depression], sets going (*a*) business-operations [(*b*) the performance of religious rites], puts a stop to all (*a*) free love-making [(*b*) unrestrained activity],—is shining'.

परोक्तिर्भेदकैः श्लिष्टैः समासोक्तिः ॥

प्रकृतार्थप्रतिपादकवाक्येन श्लिष्टविशेषणमाहात्म्यात् न तु विशेष्यस्य सामर्थ्यादपि यत् अप्रकृतस्यार्थस्याभिधानम् सा समासेन संक्षेपेणार्थद्वयकथनात् समासोक्तिः । उदाहरणम्—

लहिऊण तुज्झ बाहुप्फंसं जीए स को वि उल्लासो ।
जअलच्छी तुह विरहे ण हुज्जला दुब्बला णं सा ॥४३४॥

अत्र जयलक्ष्मीशब्दस्य केवलं कान्तावाचकत्वं नास्ति ॥

As there is nothing in the shape of Context and the rest to restrict the denotation of the words used, both, the Sun as well as the King, are equally capable of being accepted as the object described. 96.

IX—*Samāsokti*—Modal Metaphor.

Where the other object is implied by means of paronomatic differentiating adjusts, it is Modal Metaphor.

When a sentence descriptive of the object meant to be described serves to imply something else not meant to be described, through the force of adjectives used punningly—and not through any force of the object itself,—it is Modal Metaphor, '*Samāsokti*',—so called because it consists in a 'statement' (*ukti*) of two meanings, 'in brief' (*samāsena*).

Example—

'*Lahiūṇa tujjha bāhupphaṁsaṁ*
Jīe sa ko vi ullāso.
Jaa-lachchhī tuha virahe
ṇa hujjalā dubbalā ṇaṁ sā'.

'*Jayalakṣmī* (*the Glory of Victory*) who felt a peculiar exhilaration on attaining the touch of your arms, is no longer bright, on being separated from you ; in fact she is emaciated.'

निदर्शना ।

अभवन्वस्तुसंबन्ध उपमापरिकल्पकः ॥ ९७ ॥

निदर्शनं दृष्टान्तकरणम् । उदाहरणम्—

क्व सूर्यप्रभवो वंशः क्व चाल्पविषया मतिः ।
तितीर्षुर्दुस्तरं मोहादुडुपेनास्मि सागरम् ॥४३५॥

अत्र उडुपेन सागरतरणमिव मन्मत्या सूर्यवंशवर्णनमित्युपमायां पर्यवस्यति ।

यथा वा

उदयति विततोर्ध्वरश्मिरज्जावहिमरुचौ हिमधाम्नि याति चास्तम् ।
वहति गिरिरयं विलम्बिघण्टाद्वयपरिवारितवारणेन्द्रलीलाम् ।४३६।

· Here the term '*jayalakṣmī*' is so used (with such adjectives) that it expresses, not only the king's lady love, [but also the glory of victory in battle].

X—*Nidarshanā*—Illustration.

Where an impossible relation of things constitutes the similitude, it is Illustration. 97.

It is called '*nidarshanā*', because it serves the purpose of *nidarshanā*, illustrating.

Example—

'Where (on one side) is the dynasty originating from the Sun, and where (on the other) is my limited intelligence : through sheer foolishness am I desirous of crossing the ocean by means of a raft.'

Here the (impossible) statement made leads on to the Simile that—'a description of the Solar Dynasty by my intelligence would be just like the crossing ot the ocean by a raft.'

Another example—

'When (on one side) the Sun is rising with his rays

अत्र कथमन्यस्य लीलामन्यो वहतीति तत्सदृशीमित्युपमायां पर्यवसानम् ।

दोर्भ्यां तितीर्षति तरङ्गवतीभुजङ्गम्
आदातुमिच्छति करे हरिणाङ्कबिम्बम् ।
मेरुं लिलङ्घयिषति ध्रुवमेष देव
यस्ते गुणान् गदितुमुद्यममादधाति ॥४३७॥

इत्यादौ मालारूपाप्येषा द्रष्टव्या ॥९७॥

स्वस्वहेत्वन्वयस्योक्तिः क्रिययैव च सापरा ।

क्रिययैव स्वस्वरूपस्वकारणयोः संबन्धो यदवगम्यते सा अपरा निदर्शना । यथा

---

shooting upwards, and (on the other) the Moon is setting, this mountain acquires the splendour of an elephant with two bells hanging on its two sides.'

The actual acquiring of the splendour of one thing (the elephant) by the other (the mountain) being an impossibility, the statement only leads on to the Simile that the one appears *similar* to the other...

This Figure appears in the form of a 'String' also ;—*e.g.*

'O Lord ! the man that makes an attempt to describe your good qualities, (*a*) desires to cross the ocean with his arms, (*b*) wishes to catch the moon with his hands, and (*c*) to jump over the Meru mountain.' 97.

There is another kind of Illustration, where the action itself indicates the (causal) relation between itself and its cause.

Where the connection between the action itself and its cause is indicated by the action itself.—it is another kind of Illustration.

उन्नतं पदमवाप्य यो लघुहेलयैव स पतेदिति ब्रुवन् ।
शैलशेखरगतो दृषत्कणश्चारुमारुतधुतः पतत्यधः ॥४३८॥

अत्र पातक्रियया पतनस्य लाघवे सति उन्नतपदप्राप्ति-रूपस्य च संबन्धः ख्याप्यते ॥

अप्रस्तुतप्रशंसा या सा सैव प्रस्तुताश्रया ॥ ९८ ॥

अप्राकरणिकस्याभिधानेन प्राकरणिकस्याक्षेपोप्रस्तुतप्रशंसा॥९८॥

कार्ये निमित्ते सामान्ये विशेषे प्रस्तुते सति ।
तदन्यस्य वचस्तुल्ये तुल्यस्येति च पञ्चधा ॥ ९९ ॥

Example—

"When a low thing attains a high position, it will naturally fall,"—so, saying as it were, the stone-dust, on the hill-top falls down when shaken by the mild wind.'

Here it is the action of *falling* (of the stone-dust) which points to the connection between the *action of falling* and its cause, in the shape of *the low person attaining to high positions.*

XI—*Aprastutaprashaṁsā*—Indirect Description.

Where the description of an irrelevant thing points to the object meant to be described, it is Indirect Description. 98.

When the description of something not connected with the context serves to point to, imply, that which is meant to be described,—it is *Indirect Description.* 98.

It is of five kinds:—...here what is meant to be described is—(a) the effect, or (b) a cause, or (c) Universal, or (d) Particular,—what is actually spoken of is their converse (correlative); and (e) when what is meant to be described is one thing, and what is spoken of is something else of the same class. 99.

तदन्यस्य कारणादेः । क्रमेणोदाहरणम्—

याता किं न मिलन्ति सुन्दरि पुनश्चिन्ता त्वया मत्कृते
नो कार्या नितरां कृशासि कथयत्येवं सबाष्पे मयि ।
लज्जामन्थरतारकेण निपतत्पीताश्रुणा चक्षुषा
दृष्ट्वा मां हसितेन भाविमरणोत्साहस्तया सूचितः ॥४३९॥

अत्र प्रस्थानात्किमिति निवृत्तोसीति कार्ये पृष्टे कारणमभिहितम् ।

राजन्राजसुता न पाठयति मां देव्योपि तूष्णीं स्थिताः
कुब्जे भोजय मां कुमारसचिवैर्नाद्यापि किं भुज्यते ।
इत्थं नाथ शुकस्तवारिभवने मुक्तोध्वगैः पञ्जराच्
चित्रस्थानवलोक्य शून्यवलभावेकैकमाभाषते ॥४४०॥

'*Their converse*'—*i.e.* (*a*) cause and the rest. Examples in order—

(*a*) ' " O beautiful one, don't those who go out meet again ? Don't be anxious for me ; you are extremely weak ",—while, with tears, I was saying this, she, with her eyes fixed through modesty and absorbing the overflowing tears, smiled and by that smile she indicated her joy at her approaching death.'

Asked for an explanation of the *effect*, in the shape of the postponement of his projected journey, the speaker has described here the *cause* [in the shape of the beloved's perceptible determination to die on separation.]

(*b*) " O King, the princess is not teaching me to talk ; and the queens also are sitting silent. O Kubjā, feed me. Why are not the princes and ministers taking their food even at this time ?"—Thus does the parrot in the empty turrets of your enemy's houses, speak, when let out of the cage by the passers-by, it sees the figure of its master on the pictures.'

अत्र प्रस्थानोद्यतं भवन्तं ज्ञात्वा सहसैव त्वदरयः पलाय्य गताः इति कारणे प्रस्तुते कार्यमुक्तम् ।

एतत्तस्य मुखात्कियत् कमलिनीपत्रे कणं वारिणो
यन्मुक्तामणिरित्यमंस्त स जडः शृण्वन्यदस्मादपि ।
अङ्गुल्यग्रलघुक्रियाप्रविलयिन्यादीयमाने शनैः
कुत्रोड्डीय गतो ममेत्यनुदिनं निद्राति नान्तःशुचा ।।४४१।।

अत्रास्थाने जडानां ममत्वसंभावना भवतीति सामान्ये प्रस्तुते विशेषः कथितः ।

सुहृद्वधूबाष्पजलप्रमार्जनं करोति वैरप्रतियातनेन यः ।
स एव पूज्यः स पुमान्स नीतिमान्सुजीवितं तस्य स भाजनं श्रियः
।।४४२।।

What is meant to be described here is the fact that 'as soon as your enemies came to know of your projected march against them, they fled away from their houses'; and this fact is the *cause* of the *effect* that is described in the verse.

(*c*) 'What wonder is it to hear from his mouth that a certain block-head thought the water-drops upon the lotus-leaf to be so many pearls ?—Hear something more than this—when that same person proceeded to pick up the drops, they disappeared under the light pressure of his finger-tips, and since then the fool, intensely aggrieved at the thought of his pearls having flown away, goes without sleep day after day.'

What was meant to be described was the *Universal* or *general* fact that 'foolish people have even misplaced longings and affections,'—while what is actually described is a *particular* instance of it.

अत्र 'कृष्णं निहत्य नरकासुरवधूनां यदि दुःखं प्रशमयसि तत् त्वमेव श्लाघ्यः' इति विशेषे प्रकृते सामान्यमभिहितम् ।

तुल्ये प्रस्तुते तुल्याभिधाने त्रयः प्रकाराः । श्लेषः समासोक्तिः सादृश्यमात्रं वा तुल्यात् तुल्यस्य ह्याक्षेपे हेतुः । क्रमेणोदाहरणम्–

पुंस्त्वादपि प्रविचलेत् यदि यद्यधोपि
यायाद् यदि प्रणयने न महानपि स्यात् ।
अभ्युद्धरेत्तदपि विश्वमितीदृशीयं
केनापि दिक् प्रकटिता पुरुषोत्तमेन ।।४४३।।

(*d*) 'When a man wipes away the tears from the eyes of his friend's wives, by avenging himself on his enemy, then alone does he deserve to be honoured, then alone is he to be regarded as a man, as a statesman, an abode of majesty ; and then alone is his life worth something.'

What was meant to be expressed was a *particular* statement (addressed to *Narakāsura*'s (friend) that—' Then alone will you be deserving of praise, when, by killing Kṛṣṇa (who has killed Narakāsura), you will have alleged the anguish of Naraka's wives '; while what is actually expressed is a *general* statement (without reference to any particular case).

(*e*) Of that case, where while what is meant to be described is one thing, what is actually described is something else of the same class,—there are three varieties, according as the indication of one thing by another of the same class is done (1) by a Pun, or (2) by Modal Metaphor, or (3) by mere similarity.

Examples in order—

(1) 'One may deviate from the standard of manhood, he may lower himself by begging, he may even demean

येनास्यभ्युदितेन चन्द्र गमितः क्लान्तिं रवौ तत्र ते
युज्येत प्रतिकर्तुमेव न पुनस्तस्यैव पादग्रहः ।
क्षीणेनैतदनुष्ठितं यदि ततः किं लज्जसे नो मनाग्
अस्त्वेवं जडधामता तु भवतो यद् व्योम्नि विस्फूर्जसे ॥४४४॥
आदाय वारि परितः सरितां मुखेभ्यः
किं तावदर्जितमनेन दुरर्णवेन ।
क्षारीकृतं च वडवादहने हुतं च
पातालकुक्षिकुहरे विनिवेशितं च ॥४४५॥

---

himself,—he may do all this if thereby he can save the world ;—this was the way shown by the Noble Person'.

[What is meant to be described here is a certain *noble benefactor* of men, while what is described is another *noble benefactor* in the person of Viṣṇu ; and this latter is made to point to the former by means of such paronomatic expressions as are applicable to both cases.]

(2) 'O Moon, when the Sun rises, you become deprived of your lustre ; what is proper for you then is to avenge yourself, and not to *fall upon his feet* [borrow his light-rays .] If this has been done by you when you had become impoverished, then are you not ashamed ?—or, that you even now show yourself in the sky may be due to your *nervelessness* [coolness of your light].'

[What is meant to be described here is the behaviour of a certain *impoverished person* ; and this is indicated by the description of another *impoverished person* in the shape of the Moon ; and this is done through Modal Metaphor based upon the Pun involved in the words '*pāda-grahaḥ*' and '*jaḍadhāmatā*.']

(3) 'What has the wretched Ocean done with the water that he has received from the mouths of rivers ? He has rendered it brackish or poured it into the Submarine Fire, or thrown it into the innermost recesses of the Nether World.'

इयं च काचित् वाच्ये प्रतीयमानार्थानध्यारोपेणैव भवति । यथा

अब्धेरम्भः स्थगितभुवनाभोगपातालकुक्षेः
पोतोपाया इह हि बहवो लङ्घनेपि क्षमन्ते ।
आहो रिक्तः कथमपि भवेदेष दैवात् तदानीं
को नाम स्यादवटकुहरालोकनेप्यस्य कल्पः ॥४४६॥

क्वचिदध्यारोपेणैव । यथा

कस्त्वं भोः कथयामि दैवहतकं मां विद्धि शाखोटकं
वैराग्यादिव वक्षि साधु विदितं कस्मादिदं कथ्यते ।

[What is meant to be described is a *spendthrift*, and this is indicated by the description of the *spendthrift* Ocean ; and this is done through mere similarity between the two persons.]

In some cases of this last kind of Indirect Description what is implied is not necessarily imposed (or fastened) upon what is directly expressed. As in the following verse.—

'There are many people who, with the help of boats, are able to cross the ocean which has covered with water the face of the Earth and also the innermost recesses of the Nether World ; if, however, somehow or other, the ocean were by chance to become emptied, who would be able to even look at the holes and cavities in it ?'

[Here the *implied* meaning is that 'for the people it is best that the king, if wicked, should remain prosperous ;' but the directly expressed description of the ocean itself being quite apt, it is not necessary for the former to be imposed upon this latter.]

In other cases the said imposition is essential ; as for instance, in the following verse.—

'Who are you, Sir ?'—' Know me to be the fatestricken *Shākhoṭaka* tree.'—' You talk as if you were disgusted with life.'—' You have guessed rightly.'—' But why so ?'— I am going to explain : This banyan tree that lies to the

वामेनात्र वटस्तमध्वगजनः सर्वात्मना सेवते
न च्छायापि परोपकारकरणे मार्गस्थितस्यापि मे ॥४४७॥

क्वचिदंशेष्वध्यारोपेण । यथा

सोपूर्वो रसनाविपर्ययविधिः तत् कर्णयोश्चापलं
दृष्टिः सा मदविस्मृतस्वपरदिक् किं भूयसोक्तेन वा ।
सर्वं विस्मृतवानसि भ्रमर हे यद्वारणोद्याप्यसौ
अन्तःशून्यकरो निषेव्यत इति भ्रातः क एष ग्रहः ॥४४८॥

---

left of the road, is attended by all pedestrians, while to me, though I am standing on the road, does not belong even shade enough for rendering help to others.'

[What is *implied* here is the condition of a lowborn person whose gifts have been refused by a qualified recipient : and the imposition of this upon the *expressed* description of the tree is essential, since the ideas described can never belong to any such entity as the tree.]

In still other cases, there is only partial imposition ; for instance, in the following verse—

'That curious process whereby the tongue was reversed ; the fickleness of ears ; vision incapacitated by intoxication to discriminate between himself and others ;—what is the need for saying more ?—All this you have forgotten, O brother black bee ! and you still stick to this elephant, with an empty trunk [hand] ;—whence this peculiar attachment ?

[Here what is *implied* is the relation between an unappreciating master and a devoted servant ; and this is imposed upon the case described, of the elephant and the black bee]. The imposition here is only partial ; as 'the reversal of the tongue' and 'emptiness of the trunk' are not such circumstances as would justify the abandoning of the elephant by the bee ; it is only the 'fickleness of the

अत्र रसनाविपर्यासः शून्यकरत्वं च भ्रमरस्यासेवने न हेतुः कर्णचापलं तु हेतुः मदः प्रत्युत सेवने निमित्तम् ॥९९॥

निगीर्याध्यवसानं तु प्रकृतस्य परेण यत् ।
प्रस्तुतस्य यदन्यत्वं यद्यर्थोक्तौ च कल्पनम् ॥१००॥
कार्यकारणयोर्यश्च पौर्वापर्यविपर्ययः ।
विज्ञेयातिशयोक्तिः सा ॥

उपमानेनान्तर्निगीर्णस्योपमेयस्य यदध्यवसानं सैका । यथा

कमलमनम्भसि कमले च कुवलये तानि कनकलतिकायाम् ।
सा च सुकुमारसुभगेत्युत्पातपरंपरा केयम् ॥४४९॥

अत्र मुखादि कमलादिरूपतयाध्यवसितम् ।

---

ears' that would justify it; while the presence of the 'intoxicating' rut would render the elephant all the more attractive to the bee.—

[And the imposition in this case is done through the Puns involved in 'reversal of the tongue', 'fickleness of the ear' and 'emptiness of the hand']. 99.

XII—*Atishayokti*—Hyperbole.

It is to be known as the Hyperbole—(a) when the object to be described is indicated as swallowed by the other;—(b) when the object to be described is represented as another;—(c) when there is an assumption introduced by some term meaning 'if';—and (d) when there is reversal of the normal order of sequence between a cause and its effect.

(*a*) When the 'object compared' is recognised as swallowed within the 'object compared to',—it is one kind of Hyperbole. Example—

'A lotus is found in a place without water;—two blue lotuses are found in a lotus;—all these three are found on a golden creeper;—and that creeper is tender and lovely;—what a series of portentous phenomena!'

यच्च तदेवान्यत्वेनाध्यवसीयते सा अपरा । यथा

अण्णं लडहत्तणअं अण्णा विअ का वि वत्तणच्छाआ ।
सामा सामण्णपआवइणो रेहच्चिअ ण होइ ॥४५०॥

'यद्यर्थस्य' यदिशब्देन चेच्छब्देन वा उक्तौ यत् कल्पनम् (अर्थात् असंभविनोर्थस्य) सा तृतीया । यथा

राकायामकलंकं चेदमृतांशोर्भवेद्वपुः ।
तस्या मुखं तदा साम्यपराभवमवाप्नुयात् ॥४५१॥

कारणस्य शीघ्रकारितां वक्तुं कार्यस्य पूर्वमुक्तौ चतुर्थी । यथा

The *face* (and the eyes and the body) are represented as 'swallowed by' (identified with) the *lotus* (the blue lotuses and the golden creeper).

(*b*) It is the second kind of Hyperbole, when that same object (to be described) is represented 'as another', as something different. Example.—

'Her tenderness is something quite different; quite different to the brightness of her complexion; this young girl is not the creation of the ordinary Creator.'

[Here the idea expressed is that the 'tenderness' and other things are quite different from the ordinary tenderness and the rest.]

(*c*) It is the third kind of Hyperbole, when there is 'assumption',—*i.e.*, of an impossible idea through the use of 'some term meaning *if*'—*i.e.*, of the term '*yadi*' or '*chet*'.

Example—

'If the body of the Moon at night were to be spotless, then alone could her face suffer the insult of being equalled.'

(*d*) It is the fourth kind of Hyperbole, when, for the purpose of indicating the powerful efficacy of the cause, the effect is described as appearing before its time.

हृदयमधिष्ठितमादौ मालत्याः कुसुमचापबाणेन ।
चरमं रमणीवल्लभ लोचनविषयं त्वया भजता ॥४५२॥

प्रतिवस्तूपमा तु सा ॥ १०१ ॥

सामान्यस्य द्विरेकस्य यत्र वाक्यद्वये स्थितिः ।

साधारणो धर्मः उपमेयवाक्ये उपमानवाक्ये च कथितपदस्य दुष्टतयाभिहितत्वात् शब्दभेदेन यत् उपादीयते सा वस्तुनो वाक्यार्थस्योपमानत्वात् प्रतिवस्तूपमा । यथा

देवीभावं गमिता परिवारपदं कथं भजत्वेषा ।
न खलु परिभोगयोग्यं दैवतरूपाङ्कितं रत्नम् ॥४५३॥

Example—

'Mālatī's heart was occupied by the arrow of the Love-god; and it was only after that that you, O loved of women, coming within the range of her vision (occupied it).'

[The idea here expressed is that 'so powerful was the effect produced by her seeing you that she fell in love *before* she actually saw you.']

VIII—*Prativastūpamā*—Typical Comparison.

Typical Comparison is that where a single common property stands twice, in two sentences.

When the common property is mentioned, both in the sentence speaking of the 'object compared' and that speaking of the 'object compared to',—but in separate words,—since the repetition of the same words has been described as a defect,—is called, Typical Comparison, '*Prativastūpamā*', so called because the position of the 'object compared to' (*upamāna*) is occupied by what is expressed by a sentence (*vastu*).

Example.—

'Having once occupied the position of the Queen, how can she revert to the position of an attendant? Verily, a

यदि दहत्यनलोत्र किमद्भुतं यदि च गौरवमद्रिषु किं ततः ।
लवणमम्बु सदैव महोदधेः प्रकृतिरेव सतामविषादिता॥४५४॥

इत्यादिका मालाप्रतिवस्तूपमा द्रष्टव्या । एवमन्यत्राप्यनुसर्तव्यम् ॥

दृष्टान्तः पुनरेतेषां सर्वेषां प्रतिबिम्बनम् ॥ १०२ ॥

एतेषां साधारणधर्मादीनां दृष्टोन्तो निश्चयो यत्र स दृष्टान्तः ।

त्वयि दृष्ट एव तस्या निर्वाति मनो मनोभवज्वलितम् ।
आलोके हि हिमांशोर्विकसति कुसुमं कुमुद्वत्याः ॥४५५॥

एष साधर्म्येण ।

---

jewel marked with the figure of a god does not deserve to be worn.'

[The common property, 'impropriety', is mentioned in both halves of the verse, but in different words.]

In the following verse we have the 'Stringed Typical

'What is the wonder, if fire burns etc.'

(See above, stanza No. 272).

Similarly may other forms be illustrated.

XIV.—*Dṛṣṭānta*—Exemplification.

Exemplification is the reflectional representation of all these.

The '*Dṛṣṭānta*' is so called because therein is *perceived* ('*dṛṣṭa*') the 'definite recognition' ('*anta*') of 'all these'—*i.e.*, of the Common Property (the *object compared* and the *object compared to*).

Example.—

'As soon as you are seen, her heart, inflamed with love, becomes calmed; it is only in the light of the moon that the flower of the Lily-plant blooms.'

Here we have *Exemplification per similarity.*

[(*a*) The king, (*b*) the girl, (*c*) the heart, (*d*) the inflammation of love and (*e*) the becoming calm, being *reflected* respectively in, (*a*) the moon, (*b*) the lily plant, (*c*) the flower, (*d*) the withering caused by the sun's rays, and (*e*) the blooming].

वैधर्म्येण तु

तवाहवे साहसकर्मशर्मणः करं कृपाणान्तिकमानिनीषतः ।
भटाः परेषां विशरारुतामगुः दधत्यवाते स्थिरतां हि पांसवः ।।४५६।।

१००-२.

सकृद्वृत्तिस्तु धर्मस्य प्रकृताप्रकृतात्मनाम् ।
सैव क्रियासु बह्वीषु कारकस्येति दीपकम् ।। १०३ ।।

प्राकरणिकाप्राकरणिकानाम् अर्थात् उपमानोपमेयानां धर्मः क्रियादिः एकवारमेव यत् उपादीयते तत् एकस्थस्यैव समस्तवाक्यदीपनाद् दीपकम् । यथा

Exemplification *per dissimilarity* we find in the following.—

'When you, who delight in valorous deeds in battle, extended your hand towards the sword, your enemies became shattered ; it is only in the absence of the wind that dusts lie undisturbed.' 100–102.

XV—*Dīpaka*—Illuminator.

> —(*a*) *When the (common) property belonging to several objects—that to be described, as well as those not to be described,—occurs once,—and* (*b*) *when a single substantive occurs in connection with several verbs,—it is the Illuminator.* 103.

(*a*) When a 'common property',—in the shape of an *action* and so forth,—belonging to 'several objects, that to be described, as well as those not to be described',—*i.e.*, the *object compared* and the *objects compared to*,—is mentioned only once, it is Illuminator, '*Dīpaka*'; so-called because the term expressing the property, though occurring only once, 'illumines' the entire sentence.

किवणाणँ धणं णागाणं फणमणी केशराइँ सीह्वाणं ।
कुलबालिआणँ त्थणआ कुत्तो छिप्पन्ति अमुआणं ॥४५७॥

कारकस्य च बह्वीषु क्रियासु सकृद्वृत्तिर्दीपकम् । यथा

स्विद्यपि कूणति वेल्लति विचलति निमिषति विलोकयति तिर्यक् ।
अन्तर्नन्दति चुम्बितुमिच्छति नवपरिणया वधूः शयने॥४५८॥१०३

मालादीपकमाद्यं चेद्यथोत्तरगुणावहम् ।

पूर्वेण पूर्वेण वस्तुना उत्तरमुत्तरं चेदुपक्रियते तत् मालादीपकम् । यथा

संग्रामाङ्गणमागतेन भवता चापे समारोपिते
देवाकर्णय येन येन सहसा यद्यत्समासादितम् ।
कोदण्डेन शराः शरैररिशिरस्तनापि भूमण्डलं
तेन त्वं भवता च कीर्तिरतुला कीर्त्या च लोकत्रयम् ॥४५९॥

Example :—

'The wealth of misers, the head-jewel of serpents, the mane of lions, and the breasts of girls belonging to noble families,—how can these be touched until they are dead ?'

(*b*) It is *Illuminator* also when a single substantive occurs in connection with several verbs.—

Example :—

'The newly-wedded wife, when brought to the bed, perspires, shrinks, turns, moves away, closes her eyes, casts side-long glances, rejoices within herself, and longs to bestow a kiss. 103.

It is the Stringed Illuminator where what precedes imparts excellence to what follows.

If what follows is helped by what precedes it,—then we have the Stringed Illuminator.

Example.—

'*Saṅgrāmāṅgaṇamāgatena' etc.*' (See above stanza No. 229.)

नियतानां सकृद्धर्मः सा पुनस्तुल्ययोगिता ॥ १०४ ॥

नियतानां प्राकरणिकानामेव अप्राकरणिकानामेव वा । क्रमेणोदाहरणम्—

पाण्डु क्षामं वदनं हृदयं सरसं तवालसं च वपुः ।
आवेदयति नितान्तं क्षेत्रियरोगं सखि हृदन्तः ॥४६०॥

कुमुदकमलनीलनीरजालिर्ललितविलासजुषोर्दृशोः पुरः का ।
अमृतममृतरश्मिरम्बुजन्म प्रतिहतमेकपदे तवाननस्य ॥४६१॥१०४

उपमानाद्यदन्यस्य व्यतिरेकः स एव सः ।

अन्यस्योपमेयस्य व्यतिरेक आधिक्यम् ।

XVI—*Tulyayogitā.*—Equal Pairing.

The single mention of a property as belonging to a number of things of the same kind constitutes Equal Pairing 104.

'*Things of the same kind*'—(*a*) all being such as are *meant to be described,* (*i.e.* objects compared) or (*b*) all being such as are *not meant to be described* (*i. e.,* objects compared to). Examples in order.—

(*a*) '*Pāṇḍu kṣāmaṁ vadanaṁ etc.,*' (see above, stanza No. 332.)

[Here the property, *being indicative of the disease,* is common to several things, every one of which is meant to be described.]

(*b*) 'In the presence of your eyes, lovely and elegant, what is the line of white, red and blue lotuses ?—And the Nectar, the Moon and the Lotus have been subdued, at a single stroke, by your face'.

[Here the properties are described as belonging to two sets of things. Both of those to which the eyes and the *face* are compared.] 104.

XVII—*Vyatireka*—Dissimilitude.

The dissimilitude of the other to the 'object compared to' constitutes the figure of the same name.

'*Of the other*'—*i.e.,* of the object compared.

'*Dissimilitude*'—Superiority.

क्षीणः क्षीणोपि शशी भूयो भूयोभिवर्धते सत्यम् ।
विरम प्रसीद सुन्दरि यौवनमनिवर्ति यातं तु ॥४६२॥

इत्यादावुपमानस्योपमेयादाधिक्यमिति केनचिदुक्तम् तदयुक्तम् । अत्र यौवनगतास्थैर्याधिक्यं हि विवक्षितम् ॥

हेत्वोरुक्तावनुक्तीनां त्रये साम्ये निवेदिते ॥ १०५ ॥
शब्दार्थाभ्यामथाक्षिप्ते श्लिष्टे तद्वत्त्रिरष्ट तत् ।

व्यतिरेकस्य हेतुः उपमेयगतमुत्कर्षनिमित्तम् । उपमानगतमपकर्षकारणम् । तयोर्द्वयोरुक्तिः, एकतरस्य द्वयोर्वा अनुक्तिरित्यनुक्तित्रयम् । एतद्भेदचतुष्टयमुपमानोपमेयभावे शब्देन

[*Example*]—

'The Moon, though reduced again and again, really rises also again and again; but youth, O beautiful one, once gone, never returns; so cease and be propitiated'.

Here the 'superiority', belonging to 'youth' (which is the object compared), lies in its *ephemeral character* (in which point it is superior to the Moon, the object compared to). So that the assertion of some people that "this verse depicts the 'superiority" of the *object compared to* (the Moon) over the *object compared* (youth)", is not right.

It is of twenty-four kinds :—(1) *When the ground* (*of dissimilitude*) *is mentioned* ; (2-4) *the three cases where the said ground is not mentioned* ;—*each of these* (*four*) *has the similitude either expressed by word or expressed by meaning, or implied* ;—*and each of these* (*twelve*) *again occurs in a paronomatic word also.*

The ground of dissimilitude—*i.e.*, the ground of the superiority of the *object compared* and the ground of the inferiority of the *object compared to*—when both these are mentioned [it is one kind of Dissimilitude] ;—where one or the other of these, or both, are *not mentioned* [we

प्रतिपादिते आर्थेन च क्रमेणोक्ताश्चत्वार एव भेदाः। आक्षिप्ते चौपम्ये तावन्त एव। एवं द्वादश ॥ एते श्लेषेपि भवन्तीति चतुर्विंशतिर्भेदाः। क्रमेणोदाहरणम्—

असिमात्रसहायस्य प्रभूतारिपराभवे।
अन्यतुच्छजनस्येव न स्मयोस्य महाधृतेः ॥४६३॥

अत्रैव तुच्छेति महाधृतेरित्यनयोः पर्यायेण युगपद्वानपादानेन्यत् भेदत्रयम्। एवमन्येष्वपि द्रष्टव्यम्। अत्र इवशब्दस्य सद्भावाच्छाब्दमौपम्यम्।

असिमात्रसहायोपि प्रभूतारिपराभवे।
नैवान्यतुच्छजनवत्सगर्वोयं महाधृतिः ॥४६४॥

---

have the three other kinds of Dissimilitude];—we have those four kinds, when the comparison is expressed by words; another four kinds, when each of the said four has the comparison expressed by meaning ;—and yet another four kinds when each of them has the comparison only implied ;—thus there are twelve varieties (of this figure).—Each of these occurs also in paronomatic expressions (expressions with double meanings),—and thus we get the twenty-four varieties of *Dissimilitude*.

Examples in order—(1-4) 'To this person, possessed of great dignity, pride did not come,—as it does to other inferior persons, —when he suppressed his enemies with the help of his sword only.'

The person described being 'possessed of great dignity', and the other persons being 'inferior', are the grounds of Dissimilitude ;—and when either one of these is not mentioned, and when both of them are not mentioned, we have the other three varieties.—In this case, as the sentence contains the word '*iva*', the comparison is 'directly expressed by words'.

अत्र तुल्यार्थे वतिरित्यार्थमौपम्यम् ।

इयं सुनयना दासीकृततामरसश्रिया ।
आननेनाकलङ्केन जयतीन्दुं कलङ्किनम् ॥४६५॥

अत्रेवादितुल्यादिपदविरहेण आक्षिप्तैवोपमा ।

जितेन्द्रियतया सम्यग्विद्यावृद्धनिषेविणः ।
अतिगाढगुणस्यास्य नाब्जवद्भङ्गुरा गुणाः ॥४६६॥

अत्रेवार्थे वतिः । गुणशब्दः श्लिष्टः । शाब्दमौपम्यम् ॥

---

(5) 'This person, possessed of great dignity, did not become proud,—*anyatuchchhajanavat*, like other inferior persons,—when suppressed his enemies with the help of his sword only.'

Here the comparison is 'expressed by the meaning', as it is expressed by the affix '*vati*', which denotes similarity.

(6) 'This beautiful-eyed woman subdues the spotted moon with her spotless face, which has subjugated the loveliness of the lotus'.

In the absence of any such term as '*iva*', '*tulya*' and the like (which could express it), the comparison here is only 'implied'.

(7) *Jitendriyatayā samyagvidyāvṛddhaniṣeviṇaḥ*
Atigāḍhaguṇasyāsya nābjavad bhaṅgurā guṇāḥ.

'This man, possessed of unfathomable excellences and devoted to persons of sound learning, having subjugated his senses,—his *guṇas* (qualities) are not ephemeral like the *guṇas* (threads) of the lotus.'

Here the affix '*vati*' is synonymous with '*iva*' and the term '*guṇa*' contains a Pun.

अखण्डमण्डल: श्रीमान् पश्यैष पृथिवीपतिः ।
न निशाकरवज्जातु कलावैकल्यमागतः ॥४६७॥

अत्र तुल्यार्थे वतिः । कलाशब्दः श्लिष्टः ।

मालाप्रतिवस्तूपमावत् मालाव्यतिरेकोपि संभवति । तस्यापि भेदा एवमूह्याः । दिङ्मात्रमुदाह्रियते । यथा

हरवन्न विषमदृष्टिर्हरिवन्न विभो विधूतविततवृषः ।
रविवन्न चातिदुःसहकरतापितभूः कदाचिदसि ॥४६८॥

अत्र तुल्यार्थे वतिः । विषमादयश्च शब्दाः श्लिष्टाः ।

---

(8) '*Akhaṇḍamaṇḍalaḥ shrīmān pashyaiṣa pṛthivīpatiḥ*
Na nishākaravajjātu kalāvaikalyamāgataḥ'.

'Lo, this blessed Lord of the Earth, *with an unbroken stretch of empire*, has never been deprived of his *splendour*, as the *full* Moon is of its *digits*.'

Here the affix '*vati*' is used in the sense of '*iva*', and there is a pun upon the term '*kalā*.'

Just as we have the 'Stringed Typical Comparison', so it is possible to have the 'Stringed Dissimilitude' also ; of which also we may deduce the number of varieties (as in the case of simple Dissimilitude). Of these we are exemplifying only a few.

'*Haravanna viṣamadṛṣṭiḥ harivanna vibho vidhūtavitatavṛṣaḥ*
Ravivanna chātiduḥsahakaratāpitabhūḥ kadāchidasi'.

'You, O Lord, are never *viṣamadṛṣṭi*, partial,—as Hara is *viṣamadṛṣti*, possessed of *three eyes* ; you are never *vidhūtavitatavṛṣa*, one who has shaken off the all-important Dharma,—as Hari is *vidhūtavitatavṛṣa*, one who has destroyed the huge demon Vṛṣāsura ; you are never *atiduḥsahakaratāpitabhūḥ*, one who has oppressed the world with very unbearable taxes,—as the Sun is *atiduḥsaha-*

नित्योदितप्रतापेन त्रियामामीलितप्रभः ।
भास्वतानेन भूपेन भास्वानेष विनिर्जितः ॥४६९॥

अत्र ह्याक्षिप्तैवोपमा भास्वतेतिश्लिष्टः । यथा वा

स्वच्छात्मतागुणसमुल्लसितेन्दुबिम्बं
बिम्बप्रभाधरमकृत्रिमहृद्यगन्धम् ।
यूनामतीव पिबतां रजनीषु यत्र
तृष्णां जहार मधु नाननमङ्गनानाम् ॥४७०॥

---

karatāpitabhūḥ, one who has heated the Earth with his extremely unbearable rays'.

Here the affix '*vati*' is throughout used in the sense of '*iva*' and there are Puns upon the terms '*viṣama*' and the rest.

'*Nityoditapratāpena triyāmāmīlitaprabhaḥ*
Bhāsvatānena bhūpena bhāsvāneṣa vinirjitaḥ'.

'The *Bhāsvān*, Sun, who has his glory suppressed at night, has been subdued by the *bhāsvān*, resplendent, King whose glory is ever manifest'.

Here the comparison is 'implied', and there is Pun upon the term '*bhāsvān*'.

Another example of the same kind—

'*Svachchhātmatāguṇasamullasitendubimbaṁ*
Bimbaprabhādharamakṛtrimahṛdyagandham
Yūnāmatīva pibatāṁ rajanīṣu yatra
Tṛṣṇāṁ jahāra madhu nānanamaṅganānām'.

'During the nocturnal drinking bouts, though the wine allayed the desire of the young men for *drinking*, yet women's faces did not allay their desire for *kissing*;— the wine (*a*) *reflecting the bright disc of the Moon*, (*b*) *bearing the likeness of the red Bimba fruit*, and (*c*) *possessed of natural*

अत्रेवादीनां तुल्यादीनां च पदानामभावेपि श्लिष्टविशेषणैराक्षिप्तैवोपमा प्रतीयते । एवंजातीयकाः श्लिष्टोक्तियोग्यस्य पदस्य पृथगुपादानेन्येपि भेदाः संभवन्ति । तेपि अनयैव दिशा द्रष्टव्याः ॥

निषेधो वक्तुमिष्टस्य यो विशेषाभिधित्सया ॥ १०६ ॥
वक्ष्यमाणोक्तविषयः स आक्षेपो द्विधा मतः ।

विवक्षितस्य प्राकरणिकत्वादनुपसर्जनीकार्यस्य अशक्यवक्तव्यत्वमतिप्रसिद्धत्वं वा विशेषं वक्तुं निषेधो निषेध इव यः स वक्ष्यमाणविषय उक्तविषयश्चेति द्विधा आक्षेपः ।

---

fragrance; and the face, (*a*) *resembling the shining Moon*, (*b*) *with lips resembling the Bimba fruit*, and (*c*) *with natural fragrance*.'

In the absence of any such terms as '*iva*' '*tulya*' and the like, the comparison is found to be 'implied' by the epithets with double meanings.

In this manner, other varieties are also possible, even in the absence of any separate mention of words capable of being used with double meanings. These also may be illustrated in the same manner as above.

XVIII.—*Ākṣepa*—Hint.

When something desired to be said is, as if, suppressed, for the purpose of conveying a special idea, it is Hint; *and it is of two kinds, as having its subject, either* (*a*) *about to be mentioned, or* (*b*) *already mentioned.*

When something is desired to be said, and is such that cannot be entirely ignored,—and the speaker, anxious to convey (or emphasise) the idea, either (*a*) of its being something, that cannot be spoken of, or (*b*) of its being something too well known (to be spoken of),—

क्रमेणोदाहरणम्—

ए एहि किंपि कीएवि कएण णिक्किव भणामि अलमह वा ।
अविआरिअकज्जारम्भआरिणी मरउ ण भणिस्सं ॥४७१॥

ज्योत्स्ना मौक्तिकदाम चन्दनरसः शीतांशुकान्तद्रवः
कर्पूरं कदली मृणालवलयान्यम्भोजिनीपल्लवाः ।
अन्तर्मानसमास्त्वया प्रभवता तस्याः स्फुलिङ्गोत्कर-
व्यापाराय भवन्ति हन्त किमनेनोक्तेन न ब्रूमहे ॥४७२॥

---

suppresses it,—*i.e.,* he makes what appears to be a suppression of it ; and this suppression may be such as has its subject either (*a*) about to be mentioned, or (*b*) already mentioned ;—and these are two kinds of the figure *Hint*.

Exampls in order :—

(*a*) 'O ! come, I shall tell you, O cruel one ! something about a certain person ;—or no ; I shall not say it ;—when she has taken an inconsiderate step, let her die !'

[What is 'desired to be said' here is the extreme pang of separation being borne by the girl ; and in order to convey the idea that it is something indescribable, the speaker suppresses it ; and the subject is not mentioned, it is only *about to be mentioned*.]

(*b*) 'Moon-light, pearl-necklace, sandal-juice, the fluid flowing from the lunar gem, camphor, plantain-roots, bracelets of lotus-stalks and lotus-leaves—all these act like sparks of fire upon her, on account—Ah !—of yourself, who have taken possession of her heart ;—Woe to me !—what is the use of saying it ?—I shall not say it.'

[Here what is desired to be described is the love-pang of the girl under separation ; and in order to convey the idea of its being too well-known, the speaker suppresses it,—but only *after* the subject has been *already mentioned*.]

क्रियायाः प्रतिषेधेपि फलव्यक्तिर्विभावना ॥ १०७ ॥

हेतुरूपक्रियायाः निषेधेपि तत्फलप्रकाशनं विभावना । यथा

कुसुमितलताभिरहताप्यधत्त रुजमलिकुलैरदष्टापि ।
परिवर्तते स्म नलिनीलहरीभिरलोलिताप्यघूर्णत सा ॥४७३॥

१०–१०७

विशेषोक्तिरखण्डेषु कारणेषु फलावचः ।

मिलितेष्वपि कारणेषु कार्यस्याकथनं विशेषोक्तिः । अनुक्तनिमित्ता उक्तनिमित्ता अचिन्त्यनिमित्ता च ।

IX.—*Vibhāvanā*—Peculiar Causation.

Peculiar Causation consists in the mention of the effect, even though there is denial of the cause. 106–107.

When, even though the cause, in the shape of a particular action, is denied, the appearance of the effect of that cause is described, it is *Peculiar Causation.*

Example.—

'Even though unstruck by the blossoming creeper she felt pain ; even though not stung by the black bees, she turned aside ; even though not shaken by the lotus-leaves, she swerved round [all this by reason of her love-pangs.]' 10–107.

XX.—*Vishesokti*—Peculiar Allegation.

Peculiar Allegation consists in the omission to affirm the effects, even when its causes are present in full force.

When, even in the combined presence of all its causes, the effect is not affirmed, it is *Peculiar Allegation.* It is of three kinds—(*a*) having the reason (of the non-appearance of the effect) not mentioned, (*n*) having the reason mentioned and (*c*) having the reason such as is inconceivable.

क्रमेणोदाहरणम्—

निद्रानिवृत्तावुदिते द्युरत्ने सखीजने द्वारपदं पराप्ते ।
श्लथीकृताश्लेषरसे भुजङ्गे चचाल नालिङ्गनतोऽङ्गना सा ॥४७४॥

कर्पूर इव दग्धोपि शक्तिमान् यो जने जने ।
नमोस्त्ववार्यवीर्याय तस्मै मकरकेतवे ॥४७५॥

स एकस्त्रीणि जयति जगन्ति कुसुमायुधः ।
हरतापि तनुं यस्य शम्भुना न बलं हृतम् ॥४७६॥

यथासंख्यं क्रमेणैव क्रमिकाणां समन्वयः ॥ १०८ ॥

Examples in order—

(*a*) 'Though sleep had ceased, the Sun had risen, the friends had come to the door, and the lover had slackened the impetuosity of his embrace,—yet the woman did not move away from the embrace.'

[Here the reason for the non-appearance of the effect, which consists in the depth of the woman's feelings, is not mentioned.]

(*b*) 'All obeisance to the Love-god of impressible prowess, who, though consumed like camphor, is yet puissant over every individual!'

[Here we have the reason mentioned, in the shape of the 'irrepressible prowess' of the god.]

(*c*) 'Glorious is the Love-god, who single-handed conquers the three worlds, and whose power was not wrested by Shiva, when he deprived him of his body.'

[The destruction of the body would be sure to bring about the destruction of the power; and the reason, why Shiva did not do the latter when he did the former, is one that we cannot conceive of.]

XXI—*Yathāsaṅkhya*—Symmetrical.

The Symmetrical consists in the orderly connection among things mentioned in a definite order. 108.

यथा

एकस्त्रिधा वससि चेतसि चित्रमत्र
देव द्विषां च विदुषां च मृगीदृशां च ।
तापं च संमदरसं च रतिं च पुष्णन्
शौर्योष्मणा च विनयेन च लीलया च ॥४७७॥ १०८॥

सामान्यं वा विशेषो वा तदन्येन समर्थ्यते ।
यत्तु सोऽर्थान्तरन्यासः साधर्म्येणेतरेण वा ॥ १०९ ॥

साधर्म्येण वैधर्म्येण वा सामान्यं विशेषेण यत् समर्थ्यते विशेषो वा सामान्येन सोऽर्थान्तरन्यासः। क्रमेणोदाहरणम्—

निजदोषावृतमनसामतिसुन्दरमेव भाति विपरीतम् ।
पश्यति पित्तोपहतः शशिशुभ्रं शङ्खमपि पीतम् ॥४७८॥

Example—

'O Lord, how wonderful is it that, though single, you live in three ways—in the hearts (*a*) of enemies, (*b*) of learned men and (*c*) of fawn-eyed women,—producing in them, (*a*) pain, (*b*) joyous feelings and (*c*) love, through (*a*) the force of your valour, (*b*) your humility and (*c*) your amorous sportings.' 108.

XXII—*Arthāntaranyāsa*—Transition.

Where either a Universal or a Particular is supported by its converse,—either through similitude or otherwise,—it is Transition. 109.

When, either through similitude, or dissimilitude,—a Universal is supported by a Particular, or a Particular is supported by a Universal,—it is *Transition.*

Examples in order—

(*a*) 'To persons whose minds are enveloped in their own defects, even the most beautiful thing appears to

सुसितवसनालंकारायां कदाचन कौमुदी-
महसि सुदृशि स्वैरं यान्त्यां गतोस्तमभूद्विधुः ।
तदनु भवतः कीर्तिः केनाप्यगीयत येन सा
प्रियगृहमगान्मुक्ताशङ्का क्व नासि शुभप्रदः ॥४७९॥
गुणानामेव दौरात्म्याद् धुरि धुर्यो नियुज्यते ।
असंजातकिणस्कन्धः सुखं स्वपिति गौर्गलिः ॥४८०॥
अहो हि मे बह्वपराद्धमायुषा यदप्रियं वाच्यमिदं मयेदृशम् ।
त एव धन्याः सुहृदः पराभवं जगत्यदृष्ट्वैव हि ये क्षयं गताः ॥४८१॥
१०९॥

बिरोधः सोविरोधेपि विरुद्धत्वेन यद्वचः ।

---

be the reverse : a person suffering from bile sees the snow-white conch also as yellow.'

[Here a *universal* statement is supported by a *particular* case through *similarity*.]

(*b*) '*Susitavasanālankārāyām*' etc. etc.,' (see above stanza No. 266.)

[Here a *particular* statement is supported through *similarity* by a *Universal* one.]

(*c*) 'It is on account of the evil nature of good qualities that the capable person is employed in a difficult task ; the worthless bull whose shoulder is not hardened by work sleeps comfortably.'

[Here a *universal* case is supported by a *particular* one, but through *similarity*.]

(*d*) 'Oh, much harm has been done by my life that I have had to say such a disagreeable thing ! Blessed are those that have died without witnessing the calamity of their friends.'

[Here the *particular* is supported by the *universal*, through dissimilarity.] 109.

XXIII—*Virodha*—Contradiction

When something is spoken of as contradictory, even when there is no contradiction,—it is the Figure Contradiction.

वस्तुवृत्तेनाविरोधेपि विरुद्धयोरिव यदभिधानं स विरोधः ।

जातिश्चतुर्भिर्जात्याद्यैर्विरुद्धा स्याद्गुणस्त्रिभिः ॥ ११० ॥
क्रिया द्वाभ्यामपि द्रव्यं द्रव्येणैवेति ते दश ।

क्रमेणोदाहरणम्—

अभिनवनलिनीकिसलयमृणालवलयादि दवदहनराशिः ।
सुभग कुरङ्गदृशोस्या विधिवशतस्त्वद्वियोगपविपाते ॥४८२॥

गिरयोप्यनुन्नतियुजो मरुदप्यचलोब्धयोप्यगम्भीराः ।
विश्वंभराप्यतिलघुर्नरनाथ तवान्तिके नियतम् ॥४८३॥

येषां कण्ठपरिग्रहप्रणयितां संप्राप्य धाराधरस्
तीक्ष्णः सोप्यनुरज्यते च कमपि स्नेहं पराप्नोति च ।

When, as a matter of fact, there is no real contradiction between two things,—and they are spoken of as if they were contradictory,—it is the Figure *Contradiction.*

(1—4) *The Universal contradicted by the four*, (1) *Universal* [(2) *Quality,* (3) *Action and* (4) *Substance*], —(5—7) *the Quality contradicted by three* [*i.e. Quality, Action and Substance*], —(8—9) *Action contradicted by two* [*i. e. Action and Substance*] —*and* (10) *Substance contradicted by Substance ;— thus this Figure is of ten kinds.*

Examples in order—(1) [Community contradicted by Community.]

'O handsome one ! at the sudden thunderfall of your separation, fresh lotus leaves, bracelets of lotus—stalk and such other things appear to the fawn-eyed one, like heaps of flaming fuel.'

(2) [Community contradicted by Quality]—

'O King ! in your presence Mountains become devoid of height, Winds become motionless, the Ocean, devoid of depth, and the Earth, extremely light.'

तेषां संगरसङ्गसक्तमनसां राज्ञां त्वया भूपते
पांसूनां पटलैः प्रसाधनविधिर्निर्वर्त्यते कौतुकम् ।।४८४।।
सृजति च जगदिदमवति च संहरति च हेलयैव यो नियतम् ।
अवसरवशतः शफरो जनार्दनः सोपि चित्रमिदम् ।।४८५।।
सततं मुसलासक्ता बहुतरगृहकर्मघटनया नृपते ।
द्विजपत्नीनां कठिनाः सति भवति कराः सरोजसुकुमाराः ।।४८६।।
पेशलमपि खलवचनं दहतितरां मानसं सत्तत्त्वविदाम् ।
परुषमपि सुजनवाक्यं मलयजरसवत् प्रमोदयति ।।४८७।।

---

(3) [Community contradicted by Action]—

'How wonderful it is that you perform, with the dust (of the battlefield) the toilet of your enemies, whose heart is in the battle, and by obtaining the hold of whose necks your sharp sword became reddened (impassioned) and acquired smoothness (affection).'

(4) [Community contradicted by Substance]—

'It is strange that Viṣṇu, who creates, protects and destroys the universe with ease, becomes, when occasion presents itself, a small fish.'

(5) [Quality contradicted by Quality]—

'The hands of Brāhmaṇa-women, which had become hardened by the handling of the wooden mallet, in the course of household duties, have, during your reign, become soft like the lotus.'

(6) [Quality contradicted by Action]—

'The words of the wicked, even though soft, burn the hearts of wise men; and the words of gentlemen, even though harsh, are a source of joy, like the sandal-juice.'

क्रौञ्चाद्रिरुद्दामदृषद्दृढोसौ यन्मार्गणानर्गलशातपाते ।
अभून्नवाम्भोजदलाभिजातः स भार्गवः सत्यमपूर्वसर्गः ॥४८८॥

परिच्छेदातीतः सकलवचनानामविषयः
पुनर्जन्मन्यस्मिन्ननुभवपथं यो न गतवान् ।
विवेकप्रध्वंसादुपचितमहामोहगहनो
विकारः कोप्यन्तर्जडयति च तापं च कुरुते ॥४८९॥

अयं वारामेको निलय इत रत्नाकर इति
श्रितोस्माभिस्तृष्णातरलितमनोभिर्जलनिधिः ।
क एवं जानीते निजकरपुटीकोटरगतं
क्षणादेनं ताम्यत्तिमिमकरमापास्यति मुनिः ॥४९०॥

समदमतङ्गजमदजलनिस्यन्द-
तरङ्गिणीपरिष्वङ्गात् ।

---

(7) [Quality contradicted by Substance]—

'Verily, Parashurāma was a wonderful object of creation, under the uninterrupted shower of whose arrows, the Krauñcha mountain, though hard as stone, became soft like the fresh lotus.'

(8) [Action contradicted by Action]—

'*Parichchhedātītaḥ* etc., etc., (See above stanza No. 107.)

(9) [Action contradicted by Substance]—

'With our hearts restless through desire (for water and riches), we approached the Ocean, thinking it to be the one reservoir of water and also the storehouse of gems ;—but who could know that the Sage (Agastya) would hold the Ocean, with the fish and alligators fluttering in it, in his hands and quaff it off in a moment ?'

(10) [Substance contradicted by Substance]—

'O Ornament of the Earth ! when you stand on the bank of the river Gaṅgā, she becomes the Yamunā, by

क्षितितिलक त्वयि तटजुषि
शंकरचूडापगापि कालिन्दी ॥४९१॥

स्वभावोक्तिस्तु डिम्भादेः स्वक्रियारूपवर्णनम् ॥ १११ ॥

स्वयोस्तदेकाश्रययोः। रूपं वर्णः संस्थानं च। उदाहरणम्—

पश्चादङ्घ्री प्रसार्य त्रिकनतिविततं द्राघयित्वाङ्गमुच्चैर्
आसज्याभुग्नकण्ठो मुखमुरसि सटां धूलिधूम्रां विधूय।
घासग्रासाभिलाषादनवरतचलत्प्रोथतुण्डस्तुरङ्गो
मन्दं शब्दायमानो विलिखति शयनादुत्थितः क्ष्मां खुरेण ॥४९२॥
॥११०-१११॥

व्याजस्तुतिर्मुखे निन्दा स्तुतिर्वा रूढिरन्यथा।

---

contact with the rivulet of the ichor of your intoxicated elephants.' 110-111.

XXIV—*Svabhāvokti*—Natural Description.

When, of the child and other things, their own action and form are described,—it is Natural Description. 110-111.

'*Their own*'—*i. e.*, (the Action and the form) as subsisting in themselves, '*Form*'—Colour and shape.

Example.—

'The horse, rising from sleep, extends his hind legs, stretches his body enlarged by the three dips on it back, brings his mouth to his chest, with his neck curved ; and flutters his dusted mane ; his lips quivering on account of his desire for grass ; and softly neighing, he is scratching the ground with his hoofs.' 110-111.

XXV.—*Vyājastuti*—Dissembling Eulogy.

When, what, on the face of it, is praise or disparagement, turns out to be otherwise, it is Dissembling Eulogy.

The name 'Dissembling Eulogy', '*Vyājastuti*', is applied to this figure in the sense that it is a *eulogy* ('*stuti*') *in the form of, or through dissimulation* ('*vyāja*').

व्याजरूपा व्याजेन वा स्तुतिः । क्रमेणोदाहरणम्—

हित्वा त्वामुपरोधबन्ध्यमनसां मन्ये न मौलिः परो
लज्जावर्जनमन्तरेण न रमामन्यत्र संदृश्यते ।
यस्त्यागं तनुतेतरां मुखशतैरेत्याश्रितायाः श्रियः
प्राप्य त्यागकृतावमाननमपि त्वय्येव यस्याः स्थितिः ॥४९३॥

हे हेलाजितबोधिसत्त्व वचसां किं विस्तरैस्तोयधे
नास्ति त्वत्सदृशः परः परहिताधाने गृहीतव्रतः ।
तृष्यत्पान्थजनोपकारघटनावैमुख्यलब्धायशो-
भारप्रोद्वहने करोषि कृपया साहायकं यन्मरोः ॥४९४॥

सा सहोक्तिः सहार्थस्य बलादेकं द्विवाचकम् ॥ ११२ ॥

Examples in order—(*a*) [Disparagement turned into Praise]—

'O King, excepting yourself, none else is the foremost among persons whose minds are devoid of all consideration for those dependent upon you ; and apart from Lakṣmī, the Goddess, of Wealth, nowhere is shamelessness to be found : you are giving away the Wealth-goddess who has come to you in hundreds of ways, and though thus she has received the ill-treatment of being given up, she continues to reside in yourself alone'.

(*b*) [Praise turning with Disparagement]—

'O Ocean, who has easily subdued the Bodhisattva ! What is the use of many words ! There is no one who, like you, has taken the vow of benefitting others ; inasmuch as you help the desert by sharing with him the burden of ill-fame arising from its disinclination to benefit thirsty travellers.'

XXVI—*Sahokti*—Connected Description.

Where one word is expressive of two things, through the

एकार्थाभिधायकमपि सहार्थबलात् यत् उभयस्याप्यवगमकं सा सहोक्तिः । यथा

सह दिअहणिसाहिँ दीहरा सासदण्डा
सह मणिवलयेहिँ बाहधारा गलन्ति ।
तुह सुहअ विओए तीअ उब्बिग्गिरीए
सह अ तणुलदाए दुब्बला जीविदासा ॥४९५॥

श्वासदण्डादिगतं दीर्घत्वादि शाब्दम् दिवसनिशादिगतं तु सहार्थसामर्थ्यात्प्रतिपद्यते ॥११२॥

विनोक्तिः सा विनान्येन यत्रान्यः सन्न नेतरः ।

---

force of some synonym of the word 'saha' (along with),—it is Connected Description. 112.

Where, a word, which really denotative of one thing, comes, through the force of some word denoting 'along with', to bring about the idea of both things,—it is Connected Description.

Example—

'O beautiful one, at her separation from you, her breaths become long drawn out, *along with* the nights and days ; her flow of tears continue to drop, *along with* the bracelets ; and the very hope of life becomes feeble, *along with* her slender body'.

Here the properties of (*a*) 'being long drawn out' [(*b*) 'dropping' and (*c*) 'becoming feeble'] as applying to (*a*) 'breaths', [(*b*) 'tears' and (*c*) 'hope of life'] are directly expressed by the words ; but to the (*a*) 'night and days', [(*b*) 'bracelects', and (*c*) 'slender body'], they are applicable only through the force of the term 'along with'. 112.

XXVII—*Vinokti*—Privative Description.

क्वचिदशोभनः क्वचिच्छोभनः । क्रमेणोदाहरणम्—
अरुचिर्निशया विना शशी शशिना सापि विना महत्तमः ।
उभयेन विना मनोभवस्फुरितं नैव चकास्ति कामिनोः ॥४९६॥
मृगलोचनया विना विचित्रव्यवहारप्रतिभाप्रभाप्रगल्भः ।
अमृतद्युतिसुन्दराशयोयं सुहृदा तेन विना नरेन्द्रसूनुः ॥४९७॥

परिवृत्तिर्विनिमयो योर्थानां स्यात्समासमैः ॥ ११३ ॥

परिवृत्तिरलंकारः । उदाहरणम्—

लतानामेतासामुदितकुसुमानां मरुदयं
मतं लास्यं दत्त्वा श्रयति भृशमामोदमसमम् ।

That is Privative Description in which one thing, without the other, is either (a) not beautiful or (b) the contrary.

In one kind, one thing, without the other, is *not beautiful*, and in the other, it is *beautiful*.

Examples in order—

(*a*) 'Without the Night, the Moon is not beautiful; without the Moon, the Night is only dense darkness; and without both these, the love-dealings of lovers do not shine.'

(*b*) 'In the absence of the fawn-eyed one, this Prince is expert in astonishing feats of quick intelligence; and in the absence of that friend, his heart is as beautiful as the moon'.

XXVIII—*Parivṛtti*—Exchange.

When there is an interchange between equal or unequal things—it is Exchange. 113.

'*Parivṛttiḥ*'—*i.e.,* the *figure* named 'Parivṛtti', Exchange.

Example—

(*a*) 'The wind imparts graceful movement to the blossoming creepers and receives their unrivalled fragrance;

लतास्त्वध्वन्यानामहह दृशमादाय सहसा
ददत्याधिव्याधिभ्रमिरुदितमोहव्यतिकरम् ।।४९८।।

अत्र प्रथमेर्धे समेन समस्य द्वितीये उत्तमेन न्यूनस्य।

नानाविधप्रहरणैर्नृप संप्रहारे
स्वीकृत्य दारुणनिनादवतः प्रहारान्।
दृप्तारिवीरविसरेण वसुंधरेयं
निर्विप्रलम्भपरिरम्भविधिर्वितीर्णा ।।४९९।।

अत्र न्यूनेनोत्तमस्य ।।११३।।

प्रत्यक्षा इव यद्भावाः क्रियन्ते भूतभाविनः ।
तद्भाविकम् ।।

भूताश्च भाविनश्चेति द्वन्द्वः। भावः कवेरभिप्रायोत्रास्तीति

(*b*) these creepers, on the other hand, draw to themselves the eyes of travellers, and give to them pain, physical and mental, as also perplexity and nervelessness.'

Here in the former half, we have an interchange between two equal things ; and in the latter an inferior thing is exchanged for a superior one.

(*c*) 'O King ! your haughty enemies, having accepted in battle the stroke of various kinds of weapons, have made over to you this Earth in such a manner that her relationship with you shall never cease.'

Here a superior thing is exchanged for an inferior one. 113.

XXIX—*Bhāvika*—Visualisation.

When past and future things are delineated as if they were before the eyes,—it is Visualisation.

'*Bhūtabhāvinaḥ*'—'past and future'—a copulative compound.

This figure is called '*Bhāvika*' in the sense that it

भाविकम् । उदाहरणम्—

आसीदञ्जनमत्रेति पश्यामि तव लोचने ।
भाविभूषणसंभारां साक्षात्कुर्वे तवाकृतिम् ॥५००॥

आद्ये भूतस्य द्वितीये भाविनो दर्शनम् ॥

काव्यलिङ्गं हेतोर्वाक्यपदार्थता ॥ ११४ ॥

वाक्यार्थता यथा

वपुःप्रादुर्भावादनुमितमिदं जन्मनि पुरा
पुरारे न प्रायः क्वचिदपि भवन्तं प्रणतवान् ।
नमन् मुक्तः संप्रत्यहमतनुरग्रेप्यनतिभाङ्
महेश क्षन्तव्यं तदिदमपराधद्वयमपि ॥५०१॥

---

represents the poet's intention (*bhāva*).

Example—

(*a*) 'I see that there was collyrium in your eyes ;—(*b*) and I perceive your body as going to be adorned with ornaments'.

In (*a*) there is 'visualisation' of the *past* (collyrium), and in (*b*) that of the *future* (ornamentation).

XXX—*Kāvyaliṅga*—Poetical Reason.

When a reason is expressed either (*a*) *by a sentence, or* (*b*) *by a word,—it is Poetical Reason.* 114.

(*a*) The Reason expressed by a sentence—

'From my bodily incarnation I infer, O Shiva, that in my previous birth, I never bowed down to You ; and bowing down to You now, and thereby becoming liberated, I shall not have a body and hence shall not bow down to You in the future ; both these faults of mine, please pardon, O Lord.'

अनेकपदार्थता यथा

प्रणयिसखी सलीलपरिहासरसाधिगतैर्
ललितशिरीषपुष्पहननैरपि ताम्यति यत् ।
वपुषि वधाय तत्र तव शस्त्रमुपक्षिपतः
पततु शिरस्यकाण्डयमदण्ड इवैष भुजः ॥५०२॥

एकपदार्थता यथा

भस्मोद्धूलन भद्रमस्तु भवते रुद्राक्षमाले शुभं
हा सोपानपरंपरां गिरिसुताकान्तालयालंकृतिम् ।
अद्याराधनतोषितेन विभुना युष्मत्सपर्यासुखा-
लोकोच्छेदिनि मोक्षनामनि महामोहे निधीयामहे ॥५०३॥

(*b*) Reason expressed by several words.—

'Her body is such as suffers pain even on being struck with soft *Sirīsha*-flowers by her loving friends in sportive jokes ; and it is against such a body that you have raised your weapon ; so fall on your head this arm of mine, resembling the missile of the Death-God.'

[This is an instance of the reason being expressed by *several words,*—not by a *sentence,*—because it is expressed by the words '*vapuṣi shastramupakṣipataḥ*', which, in the absence of a finite verb, cannot be regarded as a complete *sentence.*]

(*c*) Reason expressed by a single word:—

'Paintings with ashes, fare thee well ! Garland of rosary, may good befall you ! Oh, for the line of steps adorning the house of Pārvatī ! Today I am being admitted by the great God, who has been propitiated by me, into that dense darkness, which is called 'Liberation', which is going to deprive me of the light of the pleasure of waiting upon you !'

एषु अपराधद्वये पूर्वापरजन्मनोरनमनम् भुजपाते शस्त्रोपक्षेपः महामोहे सुखावलोकोच्छेदित्वं च यथाक्रममुक्तरूपो हेतुः ॥११४॥

पर्यायोक्तं विना वाच्यवाचकत्वेन यद्वचः ।

वाच्यवाचकभावव्यतिरिक्तेनावगमनव्यापारेण यत् प्रतिपादनं तत् पर्यायेण भङ्ग्यन्तरेण कथनात् पर्यायोक्तम् ।

उदाहरणम्—

यं प्रेक्ष्य चिररूढापि निवासप्रीतिरुज्झिता ।
मदेनैरावणमुखे मानेन हृदये हरेः ॥५०४॥

Here, in (*a*) the omission of obeisance during the preceding and coming births is the cause of the two *faults*:—in (*b*) the raising of the weapon is the reason for the falling of the arm ; and in (*c*) the depriving of the light of pleasure is the cause of the 'dense darkness'. 114.

XXXI.—*Paryāyokta*—Periphrasis.

Periphrasis consists in such description as is independent of the ordinary denotative relation between the expressive word and the expressed meaning.

When a certain fact is described by words, through the implicative (suggestive) function,—and not through the ordinary relation between the expressive word and the expressed meaning :—it is *Periphrasis*, '*Paryāyokta*' ;—so called because what is *said* ('*ukta*') is by other *means* (*paryāya*).

Example—

'Even though long-standing, the love of residence was renounced by intoxication and self-respect, in regard respectively to the face of Airāvaṇa and the heart of Indra.'

The particle '*api*', 'even though' serves to imply that 'Airāvaṇa's face and Indra's heart became bereft

अत्र ऐरावणशक्रौ मदमानमुक्तौ जाताविति व्यङ्ग्यमपि शब्देनोच्यते। तेन यदेवोच्यते तदेव व्यङ्ग्यम् । यथा तु व्यङ्ग्यं न तथोच्यते। यथा गवि शुक्ले चलति दृष्टे 'गौः शुक्लश्चलति' इति विकल्पः। यदेव दृष्टं तदेव विकल्पयति न तु यथा दृष्टं तथा। यतोभिन्नासंसृष्टत्वेन दृष्टम् भेदसंसर्गाभ्यां विकल्पयति ॥

उदात्तं वस्तुनः संपत् ॥

संपत् समृद्धियोगः । यथा

मुक्ताः केलिविसूत्रहारगलिताः संमार्जनीभिर्हृताः
प्रातः प्राङ्गणसीम्नि मन्थरचलद्बालाङ्घ्रिलाक्षारुणाः ।

---

of intoxication and self-respect'; and this idea so suggested is the same as is directly expressed by the words themselves [the expressed meaning also being that 'intoxication and self-respect renounced their love of residing in Airāvaṇa's face and in Indra's heart']. But the *manner* in which the implication is made is not the same in which the same idea is directly expressed.

We have an analogous instance in the case where upon seeing a *white* ox *walking*, one has the complex notion 'the white ox is walking'; and here what this cognition expresses is exactly what the man had previously perceived (in the abstract); but the *manner* of the later cognition is different from that of the preceding perception : the preceding perception (being in an indeterminate form) apprehended the object (*ox*) not as distinct from and related to (the other two factors, the quality of *whiteness*, and the action of *walking*), while the subsequent cognition does actually apprehend it as so distinct and related.

XXXII.—*Udātta*—Exalted.

The Exalted consists (a) in the Exaltation of the thing; '*Exaltation*'—being endowed with prosperity.

दूराद्दाडिमबीजशङ्कितधियः कर्षन्ति केलीशुकाः
यद्विद्वद्भवनेषु भोजनृपतेस्तत् त्यागलीलायितम् ॥५०५॥

महतां चोपलक्षणम् ॥ ११५ ॥

उपलक्षणमङ्गभावः अर्थादुपलक्षणीयेर्थे। उदाहरणम्—

तदिदमरण्यं यस्मिन् दशरथवचनानुपालनव्यसनी ।
निवसन् बाहुसहायश्चकार रक्षःक्षयं रामः ॥५०६॥

न चात्र वीरो रसः तस्येहाङ्गत्वात् ॥११५॥

**तत्सिद्धिहेतावेकस्मिन् यत्रान्यत्तत्करं भवेत् ।
समुच्चयोसौ ॥**

Example—

'The pearls dropping from necklaces snapped in dalliance, which have become reddened by the foot-prints of lascivious girls walking about in the court-yard, are dusted aside with broom-sticks : mistaking them for pomegranate-seeds, the sportive parrots pick up these pearls :—that all this happens in the houses of learned men is the effect, O King Bhoja, of your munificence.'

(*b*) *It consists also in the representation of great beings as adjuncts* (*to the thing exalted*). 115

'*Adjunct*'—being subordinate,—*i.e.*, to the thing described.

Example—

'This is that same forest residing wherein Rāma, bent upon obeying the words of Dasharatha, with the help of his arms, brought about the destruction of demons.'

[Here the fact of Rāma being an adjunct, a resident of the forest, serves to *exalt* the latter ; it is the forest, which is the predominating factor [and not the Heroic Sentiment ; as this latter is itself only a subordinate factor.]

तस्य प्रस्तुतस्य कार्यस्य एकस्मिन् साधके स्थिते साधकान्तराणि यत्र संभवन्ति स समुच्चयः। उदाहरणम्—

दुर्वाराः स्मरमार्गणाः प्रियतमो दूरे मनोत्युत्सुकं
गाढं प्रेम नवं वयोतिकठिनाः प्राणाः कुलं निर्मलम् ।
स्त्रीत्वं धैर्यविरोधि मन्मथसुहृत् कालः कृतान्तोक्षमो
नो सख्यश्चतुराः कथं नु विरहः सोढव्य इत्थं शठः ॥५०७॥

अत्र विरहासहत्वं स्मरमार्गणा एव कुर्वन्ति। तदुपरि प्रियतमदूरस्थित्यादि उपात्तम् ॥

एष एव समुच्चयः सद्योगेसद्योगे सदसद्योगे च पर्यवस्यतीति

XXXIII—*Samuchchaya*—Concatenation.

(*a*) *It is Concatenation, when, while one cause conducive to the effect in question being already present, another also turns out to be conducive to it.*

I. E., when one cause conducive to the effect to be described is already present, other causes are also mentioned,—it is *Concatenation.*

Example—

'Irrepressible are the arrows of the Love-god ; my beloved is at a distance ; my mind is extremely anxious ; our love is deep ; age young ; life-breath very hard ; family pure ; the feminine character is incompatible with firmness ; the season is helpful to the Love-god ; the God of Death is incapable (of putting an end to my life); my friends are not sufficiently clever ;—how then can this cruel pang of separation be borne ?'

'The arrows of the Love-god' are enough to make the pangs of separation unbearable ;and in addition to this are mentioned the other circumstances conducive to the same effect,—such as the *beloved being at a distance* and so forth.

न पृथक् लक्ष्यते । तथाहि—

कुलममलिनं भद्रा मूर्तिर्मतिः श्रुतिशालिनी
भुजबलमलं स्फीता लक्ष्मीः प्रभुत्वमखण्डितम् ।
प्रकृतिसुभगा ह्येते भावा अमीभिरयं जनो
व्रजति सुतरां दर्पं राजन् त एव तवाङ्कुशाः ॥५०८॥

अत्र सतां योगः । उक्तोदाहरणे त्वसतां योगः ।

शशी दिवसधूसरो गलितयौवना कामिनी
सरो विगतवारिजं मुखमनक्षरं स्वाकृतेः ।
प्रभुर्धनपरायणः सततदुर्गतः सज्जनो
नृपाङ्गणगतः खलो मनसि सप्त शल्यानि मे ॥५०९॥

It is this same figure of *Concatenation* which appears in the form of (*a*) 'the combination of good things', (*b*) 'the combination of bad things' and (*c*) 'the combination of good and bad' [which three have been described by Rudraṭa and others as distinct figures of speech]. That is why these are not described by us separately. For instance, in the example quoted above, we have 'the combination of bad things'; while we have 'the combination of good things' in the following verse :—

'The family is untainted, appearance gentle, mind full of learning, the strength of arm sufficient, wealth extensive, sovereignty unimpeded ; all these circumstances are naturally agreeable ; and it is only natural that, on account of these, this man becomes arrogant ; but to you, O King, these same only serve as means of restraint.'

In the following verse, there is 'combination of good and bad', inasmuch as the fact of the 'Moon' (*good*) being 'dim' (*bad*) already being a 'dart,' several other darts are mentioned (which also are combinations of the *good* and the *bad*)—

अत्र शशिनि धूसरे शल्ये शल्यान्तराणीति शोभनाशोभनयोगः ॥

स त्वन्यो युगपद् या गुणक्रियाः ॥ ११६ ॥

गुणौ च क्रिये च गुणक्रिये च गुणक्रियाः । क्रमेणोदाहरणम्—

विदलितसकलारिकुलं तव बलमिदमभवदाशु विमलं च ।
प्रखलमुखानि नराधिप मलिनानि च तानि जातानि ॥५१०॥

अयमेकपदे तया वियोगः प्रियया चोपनतः सुदुःसहो मे ।
नववारिधरोदयादहोभिर्भवितव्यं च निरातपत्वरम्यैः ॥५११॥

कलुषं च तवाहितेष्वकस्मात्सितपङ्केरुहसोदरश्रि चक्षुः ।
पतितं च महीपतीन्द्र तेषां वपुषि प्रस्फुटमापदां कटाक्षैः ॥५१२॥

'The Moon dim during the day,—the woman with faded youth,—the tank devoid of the lotus,—the illiterate mouth of a handsome person,—the master too much attached to wealth,—the good man always in trouble,—the wicked man at the King's Court,—these are the seven darts in my heart.'

(*b*) *It is another kind of the same figure* (*Concatenation*) *when qualities and actions are* (*described as*) *simultaneous.* 116.

The compound '*guṇakriyāḥ*' is explained as meaning (1) 'two qualities', (2) 'two actions' and (3) 'quality and action'.

Examples in order :—

(1) [Concatenation of two simultaneous *qualities*]—'O King, having shattered the forces of your enemy, your army quickly became bright, [and clean] and those faces of the wicked became faded.'

(2) [Concatenation of two simultaneous *actions*]—

'This unbearable separation from my beloved has come about suddenly ; and on account of the appearance of fresh clouds the days are going to be free from heat and lovely.'

'धुनोति चासिं तनुते च कीर्तिम्' इत्यादेः 'कृपाणपाणिश्च भवान् रणक्षितौ ससाधुवादाश्च सुराः सुरालये' इत्यादेश्च दर्शनात् 'व्यधिकरणे' इति 'एकस्मिन् देशे' इति च न वाच्यम् ॥११६॥

एकं क्रमेणानेकस्मिन् पर्यायः ॥

एकं वस्तु क्रमेणानेकस्मिन् भवति क्रियते वा स पर्यायः । क्रमेणोदाहरणम्——

नन्वाश्रयस्थितिरियं तव कालकूट
केनोत्तरोत्तरविशिष्टपदोपदिष्टा ।
प्रागर्णवस्य हृदये वृषलक्ष्मणोथ
कण्ठेधुना वससि वाचि पुनः खलानाम् ॥५१३॥

---

(3) [Concatenation of *a quality and an action*]—

'O Indra [among the Lords of the] Earth! your eyes, bearing the beauty of the white lotus, [suddenly] fallen upon your enemies, became reddened, and there clearly fell upon them the glances of misfortune.'

It would not be right to assert, either that the factors 'concatenating' should subsist in different things, or that they should subsist in the same thing; because we meet with such instances of 'concatenation' as—(*a*) 'he brandishes his sword and spreads his fame' [where the substratum of both *actions* is the same, the King];—(*b*) 'you wield the sword in the battle-field, and the gods are uttering words of praise in heaven' [where the substrata of the two actions are different]. 116.

XXXIV—*Paryāya*—Sequence.

When one thing occurs successively in more than one, it is Sequence.

When one thing (1) subsists or (2) is made to appear, in several things, it is *Sequence.*

यथा वा

बिम्बोष्ठ एव रागस्ते तन्वि पूर्वमदृश्यत ।
अधुना हृदयेप्येष मृगशावाक्षि लक्ष्यते ॥५१४॥

रागस्य वस्तुतो भेदेप्येकतयाध्यवसितत्वादेकत्वमविरुद्धम् ।

तं ताण सिरिसहोअररअणाहरणम्मि हिअअमेक्करसं ।
बिम्बाहरे पिआणं णिवेसिअं कुसुमबाणेण ॥५१५॥

अन्यस्ततोन्यथा ॥

अनेकमेकस्मिन् क्रमेण भवति क्रियते वा सोन्यः ॥

---

(1) [One thin existing in several]—

'O Poison ! by whom has been ordained this successively higher series of your residences ?—First of all in the heart of the ocean, then in the throat of Śhiva, and now in the words of wicked men !'

Another example of the same kind—

'Formerly this *rāga* (redness was seen in your bimba-like lips only ; but now O fawn-eyed one, the same (*rāga* attachment, love) is perceived in your heart also.'

Though here the '*rāga*' spoken of is not exactly the same in the two cases, yet (through the sameness of sound) the two are felt to be one and the same ; hence the citing of this as an example here is not wrong.

(2) [One thing made to appear in several]—

'The hearts of the demons, that were concentrated entirely on the Wearer of the Kaustubha-jewel (when he appeared as the *Enchantress*),, were turned by the Love-god towards the bimba-like lips of their wives.

(*b*) *When the process is inverted, it is another kind (of Sequence).*

When several things successively (1) subsist, or (2) are made to appear, in one thing,—it is another kind of *Sequence*.

क्रमेणोदाहरणम्–

मधुरिमरुचिरं वचः खलानाममृतमहो प्रथमं पृथु व्यनक्ति ।
अथ कथयति मोहहेतुमन्तर्गतमिव हालहलं विषं तदेव ॥५१६॥

तद्गेहं नतभित्ति मन्दिरमिदं लब्धावकाशं दिवः
सा धेनुर्जरती नदन्ति करिणामेता घनाभा घटाः ।
स क्षुद्रो मुसलध्वनिः कलमिदं संगीतकं योषिताम्
आश्चर्यं दिवसैर्द्विजोयमियतीं भूमिं समारोपितः ॥५१७॥

अत्र एकस्यैव हानोपादानयोरविवक्षितत्वात् न परिवृत्तिः ॥

अनुमानं तदुक्तं यत् साध्यसाधनयोर्वचः ॥ ११७ ॥

पक्षधर्मान्वयव्यतिरेकित्वेन त्रिरूपो हेतुः साधनम् । धर्मिणि अयोगव्यवच्छेदो व्यापकस्य साध्यत्वम् । यथा

Examples in order—

(1) 'Strange it is that at first the words of the wicked, sweet and agreeable, clearly indicate the presence of nectar, and yet they indicate also the presence, in their heart, of poison, the source of delusion.'

(2) 'That low-walled hut,—and this palace which receives its light from heaven ; that faded cow,—and these cloud-like herds of bellowing elephants ; that mean sound of the pestle,—and this sweet music of women ; it is a wonder that this Brāhmaṇa has been transported into this condition in so very few days.'

The renouncing (of one set of things) and acceptance (of another) by the same agent is not what is meant to be emphasised here ; hence this cannot be regarded as a case of 'Exchange'.

XXXV—*Anumāna*—Inference.

It is the description of the Probans and the Probandum that costuitutes Inference. 117.

यत्रैता लहरीचलाचलदृशो व्यापारयन्ति भ्रुवं
यत् तत्रैव पतन्ति संततममी मर्मस्पृशो मार्गणाः ।
तच्चक्रीकृतचापमञ्चितशरप्रेङ्खत्करः क्रोधनो
धावत्यग्रत एव शासनधरः सत्यं सदासां स्मरः ॥५१८॥

साध्यसाधनयोः पौर्वापर्यविकल्पे न किंचिद्वैचित्र्यमिति न तथा दर्शितम् ॥११७॥

विशेषणैर्यत्साकूतैरुक्तिः परिकरस्तु सः ॥

अर्थाद्विशेष्यस्य ।

'*Probans*',—the Reason, the 'Middle Term', which fulfils the threefold condition of (1) subsisting in the 'Minor Term', (*b*) being concomitant (with the 'Major Term') and (3) being non-concomitant (with the contrary of the Major Term).

'*Probandum*'—the constant concomitant of the 'Major Term' and the 'Minor Term'.

Example.—

'*Because* the heart-piercing arrows constantly fall upon that object towards which these girls with wave-like eyes turn their eye-brows,—*therefore* (it follows that) the angry sovereign Love-god, with his hand adorned with the drawn bow and arrow, is always running before these girls.'

The mere inversion of the premises and conclusion (which has been regarded by some people as a distinct figure) does not constitute any charm ; hence it has not been described. 117.

XXXVI—*Parikara*—Insinuation.

Insinuation is description with significant epithets.

उदाहरणम्—

महौजसो मानधना धनार्चिता
धनुर्भृतः संयति लब्धकीर्तयः ।
न संहतास्तस्य न भेदवृत्तयः
प्रियाणि वाञ्छन्त्यसुभिः समीहितुम् ॥५१९॥

यद्यप्यपुष्टार्थस्य दोषताभिधानात्तन्निराकरणेन पुष्टार्थस्वीकारः कृतः तथाप्येकनिष्ठत्वेन बहूनां विशेषणानामेवमुपन्यासे वैचित्र्यमित्यलंकारमध्ये गणितः ॥

व्याजोक्तिश्छद्मनोद्भिन्नवस्तुरूपनिगूहनम् ॥ ११८ ॥

निगूढमपि वस्तुनो रूपं कथमपि प्रभिन्नं केनापि व्यपदेशेन यदपह्नूयते सा व्याजोक्तिः ।

'*Description*' of and object qualified by the said epithets.

Example—

'Archers,—brilliant, self-respecting, honoured with riches, who have made their reputation in war, neither combining nor differing among themselves,—are anxious, even at the risk of their lives, to fulfil his wishes.'

Though it is true that by the recognition of 'Irrelevancy' as a *defect*, 'relevancy' or 'significance' has already been admitted (as an *excellence*),—yet there is a certain charm brought about by the bringing together of a number of significant epithets as applying to a single object ; by reason which this has been included under 'Figures of Speech'.

XXXVII—*Vyājokti*—Artful Assertion.

Artful Assertion consists in concealing, by some artifice, the unhidden character of a thing. 118.

When the form of a thing, not explicit in itself, somehow becomes explicit,—and yet such form is, by some artifice, concealed,—it is *Artful Assertion.*

न चैषापह्नुतिः प्रकृताप्रकृतोभयनिष्ठस्य साम्यस्येहासंभवात् ।
उदाहरणम्——

शैलेन्द्रप्रतिपाद्यमानगिरिजाहस्तोपगूढोल्लसद्-
रोमाञ्चादिविसंष्ठुलाखिलविधिव्यासङ्गभङ्गाकुलः ।
हा शैत्यं तुहिनाचलस्य करयोरित्यूचिवान् सस्मितं
शैलान्तःपुरमातृमण्डलगणैर्दृष्टोवताद्वः शिवः ॥५२०॥

अत्र पुलकवेपथू सात्त्विकरूपतया प्रसूतौ शैत्यकारणतया प्रकाशितत्वादपलपितस्वरूपौ व्याजोक्तिं प्रयोजयतः ॥११८॥

किंचित् पृष्टमपृष्टं वा कथितं यत् प्रकल्पते ।
तादृगन्यव्यपोहाय परिसंख्या तु सा स्मृता ॥ ११९ ॥

This is not the same as '*Concealment*' (see above Kārikā No. 96), because in the present case there is no possibility of any similitude between the object described and that to which it is compared.

Example (of *Artful Assertion*)—

'May Shiva protect you,—he being smilingly looked upon by the ladies in the harem of the King of Mountains, when he,—having a thrill and such effects produced in himself by the touch of Pārvatī's hand offered to him by her father, and feeling confused at the consequent omission of the details of the marriage-rites,—blurted out—"Oh, how cold are the hands of the Snow-mountain!"

Here the *thrilling* and the *trembling* (the latter being among the 'other effects'),—though really appearing as the calm effects (of the feeling of Love aroused by the touch), are described here as the effects of *cold*; and as in this manner their real character is 'concealed', we have here a case of *Artful Assertion*. 118.

प्रमाणान्तरावगतमपि वस्तु शब्देन प्रतिपादितं प्रयोजनान्तराभावात् सदृशवस्त्वन्तरव्यवच्छेदाय यत् पर्यवस्यति सा भवेत्परिसंख्या। अत्र च कथनं प्रश्नपूर्वकं तदन्यथा च परिदृष्टम्। तथा उभयत्र व्यपोह्यमानस्य प्रतीयमानता वाच्यत्वं चेति चत्वारो भेदाः ॥ क्रमेणोदाहरणम्——

किमासेव्यं पुंसां सविधमनवद्यं द्युसरितः
किमेकान्ते ध्येयं चरणयुगलं कौस्तुभभृतः ।
किमाराध्यं पुण्यं किमभिलषणीयं च करुणा
यदासक्त्या चेतो निरवधिविमुक्त्यै प्रभवति ॥५२१॥

XXXVIII—*Parisaṁkhyā*—Exclusion.

Where something, either (a) asked or (b) unasked, on being mentioned, serves to exclude other things similar thereto,—it is said to be Exclusion. 119.

When a certain thing, known by other means of knowledge, is mentioned by words, and in the absence of any other purpose, serves the purpose of exclusion of other similar things,—then it is *Exclusion.* The said 'mention' is found to be preceded by (in response to), as also not preceded by, a question; and in both cases what is *excluded* may be *implied* or directly *expressed*;—thus there are four varieties of this figure.

Examples in order.—

(*a*) [Preceded by question—the Excluded implied—]

'Q. What is it that deserves to be attended upon by men? A. The excellent proximity of the Heavenly River.—Q. What is it that should be meditated upon in seclusion? A. The two feet of Viṣṇu—Q. What is it that should be honoured? A. Virtue—Q. What is it

किं भूषणं सुदृढमत्र यशो न रत्नं
किं कार्यमार्यचरितं सुकृतं न दोषः ।
किं चक्षुरप्रतिहतं धिषणा न नेत्रं
जानाति कस्त्वदपरः सदसद्विवेकम् ॥५२२॥
कौटिल्यं कचनिचये करचरणाधरदलेषु रागस्ते ।
काठिन्यं कुचयुगले तरलत्वं नयनयोर्वसति ॥५२३॥
भक्तिर्भवे न विभवे व्यसनं शास्त्रे न युवतिकामास्त्रे ।
चिन्ता यशसि न वपुषि प्रायः परिदृश्यते महताम् ॥५२४॥११९॥

यथोत्तरं चेत् पूर्वस्य पूर्वस्यार्थस्य हेतुता ।
तदा कारणमाला स्यात् ॥

---

that should be desired ? A. Mercy, by the presence whereof the mind leads on to Liberation.'

(*b*) [Preceded by question—the Excluded expressed]—

'Q. What is the real ornament in the world ? A. Reputation, not jewels.—Q. What deserves to be done ? A. The good of a gentleman, not misdeeds.—Q. What is unimpeded vision ? A. Intelleet, not the eye.—Who else, but you, know the real difference between good and evil ?'

(*c*) [Not preceded by question—the Excluded implied—]

'There is obliqueness in your mass of hair ; redness in your hands, feet and lips ;—hardness in your breasts and fickleness in your eyes.

(*d*) [Not preceded by question,—the Excluded expressed]—

'Devotion to Shiva, not to riches ; addiction to learning, not to women, the weapon of love ; anxiety for reputation, not for the body ; all this is found in nearly all good men.' 119.

उत्तरमुत्तरं प्रति यथोत्तरम् । उदाहरणम्—

जितेन्द्रियत्वं विनयस्य कारणं गुणप्रकर्षो विनयादवाप्यते ।
गुणप्रकर्षेण जनोनुरज्यते जनानुरागप्रभवा हि संपदः ॥५२५॥

"हेतुमता सह हेतोरभिधानमभेदतो हेतुः ।"

इति हेत्वलंकारो न लक्षितः । आयुर्घृतमित्यादिरूपो ह्येष न भूषणतां कदाचिदर्हति वैचित्र्याभावात् ।

अविरलकमलविकासः सकलालिमदश्च कोकिलानन्दः ।
रम्योयमेति संप्रति लोकोत्कण्ठाकरः कालः ॥५२६॥

XXXIX—*Kāraṇamālā*—The String of Causes.

Where (among a number of things mentioned), each preceding one appears as the cause of each succeeding one,—it is the String of Causes.

'*Yathottaram*',—of each of the succeeding.

Example—

'Control over the senses is the cause of good character; excellence of qualities is obtained from good character; by the excellence of qualities people become attached; and the attachment of the people brings about prosperity.'

The figure 'Hetu', 'Cause', defined (by Udbhaṭa) as consisting in 'the delineation of the affect as not different from the cause',—has not been mentioned here, because such an identification, being of the nature of statements like 'Butter is longevity', can never be an ornament of speech, (a Figure of Speech), because there is no charm in it. In the example also that has been cited of the said figure,—

'*Aviralakamalavikāsaḥ*
Sakalālimadashcha kokilānandaḥ
Ramyoyameti samprati
Lokotkaṇṭhākaraḥ kālaḥ.'

इत्यत्र काव्यरूपतां कोमलानुप्रासमहिम्नैव समाम्नासिषुर्न पुनर्हेत्वलंकारकल्पनयेति पूर्वोक्तकाव्यलिङ्गमेव हेतुः ॥

क्रियया तु परस्परम् ॥ १२० ॥

वस्तुनोर्जननेऽन्योन्यम् ॥

अर्थयोरेकक्रियामुखेन परस्परं कारणत्वे सति अन्योन्यनामा अलंकारः । उदाहरणम्--

हंसाणं सरेंहि सिरी सारिज्जइ अह सराण हंसेहिँ ।
अण्णोण्णं विअ एए अप्पाण्णं णवर गरुअन्ति ॥५२७॥

अत्रोभयेषामपि परस्परजनकता मिथःश्रीसारतासंपादनद्वारेण ॥

'Now is come the lovely season, which bears the beauty of dense lotuses, during which the black bees are humming in exuberant joy, which is a source of felicity to the cuckoo, and brings longings in the minds of men'.

Here the presence of poetical charm has been declared to lie in the presence of the soft Alliteration, and not in that of any such Figure of Speech as *Cause*.

As a matter of fact, this Figure 'Cause' is the same as what has been described above as 'Poetical Reason'.

XL—*Anyonya*—Reciprocal.

Text.—When two things are productive of each other, through an action,—it is the Reciprocal.

When through a single action, two things appear as the cause of each other,—it is the Figure called 'Reciprocal'.

Example.—

'Tanks add beauty to the lakes, and the lakes add beauty to the swans; these two only serve to improve each other.'

[The छाया of विअ is given as एव in Vāma, nācārya. In the translution the word has been omitted.]

Here the two things spoken of are the 'cause' of each other through the common action of 'beautifying'.

उत्तरश्रुतिमात्रतः ॥

प्रश्नस्योन्नयनं यत्र क्रियते तत्र वा सति ॥ १२१ ॥

असकृद् यदसंभाव्यमुत्तरं स्यात् तदुत्तरम् ।

प्रतिवचनोपलम्भादेव पूर्ववाक्यं यत्र कल्प्यते तदेकं तावदुत्तरम् । उदाहरणम्—

वाणिअअ हत्थिदन्ता कुत्तो अम्हाण वग्घकित्ती अ ।
जाव लुलिआलअमुही घरम्मि परिसक्कए सोण्हा ॥५२८॥

हस्तिदन्तव्याघ्रकृत्तीनामहमर्थी ताः मूल्येन प्रयच्छेति क्रेतुर्वचनम् अमुना वाक्येन समुन्नीयत ॥

न चैतत् काव्यलिङ्गम् उत्तरस्य ताद्रूप्यानुपपत्तेः । नहि प्रश्नस्य प्रतिवचनं जनको हेतुः । नापीदमनुमानम् एकधर्मिनिष्ठतया साध्यसाधनयोरनिर्देशादित्यलंकारान्तरमेवोत्तरं साधीयः ।

XLI—*Uttara*—Answer.

(*a*) *When from the hearing of only the answer, the presumption of the question is made,—*(*b*) *or when the question being there, an inconceivable answer is given, and this more than once,—it is Answer.*

(*a*) It is one kind of *Answer*, where the statement embodying the question is presumed from the hearing of the answer.

Example—

'O trader, whence could we have ivory or tiger-skins' so long as my daughter-in-law with lovely locks lives in my house ?'

[Here the implication is that my son does not go out for hunting.]

The assertion here made leads to the presumption that it is in answer to the request of a likely purchaser to the following effect—'I am seeking for ivory and tiger-skins, give them to me and receive their price'

प्रश्नादनन्तरं लोकातिक्रान्तगोचरतया यत् असंभाव्यरूपं प्रतिवचनं स्यात् तत् अपरमुत्तरम् । अनयोश्च सकृदुपादाने न चारुताप्रतीतिरित्यसकृदित्युक्तम् । उदाहरणम्—

का विसमा देव्वगई किं लब्भं जं जणो गुणग्गाही ।
किं सोक्खं सुकलत्तं किं दुक्खं जं खलो लोओ ।।५२१।।

प्रश्नपरिसंख्यायामन्यव्यपोहे एव तात्पर्यम् । इह तु वाच्ये एव विश्रान्तिरित्यनयोर्विवेकः ।।

This figure is not the same as 'Poetical Reason'; because the nature of the figure 'Answer' is not the same as that of Poetical Reason, as the *Answer* here is not the productive cause of the *question* (as it is in *Poetical Reason*).

Nor is it the same as 'Inference', as it does not involve any mention of the Probans and Probandum as subsisting in a single substratum (as it is in *Inference*).

For these reasons it is best to regard this *Answer* as a distinct Figure of Speech.

(*b*) It is the second kind of *Answer* when, after the statement of the question, there follows an answer which, being beyond the reach of ordinary comprehension, is 'inconceivable'.—As the single mention of such question and answer would have no charm, it is added '*this more than once*'.

Example—

'What is perverse? The ways of destiny.—What is difficult to obtain? Appreciative men.—What is happiness? A good wife.—What is unhappiness? The presence of wicked men'.

In the 'Exclusion with question', what is aimed at is only the exclusion of other things while in the present figure the import rests entirely in the expressed meaning only;—herein lies the difference between these two Figures.

कुतोपि लक्षितः सूक्ष्मोप्यर्थोन्यस्मै प्रकाश्यते ॥ १२२ ॥
धर्मेण केनचिद् यत्र तत् सूक्ष्मं परिचक्षते ॥

कुतोपि आकारादिङ्गिताद्वा सूक्ष्मस्तीक्ष्णमतिसंवेद्यः ॥

उदाहरणम्—

वक्त्रस्यन्दिस्वेदबिन्दुप्रबन्धैर्दृष्ट्वा भिन्नं कुङ्कुमं कापि कण्ठे ।
पुंस्त्वं तन्व्या व्यञ्जयन्ती वयस्या स्मित्वा पाणौ खड्गलेखां
लिलेख ॥५३०॥

अत्र आकृतिमवलोक्य कयापि वितर्कितं पुरुषायितम् असिलतालेखनेन वैदग्ध्यादभिव्यक्तिमुपनीतम् पुंसामेव कृपाणपाणिता योग्यत्वात् ॥

यथा वा

संकेतकालमनसं विटं ज्ञात्वा विदग्धया ।
ईषन्नेत्रार्पिताकूतं लीलापद्मं निमीलितम् ॥५३१॥

LXII.—*Sūkṣma*—Subtle.

Where a subtle fact somehow noticed, is expressed to another person, by means of some property,—it is the Subtle.

'*Somehow*'—Through appearance of gestures and so forth.

'*Subtle*'—Cognisable only by persons with keen intelligence.

Example—

'A certain friend, noticing the *kuṅkuma* paint on her neck blurred by perspiration from the girl's face, smiled and painted the sword in her hand, with a view to indicate her male character.'

What is depicted here is that on seeing the appearance of the girl, her friend understood that she had behaved like a male ; and this idea she very cleverly expressed to her by the painting of the sword,—the proper place for the sword being in the hand of a male only.

अत्र जिज्ञासितः संकेतकालः कयाचिदिङ्गितमात्रेण विदितो निशासमयशंसिना कमलनिमीलनेन लीलया प्रतिपादितः ॥

उत्तरोत्तरमुत्कर्षो भवेत्सारः परावधिः ॥ १२३ ॥

परः पर्यन्तभागः अवधिर्यस्य धाराधिरोहितया तत्रैवोत्कर्षस्य विश्रान्तेः । उदाहरणम्—

राज्ये सारं वसुधा वसुधायां पुरं पुरे सौधम् ।
सौधे तल्पं तल्पे वराङ्गनानङ्गसर्वस्वम् ॥५३२॥१२३॥

भिन्नदेशतयात्यन्तं कार्यकारणभूतयोः ।
युगपद्धर्मयोर्यत्र ख्यातिः सा स्यादसंगतिः ॥ १२४ ॥

Another example—

'The clever girl, noticing from the meaning glances of her lover that he was desirous of knowing the time of assignation, closed up the lotus with which she was playing'.

Having noticed, from a mere gesture, that the time for assignation was what was sought after, the girl very gracefully gave him the information by the *closing of the lotus*, which pointed to the *night* as the time.

XLIII.—*Sāra*—Climax.

Climax is the successive rising in the excellence of things to the highest pitch. 121-23.

'*Parāvadhi*',—that of which the '*para*' *highest pitch*, is the '*avadhi*', '*limit*; it is at that limit that the excellence, rising by degrees, rests.

Example—

'The Earth is the essence of the kingdom ; the city, of the Earth ; the palace, of the city ; the bed, of the palace ; and of the bed, the lovely woman, the all-in-all of the Love-god. 123.

इह यद्देशं करणं तद्देशमेव कार्यमुत्पद्यमानं दृष्टम् यथा धूमादि। यत्र तु हेतुफलरूपयोरपि धर्मयोः केनाप्यतिशयेन नानादेशतया युगपदवभासनं सा तयोः स्वभावोत्पन्नपरस्पर-संगतित्यागात् असंगतिः। उदाहरणम्––

जस्सेअ वणो तस्सेअ वेअणा भणइ तं जणो अलिअं।
दन्तक्खअं कवोले बहुए वेअणा सवत्तीणं ॥५३३॥

एषा च विरोधबाधिनी न विरोधः भिन्नाधारतयैव द्वयोरिह विरोधितायाः प्रतिभासात्। विरोधे तु विरोधित्वम् एकाश्रय-निष्ठमनुक्तमपि पर्यवसितम् अपवादविषयपरिहारेणोत्सर्गस्य व्यवस्थितेः। तथा चैवं निर्दशितम् ॥१२४॥

XLIV.—*Asaṅgati*—Disconnection.

When there is representation of two properties, which bear to each other the relation of cause and effect, as subsisting, at the same time, in totally different places,—it is Disconnection. 124.

As a rule, the effect is found to appear in the same place as its cause ; *e.g.*, the smoke (is found in the same place as fire)); under the circumstances if two properties, one of which is the cause and the other its effect, are described as appearing, at the same time, in different places,—on account of some peculiar circumstance,—it is the figure *Disconnection*, '*Asaṅgati*',—so called because it involves the abandoning of the natural *connection*, '*saṅgati*', between the cause and its effect.

Example—

'What people say as to the pain belonging to the person who has the sore is not true ; the cut of the teeth is on the cheek of the newly wedded wife, while the pain appears in her co-wives.'

समाधिः सुकरं कार्यं कारणान्तरयोगतः ।।

साधनान्तरोपकृतेन कर्त्रा यत् अक्लेशेन कार्यमारब्धं समाधीयते स समाधिर्नाम । उदाहरणम्—

मानमस्या निराकर्तुं पादयोर्मे पतिष्यतः ।
उपकाराय दिष्टचेदमुदीर्णं घनगर्जितम् ।।५३४।।

Though it does imply an inconsistency (which is a form of Contradiction), yet the figure is not the same as 'Contradiction), as in this the 'inconsistency' appears only in the form of two things appearing in two distinct substrata; while in 'Contradiction', the inconsistency really lies in two things subsisting in the same substratum; though this fact has not been stated (in the definition of 'Contradiction' given before), —that it is so is clear from the fact that what is of wider application (in the present case, 'contradiction') is made applicable to only those cases that do not come under what is of narrower application ('Disconnection', in the present case.)

[Hence it is that when 'disconnection' is found to be applicable to cases where the two things are represented as subsisting in *different* substrata, it is only right that the scope of 'contradiction' should be restricted to cases where they are described as subsisting in the same substratum.]

And it is under this understanding that examples have been cited above (of the figure of 'Contradiction.')
124.।।

XLV.—*Samādhi*—Convenience.

When, through the help of other causes, the fulfilment of an effect is described as becoming easier,—it is Convenience.

When a certain work, commenced by an agent (with one set of accessories), becomes accomplished without much trouble, with the help of other accessories,—it is the figure named 'Convenience'.

समं योग्यतया योगो यदि संभावितः क्वचित् ॥ १२५ ॥

इदमनयोः श्लाघ्यमिति योग्यतया संबन्धस्य नियतविषय-मध्यवसानं चेत्तदा समम् तत् सद्योगेसद्योगे च ॥

उदाहरणम्—

धातुः शिल्पातिशयनिकषस्थानमेषा मृगाक्षी
रूपे देवोप्ययमनुपमो दत्तपत्रः स्मरस्य ।
जातं दैवात्सदृशमनयोः संगतं यत् तदेत-
च्छृङ्गारस्योपनतमधुना राज्यमेकातपत्रम् ॥५३५॥
चित्रं चित्रं बत बत महच्चित्रमेतद्विचित्रं
जातो दैवादुचितरचनासंविधाता विधाता ।

Example.—

'As I was going to fall on her feet, with a view to pacifying her indignant feelings, luckily the thundering of clouds appeared for the purpose of helping me'.

XLVI.—*Sama*—Compatible.

When the connection (between two things) is considered to be right and proper,—it is the Compatible. 125.

When the connection between any two definite things is regarded as right and proper,—the idea being that 'this is commendable'—it is the *Compatible.* It is of two kinds,—(*a*) where the connection is between two good things, and (*b*) where the connection is between two bad things.

Examples—

(*a*) 'This fawn-eyed one is the touch-stone of the excellence of the creator's art ; your Majesty, being unrivalled in beauty, have relegated the Love-God to a lower position ; that a proper connection between these two has luckily come about constitutes the undisputed sovereignty of Love'.

यन्निम्बानां परिणतफलस्फीतिरास्वादनीया
यच्चैतस्याः कवलनकलाकोविदः काकलोकः ॥५३६॥

क्वचिद्यदतिवैधर्म्यान्न श्लेषो घटनामियात् ।
कर्तुः क्रियाफलावाप्तिर्नैवानर्थश्च यद्भवेत् ॥ १२६ ॥
गुणक्रियाभ्यां कार्यस्य कारणस्य गुणक्रिये ।
क्रमेण च विरुद्धे यत् स एष विषमो मतः ॥ १२७ ॥

द्वयोरत्यन्तविलक्षणतया यत् अनुपपद्यमानतयैव योगः प्रतीयते (१) यच्च किंचिदारभमाणः कर्ता क्रियायाः प्रणाशात् न केवलमभीष्टं यत् फलं न लभेत यावदप्रार्थितमप्यनर्थं विषय-मासादयेत् (२) तथा सत्यपि कार्यस्य कारणरूपानुकारे तत्

(*b*) 'Strange, strange, extremely strange is this that the Creator has, by chance, been the ordainer of one compatible phenomenon that when the large quantities of Nimba-berries had to be eaten, the beings selected as expert in eating them were the crows'. 125.

XLVII.—*Viṣama*—Incongruous.

> *Where—(a) between two things no compatibility can come about, by reason of extreme dissimilitude,—(b) where the agent does not obtain the fruit of his action, but comes by an adverse effect,—(c) (d) where the quality and action of the cause are incompatible respectively, with the quality and action of the effect,—it is held to be the Incongruous.* 126—7.

(*a*) In a case where the two things are so entirely incompatible, that any connection between them is conceived of as purely impossible ;—(*b*) where, the Agent, commencing an act, does not only fail, by reason of the failure of his operations, to obtain the fruit that he sought to obtain from that act, but, on the contrary, ob-

तयोर्गुणौ क्रिये च परस्परं विरुद्धतां व्रजतः (३।४) स समविपर्ययात्मा चतूरूपो विषमः ॥

क्रमेणोदाहरणम्—

शिरीषादपि मृद्वङ्गी क्वेयमायतलोचना ।
अयं क्व च कुकूलाग्निकर्कशो मदनानलः ॥५३७॥
सिंहिकासुतसंत्रस्तः शशः शीतांशुमाश्रितः ।
जग्रसे साश्रयं तत्र तमन्यः सिंहिकासुतः ॥५३८॥
सद्यः करस्पर्शमवाप्य चित्रं रणे रणे यस्य कृपाणलेखा ।
तमालनीला शरदिन्दुपाण्डु यशस्त्रिलोक्याभरणं प्रसूते ॥५३९॥
आनन्दममन्दमिमं कुवलयदललोचने ददासि त्वम् ।
विरहस्त्वयैव जनितस्तापयतितरां शरीरं मे ॥५४०॥

---

tains an adverse effect, which he never desired ;—and (*c*) (*d*), where, even though the effect resembles the cause, yet their qualities and actions are mutually contradictory ;—this is the four-fold *Incongruous*, '*Viṣama*', so called because it is the reverse of 'congruity' (*Sama*).

Examples in order—

(*a*) 'Where on one side is the large-eyed one, with body more tender than the *Shirīṣa* flower, and where, on the other, is the fire of love, terrible as straw-fire'.

'The hare, fearing the *son of Simhikā* (lioness) took refuge under the Moon ; and yet there also it was swallowed by another *son of Simhikā* (Rāhu)'.

(*c*) 'It is strange that touched in battle by his hand his sword, black like the *Tamāla* tree, brings forth fame, white like the autumnal moon which adorns the three worlds'.

(*d*) 'O lotus-eyed one, thou impartest extreme joy, and yet the separation, brought about by thee, consumes my body'.

अत्रानन्ददानं शरीरतापेन विरुध्यते ।

एवम्

विपुलेन सागरशयस्य कुक्षिणा भुवनानि यस्य पपिरे युगक्षये ।
मदविभ्रमासकलया पपे पुनः स पुरस्त्रियैकतमयैकया दृशा॥५४१॥

इत्यादावपि विषमत्वं यथायोगभवगन्तव्यम् ॥१२७॥

महतोर्यन्महीयांसावाश्रिताश्रययोः क्रमात् ।
आश्रयाश्रयिणौ स्यातां तनुत्वेऽप्यधिकं तु तत् ॥ १२८ ॥

आश्रितम् आधेयम् आश्रयस्तदाधारः । तयोर्महतोरपि विषये तदपेक्षया तनू अप्याश्रयाश्रयिणौ प्रस्तुतवस्तुप्रकर्षविवक्षया यथाक्रमं यत् अधिकतरतां व्रजतः । तदिदं द्विविधम् अधिकं नाम ।

Here the action of *imparting joy* (belonging to the cause, the *woman)* is incompatible with the *consuming of the body* (which is the action of the *separation*, the effect produced by that woman.)

Similarly, the same *Incongruity* may be traced also in such verses as the following—

'The Being who sleeps in the ocean, by whose extensive stomach the worlds had been swallowed, at the time of dissolution, was swallowed (so to say) by a certain citizen, with her eye only partially opened through the intoxication of love'. 126-27.

XLVIII—*Adhika*—the Exceeding.

> *When of the Container and the Contained, both of which are large, the respective Contained and Container, though really smaller, are described as larger,—it is the Exceeding.* 128.

'*Ashrita*' is the Contained, and '*Ashraya*' is its Container; when, both of them being large, their respective Container and Contained, though really smaller than the former, are described as larger,—for the purpose

क्रमेणोदाहरणम्--

अहो विशालं भूपाल भुवनत्रितयोदरम् ।
माति मातुमशक्योपि यशोराशिर्यदत्र ते ॥५४२॥

युगान्तकालप्रतिसंहृतात्मनो जगन्ति यस्यां सविकाशमासत ।
तनौ ममुस्तत्र न कैटभद्विषस्तपोधनाभ्यागमसंभवा मुदः ॥५४३॥
॥१२८॥

प्रतिपक्षमशक्तेन प्रतिकर्तुं तिरस्क्रिया ।
या तदीयस्य तत्स्तुत्यै प्रत्यनीकं तदुच्यते ॥ १२९ ॥

न्यक्कृतिपरमपि विपक्षं साक्षान्निरसितुमशक्तेन केनापि यत् तमेव प्रतिपक्षमुत्कर्षयितुं तदाश्रितस्य तिरस्करणम् तत् अनीकप्रतिनिधितुल्यत्वात् प्रत्यनीकमभिधीयते । यथा अनीके

---

of delineating the superiority of the object described,—this constitutes the two kinds of the figure 'Exceeding'.

Examples in order—

(*a*) 'O King, the inside of the three worlds is really extensive, inasmuch as the mass of your fame, though really too large to be contained, becomes contained in it'.

(*b*) 'Viṣṇu,—in whom, when he had withdrawn himself at the time of the cosmic dissolution, the worlds became freely contained,—could not contain in his body the joy produced by the arrival of the saint'. 128.

XLIX—*Pratyanīka*—Hostile.

It is the Hostile, when a person, unable to injure his enemy, is described as offering an insult to a relative of that enemy,—such description tending to eulogise this latter. 129.

A man has an enemy who is ever insulting him, and whom he himself is unable to injure; under the circumstances, if he offers an insult to some one else de-

अभियोज्ये तत्प्रतिनिधीभूतमपरं मूढतया केनचिदभियुज्यते तथेह प्रतियोगिनि विजेये तदीयोन्यो विजीयते इत्यर्थः ।
उदाहरणम्—
त्वं विनिर्जितमनोभवरूपः सा च सुन्दर भवत्यनुरक्ता ।
पञ्चभिर्युगपदेव शरैस्तां तापयत्यनुशयादिव कामः ॥५४४॥
यथा वा
यस्य किंचिदपकर्तुमक्षमः कायनिग्रहगृहीतविग्रहः ।
कान्तवक्त्रसदृशाकृतिं कृती राहुरिन्दुमधुनापि बाधते ॥५४५॥
इन्दोरत्र तदीयता संबन्धिसंबन्धात् ॥१२९॥

---

pendant upon that enemy,—which action of his tends to add to the prestige of this latter,—it is called the figure 'Hostile', '*Pratyanīka*';—so called because it is analogical to the case of the 'substitute of an army (*anīka*).—Just as, having to fight with an army, one, through ignorance, fights with something else that appears in itself,—so, in the case in question, the enemy being the person to fight, the person goes out to fight a relation of his.

Example.—

'You are one who have subdued the beauty of the Love-god, and O beautiful one, she is attached to you ; for this reason the Love-god, though hated as it were, strikes her simultaneously with all his five arrows'.

Another example—

'Being unable to injure Viṣṇu himself,—with whom his enmity was brought about by the cutting off of the head,—Rāhu even now, continues to attack the Moon, who resembles the beautiful face of Viṣṇu'.

The moon in this case, though not related directly to Viṣṇu, is represented as related to him indirectly—*i. e.*, being related to the face which is directly related to Viṣṇu. 129.

समेन लक्ष्मणा वस्तु वस्तुना यन्निगूह्यते ।
निजेनागन्तुना वापि तन्मीलितमिति स्मृतम् ॥ १३० ॥

सहजम् आगन्तुकं वा किमपि साधारणं यत् लक्षणम् तद्द्वारेण यत् किंचित् केनचिद्वस्तु वस्तुस्थित्यैव वलीयस्तया तिरोधीयते तत् मीलितमिति द्विधा स्मरन्ति ॥

क्रमेणोदाहरणम्——
अपाङ्गतरले दृशौ मधुरवक्रवर्णागिरो
विलासभरमन्थरा गतिरतीव कान्तं मुखम् ।
इति स्फुरितमङ्गके मृगदृशःस्वतो लीलया
तदत्र न मदोदयः कृतपदोपि संलक्ष्यते ॥५४६॥

अत्र दृक्तरलतादिकमङ्गस्य लिङ्गं स्वाभाविकं साधारणं च महोदयेन तत्राप्येतस्य दर्शनात् ।

L. *Mīlita*—The Obscured

When one thing is obscured by another, through a common characteristic, innate or adventitious,—it is the Obscured. 130.

Between two things there is a certain common characteristic, which may be either (*a*) innate or (*b*) adventitious ;—through this, when one of those things is obscured, (hidden from view) by the other, by reason of this latter being naturally more powerful,—this is the figure *Obscured*, which they declare to be of two kinds ; of which the following are the respective examples—

(*a*) [The obscuring being done through an innate characteristic]—

'The eyes are tremulous in the corners ; words sweet and artful, the movement graceful and languid, the face extremely light ;—all this has appeared naturally in the tender body of the fawn-eyed one through lasciviousness ; so that no sign of intoxication is perceptible in her body'.

ये कन्दरासु निवसन्ति सदा हिमाद्रेस्
त्वत्पातशङ्कितधियो विवशा द्विषस्ते ।
अप्यङ्गमुत्पुलकमुद्वहतां सकम्पं
तेषामहो बत भियां न बुधोप्यभिज्ञः ॥५४७॥

अत्र तु सामर्थ्यादवसितस्य शैत्यस्य आगन्तुकत्वात्तत्प्रभवयोरपि कम्पपुलकयोस्तादृप्यं समानता च भयेष्वपि तयोरुपलक्षितत्वात् ॥१३०॥

स्थाप्यतेपोह्यते वापि यथापूर्वं परं परम् ।
विशेषणतया यत्र वस्तु सैकावली द्विधा ॥ १३१ ॥

The tremulousness of the eyes and the other signs are natural characteristics, common to lasciviousness and intoxication,—all of them being found in the latter also.

[And through these, the more powerful, *i. e.*, better known, lasciviousness, serves to obscure, hide from view, the intoxication.]

(*b*) [Where the obscuring is done through adventitious characteristics.]—

'When, with minds full of fear of being attacked by you, your helpless enemies are living in the caves of the Himālaya,—even though they have their bodies thrilled and shivering, their fright is not perceptible even to the most intelligent'.

The feeling of *cold*, which is implied by the force of the character of the Himālaya, is something *adventitious* (not *innate* to the body); and hence *thrill* and the *shivering* also, which are effects of that feeling, are *adventitious conditions*; and these are 'common', being found to be present in the case of *fear* also.

[And here the more apparent thing, the cold due to the Himālaya, serves to obscure the other thing, fear.] 130

पूर्वं पूर्वं प्रति यथोत्तरस्य वस्तुनो वीप्सया विशेषणभावेन यत् स्थापनं निषेधो वा संभवति सा द्विधा बुधैरेकावली भण्यते ।

क्रमेणोदाहरणम्—

पुराणि यस्यां सवराङ्गनानि वराङ्गना रूपपुरस्कृताङ्गयः ।
रूपं समुन्मीलितसद्विलासमस्त्रं विलासः कुसुमायुधस्य ।।५४८।।

न तज्जलं यन्न सुचारुपङ्कजं
न पङ्कजं तद् यदलीनषट्पदम् ।
न षट्पदोसौ कलगुञ्जितो न यो
न गुञ्जितं तन्न जहार यन्मनः ।।५४९।।

LI—*Ekāvalī*—Necklace.

Where [among a number of things] the succeeding thing is either (a) affirmed or (b) denied, as qualifying the preceding things,—it is the Necklace, which is of two kinds. 131

When among a number of things, when one succeeding thing after another, is found to be either (*a*) affirmed or denied, as belonging to the preceding,—it is the figure which the learned call 'Necklace'; and this is of two kinds, of which the following are the respective examples.

(*a*) [Where there is affirmation.]—

'The city there contained excellent women ; the excellent women were adorned with beauty ; their beauty was teeming with lasciviousness : and lasciviousness is the weapon of the Love-god'.

(*b*) [Where there is denial.]—

'It is not water which does not contain beautiful lotuses ; it is not lotus which does not contain the hidden black bee ; it is not a black bee which hums not sweetly ;

पूर्वत्र पुराणां वराङ्गनाः तासामङ्गविशेषणमुखेन रूपम् तस्य विलासाः तेषामप्यस्त्रमित्यमुना क्रमेण विशेषणं विधीयते। उत्तरत्र प्रतिषेधेप्येवं योज्यम् ॥१३१॥

यथानुभवमर्थस्य दृष्टे तत्सदृशे स्मृतिः।
स्मरणम् ॥

यः पदार्थः केनचिदाकारेण नियतः यदा कदाचित् अनुभूतोभूत् स कालान्तरे स्मृतिप्रतिबोधाधायिनि तत्समाने वस्तुनि दृष्टे सति यत् तथैव स्मर्यते तत् भवेत् स्मरणम्।

---

and it is no humming which does not captivate the heart'.

In the former example (*a*) we have the *affirmation* of a series of qualifications *viz.*, the excellent women, of the city,—the beauty of the women through their body,—lascivious graces of the beauty,—and the *character of weapon* of the graces. And in the latter example (*b*) we have a denial of a series of qualifications, which can be similarly explained. 131.

LII.—*Smaraṇa*—Reminiscence.

When on the perception of a thing similar to it, there is remembrance of an object as previously perceived,—it is Reminiscence.

When a certain object, with a certain well-defined character, has been perceived at some time,—and, at some subsequent time, on the perception of a thing similar to it, which serves to arouse the impression conducive to remembrance, if it becomes remembered just as it had been perceived before,—this would constitute *Reminiscence*.

उदाहरणम्—

निम्ननाभिकुहरेषु यदम्भः प्लावितं चलदृशां लहरीभिः ।
तद्भवैः कुहरुतैः सुरनार्यः स्मारिताः सुरतकण्ठरुतानाम् ॥५५०॥

यथा वा

करजुअगहिअजसोआत्थणमुहविणिवेसिआहरपुडस्स ।
समरिअपञ्चजण्णस्स णमह कण्हस्स रोमाञ्चं ॥५५१॥

भ्रान्तिमानन्यसंवित्तत्तुल्यदर्शने ॥ १३२ ॥

तदिति अन्यत् अप्राकरणिकं निर्दिश्यते । तेन समानम् अर्थादिह प्राकरणिकम् आश्रीयते । तस्य तथाविधस्य दृष्टौ सत्यां यत् अप्राकरणिकतया संवेदनं स भ्रान्तिमान् ।

Example—

'When the ripples of water flowed into the deep navels of the girls with tremulous eyes, the celestial damsels were reminded, by the cooing sound therein produced, of the cooing issuing from their own throats during dalliance'.

Another example—

"Bow down to the thrill in Kṛṣṇa's body, which appeared at the recollection of his *Pāñchajanya* Conch, at the time when he held with his hands Yashodā's breasts with his lips at the nipples'.

LIII.—*Bhrāntimān*—Illusion.

When there is cognition of another thing, at the sight of a thing similar to it,—it is Illusion. 132.

'*It*' and the term '*another thing*', refer to something not forming the subject of the statement; —what is 'similar to it' is, in the present context, the thing that forms the subject-matter of the statement;—when at '*sight*', or perception of this latter, there appears

न चैष रूपकं प्रथमातिशयोक्तिर्वा तत्र वस्तुतो भ्रमस्याभावात् इह च, अर्थानुगमनेन संज्ञायाः प्रवृत्तेः तस्य स्पष्टमेव प्रतिपन्नत्वात् । उदाहरणम्—

कपाले मार्जारः पय इति करान् लेढि शशिनस्
तरुच्छिद्रप्रोतान् बिसमिति करी संकलयति ।
रतान्ते तल्पस्थान् हरति वनिताप्यंशुकमिति
प्रभामत्तश्चन्द्रो जगदिदमहो विप्लवयति ॥५५२॥

आक्षेप उपमानस्य प्रतीपमुपमेयता ।
तस्यैव यदि वा कल्प्या तिरस्कारनिबन्धनम् ॥ १३३ ॥

---

a cognition (idea) of it as the 'other',—*i. e.*, the thing not forming the subject of the statement,—it is the figure '*Illusion*'.

This is not the same as either *Metaphor* or *Hyperbole*; as in these latter there is no real *illusion*, while in the present instance, the illusion is manifest, as is clear from the fact that the name 'Illusion' is applied to it in the literal sense.

'When the cat sees the moon's rays in the bowl, it mistakes them for milk and proceeds to lap it; when the elephant sees them entering through the interstices in the trees, it mistakes them for the lotus-stalk, and proceeds to collect them; when the woman sees them on her bed, at the end of dalliance, she mistakes them for her cloth and proceeds to pick them up :—Thus the moon, maddened with his resplendence, deludes the whole world'. 132.

LIV. *Pratīpa*—The Converse.

(a) Where there is discarding of the object compared to, or (b) where that object itself is treated, with a view to its being condemned, as the object compared,—it is the Converse. 133.

अस्य धुरं सुतरामुपमेयमेव वोढुं प्रौढमिति कैमर्थ्येन यत् उपमानमाक्षिप्यते यदपि तस्यैवोपमानतया प्रसिद्धस्य उपमानान्तरविवक्षयानादरार्थमुपमेयभावः कल्प्यते तत् उपमेयस्योपमानप्रतिकूलवर्तित्वात् उभयरूपं प्रतीपम् । क्रमेणोदाहरणम्—

लावण्यौकसि सप्रतापगरिमण्यग्रेसरे त्यागिनां
देव त्वय्यवनीभरक्षमभुजे निष्पादिते वेधसा ।
इन्दुः किं घटितः किमेष विहितः पूषा किमुत्पादितं
चिन्तारत्नमदो मुधैव किममी सृष्टाः कुलक्ष्माभृतः ॥५५३॥

ए एहि दाव सुन्दरि कण्णं दाऊण सुणसु वअणिज्जं ।
तुज्झ मुहेण किसोअरि चंदो उअमिज्जइ जणेण ॥५५४॥

(*a*) When the *object compared* is 'discarded' as being superfluous, the idea being that its functions can be easily served by the *object compared* itself;—or (*b*) when what is known as the *object compared* to is treated as the *object compared*, with a view to its being condemned in favour of another *object compared to*;—these two conditions constitute the two kinds of Converse, '*Pratīpa*';—so called because the *object compared* stands here as inimical (*pratikūla*) to the *object compared to.*

Examples in order—

(*a*) 'O King, after the Creator had created you, the receptacle of beauty, endowed with supreme glory, foremost among the generous, and capable of bearing the burden of supporting the Earth,—why did he create the Moon? For what purpose was the Sun created? Why too was the Desire-gem produced? and why were the leading Mountains created without any purpose?'

[Here all the objects compared to have been discarded as useless.]

(*b*) 'Come, O beautiful one, and just lend your ears

अत्र मुखेनोपमीयमानस्य शशिनः स्वल्पतरगुणत्वात् उपमित्यनिष्पत्त्या 'वअणिज्जं' इति वचनीयपदाभिव्यङ्ग्यस्तिरस्कारः ।

क्वचित्तु निष्पन्नैवोपमितिक्रिया अनादरनिबन्धनम् । यथा

गर्वमसंवाह्यमिमं लोचनयुगलेन किं वहसि मुग्धे ।
सन्तीदृशानि दिशि दिशि सरस्सु ननु नीलनलिनानि ॥५५५॥

इहोपमेयीकरणमेवोत्पलानामनादरः ।

अनयैव रीत्या यत् असामान्यगुणयोगात् नोपमानभावमपि अनुभूतपूर्वि तस्य तत्कल्पनायामपि भवति प्रतीपमिति प्रत्येतव्यम् । यथा

---

to hear the calumny that is spreading : O slender-waisted one, people are comparing the Moon to your face !'

The idea here is that the Moon which is compared to the face being possessed of inferior qualities, the comparison is not correctly accomplished, and this contempt (for the Moon) is suggested by the word 'calumny'.

In some cases, the contempt is indicated by a comparison that is correctly accomplished. For instance, in the following—

'O deluded one, wherefore do you entertain boundless pride on account of your eyes ? There are in the lakes on all sides, blue lotuses which are like them'.

Here the contempt for the lotuses consists in their being made the *objects compared.*

In the same manner, when an object, possessed of a unique property, not belonging to any other thing, and hence never recognised as similar (*i.e.*, bearing comparison) to anything,—is represented as an object to which something is compared,—this also is to be regarded as an instance of the figure, *Converse*. For instance, in the following.—

अहमेव गुरुः सुदारुणानाम्
इति हालाहल तात मा स्म दृप्यः ।
ननु सन्ति भवादृशानि भूयो
भुवनेस्मिन् वचनानि दुर्जनानाम् ॥५५६॥

अत्र हालाहलस्योपमानत्वमसंभाव्यमेवोपनिबद्धम् ॥

प्रस्तुतस्य यदन्येन गुणसाम्यविवक्षया ।
ऐकात्म्यं बध्यते योगात्तत्सामान्यमिति स्मृतम् ॥ १३४ ॥

अतादृशमपि तादृशतया विवक्षितुं यत् अप्रस्तुतार्थेन संपृक्तमपरित्यक्तनिजगुणमेव तदेकात्मतया निबध्यते तत् समानगुणनिबन्धनात् सामान्यम् ।

'O Poison, don't you, my friend, be puffed up at the idea that you are the greatest of terrible things : verily there abound in this world the words of the wicked, which are just as terrible as yourself'.

Here the Poison is represented as the *object compared to*, and this character of it is something entirely inconceivable. 133.

LV. *Sāmānya*—Identification.

Where, with a view to delineate the presence of common properties, the object described is represented as identical with another, through its connection with this latter,—it is held to be Identification. 134.

When the speaker desires to describe an object as similar to another, to which it is not really similar,—and represents it, through its connection with that object, as identical with it,—though not renouncing its own qualities,—it is *Identification, 'Sāmānya'*;—so called because it is based upon the presence of *identical* (*samāna*) properties.

Example—

'The women repining for their lovers,—having

उदाहरणम्—

मलयजरसविलिप्तनवो नवहारलताविभूषिताः
सिततरदन्तपत्र कृतवक्त्ररुचो रुचिरामलांशुकाः।
शशभृति विततधाम्नि धवलयति धरामविभाव्यतां गताः।
प्रियवसतिं प्रयान्ति सुखमेव निरस्तभियोभिसारिकाः ॥५५७॥

अत्र प्रस्तुततदन्ययोरन्यूनानतिरिक्ततया निबद्धं धवलत्वमेकात्मताहेतुः। अत एव पृथग्भावेन न तयोरुपलक्षणम्। यथा वा

वेत्रत्वचा तुल्यरुचां वधूनां कर्णाग्रतो गण्डतलागतानि।
भृङ्गाः सहेलं यदि नापतिष्यन् कोवेदयिष्यन्नवचम्पकानि ॥५५८॥

अत्र निमित्तान्तरजनितापि नानात्वप्रतीतिः प्रथमप्रतिपन्नमभेदं न व्युदसितुमुत्सहते प्रतीतत्वात्तस्य प्रतीतेश्च बाधायोगात् ॥

---

their body smeared with sandal-paint, adorned with new pearl-necklaces, their faces shining through white paint, and clothed in clean white clothes,—become undistinguishable when the moon with its rays has whitened the Earth, and thus proceed to the house of their lovers comfortably and fearlessly'.

Here the ground of *identification* consists in the quality of *whiteness*, which is represented as being of the same degree as—neither more nor less than,—that in the object described (the women) and the other thing (moonlight); and for this reason the two objects themselves are not recognised as distinct.

Another example—

'Who could have recognised the *champaka*-flowers hanging from their ears over the cheeks of young women, with complexion like the cane-bark,—if the black bees had not gracefully hovered over them?'

Here the cognition of difference, though produced by other causes (the hovering of the bees), is not able to

विना प्रसिद्धमाधारमाधेयस्य व्यवस्थितिः ।
एकात्मा युगपद्वृत्तिरेकस्यानेकगोचरा ॥ १३५ ॥
अन्यत् प्रकुर्वतः कार्यमशक्यस्यान्यवस्तुनः ।
तथैव करणं चेति विशेषस्त्रिविधः स्मृतः ॥ १३६ ॥

प्रसिद्धाधारपरिहारेण यत् आधेयस्य विशिष्टा स्थितिरभिधीयते स प्रथमो विशेषः ।

उदाहरणम्—

दिवमप्युपयातानामाकल्पमनल्पगुणगणा येषाम् ।
रमयन्ति जगन्ति गिरः कथमिह कवयो न ते वन्द्याः ॥५५९॥

---

shake off the identity perceived before (the mention of the distinguishing bees); for the simple reason that this identity has been recognised, and what has been recognised once cannot be completely set aside. 134.

LVI—*Vishesa*—Extraordinary.

> *(a) When the contained is represented as existing without its recognised container,—(b) when one thing is represented as subsisting, in the same form, and at the same time, in several things;—and (c) where, while a person is engaged in the doing of one thing, he is described as accomplishing, in the same manner, a different thing, which (in reality) is not capable of being accomplished (by that same effort);—it constitutes what has been described as the figure Extraordinary with its three varieties.* 135-36.

(*a*) When the recognised *container* or receptacle of a thing, is omitted, and the *contained* is described as subsisting in a peculiar manner (*i. e.*, without a receptacle),—it is the first variety of the *Extraordinary*.

एकमपि वस्तु यत् एकेनैव स्वभावेन युगपदनेकत्र वर्तते स द्वितीयः। उदाहरणम्—

सा वसइ तुज्झ हिअए सा च्चिअ अच्छीसु सा अ वअणेसु।
अह्मारिसाण सुन्दर ओसासो कत्थ पावाणं ॥५६०॥

यदपि किंचिद्रभसेन आरभमाणस्तेनैव यत्नेनाशक्यमपि कार्यान्तरमारभते सोपरो विशेषः। उदाहरणम्—

स्फुरदद्भुतरूपमुत्प्रतापज्वलनं त्वां सृजतानवद्यविद्यम्।
विधिना ससृजे नवो मनोभूर्भुवि सत्यं सविता बृहस्पतिश्च॥५६१॥

यथा वा

Example—

'Wherefore should the poets not be regarded as objects of reverence,—whose words, grand with infinite beauty, continue to rejoice the worlds, to the very end of the cycle, even after the poets themselves have departed to heaven?'

(*b*) When a single thing is described as subsisting in the same form, in several things simultaneously,—it is the second kind of the *Extraordinary*. Example—

'She resides in your heart, in your eyes and in your words; where can there be any room for wretched beings like myself?'

(*a*) It is another kind of the *Extraordinary* where a person, proceeding in a hurry to do something, is described as accomplishing another thing, which is not capable of being accomplished by the same effort. Example—

'When the Creator was creating you, with your resplendent form, dazzling glory and flawless learning,—he actually created a new Love-god, a new Sun and a new Bṛhaspati on the Earth'.

गृहिणी सचिवः सखी मिथः प्रियशिष्या ललिते कलाविधौ।
करुणाविमुखेन मृत्युना हरता त्वां बत किं न मे हृतम् ॥५६२॥

सर्वत्र एवंविधविषयेतिशयोक्तिरेव प्राणत्वेनावतिष्ठते तां विना प्रायेणालंकारत्वायोगात्। अत एवोक्तम्

"सैषा सर्वत्र वक्रोक्तिरनयार्थो विभाव्यते।
यत्नोस्यां कविना कार्यः कोलंकारोनया विना ॥ इति ॥

स्वमुत्सृज्य गुणं योगादत्युज्ज्वलगुणस्य यत्।
वस्तु तद्गुणतामेति भण्यते स तु तद्गुणः ॥ १३७ ॥

वस्तु तिरस्कृतनिजरूपं केनापि समीपगतेन प्रगुणया स्वगुणसंपदोपरक्तं तत्प्रतिभासमेव यत्समासादयति स तद्गुणः। तस्याप्रकृतस्य गुणोत्रास्तीति।

Another example of the same—

'When cruel Death deprived me of you—who were my wife, counsellor, confidante and beloved pupil in the graceful arts,—oh ! what is there that he did not deprive me of ?'

In all these cases (of the Extraordinary), artistic expression forms the very essence ; as without it they would almost cease to be ornamental (figures of speech) at all. It is for this reason that the following statement has been made (by Bhāmaha and others)—'Artistic expression is present everywhere ; it is by this that meanings become beautified ; it is on this that the poet should concentrate his effort ; what figure of speech can there be without this ?' 136.

LVII—*Tadguṇa*,—Quality borrowing.

When a thing, through contact with another possessed of extremely brilliant qualities, renounces its own quality and takes up the qualities of that other thing,—it is Quality-borrowing. 137.

उदाहरणम्——

विभिन्नवर्णा गरुडाग्रजेन सूर्यस्य रथ्याः परितः स्फुरन्त्या ।
रत्नैः पुनर्यत्र रुचा रुचं स्वामानिन्यिरे वंशकरीरनीलैः ॥५६३॥

अत्र रवितुरगापेक्षया गरुडाग्रजस्य तदपेक्षया च हरिन्मणीनां प्रगुणवर्णता ॥१३७॥

तद्रूपाननुहारश्चेदस्य तत् स्यादतद्गुणः ।

यदि तु तदीयं वर्णं संभवन्त्यामपि योग्यतायाम् इदं न्यूनगुणं न गृह्णीयात् तदा भवेदतद्गुणो नाम ।

When a thing, on contact with another thing, has its own character obscured by the superiority of the brilliant qualities of the other, and acquires a semblance of that thing, it is the figure *Quality-borrowing*, '*Tadguṇa*'—so called because there is borrowing of the *quality* ('*guṇa*') *of that*, ('*tat*'), the thing other than the one described.

Example—

'The sun's horses, having their colour altered by the wide-spreading splendour of Aruṇa, (the Sun's charioteer, the brother of Garuḍa), were brought back to their own colour by the gems, green like the bamboo-sprout'.

Here the green gems are described as possessed of more brilliant qualities than Aruṇa, whose qualities are more brilliant than those of the Sun's horses.

LVIII.—*Atadguṇa*—Non-borrowing of Qualities.

If, however, there is no absorbing by the one from the other, it is the Non-borrowing of qualities.

In a case, where the thing with inferior qualities does not absorb the form of the other thing,—even when such absorption is possible,—then it is the figur named 'Non-borrowing of Qualities'.

उदाहरणम्—

धवलोसि जहवि सुन्दर तह वि तुए मज्झ रञ्जिअं हिअअं ।
राअभरिएवि हिअए सुहअ णिहित्तो ण रत्तोसि ॥५६४॥

अत्रातिरक्तेनापि मनसा संयुक्तो न रक्ततामुपगत इत्यतद्गुणः ।

किंच तदिति अप्रकृतम् अस्येति च प्रकृतमत्र निर्दिश्यते । तेन यत् अप्रकृतस्य रूपं प्रकृतेन कुतोपि निमित्तात् नानुविधीयते सोतद्गुण इत्यपि प्रतिपत्तव्यम् । यथा

गाङ्गमम्बु सितमम्बु यामुनं कज्जलाभमुभयत्र मज्जतः ।
राजहंस तव सैव शुभ्रता चीयते न च न चापचीयते ॥५६५॥

Example—

'Though you are yourself white (fair), yet you have made my heart *red* (affected by love) ; but though enshrined in my heart which is full of *redness* (love), you have not been *reddened* (made to love)'.

Here the expression of the idea that 'though the *man*, even in contact with very much *reddened* mind, has not become red' involves the figure of 'Non-borrowing of Qualities'.

In the text, the pronoun '*tat*', ('the one') may stand for the object other than the one described, and '*asya*', ('the other') for the object described ; so that the definition may also be taken to mean that when, for some reason the character of the *other object* is not absorbed by the *object described*, then it is the *Non-borrowing of Qualities.*

For example—

'O Chief of Swans, when you dip into the white water of the *Gaṅgā*, or in the black water of the *Yamunā*, your own whiteness becomes neither increased nor decreased'.

यद्यथा साधितं केनाप्यपरेण तदन्यथा ॥ १३८ ॥
तथैव यद्विधीयेत स व्याघात इति स्मृतः ।

येनोपायेन यत् एकेनोपकल्पितम् तस्यान्येन जिगीषुतया तदुपायकमेव यत् अन्यथाकरणम् स साधितवस्तुव्याहतिहेतुत्वात् व्याघातः । उदाहरणम्—

दृशा दग्धं मनसिजं जीवयन्ति दृशैव याः ।
विरूपाक्षस्य जयिनीस्ताः स्तुवे वामलोचनाः ॥५६६॥

सेष्टा संसृष्टिरेतेषां भेदेन यदिह स्थितिः ॥ १३९ ॥

एतेषां समनन्तरमेवोक्तस्वरूपाणां यथासंभवमन्योन्यनिर-

LIX.—*Vyāghāta*—Frustration.

When one thing, which has been accomplished, in one way, by one person, is turned otherwise in that same way, by another,—that is called 'Frustration'.

One man having accomplished a certain object by a certain means,—if that same object is made, by that same means, to become otherwise, by another person,—it is the figure 'Frustration', '*Vyāghāta*';—so called because it is based upon the *frustration* (*vyāhati*) of something that has been accomplished.

Example—

'We eulogise the women who revivify, by their glances, the Love-god, who was burnt by Shiva, by his glance,—and who are thus superior to this latter god'.

LX.—*Samsṛṣṭi*—Collocation of Figures.

When these (figures) are present, distinctly from one another, it is Collocation. 138-39.

When the figures of speech described above are present,—as far as possible independently of one another,—in one substratum,—either (*a*) in the word or (*b*)

पेक्षतया यत् एकत्र शब्दभागे एव अर्थविषये एव उभयत्रापि वा अवस्थानम् सा एकार्थसमवायस्वभावा संसृष्टिः ।

तत्र शब्दालंकारसंसृष्टिर्यथा

वदनसौरभलोभपरिभ्रमद्भ्रमरसंभ्रमसंभृतशोभया ।
चलितया विदधे कलमेखलाकलकलोलकलोलदृशान्यया ।।५६७।।

अर्थालंकारसंसृष्टिस्तु

लिम्पतीव तमोऽङ्गानि वर्षतीवाञ्जनं नभः ।
असत्पुरुषसेवेव दृष्टिर्विफलतां गता ।।५६८।।

पूर्वत्र परस्परनिरपेक्षौ यमकानुप्रासौ संसृष्टिं प्रयोजयतः उत्तरत्र तु तथाविधे उपमोत्प्रेक्षे ।

---

in the meaning or (*c*) in both,—it is called 'Collocation', because it consists in the *co-existence* of several in one thing.

(*a*) In the following we have the Collocation of two *verbal* figures of speech—

'*Vadanasaurabhalobhaparibhramad-*
bhramarasaṁbhramasaṁbhṛtashobhayā.
Chalitayā vidadhe kalamekhalā
kalakalo lakaloladṛshānyayā.'

'The sweet sound of the girdle-zone was produced by another woman, with her eyes tremulous by reason of her hanging locks tossing about, and her beauty enhanced by the flurry caused by the black bees hovering about her, having been attracted by the sweet fragrance of her mouth'.

(*b*) The Collocation of an Ideal and a Verbal Figure of Speech, we have in the verse—

'*Limpatīva tamoṅgāni etc.*' (see above, stanza No. 417).

In the former verse (*a*) we have the Collocation brought about by the verbal figures Alliteration and Chime, which

शब्दार्थलिंकारयोस्तु संसृष्टिः ।

सो णत्थि एत्थ गामे जो एअं महमहन्तलाअण्णं ।
तरुणाण हिअअलूडिं परिसक्कन्तीं णिवारेइ ॥५६९॥

अत्रानुप्रासो रूपकं चान्योन्यानपेक्षे। संसर्गश्च तयोरेकत्र वाक्ये छन्दसि वा समवेतत्वात् ॥१३९॥

अविश्रान्तिजुषामात्मन्यङ्गाङ्गित्वं तु संकरः ।

एते एव यत्रात्मनि अनासादितस्वतन्त्रभावाः परस्परम् अनुग्राह्यानुग्राहकतां दधति स एषां संकीर्यमाणस्वरूपत्वात् संकरः ।

---

stand independent of each other ; and in the latter (*b*), by the two ideal figures, Simple and Poetic Fancy, standing independently of each other.

(*c*) As an example of the Collocation of a Verbal and Ideal figure of speech, we have the following—

'*So ṇatthi ettha gāme jo eaṁ mahamahantalāaṇṇaṁ.*
Taruṇāṇa hiaalūḍiṁ parisakkantīṁ ṇivārei.'

'There is no one in this village who could restrain this young woman loitering about with her exuberant charm, captivating the hearts of young men'.

Here we have Alliteration and Metaphor, independently of each other, and there is connection between these,—as they both occur in the same sentence or the same verse. 139.

LXI.—*Saṅkara.*—Commixture.

(*a*) *When, however, there is a relation of subserviency among the said figures of speech, which are incapable of independent existence by themselves,—then it is Commixture.*

उदाहरणम्—

आत्ते सीमन्तरत्ने मरकतिनि हृते हेमताटङ्कपत्रे
लुप्तायां मेखलायां झटिति मणितुलाकोटियुग्मे गृहीते ।
शोणं बिम्बोष्ठकान्त्या त्वदरिमृगदृशामित्वरीणामरण्ये
राजन् गुञ्जाफलानां स्रज इति शबरा नैव हारं हरन्ति ॥५७०॥

अत्र तद्गुणमपेक्ष्य भ्रान्तिमता प्रादुर्भूतम् तदाश्रयेण च तद्गुणः सचेतसां प्रभूतचमत्कृतिनिमित्तमित्यनयोरङ्गाङ्गिभावः । यथा वा

When these same figures, incapable of attaining independent existence by themselves, bear to one another the relation of helper and helped (*i. e.*, when one helps to sustain the other), it is *Commixture*, '*Saṅkara*';—so called because it involves a *mixing up* of the figures.

Example—'O King, when the wives of your enemies are wandering about in the forest, the foresters wrest from them emerald crown-jewel, take away the golden ear-ornament, snap away the girdle-zone and quickly remove the jewelled anklets ; but on seeing the necklace of pearls, which has become reddened by the reflection of the red colour of their Bimba-like lips, they take it to be only a string of red berries and therefore do not take it'.

Here the figure 'Illusion' appears as based upon 'Quality-borrowing', and *vice versa* ; and this commingling of the two figures is felt by persons possessed of poetic sensibility to be extremely charming ; and hence it is found that there is 'mutual subserviency' between the two.

जटाभाभिर्भाभिः करधृतकलङ्काक्षवलयो
वियोगिव्यापत्तेरिव कलितवैराग्यविशदः ।
परिप्रेङ्खत्तारापरिकरकपालाङ्किततले
शशी भस्मापाण्डुः पितृवन इव व्योम्नि चरति ॥५७१॥

उपमा रूपकम् उत्प्रेक्षा श्लेषश्चेति चत्वारोत्र पूर्ववत् अङ्गाङ्गितया प्रतीयन्ते ।

कलङ्क एवाक्षवलयमिति रूपकपरिग्रहे करधृतत्वमेव साधकप्रमाणतां प्रतिपद्यते । अस्य हि रूपकत्वे तिरोहितकलङ्करूपम्

Another example of the same—

'*Jaṭābhābhirbhābhiḥ karadhṛtakalaṅkākṣabalayo*
Viyogivyāpatteriva kalitavairāgyavishadaḥ
Paripreṅkhattārāparikarakapālāṅkitatale
Shashī bhasmāpāṇḍuḥ pitṛvana iva vyomni charati'.

'The Moon roams in the sky, which has its surface marked by skulls in the shape of the moon and stars, as if it were in a crematorium,—shining, as he does, with the colour of the knotted hair,—*wearing* in his hand (rays) the bracelet of rosary-beads, in the shape of the black mark,—having attained the purity (whiteness) of dispassion (freedom from redness) consequent upon the trouble brought upon separated lovers (the destruction of the objects of sense),—and is white like (with) ashes'.

Here the four Figures, Simile, Metaphor, Poetical Fancy, and Pun appear, as in the foregoing verse, to be 'mutually subservient'.

When we expound the expression '*Kalaṅkākṣabalaya*' *as* '*Kalaṅka eva akṣabalayam*', (the black mark itself being 'the bracelet of rosary-beads'), and as such involving the figure of Metaphor,—the n the fact of 'being held in the hand (rays)' is to be regarded as the basis justifying that

अक्षवलयमेव मुख्यतयावगम्यते तस्यैव च करग्रहणयोग्यतायां सार्वत्रिकी प्रसिद्धिः। श्लेषच्छायया तु कलङ्कस्य करधारणम् असदेव प्रत्यासत्त्या उपचर्य योज्यते शशाङ्केन केवलं कलङ्कस्य मूर्त्यैव उद्वहनात्। कलङ्कोक्षवलयमिवेति तु, उपमायां कलङ्कस्य, उत्कटतया प्रतिपत्तिः। न चास्य करधृतत्वं तत्त्वतोस्तीति मुख्येप्युपचार एव शरणं स्यात्।

एवंरूपश्च संकरः शब्दालंकारयोरपि परिदृश्यते। यथा

Metaphor ; and in this Metaphor it is the 'bracelet of rosary-beads' which appears as the predominant factor, entirely hiding from view the 'black mark' ; as it is the *bracelet* (and not the *black mark*) that is universally known as '*Karadhṛta*', 'worn in the hand'; this latter factor, of being '*Karadhṛta*',—though really not present in the case of the *black* mark—is imposed upon it figuratively, through the force of the Pun (upon the word '*kara*', which means both *hand* and *rays*) aided by the proximity (of the lunar disc),—since it is only on his disc that the Moon wears the black mark.

If, on the other hand, the expression '*Kalaṅkākṣabalaya*' is expounded as '*Kalaṅkaḥ askṣabalayam iva*', ('the black mark which is like the bracelet of rosary-beads'),—thus involving a Simile (not a Metaphor),—then it is the 'black mark' that comes to be recognised most obtrusively (as the principal factor) ;—but even so, as it is not possible for this *mark* to be '*karadhṛta*' (worn in the hand),—if it is the predominant factor, for the application of this epithet, it would have to be dependent entirely upon the said figurative indication (based upon Pun).

Commixture of this kind is met with between *verbal* figures also. As for example, in the following—

राजति तटीयमभिहतदानवरासातिपातिसारावनदा ।
गजता च यूथमविरतदानवरा सातिपाति सारा वनदा ।।५७२।।

अत्र यमकामनुलोमप्रतिलोमश्च चित्रभेदः पाददृयगते परस्परापेक्षे।

एकस्य च ग्रहे न्यायदोषाभावादनिश्चयः ॥ १४० ॥

द्वयोर्बहूनां वा अलंकाराणामेकत्र समावेशेपि विरोधात् न यत्र युगपदवस्थानम् न चैकतरस्य परिग्रहे साधकम् तदितरस्य वा परिहारे बाधकमस्ति येनैकतर एव परिगृह्येत स निश्चयाभावारूपो द्वितीयः संकरः समुच्चयेन संकरस्यैवाक्षेपात् ।

'*Rājati taṭīyamabhihatadānavarāsātipātisārāvanaḍa*
Gajatā cha yūthamaviratadānavarā sātipāti sārā vanadā.'

'This place is glorious, where the roaring of demons has been subdued and which is adorned with fast-flowing murmuring rivers ; and this elephant-herd protects itself, glorious with the uninterrupted flow of the ichor, powerful and destroying thé forest'.

Here *Chime* and the *Fanciful* with convertible parts, are contained in the two feet, and are dependent upon each other.

(b) When there is no reason in support of, nor any objection against, the recognition of any one (to the exclusion of the likely figures), there is Uncertainty (which forms the second variety of Commixture). 140.

When two or more figures of speech are found together, and by reason of incompatibility, all of them cannot be admitted simultaneously,—nor is there any reason for accepting any one of them, nor is there any objection against the exclusion of others, by virtue of which any one only could be admitted,—then there is

उदाहरणम्—

जह गहिरो जह रअणणिब्भरो जह अ णिम्मलच्छाओ ।
तह किं विहिणा एसो सरसवाणीओ जलणिही ण किओ ॥५७३॥

अत्र समुद्रे प्रस्तुते विशेषणसाम्यादप्रस्तुतार्थप्रतीतेः किमसौ समासोक्तिः किम् अब्धेरप्रस्तुतस्य मुखेन कस्यापि तत्सभगुणतया प्रस्तुतस्य प्रतीतेः इयमप्रस्तुतप्रशंसा इति सदेहः। यथा वा

नयनानन्ददायीन्दोर्बिम्बमेतत्प्रसीदति ।
अधुनापि निरुद्धाशमविशीर्णमिदं तमः ॥५७४॥

अत्र किं कामस्योद्दीपकः कालो वर्तते इति भङ्ग्यन्तरेणाभिधानात् पर्यायोक्तम्। उत वदनस्येन्दुबिम्बतया अध्यवसानात्

Uncertainty; and this is to be regarded as the second variety of *Commixture*;—this being the implication of the collective particle '*cha*' (in the text), which is meant to connect the 'commixture' with the present text.

For example, in the following verse—'Hot is it that the ocean was not made sweet-watered, by the Creator, as it was made deep, rich in gems and bright ?'

Here it is uncertain what figure is meant to be expressed; either (*a*) *Modal Metaphor*—involving the recognition of an *object not meant to be described* (the King), when what is actually described is the Ocean,—or (*b*) *Indirect Description*, involving the recognition of the *object to be described* (the King), through the mention of an *object not meant to be described* (the Ocean), which the former resembles.

Or, another example (of Uncertainty), in the following verse.—

'This disc of the moon, which is a source of joy to the eye, is shining; and yet even now this darkness, pervading all quarters, stands unpierced'.

अतिशयोक्तिः किं वा। एतदिति वक्त्रं निर्दिश्य तद्रूपारोपवशात् रूपकम्। अथवा तयोः समुच्चयविवक्षायां दीपकम्। अथवा तुल्ययोगिता। किमु प्रदोषसमये विशेषणसाम्यादाननस्यावगतौ समासोक्तिः। आहोस्वित् मुखनैर्मल्यप्रस्तावात् अप्रस्तुतप्रशंसा इति बहूनां संदेहादयमेव संकरः।

यत्र तु न्यायदोषयोरन्यतरस्यावतारः तत्र एकतरस्य निश्चयात् न संशयः॥

न्यायश्च साधकत्वम् अनुकूलता दोषोपि बाधकत्वं प्रतिकूलता। तत्र

Here it is *Uncertain,* whether what is meant is—(*a*) the indirect assertion of the fact that 'the time favourable for the manifestation of love has arrived',—thus involving the Figure of *Periphrasis* ;—or (*b*) the recognition of the Face of the girl as the Moon,—thus involving the figure *Hyperbole* ;—or (*c*) the imposition of the character of the Moon upon the *Face,* referred to by the pronoun 'this',—thus involving the figure of *Metaphor* ;—or (*d*) the combination of both (Face and Moon),—thus involving the figure of *Illuminator*)—or (*e*) the figure of *Equal Pairing* (both Face and Moon being meant to be described) ;—or (*f*) the cognition of the face, through common qualifications and the mention of the evening-time,—thus involving the figure of *Modal Metaphor* ;—or (*g*) the introduction of the description of the face,—thus involving the figure of *Indirect Description.*

Thus, there being an uncertainty pertaining to several figures, this is an instance of the *Uncertain Commixture.*

In cases where there are reasons for or against the admission of any one of the figures involved, there is certainty with regard to that one ; so that in that case there is no *uncertainty.*

सौभाग्यं वितनोति वक्त्रशशिनो ज्योत्स्नेव हासद्युतिः ॥५७५॥

इत्यत्र मुख्यतया अवगम्यमाना हासद्युतिर्वक्त्रे एवानुकूल्यं भजते इत्युपमायाः साधकम्। शशिना तु न तथा प्रतिकूलेति रूपकं प्रति तस्या अबाधकता।

वक्त्रेन्दौ तव सत्ययं यदपरः शीतांशुरभ्युद्यतः ॥५७६॥

इत्यत्रापरत्वमिन्दोरनुगुणं न तु वक्त्रस्य प्रतिकूलमिति रूपकस्य साधकतां प्रतिपद्यते न तूपमाया बाधकताम्।

राजनारायणं लक्ष्मीस्त्वामालिङ्गति निर्भरम् ॥५७७॥

The term '*nyāya*' (in the text) stands for *reasons for*, that is, favourable to, something ; and '*doṣa*' for *reasons against*, opposed to, something.

(*a*) In the following passage—'the brightness of the smile like moonlight, lends gracefulness to the face-moon', —what is recognised as the predominant factor is the 'brightness of smile.', and this is favourable to the description being applicable to the face ; and hence it serves as the reason for the definite recognition of the figure of *Simile* (in the expression 'face-moon') ; and as regards the application of the description to the moon, also, the said circumstance (of the *brightness of Simile* being the predominant factor) is not altogether unfavourable ; and hence it cannot be regarded as a *reason for* the admission of the figure of *Metaphor* (in the same expression 'Face-moon'.)—

(*b*) But in the passage—'that this other moon should appear while your face-moon is already present',—the epithet 'other' is favourable to the *moon* being taken as the object described, but not entirely unfavourable to the

इत्यत्र पुनरालिङ्गनमुपमां निरस्यति सदृशं प्रति परप्रेयसीप्रयुक्तस्यालिङ्गनस्यासंभवात् ।

पादाम्बुजं भवतु नो विजयाय मञ्जु-
मञ्जीरशिञ्जितमनोहरमम्बिकायाः ॥५७८॥

इत्यत्र मञ्जीरशिञ्जितम् अम्बुजे प्रतिकूलम् असंभवादिति रूपकस्यबाधकम् न तु पादेनुकूलमित्युपमायाःसाधकममिधयते विघ्युपमर्दिनो बाधकस्य तदपेक्षयोत्कटत्वेन प्रतिपत्तेः ॥

एवमन्यत्रापि सुधीभिः परीक्ष्यम् ॥१४०॥

---

face being so taken; and hence it becomes a *reason for* the admission of *Metaphor*, but not a *reason against* that of Simile.

(*c*) In the passage—'The Goddess of Wealth firmly embraces you, the *King-Viṣṇu*',—the mention of 'embracing' excludes the *Simile*, as it is not possible (right) for the wife of one person to 'embrace' another who may be *similar* to him.

(*d*) In the passage—'may the lotus-feet of Ambikā, lovely on account of the jingling of the anklets, ordain your victory',—the 'jingling' is unfavourable to the description applying to the *lotus* whose *jingling* is impossible and as such, it is a *reason against* the admission of *Metaphor*; we do not regard it as a *reason for* the admission of the Simile, on the ground of its being favourable to its applying to the feet,—because the fact of its being a negative *reason against* (Metaphor) is more obtrusively recognised than that of its being an affirmative *reason for* Simile.

Similar deductions may be made by the learned in other cases also.

स्फुटमेकत्र विषये शब्दार्थालंकृतिद्वयम् ।
व्यवस्थितं च

अभिन्ने एव पदे स्फुटतया . यत् उभावपि शब्दार्थालंकारौ व्यवस्थां समासादयतः सोप्यपरः संकरः । उदाहरणम्——

स्पष्टोल्लसत्किरणकेसरसूर्यबिम्ब-
विस्तीर्णकर्णिकमथो दिवसारविन्दम् ।
श्लिष्टाष्टदिग्दलकलापमुखावतार-
बद्धान्धकारमधुपावलि संचुकोच ॥५७९॥

अत्र एकापदानुप्रविष्टौ रूपकानुप्रासौ ॥

तेनासौ त्रिरूपः परिकीर्तितः ॥ १४१ ॥

(*c*) *Also, when, in a single word, both the Verbal and the Ideal Figures of Speech are clearly manifest.*

When in one and the same word, both, the Verbal and the Ideal Figures of Speech obtain a clear footing,—it is another (third) kind of *Commixture.*

Example—

'*Spaṣṭollasatkiraṇakesarasūryabimba—*
Vistīrṇakarṇikamatho divasāravindam
Shliṣṭāṣṭadigdalakalāpamukhāvatāra—
Baddhāndhakāramadhupāvali sañchukocha'.

'The Day-lotus, with the Sun for its pericarp of which the shooting rays are the filaments,—enveloping the Night-bee embracing the eight quarters, has become contracted'.

Here we have the *Commixture* of *Alliteration* and *Metaphor* in single words (in the shape of the two long compounds).

Thus this (Commixture) has been described as having three forms. 141.

तदयमनुग्राह्यानुग्राहकतया संदेहेन एकपदप्रतिपाद्यतया च व्यवस्थितत्वात्त्रिप्रकार एव संकरो व्याकृतः। प्रकारान्तरेण तु न शक्यो व्याकर्तुम् आनन्त्यात्तत्प्रभेदानामिति प्रतिपादिताः शब्दार्थोभयगतत्वेन त्रैविध्यजुषोलंकाराः ॥

कुतः पुनरेष नियमो यदेतेषां तुल्येपि काव्यशोभातिशयहेतुत्वे कश्चिदलंकारः शब्दस्य कश्चिदर्थस्य कश्चिच्चोभयस्य इति चेत्। उक्तमत्र यथा काव्ये दोषगुणालंकाराणां शब्दार्थोभयगतत्वेन व्यवस्थायामन्वयव्यतिरेकावेव प्रभवतः निमित्तान्तरस्याभावात्। ततश्च योलंकारो यदीयान्वयव्यतिरेकावनुविधत्ते स तदलंकारो व्यवस्थाप्यते इति ।

Thus has been described *Commixture* in its three forms—(1) that in which one figure aids, and is subservient to, the other, (2) where the predominance of one or the other is doubtful, and (3) where both figures manifest themselves in single words.

Any other method of sub-dividing it is not advisable, as the number of such divisions would be endless.

Thus have been described all the Figures of Speech, classified under three heads—as pertaining to the word, to the idea and to both.

Question.—" All Figures of Speech equally being only the means of lending charm to poetry, wherefore should there be any such restriction as that some figures belong to Words, others to Ideas, and others again to both Words and Ideas ?"

Our answer to this is as follows :—It has already been explained that in Poetry, Defects,Excellences and Figures of Speech are attributed to Words, Ideas or both, entirely on the basis of positive and negative concomitance ; as

एवं च यथा पुनरुक्तवदाभासः परंपरितरूपकं चोभयोर्भावा-भावानुविधायितया, उभयालंकारौ तथा शब्दहेतुकार्थान्तरन्यास-प्रभृतयोपि द्रष्टव्याः । अर्थस्य तु तत्र वैचित्र्यम् उत्कटतया प्रतिभासते, इति वाच्यालंकारमध्ये वस्तुस्थितिमनपेक्ष्यैव लक्षिताः ॥

योलंकारो यदाश्रितः स तदलंकार इत्यपि कल्पनायाम् अन्वयव्यतिरेकावेव समाश्रयितव्यौ । तदाश्रयणमन्तरेण विशिष्ट-स्याश्रयाश्रयिभावस्याभावादित्यलंकाराणां यथोक्तनिमित्त एव परस्परव्यतिरेको ज्यायान् ॥१४१॥

---

there can be no other determining basis ; consequently a Figure of Speech is attributed to one or the other according as it is concomitant, positively as well as negatively, with that. So the *Semblance of Repetition* and the *Consequential Metaphor* are attributed to both Word and Idea, because their presence or absence is dependent upon the presence and absence of both. Similarly with the 'Transition' based upon words and other Figures of speech ; even so however the real state of things has been ignored, and these latter have been classed among *Ideal* figures, simply because what shines forth in them most prominently is the charm of the Idea expressed.

Even if we accept the principle that ' a figure is to be attributed to that on which it rests ', the ultimate criterion to be adopted will have to be the before-mentioned ' positive and negative concomitance ', especially because in the absence of these latter there can be no idea of the figures subsisting in anything For these reasons it is best to accept the said distinction among Figures of Speech entirely on the basis of the said ' concomitance '. 141.

एषां दोषा यथायोगं संभवन्तोपि केचन ।
उक्तेष्वन्तर्भवन्तीति न पृथक् प्रतिपादिताः ॥ १४२ ॥

तथाहि—अनुप्रासस्य प्रसिद्ध्यभावो वैफल्यं वृत्तिविरोध इति ये त्रयो दोषाः। ते प्रसिद्धिविरुद्धताम् अपुष्टार्थत्वम् प्रतिकूलवर्णतां च यथाक्रमं न व्यतिक्रामन्ति तत्स्वभावत्वात्। क्रमेणोदाहरणम्—

चक्री चक्रारपङ्क्तिं हरिरपि च हरीन् धूर्जटिर्धूर्ध्वजाग्रान्
अक्षं नक्षत्रनाथोरुणमपि वरुणः कूबराग्रं कुबेरः ।
रंहः संघः सुराणां जगदुपकृतये नित्ययुक्तस्य यस्य
स्तौति प्रीतिप्रसन्नोन्वहमहिमरुचेः सोवतात्स्यन्दनो वः ॥५८०॥

Defects are possible in connection with these (Figures) also ; but they are such as are likely to be included among these already described ; hecnce they are not dealt with separately. 142.

For instance, in connection with Alliteration, three defects have been cited (by the older writers) as specially noticeable ; these are—(1) absence of general recognition, (2) uselessness and (3) incompatibility of diction ; and these do not differ in character respectively from (1) being opposed to accepted notions, (2) Irrelevancy and (3) Discordance of letters ; as they have the same character as these. Examples in order—

(1) [*Absence of General Recognition*]—

'*Chakrī chakrārapaṅktiṁ harirapi cha harīn, dhūrjaṭirdhūrdhvajāgrān*
Akṣaṁ nakṣatranāthoruṇamapi varuṇaḥ, kūbarāgraṁ kuberaḥ
Raṁhaḥ saṁghaḥ surāṇāṁ jagadupakṛtaye nityayuktasya yasya
Stauti prītiprasannonvahamahimarucheḥ sovatātsyandano vaḥ.'

अत्र कर्तृकर्मप्रतिनियमेन स्तुतिः अनुप्रासानुरोधेनैव कृता न पुराणेतिहासादिषु तथा प्रतीतेति प्रसिद्धिविरोधः ॥

भण तरुणि रमणमन्दिरमानन्दस्यन्दिसुन्दरेन्दुमुखि ।
यदि सल्लीलोल्लापिनि गच्छसि तत् किं त्वदीयं मे ॥५८१॥
अनणुरणन्मणिमेखलमविरतशिञ्जानमञ्जुमञ्जीरम् ।
परिसरणमरुणचरणे रणरणकमकारणं कुरुते ॥५८२॥

'May that chariot of the Sun bent upon benefitting the world, protect you, whose line of spokes is daily recognised with pleasure by Viṣṇu, the horses by Indra, the banners by Shiva, the wheel by the Moon, the driver Aruṇa by Varuṇa, the poles by Kubera and the speed by the hosts of gods !'

The series of Agents and the Acts attributed to them here are all such as have been assumed for the purposes of Alliteration, and no such acts are found to have been described in the Itihāsas or Purāṇas. So that this is only a case of 'contraxity to prevailing notions'.

(2) [*Uselessness*]—

'*Bhaṇa taruṇi ramaṇamandiramānandasyandi-sundarendumukhi*
Yadi sallīlollāpini gachchasi tat kiṁ tvadīyaṁ me
Anaṇuraṇanmaṇimekhalamaviratashiñjānamañju-mañjīram
Parisaraṇamaruṇacharaṇe raṇaraṇakamakā-raṇam kurute.'

'O young girl, with face as bright as the joyous moon, who converse sweetly and whose feet are red ! at the time that you are going to your husband, your movement, accompanied by the tingling girdlezone and jingling anklets, produce without reason, a peculiar anxiety in my heart ;—tell me why this is so'.

अत्र वाच्यस्य विचिन्त्यमानं न किंचिदपि चारुत्वं प्रतीयते, इत्यपुष्टार्थतैवानुप्रासस्य वैफल्यम् ।।

अकुण्ठोत्कण्ठया इति अत्र शृङ्गारे परुषवर्णाडम्बरः पूर्वोक्तरीत्या विरुध्यते इति परुषानुप्रासोत्र प्रतिकूलवर्णतैव वृत्तिविरोधः ।।

यमकस्य पादत्रयगतत्वेन यमनमप्रयुक्तत्वं दोषः ।। यथा

भुजङ्गमस्येव मणिः सदम्भा ग्राहावकीर्णेव नदी सदम्भाः ।
दुरन्ततां निर्णयतोपि जन्तोः कर्षन्ति चेतः प्रसभं सदम्भाः ।।५८३।।

The idea expressed here is one in which, however much we ponder over it, we perceive no charm; hence the 'uselessness' of the Alliteration is only what has been described above as 'Irrelevancy'.

(3) [*Incompatibility of Diction*]—

'*Akuṇṭhotkaṇṭhayā &c., &c.*, (see above, stanza No. 207).

Here, the bombast of harsh words is incompatible with the delineation of the Erotic Passion, in accordance with what has been said before (in Chapter VII); so that the defect of 'incompatibility of diction' in this Alliteration is nothing more than the presence of 'discordant letters'.

The presence of chiming in three feet of a verse, which has been mentioned as a defect in connection with *Chime*, is only 'opposition to usage'; *e. g.*, in the following verse—

'Bhujaṅgamasyeva maṇiḥ sadambhā
Grābhāvakīrṇeva nadī sadambhāḥ
Durantatānnirṇayatopi jantoḥ
Karṣanti chetaḥ prasabhaṁ sadambhāḥ.'

उपमायाम् उपमानस्य जातिप्रमाणगतन्यूनत्वम् अधिकता वा तादृशी अनुचितार्थत्वं दोषः। धर्माश्रये तु न्यूनाधिकत्वे यथाक्रमं हीनपदत्वमधिकपदत्वं च न व्यभिचरतः॥ क्रमेणोदाहरणम्–

चण्डालैरिव युष्माभिः साहसं परमं कृतम् ॥५८४॥
वह्निस्फुलिङ्ग इव भानुरयं चकास्ति ॥५८५॥
अयं पद्मासनासीनश्चक्रवाको विराजते।
युगादौ भगवान् वेधा विनिर्मित्सुरिव प्रजाः ॥५८६॥

'Deceitful people, though bearing testimony to their wicked heart, yet succeed in attracting the hearts of simple people,—just as is done by the pure and brilliant hood-gem of the serpent, and by the clear-watered streams full of alligators'.

The defect mentioned in connection with Simile is the inferiority or superiority of the *object compared to* (to the *object compared*), in point of kind and degree ;—and this is only what has been described as 'Impropriety' of meaning ;—while the inferiority and superiority as regard the properties (of the two objects) do not differ from what has been described as 'deficiency of words' or 'redundancy of words'.

For Example—

(1) [*Inferiority in kind*]—

'You took a very bold step, *like Chaṇḍālas*'

(2) [*Inferiority in degree*]—

'The Sun is shining like a spark of fire'.

(3) [*Superiority in kind*]—

'This Chakravāka bird, seated on the lotus-seat, looks beautiful,—just like the revered Creator going to create the people at the beginning of the cycle'.

पातालमिव ते नाभिः स्तनौ क्षितिधरोपमौ ।

वेणीदण्डः पुनरयं कालिन्दीपातसंनिभः ॥५८७॥

अत्र चण्डालादिभिरुपमानः प्रस्तुतोर्थोत्यर्थमेव कदर्थित इत्यनुचितार्थता ॥

स मुनिर्लाञ्छितो मौञ्ज्या कृष्णाजिनपटं वहन् ।

व्यराजन्नीलजीमूतभागाश्लिष्ट इवांशुमान् ॥५८८॥

अत्रोपमानस्य मौञ्जीस्थानीयस्तडिल्लक्षणो धर्मः केनापि पदेन न प्रतिपादित इति हीनपदत्वम् ॥

स पीतवासाः प्रगृहीतशार्ङ्गो मनोज्ञभीमं वपुराप कृष्णः ।

शतह्रदेन्द्रायुधवान्निशायां संसृज्यमानः शशिनेव मेघः ॥५८९॥

अत्रोपमेयस्य शङ्खादेरनिर्देशे शशिनो ग्रहणमतिरिच्यते इत्यधिकपदत्वम् ॥

---

(4) [*Superiority in degree*]—

'Thy navel is like the nether regions, thy breasts are like mountains and thy looks like the stream of the Yamunā'.

In all these instances, the objects described, by being compared to the things mentioned, have been very much depreciated ; and this involves the defect of 'impropriety of meaning' (already described in Chap. VII.)

In the passage—'The sage, wearing the girdle and the skin of the antelope, appeared like the sun interspersed among masses of blue clouds',—it is found that in connection with the *object compared to* (the Sun), nothing (like the lightning, for instance) has been mentioned as corresponding to the 'girdle' of the *object compared* ; and this is only a 'deficiency of words'.

In the passage—'Kṛṣṇa, dressed in yellow cloth and holding his bow assumed a body at once beautiful and terrible,—like the nocturnal cloud accompanied by lightning and the rainbow and the Moon',—in the absence

लिङ्गवचनभेदोपि उपमानोपमेययोः साधारणं चेत् धर्ममन्यरूपं कुर्यात्। तदा एकतरस्यैव तद्धर्मसमन्वयावगतेः सविशेषणस्यैव तस्योपमानत्वमुपमेयत्वं वा प्रतीयमानेन धर्मेण प्रतीयते इति प्रक्रान्तस्यार्थस्य स्फुटमनिर्वाहादस्य भग्नप्रक्रमरूपत्वम्। यथा—

चिन्तारत्नमिव च्युतोसि करतो धिङ्मन्दभाग्यस्य मे ॥५९०॥

---

of any mention of the *conch* and other things in connection with the *object compared* (Kṛṣṇa), the mention of the *moon* is superfluous ; and this involves the defect of 'Redundancy' (already described under chapter VII).

Further, the diversity in gender and number, of the *object compared* and that *compared to* (which has been described as a defect of Simile),—if it bring about some diversity in the form of the word mentioning the common property, it is only the defect which has been described as 'Broken Uniformity ;' because in such a case the said property belonging to only one of the two objects, the objects could be regarded either as 'the object compared' or 'the object compared a to' on the basis of that property only in a qualified (and not original) form ; and this would mean that the idea started with could not be sustained. For example, in the following instances—

(*a*) '*Chintāratnamiva chyutosi karato dhin̄ mandabhāgyasya me*'

'You are fallen from my hands, like the *Chintāmaṇi*,—unlucky that I am !' [where the past-participle '*chyutaḥ*' being in the masculine gender, can be construed only with the man described, and not with '*ratnam*', which is in the neuter gender,[;—and also in the passage—(*b*) '*Saktavo*

सक्तवो भक्षिता देव शुद्धाः कुलवधूरिव ॥५९१॥

यत्र तु नानात्वेपि लिङ्गवचनयोः सामान्याभिधायि पदं स्वरूपभेदं नापद्यते न तत्रैतद्दूषणावतारः उभयथापि अस्य अनुगमक्षमस्वभावत्वात् । यथा

गुणैरनर्घ्यैः प्रथितो रत्नैरिव महार्णवः ॥५९२॥
तद्वेषोसदृशोन्याभिः स्त्रीभिर्मधुरताभृतः ।
दधते स्म परां शोभां तदीया विभ्रमा इव ॥५९३॥

---

bhakṣitā deva shuddhāḥ kulavadhūriva,—'The clean barley-meal was eaten, like pure women',—[where the past-participle '*bhakṣitāḥ*' in the plural number cannot be construed with '*kulavadhūḥ*' in the singular.]

In those cases however where, even when there is diversity of gender and number, there is no consequent alteration in the word denoting the common property,—it does not involve the said defect; as the common property remains capable of being connected with both the objects concerned. For example, in the following passages—(*a*) '*Guṇairanarghyaiḥ prathito ratnairiva mahārṇavaḥ*' [He is famous for his valuable qualities, as the ocean for his gems] [where though the genders of the nouns '*ratnaiḥ*' and '*guṇaiḥ*' are different, yet that does not make any difference in the form of the connected word '*prathitaḥ*'];—or in the passage—(*b*) '*Tadveṣo' sadṛshonyābhiḥ strībhirmadhuratābhṛtaḥ dadhate sma parāṁ shobhāṁ tadīyā vibhramā iva*'—Her apparel was lovely as her graces, sweet and unequalled by other women'; [where the compounds ending with '*sadṛshaḥ*' and '*bhṛtaḥ*' are such as can be made applicable to both nouns '*veṣaḥ*', singular and '*vibhramāḥ*', plural.]

कालपुरुषविध्यादिभेदेपि न तथा प्रतीतिरस्खलितरूपतया विश्रान्तिमासादयतीत्यसावपि भग्नप्रक्रमतयैव व्याप्तः। यथा

अतिथिं नाम काकुत्स्थात् पुत्रमाप कुमुद्वती ।
पश्चिमाद् यामिनीयामात् प्रसादमिव चेतना ॥५९४॥

अत्र चेतना प्रसादमाप्नोति न पुनरापेति कालभेदः ।

प्रत्यग्रमज्जनविशेषविविक्तमूर्तिः
कौसुम्भरागरुचिरस्फुरदंशुकान्ताः ।
विभ्राजसे मकरकेतनमर्चयन्ती
बालप्रबालविटपप्रभवा लतेव ॥५९५॥

Diversity in Tense, Person, and the Imperative and other endings interferes with the clear comprehension of the idea ; so that this also would be included under 'Broken Uniformity'. For example, in the passage—'*Atithiṁ nāma kākutsthāt putramāpa kumudvatī, pashchimād yāminīyāmāt prasādamiva chetanā*'—'Kumudvatī obtained from Kākutstha, the son named '*Atithi*'—just as Intellect obtains enlightenment from the last quarter of the night',—where the verb as applying to the *Intellect* should be in the *present* tense—'*āpnoti*',—and not in the *past*, '*āpa*' ; hence here we have diversity of tense (which mars the *clear* comprehension of the Simile).

And in the following passage—

'*Pratyagramajjanavisheshaviviktamūrtiḥ*
kausumbharāgaruchirasphuradamshukāntā
vibhrājase makaraketanamarchayantī
bālaprabālaviṭapaprabhavā lateva',

'Having the body brightened by a fresh bath and clothed in a dress coloured red with *Kusumbha*, while thou art worshipping the Love-god, thou shinest like a creeper growing out of the branch of a tree with fresh leaves',—the proper verb with '*latā*' would have been '*vibhrājate*', in the third person ; and as this would

अत्र लता विभ्राजते न तु विभ्राजसे इति संबोध्यमाननिष्ठस्य परभागस्य असंबोध्यमानविषयतया व्यत्यासात् पुरुषभेदः ।

गङ्गेव प्रवहतु ते सदैव कीर्तिः ॥५९६॥

इत्यादौ च गङ्गा प्रवहति न तु प्रवहतु इति अप्रवृत्तप्रवर्तनात्मनो विधेः । एवंजातीयकस्य चान्यस्यार्थस्य उपमानगतस्यासंभवाद्विध्यादिभेदः ॥

ननु समानम् उच्चारितं प्रतीयमानं वा धर्मान्तरमुपादाय पर्यवसितायाम् उपमायाम् उपमेयस्य प्रकृतधर्माभिसंबन्धान्न कश्चित्कालादिभेदोस्ति। यत्राप्युपात्तेनैव सामान्यधर्मेण उपमा अवगम्यते यथा "युधिष्ठिर इवायं सत्यं वदति" इति तत्र युधिष्ठिर

---

mean a change consequent upon the last portion of the verb referring to the person addressed being applied to an object not addressed ; and thus there comes about a diversity in the Person.

In the passage '*Gaṅgevā pravahatu te sadaiva kīrtiḥ*'—'May your reputation flow on for ever like the Gaṅgā'—the form of the verb applicable to 'Gaṅgā' would be '*pravahati*' and not '*provahatu*' ; so that the text involves the diversity of the Imperative, whose function lies in urging that which is not already engaged in the work (which in this case is the 'Reputation', and not the *Gaṅgā*, which is always flowing).

Many such diversities of the injunctive and other factors are possible, as most of them are not applicable to the *object compared to.*

An objection is raised—" As a matter of fact, the conditions of the Simile are fulfilled when a property common to the two objects has been comprehended, either as expressed by the words uttered or implied ; and when the

इव सत्यवाद्ययं सत्यं वदतीति प्रतिपत्स्यामहे। सत्यवादी सत्यं वदतीति च न पौनरुक्त्यम् आशङ्कनीयम् रैपोषं पुष्णातीतिवत् युधिष्ठिर इव सत्यवदनेन सत्यवाद्ययमित्यर्थावगमात्। सत्यमेतत् किं तु स्थितेषु प्रयोगेषु समर्थनमिदं न तु सर्वथा निरवद्यम् प्रस्तुतवस्तुप्रतीतिव्याघातादिति सचेतस एवात्र प्रमाणम्॥
असादृश्यासंभवावप्युपमायाम् अनुचितार्थतायामेव पर्यवस्यतः।

---

object compared is found to be possessed of this property, there is nothing objectionable in any diversity that there may be as regards the tense and other details. Even in cases where the Simile is comprehended through a directly expressed common property,—*e. g.*, in such expressions as 'he tells the truth like Yudhiṣṭhira',—the idea we derive from it is that—'this person, who is as truthful as Yudhiṣṭhira, tells the truth'. It need not be argued against this that such an expression as 'the truthful man tells the truth' involves a tautology.—Because the idea derived is that 'by telling the truth this man is truthful like Yudhiṣṭhira'; and this stands on the same footing as such (seemingly tautological) expressions as '*raipoṣaṁ puṣṇāti*', 'he develops with the development of wealth".

All this is quite true. But this can be a justification only for such expressions as are actually found in standard works; but such usage cannot be regarded as entirely unobjectionable; for in reality it does mar the due comprehension of the thing meant to be described.

On this point the only right judges are persons endowed with poetic sensibility.

As regards the defects of 'absence of similitude'

यथा

ग्रथ्नामि काव्यशशिनं विततार्थरश्मिम् ।।५९७।।

अत्र काव्यस्य शशिना अर्थानां च रश्मिभिः साधर्म्यं कुत्रापि न प्रतीतमित्यनुचितार्थत्वम् ।

निपेतुरास्यादिव तस्य दीप्ताः
शरा धनुर्मण्डलमध्यभाजः ।
जाज्वल्यमाना इव वारिधारा
दिनार्धभाजः परिवेषिणोर्कात् ।।५९८।।

अत्रापि ज्वलन्त्योम्बुधाराः सूर्यमण्डलात् निष्पतन्त्यो न संभवन्तीत्युपनिबध्यमानोर्थोनौचित्यमेव पुष्णाति ।।

उत्प्रेक्षायामपि संभावनं ध्रुवेवादय एव शब्दा वक्तुं सहन्ते न यथाशब्दोपि केवलस्यास्य साधर्म्यमेव प्रतिपादयितुं पर्याप्तत्वात् तस्य चास्यामविवक्षितत्वादिति तत्राशक्तिरस्यावाचकत्वं दोषः । यथा

---

and ' impossibility ', which have been attributed to Simile,—these are included under the ' Impropriety of Meaning '. For example, in the expression ' I am stringing the moon of poetry with the rays of ideas ',—Poetry is described as similar to the Moon, and Ideas to the rays ; while as a matter of fact, no such similarity is known to any one ; hence here we have the defect of the ' Impropriety of meaning '.

Similarly in the following verse—' Out of the mouth of the king who was occupying the centre of the bow-circle, there fell resplendent arrows, like the flaming showers of rain from the encircled Sun occupying the meridian sky ;'—the ' falling of the flaming showers of rain out of the solar disc ' is an impossible phenomenon ; hence the expression of such an idea only serves to lend support to the idea that it is ' improper '.

In Poetical Fancy also, the fancy or imagination or

उद्ययौ दीर्घिकागर्भान्मुकुलं मेचकोत्पलम् ।
नारीलोचनचातुर्यशङ्कासंकुचितंय था ॥५९९॥

उत्प्रेक्षितमपि तात्त्विकेन रूपेण परिवर्जितत्वात् निरुपाख्य-प्रख्यम् । तत्समर्थनाय यत् अर्थान्तरन्यासोपादानम् तत् आलेख्य-मिव गगनतलेत्यन्तमसमीचीनमिति निर्विषयत्वमेतस्य । अनुचि-तार्थतैव दोषः । यथा

---

assumption can be expressed by only such things as '*dhruva*' '*iva*' and so forth,—and not such terms as '*yathā*' and the like ; as all that the latter, by itself, signifies is the presence of a common property, which is not intended to be expressed in Poetical Fancy. Hence whenever the assumption involved in this latter figure is expressed by '*yathā*' or some such word, it involves the defect of 'In-expressiveness'. For example, in the following verse,—

'The tender lotus-bud rose from amidst the tank,—shut up as being afraid of the superior elegance of the girl's eyes';—[where the term '*yathā*', 'as', is not expressive of the idea of 'as it were', which is what the Poetic Fancy requires].

Another defect attributed to the Figure of *Poetic Fancy* is 'objectlessness' ('*nirviṣayatva*'), which has been found in those cases of Poetic Fancy where what is *imagined* (fancied, or assumed) having no real existence, and hence being as good as non-existent,—a 'Transition' is put forward for its justification, and this 'Transition' is as improper as painting in the sky.—But here also the defect is that of 'Improper Signification'. For example, in the following verse—

दिवाकराद्रक्षति यो गुहासु लीनं दिवा भीतमिवान्धकारम् ।
क्षुद्रेपि नूनं शरणं प्रपन्ने ममत्वमुच्चैः शिरसामतीव ॥६००॥

अत्राचेतनस्य तमसो दिवाकरात्त्रास एव न संभवतीति कुत एव तत्प्रयोजितमद्रिणा परित्राणम् । संभावितेन तु रूपेण प्रतिभासमानस्यास्य न काचिदनुपपत्तिरवतरतीति व्यर्थ एव तत्समर्थनायां यत्नः ।

साधारणविशेषणवशादेव समासोक्तिरनुक्तमपि उपमानविशेषं प्रकाशयतीति तस्यात्र पुनरुपादाने प्रयोजनाभावात् अनुपादेयत्वं यत् तत् अपुष्टार्थत्वं पुनरुक्तं वा दोषः । यथा

'Who, during the day, protects, from the sun, Darkness, which, is as it were, afraid and hidden among the caves : Persons with *magnanimity* (high heads) sympathise even with an insignificant thing that seeks shelter with them'.

Here, in the first place, it is not possible for *Darkness*, which is an insentient thing, to have any fear from the sun ; wherefore then could there be any *protection* by the mountain, incited by that fear ? And yet there is no incongruity in the imaginary semblance of fear (which is all that the Poetic Fancy has set forth) ; so that the attempt (made in the second line) to justify the preceding statement (by means of 'Transition') is entirely unnecessary.

Another defect attributed to the figure of *Modal Metaphor* is '*anupādeyatva*', 'unmentionability', which has been found in cases where,—the particular *object compared to*, which is not expressly stated, is indicated by the figure (Modal Metaphor), through the force of common epithets,—yet the said object is mentioned again, for which really there is no use at all. This however,

स्पृशति तिग्मरुचौ ककुभः करैर्दयितयेव विजृम्भिततापया ।
अतनुमानपरिग्रहया स्थितं रुचिरया चिरयापि दिनश्रिया ॥६०१॥

अत्र तिग्मरुचेः ककुभां च यथा सदृशविशेषणवशेन व्यक्तिविशेषपरिग्रहेण च नायकतया नायिकात्वेन च व्यक्तिः, तथा ग्रीष्मदिवसश्रियोपि प्रतिनायिकात्वेन भविष्यतीति किं दयितयेति स्वशब्दोपादानेन ॥

श्लेषोपमायास्तु स विषयः यत्रोपमानस्योपादानमन्तरेण साधारणेष्वपि विशेषणेषु न तथा प्रतीतिः । यथा

---

is the same as the defect of either 'Irrelevancy' or 'Tautology' (already described under chapter VII). For example, in the following verse,—

'*Spṛshati tigmaruchau kakubhaḥ karair*
Dayitayeva vijṛmbhitatāpayā
Atanumānaparigrahayā sthitaṁ
Ruchirayā chirayāpi dinashriyā'.

'On the sun touching the quarters with his *hands* (rays), day-light oppressed with *grief* (heat), continued to be *indignant for a long time* (of long duration), just like a girl beloved of him'.

Here, through the force of the common epithets, and through the choice of the genders of the nouns used, it is clearly indicated that the Sun is the lover and the quarters, the loved woman ; equally clearly would it also be indicated that the Summer Day-light is the rival-beloved ; so that where was the use of his being mentioned directly by the term '*dayitayā*' 'girl beloved' ?

[It would not be right to contend that the use of the addition of the word in question serves to make the figure the *Punning Simile* ; because [as a matter of fact, it is a case of *Punning Simile* where, even on the mention of the

स्वयं च पल्लवाताम्र भास्वत्करविराजिता ।
प्रभातसंध्येवास्वापफलल्गुब्धेहितप्रदा ॥६०२ ॥ इति॥

अप्रस्तुतप्रशंसायामपि उपमेयम् अनयैव रीत्या प्रतीतं न पुनः प्रयोगेण कदर्थतां नेंयम् । यथा

आहूतेषु विहंगमेषु मशको नायान् पुरो वार्यते
मध्येवारिधि वावसंस्तृणमणिर्धत्ते मणीनां रुचम् ।
खद्योतोपि न कम्पते प्रचलितुं मध्येपि तेजस्विनां
धिक् सामान्यमचेतनं प्रभुमिवानामृष्टतत्त्वान्तरम् ॥६०३॥

अत्र अचेतनस्य प्रभोरप्रस्तुतविशिष्टसामान्यद्वारेणाभिव्यक्तौ न युक्तमेव पुनः कथनम् ॥

---

common properties, the Simile is not comprehended, unless the *object compared to* is also mentioned. For example, in the verse,—'*Svayañcha pallavātāmra etc. etc.*' (See above, stanza No 377), [where, if the 'dawn' had not been mentioned, the Simile could not have been grasped].

Similarly in the figure *Indirect Description* also, the *object compared* should be comprehended in the same manner (*i. e.* by the force of common epithets), and should not be degraded by being directly mentioned. For example, in the following verse.—

'On *flying objects* being invited, even the mosquito, if it comes, is not prevented ; even the coral lying in the bed of the ocean bears the splendour of a *gem* ; the firefly also is not excluded from among *shining objects* ;—fie upon this unintelligent and indiscriminate classification, which resembles a dull and unappreciative master ',—the *unintelligent master* being already indicated by the mention of such common properties as are not meant to be described,—it was not right to mention him by name.

तदेतलंकारदोषाः यथासंभाविनोन्येप्येवंजातीयकाः पूर्वोक्तयैव दोषजात्या अन्तर्भाविताः न पृथक् प्रतिपादनमर्हन्तीति संपूर्णमिदं काव्यलक्षणम् ॥१४२॥

इत्येष मार्गो विदुषां विभिन्नोप्यभिन्नरूपः प्रतिभासते यत् ।
न तद्विचित्रं यदमुत्र सम्यग्विनिर्मिता संघटनैव हेतुः ॥ १ ॥

इति काव्यप्रकाशेर्थालंकारनिर्णयो नाम दशम उल्लासः ॥

॥ समाप्तश्चायं काव्यप्रकाशः ॥

॥ समाप्तोयं ग्रन्थः ॥

Thus it is found that the defects that have been attributed (by older writers) Figures of Speech, as also other similar defects, are all included among the general defects already described (under Chapter VII) ; and as such, they should not be described separately 142.

Thus is the Exposition of Poetry concluded.

That this high-way (of Rhetoric), though divergent, through the agency of learned writers, yet appears to be one, is nothing strange ; as the reason for this lies in a properly planned collation. [Or, that this work, though composed by different authors, yet appears as one organic whole, is nothing strange ; as the reason for this lies in a properly planned execution of the work.]

Thus ends Chapter X of the Kāvyaprakāsha dealing with Ideal Figures of Speech

END

Alphabetical Index of Sanskrit Terms

Pages

Pages

Pages

Appendices

Prepared under the direction of
Prof. S. M. Mukhopadhyaya.

APPENDIX A

Sanskrit Versions of Prakrit Verses

P. 10, L. 3	मातर्गृहोपकरणमद्य खलु नास्तीति साधितं त्वया । तद्भण किं करणीयमेवमेव न वासरः स्थायी ॥ ६ ॥
P. 10, L. 7.	साधयन्ती सखि सुभगं क्षणे क्षणे दूनाऽसि मत्कृते । सद्भावस्नेहकरणीयसदृशकं तावद्विरचितं त्वया ॥ ७ ॥
P. 11, L. 4.	पश्य निश्चलनिष्पन्दा विसिनीपत्रे राजते बलाका । निर्मलमरकतभाजनपरिस्थिता शंखशुक्तिरिव ॥ ८ ॥
P. 38, L. 2.	एतावन्मात्रस्तनिका एतावन्मात्राभ्यामक्षिपत्राभ्याम् । एतावन्मात्रावस्था एतावन्मात्रैर्दिवसैः ॥११॥
P. 41, L. 3.	अतिपृथुलं जलकुम्भं गृहीत्वा समागतास्मि सखि त्वरितम् । श्रमस्वेदसलिलनिःश्वासनिःसहा विश्राम्यामि क्षणम् ॥१३॥
P. 41, L. 6.	औन्निद्रयं दौर्बल्यं चिन्तालसत्वं सनिःश्वसितम् । मम मन्दभागिन्याः कृते सखि त्वामप्यहह परिभवति ॥१४॥
P. 43, L. 1.	तदा मम गण्डस्थलनिमग्नां दृष्टिं नानैषीरन्यत्र । इदानीं सैवाहं तौ च कपोलौ न च सा दृष्टिः ॥१६॥
P. 44, L. 2.	नुदत्यनार्द्रमनाः श्वश्रूर्मां गृहभरे सकले । क्षणमात्रं यदि संध्यायां भवति न वा भवति विश्रामः ॥१८॥
P. 44, L. 5.	श्रूयते समागमिष्यति तव प्रियोऽद्य प्रहरमात्रेण । एवमेव किमिति तिष्ठसि तत् सखि सज्जय करणीयम् ॥१९॥
P. 45. L. 6.	गुरुजनपरवश प्रिय किं भणामि तव मन्दभागिनी अहकम् । अद्य प्रवासं व्रजसि व्रज स्वयमेव श्रोष्यसि करणीयम् ॥२१॥
P. 80, L. 3.	पथिक नात्र स्त्रस्तरमस्ति मनाक् प्रस्तरस्थले ग्रामे । उन्नतपयोधरं प्रेक्ष्य यदि वससि तदा वस ॥५८॥
P. 82, L. 4.	अलसशिरोमणिर्धूर्तानामग्रिमः पुत्रि धनसमृद्धिमयः । इति भणितेननताङ्गी प्रफुल्लविलोचना जाता ॥६०॥
P. 84, L. 9.	केशेषु बलात्कारेण तेन च समरे जयश्रीर्गृहीता । यथा कन्दराभिर्विधुरास्तस्य वृढं कण्ठे संस्थापिता ॥६५॥
P. 85, L. 6.	गाढालिङ्गनरभसोद्यते दयिते लघु समपसरति । मनस्विन्याः मानः पीडनभीत इव हृदयात् ॥६६॥

P. 86. L. 1. या स्थविरमिव हसन्ती कविवदनाम्बुरुहबद्धविनिवेशा ।
दर्शयति भुवनमण्डलमन्यदिव जयति सा वाणी ।।६७।।

P. 86. L. 6. ये लङ्कागिरिमेखलासु स्खलिताः संभोगखिन्नोरगी-
स्फारोत्फुल्लफणावलीकवलने प्राप्ता दरिद्रत्वम् ।
त इदानीं मलयानिला विरहिणीनिःश्वाससंपर्किणो
जाता झटिति शिशुत्वेऽपि बहलास्तारुण्यपूर्णा इव ।।६८।।

P. 87, L. 3. सखि विरचय्य मानस्य मम धीरत्वेनाश्वासम् ।
प्रियदर्शनविशृङ्खलक्षणे सहसेति तेनापसृतम् ।।६९।।

P. 87, L. 7. आर्द्रार्द्रकरजरदनक्षतैस्तव लोचनयोर्मम दत्तम् ।
रक्तांशुकं प्रसादः कोपेन पुनरिमे नाक्रान्ते ।।७०।।

P. 88, L. 4. महिलासहस्रभरिते तव हृदये सुभग सा अमान्ती ।
अनुदिनमनन्यकर्मा अङ्गं तनुकमपि तनयति ।।७१।।

P. 92, L. 5. खलव्यवहारा दृश्यन्ते दारुणा यद्यपि तथापि धीराणाम् ।
हृदयवयस्यबहुमता न खलु व्यवसाया विमुह्यन्ति ।।७४।।

P. 97, L. 1. तव वल्लभस्य प्रभात आसीदधरो म्लानकमलदलम् ।
इति नववधूः श्रुत्वा करोति वदनं महीसंमुखम् ।।८३।।

P. 97, L. 6. रात्रीषु चन्द्रधवलासु ललितमास्फाल्य यश्चापम् ।
एकच्छत्रमिव करोति भुवनराज्यं विजृम्भमाणः ।।८४।।

P. 98, L. 8. वार्यमाणोऽपि पुनः संतापकदर्थितेन हृदयेन ।
स्तनभरवयस्येन विशुद्धजातिर्न चलत्यस्या हारः ।।८६।।

P. 99, L. 2. स मुग्धश्यामलाङ्गो धम्मिल्लः कलितललितनिजदेहः ।
तस्याः स्कन्धाद्बलं गृहीत्वा स्मरः सुरतसंगरे जयति ।।८७।।

P. 99, L. 8. नवपूर्णिमामृगाङ्कस्य सुभग कस्त्वमसि भण मम सत्यम् ।
का सौभाग्यसमग्रा प्रदोषरजनीव तवाद्य ।।८८।।

P. 100, L. 3. सखि नवनिधुवनसमरेऽङ्कपालीसख्या निबिडया ।
हारो निवारित एवोच्छिद्यमाणस्ततः कथं रमितम् ।।८९।।

P. 101, L. 1. प्रविशन्ती गृहद्वारं विवलितवदना विलोक्य पन्थानम् ।
स्कन्धे गृहीत्वा घटं हा हा नष्ट इति रोदिषि सखि किमिति ।।९०।।

P. 101, L. 6. विशृङ्खलां त्वां सखि दृष्ट्वा कुटेन तरलतरदृष्टिम् ।
द्वारस्पर्शमिषेण चात्मा गुरुक इति पातयित्वा विभिन्नः ।।९१।।

P. 102, L. 3. ज्योत्स्नया मधुरसेन च वितीर्णतारुण्योत्सुकमनाः सा ।
वृद्धापि नवोढेव परवधूरहह हरति तव हृदयम् ।।९२।।

P. 105, L. 6. रतिकेलिहृतनिवसनकरकिसलयरुद्धनयनयुगलस्य ।
रुद्रस्य तृतीयनयनं पार्वतीपरिचुम्बितं जयति ॥९७॥

P. 108, L. 6. ग्रामरुहास्मि ग्रामे वसामि नगरस्थितिं न जानामि ।
नागरिकाणां पतीन् हरामि या भवामि सा भवामि ॥१०१॥

P. 109, L. 5. तेषां गुणग्रहणानां तासामुत्कण्ठानां तस्य प्रेम्णः ।
तासां भणितीनां सुन्दर ईदृशं जातमवसानम् ॥१०२॥

P. 117, L. 2. क्षणप्राघुणिका देवर जायया सुभग किमपि ते भणिता ।
रोदिति गृहपश्चाद्भागवलभीगृहेऽनुनीयतां वराकी ॥१११॥

P. 132, L. 2. वानीरकुञ्जोड्डीनशकुनिकोलाहलं शृण्वन्त्याः ।
गृहकर्मव्यापृताया वध्वाः सीदन्त्यङ्गानि ॥१३२॥

P. 151, L. 4. कस्य वा न भवति रोषो दृष्ट्वा प्रियाया सव्रणमधरम् ।
सभ्रमरपद्माघ्रायिणि वारितवामे सहस्वेदानीम् ॥१३५॥

P. 154, L. 6. श्वश्रूरत्र निमज्जति अत्राहं दिवसके प्रलोकय ।
मा पथिक राज्यन्धक शय्यायामावयोर्निमङ्क्ष्यसि ॥१३६॥

P. 156, L. 3. विपरीतरते लक्ष्मीर्ब्रह्माणं दृष्ट्वा नाभिकमलस्थम् ।
हरेर्दक्षिणनयनं रसाकुला झटिति स्थगयति ॥१३७॥

P. 158, L. 4. भ्रम धार्मिक विश्रब्धः स शूनकोऽद्य मारितस्तेन ।
गोदानदीकच्छकुञ्जवासिना दृप्तसिंहेन ॥१३८॥

P. 213, L. 6. यत् परिहर्तुं तीर्यते मनागपि न सुन्दरत्वगुणेन ।
अथ केवलं यस्य दोषः प्रतिपक्षैरपि प्रतिपन्नः ॥२१६॥

P. 273, L. 2. पुष्पोत्करं कलमभक्तनिभं वहन्ति
ये सिन्धुवारविटपा मम वल्लभास्ते ।
ये गालितस्य महिषीदध्नः सदृक्षा
स्तेऽकिं च मुग्धविचकिलप्रसूनपुञ्जाः ॥ ३०९ ॥

P. 277, L. 1. तदा जायन्ते गुणाः यदा ते सहृदयैर्गृह्यन्ते ।
रविकिरणानुगृहीतानि भवन्ति कमलानि कमलानि ॥३१५॥

P. 278, L. 7. भवाम्यपहस्तितरेखो निरङ्कुशोऽथ विवेकरहितोऽपि ।
स्वप्नेऽपि त्वयि पुनः प्रतीहि भक्तिं न प्रस्मरामि ॥३२०॥

P. 283, L. 9. निभृतरमणे लोचनपथे पतिते गुरुजनमध्ये ।
सकलपरिहारहृदया वनगमनमेवेच्छति वधूः ॥३२८॥
चित्ते विघटते...३४४
मम देहि रसं धर्मे तमोवशाम् आशां गमागमात् हर नः ।
हरवधुः शरणं त्वं चित्तमोहोऽपसरतु मे सहसा ॥३७२॥

P. 302, L. 7. चित्ते विघटते न त्रुट्यति सा गुणेषु
शय्यासु लुठति विसर्पति दिङ्मुखेषु ।
वचने वर्तते प्रवर्तते काव्यबन्धे
ध्यानेन त्रुट्यति चिरं तरुणी प्रगल्भा ।। ३४३ ।।

P. 357, L. 2. सकलकरणपरविश्रामश्रीवितरणं न सरसकाव्यस्य ।
दृश्यतेऽथ वा निशम्यते सदृशमंशांशमात्रेण ।।४००।।

P. 361, L. 2. टुण्टुणायमानो मरिष्यसि कण्टककलितानि केतकीवनानि ।
मालतीकुसुमसदृक्षं भ्रमर भ्रमन् न प्राप्स्यसि ।।४०७।।

P. 371, L. 1. यस्य रणान्तःपुरे करे कुर्वतो मण्डलाग्रलताम् ।
रससंमुख्यपि सहसा पराङ्मुखी भवति रिपुसेना ।।४२२।।

P. 380, L. 5. लब्ध्वा तव बाहुस्पर्शं यस्याः स कोऽप्युल्लासः ।
जयलक्ष्मीस्तव विरहे न खलूज्ज्वला दुर्बला ननु सा ।।४३४।।

P. 391, L. 2. अन्यत्सौकुमार्यम् अन्यैव च कापि वर्तनच्छाया ।
श्यामा सामान्यप्रजापतेः रेखैव च न भवति ।।४५०।।

P. 395, L. 1. कृपणानां धनं नागानां फणमणिः केसरा सिंहानाम् ।
कुलबालिकानां स्तनाः कुतः स्पृश्यन्तेऽमृतानाम् ।।४५७।।

P. 403, L. 2. ए एहि किमपि कस्या अपि कृते निष्कृप भणामि अलमथ वा ।
अविचारितकार्यारम्भकारिणी म्रियतां न भणिष्यामि ।।४७१।।

P. 413, L. 3. सह दिवसनिशाभिर्दीर्घाः श्वासदण्डाः
सह मणिवलयैर्बाष्पधारा गलन्ति ।
तव सुभग वियोगे तस्या उद्विग्नायाः
सह च तनुलतया दुर्बला जीविताशा ।।४९५।।

P. 425, L. 5. तत्तेषां श्रीसहोदररत्नाभरणे हृदयमेकरसम् ।
बिम्बाधरे प्रियाणां निवेशितं कुसुमबाणेन ।।५१५।।

P. 433, L. 8. हंसानां सरोभिः श्रीः सार्यते अथ सरसां हंसैः ।
अन्योन्यमेव एते आत्मानं केवलं गरयन्ति ।।५२७।।

P. 434, L. 5. वाणिजक हस्तिदन्ताः कुतोऽस्माकं व्याघ्रकृत्तयश्च ।
यावत् लुलितालकमुखी गृहे परिष्वक्कते स्नुषा ।।५२८।।

P. 435, L. 4. का विषमा दैवगतिः किं लब्धव्यं यत् जनो गुणग्राही ।
किं सौख्यं सुकलत्रं किं दुःखं यत् खलो लोकः ।।५२९।।

P. 438, L. 5. यस्यैव व्रणस्तस्यैव वेदना भणति तज्जनोऽलीकम् ।
दन्तक्षतं कपोले वध्वाः वेदना सपत्नीनाम् ।।५३३।।

P. 452, L. 9, अयि एहि तावत् सुन्दरि कर्णं दत्त्वा श्रृणुष्व वचनीयम् ।
तव मुखेन कृशोदरि चन्द्र उपमीयते जनेन ।।५५४।।

P. 457, L. 3. सा वसति तव हृदये सैवाक्षिषु सा च वचनेषु ।
अस्मादृशीनां सुन्दर अवकाशः कुत्र पापानाम् ।।५६०।।

P. 460, L. 2. धवलोऽसि यद्यपि सुन्दर तथापि त्वया मम रञ्जितं हृदयम् ।
रागभरितेऽपि हृदये सुभग निहितो न रक्तोऽसि ।।५६४।।

P. 463, L. 2. स नास्त्यत्र ग्रामे य एनां महमहायमानलावण्याम् ।
तरुणानां हृदयलुण्ठाकीं परिष्वक्कमाणां निवारयति ।।५६९।।

P. 468, L. 2. यथा गभीरो यथा रत्ननिर्भरो यथा च निर्मलच्छायः ।
तथा किं विधिना एष सरसपानीयो जलनिधिर्न कृतः ।।५७३।।

APPENDIX B

Index of the illustrative verses occurring in the Kāvyaprakāśa

Verse No.		Verse References.
१३	अइपिहुलं जलकुंभं	हा० गा० स० 989; श्री० का० प० 3; गो० का० प्र० P. 49.
२५१	अकलिततपस्तेजोवीर्यं	भ० म० वी० च० II. 30; गो० का० प्र० P. 230.
२०७	अकुण्ठोत्कण्ठया पूर्णं	श्री० का० प० 107, 325; गो० का० प्र० P. 204.
४६७	अखण्डमण्डलः श्रीमान्	गो० का० प्र० P. 348; भो० स० कं० आ, I. 12; सु० र० भा० 103/62.
४५०	अण्णं लडहत्तणअं	हा० गा० स०969; रु० अ० स० P. 39. ज० व० ल० 315; कु० व० जी० I.66.
७२	अतन्द्रचन्द्राभरणा	श्री० का० प० 49; गो० का० प्र० P. 109 सु० र० भा० 253/5.
५९४	अतिथिं नाम काकुत्स्थात्	श्री० का० प० 337; गो० का० प्र० 399; का० र० व० XVII. 1.
२०२	अतिपेलवमतिपरिमित	श्री० का० प० 102; गो० का० प्र० P. 202; सु० र० भा० 57/134.
२५५	अतिविततगगनसरणि	श्री० का० प० 126; गो० का० प्र० P. 232; सु० न० भा० 27/3.
१३६	अत्ता एत्थ णिमज्जइ	हा० गा० स० VII. 67. P. 339; आ० ध्व० आ० P. 24; गो० का० प्र० P. 55.
३९४	अत्यायतैर्नियमकारिभि	शि० क० अ० I.39; गो० का० प्र० P. 311; सु० र० भा० 110/143.

११८ अत्युच्चाः परितः स्फुरन्ति — पञ्चाक्षरी; भो० स० क० ग्रा० III. 37; गो० का० प्र० P. 136; श्र० कु० का० 102; सु० र० भा० 110/232.

११५ अत्रासीत्फणिपाश — रा० बा० रा० X. 20; गो० का० प्र० P. 181.

१५८ अत्रिलोचनसंभूत — गो० का० प्र० P. 181; श्री० का० प०. 88; सु० र० भा० 188/41.

१२८ अदृष्टे दर्शनोत्कण्ठा — गो० का० प्र० P. 143; श्री० का० प० 69; सु० र० भा० 291/1.

२३८ अद्यापि स्तनशैलदुर्ग — वे० प० वे० 5; ह० ना II, 41; वसुकल्पस्य; भो०स० कं०ग्रा०; श्री० का० प० 118; गो० का० प्र० P. 223.

३४५ अद्रावत्र प्रज्ज्वलत्यग्निरुच्चैः

२२३ अधिकरतलतल्पं — श्री० का० प० 114; कु० व० जी० I. 109; गो० का० प्र० P. 212; सु० र० भा० 286/12.

१४१ अनङ्गमङ्गलगृहा — श्री० का० प० 73, 94; गो० का० प्र० P. 171; सु० र० भा० 259/72.

३४७ अनङ्गरङ्गप्रतिमं तदङ्गं — श्री० का० प० 179; गो० का० प्र० P. 284.

५८२ अनणुरणन्मणि — र० का० श्र० II. 23; कु० व० जी० I. 10; गो० का० प्र० P. 396.

३६४ अनन्तमहिमव्याप्त — ग्रा० दे० श० I; गो० का० प्र० P. 293.

२६८ अनन्यसदृशं यस्य — गो० का० प्र० P. 240.

४१० अनयेनेव राज्यश्रीः — श्री० का० प० 222; गो० का० प्र० P. 319.

४१२ अनवरतकनकवितरण — गो० का० प्र० P. 319.

३८२ अनुरागवती सन्ध्या — ग्रा० ध्व० ग्रा० I.9; गो० का प्र० P. 302. सु० र० भा० 91/35.

२९८ अन्त्रप्रोतबृहत्कपाल — भ० म० वी० च० I.35; गो० का० प्र० P. 253; सु० र० भा० 366/5.

२० अन्यत्र यूयं कुसुमावचायं	गो० का० प्र० P. 53; सु० र० भा० 334/106.
३३ अन्यत्र व्रजतीति का	गो० का० प्र० P. 80; सु० र० भा० 358/77.
२१८ अन्यास्ता गुणरत्नरोहण	गो० का० प्र० P. 210; सु० र० भा० 111/250.
३४१ अपसारय घनसारं	दा० कु० म० 102; गो० का० प्र० P. 275; सु० र० भा० 275/7; व० सु० भा० 1071.
३५६ अपसारय घनसारं	दा० कु० म० 102; गो० का० प्र० P. 275; सु० र० भा० 275/7; व० सु० भा० 1071.
५४६ अपाङ्गतरले दृशौ	गो० का० प्र० P. 380; रु० भ्र० स० P. 94; सु० र० भा० 253/27.
१८४ अपाङ्गसंसर्गितरङ्गितं	गो० का० प्र० P. 193; सु० र० भा० 304/3.
२८७ अपूर्वमधुरामोद	गो० का० प्र० P. 250.
२३३ अप्राकृतस्य चरितातिशयैः	भ० म० वी० च० II. 39; गो० का० प्र० P. 121; सु० र० भा० 360/28.
४४६ अब्धेरम्भः स्थगित	गो० का० प्र० P. 340; सु० र० भा० 248/95.
४८२ अभिनवनलिनीकिसलय	श्री० का० प० 267; गो० का० प्र० P. 353.
५६ अमितः समितः प्राप्तैः	गो० का० प्र० P. 99; सु० र० भा० 102/36; वि० सा० द० IV. 7.
४३२ अमुष्मिँल्लावण्यामृत	गो० का० प्र० P. 333; सु० र० भा० 268/362; व० सु० भा० 1558.
९६ अमुं कनकवर्णाभं	म० भा० शा० प० Ch. 153, Sl. 65(?) श्री० का० प० 54; गो० का० प्र० P. 121.
२१५ अमृतममृतं कः सन्देहः	वा० का० भ्र० सू० वृ० III. 2. 10; श्री० का० प० 110; गो० का प्र०

P. 209; सु० र० भा० 252/50.

५११ अयमेकपदे तया वियोगः	का० वि० उ० IV. 10; ध्व० आ० P. 156; कु० व० जी० II. 109; श्री० का० प० 101; गो० का० प्र० P. 365.
५८६ अयं पद्मासनासीनः	भा० का० II. 25; वा० का० अ० सू० वृ० IV. 2. 11; भो० स० क० आ० I. 61; श्री० का० प० 329; गो० का० प्र० P. 397.
४१८ अयं मार्तण्डः किं स खलु	रु० अ० स० P. 30; गो० का० प्र० P. 325.
४९० अयं वारामेको निलय	भ० श० 108; रु० अ० स० P. 72; गो० का० प्र० P. 356; सु० र० भा० 216/33.
११६ अयं स रशनोत्कर्षी	म० भा०, स्त्री०, Ch. 24. Sl. 19; गो० का० प्र० PP. 135, 271.
३३६ अयं स रशनोत्कर्षी	" " " "
३७३ अयं सर्वाणि शास्त्राणि	गो० का० प्र० P. 296.
४०८ अरातिविक्रमालोक	गो० का० प्र० P. 317.
३८९ अरिवधदेहशरीरः	उ० का० अ० सा० सं० I; गो० का० प्र० P. 306.
४९६ अरुचिर्निशया विना	गो० का० प्र० P. 358; सु० र० भा० 175/931.
२८३ अरे रामाहस्ताभरण	का० वि० उ० ?; श्री० का० प० 143; गो० का० प्र० P. 248.
२७७ अर्थित्वे प्रकटीकृतेऽपि	म० वी० च० II. 9; श्री० का० प० 138; गो० का० प्र० P. 244.
३६९ अलङ्कारः शङ्काकर	सु० र० को० No. 1344; गो० का० प्र० P. 295; सु० र० भा० 93/94; धर्मकीर्तिः; कवस; विका 58.

१९७	अलमतिचपलत्वात्	धर्मकीर्त्तिः; क० व० स० ; बि० का० 58; गो० का० प्र० P. 280; शा० प० No. 566; सु० र० भा० 252/44.
५०	अलसशिरोमणि धुत्ताणं	हा० गा० स० 970; श्री० का० प० 41; गो० का० प्र० P. 102; गो० का० प्र० P. 102.
९३	अलं स्थित्वा स्मशाने	म० भा० शा० आ प० Ch. 153, Sl. 11; गो० का० प्र० P. 121.
४२७	अलौकिकमहालोकः	गो० का० प्र० P. 331.
१४८	अवन्ध्यकोपस्य	भा० कि० अ० I. 33; गो० का० प्र० P. 175; सु० र० भा० 152/40.
४३०	अवाप्तः प्रागल्भ्यं	गो० का० प्र० P. 332; सु० र० भा० 304/158.
३९५	अवितथमनोरथपथ	गो० का० प्र० P. 312.
५२६	अविरलकमलविलासः	रु० का० अ० VII. 83; श्री० का० प० P. 293; गो० का० प्र० P. 372; सु० र० भा० 331/13.
१२०	अविरलकरवाल	गो० का० प्र० P. 127; वि० सा० द० X. 94; सु० र० भा० 104/94.
२७०	अष्टाङ्गयोगपरिशीलन	गो० का० प्र० P. 240.
४०२	असितभुजगभीषणा	गो० का० प्र० P. 347.
४६३	असिमात्रसहायस्य	गो० का० प्र० P. 347.
४६४	असिमात्रसहायोऽपि	गो० का० प्र० P. 347.
१२२	असोढ़ा तत्कालोल्लसद	गो० का० प्र० P. 137; सु० र० भा० 5/50; अ० कु० का० 60.
१९०	असौ मरुच्चुम्बित	म० व्य० वि० P. 206; ह० ना० VI. 4;. वे० प० वे० 5; गो० का० प्र० P. 196; सु० र० भा० 331/51.
३५९	अस्त्रज्वालावलीढप्रति	भ० वे० सं० III. 7; गो० का० प्र० P. 236; सु० र० भा० 361/50.
२८६	अस्याः कर्णावतंसेन	वा० का० अ० सू० वृ० II. 2. 14; गो० का० प्र० P. 249.

४२० अस्याः सर्गविधौ	का० वि० उ० I. 8; व० सु० आ० 1467; शा० प० No 3268; कु० व० जी० III. P. 140; रु० अ० स० P. 40; गो० का० प्र० P. 326; भा० स० क० आ० 175; ध० द० रू० IV. 2; वि० सा० द० P. 156; सु० र० भा० 254/42.
५५६ अहमेव गुरुः सुदारुणाना	गो० का० प्र० P. 384; सु० र० भा० 59/204.
३५३ अहो केनेदृशी बुद्धिः	रु० अ० स० P. 99; गो० का० प्र० P. 287; सु० र० भा० 205/3.
५४२ अहो विशालं भूपाल	द० का० आ० II. 297; श्री० का० प० 304; गो० का० प्र० P. 378; सु० र० भा० 134/6.
४८१ अहो हि मे बह्वपराद्ध	रु० अ० स० P. 65; गो० का० प्र० P. 353.
४४ अहौ वा हारे वा	उत्पलराजः; गो० का० प्र० P. 90; क्षे० औ० वि० च० 16; सु० र० भा० 368/40.
३७ आकुञ्च्य पाणिमशुचिं	गो० का० प्र० P. 80; सु० र० भा० 364/43.
३९८ आकृष्टकरवालोऽसौ	गो० का० प्र० P. 313.
१२५ आगत्य सम्प्रति वियोग	श्री० का० प० 67; गो० का० प्र० P. 140; सु० र० भा० 327/7.
२७८ आज्ञा शक्रशिखामणि	रा० बा० रा० I. 36; श्री० का० प० 139; गो० का० प्र० P. 245.
५७० आत्ते सीमन्तरत्ने	हनुमत्कविकृत-खण्डप्रशस्तिः; गो० का० प्र० P. 390; सु० र० भा० 133/43.
३०७ आत्मारामा विहितरतयो	भ० वे० सं० I. 23; गो०, का० प्र० P. 257.
३८३ आदाय चापमचलं	गो० का० प्र० P. 302; सु० र० भा० 4/24.

४४५ आदाय वारि परितः — Cited by Kṣemendra in his औचित्यविचारचर्चा as belonging to भट्टेन्दुराज; गो० का० प्र० P. 339; सु० र० भा० 216/17.

२०० आदावञ्जनपुञ्जलिप्त — गो० का० प्र० P. 201; सु० र० भा० 291/93.

९५ आदित्योऽयं स्थितो — म० भा०, शा० प० ch. Sl 19; गो० का० प्र० P. 121.

५४० आनन्दममन्दमिमं — रु० का० अ० IX. 47; गो० का० प्र० P. 378; सु० र० भा० 278/23.

१६२ आनन्दसिन्धुरति — गो० का० प्र० P. 183.

४२६ आलानं जयकुञ्जरस्य — भट्टश्यामलः; म० व्य० वि० P. 350; श्री० का० प० 234; गो० का० प्र० P. 330; सु० र० भा० 109/211.

१५४ आलिङ्गितस्तत्रभवान् — श्री० का० प० 84; गो० का० प्र० P. 179.

३२३ आलोक्य कोमलकपोल — गो० का० प्र० P. 263.

५०० आसीदञ्जनमत्रेति — श्री० का० प० 277; गो० का० प्र० P. 360.

६७३ आहूतेषु विहङ्गमेषु — भ० श० 69; गो०का० प्र० P. 402; भ० श० 69; सु० र० भा० 180/1053.

२२२ इदमनुचितमक्रमश्च — गो० का० प्र० P. 212; भ० शृं० श० 27; सु० र० भा० 205/7

२६४ इदं ते केनोक्तं कथय — गो० का० प्र० P. 238.

४१९ इन्दुः किं क्व कलंकः — रु० अ० स० P. 30; गो० का० प्र० P. 326; सु० र० भा० 312/22.

४६५ इयं सुनयना दासीकृत — उ० का० अ० सा० सं०; श्री० का० प० 255; गो० का० प्र० P. 347; सु० र० भा० 262/168.

८ उअ णिच्चलणिप्पन्दा — हा० गा० स० I. 4; श्री० का० प० 9; गो० का० प्र० P. 19.

१८७ उत्कम्पिनी भयपरि	मा० ता० व० II. 16; गो० का० प्र० P. 104; ह० र० आ० ?; आध्वआ P. 131;
४२ उत्कृत्योत्कृत्य कृत्ति	भ० मा० मा० V. 16; श्री० का० प० 28; गो० का० प्र० P. 83; सु० र० भा० 366/7
३०४ उत्तानोच्छूनमण्डूक	श्री० का० प० 155; गो० का० प्र० P. 256; सु० र० भा० 371/119.
१४७ उत्फुल्लकमलकेसर	ह० ना० आ० I. 14; गो० का० प्र० P. 175.
५२ उत्सिक्तस्य तपः परा	भ० म० वी० च० II. 16; गो० का प्र० P. 95.
४३६ उदयति विततोर्ध्वरश्मि	मा० शि० व० IV. 20; गो० का० प्र० P. 336; सु० र० भा० 327/5.
४३३ उदयमयते दिङ्मालिन्यं	श्री० का० प० 237; गो० का० प्र० P. 334; सु० र० भा० 327/18.
२४४ उदेति सविता ताम्र	श्री० का० प० 123; गो० का० प्र० P. 227.
१७ उद्देशोऽयं सरसकदली	कु० व० जी० I. 93; गो० का० प्र० P. 52
५९९ उद्ययौ दीर्घिकागर्भात्	श्री० का० प० 340; गो० का० प्र० P. 401.
४३८ उन्नतं पदमवाप्य यो लघुः	श्री० का० प० 242; गो० का० प्र० P. 336; सु० र० भा० 59/214.
११४ उन्निद्रकोकनदरेणु	कु० व० जी० II. 3; शा० प० 3736; गो० का० प्र० P. 134; सु० र० भा० 327/8
४१६ उन्मेषं यो मम न सहते	गो० का० प्र० P. 323; सु० र० भा० 313/60
२४ उपकृतं बहु तत्र	अ० ध्व० आ० लो० P. 56; श्री० का० प० 8; गो० का० प्र० P. 58.
२६५ उपपरिसरं गोदावर्याः	गो० का० प्र० P. 239.

५५२ कपाले मार्जारः पय	भासकविः; गो० का० प्र० P. 382; व०सु० आ०; भो० स० क० आ० III. 38; सु० र० को० 905; शा० प०; सु० र० भा० 301/79.
४४९ कमलमनम्भसि	शङ्करगणः; रु० अ० सं० P. 39; म० व्य० वि० P. 387; गो० का० प्र० P. 341; सु० र० भा० 363/10.
४१५ कमलेव मतिर्मतिरिव	श्री० का० प० 225; गो० का० प्र० P. 323; वि० सा० द० X. 27; सु० र० भा० 104/83.
५५१ करजुअगहिअजसोआ	हा० गा० स० 974; गो० का० प्र० P. 382.
३९९ करवाल इवाचारस्तस्य	गो० का० प्र० P. 314.
१९१ करवालकरालदो सहायो	गो० का० प्र० P. 197.
३०३ करिहस्तेन संबाधे	श्री० का० प० 154; गो० का० प्र० P.256.
४७५ कर्पूर इव दग्धोऽपि	रु० अ० स० P. 74; रा० बा० रा० III. 11; गो० का० प्र० P. 351; सु० र० भा० 250/5.
३२५ कर्पूरधूलिधवल	गो० का० प्र० P. 264; सु० र० भा० 273/10.
५१२ कलुषं च तवाहितेष्व	वि० सा० द० X. 85; सु० र० भा० 104/90.
१९४ कल्याणानां त्वमसि महसां	भ० मा० भा० I. 4.
२७६ कल्लोलवेल्लितदृषत्	भागवतत्रिविक्रमः; कु० व० जी० I. 25, P. 16; भ० श० 62; व० सु० आ० 866; सु० र० भा० 216।19; श्री० का० प० 137; गो० का० प्र० P. 244.
४४७ कस्त्वं भोः कथयामि	अ० ध्व० आ० लो० III. 51; रु० अ० स० P. 64; गो० का० प्र० P. 340; शा० प० No. 1046; सु० र० भा० 242/171.

२०५ कस्मिन्कर्मणि सामर्थ्यं — श्री० का० प० 106; गो० का० प्र० P. 203.

२२४ कः कः कुत्र न घुर्घुरायित — श्री० का० प० 115; सु० र० भा० 231/48; गो० का० प्र० P. 213.

१३५ कस्स व ण होइ रोसो — अ० ध्व० आ० लो० I. P. 23; हा० गा० स० 886; गो० का० प्र० P. 160.

२४९ काचित्कीर्णा रजोभिः — मा० शि० व० XV. 96; गो० का० प्र० P. 229; सु० र० भा० 126/22.

१८५ कातर्यं केवला नीतिः — का० र० वं० XVII. 47; गो० का० प्र० P. 194.

५२९ का विसमा देव्वगई — हा० गा० स० 975; श्री० का० प० 296; गो० का० प्र० P. 373.

५२१ किमासेव्यं पुंसां — रु० अ० स० P. 87; गो० का० प्र० P. 371; सु० र० भा० 17/1985.

२३९ किमिति न पश्यसि कोपं — रु० का० अ० VI. 42; गो० का० प्र० P. 224.

२०६ किमुच्यतेऽस्य भूपाल — गो० का० प्र० P. 203; श्री० का० प० 106.

४५७ किवणाणँ धणं णाआणं — हा० गा० स० 976; श्री० का प० 262; गो० का० प्र० P. 344.

४२९ किसलयकरैर्लतानां — रु० का० अ० VIII. 50; गो० का० प्र०P. 331.

५२२ किं भूषणं सुदृढमत्र — गो० का० प्र० P. 371; वि० सा० द० X. 82; सु० र० भा० 176/948.

१९५ किं लोभेन विलंघितः — म० व्य० वि० P. 253; ध० द० रू० III. 29; भ० उ० रा० च० ?; गो० का० प्र० P. 199.

४६१ कुमुदकमलनीलनीरः — गो० का० प्र० P. 346.

४२३ कुरङ्गीवाङ्गानि स्तिमितयति — अ० ध्व० आ० लो० P. 211; अ० अ० भा० III. P. 150; गो० का० प्र० P. 328; सु० र० भा० 310/3; सू० मु० 51.15.

५०८ कुलममलिनं भद्रा मूर्तिः	भा० स० क० आ० V. 368; गो० का० प्र० P. 364.
१७३ कुविन्दस्त्वं तावत्पटयसि	गो० का० प्र० P. 188; सु० र० भा० 135/30.
४७३ कुसुमितलताभिरहता	श्री० का० प० 262; ो० का० प्र० P. 350; सु० र० भा० 275/13.
३९ कृतमनुमतं दृष्टं वा यैः	भ० वे० सं०, III. 24; श्री० का० प० 22; गो० का० प्र० P. 81; सु० र० भा० 366/4.
२५८ कृतमनुमतं दृष्टं वा यैः	" " "
१०८ कृतं च गर्वाभिमुखं	र० अ० स० P. 45; गो० का० प्र० P. 128; सु० र० भा० 105/118.
६५ केसेसु बलामोडिव	हा० गा० स० 971; श्री० का० प० 46; गो० का० प्र० P. 105.
६४ कलासस्य प्रथमशिखरे	श्री० का० प० 45; गो० का० प्र० P. 64; सु० र० भा० 136/34.
११७ कैलासालयभाल	गो० का० प्र० P. 135; सु० र० भा० 12/39.
५२३ कौटिल्यं कचनिचये	र० का० अ० VII. 81; श्री० का० प० 291; गो० का० प्र० P. 371; सु० र० भा० 312/24.
३३८ कामन्त्यः क्षतकोमला	आ० ध्व० आ० III. 20, P. 169; अ० ध्व० आ० लो० III. 20; गो० का० प्र० P. 272; सु० र० भा० 132/29.
२२५ क्रेङ्कारः स्मरकार्मुकस्य	श्री० का० प० 116; गो० का० प्र० P. 214. सु० र० भा० 26/202.
३२९ क्रोधं प्रभो संहर	का० कु० स० III, 32; गो० का० ० P. 266.
४८८ क्रौञ्चाद्रिरुद्दामदृषद्‌दृढौं	गो० का० प्र० P. 355.
४३५ क्व सूर्यप्रभवो वंशः	का० रं० वं० I. 2; श्री० का० प० 239; गो० का० प्र० P. 335.

५३ क्वाकार्यं शशलक्ष्मणः	का० वि० उ० IV. 4; रु० अ० स० P. 106; श्री० का० प० 39; गो० का० प्र० P. 96; सु०र० भा० 281/113.
३३१ क्वाकार्यं शशलक्ष्मणः	" " "
८२ क्षणदासावक्षणदा	सु० र० भा० 103/74.
३४० क्षिप्तो हस्तावलग्नः	अ० श०, 2; श्री० का० प० 172; गो० का० प्र० P. 273; सु०र०भा० 8/109.
४६२ क्षीणः क्षीणोऽपि शशी	रु० का० अ० VII, 90; अ० स० P. 48; गो० का० प्र० P. 347; व० सु० आ० 161; सु० र० भा० 305/11.
४० क्षुद्राः संत्रासमेते	ह० ना० XI. 2; श्री० का० प० 26; गो० का० प्र० P. 82; व० सु० आ० 2283; सु० र० भा० 361/49.
१११ खणपाहुणिआ देअर	हा० गा० स० 963; अ० ध्व० आ० लो० III; श्री० का० प० 60.
७४ खलववहारा दीसन्ति	गो० का० प्र० P. 111; हा० गा० स० 978.
४५८ खिद्यति कूणति वेल्लति	सु० र० भा० 317/3.
५९६ गङ्गेव प्रवहतु ते	श्री० का० प० 339.
१२७ गच्छाम्यच्युत दर्शनेन	गो० का० प्र० P. 142; अ० कु० का० 155; सु० र० भा० 24/154.
५५५ गर्वमसंवाह्यमिमं	रु० का० अ० VIII. 78; गो० का० प्र० P. 384.
५६५ गाङ्गमम्बु सितमम्बु	रु० अ० स० P. 96; सुरभिः; श्री० का० प० 317; गो० का० प्र० P. 388; सु० र० भा० 221/12.
६३ गाढकान्तदशनक्षत	श्री० का० प० 44; गो० का० प्र० P. 104; वि० सा० द० IV. 9; सु० र० भा० 104/85.

६६ गाढालिङ्गणरहसुज्जुअम्मि	हा० गा० स० 934; गो० का० प्र० P. 106.
१०१ गाहारुहम्मि गामे	हा० गा० स० 705.
३९६ गाम्भीर्यगरिमा तस्य	गो० का० प्र० P. 312.
२५० गाहन्तां महिषा निपान	का० प्र० श० II. 6; मं० व्य० वि०; गो० का० प्र० P. 229; सु० र० भा० 141/1.
४८३ गिरयोऽप्यनुन्नतियुजो	गो० का० प्र० P. 354; सु० र० भा० 103/76.
४८० गुणानामेव दौरात्म्यात्	भो० स० क० आ० IV. 125; श्री० का० प० 266; गो० का० प्र० P. 352; सु० र० भा० 234/140.
५९२ गुणैरनर्घ्यैः प्रथितो	श्री० का० प० 335.
२१ गुरुअणपरवस पिअ	हा० गा० स० 851; गो० का० प्र० P. 79.
३५४ गुरुजनपरतन्त्रतया	श्री० का० प० 191; गो० का० प० P. 283.
५६२ गृहिणी सचिवः सखी	का० र० व० VIII. 67; श्री० का० प० 21; गो० का० प्र० P. 386; सु० र० भा० 362/15.
२६६ गृहीतं येनासीः परिभव	भ० वे० सं०, III. 19; श्री० क० प० 131; गो० का० प्र० P. 237.
१६८ गोरपि यद्वाहनतां	गो० का० प्र० P. 186.
५९७ ग्रथ्नामि काव्यशशिनं	वा० का० अ० सू० वृ० II. 4. 16.
३ ग्रामतरुणं तरुण्याः	रु० का० अ०, VII. 39; श्री० का० प० 11; गो० का० प्र० P. 14; सु० र० भा० 352/20.
४१ ग्रीवाभङ्गाभिरामं	का० अ० श० I. 7; कु० व० जी० III. 31; गो० का० प्र० P. 83; श्री० का० प० 27.
३९० चकासत्यङ्गनारामाः	श्री० का० प० 207; गो० का० प्र० P. 306.

५७० जटाभाभिर्भाभिः करधृत	गो० का० प्र० P. 390.
१२४ जनस्थाने भ्रान्तं	भट्टवाचस्पतिः; श्री० का० प० 66; गो० का० प्र० P. 139.
४२२ जस्स रणन्तेउरए करे	हा० गा० स०, 980; गो० का० प्र० P. 328.
५३३ जस्सेअ वणो तस्से अ	हा० गा० स० 981; श्री० का० प० 168; गो० का० प्र० P. 375.
५७३ जह गहिरो जह रअण	हा० गा० स० 976; गो० का० प्र० P. 392.
२१६ जं परिहरिउं तीरइ	आ० वि० बा० ली० ?; हा० गा० स० 979; गो० का० प्र० P. 209.
६७ जा ठेरं व हसन्ती	हा० गा० स० 982; गो० का० प्र० P. 106.
४७ जाने कोपपराङ्मुखी	व० सु० आ०; शा० प०; गो० का० प्र० P. 92; श्री० का० प० 33.
४६६ जितेन्द्रियतया सम्यक्	गो० का० प्र० P. 348.
३१६ जितेन्द्रियत्वं विनयस्य	व० सु० आ०; श्री० का० प० 162; गो० का० प्र० P. 261; गो० का प्र० P. 372.
५२५ जितेन्द्रियत्वं विनयस्य	,, ,, ,,
१६४ जुगोपात्मानमत्रस्तः	का० र० व० I. 21; गो० का० प्र० P. 184.
६८ जे लंकागिरिमेहलासु	रा० क० म०, I. 19; गो० का० प्र० P. 107.
९२ जोह्नाइ महुरसेन	हा० गा० स० 984; गो० का० प्र० P. 120.
२८९ ज्याबन्धनिष्पन्दभुजेन	का० र० व०, VI. 40; कु० व० जी०, I. 80; गो० का० प्र० P. 250.
४२१ ज्योत्स्नाभस्मच्छुरणधवला	रु० अ० स० P. 33 ?; गो० का० प्र० P. 327.
४७२ ज्योत्स्ना मौक्तिकदाम	गो० का० प्र० P. 349.

४११ ज्योत्स्न्येव नयनानन्दः	गो० का० प्र० P. 319.
४०७ ढुण्ढुण्णन्तो मरिहसि	हा० गा० स० 979; अ० ध्व० आ० लो० P. 116; श्री० का० प० 220; गो० का० प्र० P. 316.
८८ णवपुण्णिमामिअंकस्स	हा० गा० स० 986; गो० का० प्र० P. 118.
३२८ णिहुअरमणम्मि लोअण	हा० गा० स० 987; गो० का० प्र० P. 265.
१८ णोल्लेइ अणोल्लमणा	हा० गा० स० 875; गो० का० प्र० P. 52.
१६ तइआ मह गंडत्थल	हा० गा० स० 939; गो० का० प्र० P. 51.
२१२ तत उदित उदाहारहारि	गो० का० प्र० P. 207.
४०१ ततः कुमुदनाथेन	म० भा० द्रो० Ch. 184; Sl. 46; श्री० का० प० 216; गो० का० प्र० P. 315.
३५५ ततोऽरुणपरिस्पन्द	कु० व० जी० I. 19; रा० का० मी० P. 67; वाल्मीकिः; व० सु० आ० 2153; श्री० का० प० 193; गो० का० प्र० P. 289.
५१५ तं ताण सिरिसहोअर	आ० वि० बा० ली०; गो० का० प्र० P. 367.
१५ तथाभूतां दृष्ट्वा	भ० वे० सं० I. 11; श्री० का० प० 5; गो० का० प्र० P. 50.
२२० तथाभूतां दृष्ट्वा	भ० वे० सं० I. 11; श्री० का० प० 5; गो० का० प्र० P. 50; गो० का० प्र० P. 250.
८० तदप्राप्तिमहादुःख	? वि० पु०; गो० का० प्र० P. 114.
५०६ तदिदमरण्यं यस्मिन्	रु० का० अ० VII. 104; गो० का० प्र० P. 363.
१९८ तद्गच्छ सिध्द्यै कुरु	का० कु० सं० III. 18; श्री० का० प० 152; गो० का० प्र० P. 200.

५१७ तद्गेहं नतभित्ति — आ० ध्व० आ० P. 158; अ० ध्व० आ० लो० III. 16; गो० का० प्र० P. 367.

५९३ तद्वेषोऽसदृशोऽन्याभिः — श्री० का० प० 336; गो० क० प्र० P. 398.

३९१ तनुवपुरजघन्योऽसौ — गो० का० प्र० P. 307.

१४६ तपस्विभिर्या सुचिरेण — म० व्य० वि० P. 203 (P. 251 Chowkhamba); श्री० का० प० 78; गो० का० प्र० P. 174.

११० तरुणिमनि कलयति — म० व्य० वि० ? ; श्री का० प० 59; गो० का० प्र० P. 129.

४०९ तरुणिमनि कृतावलोकना — गो० का० प्र० P. 317.

४५६ तवाहवे साहसकर्म — गो० का० प्र० P. 344.

१७९ तस्याधिमात्रोपायस्य — गो० का० प्र० P. 190.

५० तस्याः सान्द्रविलेपन — अ० श० 26; गो० का० प्र० P. 94.

१०२ ताणं गुणग्गहणाणं — हा० गा० स० 940; गो० का० प्र० P. 125.

३२२ तामनङ्गजयमङ्गलश्रियं — श्री० का० प० 166; गो० का० प्र० P. 263.

१८० ताम्बूलभृतगल्लोऽयं — गो० का० प्र० P. 191.

३१५ ताला जाअंति गुणा — कु० व० जी० II. 26; म० व्य० वि०; हा० गा० स० 989; अ० ध्व० आ० लो० P. 62; आ० वि० बा० ली०; गो० का० प्र० P. 58.

५५ तिग्मरुचिरप्रतापः — गो० का० प्र० P. 99.

३११ तिष्ठेत्कोपवशात्प्रभाव — का० वि० उ० IV. 9; श्री० का० प० 159; गो० का० प्र० P. 259.

१४५ तीर्थान्तरेषु स्नानेन — रु० अ० स० P. 76; श्री० का० प० 76; गो० का० प्र० P. 174.

८३ तुह वल्लहस्स गोसम्मि — हा० गा० स० 998; गो० का० प्र० P. 116.

१४० ते दृष्टिमात्रपतिताः — गो० का० प्र० P. 167.

१७६ तेऽन्यैर्वान्तं समश्नन्ति — गो० का० प्र० P. 189.

२४६ ते हिमालयमामन्त्र्य	का० कु० सं० VI. 94; गो० का० प्र० P. 227.
२२८ त्वमेवंसौन्दर्या स च	भ० मा० मा०; म० व्य० वि० ; वा० का० अ० सू० वृ० III. 2.12; गो० का० प्र० P. 216.
४५५ त्वयि दृष्ट एव तस्याः	श्री० का० प०251;गो०का०प्र०P.343.
२३५ त्वयि निबद्धरतेः प्रिय	का० वि० उ० IV. 55; श्री० का० प० 112.
३१ त्वं मुग्धाक्षि विनैव	अ० श० 23; गो० का० प्र० P. 76.
५४४ त्वं विनिर्जितमनोभव	श्री० का० प० 306; गो० का० प्र० P. 379.
२३ त्वामस्मि वच्मि विदुषां	रु० का० अ० VI. 15; गो० का० प्र० P. 58.
३६ त्वामालिख्य प्रणयकुपितां	का० मे० दू० उ० 44; श्री० का० प० 19;गो० का० प्र० P. 79;सु०र०भा० 292/54.
३३७ दन्तक्षतानि करजैश्च	अ० ध्व० आ० लो० III. 43; गो० का० प्र० P. 271.
६२ दर्पान्धगन्धगज	शि० क० अ० I. 37; श्री० का० प० 43; गो० का० प्र० P. 103.
५५९ दिवमप्युपयातानां	रु० का० अ० IX. 6; गो० का० प्र० P. 385.
६०० दिवाकराद्रक्षति यो	का० कु० सं० I. 12; गो० का० प्र० P. 401.
२९६ दीधीङ्वेवीङ्समः कश्चित्	श्री० का० प०43;गो०का०प्र०P. 253.
५०७ दुर्वाराः स्मरमार्गणाः	भट्टशंकुकः; शा० प०; सु० र० भा०. 285/34.
२९ दूरादुत्सुकमागते	अ० श०, 44; गो० का० प्र० P. 72.
५६६ दृशा दग्धं मनसिजं	रु० अ० स० P. 80; रा० वि०भ० I. 4; श्री० का० प० 271; गो० का० प्र० P. 388.
३७९ देव त्वमेव पाताल	

४५३ देवीभावं गमिता	वा० का० अ० सू० वृ०, IV. 2. 4; ह० र० आ०; श्री० का० प० 250; गो० का० प्र० P. 343.
२०८ देशः सोऽयमरातिशोणित	भ० वे० सं०, III. 33; म० व्य० वि०; गो० का० प्र० P. 205.
२६ दैवादहमद्य तया	रु० का० अ० VII. 29; गो० का० प्र० P. 64.
४३७ दोर्भ्यां तितीर्षति तरङ्ग	श्री० का० प० 241; गो० का० प्र० P. 336.
१८६ द्वयं गतं संप्रति	का० कु० सं० V. 71; कु० व० जी० I. 23; म० व्य० वि०, P. 40; श्री० का० प० 117; गो० का० प्र० P. 230.
२५२ द्वयं गतं संप्रति	" " " "
२२ द्वारोपान्तनिरन्तरे	गो० का० प्र० P. 54; सुरभा 304/6.
३९७ धन्यस्यानन्यसामान्य	गो० का० प्र० P. 313.
६१ धन्यासि या कथयसि	शा० प०; विज्जिका; श्री० का० प० 42; गो० का० प्र० P. 102.
१८२ धम्मिल्लस्य न कस्य	वा० का० अ० सू० वृ० II. 1.22; श्री० का० प० 95; गो० का० प्र० P. 192.
५६४ धवलोसि जह वि	हा० गा० स० 665, VII. 64; रु० अ० स० P. 96; गो० का० प्र० P. 383.
५३५ धातुः शिल्पातिशय	गो० का० प्र० P. 376.
२१० धीरो विनीतो निपुणो	गो० का० प्र० P. 206.
४१४ न केवलं भाति नितान्त	गो० का० प्र० P. 322.
९४ न चेह जीवितः कश्चित्	श्री० का० प० 52; गो० का० प्र० P. 121.
५४९ न तज्जलं यन्न सुचारु	भ० का०, II. 19; श्री० का० प० 309; गो० का० प्र० P. 381.
१६७ न त्रस्तं यदि नाम	भ० म० वी० च० II. 28; गो० का० प्र० P. 185.
५१३ नन्वाश्रयस्थितिरियं	भ० श० 4; रु० अ० स० P. 85; गो० का० प्र० P. 366.
५७४ नयनानन्ददायीन्दोः	क्षे० औ० वि० च०, P. 46; श्री० का० प० 320; गो० का० प्र० P. 392.

१६३	नवजलधरः सन्नद्धोऽयं	गो० का० प्र० P. 184; का० वि० उ० IV. 7; म० व्य० वि०
२४३	नाथे निशाया नियतेः	श्री० का० प० 122; गो० का० प्र० P. 226.
४९९	नानाविधप्रहरणैर्नृप	गो० का० प्र० P. 359.
३५२	नारीणामनुकूलमाचरसि	गो० का० प्र० P. 283.
६८१	नाल्पः कविरिव स्वल्प	
४७८	निजदोषावृतमनसां	श्री० का० प० 265; गो० का० प्र० P. 352.
४६९	नित्योदितप्रतापेन	गो० का० प्र० P. 348.
४७४	निद्रानिवृत्तावुदिते	गो० का० प्र० P. 350.
५९८	निपेतुरास्यादिव तस्य	गो० का० प्र० P. 400.
५५०	निम्ननाभिकुहरेषु यदम्भः	श्री० का० प० 310; गो० का० प्र० P. 382.
४२८	निरवधि च निराश्रयं च	वा० का० अ० सू० वृ०; III. 4. 32. गो० का० प्र० P. 311.
५७	निरुपादानसंभार	नारायणभट्टः०; स्तवचिन्तामणिः; गो० का० प्र० P. 99.
३०५	निर्वाणवैरदहनाः	म० वे० सं० I. 7; श्री० का० प० 156; गो० का० प्र० P. 257.
८५	निशितशरधिया	गो० का० प्र० P. 117.
२	निःशेषच्युतचन्दनं	अ० श०, 105; श्री० का० प० 10; गो० का०प्र०P. 12; ज० सू० मु०; व० सु० आ०; शा० प०.
१८३	न्यक्कारो ह्ययमेव मे	ह० ना० IX. 55; अ० ध्व० आ० लो० P. 153; श्री० का० प० 96; गो० का० प्र० P. 192.
९९	पथि पथि शुकचञ्चु	सु० र० भा० 333/85.; रु० अ० स० P. 75; गो० का० प्र० P. 123.
५८	पंथिअ ण एत्थ	ज० व० ल० 494; हा० गा० स० 879; गो० का० प्र० P. 100.
२४०	परापकारनिरतैः	गो० का० प्र० P. 224.

१०७ परिच्छेदातीतः	भ० मा० मा० I. 30; गो० का० प्र० P. 123.
४८९ परिच्छेदातीतः	भ० मा० मा० I. 30; गो० का० प्र० P. 356.
४०६ परिपन्थिमनोराज्य	गो० का० प्र० P. 316.
२८ परिमृदितमृणालीम्लान	भ० मा० मा० I. 22; गो० का० प्र० P. 72.
३४९ परिम्लानं पीनस्तनजघन	का० र० व०.II. 12; गो० का० प्र० P. 284.
३२६ परिहरति रतिं मतिं	गो० का० प्र० P. 264.
९० पविसंती घरवारं	हा० गा० स० 880; गो० का० प्र० P. 119.
४९२ पश्चादङ्घ्री प्रसार्य	बा० हृ० च०, III. 5; गो० का० प्र० P. 356.
१२३ पश्येत्कश्चिच्चलचपल	गो० का० प्र० P. 138
३३२ पाण्डु क्षामं वदनं	ध्व० ध्व० आ० लो० P. 166; श्री० का० प० 254; गो०का०प्र० P. 238.
४६० पाण्डु क्षामं वदनं	ध्व० ध्व० आ० लो० P.166; श्री० का० प० 254; गो० का० प्र० P. 238; गो० का० प्र० P. 346.
५८७ पातालमिव ते नाभिः	वा० का० अ० सू० वृ० IV.2. 11; श्री० का० प० 330; गो०का०प्र० P. 397.
५७८ पादाम्बुजं भवतु नो	पञ्चस्तवी III. 1.
१७७ पितृवसतिमहं व्रजामि	श्री० का० प० 83; गो० का० प्र० P. 140.
५४८ पुराणि यस्यां सवराङ्गनानि	प० न० सा० च० I.22; स० अ० स० P. 81; श्री० का० प० 308; गो० का० प्र०P.381.
४४३ पुंस्त्वादपि प्रविचलेत्	भ० श० 79; गो० का० प्र० P. 339.
३०६ पृथुकार्तस्वरपात्रं	सु० र० को० No. 1644; गो० का० प्र० P. 257.
३७० ,, ,,	गो० का० प्र० P. 294.

९८	प्रेयान् सोऽप्यमप्राकृत	वा० का० अ० सू० वृ० III. 2. 15; श्री० का० प० 56; गो० का० प्र० P. 122.
३५१	प्रौढ़च्छेदानुरूपोच्छलन	छलितरामम्; गो० का० प्र० P. 285.
३०९	फुल्लुक्करं कलमकूरणिहं	रा० क० म०, I. 19; गो० का० प्र० P. 258.
४३१	बत सखि कियदेतत्	गो० का० प्र० P. 333.
११९	बन्दीकृत्य नृप द्विषां	सुरभा 112/268.
५१४	बिम्बोष्ठ एव रागस्ते	प० न० सा० च० VI. 60; गो० का० प्र० P. 367.
१३०	ब्राह्मणातिक्रमत्यागो	गो० का० प्र० P. 143; भ० म० वी० च० II. 8; श्री० का० प० 71.
३७१	भक्तिप्रह्वविलोकन	भागवतामृतवर्धनः; व० सु० आ०; म० व्य० वि० II. 92. p. 362 (P. 421 Chow-); गो० का० प्र० P. 295.
५२४	भक्तिर्भवे न विभवे	रु० अ० स० P. 87; गो० का० प्र० P. 271.
५८१	भण तरुणि रमण	कु० व० जी० I. 9; II.20; रु० का० अ० II. 22; गो० का० प्र० P. 396.
१२	भद्रात्मनो दुरधिरोह	शि० क० अ० I.38; श्री० का० प० 1; गो० का० प्र० P.46.
१३८	भम धम्मिअ वीसद्धो	हा० गा० स० 175 (II.75.) म० व्य० वि० P. 400; श्री० का० प० 2; गो० का० प्र० P. 164.
५०३	भस्मोद्धूलन भद्रमस्तु	गो० का० प्र० P. 361.
३८७	भासते प्रतिभासार	रु० अ० स० P. 20; श्री० का० प० 205; गो० का० प्र० P. 305.
७८	भुक्तिमुक्तिकृदेकान्त	गो० का० प्र० P. 113.
५८३	भुजङ्गमस्येव मणिः	गो० का० प्र० P. 397.
१७५	भूपतेरुपसर्पन्ती	गो० का० प्र० P. 189.
२६०	भूपालरत्न निर्दैन्य	श्री० का० प० 126; गो० का० प्र० P. 236.

१०६ भूयो भूयः सविध	भ० मा० मा०, I. 30; गो० का० प्र० P. 126.
३३४ भूरेणुदिग्धान्नवपारि	आ० ध्व० आ० III. P. 178; अ० ध्व० आ० लो० III P. 178; गो० का० प्र० P. 270.
१२६ भ्रमिमरतिमलस	आ० ध्व० आ० II. 3; अ० ध्व० आ० लो० PP. 237, 368; रु० अ० स० P, 27; श्री० का० प० 68; गो० का० प्र० P. 141.
४१३ मतिरिव मूर्तिर्मधुरा	श्री० का० प० 223; गो० का० प्र० P. 320.
१३१ मथ्नामि कौरवशतं	भ० वे० सं० I. 15; अ० ध्व० आ० लो० P. 213; श्री० का० प० 72; गो० का० प्र० P. 144.
३६८ मधुपराजिपराजित	र० ह० वि० III. 57; गो० का० प्र० P. 294.
५१६ मधुरिमरुचिरं वचः	श्री० का० प० 286; गो० का० प्र० P. 367.
३४२ मनोरागस्तीव्रं विषमिव	भ० मा० मा० II. 1; श्री० का० प० 174; गो० का० प्र० P. 276.
३५० मन्थायस्तार्णवाम्भः प्लुत	भ० वे० सं० I. 22; गो० का० प्र० P. 285.
५५७ मलयजरसविलिप्त	रु० अ० स० P. 95; वा० का० अ० सू० वृ० IV. 3. 10; गो० का० प्र० P. 385.
२२६ मसृणचरणपातं	रा० बा० रा० VI. 36; गो० का० प्र० P. 214.
३७२ महदेसुरसंघम्मे	हा० गा० स० 991; आ० दे० श०; गो० का० प्र० P. 296.
२४२ महाप्रलयमारुत	भ० वे० सं० III. 4; श्री० का० प० 120; गो० का० प्र० P. 225.

७१ महिलासहस्सभरिए	हा० गा० स० II. 82; रु० अ० स० P. 36; गो० का० प्र० P. 108.
२४७ महीभृतः पुत्रवतोऽपि	का० कु० सं०, I. 27; गो० का० प्र० P. 227.
५१९ महौजसो मानधनाः	भा० कि० अ० I. 19; श्री० का० प० 288; गो० का० प्र० P. 369.
६ माए घरोवअरणं	हा० गा० स० 889; गो० का० प्र० P. 18.
२९९ मातङ्गाः किमु वल्गितैः	गो० का० प्र० P. 254.
३८५ माता नतानां संघट्टः	रु० का० अ०, V. 7; गो० का० प्र० P. 304.
१३३ मात्सर्यमुत्सार्य	भ० शृ० श० 36; गो० का० प्र० P. 159.
२६२ मात्सर्यमुत्सार्य	भ० शृ० श० 36; गो० का० प्र० P. 237
५३४ मानमस्या निराकर्तुं	द० का० आ० II. 299; रु० अ० स० P. 92; श्री० का० प० 299; गो० का० प्र० P. 376.
३८४ मारारिशक्ररामेभ	रु० का० अ० V. 6, 7; गो० का० प्र० P. 303.
३४४ मित्रे क्वापि गते सरोरुह	प्रवरसेनः; श्री० का० प० 176; गो० का० प्र० P. 277.
५०५ मुक्ताः केलिविसूत्रहार	रु० अ० स० P. 103; श्री० का० प० 281; गो० का० प्र० P. 363.
९ मुखं विकसितस्मितं	अ० ध्व० आ० लो० P. 63; गो० का० प्र० P. 36; शाप 3277; सुरभा 256/35.
७६ मुग्धे मुग्धतयैव	अ० श० 70; गो० का० प्र० P. 112.
१५९ मूर्ध्नामुद्वृत्तकृत्ता	ह० ना० VIII; श्री० का० प० 89; गो० का० प्र० P. 182.
३४८ मूर्ध्नामुद्वृत्तकृत्ता	" " "
२९५ मृगचक्षुषमद्राक्षम्	श्री० का० प० 147; गो० का० प्र० P. 252.

४९७ मृगलोचनया विना	रु० अ० स० 50; गो० का० प्र० P. 358.
१५३ मृदुपवनविभिन्नो	का० वि० उ० IV. 22; गो० का० प्र० P. 178.
४०४ मृधे निदाघघर्मांशु	श्री० का० प० 218; गो० का० प्र० P. 315.
५०४ यं प्रेक्ष्य चिररूढापि	गो० का० प्र० P. 362; उ० का० अ० सा० स० उ० वि० P. 44; मेण्ठकृतं हयग्रीववधम् ।
१ यः कौमारहरः	शीलाभट्टारिका; क० व० स० 508; रुय्रस P. 74; विसाद I, line 5, P. 14. शा० प०; गो० का० प्र० P. 9. I.2; सु० र० भा०; 353/42. गो०
२०३ यः पूयते सुरसरिन्मुख	का० प्र० P. 203.
१९३ यत्त्वन्नेत्रसमानकान्ति — यत्तदूर्जितमत्युग्रं	भ० वे० सं० I. 13; म० व्य० वि०; गो० का० प्र० P. 198.
२७३ यत्रानुल्लिखितार्थमेव	कु० व० जी०, I. 29, P. 18; श्री० का० प० 134; गो० का० प्र० P. 242.
५१८ यत्रैता लहरीचलाचलदृशः	रु० अ० स० P. 83; श्री० का० प० 287; गो० का० प्र० P. 368.
१४३ यथायं दारुणाचारः	श्री० का० प० 75; गो० का० प्र० P.173.
२९७ यदा त्वामहमद्राक्षम्	श्री० का० प० 149; गो० का० प्र० P. 253.
३६५ यदानतोऽयदानतो	आ० दे० श० 49; श्री० का० प० 197; गो० का० प्र० P. 293.
२७२ यदि दहत्यनलोऽत्र	आ० दे० श०; श्री० का० प० 185; गो० का० प्र० P. 241.
४५४ यदि दहत्यनलोऽत्र	गो० का० प्र० P. 343.
३१२ यद्वञ्चनाहितमतिर्बहु	अ० ध्व० आ० लो०: III. 16; गो० का० प्र० P. 260.

२४५ यशोऽधिगन्तुं सुख	भा० किं० अ० III. 40; गो० का० प्र० P. 227.
१९९ यश्चाप्सरोविभ्रम	का० कु० सं० I. 4; श्री० का० प० 99; गो० का० प्र० P. 200.
५४५ यस्य किंचिदपकर्तुं	रु० अ० सं० P. 93; मा० शि० व० XIV. 78; गो० का० प्र० P. 379.
३५७ यस्य न सविधे दयिता	श्री० का० प० 161; गो० का० प्र० P. 290
७३ यस्य मित्राणि मित्राणि	गो० का० प्र० P. 111.
११३ यस्यासुहृत्कृततिरस्कृति	गो० का० प्र० P. 133.
४३९ याताः किं न मिलन्ति	अ० श० 10; गो० का० प्र० P. 337.
१४५ यावकरसार्द्रपाद	श्री० का० प० 77; गो० का० प्र० P. 174.
५४३ युगान्तकालप्रतिसंहृता	मा० शि० व० I. 23; श्री० का० प० 305; गो० का० प्र० P. 379.
५४७ ये कन्दरासु निवसन्ति	रु० अ० स० P. 94; गो० का० प्र० P. 380.
३०२ येन ध्वस्तमनोभवेन	चन्द्रक; व० सु० आ०; अ० ध्व० आ० लो० II. 21, 22; म० व्य० वि० P. 94; कु० व० जी०; श्री० का० प० 153; गो० का० प्र० P. 255.
१८९ ये नाम केचिदिह	भ० मा० मा० I. 7; म० व्य० वि० P. 200; गो० का० प्र० P. 196.
४४४ येनास्यभ्युदितेन चन्द्र	गो० का० प्र० P. 339.
४८४ येषां कण्ठपरिग्रह	गो० का० प्र० P. 354.
२२७ येषां तास्त्रिदशेभदान	म० व्य० वि०; श्री० का० प० 124; गो० का० प्र० P. 215.
१०४ येषां दोर्बलमेव दुर्बल	गो० का० प्र० P. 126.
१९२ योऽविकल्पमिदमर्थं	म० व्य० वि० P. 208; गो० का० प्र० P. 197.
३७६ योऽसकृत्परगोत्राणां	श्री० का० प० 201; गो० का० प्र० P. 297.

९७	रइकेलिहिअणिअरण	हा० गा० स० V. 53; कु० व० जी० I. 58; म० व्य० वि०; व० ल० 607; श्री० का० प० 55; गो० का० प्र० P. 122.
३००	रक्ताशोक कृशोदरी क्व	का० वि० उ० IV; श्री० का० प० 151; गो० का० प० P. 254.
३१९	रक्ताशोक कृशोदरी क्व	का० वि० उ० IV; श्री० का०प० 151; गो० का० प० P. 245.
३७४	रजनिरमणमाले:	
३८८	रसासार रसा सार	रु० का० अ० III. 399; श्री० का० प० 206; गो० का० प्र० P. 303.
८४	राईसु चंदधवलासु	हा० गा० स० 992; गो० का० प्र० P. 116.
४५१	राकायामकलङ्कं चेत्	गो० का० प्र० P. 342.
१५६	राकाविभावरीकान्त	श्री० का० प० 86; गो० का० प्र० P. 180.
४९	राकासुधाकरमुखी	श्री० का० प० 34; गो० का० प्र० P. 94.
५७२	राजति तटीयमभिहत	र० ह० वि० V. 137; गो० का० प्र० P. 391.
५७७	राजनारायणं लक्ष्मी:	उ० का० अ० सा० स० उ० वि० P. 46.
४४०	राजन्राजसुता न पाठयति	रु० अ० स० P. 63; गो० का० प्र० P. 338.
२११	राजन्विभान्ति भवत:	श्री० का० प० 109; गो० का० प्र० P. 207.
५३२	राज्ये स्सारं वसुधा	रु० का० अ० VII. 97; गो० का० प्र० P. 375.
२५४	राममन्मथशरेण ताडिता	का० र० व० XI. 20; गो० का० प्र० P. 232.
१०९	रामोऽसौ भुवनेषु	विशाखदत्त:; कु० व० जी० I. 43; II. 30; भो० स० क० आ० P. 341.

		श्री० का० प० 58; राघवानन्दम्; गो० का० प्र० P. 128.
७७	रुधिरविसरप्रसाधित	गो० का० प्र० P. 113.
१०३	रे रे चञ्चललोचनाञ्चित	गो० का० प्र० P. 125.
२४१	लग्नं रागावृत्ताङ्ग्या	वे० प० वे० II; गो० का० प्र० P. 224.
२५३	लग्नं रागावृत्ताङ्ग्या	वे० प० वे० II; गो० का० प्र० P.247.
२८०	लग्नं रागावृत्ताङ्ग्या	वे० प० वे० II; गो० का० प्र० P.247.
२८४	लग्नं रागावृत्ताङ्ग्या	वे० प० वे० II; गो० का० प्र० 247.
२३७	लग्नः केलिकचग्रह	गो० का० प्र० P. 223.
४९८	लतानामेतासामुदित	गो० का० प्र० P. 359.
४३४	लहिऊण तुज्झ बाहुप्फंस	हा० गा० स० 428; श्री० का० प० 238; गो० का० प्र० P. 334.
७५	लावण्यं तदसौ कान्तिः	श्री० का० प० 5; गो० का० प्र० P.112.
५५३	लावण्यौकसि सप्रताप	खण्डप्रशस्तिः; गो० का० प्र० P. 383.
१००	लिखन्नास्ते भूमिं	अ० श० 6; श्री० का० प० 57; गो० का० प्र० P. 124.
४१७	लिम्पतीव तमोङ्गानि	शू० मृ० श० I. 32; भा० चारुदत्त I. 19; भा० बालचरित I. 15; श्री० का० प० 318; गो० का० प्र० P. 324.
५६८	लिम्पतीव तमोङ्गानि	श० मृ० श० I. 32; भा० चारुदत्त I. 19; भा० बाल चरित I. 15; श्री० का० प० 318; गो० का० प्र० P. 324; गो० का० प्र० P. 389.
१५२	लीलातामरसाहतो	अ० श० 70; गो० का० प्र० P. 178.
५३०	वक्त्रस्यन्दिस्वेदबिन्दु	रु० अ० स० P.97; श्री० का० प० 297; गो० का० प्र० P. 474.
२७४	वक्त्राम्भोजं सरस्वत्यधि	व० भो० प्र० 230, P. 51; श्री० का० प० 135; गो० का० प्र० P. 243.
५७६	वक्त्रेन्दौ तव सत्ययं	ह० र० आ० III. 23 cd;
५६७	वदनसौरभलोभ	मा० शि० ब० VI. 14; गो० का० प्र० P. 389.

३५८ वदनं वरवर्णिन्यास्तस्याः	श्री० का० प० 194; गो० का० प्र० P. 290.
३१३ वद वद जितः स शत्रुः	रु० का० अ० VI. 30; श्री० का० प० 160; गो० का० प्र० P. 260.
५०१ वपुःप्रादुर्भावादनु	मुञ्जः; सु० र० को० 36; गो० का० प्र० P. 360.
१६१ वपुर्विरूपाक्षमलक्ष्य	का० कु० सं० V. 12; गो० का० प्र० P. 183.
१८१ वस्त्रवैदूर्यचरणैः	श्री० का० प० 37; गो० का० प्र० P. 191.
५८५ वह्निस्फुलिङ्ग इव	भो० स० क० आ० I. 51; वा० का० अ० सू० वृ० IV. 2; श्री० का० प० 328.
५२८ वाणिअअ हत्थिदन्ता	हा० गा० स० 951; अ० ध्व० आ० लो० III. 17; गो० का० प्र० P. 373.
१३२ वाणीरकुडंगुड्डीण	हा० गा० स० 876; अ० ध्व० आ० लो० P. 116-120; गो० का० प्र० P. 144.
२८२ वाताहरतया जगत्	भ० श० 87; श्री० का० प० 142; गो० का० प्र० P. 248.
८६ वारिज्जन्तो वि पुणो	हा० गा० स० 994; गो० का० प्र० P. 117.
२१७ विकसितसहकारतार	गो० का० प्र० P. 210.
५१० विदलितसकलारिकुलं	रु० का० अ० VII. 28; गो० का० प्र० P. 365.
२८८ विदीर्णाभिमुखाराति	वा० का० अ० सू० वृ० II. 2.13; गो० का० प्र० P. 250.
४२५ विद्वन्मानसहंस	रु० अ० स० P. 27; श्री० का० प० 233; गो० का० प्र० P. 329.
२६९ विधाय दूरे केयूर	गो० का० प्र० P. 240.
२०४ विनयप्रणयैककेतनं	श्री० का० प० 104; गो० का० प्र० P. 203.

३६१	विनायमेनो नयता	रु० अ० का० अ० III. 5; गो० का० प्र० P. 292.
५	विनिर्गतं मानदमात्म	मेण्ठ कृतं हयग्रीववधम्; गो० का० प्र० P. 16.
२४८	विपदोऽभिभवन्त्यविक्रमं	भा० कि० अ० II. 14; म० व्य० वि०; गो० का० प्र० P. 228.
१३७	विपरीअरए लच्छी	हा० गा० स० 816; ज० व० ल० 611.
५४१	विपुलेन सागरशयस्य	मा० शि० व० XIII. 40; गो० का० प्र० P. 378.
५६३	विभिन्नवर्णा गरुडा	गो० का० प्र० P. 378; मा० शि० व० IV. 14; श्री० का० प० 316.
३३५	विमानपर्यङ्कतले	आ० ध्व० आ० III P. 178; अ० ध्व० आ० लो० III, P. 178; गो० का० प्र० P. 271.
२७	वियदलिमलिनाम्बु	गो० का० प्र० P. 71.
९१	विहलं खलं तुमं सहि	हा०गा०स० 880; गो०का०प्र०P. 119.
२१३	वेगाडुड्डीय गगने	गो० का० प्र० P. 203.
५५८	वेत्रत्वचा तुल्यरुचां	श्री० का० प० 311; गो० का० प्र० P. 385; सुरभा 223/64.
२५३	शक्तिर्निस्त्रिशजेयं तव	गो० का० प्र० P. 231 ; वसुआ 2596; सुरभा 148/80.
५९	शनिरशनिश्च तमुच्चैः	श्री० का० प० 40; गो० का० प्र० P. 101; सुरभा 103/73.
१५७	शरत्कालसमुल्लासि	गो० का० प्र० P. 180; सुरभा 262/165.
५०९	शशी दिवसधूसरो	भ० नी० श० 45; गो० का० प्र० P. 364; सुरभा 177/993.
५३७	शिरीषादपि मृद्वङ्गी	प० न० सा० च०, I. 28; श्री० का० प० 302; गो० का० प्र० P. 377.
३०१	शीर्णघ्राणाङ्घ्रिपाणीन्	म० सू० श० 6; गो० का० प्र० P. 255.
३०	शून्यं वासगृहं	अ० श० 77; श्री० का० प० 15; गो० का० प्र० P. 75.

३६२ स त्वारम्भरतोऽवश्य	रु० का० अ० III. 18; गो० का० प्र० P. 293 .
३६३ सत्त्वारम्भरतोऽवश्य	रु० क ० अ० III. 19.
२५६ सदा मध्ये यासामियमभृत	श्री० का० प० 127; गो० का० प्र० P. 234.
२६७ सदा स्नात्वा निशीथिन्यां	श्री० का० प० 132; गो० का० प्र० P. 239.
५३९ सद्यः करस्पर्शमवाप्य	प० न० सा० च० I. 62; श्री० का० प० 269; गो० का० प्र० P. 378.
३८० सद्वंशमुक्तामणिः	
३६० सन्नारीभरणोपाय	रु० का० अ० X. 27; गो० का० प्र० P. 292.
५८९ स पीतवासाः प्रगृहीत	भा० का० अ० II. 58; श्री० का० प० 332; गो० का० प्र० P. 397.
४९१ समदमतङ्गजमदजल	गो० का० प्र० P. 356.
५८८ स मुनिर्लाञ्छितो	वा० का० अ० सू० वृ० IV. 2.9; श्री० का० प० 331; गो० का० प्र० P. 397.
३२४ संप्रहारे प्रहरणैः	श्री० का० प० 167.
१५५ सम्यग्ज्ञानमहाज्योतिः	गो० का०प्र० P. 179; श्री० का०प० 85.
३८६ सरला बहुलारम्भ	रु० का० अ० V. 19; गो० का० प्र० P. 304; सु० र० भा० 205/9.
३६६ सरस्वति प्रसादं मे	आ० दे० रा० 50; गो० का०प्र० P. 293; सु० र० भा० 205/51.
१८१ स रातु वो दुश्च्यवनो	गो० का० प्र० P. 188.
३७५ सर्वस्वं हर सर्वस्य	गो० का० प्र० P. 297.
४०५ सवितृ विधवति विधुरपि	श्री० का० प० 219; गो० का० प्र० P. 316; सु० र० भा० 171/800.
३२१ सव्रीडा दयितानने	श्री० का० प० 164; गो० का० प्र० P. 262; सु० र० भा० 12/41
३३५ सशोणितैः क्रव्यभुजां	गो० का० प्र० P. 271.

३६७ ससार साकं दर्पण	रु० का० अ०III. 35; गो० क० प्र० P. 294; सु० र० भा० 205/6.
४९५ सह दिअहणिसाहिं	रा० क० म० II. 9; गो० का० प्र० P. 358.
८९ सहि णवणिहुवणसमरम्भि	हा० गा० स० 996; गो० का० प्र० P. 118.
६९ सहि विरइऊण माणस्स	हा० गा० स० 936; गो० का० प्र० P. 108.
१२१ साकं कुरङ्गकदृशा	गो० का० प्र० P. 137; सु० र० भा० 105/142.
१६९ सा दूरे च सुधा	श्री० का० प० 93; गो० का० प्र० P. 186.
१५१ साधनं सुमहद्यस्य	श्री० का० प० 81; गो० का० प्र० P. 177; सु० र० भा० 79/12.
१८८ साधु चन्द्रमसि पुष्करैः	अ० रा० च० II. 95; गो० का० प्र० P. 195; ज० सू० मु० 53/34; सु० र० भा० 262/178.
३४ सा पत्युः प्रथमापराध	अ० श० 29; गो० का० प्र० P. 78; सु० र० भा० 358/64.
७२ सायकसहायबाहोः	गो० का० प्र० P. 188; सु० र० भा० 189/55.
७९ सायं स्नानमुपासितं	गो० का० प्र० P. 114; सु० र० भा० 293/12.
५६० सा वसइ तुज्झ हिअए	हा० गा० स० 947; श्री० का० प० 314; गो० का० प्र० P. 386.
७ साहेन्ती सहि सुहअं	हा० गा० स० 840; गो० का० प्र० P.19.
३१४ सितकरकररुचिरविभा	श्री० का० प० 195; गो० का० प्र० P. 260; गो० का० प्र० P. 290.
३५९ सितकरकररुचिरविभा	" " "
५३८ सिंहिकासुतसंत्रस्तः	श्री० का० प० 303; गो० का० प्र०

१६५ सुधाकरकराकर	श्री० का० प० 90; गो० का० प्र० P. 185; शा० प० 1102; सु० र० भा० 218/67.
१७८ सुरालयोल्लासपरः	गो० का० प्र० P.190.
१९ सुव्वइ समागमिस्सदि	हा० गा० स० 962; गो० का० प्र० P.53.
२६६ सुसितवसनालंकारायां	श्री० का० प० 121; गो० का० प्र० P. 239; सु० र० भा० 136/38.
४७९ सुसिवसनातलंकारायां	" " "
४४२ सुहृद्वधूवाष्पजल	उ० का० अ० सा० सं० उ० वि० P. 43; गो० का० प्र० P. 338.
४८५ सृजति च जगदिदमवति	गो० का० प्र० P. 355; सु० र० भा० 91/45.
२५ सेयं ममाङ्गेषु सुधारस	शंकुक; गो० का० प्र० P. 64; सु० र० भा० 273/6.
५६९ सो णत्थि एत्थ गामे	हा० गा० स० 997; गो० का० प्र० P. 389.
१७० सोऽध्यैष्ट वेदान्	भ० का० I. 2; गो० का० प्र० P. 187.
४४८ सोऽपूर्वो रसनाविपर्यय	भ० श० 18; गो० का० प्र० P. 341; सु० र० भा० 224/110.
८७ सो मुद्धसामलंगो	हा०गा०स० 998; आ० वि० बा० ली०; गो० का० प्र० P. 118.
२९१ सौन्दर्यसंपत् तारुण्यं	गो० का० प्र० P. 250.
४२४ सौन्दर्यस्य तरङ्गिणी	गो० का० प्र० P. 329.
५७५ सौभाग्यं वितनोति	श्री० का० प० 321.
४८ स्तुमः कं वामाक्षि	श्री० का० प० 33; गो० का० प्र० P. 93; सु० र० भा० 313/64.
३७८ स्तोकेनोन्नतिमायाति	श्री० का० प० 202; गो० का० प्र० P. 299. प० तं० I. 161; सु० र० भा० 54/23.
११२ स्निग्धश्यामलकान्ति	आ० ध्व० आ० II; गो० का० प्र० P.131; ध्व० आ० लो० II. 1, PP. 61-62;

	ह० ना० V. 7, प्रतिहारेन्दुराज on उद्भट, P. 86; कु० व० जी० I. 42; P. 30; अ० वृ० मा० P. 11.
५७९ स्पष्टोल्लसत्किरण	र० ह० वि० XIX. 1; म० व्य० वि०; गो० का० प्र० P. 394.
६०१ स्पृशति तिग्मरुचौ	र० ह० वि० III. 37; गो० का० प्र० P. 401 ; सु० र० भा० 336/38.
२२१ स्फटिकाकृतिनिर्मलः	गो० का० प्र० P. 210.
५६१ स्फुरदद्भुतरूपमुत्प्रताप	श्री० का० प० 315; गो० का० प्र० P. 386; सु० र० भा० 104/89.
१६० स्रस्तां नितम्बादव	का० कु० सं० III. 55; गो० का० प्र० P. 182; सु० र० भा० 268/381.
४ स्वच्छन्दोच्छलदच्छ	गो० का० प्र० P. 15; सु० र० भा० 9/131.
४७० स्वच्छात्मतागुणसमु	गो० का० प्र० P. 348.
२६१ स्वपिति यावदयं निकटे	श्री० का० प० 130; गो० का० प्र० P. 237.
३९२ स्वप्नेऽपि समरेषु त्वां	गो० का० प्र० P. 311.
३७७ स्वयं च पल्लवाताम्र	उ० का० अ० सा० सं० IV. 15; गो० का० प्र० P. 298.
६०२ स्वयं च पल्लवाताम्र	उ० का० अ० सा० सं० IV. 15; गो० का० प्र० P. 402.
३४६ स्वर्गप्राप्तिरनेनैव	
२८५ हन्तुमेव प्रवृत्तस्य	भा० का० अ० I.41.
४६ हरत्यघं संप्रति हेतु	मा० शि० व० I. 26; गो० का० प्र० P. 91.
४६८ हरवत्र विषमदृष्टिः	श्री० का० प० 256.
११९ हरस्तु किंचित्परिवृत्त	का० कु० सं० III. 67; श्री० का० प० 70.
५२७ हंसाणं सरेहिं सिरी	हा० गा० स० 953; गो० का० प्र० P. 372.
१४९ हा धिक् सा किल	गो० का० प्र० P. 179.
२१९ हा नृप हा बुध हा कवि	गो० का० प्र० P.210.

३८ हा मातस्त्वरितासि	नारायणभट्टः; गो० का० प्र० P. 81; सु० र० भा० 362/37.
४९३ हित्वा त्वामुपरोध	गो० का० प्र० P. 357.
३२० हुमि अवहत्थिअरेहो	आ० वि० बा० ली०; अ० ध्व० आ० लो० P. 152.
४५२ हृदयमधिष्ठितमादौ	कु० म० 96, P. 23; श्री० का० प० 248; गो० का० प्र० P. 342.
४९४ हे हेलाजितबोधिसत्त्व	कु० व० जी० I. 90; वाक्यपदीयटीका पुञ्जराजकृता II. 249; रु० अ० स० P. 67; गो० का० प्र० P. 357.

APPENDIX C

Index of the first and second lines of the Kārikās of the Kāvyaprakāśa

अर्थान्तरैकवाचकं भवन्मतमनभिहितवाच्यम् । 54a
अलङ्कारोथ वस्त्वेव शब्दाद्यत्रावभासते ॥ 38b
अविमृष्टविधेयांशं विरुद्धमतिकृत्समासगतमेव ॥ 51b
अविवक्षितवाच्यो यस्तत्र वाच्यं भवेद्ध्वनौ । 24a
अविश्रान्तिजुषामात्मन्यङ्गाङ्गित्वं तु संकरः । 140a
असकृद् यदसंभाव्यमुत्तरं स्यात् तदुत्तरम् । 122a
आक्षेप उपमानस्य प्रतीपमुपमेयता । 133a
आलस्यं चैव दैन्यं च चिन्ता मोहः स्मृतिर्धृतिः ॥ 31b
आवृत्तिर्मध्यवृत्तिर्वा माधुर्ये घटना तथा ॥ 74b-
आश्रयाश्रयिणौ स्यातां तनुत्वेप्यधिकं तु तत् ॥ 128b
आश्रयैक्ये विरुद्धो यः स कार्यो भिन्नसंश्रयः । 64a
आह्लादकत्वं माधुर्यं शृंगारे द्रुतिकारणम् ॥ 68b
इदमुत्तममतिशयिनि व्यङ्ग्ये वाच्याद्ध्वनिर्बुधैः कथितः ॥ 4b
उक्तेष्वन्तर्भवन्तीति न पृथक् प्रतिपादिता ॥ 142b
उत्कर्षहेतवस्ते स्युरचलस्थितयो गुणाः ॥ 66b
उत्तरोत्तरमुत्कर्षो भवेत्सारः परावधिः ॥ 123b
उदात्तं वस्तुनं सम्पत् महतां चोपलक्षणम् ॥ 115b
उपकुर्वन्ति तं सन्तं येङ्गद्वारेण जातुचित् । 67a
उपमानाद्यदन्यस्य व्यतिरेकः स एव सः । 105a
उपमानानुपादाने वाक्यगाथ समासगा ॥ 88b
उपमानोपमेयत्वे एकस्यैवैकवाक्यगे । 91a
उपादानं लक्षणं चेत्युक्ता शुद्धैव सा द्विधा ॥ 10b
उभयोपयोगिनः स्युः शब्दाद्यास्तेन तेष्वपि सः ॥ 49b
एकं क्रमेणानेकस्मिन् पर्यायोन्यस्ततोन्यथा । 117a
एकस्य च ग्रहे न्यायदोषाभावादनिश्चयः ॥ 140b
एकात्मा युगपद्वृत्तिरेकस्यानेगोचरा । 135b
एकार्थतेव शब्दस्य तथा शब्दार्थयोरयम् ॥ 86b
एवमप्यनवस्था स्याद् या मूलक्षयकारिणी । 17a
एषां दोषा यथायोगं संभवन्तोपि केचन । 142a
एषां भेदा यथायोगं वेदितव्याश्च पूर्ववत् ॥ 46b
ऐकात्म्यं बध्यते योगात्तत्सामान्यमिति स्मृतम् ॥ 134b
ओजः प्रकाशकैस्तैस्तु परुषा कोमला परैः ॥ 80b

तत्सिद्धिहेतावेकस्मिन् यत्रान्यत्तत्करं भवेत् । 116a
तथैव करणं चेति विशेषस्त्रिविधः स्मृतः ॥ 136b
तथैव यद्विधीयेत स व्याघात इति स्मृतः । 139a
तद्भाविकं काव्यलिङ्गं हेतोर्वाक्यपदार्थता ॥ 114b
तद्भूर्लाक्षणिकस्तत्र व्यापारो व्यञ्जनात्मकः । 14a
तददोषौ शब्दार्थौ सगुणावनलंकृती पुनः क्वापि । 4a
तदन्यस्य वचस्तुल्ये तुल्यस्येति च पञ्चधा ॥ 99b
तदा कारणमाला स्यात् क्रियया तु परस्परम् ॥ 120b
तद्युक्तो व्यञ्जकः शब्दो यत्सोऽर्थान्तरयुक् तथा । 20a
तद्रूपकमभेदो य उपमानोपमेययोः । 93a
तद्रूपाननुहारश्चेदस्य तत् स्यादतद्गुणः । 138a
तद्वद् धर्मस्य लोपे स्यान्न श्रौती तद्धिते तथा । 88a
तस्यैव यदि वा कल्प्या तिरस्कारनिबन्धनम् ॥ 133b
तादृगन्यव्यपोहाय परिसंख्या तु सा स्मृता ॥ 119b
तेन नार्थगुणा वाच्याः प्रोक्ताः शब्दगुणाश्च ये । 73a
त्रयस्त्रिंशदमी भावाः समाख्यातास्तु नामतः ॥ 34b
त्रासश्चैव वितर्कश्च विज्ञेया व्यभिचारिणः । 34a
दीप्त्यात्मविस्तृतेर्हेतुरोजो वीररसस्थितिः ॥ 69b
दुष्टं पदं श्रुतिकटु च्युतसंस्कृत्यप्रयुक्तमसमर्थम् । 50a
दृष्टान्तः पुनरेतेषां सर्वेषां प्रतिबिम्बनम् ॥ 102b
धर्मेण केनचिद् यत्र तत् सूक्ष्मं परिचक्षते । 123a
धर्मोपमानयोर्लोपे वृत्तौ वाक्ये च दृश्यते । 90a
न दोषः स्वपदेनोक्तावपि संचारिणः क्वचित् । 63a
न प्रयोजनमेतस्मिन् न च शब्दः स्खलद्गतिः ॥ 16b
नवरसरुचिरां निर्मितिमादधती भारती कवेर्जयति ॥ 1b
नाभिधा समयाभावाद्धेत्वभावान्न लक्षणा ॥ 15b
नाम्नः स वृत्त्यवृत्त्योश्च तदेवं पञ्चधा मतः ॥ 82b
निगीर्याध्यवसानं तु प्रकृतस्य परेण यत् । 100a
निजेनागन्तुना वापि तन्मीलितमिति स्मृतम् ॥ 130b
नियतानां सकृद्धर्मः सा पुनस्तुल्ययोगिता ॥ 104b
नियतारोपणोपायः स्यादारोपः परस्य यः । 95a
नियतिकृतनियमरहितां ह्लादैकमयीमनन्यपरतन्त्राम् । 1a
निर्वेदग्लानिशङ्काख्यास्तथासूया मदश्रमाः । 31a

व्याप्नोत्यन्यत् प्रसादोसौ सर्वत्र विहितस्थितिः । 71a
व्रीडा चपलता हर्ष आवेगो जड़ता तथा । 32a
शक्तिर्निपुणता लोकशास्त्रकाव्याद्यवेक्षणात् । 3a
शब्दचित्रं वाच्यचित्रमव्यङ्ग्यं त्ववरं स्मृतम् ॥ 5b
शब्दप्रमाणवेद्योर्थो व्यनक्त्यर्थान्तरं यतः । 23a
शब्दार्थचित्रं यत्पूर्वं काव्यद्वयमुदाहृतम् । 48a
शब्दार्थाभ्यामथाक्षिप्ते श्लिष्टे तद्वत्त्रिरष्ट तत् । 106a
शब्दार्थोभयभूरेको भेदा अष्टादशास्य तत् ॥ 41b
शब्दार्थोभयशक्त्युत्थस्त्रिधा स कथितो ध्वनिः । 38a
शाब्दस्तु लाटानुप्रासो भेदे तात्पर्यमात्रतः ॥ 81b
शुष्केन्धनाग्निवत् स्वच्छजलवत्सहसैव यः ॥ 70b
शृङ्गारहास्यकरुणरौद्रवीरभयानकाः । 29a
श्लिष्यन्ति शब्दाः श्लेषोसावक्षरादिभिरष्टधा ॥ 84b
श्लेषः स वाक्य एकस्मिन् यत्रानेकार्थता भवेत् ॥ 96b
श्लेषेण काक्वा वा ज्ञेया सा वक्रोक्तिस्तथा द्विधा ॥ 78b
श्रुतिमात्रेण शब्दात्तु येनार्थप्रत्ययो भवेत् । 76a
श्रौता आर्थाश्च ते यस्मिन्नेकदेशविवर्ति तत् । 94a
श्रौत्यार्थी च भवेद्वाक्ये समासे तद्धिते तथा ॥ 87b
संकरेण त्रिरूपेण संसृष्ट्या चैकरूपया । 44a
संकेतितश्चतुर्भेदो जात्यादिर्जातिरेव वा । 8a
संचार्यादेर्विरुद्धस्य बाध्यस्योक्तिर्गुणावहा ॥ 63b
संदिग्धो निर्हेतुः प्रसिद्धिविद्याविरुद्धश्च । 56a
संनिधानादिबोधार्थं स्थितेष्वेतत् समर्थनम् ॥ 58b
संभावनमथोत्प्रेक्षा प्रकृतस्य समेन यत् । 92a
संयोगाद्यैरवाच्यार्थधीकृद्व्यापृतिरञ्जनम् ॥ 19b
सकृद्वृत्तिस्तु धर्मस्य प्रकृताप्रकृतात्मनाम् । 103a
सद्यः परनिर्वृतये कान्तासंमिततयोपदेशयुजे ॥ 2b
सन्दिग्धतुल्यप्राधान्ये काक्वाक्षिप्तमसुन्दरम् ॥ 45b
सन्दिग्धमप्रतीतं ग्राम्यं नेयार्थमथ भवेत् क्लिष्टम् । 51a
समं योग्यतया योगो यदि संभावितः क्वचित् ॥ 125b
समस्तवस्तुविषयं श्रौता आरोपिता यदा ॥ 93b
समाधिः सुकरं कार्यं कारणान्तरयोगतः । 125a
स मुख्योर्थस्तत्र मुख्यो व्यापारोभिधोच्यते ॥ 8b

ABBREVIATIONS

अराच —Abhinanda's Rāmacarita, Gaekwad's Oriental Series. 1929.

अअभा —Abhinavagupta's Abhinavabhāratī, Gaekwad's Oriental Series. 1926;1934.

अध्वआलो —Abhinavagupta's Dhvanyālokalocana, Nirnaya-Sagar Press. 1928.

अकुका —Appayyadīkṣita's Kuvalayānandakārikā, Nirnaya Sagar Press. 1927.

अपु —Agnipurāṇa. Published by Mansukhrai More, Calcutta.

अश —Amaruśataka, (also Sṛṅgāraśataka) Nirnaya Sagar Press. 1954.

आदेश —Ānandavardhana's Deviśataka, Kāvyamālā IX. Nirnaya Sagar Press.

आध्वआ —Ānandavardhana's Dhvanyāloka, Nirnaya Sagar Press. 1928.

उकाअसासं —Udbhaṭa's Kāvyālaṅkārasārasaṅgraha. Bombay Sanskrit and Prakrit Series. No. LXXIX. 1925.

कुवजी —Kuntaka's Vakroktijīvita, Ed. S. K. De. Pub. K. L. Mukhopadhyaya. Calcutta.

कारवं —Kālidāsa's Raguvaṁśa, Nirnaya Sagar Press. 1948.

काकुसं —Kālidāsa's Kumārasaṁbhava, Nirnaya Sagar Press. 1927.

कामेदूउ —Kālidāsa's Meghadūta, Uttaramegha. Nirnaya Sagar Press. 1935.

काअश —Kālidāsa's Abhijñānaśakuntala, Nirnaya Sagar Press. 1922.

कामाअ —Kālidāsa's Mālavikāgnimitra. Nirnaya Sagar Press. 1924.

काविउ —Kālidāsa's Vikramorvaśīya. Nirnaya Sagar Press. 1922.

क्षेऔविच —Kṣemendra's Aucityavicāracarcā, Kāvyamālā I. Nirnaya Sagar Press.

गोकाप्र —Govindaṭhakkura's Kāvyapradīpa, Nirnaya Sagar Press. 1912.

जरग —Jagannātha's Rasagaṅgādhara, Nirnaya Sagar Press. 1930.

जसूमु —Jalhaṇa's Sūktimuktāvali, Gaekwad's Oriental Series. 1925.

दकाआ —Daṅḍin's Kāvyādarśa, Jībānanda Vidyāsāgara. 1925.

दाकुम —Dāmodaragupta's Kuṭṭanīmata, Gujrati Printing Press. 1924.

धदरु —Dhanañjaya's Daśarūpaka, Gujrati Printing Press. 1927.

धदरूअ —Dhanika's Daśarūpakāvaloka, Gujrati Printing Press. 1927.

नापलम —Nāgeśabhaṭṭa's Paramalaghumañjūṣā, Chowkhamba.

पमभा —Patañjali's Mahābhāṣya, Chowkhamba.

पनसाच —Padmagupta alias Parimala's Navasāhasāṅkacarita, Bombay Sanskrit and Prakrit Series.

पुवाप —Puṇjarāja's commentary on the Vākyapadīya.

बभोप्र —Ballāla's Bhojaprabandha, Nirnaya Sagar Press. 1932.

बाहच —Bāṇa's Harṣacarita, Nirnaya Sagar Press. 1925.

भवेस —Bhaṭṭanārāyaṇa's Veṇīsaṁhāra, Nirnaya Sagar Press. 1925.

भउच —Bhavabhūti's Uttararāmacarita, Nirnaya Sagar Press. 1925.

भमवीच —Bhavabhūti's Mahāvīracarita, Nirnaya Sagar Press. 1926.

भमामा —Bhavabhūti's Mālatimādhava, Nirnaya Sagar Press, 1926.

भनाशा —Bharata's Nāṭyaśāstra, Kashi Sanskrit Series No. 60. 1929.

भउकाअसासंवृ—Bhaṭṭenduräja's commentary on Udbhaṭa's Kāvyālaṅkārasarasaṅgraha, Bombay Sanskrit and Prakrit Series. 1925.

भाकाअ —Bhāmaha's Kāvyālaṅkāra, Kashi Sanskrit Series.

भाकिअ —Bhāravi's Kirātārjunīya, Nirnaya Sagar Press. 1942.

भनीश —Bhartṛhari's Nītiśataka, Subhāṣitatriśatī, Nirnaya Sagar Press. 1957.

भश —Bhallaṭaśataka, Kāvyamālā IV, Nirnaya Sagar Press.

भवैश —Bhartṛhari's Vairāgyaśataka, Subhāṣitatriśatī, Nirnaya Sagar Press. 1957.

भशृश —Bhrtṛhari's Śṛṅgāraśataka, Subhāṣitatriśatī, Nirnaya Sagar Press. 1957.

भोशृप्र —Bhoja's Sṛṅgāraprakāśa.

भका —Bhaṭṭikāvya. Nirnaya Sagar Press. 1920

भोसकआ —Bhoja's Sarasvatīkaṇṭhābharaṇa. Nirnaya Sagar Press. 1934.

मशव्यावि —Mammaṭa's Śabdavyāpāravicāra. Nirnaya Sagar Press. 1916

मसूश —Mayūra's Sūryaśataka, Nirnaya Sagar Press. 1927.

मव्यवि —Mahimabhaṭṭa's Vyakt viveka, Trivandrum Sanskrit Series. 1909.

माशिव —Māgha's Śiśupālavadha, Nirnaya Sagar Press.

मुअवृमा —Mukulabhaṭṭa's Abhidhāvṛttimātṛkā, Nirnaya Sagar Press. 1916.

मभा —Mahābhārata, Gita Press.

रहवि —Ratnākara's Haravijaya, Nirnaya Sagar Press. 1914.

राकामी —Rājaśekhara's Kāvyamīmāmsā, Gaekwad's Oriental Series. 1934.

राकम —Rājaśekhara's Karpūramañjarī, Kāvyamālā, No. IV., Nirnaya Sagar Press. 1927.

राबारा —Rājaśekhara's Bālarāmāyaṇa. Jībānanda Vidyāsāgara, Calcutta. 1884.

राविभ —Rājaśekhara's Viddhaśālabhañjikā, Jībānanda Vidyāsagara, Calcutta. 1883.,

रुकाअ — Rudraṭa's Kāvyālaṅkāra, Nirnaya Sagar Press. 1909.

रुअस —Ruyyaka's Alaṅkārasarvasva. Ed. Gauīrnātha Pāṭhaka. Banaras. 1926.

वसुआ —Vallabhadeva's Subhāṣitāvali, Bombay Sanskrit and Prakrit Series.

वेपवे —Veṇidatta's Padyaveṇī, Calcutta.

वाकाअसूवृ —Vāmana's Kāvyālaṅkārasūtravṛtti, Vani Vilas Press. 1909.

विमुरा —Viśākhadatta's Mudrārākṣasa. Ed. K. T. Telang, Nirnaya Sagar Press. 1935.

विप्रय —Vidyānātha's Pratāparudrīya, Balamanorama Press. 1950.

विसाद —Viśvanātha's Sāhityadarpaṇa, Nirnaya Sagar Press. 1931.

विपु —Viṣṇupurāṇa, Gita Press, Gorakhpur.

शूमृश —Śūdraka's Mṛcchakaṭika, Nirnaya Sagar Press. 1916.

शाप —Śārṅgadharapaddhati, Bombay Sanskrit and Prakrit Series. 1888.

शिकअ —Śivasvāmin's Kapphinābhyudaya, Lahore. 1937.

श्रीकाप —Srivatsalāñchanācārya's Kāvyaparīkṣā, Mithilā Institute, Darbhanga.

सुरभा —Subhāṣitaratnabhāṇḍāgāra, Nirnaya Sagar Press. 1952.

हनाआ —Harṣa's Nāgānanda, Jībānanda Vidyāsāgara, Calcutta.

हरआ —Harṣa's Ratnāvali, Nirnaya Sagar Press. 1925

हमना —Hanumatkavi's Mahānāṭaka. (Also Hanumannāṭaka). Jībānanda Vidyāsāgara. Calcutta, 1939.

हागास —Hāla's Gāthāsaptaśatī, Nirnaya Sagar Press.

हेकाअ —Kāvyānuśāsana of Hemacandra, Kāvyamālā, Nirnaya Sagar Press.